AF505496

Monumental Shadows

On museums, memory and the making of history

Kaph Books

Art Jameel

Monumental Shadows
On Museums, Memory and the Making of History

Published by Kaph Books and Art Jameel

Editor: Nora Razian
Managing Editor: Lucas Morin
Publication Design: Clara Sancho

With contributions by:
Pio Abad, Basel Abbas and Ruanne Abou-Rahme, Rand Abdul Jabbar,
Nora Al-Badri, Anahi Alviso-Marino, Noah Angell, Ariella Aïsha Azoulay,
Omar Berrada, Antonia Carver, Haytham El Wardany, Faustin Linyekula,
Jumana Manna, Bonaventure Soh Bejeng Ndikung, Marian Pastor Roces,
Gala Porras-Kim, Michael Rakowitz, Nora Razian, Uzma Z. Rizvi, Alya Sebti,
Dima Srouji, Akram Zaatari

English to Arabic translation: The Archilogue (all texts unless noted)
Arabic to English translation: Nariman Youssef ('The A in Qaf',
Haytham El Wardany)
French to Arabic translation: The Archilogue ('Releasing History',
Omar Berrada and Faustin Linyekula)

Arabic copy-editing: Abu Bakr Al Ani, Ban Kattan
Arabic proofreading: Mohamed Hamdan (Kaph Books)
English copy-editing: Muriel Kahwagi
English proofreading: Zeina Assaf (Kaph Books)

Additional layouts: Romy Bitar ('A Monument Once Called "Kuwaiti Women,
Giving and Sacrifice"', Anahi Alviso-Marino, and 'Sebastia: A Vignette of
Apartheid from Below', Dima Srouji)

Special thanks to Fady Jameel, the Art Jameel team, ifa-Gallery, SAVVY
Contemporary and Various & Gould

Typefaces: 29LT Zarid Display, 29LT Zarid Text and 29LT Okaso
by 29Letters Type Foundry

Papers: Wibalin Natural Plum (cover), Wibalin Natural Basalt (endpaper),
Rainbow Yellow and Fedrigoni Arena 90 gsm

Printed in Belgium by die Keure

ISBN: 978-614-8035-45-6

First edition, 2023
© 2023 Kaph Books, Art Jameel, and the authors

All rights reserved. The reproduction of this publication in whole or in part,
in any form by any electronic, mechanical or other means, including
photocopying or recording or in any information storage or retrieval system,
is prohibited without the prior consent of the publisher and Art Jameel.

This book has been published in conjunction with the exhibition:

Phantom Limb
with Pio Abad and Frances Wadsworth Jones, Rand Abdul Jabbar, Kader Attia,
Benji Boyadgian, Ali Cherri, Decolonizing Architecture, Forensic Architecture,
Jumana Manna, Théo Mercier, Khalil Rabah, Rayyane Tabet and Akram Zaatari
Curated by Nora Razian

Jameel Arts Centre
9 October 2019 – 15 February 2020

Published and distributed by
Kaph Books
Gouraud Street, Gemmayze
Renno Building, 3rd floor
Beirut, Lebanon
kaphbooks.com

Art Jameel
Jameel Arts Centre
Dubai, United Arab Emirates
artjameel.org

Available through
Les presses du réel, Dijon
lespressesdureel.com

Idea Books, Amsterdam
ideabooks.nl

ARTBOOK LLC, New York
D.A.P. | Distributed Art Publishers, Inc.
artbook.com

CIEL Book Distribution, Beirut and Dubai
ciel.me

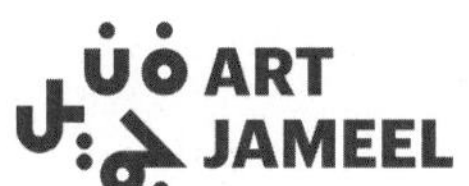
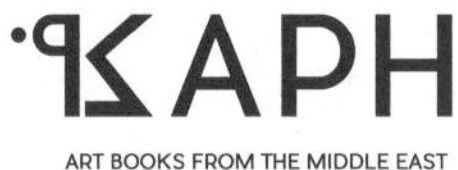

ANTONIA CARVER

Foreword

Monumental Shadows accompanies and emerges from Art Jameel's long engagement with material heritage and ideas around preservation, destruction, reconstruction and re-creation. What began initially as a focus on artisanship and the built environment – through the running of craft legacy schools in Jeddah and Cairo, as well as community-led documentation and architectural projects further afield – has over the past five years expanded into a robust programme of exhibitions, talks and seminars. Internally, and by 'thinking in public' with – and learning from – contemporary artists and other collaborative practitioners, we have attempted to interrogate and unravel the notion of 'heritage' as a singular term, addressing museology, archaeology, memory, and the making and unmaking of multiple histories. A series of exhibitions and commissions, often sparked by or running alongside Jameel Library research projects, included *Phantom Limb* at Jameel Arts Centre in Dubai, in 2019, through which the seed for this rich publication was planted, followed by solo exhibitions by Michael Rakowitz and Hiwa K.

Monumental Shadows is located within a global context of ever-more urgent conversations that examine museum practices, history-making and the consequences of dispos-session and conflict on material heritage, looking for new ways forward. The past decade has seen some significant milestones, such as the 2018 Sarr-Savoy report, which has led to an (uneven, unfinished, currently somewhat gestural) accelerated pace of restitution from some Western museums, and the 2020 wave of protests that led to the dismantling of select monuments honouring contested historical figures in Europe and North America.

The first such publication of its kind, *Monumental Shadows* focuses on the region Art Jameel is grounded in, one which is particularly scarred by both histories of nation-building through archaeology and the large-scale destruction of objects and sites of significance. While most contributions engage with West Asia, notably Iraq, Lebanon, Palestine and the Gulf, others offer far-reaching global perspectives, exploring how various cultures, practices and institutions read, experience, and claim ownership of heritage.

Monumental Shadows compiles and builds on years of research and conversations that emerged out of the exhibition-making process. It features a breadth of tones and formats, ranging from academic texts to interviews, visual essays, and literary fiction. Published in collaboration with Kaph Books in Beirut, this bilingual volume also highlights Art Jameel's commitment to commissioning original writing in, and translating content into, Arabic, making such scholarship accessible to all our audiences.

These conversations were further enriched by international institutional collaborations: notably with SAVVY Contemporary and ifa-Gallery in Berlin, with whom we developed the interdisciplinary programme *For the Phoenix to Find Its Form in Us* in 2021. We are particularly thankful to their respective directors at the time, Bonaventure Soh Bejeng Ndikung and Alya Sebti, who reflected on this collaboration in the following pages.

The Art Jameel team, across the board, has been and is a part of these ongoing explorations into heritage and the material; I thank them all, and in particular, Nora Razian, who with Rahul Gudipudi and Lucas Morin, has led on the curation, conceptualisation and production of this thematic strand and this book. We are grateful to the many artists, writers, researchers and curators who were part of this journey, for their insightful and nourishing exchanges on the theme over the years. Some of those conversations were expanded on in this volume, others took shape as projects, artworks, exhibitions, texts and lectures that followed their own path. All are part of Art Jameel's broad, communal commitment to exploring what heritage means to us today in thought-provoking and timely ways.

Antonia Carver

Director
Art Jameel

NORA RAZIAN

Introduction

October 2019 marked the opening of the exhibition *Phantom Limb*[1] at the Jameel Arts Centre in Dubai. Bringing together works from 13 artists and collectives from West Asia and beyond, the exhibition raised pressing questions about the weaponisation of heritage, construction of foundational myths, and legacies of colonial violence upheld through the administration and legislation of material culture. The exhibition sought to perform an 'archaeology in reverse', a tracing backwards from the object to the entangled network of hands, legislations, and discursive frameworks that inscribed it within the rarified realm of 'heritage'.

The space of material heritage, and its attendant disciplines of archaeology and museology, have long been sites for the assertion of historical narratives, tools for substantiating territorial claims, and the stage onto which national and ethnic identities are projected. However, much has changed in the tenor and tone of public debate. Fuelled by global movements demanding social justice, an end to racism, and the restoration of dignity, debates on the restitution of cultural artefacts have seeped out of the halls of UNESCO and the arena of national politics and into the political zeitgeist, becoming ever more insistent. These ongoing global movements identify statues, monuments, and sites of commemoration as focal points that serve to uphold and perpetuate histories of violence, oppression, and discrimination tied to racialisation and colonial power structures. Those calling for the dismantling or renaming of these sites 'recognize the histories of forgetting that underpin their making, they can see clearly how monuments have been often weaponized in the ongoing battles around race and nation.'[2] As archaeologist Yannis Hamilakis eloquently reminds us, 'The toppling of these statues is not a symbolic "killing" of the men [...] depicted, but rather an attempt to mobilize their figures in the service of a powerful political performance. This performance aims to redirect our attention to the unfinished histories that should haunt us all, inviting us at the same time to embrace an ontology of life that is guided by such haunting.'[3]

It is a desire to engage with this 'haunting' that informs the putting together of this publication and the exhibition preceding it. The essays, texts, and visual contributions presented here expand on conversations put forward in the exhibition *Phantom Limb*, which called into question the foundations on which modern understandings of material heritage have been built. Decolonizing Architecture's project *Refugee Heritage* (2015 – 2021) put forward a case for the inscription of the Dheisheh refugee camp in Bethlehem as a UNESCO World Heritage Site, engaging with the potential of heritage discourse to be mobilised as an agent of political transformation, while Kader Attia's film *Reflecting Memory* (2016) explored notions of repair in the context of the post-colonial state. The history of the discipline of archaeology was put into question in many of the works, including Rayyane Tabet's *Orthostates* (2017 – ongoing) which brought to light the legislative murkiness once governing the removal of finds, as do Akram Zaatari's haunting photographs of Osman Hamdi Bey's Ottoman-era excavation in the south of Lebanon.

Bringing together contributions from the fields of literature, dance, archaeology, art history, and the visual arts, *Monumental Shadows* continues to engage with these pressing questions, while offering varied perspectives on how we might engage with the past and its residues. While the intention of the publication was to have various forms of contributions in dialogue throughout, for practical reasons related to publishing a single version in Arabic and English, essays and interviews lead the publication, while the visual essays are grouped at the centre.

Noah Angell's text 'Museums Breed Ghosts' draws on his years-long engagement with curatorial staff and night-time security personnel at the British Museum, which with over eight million holdings is one of the largest encyclopaedic museums in the world. Along with ample gallery spaces, the British Museum runs vast storage spaces holding archaeological finds, objects, and artefacts from around the world as well as over 6,000 human remains. Angell brings together testimonials of nocturnal hauntings, unsettled objects, and unruly ghosts, while ruminating on what would be at stake for the museum were it to engage seriously with these events.

In a similar vein, **Gala Porras-Kim**'s 'Letters to Museum Directors' petitions, on behalf of parched and dehydrated objects and human remains sequestered in storage spaces, for their return to their humid and life-filled environments. Porras-Kim suggests that instead of preservation, museums might actually be complicit in destruction, by severing objects and subjects from the contexts and communities that nurture them.

In the absence of access – to objects, archives and sites that have been destroyed or looted – what might be the role of artists, curators and writers in creating public platforms for remembrance? How can speculation and imagination enable the re-reading and re-claiming of lost and silenced histories? In **Faustin Linyekula**'s conversation with curator and writer **Omar Berrada**, the acclaimed dancer and choreographer discusses his performance *Banataba* (2017) at the Metropolitan Museum of Art in New York. The conversation touches on the often-painful practice of attempting to recall one's history through engaging with a community's alienated objects, as one step towards suturing the many wounds left by histories of violent colonialism and extraction. As author and activist **Ariella Aïsha Azoulay** reminds us in *Potential History: Unlearning Imperialism* (2020), an excerpt of which appears in the Arabic version of this publication, 'We can no longer accept the imperial reduction of art making to the production of objects with museum value and market price, which, stripped of their context, are rendered tautological: an art object is an art object is an art object. Instead we must recognize these objects as relics of destroyed worlds and in them the inscribed rights that can be actualized in the presence of those from whom they were separated or from their descendants.'[4] In the excerpt reprinted here, Azoulay critically engages with *Lanier v Harvard* – a lawsuit brought against Harvard by Tamara Lanier, who argued for the handing over of slavery-era photos of her ancestors held in the university's collection, as an example of how we can begin to rethink relationships between objects, people, and the institutions that hold them.

The 'ruin', historically constructed as a romantic space integral to the formation of notions of European modernity, becomes a site for the reclamation of agency and community empowerment in the work of artist duo **Basel Abbas and Ruanne Abou-Rahme**. Their visual essay 'And yet my mask is powerful' draws from a larger body of work of the same name, where 3D printed copies of Neolithic masks – excavated in the West Bank in Palestine and now sequestered in private collections and at the Israel Museum – are worn by Palestinian youth while visiting, walking through, eating, dancing and singing in the ruins of their destroyed villages. As the artists write, 'The destroyed sites emerge not just as places of ruin or trauma, but appear full of an unmediated vitality.'[5] This active engagement with the ruin and processes of ruination is, as Ann Laura Stoler writes, a way 'to emphasize less the artefacts of empire as dead matter or remnants of a defunct regime than to attend to their reappropriations, neglect and strategic and active positioning within the politics of the present.'[6]

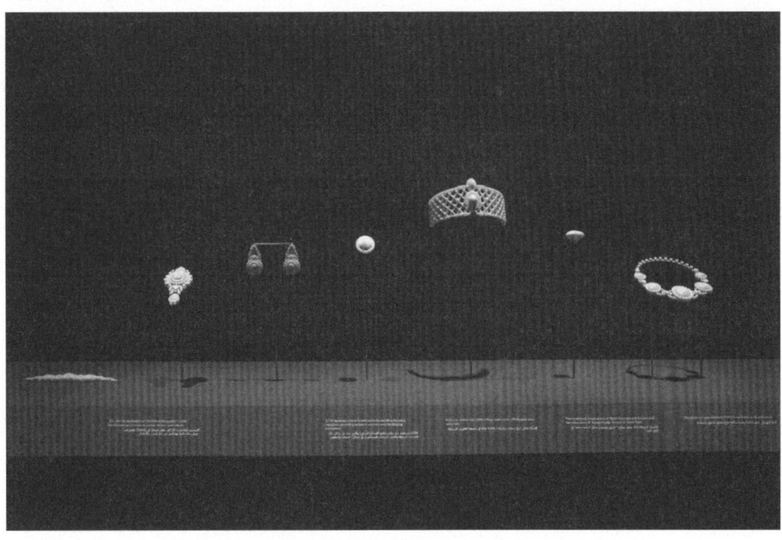

Pio Abad and Frances Wadsworth Jones, *The Collection of Jane Ryan and William Saunders*, Jameel Arts Centre, 2019.
Courtesy of Art Jameel. Image credit: Daniella Baptista.

The urgent and often emotional debate around the circulation and exhibition of material culture and archaeological artefacts, while a pertinent global issue, is one that is keenly felt within the context of West Asia. Long histories of occupation and conflict have simultaneously fuelled the excavation and dispersal of artefacts as well as the global antiquities market. Over half of the 15,000 artefacts looted from the Iraq Museum in Baghdad in 2003 remain missing, while in Syria hundreds of archaeological sites, museums and historic monuments have been damaged and looted since the onset of the civil war in 2011. One need only consult Interpol's list of stolen artefacts – which can also be read as an inventory of recent and current conflicts – to ascertain the full breadth of the illicit antiquities trade, estimated to have a yearly turnover of $10 billion.[7] **Nora Al-Badri**'s visual essay 'Babylonian Visions: Neuronal Ancestral Sculptures Series' deploys the concept of *technoheritage* – the intersection of technology and cultural heritage – to complicate notions of ownership and copyright in relation to museum collections. Training an AI with 10,000 images from the holdings of five different museums with the largest collections of Mesopotamian, Neo-Sumerian and Assyrian artefacts,

Al-Badri creates a database of new objects that speak to the desire to recreate what has been lost while querying what the future of material heritage in the digital age might look like.

Archaeology, a discipline long critiqued as a hand-maiden to colonial pursuits, was fundamental in shaping desires for, and consumable images of, the 'other' through the production of romantic ruins and the extension of the logic of salvation and preservation thrust onto both the landscape and its occupants. In her opening essay 'Still Life', archaeologist **Uzma Z. Rizvi** dives into the colonial mechanism at the core of archaeology – the division, categorisation and articulation of linear time – and with that, the measuring of distance from the past as a marker of modernity and progress; arguing instead for the emancipatory power of stillness. Drawing on references from modern and contemporary art, as well as photographs of labourers at archaeological sites in the early 20th century, Rizvi argues that the act of refusal in stillness 'engages with what has been a core premise of decolonial praxis.'

The stillness – of the photograph and in the act of watching – is the starting point of artist **Akram Zaatari**'s 'A Second Reading', a close examination of photographs taken and letters written by Osman Hamdi Bey in relation to events surrounding his 1887 excavation of 17 sarcophagi in Sidon, southern Lebanon. Osman Hamdi Bey was an artist, archaeologist, and the founder of the Imperial Museum in Constantinople, the first archaeological museum under the Ottoman Empire. He is also credited with establishing the Ottoman Archaeology Law in 1884, the first legislation governing the excavation and exportation of archaeological finds within the empire.

The interlinking of colonial and archaeological pursuits was most apparent in the Levant, and in particular in Palestine, where the field of archaeology was, and continues to be, a politicised tool for producing historical 'facts' that are, in turn, used as evidence legitimising the continued occupation and settlement of Palestinian territories.[8]

In **Dima Srouji**'s visual essay 'Sebastia: A Vignette of Apartheid from Below', we are drawn into the daily struggle of residents from the ancient town of Sebastia in Palestine – one of the longest continually inhabited places in the West Bank – to keep hold of its heritage, its land and its dignity. In conversation with local expert and activist Zaid Azhari, Srouji traces the origin of the town's struggle to a 1908 Harvard University-led excavation of its archaeological site.

Archives are never neutral spaces; they reproduce dominant power structures and social configurations. What does it mean to look at public spaces, monuments, and even given names as alternative archives and sites of collective learning and unlearning? Founder and artistic director of SAVVY Contemporary **Bonaventure Soh Bejeng Ndikung** and curator and ifa-Gallery director **Alya Sebti**'s conversation weaves through their respective practices, interrogating structures and modes of knowledge production. They pick up some of the questions put forward during the exhibition and symposium 'For the Phoenix to Find its Form in Us: On Restitution, Rehabilitation, and Reparation'[9] which took place in Berlin in August 2021 in collaboration with Art Jameel and their respective institutions.

The monument as archive is further explored in scholar and researcher **Anahi Alviso-Marino**'s visual essay 'A Monument Once Called *Kuwaiti Women, Giving and Sacrifice*'. Working from the archives of artist Khalifa Qattan, Alviso-Marino probes into the troubled history of a monument initially commissioned to commemorate female martyrs and resistance fighters during the 1990 Iraqi invasion of Kuwait, drawing attention to contested public spaces and sites of memory within shifting political contexts.

Heritage and inheritance share the same etymology and meaning – to be bequeathed something of value from others. In their contemporary usage, they imply a shift in scale, from the monumental and national to the intimate and emotional. Yet, it is in the intimate and personal spaces of intergenerational exchange that the act of passing on is negotiated daily; in the accumulation of keepsakes from a land lost, in the act of preparing food or consuming a meal together. These intimate inheritances accumulate to form a larger map of geopolitical tensions, exiles, longings and desires, as well as shared communities of hope and resistance.

In artists **Michael Rakowitz** and **Rand Abdul Jabbar**'s contributions, the diasporic home and the objects, foods and shared rituals it contains become surrogates for a lost Iraqi homeland and portals to wider reflections on intergenerational transmissions of knowledge and memory.

In **Jumana Manna**'s essay 'Where Nature Ends and Settlements Begin', the seemingly simple act of foraging wild plants around the Shu'fat Valley in East Jerusalem belies a multigenerational struggle to preserve ties to the land and ensure the continuation of Palestinian culinary and agricultural traditions, raising important questions around the tactical use of environmental legislation in the context of Palestine/Israel.

The obfuscation or altering of lines of inheritance is a well-known tactic of those seeking to lay claim to power. Artist **Pio Abad** and curator and author **Marian Pastor-Roces** discuss the politics of cultural and ethnolinguistic heritage in the Philippines, appropriated inheritance in the context of a corrupt post-colonial state, and the inheritance of hope that continues to drive their respective, politically committed practices.

The final piece of writing in this publication is a fictional short story by author **Haytham El Wardany**. 'The A in Qaf' follows the journey of two elephants, Vastator and Natator, who arrive from a future in which vowels had disappeared from language, leading to death and despair in their homeland. Guided by the hope that they would find vowels elsewhere, they reach a troubled land where speech itself is severely punished.

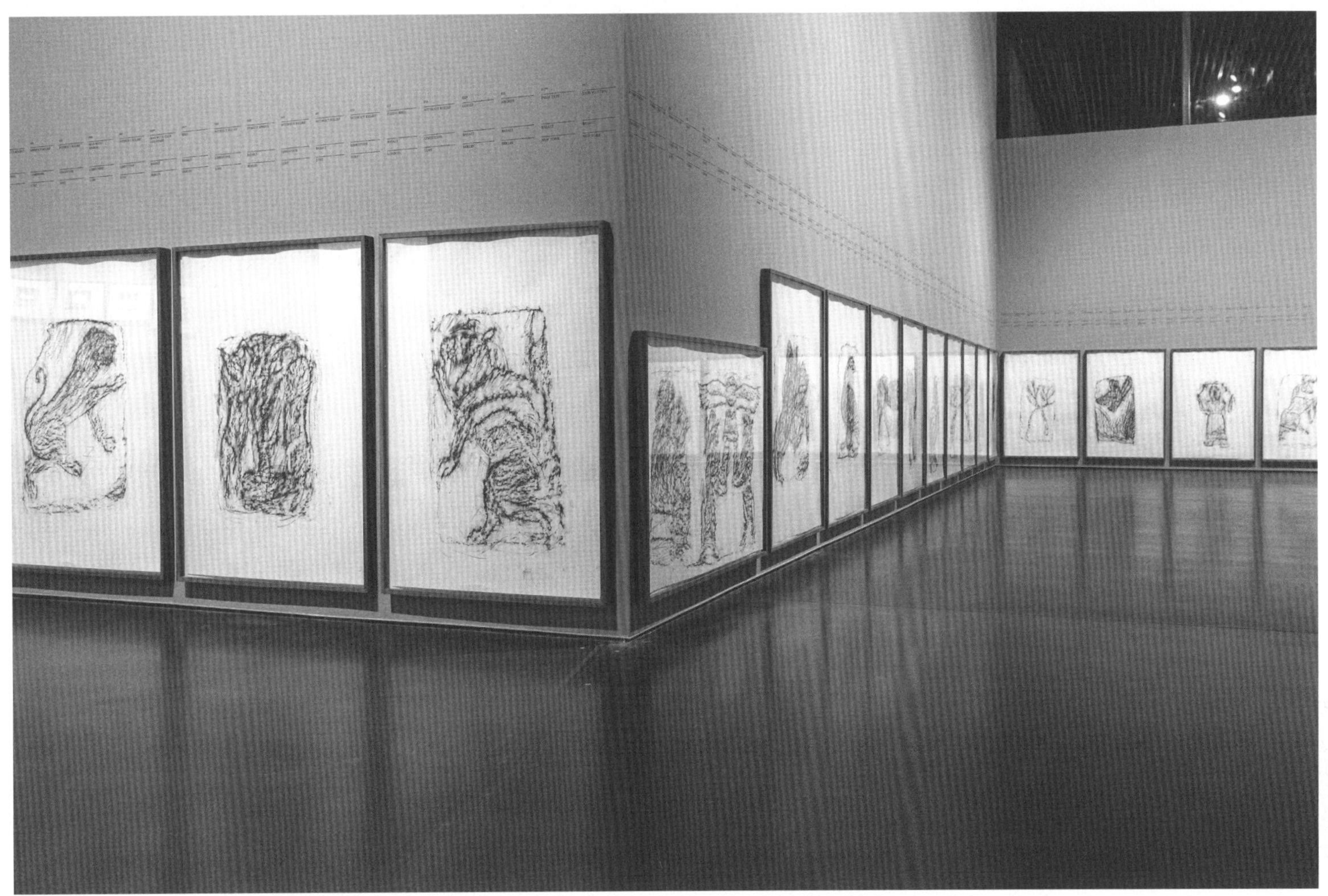

Rayyane Tabet, *Orthostates*, Jameel Arts Centre, 2017-2019. Courtesy of Art Jameel. Image credit: Daniella Baptista.

The title of this publication is indebted to the work of Berlin-based artist duo **Various&Gould**, and their ongoing engagement with the monumental shadows of German imperialism, both within and outside Germany. Together with SAVVY's *Colonial Neighbours*, they created a series of participatory projects in public spaces, taking memorialised figures from colonial-era Germany 'off the pedestal' by creating paper mouldings of monuments that were then used in performances highlighting their historical continuity with social and political issues in the present.

While many of the contributions brought together here deal with histories of struggle and their aftermath, they all celebrate the ability of objects, places and sites of commemoration to resonate with meaning across time. At the same time, many propose a more expansive and de-centred approach to caring for 'heritage' and for engaging meaningfully with the web of relations that each site or object sits within. In order to seriously think through the question of whether and how museum structures can be decolonised, reimagined and remain relevant for generations to come, we must also think seriously about questions of ownership, care, repair and reparations – whether financial or otherwise. We hope that the voices brought together here offer insights into possible ways forward while raising timely questions on what the future of museums might allow.

1   *Phantom Limb*, Jameel Arts Centre, Dubai, 9 October 2019 – 15 February 2020.
    With works by Rand Abdul Jabbar, Pio Abad and Frances Wadsworth Jones,
    Kader Attia, Benji Boyadgian, Ali Cherri, Decolonizing Architecture, Forensic
    Architecture, Jumana Manna, Théo Mercier, Khalil Rabah,
    Rayyane Tabet, and Akram Zaatari. https://jameelartscentre.org/whats-on/
    phantom-limb/

2   Raphael Greenberg and Yannis Hamilakis, *Archeology, Nation, And Race*
    (Cambridge, Cambridge University Press, 2022), p. 152.

3   Yannis Hamilakis, 'Learning from the "Vandals": Histories of Forgetting',
    LA Review of Books, 26 June 2020. https://lareviewofbooks.org/short-takes/
    learning-vandals-histories-forgetting/

4   Ariella Aïsha Azoulay, *Potential History: Unlearning Imperialism*
    (London, Verso, 2019), p. 142.

5   From the artists' website, accessed 10 November 2022.
    https://baselandruanne.com/And-yet-my-mask-is-powerful-Part-2

6   *Imperial Debris: On Ruins and Ruination*, ed. Ann Laura Stoler, Durham,
    Duke University Press, 2013, p. 11.

7   Nada El Sawy, Sinan Mahmoud, and Mina Aldroubi, 'Stealing from history:
    Inside the multimillion-dollar illegal trade in artefacts from the Middle
    East', *The National*, accessed 20 May 2022. https://www.thenationalnews.
    com/weekend/2022/05/20/inside-the-multimillion-dollar-illegal-trade-of-
    artefacts-from-the-middle/

8   For a thorough study of the role of archaeology as a tool of occupation, see
    Nadia Abu El-Haj, *Facts on the Ground: Archaeological Practice and Territorial
    Self-fashioning in Israeli Society* (Chicago, University of Chicago Press, 2001);
    Also, since 1967, Israel has used archaeological excavations as a pretext for
    territorial claims in the West Bank and Gaza. See the sources below:

    https://www.thenational.ae/world/mena/palestinians-say-east-jerusalem-
    archaeology-project-inaugurated-by-us-is-fake-1.881837
    https://www.msn.com/ar-eg/news/other/what-happened-to-gaza-s-apollo-
    statue/ar-AA2sLM
    https://www.theguardian.com/world/2010/may/26/jerusalem-city-of-david-
    palestinians-archaeology

9   For more information, see:
    https://savvy-contemporary.com/en/events/2021/phoenix-invocations/

Biographies

PIO ABAD

b. 1983, lives and works in London, United Kingdom.

Deeply informed by the modern history of the Philippines, Pio Abad's work reflects on the role of family as archive and agent, employing strategies of appropriation to mine alternative or repressed historical events, unravel official accounts, and draw out threads of complicity between incidents, ideologies, and people.

BASEL ABBAS AND RUANNE ABOU-RAHME

b. 1983, live and work in New York, USA.

Artists Basel Abbas and Ruanne Abou-Rahme work together across a range of mediums, including sound, image, text, installation, and performance. Their largely research-based practice engages with the intersections of performativity, political imaginaries, the body, and virtuality.

RAND ABDUL JABBAR

b. 1990, lives and works in Abu Dhabi, UAE.

Rand Abdul Jabbar borrows from and reconstructs the ephemera of place, history, and memory, employing design, sculpture, and installation as her primary mediums of operation. Examining and engaging with historical, cultural, and archaeological narratives, she interrogates the fragility of tangible heritage to create and compose forms that draw on artefacts, architecture, and mythology.

NORA AL-BADRI

b. 1984, lives and works in Berlin, Germany.

Nora Al-Badri is a German-Iraqi multi-disciplinary and conceptual media artist. Her research-based works are paradisciplinary, post-colonial, and post-digital. Her practice focuses on the politics and the emancipatory potential of new technologies, such as machine intelligence or data sculpting, non-human agency, and transcendence.

ANAHI ALVISO-MARINO

lives and works in Paris, France.

Anahi Alviso-Marino is a political scientist interested in the sociological lives of public sculptures created by artists across cities of the Arabian Peninsula. Her methodological approach lies at the intersection of social sciences and artistic practice. She has conducted fieldwork in Yemen, Kuwait, Oman, and the United Arab Emirates, focusing on archival research and the study of monumental public artworks.

NOAH ANGELL

b. 1980, lives and works in Berlin, Germany.

Noah Angell is a writer and artist who works with the transmission of oral traditions, including storytelling and song. He is currently working on his first book, *Ghosts of the British Museum*. Since 2016, Angell has collected testimonies from current and former British Museum staff that describe unquiet objects and unruly human remains that contest the conditions of their storage and display.

ARIELLA AÏSHA AZOULAY

b. 1962, lives and works in Providence, USA.

Ariella Aïsha Azoulay is a curator, filmmaker, and Professor of Modern Culture and Media in the Department of Comparative Literature at Brown University. Her work focuses on the violence of imperial boundary-making, suggesting a hitherto under-recognised relationship between documented cultural artefacts and undocumented migrants.

OMAR BERRADA

b. 1980, lives and works in New York, USA.

Omar Berrada is a writer, curator, and the director of Dar al-Ma'mûn, a library and artists residency in Marrakesh. His work focuses on the politics of translation and intergenerational transmission. He currently teaches at The Cooper Union's School of Art in New York City, where he co-organises the Intra-Disciplinary Seminar (IDS) lecture series.

HAYTHAM EL WARDANY

b. 1972, lives and works in Berlin, Germany.

Haytham El Wardany is a writer, translator, and the author of *How to Disappear* (2013) and (2017). Combining fragments of poetry, philosophical reflection, and storytelling, El Wardany destabilises the active/passive binary that is foundational to our perception of political resistance, instead circling around a subject rife with metaphor.

FAUSTIN LINYEKULA

b. 1974, lives and works in Kisangani, Democratic Republic of the Congo.

Faustin Linyekula is a dancer, choreographer, and stage director. In 1997, he founded Gàara, Kenya's first contemporary dance company. In 2001, he founded Studios Kabako, a platform for dance and theatre located in Kinshasa with a mission to promote cultural dialogue, research, and artistic creation.

JUMANA MANNA

b. 1987, lives and works in Berlin, Germany.

Jumana Manna is a visual artist and filmmaker, who was raised in Jerusalem. Her work explores the ways in which power is articulated, focusing on the body, land, and materiality in relation to colonial inheritances and histories of place. Through sculpture, filmmaking, and writing, Manna deals with the paradoxes of preservation practices, particularly within the fields of archaeology, agriculture, and law.

BONAVENTURE SOH BEJENG NDIKUNG

b. 1977, lives and works in Berlin, Germany.

Prof. Dr. Bonaventure Soh Bejeng Ndikung is a curator, writer, and biotechnologist. He is the director of Haus der Kulturen der Welt (HKW) in Berlin. He is the founder and former artistic director of SAVVY Contemporary in Berlin and was the artistic director of Sonsbeek20–24, a quadrennial contemporary art exhibition in Arnhem, the Netherlands.

MARIAN PASTOR ROCES
lives and works in Manila, the Philippines.

Marian Pastor Roces is a Filipina independent curator, art historian, and critic of institutions. Published internationally, her critical writing is sustained by an enduring engagement with social justice concerns in museology, clothing, cities, contemporary art, and cultural change.

GALA PORRAS-KIM
b. 1984, lives and works in Los Angeles, USA.

Gala Porras-Kim is an artist. Her research-based practice considers how sounds, language, and history are represented through methodologies of linguistics and conservation.

MICHAEL RAKOWITZ
b. 1973, lives and works in Chicago, USA.

Michael Rakowitz is an Iraqi-American artist working at the intersection of problem-solving and troublemaking.

NORA RAZIAN
b. 1980, lives and works in Dubai, UAE.

Nora Razian is Head of Exhibitions at Art Jameel, where she curates exhibitions and oversees the global exhibitions programme. Previously, she was Head of Exhibitions and Programmes at the Sursock Museum, Beirut (2015 – 2017) where she spearheaded the museum's reopening programme following a seven-year closure; and Curator of Public Programmes at Tate, London (2009 – 2015).

UZMA Z. RIZVI
b. 1973, lives and works in Brooklyn, USA.

Uzma Z. Rizvi is Associate Professor of Anthropology and Urban Studies at Pratt Institute, New York City. Rizvi's work interweaves archaeology with cultural criticism, philosophy, critical theory, art, and design.

ALYA SEBTI
b. 1983, lives and works in Berlin, Germany.

Alya Sebti is the director of the ifa-Gallery Berlin (Institute for Foreign Cultural Relations). She has written and lectured extensively on art and the public sphere, biennials, and transcultural art practices.

DIMA SROUJI
lives and works in Ramallah, Palestine.

Dima Srouji is an architect and visual artist. Her work explores the ground as a deep space of rich cultural weight, where imaginary liberation is possible. She founded Hollow Forms Studio in 2016.

AKRAM ZAATARI
b. 1966, lives and works in Beirut, Lebanon.

Akram Zaatari is an artist whose practice explores a range of interconnected themes, subjects, and practices related to excavation, political resistance, the lives of former militants, the legacy of an exhausted left, the circulation of images in times of war, and letters that have been lost, found, buried, discovered, or otherwise delayed in reaching their destinations.

Texts and interviews

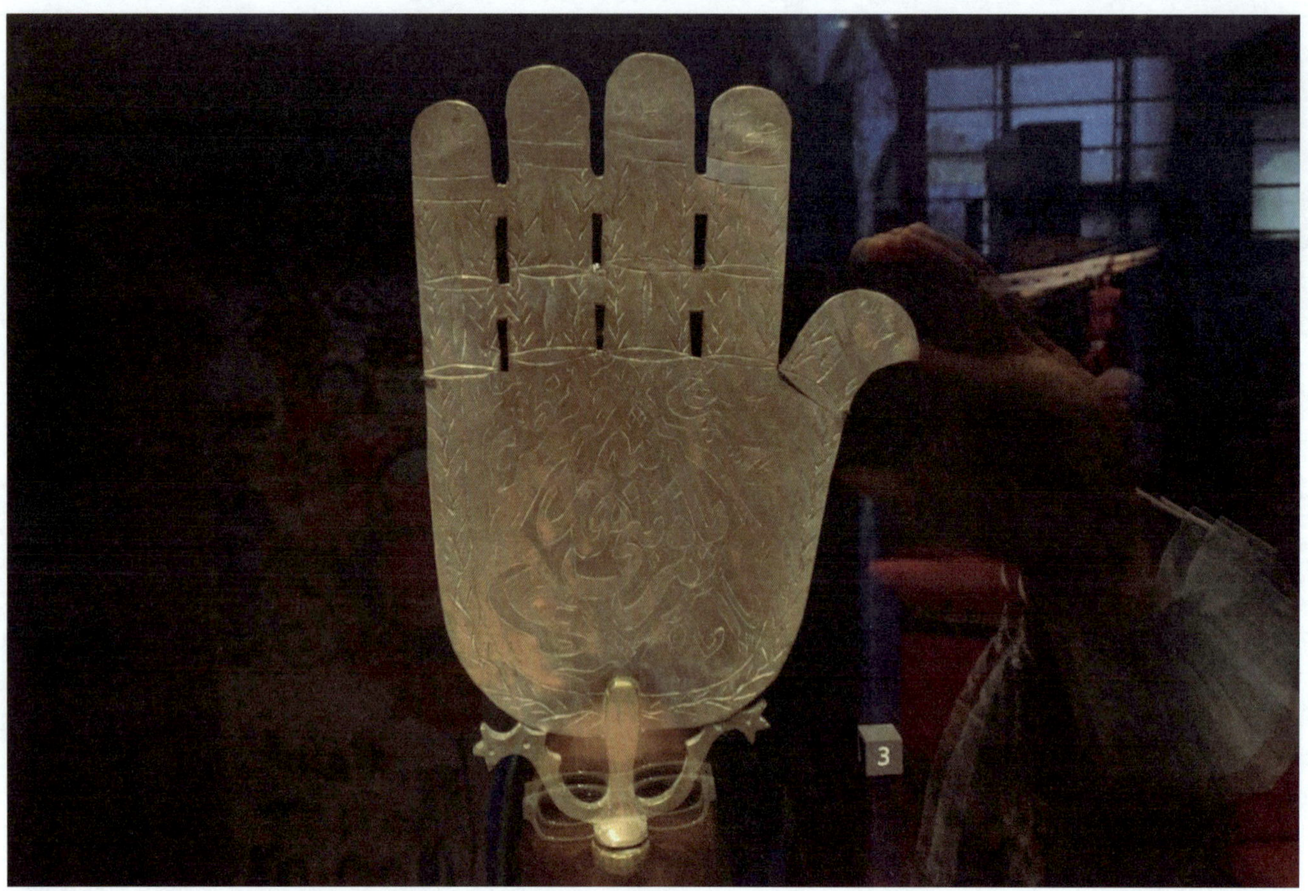

Processional standard ('Alam), Iran, early 20th century. 71.1991.281.120. White metal, 29×18×2.5 cm.
Musée du Quai Branly collection. Courtesy of the author, 2022.

Uzma Z. Rizvi

Still Life

Every time I walk into a museum, I am startled and unsure.

I see facets of myself within everything kept behind glass. The glass reflects the ways by which I am held in place by a logic at the root of archaeological practice: a colonial logic that holds me in place as the archaeologist, and the artefact as an object to be studied. The glass between us barely contains the artefacts' dismay and reflects my shame in having to see them all on display, again.

As I walk through museums, I am reminded of films like *Les statues meurent aussi* (1953)[1] and *Somniculus* (2017).[2] My heart stills to recognise the lives that these films draw our attention to within the museum. In those spaces, there is stillness, an almost quiet recognition. We, the artefact and I, become so still that one may think we are inanimate – perhaps, sleeping. I find in this slowness, this quietness, this stillness, something intentional and decolonial to its core.

Slowness allows for a pragmatic approach to a critical engagement speaking back to the requirements of supermodernity.[3] Rather than giving in to the acceleration of history, a slow praxis provides the space for many interpretations. The idea of still life is a paradox in and of itself, one that belies its modern desire to control through representation. On the National Gallery in London's website, the definition of still life starts off with the inanimacy of objects:

> Inanimate objects such as fruit, flowers, food and everyday items are painted as the main focus of interest in still lifes. The term derives from the Dutch 'stilleven', which became current from about 1650 as a collective name for this type of subject matter. Still-life painting...was particularly popular in the Netherlands during the 17th century and was often associated with material decay and the futility of worldly life.[4]

1   Alain Resnais, Chris Marker, and Ghislain Cloquet, *Les statues meurent aussi* (Statues Also Die), France: Présence Africaine, Tadié Cinéma, 1953.

2   Ali Cherri, *Somniculus*, Paris: Jeu de Paume, Fondation Nationale des Arts Graphiques et Plastiques, and CAPC Musée d'art contemporain de Bordeaux, 2017, HD video, 14 min 40 sec.

3   Alfredo González-Ruibal, 'Time to Destroy: An Archaeology of Supermodernity', *Current Anthropology*, no. 49 2008, pp. 247-279.

4   'Glossary: Still lives', National Gallery, accessed 7 June 2022. https://www.nationalgallery.org.uk/paintings/glossary/still-lives

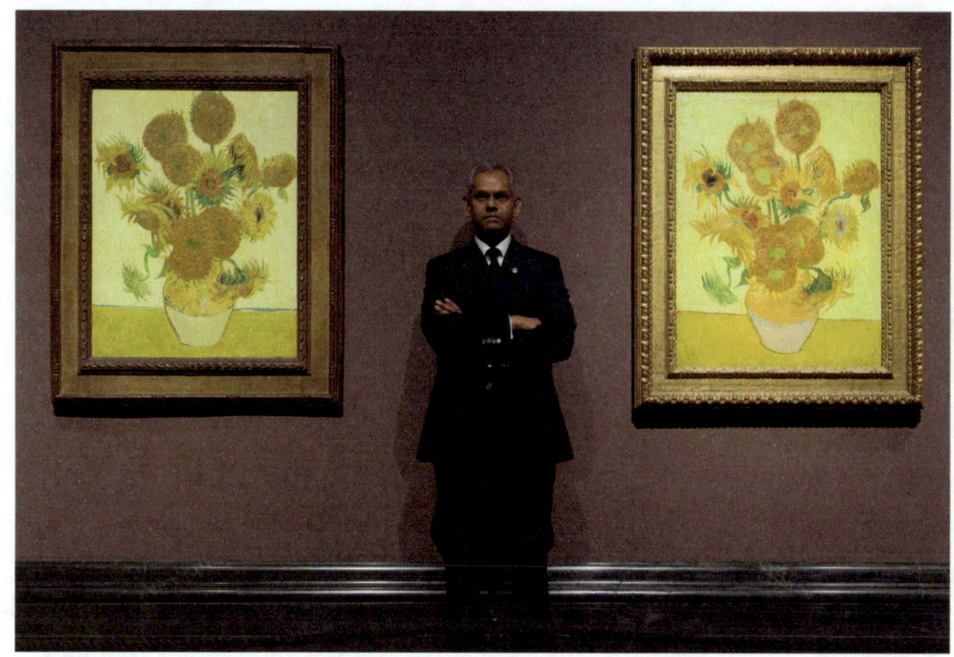

Leon Neal/AFP. A gallery supervisor poses for photographs with two versions of Dutch artist Vincent van Gogh's *Sunflowers* paintings at the National Gallery in London on 24 January 2014. Brought together for the first time in 65 years, the National Gallery's own *Sunflowers* (1888) is joined by the Van Gogh Museum's *Sunflowers* (1889) until 27 April 2014. Digital photograph. Courtesy of AFP Photo.

It is this assumption, insistence, and matter-of-factness of inanimacy that I dwell upon. A well-circulated image in 2014 was that of Vincent van Gogh's 1888 (left) and 1889 (right) versions of the *Sunflowers* series. Reports spoke of how these two paintings were reunited after 65 years.[5] There was a lot of excitement, as if they were twins separated at birth. I consider these forms of representation, still lifes – both the sunflowers and the guard standing between them.

The fields of art and anthropology intersect once photography, in particular scientific photography, enters our discursive spaces. Daguerreotype – a truly slow practice – emerged as a way to capture the notion of still life more accurately. In what seems to be bustling with animacy, narrative, and meaning is Louis Daguerre's daguerreotype *Intérieur d'un cabinet de curiosité* also known as *L'Atelier de l'artiste* (The Artist's Studio)(1837), in which the space of a certain kind of existence is documented. Each piece in this image has stories in the multiples. It is as if the stillness is overflowing out of the frame and into our imaginations. To have images within images, to have pathos and expression captured by this early technology, belies the colonial desire to control, to hold, to capture that feeling and the memory of a space within which dreams unfold. With these early images, the paradox of still life is set.

These one-of-a-kind photographic images on a highly polished silver-plated sheet of copper sensitised with iodine vapours, exposed in a large box camera, developed in mercury fumes and stabilised (or fixed) with salt water or 'hypo' (sodium thiosulphate), were remarkable not only because of their ability to capture. This process created a visual record as a fact, particularly as a way to document

5   'The 10 Most Expensive Paintings on Public Display', *Business Insider*, accessed 7 June 2022. https://www.businessinsider.com/the-10-most-expensive-paintings-on-public-display-2014-2.

Uzma Z. Rizvi

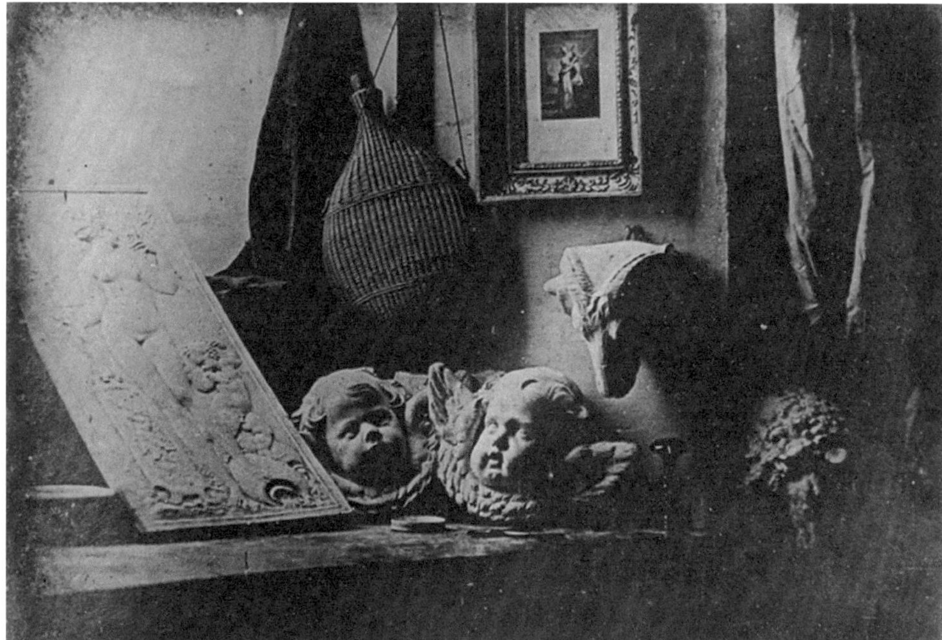

Louis Daguerre. *Intérieur d'un cabinet de curiosité (Interior of a Cabinet of Curiosities)*, 1837. Daguerreotype, 16.5×23 cm. Collection of the Société française de photographie.

non-textual information. Anthropologists began to use these techniques to study and create the image of the 'other'. Notably, the photographic collections from Harvard's Peabody Museum contain early forms of ethnographic documentation. In particular, daguerreotypes commissioned in 1850 by Swiss naturalist Louis Agassiz and photographed by Lorenzo G. Chase created the image as a form of collection, as a form of documentation, as a form of object-making. This visual construction of otherness seamlessly merged with the technical and aesthetic choices of still life.

In *From Here I Saw What Happened and I Cried* (1995 – 1996), artist Carrie Mae Weems revealed how these 1850 daguerreotypes were intended as visual evidence to support Agassiz's theories of the racial inferiority of Africans and to prepare a taxonomy of physical types in the enslaved population. As a gesture of reappropriation and critique, Weems utilised the daguerreotypes that she found at the Peabody Museum and Harvard University archives as a backdrop against which she placed a reflective glass with etched text.[6] Her critique forces us to see our own reflections, and thus, our complicity, as we peer in to see the piece. What does it mean to operate within these systems of violence? What does it mean to be complicit with slow and systematic forms of ongoing inequity and dispossession in and under the guise of scientific knowledge production?

In 'Visions of a discipline', anthropologist Ashish Chadha focuses on the epistemological similarities between the construction of archaeological knowledge, archaeological evidence, and the nature of archaeological representation, particularly within the archive of 20th-century British archaeologist Mortimer Wheeler.[7] Simply put, the brown bodies in Wheeler's frame are only used for scale. Chadha

6   For a brilliant reading of this work, see Eunsong Kim, 'Found, Found, Found, Lived, Lived, Lived', *Scapegoat*, no. 9, Eros, 2016, pp. 53-60.
For additional context, see 'Case Review: Lanier v. Harvard (2021)', Center for art law, accessed 18 August 2022. https://itsartlaw.org/2021/07/27/case-review-lanier-v-harvard-2021/

7   Ashish Chadha. 'Visions of a Discipline: Sir Mortimer Wheeler and the archaeological method in India (1944-1948)', *Journal of Social Archaeology*, no. 2, 2002, pp. 378-401.

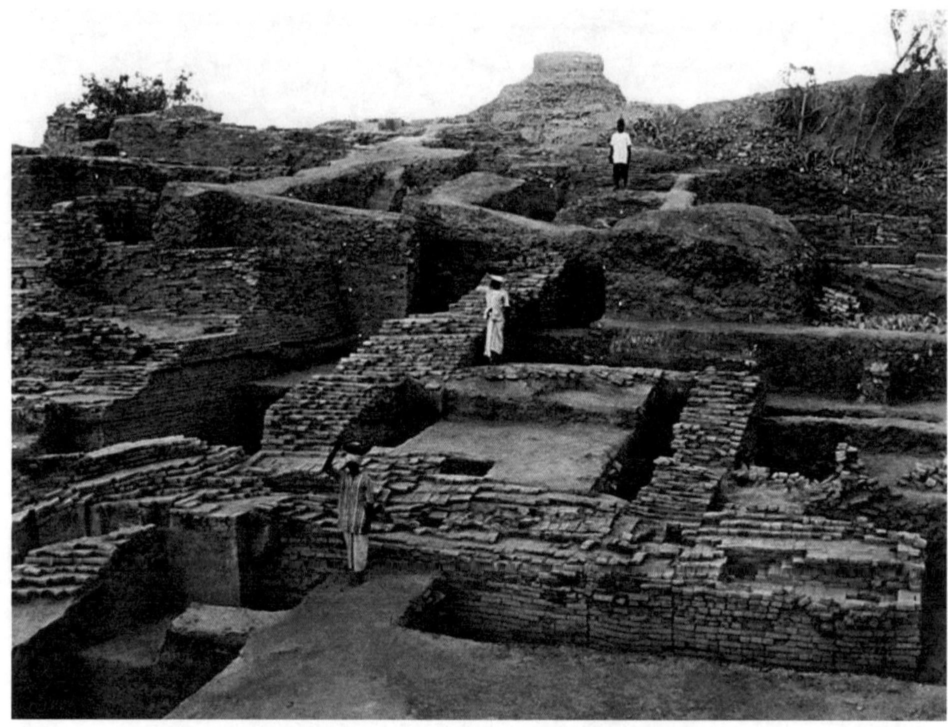

Mortimer Wheeler. *REM Granary, Western Edge of Citadel, Mohenjo-daro* [122 A], 1950. Courtesy of Harappa.com.

argues that through these photographs, Wheeler deftly brings together the disciplinary ideologies of the colonial, scientific, and military projects. And significant to the argument I am putting forward, Chadha argues that this was articulated by appropriating the ideas of an epistemic marker and ethnic marker as visual tropes. This approach to archaeological documentation makes the bodies into objects, inanimate and controlled through a colonial gaze.

These visual forms of marking link colonial ways of seeing and documenting to contemporary visual tropes in forms of reporting – and here I will ask that you recall the image of Van Gogh's paintings flanking the brown body of the gallery security guard.[8] I am also thinking carefully about Ariella Aïsha Azoulay's recommendation in *The Civil Contract of Photography* (2008) that we should not just look at photographs but 'watch them'.[9] As you watch these photographs, narratives begin to fill in the spaces, and I can hear the ways through which Wheeler admonishes workers on the site. He documented his own militaristic control in the 1948 edition of *Ancient Pakistan*, where he details how best to deal with labourers – those so-called 'lazy natives' who like to nap under baskets behind the mound. His article can be read as a handbook to discipline the slow and reticent labourer as an archaeological excavation method. These methods are a part of the modernisation of the scientific project.

In Egypt, modernisation was understood as a mode of colonial control and visuality. During the 1919 revolution against British occupation, protests were directed, among other demands, against newly installed electric streetlights, which were

8   This also links to my recent work on the colonial archival film footage from the United Arab Emirates, the body of the guard and the labour as epistemic and ethnic markers of control. See: 'The Chowkidar: Epistemic Markers and Transnational Labor Flows', in *Currency: A Critical Reader*, ed. Oluremi C. Onabanjo, Hatje Cantz, 2022, 8th edition of the Triennial of Photography of Hamburg.

9   Ariella Aïsha Azoulay, *The Civil Contract of Photography*, New York, Zone Books, 2008.

                                                                Uzma Z. Rizvi

seen as an oppressive measure to impose order through nighttime visibility. In 1945, Egyptian author Albert Cossery published a brilliant satire titled *Laziness in the Fertile Valley*, calling out the implications of modernisation in Egypt after the Unilateral Declaration of Egyptian Independence in 1922, in which the United Kingdom recognised Egypt as a sovereign nation.[10] Cossery's novel confronts the stereotype of the 'lazy native', recasting it within the discursive and political realm of resistance and rebellion. At the heart of this novel is the idea that modernity is not always progressive or moral. In fact, it can be at times, as Cossery argues, profoundly anti-humanistic. His work brings us to the consideration of slowness as resistance.

In an early part of the book, Cossery sets this up with an encounter between one of the protagonists, Serag, and a young boy:

> Once more Serag looked at the child. This time he felt a shock in his chest. His legs gave way under him as though they had been cut. The child continued his hunt within an increased frenzy. It was no longer a human thing; it was as though a demonic force were attacking the void with fury. Serag looked at the boy without believing in him. He was seized by an imperative need for sleep. But how to sleep before this absurd and annihilating vision? At bottom, the thing that terrified him the most in this mad agitation was the mystery that it seemed to conceal – the mystery of a monstrous universe, filled with men overwhelmed by work and succumbing under the strain. He couldn't be wrong about this. Serag recognized in the child's insane frenzy all the signs of a laboring and trapped humanity.

As a response to frenetic, insane, absurd, and even demonic energy, Cossery stills his protagonist. Using that as a rhetorical gesture, he provides insight into the critique where stillness becomes that place between frenzy and sleep.

Rebecca Solnit's 2007 piece *Finding Time* ends with this realisation: 'Ultimately, I believe that slowness is an act of resistance, not because slowness is a good in itself but because of all that it makes room for, the things that don't get measured and can't be bought.'[11] To me, this engages with what has been a core premise of decolonial praxis. Within that space of what cannot be measured nor bought, slowing down provides the brown bodies labouring in images the capacity to resist being that epistemic marker of scale. As such, the bodies that Wheeler describes as lazy and sleeping behind the mounds are bodies in resistance. They are claiming their right to be human. To be still. To be life.

Slowness opens up space to become still to watch these images and to listen to their quiet stillness. As Tina Campt has reminded us in *Listening to Images* (2017): 'Quiet is not an absence of articulation or utterance. Quiet is a modality that surrounds and infuses sound with impact and affect, which creates the possibility for it to register as meaningful.'[12] Campt's work allows one to find meaning in stillness. It leads us to listen to what we have been conditioned to see as silent as a form of quietness, opening the space to consider quiet things as resistant, and thus, full of a different agency. The narrative of discursive and archaeological

10 Albert Cossery, *Laziness in the Fertile Valley*, trans. William Goyen, New York, New Directions Publishing, 1945, 2013.

11 Rebecca Solnit, 'Finding Time', *Orion Magazine*, accessed 7 June 2022. https://orionmagazine. org/article/a-fistful-of-time/

12 Tina Campt, *Listening to Images*, Durham, Duke University Press, 2017.

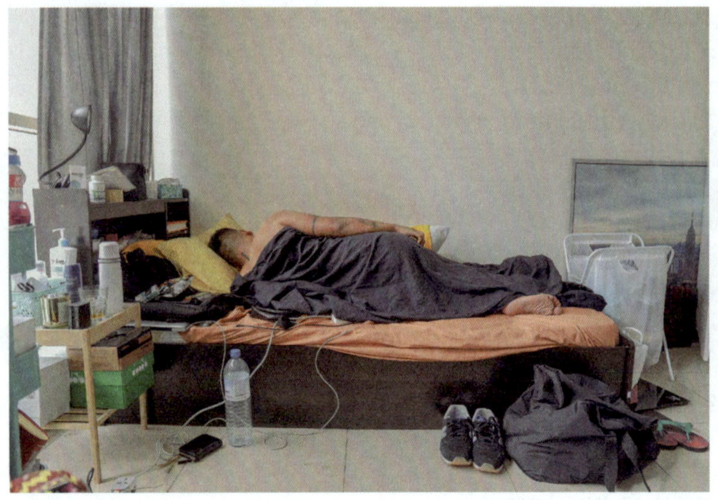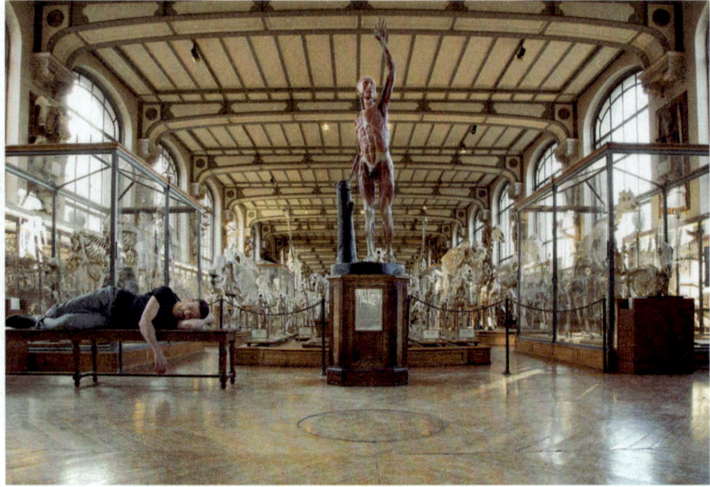

Left: Augustine Paredes. *How to Slouch When Sleeping*, 2018. Photographic print. Courtesy of the artist.
Right: Ali Cherri. *Still Life*, 2017. Lightbox, Duratrans photographic print, 150×95 cm. Courtesy of the artist and Galerie Imane Farès.

representation may be recognised as having a contemporary context of quietness, a sonic form that one has to learn what to listen for or to.

And so, we are still. And keen to learn, to know how to reclaim life from stillness. But who we are and where we come from influences how we understand and see what we hear. It is also the same space that suddenly muddles the context all around us. What remains is the stillness of our bodies in particular spaces, anchored to our histories. Those histories, when placed in museums, become spotlessly clean and articulate, even though we all know that life itself is messy, loud, queer, and uncivilised. We see the shadows of the museum ooze beyond their walls and creep their way into white cube propriety. For *othered* bodies, like my own, we see how the ethnographic markers from the museums find their way onto us as we walk through the art world and the academy. This is why, perhaps, stillness appeals to our senses.

As Cossery alluded to, stillness is that space between sleep and frenzy. It is a position of insight. The museum may capture our bodies in that stillness; behind the glass; on the shelf; maybe on a bench; maybe on a bed, as in Augustine Paredes's still self-portrait *How to Slouch When Sleeping* (2018). But sleep is not inanimate. Rather, this stillness holds an emancipatory power. We may recognise stillness as a decolonial and queering instance as it is in that space that we become multiple and non-normative. We are the artefacts behind the glass; we are the ceramic bowls; we are the beaded designs; and we are the bodies you put into the closets and in storage. We are the researcher. We are the artefacts.

Look again when you come to the museum, and you will see us, still. You will see us in our new habitats, sharing space with otherness. If you slow down long enough, you might see our bodies and lives and work not as markers or approximations, nor as measurements of ethnicity, race, sexuality, or class. Nor might you appropriate our image for epistemic fodder about the *other*.

Uzma Z. Rizvi

Instead, in our slowness, we will create meaning for what you see. In this space, we lay waiting, messy and uncivilised, all at once. We continue to be dismayed at being held in place, at being held within this stillness. Can you hear us asking, when will this violence of collection end? Can you feel our dismay through the glass as you walk by?

This is where you see us as *Still Life*.

Faustin Linyekula and Omar Berrada

Releasing History

In 2017, dancer-choreographer Faustin Linyekula premiered *Banataba* at the Metropolitan Museum of Art in New York (Met).[1] The work emerged from his encounter with a statue in the museum's storerooms, which took him on a physical and spiritual journey to his ancestors' village in the Democratic Republic of Congo (DRC), and an ongoing reflection on looted pasts and mended futures. I wanted to take *Banataba* as a point of entry into a discussion about restitution. As always with Faustin, who likes to introduce himself as a storyteller, the conversation took many turns. We recorded it in August 2021, in French, via Zoom. I was in Casablanca visiting my parents; Faustin was in Düsseldorf presenting *Statue of Loss*, another choreographic work on colonial remains.[2]

OMAR BERRADA

I'd like to begin by sharing the opening lines of an essay titled 'Waste', which appeared in 1967 in the Moroccan journal *Souffles*. It was written by the poet Abdellatif Laâbi, the journal's founder, who was 25 years old at the time. This is how it starts:

'For over half a century, the history of Moroccan art has been a European speciality, monopolised by Western science.'

There's little point here to joining the debate that, when examining recent endeavours by Moroccans to reconsider our art, sees nothing but an artificial curiosity sparked by reading foreign analyses and criticism. The interest we might take in our art, however belated, in no way reflects a fascination with folklore, nor is it a bourgeois imitation of the thirst foreigners have developed for it. If European specialists or mere collectors have awakened our interest in our own art, it does not mean that our curiosity will only extend as far as competing in the hunt for treasures or a chauvinistic admiration for our artistic traditions. On the contrary,

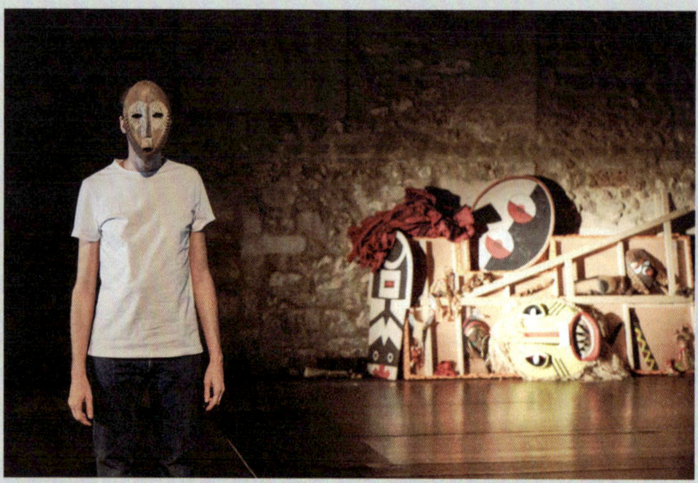

Faustin Linyekula, *Histoire(s) du théâtre II*, 2019.
Image credit: Agathe Poupeney.

understanding and valorising that heritage is part of a desire for its complete retrieval, which is essential for our restructuring.[3]

FAUSTIN LINYEKULA

That makes me think of the *Kongo: Power and Majesty* exhibition held at the Metropolitan Museum in 2015, with totemic power sculptures called Nkisi.[4] I was passing through New York at the time, and was rather sad when I left the museum. The written archives available in the Congo date back 150 or 200 years at most, and they're the victor's archives, completely biased. And yet, our ancestors did invent a kind of writing; they tried to pass down history through sculptures like the ones displayed at the Met. The museum had gathered pieces from collections scattered throughout the world, but there was no way for a Congolese kid to access that archive. The tools we use to express or try to make sense of who we are, even slightly, remain at the sole disposal of a small group of privileged individuals in the West. That's the perspective from which I understand the 'desire for complete retrieval, essential for our restructuring' that Laâbi talks about.

How is restructuring possible when we no longer have access to those archives? Under these conditions, how can we inhabit this territory that's supposedly ours? I'm reminded of a quote from Adonis: 'How can I walk towards myself, towards my people, when my blood is fire, my history a heap of ruins?'[5] I wonder if gaining access to those archives might be a possible response. Can a full knowledge and understanding of all that art

respond to the dismemberment, the dislocation, the ruin? I can't claim so with absolute certainty but at least we could begin the journey.

OB Laâbi also said that this is only one step on the path to reconstruction. Since you're talking about archives, I want to point out that the passage I quoted comes from a section of the essay that's titled 'Releasing History'. As if to say that history – our history – was imprisoned, or that it was interrupted.

FL Or held hostage. At some point, Europe decreed that other people had no history, that the history of the 'other' began with the arrival of Europeans. And even today, we look at ourselves with a European gaze. This is painfully evident in the academic milieu of francophone Africa. When an African talks about Africa, I'll often get the feeling that a European is speaking through them. How can we 'release' that history? How can we emancipate ourselves from a gaze that was constructed for us?

In the DRC, today still, history textbooks teach us that the mouth of the Congo River was discovered in 1482 by Diogo Cão, a Portuguese explorer. If you go to the Royal Museum for Central Africa in Tervuren, Belgium, you'll be confronted with a narrative according to which there was nothing but chaos until civilisation arrived, via King Leopold II's envoys. We were saved from the Arab slave trade and finally became a part of history. How can we let go of that history, how can we release or liberate it? When Belgium eventually announced that it was willing to return stolen cultural objects to the Congo, we were told we weren't ready to receive them yet – in other words, we didn't have the museums to host them.

And this is where I start asking myself: 'Aren't we in fact just rewriting European history on African soil?' Four years ago, when I went to Banataba, the village where my maternal grandfather was born, I was surprised to see that the sculptures there weren't always thought to be precious objects. A sculpture was just a piece of wood in the corner of a room. A piece of wood impacted by the elements: humidity, tiny bugs… Dogs would rub against them. And then comes the moment when a ceremony takes place. You bring out the piece of wood, you activate it, and then – it becomes magical. These objects aren't magical all the time. They're only magical once they've been activated. What does it mean when we talk about restitution, about repatriating these objects to museums where, once again, only a select few can access them? If these are the archives, we need to fully rediscover our own experience, how can they be accessed when they're in the National Museum of Kinshasa? If we're still dealing with a museum structure, have we really liberated history?

There were similar instincts during the independence movements, in Guinea, for example. Sékou Touré believed that one of the newly independent nation's worst enemies wasn't so much neo-colonialism as it was tribalism. His question was: 'How can we move past tribalism? How can we teach the people what it means to be Guinean?' His response was: 'Let's create a national ballet.' But what is a national ballet? A space where all the country's various dances and music are gathered, and by the mere virtue of being brought together, there will no longer be the Baluba dance, the Lokele dance, etc., but the national dance instead. As a dancer, I find it fascinating that a nation-building project could be conceived of as occurring in and through the body. It could have been a tremendous testing ground. Except that, like all politicians, he wasn't there to ask questions. He wanted to dictate answers to the body. It wasn't a matter of wondering, 'What does it mean to be Guinean?' but about saying: '"This" is what it means to be Guinean.' I also find it fascinating that he decided to call it a 'ballet' because you can't get any more Western than that. Mobutu did the same thing later on. The search for what is authentically Guinean or Zairian occurred by way of a structure that reproduced the colonial legacy. They built theatres with stages in frontal configurations.

FL That's the dark side of restitution. African countries are racing to build new museums so they can convince Europeans that they deserve to have their objects returned. We're still good little students. And on top of that emulation, there's also, as you alluded to, a form of classism. Ultimately, that's what independence was: nations established within colonial borders became the exclusive domains of local bourgeois elites subservient to European interests. Frantz Fanon warned us, but we're in the thick of it. The African elites that insist on having museums full of objects in their countries are the same people who can easily go see them in Europe or the United States. The risk is, by cannibalising

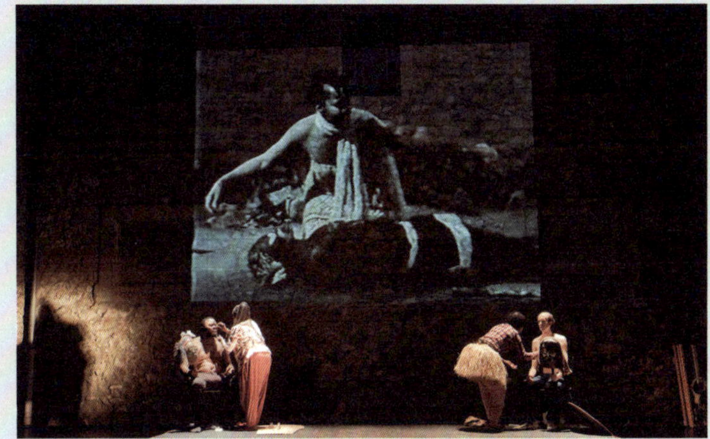
Faustin Linyekula, *Histoire(s) du théâtre II*, 2019.
Image credit: Agathe Poupeney.

the process of restitution, that copycat desire for the museum institution ultimately hinders the larger project of the 'complete retrieval' of ourselves and our experiences.

FL That's true of language, too. For example, the DRC is a country where public life is structured in French. You'll often hear that the Congo is the largest French-speaking country. But the percentage of people with a solid grasp of French doesn't exceed 20% of the population. What does it mean to structure public life in a language that excludes the staggering majority of people? It becomes a way for the francophone elite who hold power to continue to benefit from it for their own profit. For example, in parliament, there might be a deputy with important things to say. But because he cannot speak French and is forced to clamber through the language, he expresses himself badly. The others, like kids in a playground, will start laughing and all his words will literally drown in the language. There's a reason we have this popular expression in Lingala: 'Français nde eboma mboka oyo.' Literally, 'It's the French language that killed this country.' The worst part is that I belong to that elite as well and, in a way, I benefit, too.

OB Let's talk about your show *Banataba*. It all began with an invitation to use the collections at the Metropolitan Museum as inspiration. But that trip to New York sent you back to the Congo under very specific, personal circumstances. I'd love for you to tell me a little more about that trip and the show that came out of it, and notably about the statue in pieces that you dance with.

FL To respond, I need to go back to that awareness of the ruins I mentioned earlier. Wherever I go, I feel like I'm always looking for the Congo, because I know that there are many little pieces of it that have been scattered throughout the world. And since I belong to the privileged elite that can travel anywhere, even though borders are growing taller and taller, I keep trying. Every time, the action is twofold: I leave to find the Congo outside of me, but also the Congo inside of me. Congo as a physical space, but also, simultaneously, an imaginary space that I've been trying to understand for many years, and which continues to elude me. At the Metropolitan, I found a wooden statue in storage, with the label 'Lengola people', which is my mother's tribe. I couldn't have found anything closer to home. They say all statues that went through a ceremony contain souls. But this was the only statue from the Lengola people in the museum. What must it be like for it to be thousands of miles away from home, all alone?.

I called my mother from New York and told her, 'I just found something extraordinary here and I'd like to make a trip to Banataba, where I've never been.' She told me, 'You went there when you were one year old. It was 1975 and even I haven't gone back since.' I asked, 'Why don't you come with me?' We made the trip. I brought photos of the sculpture from the Met. For me, the most important thing was to find out if there were still people in the village who remembered that kind of sculpture. Were these sculptures still present in people's lives there or had they completely disappeared?

I told myself that if there were people for whom this was still important and who knew how to make them, I could bring a sculpture from Banataba to New York, and that way the sculpture at the Met would have some company. But I couldn't, of course, because right away the museum said: 'No, you can't bring in an object like that as a work of art; that's impossible. But if you tell us that it's a stage prop and not a piece of art, then it can come into the museum.' And so, at least for as long as we remained in the museum performing the show, I could tell myself that there was another Lengola presence in one of the galleries and maybe they could communicate with one another.

Except that the sculpture I brought back hadn't gone through a ceremony. Back home, when a sculptor produces a work, sometimes it's meant to serve in a ritual. After a ritual, that work is invested with power. It might even be inhabited by a soul. When I went back to Banataba, there was a ceremony during which a sculpture that I had bought from a local artist was invested with power. The ceremony was an initiation ritual, so that I would be allowed to sit with the elders of my village. But I said to myself, 'Given that everything of value in our country has been taken abroad, for many centuries, what would it mean for me to bring back this sculpture to the Met or other museums where this project might be staged? Am I not perpetuating the pillage myself? Wouldn't it be best to leave this sculpture in Banataba in the safekeeping of my uncle André, the clan chief?'

Which is what I did. But since I was attached to the idea of bringing a sculpture that came from the Lengola people to the Met, I had another one made, without going through a ceremony, telling myself that since it was a tree that had been cut down in that region, that was hand-sculpted there, that had heard voices there, it might still tell stories to the other sculpture that was in New York. So, on one hand, it's a precious object, but at the same time, I know it's just a piece of wood, because it didn't go through a ceremony. Plus, it's a sculpture that can be taken apart and put back together, meaning that: during the performance, we are reconstructing that history; we're reinventing it.

This brings to mind my show *Histoire(s) du théâtre II* (History/ies of Theatre II), for which I spoke to elders who had participated in Mobutu's establishment of the National Ballet of Zaire, in 1974.[6] Ultimately, you realise that what had been sold to us as the authentic image of the people was a construct and that we are still constructing who we are, using scattered elements that we collect. For the National Ballet of Zaire's first performance, which was called *L'épopée de Lyanja* (The Epic of Lyanja), Mobutu used the creation myth of a specific people, the Mongo people, to make a creation myth for all the people of Zaire. In a way, Lyanja is the alter ego of Mobutu, who is the father of the nation. The elders told me that for certain dances, they no longer remembered how they'd been done in the village, so they invented them. But you never invent something from nothing; you reconstruct. You reconstruct from the pieces you have.

OB There exists a very colonial fetishism for authenticity: cultural phenomena must remain as they were found, because it's assumed they were always

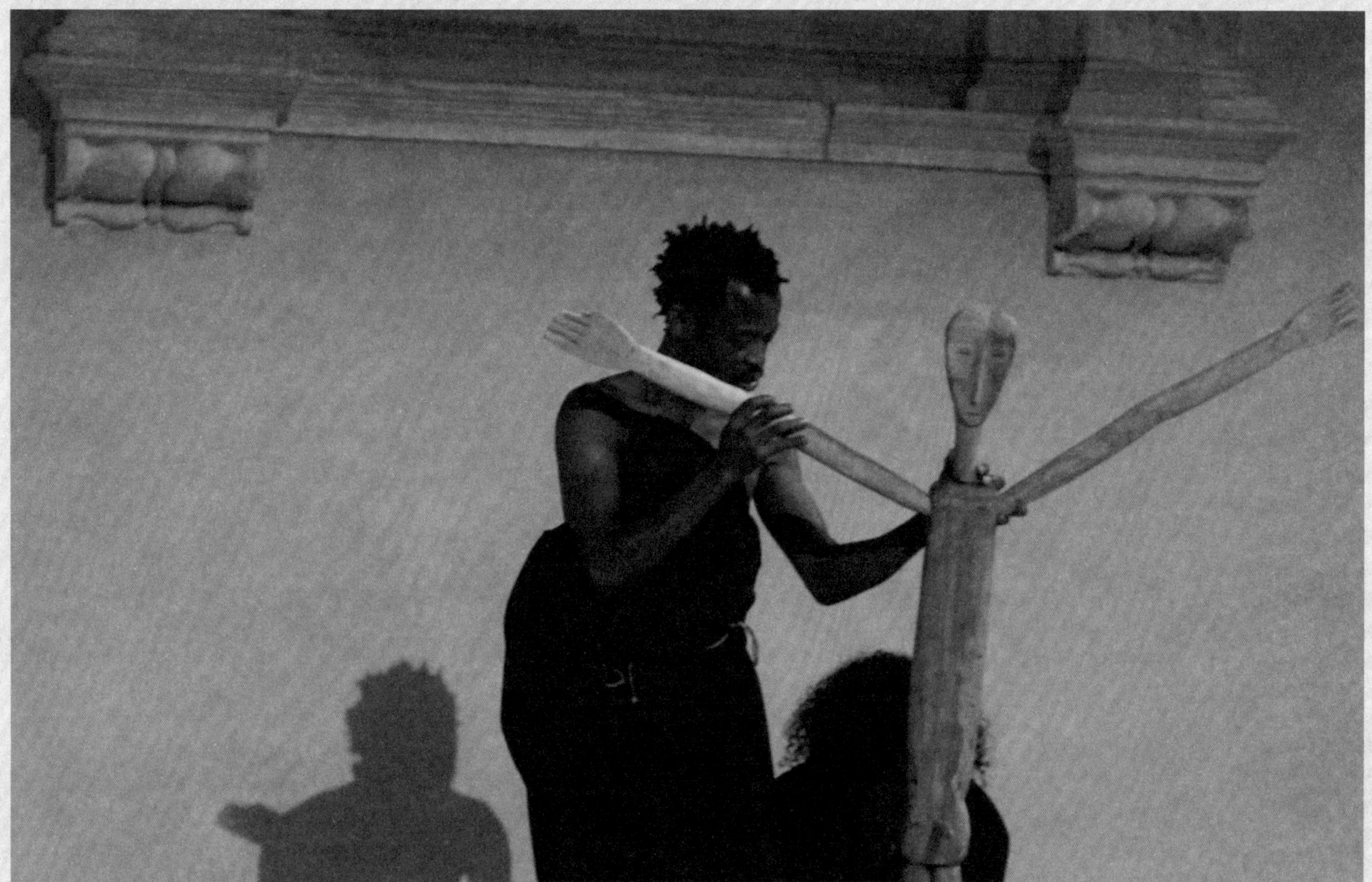

Faustin Linyekula, *Banataba*, 2017. Courtesy of Studios Kabako.

like that, that they never changed or evolved. This can be seen in museographic modes of display. The way in which objects are placed behind glass, as well as how the descriptions of works are written, confines them to rigid meanings. Here, again, is a way to 'release history': let the object live, recognise that cultures change. I've worked a little with Amazigh jewellery in the Maghreb. Many colonial anthropologists were scandalised by the habit people in the villages had of melting their jewels to make new ones out of the metal of old ones. As a result, certain jewels they would have liked to protect (lock up) in a museum were difficult to find.

FL That negates the death that has always been a part of the cycle of those objects. The people who made them knew they weren't eternal, that at a given moment, they would die, disappear, and that there would be others, made differently. Every generation rewrites this history, adds a paragraph. Release history, indeed…

OB Smash the glass! I'm reminded of Dan Hicks' recent book, *The Brutish Museums*, an in-depth look at the Benin bronzes and the urgency of their restitution.[7] I was struck by a phrase in the book that I think will speak to you as a dancer. At one point, talking about pillaged objects, he says that they are 'unfinished events'. I'm mentioning the term here with *Banataba* in mind. What is an object in a museum as compared with an object on stage, even if the stage is itself in the museum? Can the performance summon another type of presence or life from objects?

FL In *Banataba*, the object is only activated during the performance, and even then, not the entire performance: there's a specific moment when we do something with it. After that, it's wrapped up and goes back into storage until the next performance. It's kept someplace that's not climate-controlled: over time, the wood loses more and more of its water and the pieces don't fit together so easily anymore.

The only moment when the object can be considered sacred is when we activate it on stage. Otherwise, it's just a piece of wood living its life and maybe one day it won't be usable at all. We staged the performance a month and a half ago in Marseille; a few of the statue's fingers were already broken and couldn't be fixed. In time, I might have to go back to the village to have another one made. In any case, the fact that it will never be a sacred object, once and for all, takes away the weight of knowing that it's precious. The object is a partner that I need so I can say what I have to say. Unlike Moya Michael, the dancer I share the space with, the object can be replaced. If Moya can't be there, I perform alone, but if the piece gets broken, I have another one made. I don't know if that answers the question. In 'unfinished events', I hear the need for an object to be situated within its cycle, which also entails its death.

OB I really like your insistence on incorporating death into this history, death as part of life. I'm not sure the idea is as present among European commentators, even decolonial ones.

FL Maybe it comes from living at least part of the year in the Congo, where there's always something to remind me of the presence of death. It's not that we're not afraid of it, just that we negotiate with it more serenely. Death is not an endpoint. Nowadays, many parts of the world are catching up with us on this, by incorporating uncertainty and death into daily life.

There's a word in Lingala, *lobi*, that means 'yesterday', but it also means 'tomorrow'. Time isn't linear. It goes in a circle, it goes through us, ancestors are foetuses and vice versa. We live with that kind of awareness of our ancestors, but also awareness of the foetus. At least we 'should' live with it; it would help us break out of the cycle of constant destruction... I tell myself that if people were aware of this notion of time – *lobi*: yesterday is tomorrow; tomorrow is yesterday – they wouldn't be afraid of those objects disappearing, of the fact that metal can be melted. Yesterday's soul has taken the form of today, but it's the same jewel that I received from my grandmother. I made something new out of it and I imagine that my grandmother received it from someone else. Before the arrival of European ethnologists who wanted to fossilise everything in time, that was the prevailing cycle.

OB Which doesn't mean that there's no loss or there's no aggression, or injustice, or something to repair.

FL Can we repair the aggressions of the past? Loss is there and people need to be made aware of that loss. When you're wounded, even if you get stitched up, the scar remains. How should we look at the scar? How can we build from that scar? That's the most important element for me.

OB Is that what you mean when you talk about searching everywhere for the Congo, searching everywhere for scattered pieces of the Congo? Is it to look at the scar? To create a scar?

FL It's to reinvent my Congo, while asking myself what I can do with the pieces. Maybe understanding at what temperature that metal can melt, while saving my own energy, would allow me to reinvent my Congo, and to reinvent myself, on the inside. I'm also thinking about my children. What can I pass down to them? How can I build them a small sanctuary out of these ruins? This mirror broke into shards so small that it's impossible to find them all. But I can at least try to gather as many as I can. That way, I can say: 'Here's a small sanctuary for you. I hope you can make something of it.'

OB I don't know if you followed, a few years ago, what was called in the United States the 'migrant caravan'. People from Guatemala, Honduras, and elsewhere were making their way on foot to the US-Mexican border. Meanwhile, Trump was making belligerent statements about them, warning that they would be met with force at the border. This was around the time of Felwine Sarr and Bénédicte Savoy's report about the restitution of African heritage,[8] and not too long after the release of the movie *Black Panther* (2018), which has that famous scene in the 'Museum of Great Britain', where the character Killmonger, after a confrontation with the museum director, leaves with an object that was stolen from his ancestors. Ariella Aïsha Azoulay evokes these simultaneous realities in an article in which she identifies the aberrant contrast that exists between 'undocumented' people subjected to maltreatment at the border, and the objects from their regions of origin, which are 'well documented' and treated with care in museums.[9] She demands that this forced separation be refused, and that the migrant caravan be seen as a kind of counter-expedition through which people from Latin America long deprived of their cultural heritage be reunited with the objects that were taken from them. She says that this proximity, this possibility for reunion, far from a transgression, should be a right.

Beyond the restitution of objects, she's essentially calling for the abolition of borders.

FL There's an interview with Stuart Hall where he says that when he arrived to England in 1951, someone asked him, 'Why are you here?' He answered something to the effect of: 'I'm here to complete the colonial journey. You started out in the 15th century. In the 20th century, I'm completing the last leg. You shaped my life. I came to look you in the eye.' Ultimately, for me, it's less about reuniting with objects than with what fundamentally shaped us. Deep down, we're not foreigners here. The idea of a reunion, of a dialogue, even if difficult, with what has shaped us, strikes me as a very beautiful idea. It's not because you give military-esque speeches, and build higher and higher walls on the borders that people will stop moving around. They will continue to move around. And for lots of them, tough luck if they end up in the Mediterranean or the Atlantic: they will still try. You can't stop it. I can't judge it or say if it's a good thing or not; I'm just noting that the movement exists. It never occurred to me to link this to being reunited with something so profound, to remove it from a purely economic reasoning. We're wandering, unknowingly, in search of ourselves, and these selves are perhaps more likely to be found in Europe or the United States than in the places where our passports are from.

Maybe all the objects in museums play a role for those wandering souls that must be released, just like history must be released. It's a very beautiful image. Can you imagine: all the souls wandering north to south, south to north, and who might meet somewhere? Maybe all the men and women moving around today, when they encounter those objects, will find a way to reactivate and liberate them. For *Banataba*, I told myself: 'If I bring my sculpture back to the Met, since I know that sculptures speak, I'd just like to hear the sculpture at the Met talk about life before, on Lengola land, and the new statue tell it about life today, post-war, post-crisis, post-war, post-crisis…' But before that, there was this

wandering movement. Which could be quite beautiful in a movie. It would be a horror movie, but one where there are no zombies eating children. Instead, these zombies recognise one another and, in the end, find a way to release themselves, to liberate themselves from history, and finally, in the end, to 'finish the events'.

OB I like the fact that finishing the events is a task performed by zombies that recognise each other. In other words, it's not an ending, it's not something that comes to a close.

FL On the contrary, it opens up possibilities. I just hope that the objects that are starting to return to the continent can allow for new possibilities to emerge. Simply that. It would be such a shame if they returned only to be locked up, as some of them were, in Europe, for centuries.

1 Faustin Linyekula, *Banataba [new work]*, Crossing the Line Festival, The Metropolitan Museum of Art, New York, 9–12 September, 2017.

2 Faustin Linyekula, *Statue of Loss*, tanzhaus nrw, Düsseldorf, 12–13 August 2021.

3 Abdellatif Laâbi, 'Le gâchis', *Souffles*, no. 7-8, 1967, p. 1.

4 *Kongo: Power and Majesty*, 18 September 2015–5 January 2016, The Metropolitan Museum of Art, New York.

5 Adonis, 'The Pearl', translated by Abdullah al-Udhari, *Victims of a Map: A Bilingual Anthology of Arabic Poetry*, ed. Adūnīs, Mahmud Darwīsh, and Samih Qāsim, London, Saqi Books, 1984.

6 Faustin Linyekula, *Histoire(s) du théâtre II*, Festival d'Avignon, Avignon, 18–22 July 2019. https://festival-avignon.com/fr/edition-2019/programmation/histoire-s-du-theatre-ii-2934

7 Dan Hicks, *The Brutish Museums*, London, Pluto Press, 2020.

8 Felwine Sarr and Bénédicte Savoy, *The Restitution of African Cultural Heritage. Toward a New Relational Ethics*, November 2018. http://restitutionreport2018.com/

9 Ariella Aïsha Azoulay, 'Understanding the Migrant Caravan in the Context of Imperial Plunder and Dispossession', *Hyperallergic*, 29 November 2018, https://hyperallergic.com/473575/understanding-the-migrant-caravan-in-the-context-of-imperial-plunder-and-dispossession/

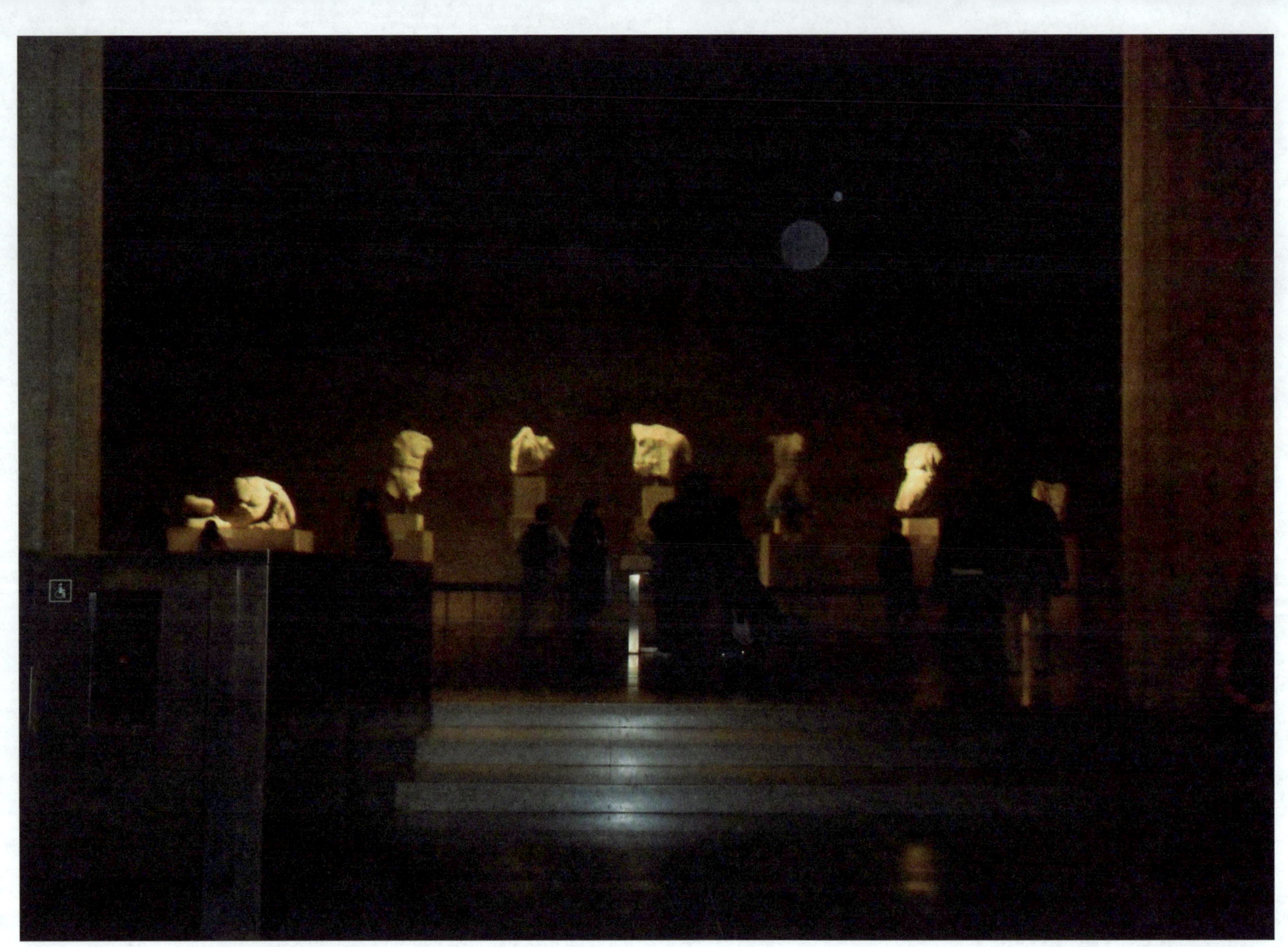

Noah Angell

NOAH ANGELL

Museums Breed Ghosts

We accordingly went out, and, after pillaging it, burned the whole place, destroying in a Vandal-like manner most valuable property which would not be replaced for four millions… You can scarcely imagine the beauty and magnificence of the places we burnt. It made one's heart sore to burn them; in fact, these palaces were so large, and we were so pressed for time, that we could not plunder them carefully. Quantities of gold ornaments were burnt, considered as brass. It was wretchedly demoralising work… Everybody was wild for plunder.[1]

Museums breed ghosts. Colonial and ethnological museums, in particular, are especially prone to hauntings. It is a matter of consensus across cultures that hauntings arise from unaddressed trauma, festering in its prolonged irresolution, and made worse by ongoing injustice in the world of the living. Perhaps it's the acquisition methods common to such museums – whose collections have largely been built via processes of extraction and estrangement, including violence, theft, and fraud – that cause ghosts to proliferate within them.

I came to grasp this relationship between museums and hauntings after collecting oral accounts of ghost stories from employees of the British Museum. Established in 1754 as the world's first national museum, it still stands today

All images courtesy of the author.

1   Testimony from Major Charles Gordon, who on 18 October 1860, as part of a joint Anglo-French army, looted and burned down the Summer Palace in Beijing during the Opium Wars, under the eighth Earl of Elgin. Demetrius Charles de Kavanagh Boulger, *The Life of Gordon*, London, 1896, pp. 45-46.

as a palatial trophy case of colonial loot. Since 2016, I've collected accounts from overnight security staff, visitor services, storage assistants, collections managers, administrators, curators, visiting researchers, and sundry other staff. I consistently found that material heritage retains centuries-old sense-impressions and ritual functions, and that objects and human remains in the museum are restless. Moreover, the conflicts that uprooted these objects and brought them into the museum are still playing out in ways that startle museum staff and visitors, a phenomenon whispered about throughout the museum world, but routinely ignored as a matter of policy.

My upcoming book, based upon testimonies that I have gathered from museum workers for years, is structured in part as an oral history to ensure that the interview material loses none of the tensity of its telling. By documenting these stories, the lived experience of museum workers is fossilised in its fluidity as the internal folklore of the museum, circulated at the pub and in museum corridors. The aim of this project is to denaturalise the museum and to catalyse a rethinking of this institution: away from the conception of the museum as a sterile setting for objects pacified behind glass, and towards that of active, destabilising presences, commingling in ways which cannot be easily accounted for.

If I told you, dear reader, that I have a few human corpses stashed away in my basement, you would think I was a psychopath, and rightfully so. Scaling that up, we know that the British Museum holds thousands of corpses and human remains, ranging from elaborately prepared and ritually ornamented mummies to loose skull and bone fragments. Human remains and contested objects held in colonial museums are, in many ways, prisoners of war. It is not at all unheard of for human remains to figure into prisoner exchanges of warring or once-warring nations. These thousands of people are held captive, denied rest, and return, out of the continued tradition of showcasing the bodies of those conquered by an imperial power and as a materialisation of the refusal or inability to accept the loss of an empire. Thus, when Prokopis Pavlopoulos, former President of Greece, branded the British Museum a 'murky prison'[2] over its obstinate refusal to repatriate the Parthenon Marbles, he spoke of a reality familiar to many museum workers.

According to some of the accounts I have gathered, a worker of formidable stature was ejected from the Sutton Hoo gallery by an unseen presence, thrown through the air and left to land on their backside. Music is known to mysteriously emanate from the dome of the Nereid Monument after hours. In a certain section of the basement, not one but two curators spoke of being hit in the head with an airborne pebble when absolutely no one else was around. Balls of light have appeared on CCTV night after night, rocketing around the entrance to the travelling exhibition *Germany: Memories of a Nation*, only to disappear with the exhibition once it moved on. Visitors have photographed strange personages reflected in glass cases and hovering in mid-air in the gallery. Some spectres only appear in photographs; others only on CCTV. This disparity brings to mind the lessons of molecular physics, where the density of materials registers differently depending on the instruments used in imaging them, calling into question our understanding of objects and their solidity.

2   Nick Squires, 'Greek president brands British Museum a "murky prison" for Elgin Marbles,' *The Telegraph*, 15 April 2019. https://www.telegraph.co.uk/news/2019/04/15/greek-president-brands-british-museum-murky-prison-elgin-marbles/

Some spectres are so commonplace that they are acknowledged almost as one would a co-worker. Some wraiths are associated with genocides; others with human remains or contested objects. Other encounters speak to more subtle forms of attachment and resonance, having no apparent traumatic association.

Some of these accounts suggest that the hauntings at the British Museum are not only related to objects held by the museum, but in some cases, to the site itself. There have been numerous deaths on site, including workers and visitors, since the museum was established over 250 years ago. It has been continuously occupied, with directors, curators, servants, and others living in quarters in the back of house, and security personnel patrolling at all hours. Before its current incarnation, the building we now know as the British Museum was Montagu House, a flamboyant aristocratic home, with the gallows at Holborn situated nearby – a space for the public showing of those sentenced and hanged. Prior to Montagu House, the site of the present-day British Museum was farmland. Accounts suggest that the farmers and farmhands who once worked this soil went to the grave harbouring resentment at their displacement, another resonance found deep within the Museum's psychic foundations.

Every museum worker who encounters the phenomenon of hauntings does so at the level of their labour. Curators and collections managers tell of unquiet objects in restricted-access storage areas. Security staff speak about alarms and lights inexplicably going off on their nightly patrols. Visitor services tell us of encounters that leave visitors shaken, as well as anomalous events that take place within the routine opening and closing of the museum.

There is a class divide in the understanding and telling of these events. Security and visitor services are overwhelmingly working-class; natural-born storytellers, charismatic and concise, with a keen sense of dramaturgy and timing. Curators tend to theorise at great length, citing historical precedent while avoiding claims of direct experience. There is a sense that they enjoy flirting with the suggestion of being not only the keepers of objects, but also of spirits. However, most wouldn't wish to erode their own credibility, or undermine the institutional line by characterising these presences as anything more than a slight, whimsical theoretical possibility. By contrast, overnight security staff take seriously their duty to spot intruders and secure the building. Furthermore, they patrol in pairs, and therefore, have credible witnesses corroborating their encounters.

Phil Heary, a veteran of visitor services who's spent nearly 30 years in the department, elaborates on this point of one's vocation shaping their experience of the museum:

> The curators are so cocooned in their own environments, sometimes they don't realise what goes on around them, you know? That's no disrespect to them as people, I mean they're very academically clever, but street-wise – they're not streetwise. You know, they could talk you to death about a certain stone or a certain sculpture down there, but if you ask them anything about what's happening in the world today, about modern society, they wouldn't know... They never really get involved with the galleries.

When Heary invokes being streetwise and adds that the curators 'never really get involved with the galleries', he was nodding in the direction of the subject of our inquiry – ghosts. The curators stay sequestered in the back of house, so while they may be involved in the research that readies objects for cataloguing or exhibition, they are not present to observe the objects' behaviour on the museum floor or to hear visitors' impressions of these objects.

Irving Finkel, Assistant Keeper of Ancient Mesopotamian script, languages and cultures in the Middle East Department at the British Museum, concurs:

> Security go around the building after dark, and the museum is like a madding crowd, whatever 'madding' means. It's a complete melee during the day; it's like Holborn tube station. If there was anything subtle, on any kind of wavelength that came off objects in the galleries, it would be trampled underfoot and swallowed forever. At night, when there's nobody here, it's a whole different kettle of fish. When you have shadowy sculptures and you walk down the gallery, and it's just your footfall and it's two in the morning, then a person is much more inclined to look at things in the cases and wonder about them, and all that. If that is something which can be registered by those people, that will be when it happens.

While most museum workers I've interviewed do not self-identify as believing in ghosts, they all seem to agree that 'objects hold energy', a formulation that encompasses and bypasses questions of belief. As one visitor services worker put it: 'When you play a violin, the violin retains your energy, or the energy of people who've played the violin before.' Another points out that many of 'these things are designed to have some kind of resonance.' A couple of museum workers have identified themselves as adherents of the 'stone tape theory' – a reference to the BBC television drama *The Stone Tape* (1972). Stone tape theory is the idea that not only objects, but also buildings – in this case, the British Museum – operate as recording devices. They absorb experiences, particularly traumatic events that take place inside the building, which are later aired or replayed at unpredictable intervals.

Suppose we accept that 'objects hold energy', that every object is in some sense a vessel, carrying within it traces of the place it was removed from; of the energy invested by those who cared for or used it; of its function; and of the upheaval that brought it into the museum. We could begin to understand the museum in continuity with, and not artificially cordoned off from, the rest of the world. When we consider the British Museum as a monument to the empire, to the systems of classification and subjugation that were birthed and that solidified during the colonial period, these battles and disturbances still playing out inside the British Museum take on a new life.

When trustees refuse to heed repatriation requests, while at the same time approving sponsorships from British Petroleum, another extractive colonial-era institution, they leave those responsible for the museum's security in the untenable position of policing ghosts. These stories continually invoke the carceral element of the museum – a prison of sentient objects, with odd cellmates trafficked in from across the globe, sharing cramped conditions of confinement and non-consensual display. Security and visitor services workers who are aware of this dynamic tend to be sympathetic towards those locked in their workplace and, in some cases, this discovery deepens their sense of duty as a caretaker.

One warder who experienced several distressing incidents in the Upper Egypt gallery confessed that they disapprove of excavating and displaying human remains, an operation they called sacrilegious as it is 'mixing the spirits up'. Another welcomed those who are now in residence in the museum with hospitality:

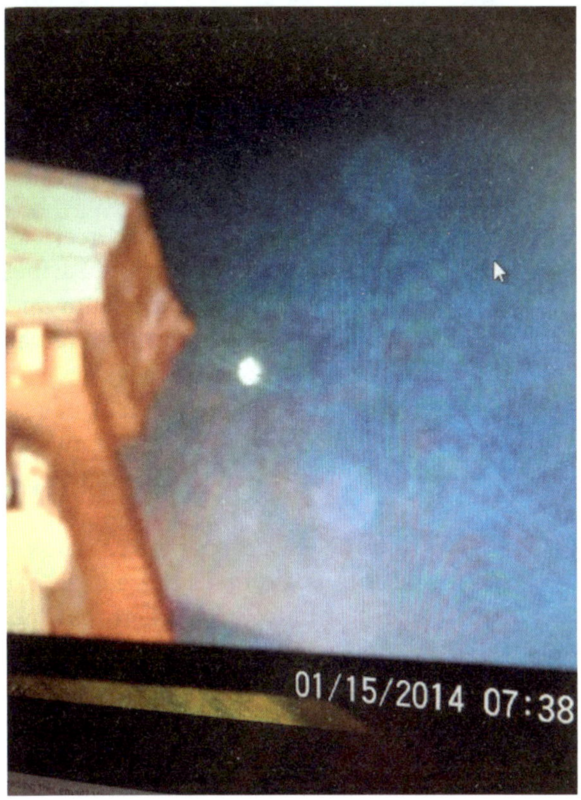

> At the end of the day, obviously we've got a vast amount of objects in this place from different places around the world. You know, I'm really not surprised if someone attached to that object was to come with it. I couldn't blame them to be quite honest. So, I'm happy to have them here.

Some security warders speak to human remains while on nightly patrol, asking them if they are all right. I have even heard of them covering a certain corpse in the early hours:

> There was a sense that it wasn't just about conservation, that it was about almost like tucking somebody up, like you would a child, you know, you're putting them to bed. And they used to say goodnight to him.

Those with previous experience in security may have held positions working in an office lobby, or perhaps working the door at a music venue – although in earlier times I'm told security and visitor services were populated mainly by ex-military and police. Visitor services staff may have previously held customer service positions. In many cases, they are art students or art historians, or simply people who would like to spend more time with the artefacts. None of them anticipated that their new role would have this dimension, as keepers of an underworld of spirit-presences shadowing the objects and permeating the museum – it is not something that is covered in their training. I have also heard of a few museum workers who, unable to shake their disquietude, quit their post at the British Museum after such incidents.

The paradigm shift suggested by this body of testimony is simple, yet its implications are many and far-reaching: that objects speak.

The discourse around repatriation often treats articles of material heritage as pawns between nation-states, brokered in the context of an already-troubled history. Repatriation requests are often dismissed as complaints about a state of affairs settled long ago, only to be revived by a new crop of opportunistic politicians and activists, e.g., 'The Greeks are moaning about the Elgin Marbles again.' But what if we accept that the Parthenon Marbles themselves are moaning, that restless objects fill the museum and protest the conditions of their display? What if we accept that human remains are animate for as long as their internment lasts – as long as they are kept from rest? What are we – museumgoers, museum professionals, and custodians of sites holy and profane – to do with this poly-phony of protestations? If museums took seriously the agency of the objects they claim to care for, how would this change the way they operate?

'How are we to re-imagine the museum?' is a question frequently put forth by museum professionals these days. Talk of decolonisation is increasingly on the tongues of museum workers, but museums may be too bound up in the colonial project to be decolonised in any meaningful sense. 'How to re-imagine the museum?' is a linguistic frame that delimits the dismantling of imperial institutions.[3] It is paramount that we understand this line of questioning as secondary to the more pressing question of how we shall collectively configure and inhabit a more just world. One could just as easily ask, 'How will all the dead who are currently held in museum storage be freed and honoured with a proper burial in their home country?' Perhaps, to begin with, it is a matter of listening to the objects rather than looking at them.

The imperial gaze, built into the very core of colonial museums such as the British Museum, denies the agency of objects and the role of material heritage in providing communities with social cohesion through shared meaning and regular, focused moments of togetherness. This imperial gaze haunts us all, albeit unevenly – an obscured force spawning racism and nationalism, ensuring that some of us are seen as backwards or underdeveloped. This imperial gaze is a form of ideological blindness, upheld by a Eurocentric training in archaeology, anthropology, art history, and related fields. To the specialists tasked with making sense of museum collections, imperial violence becomes illegible. While for those European powers that have scrambled for the rest of the world's resources from the colonial period to the present, the removal and exhibition of material heritage is a show of strength. It is a means of disempowering a people by ridding them of objects whose power could be harnessed to resist imperial subjugation, extraction, and violence. To be displayed in the ethnological museum, material heritage is flattened out, made into an image and put forth as a fragment of an outmoded or lost world.

Perhaps, to put an object in a museum is to make a ghost of it. Perhaps, by attempting (and failing) to force a split between an article of material heritage and its rightful place, its attendant people and its utility in the world, this displacement produces ghosts. Folklore abounds with orphans, widows, soldiers, sailors, and voyagers, those mistreated, separated from loved ones, or unable to return home, who now haunt others. Since colonial museums cannot exist independently of the mass displacement of material heritage, these oral accounts I have gathered lead me to consider that this system of uprooting and display

3   Ariella Aïsha Azoulay, *Potential History: Unlearning Imperialism*, London, Verso Books, 2019.

Noah Angell

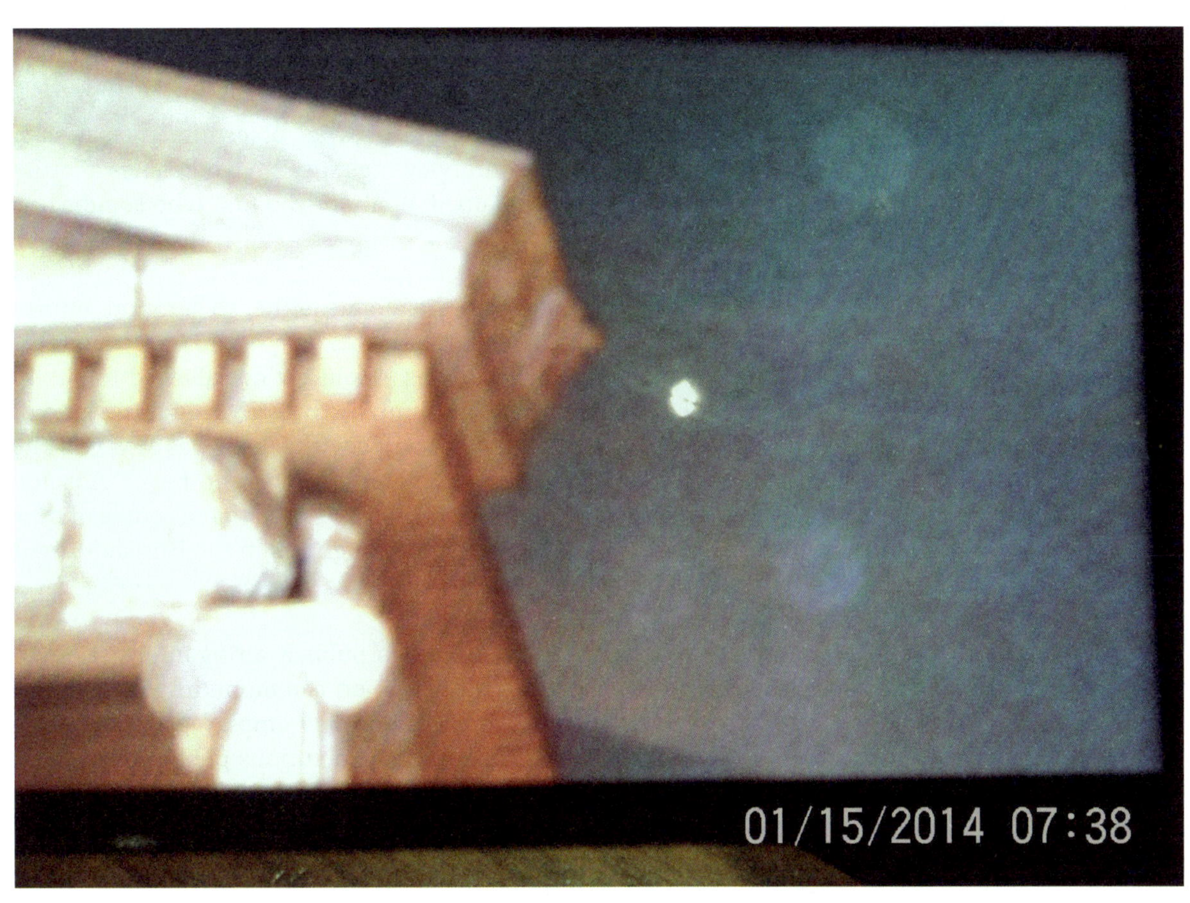

01/15/2014 07:38

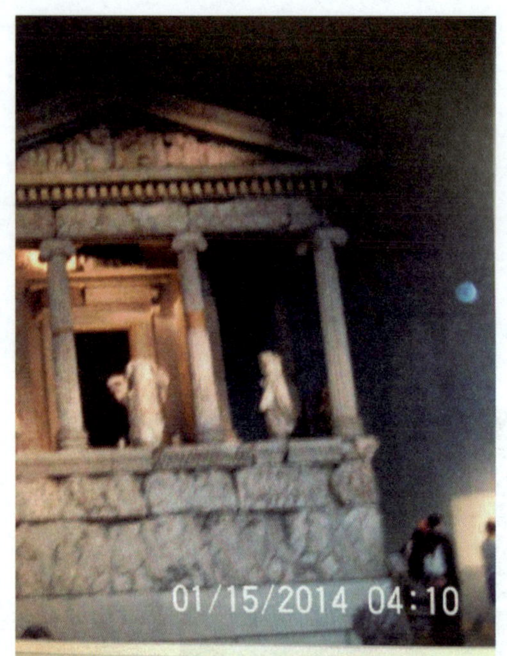

by agents of empire yields ghosts. The museum's failed attempt at separating objects from their place of origin seems to backfire, leaving nerve endings dangling but not altogether severed, reaching out for connection and left to wander and agitate in the halls of the museum, the dwelling place of the dispossessed.

While many of the articles of material heritage in the museum are inarguably ancient, these ghosts are not voices from, or of, the past. They speak to us in the present. The objects currently housed within the British Museum will outlast this imperial gaze and, in this persevering, they are more integral to our collective futures than the building they inhabit. Meanwhile, the British Museum itself has fast become an anachronism, a relic of the colonial period, of a bygone world of British power. The stories I have collected testify to this friction between a near infinity of powerful, dislocated objects and their unfit, temporary holding cell.

That the British Museum is afraid of what objects might say is something I uncovered in the course of interviewing museum workers. As a former employee of the British Museum explained, I am not the first who sought to collect such stories:

> I approached the (former) directorate, either to get more information from them, or to run it by them that it was okay. In no uncertain terms, they told me I was not to do this. I was absolutely not allowed to publish anything to do with ghosts in the museum because it was not the kind of thing that they wanted their name associated with. There was also, you know, security elements, and they forbade me in no uncertain terms. Absolutely forbade me, and I then heard from members of staff, that a couple of other members of staff had tried to write books on ghosts in the British Museum and they were told the same thing.

Despite this prohibition on employees' publicly airing information on the ghosts in the British Museum, at an orientation ceremony in 2018, the current Director Hartwig Fischer told a room full of new employees: 'We're here because of the spirits.' More recently, Fischer made a curious public admission: 'I had once the visit of the Ooni of Ife, the spiritual head of the Yoruba. And he came to the museum,' Fischer recalls. 'And he called the museum a house of spirits, and said that, while he was there, he could communicate with the spirits of all times and from all regions of the world.'[4]

In just a few words, Fischer's acknowledgement of spirits in the museum broadened the bounds of the current debate around museums significantly. It's not only objects that are held by the British Museum in contravention of the will of their communities of origin. By Fischer's admission, ancestral spirits inseparable from those objects are being held there, too. The abundant haunted-ness of the museum is not a side effect of housing these collections as I had initially supposed, but part of the museum's purpose, as the director conveyed to his employees upon initiation. This admission seems to betray an imperial fantasy that real power consists not only in the mere possession of others' heritage objects, but the agency present within those objects. Possessing these objects is a means of capturing and holding others' spiritual power. Alternatively, it is possible to read

4   British Museum Events, 'British Museum Youth Collective presents: Quizzing the British Museum's Director,' YouTube, 14 April 2021. https://www.youtube.com watch?v=0GApxVRsmLQ&t=746s&ab_

Noah Angell

Fischer's statement about spirits in the museum as paternalistic. When the British Museum claims that the Benin Bronzes are too fragile to travel back to Nigeria, they imply that the communities who produced these objects don't have the tools or the knowledge to care for them.[5]

To maintain a prohibition on public discussion of ghosts in the museum while the director privately assures museum workers that these ghosts exist belies an uneasy possessiveness. This schism reads as an admission that objects speak, but that the museum is afraid of what they might say. Therefore, the objects' speech is to be suppressed. What if the objects agreed with those whose worlds survived the British Empire, who say that these objects belong under the care of those outside of the museum, that public exhibition or even archival preservation are inappropriate? While repatriation may not be the solution in every case, it is what the museum fears most, as it would lead to not only the dissolution of certain collections, but to the unravelling of one of the British Empire's last, most visible outposts.

The British Museum's refusal to give up these ghosts, to acknowledge the violence foundational to its collections, or the still-smouldering palaces left in the wake of those 'wild for plunder', continues to cause unquantifiable harm. These conflicts persist, not only amongst trustees, politicians, activists, and academics, but also among ghosts, warders, and unsuspecting museumgoers, in the galleries and storage facilities of colonial museums across the world.

5 'The British are very good at telling you, "We are looking after it. If you'd been looking after it, it would have been stolen by now."' Quote by David Omoregie. Alex Marshall, 'This Art Was Looted 123 Years Ago. Will It Ever Be Returned?' *The New York Times*, 23 January 2020. https://www.nytimes.com/2020/01/23/arts/design/benin-bronzes.html

In Conversation Bonaventure Soh Bejeng Ndikung and Alya Sebti

ALYA SEBTI

I remember our very first encounter. We met in 2012 during the exhibition *There is no wind on the moon* that you curated at SAVVY Contemporary, when it was located at Richardplatz in Neukölln. I was taking a summer course at the Goethe Institute back then, and among my classmates were Maria Iorio and Raphael Cuomo, who also happened to be participating in your exhibition. They were always saying, 'Bona, Bona, Bona, Bona' – one day, I came by to see the exhibition, and that's how I met the famous 'Bona'. That's how I met you. It was a beautiful beginning of so many adventures to come. Soon after, we embarked on the 2014 Marrakesh Biennale. There, the title of your show was fun and unforgettable: *If You're So Smart, Why Ain't You Rich?* It's been ten years since we started this ongoing convertsation, and it's always a pleasure to pick up the threads.

I looked again at the curatorial statement you wrote for *There is no wind on the moon*, and noticed you were already talking about the materiality of the archive. You kind of brought sexy back when talking about archives in Berlin. Since then, everyone has been talking about archives, archives, and archives again. I'd like to start this conversation by asking, why do you think the archive is so important?

BONAVENTURE SOH BEJENG NDIKUNG

I think archives are some of the most contested spaces of all time, not just our time. The space of the archive is one in which power is constructed, cultivated, and disseminated. Archives are not innocent spaces because they're made, consciously, to include certain people and histories, and to exclude others. From the very onset of our work at SAVVY Contemporary, we wanted to reflect on what archives perform, as opposed to what they are – in other words, we wanted to think about the performativity of the archive.

Life is very much in an archive. We wanted to look at the hierarchies that are created within archival structures. Do we really need to strive towards being part of existing archives that are meant to denigrate us, to keep us out, to exclude us, so to speak? Or should we look for other kinds of archives? If we have to find knowledge about ourselves, where do we go to? We looked at the body, the site of discourse; we looked at the knowledge that can be found on the street. We were looking at public space as an archive; looking at monuments as archives; looking at names; looking at our names. What does 'Alya' mean, for instance? What does 'Sebti' mean? Why do we call ourselves in such ways? The question isn't only 'Why were these names given to us?' but 'How do these names shape us?' How can we look at proverbs as archival spaces, as well?

A plethora of projects have been born out of these questions. Another thing that concerned us was the fact that, as powerful as archives might seem, and as much as they determine much of what we are meant to be, some archival spaces have also become redundant. The question was, how can we revitalise certain archival spaces, and let others die. This is an integral part of our project, and the lecture I did in 2019 in Istanbul, called 'Apoptotic Archive', was centred on that: an archive which, like a living cell, can self-destruct to make room for other archives or other forms of knowledge. This is where our interest in the archive comes from, and I don't think our work here is done. In the coming years, we will continue thinking about these notions and unpacking them, and tighten our grasp on what it means to be thinking of the archives of the future. The battlefield is no longer on the streets; it's in the archives.

AS You always encouraged me to write, and stressed the importance of writing and of not leaving it up to others to tell our own stories. You put this constant emphasis on who writes stories, but also who erases them, and who decides whose stories are told and heard (or unheard); on how important it is to take back that space of writing, and to leave an enduring mark behind. Exhibitions come and go, but texts stay. In your texts, you never shy away from complexity while keeping the message and the language accessible. You open them up and flesh them out, exposing their many

layers, always with an acute awareness that these documents belong to a future archive. Whether it is a written piece or a sonic element that can be shared and disseminated in the future: all of these will remain.

And you do the same: that's how I understand your project, *Untie to Tie*. When you unpack colonial legacies, what do you find at their core? If the question is the tie, how do you untie it? When you were working on this project, I was thinking about unlearning as a means to learn. We cannot simply continue building on certain things; we need to undo them to be able to redo them; meaning, we need to be able to dismantle a narrative in order for us to rewrite a new one. What is out there? How do we untie it; unpack it; unravel it? Only then, can we start putting the pieces together. I think it applies to you, as well, which is something I deeply admire about you. The exhibition practice that we've all cultivated in the past few years has revolved around precisely that: working with artists as storytellers, with different narratives. This multiplicity of stories and perspectives that come together in the opportunities we've had to tell our stories is something I also see in your practice.

AS Thank you. I learned so much from you. When I started the *Untie to Tie* programme at ifa-Gallery Berlin, I had been frequenting SAVVY Contemporary for several years, and felt empowered to work on something like that in the framework of a German institution. You paved the way for this to be possible for me, to go way beyond a cosmetic discursive level, and to probe and question – for several years within a German institution – what it means to talk about colonial legacies today. You made it possible, in the heated moment of talking about restitution, to look at this very institution, and to say 'What does it mean to talk about restitution?' And that is what we managed to do, with you for SAVVY Contemporary, and with Nora Razian and Rahul Gudipudi for Art Jameel, for the project *For the Phoenix to Find its Form in Us* (2021). The way you talk about restitution, going beyond the objects themselves, has been really powerful. I'm not going to say 'in the past' because this is not a past project, but an ongoing conversation.

I'd like to expound on the project's title, *For the Phoenix to Find its Form in Us. On Restitution, Rehabilitation, and Reparation*. We mention restitution, but not only. Could you tell us more about the three words in the subtitle?

BSBN

The subtitle, *On Restitution, Rehabilitation, and Reparation*, was an effort to open that space. Since this pressing urge to talk about restitution started – significantly so, since Emmanuel Macron's 2017 speech in Ouagadougou – I was under the impression that everybody, every Dick, Tom, and Harry, wanted to say something about restitution. And of course, we should all be talking about it, but what are we actually talking about when we talk about restitution? It felt like these conversations weren't necessarily serving our purposes, but rather serving the purposes of the institutions that were at fault and being criticised. A lot of these institutions hijacked the debate, and rode the wave of the conversation, so to speak. With our project, we needed to take stock, and make a kind of *état des lieux*, assess the situation at hand. So, I started thinking about the meaning of restitution. Are we just talking about objects? The obvious answer is yes, but more than that, we are also talking about subjects. We are talking about beings that have been mistaken for objects, while a lot of them have subjectivity. How is restitution possible when we consider the complexity of these subjectivities?

Some of these so-called objects were vilified and demonised, called fetishes and all kinds of derogatory names. This led to devastating situations in places like Cameroon or Nigeria, where a Christian priest recently set fire to several sacred beings, claiming that they were serving the devil. People not only witnessed this barbaric ritual but also joined forces with the priest. How de-territorialised and brainwashed must you be to take part in something like this? We have to start by decolonising the mind. The question then becomes, how do we think? We need to be able to restitute that person's dignity for them to see value in what is being taken away.

It's not just about bringing a 'thing' back to its people; it's also giving them back their dignity. I've been on too many panels – I no longer attend them now, I try to avoid them as much as possible to keep my blood pressure low – where sometimes panellists will say: 'If you send these objects back to Asia, to Africa or to the Americas, the people there wouldn't be able to take care of them.' How do you intrude into someone's home, someone who's been taking very good care of a given object for 1,000 or 2,000 years, take this object and put it in a glass box, and then claim that this person doesn't know how to take care of it? This kind of infantilisation is at the core of the colonial enterprise. It makes people lose their dignity.

Then we played around with the notion of rehabilitation. As soon as time and space change, it is no longer possible to return, because you cannot turn back the hands of time. We need to think of rehabilitation; of giving these beings another habitat; of finding a way of accommodating and situating them within particular contexts. There's a great deal of work that has to be done there.

Then comes the question of the reparation of all that has been destroyed, of all the open wounds – because people are walking wounds. The postcolonial being bears many wounds, many scars, and needs to think of healing processes. A kind of reparation must be done; but how do you value that? Reparation is also financial, and we cannot underestimate or ignore that. We forget the economic aspect of all of this. That is what I wrote in the essay 'Ceux qui sont morts ne sont jamais partis'. By taking certain beings away from people, you deprive them of their being-in-the-world. You cannot repay that without compensating them, especially if, for decades or centuries, you've kept these beings in your museums and have generated economic value from them. People travel from around the world to see things in museums, like here, in the centre of Berlin. It's not just the admission fee you pay to enter the museum. It's also the whole economic sector: paying for a flight, paying for a hotel room, and so forth, just to see that. You've made a fortune from all this exploitation; that is extractivism of its finest sort. We cannot hold a debate about reparation without talking about financial reparations.

AS

I would like to go back to the text you mentioned, 'Ceux qui sont morts ne sont jamais partis', which was published in *South as a State of Mind* with the title, 'Those Who Are Dead Are Never Gone'. In the context of the Berlin Humboldt Forum, built where East Germany's Palast der Republik used to stand, you wrote about architecture as a tool for the erasure of history, and constructions as architectural erasers. When talking about restitution, it is fundamental to investigate the architectural dimension, the erasure of architectural knowledge, and how whole cities have been erased and reconstructed in such ways that communities have completely lost their dignity. How do we talk about restitution then? What are we going to bring back?

BSBN

We just came back from a trip to Bandjoun in Cameroon. Cameroon is experiencing much hardship at the moment; the part of the country that I come from has been at war for the past five or so years. At Bandjoun Station, the space of artist Barthélémy Toguo, we invited some 40 people from that region and other parts of the country – scholars, artists, etc. We were commemorating the 50th anniversary of the publishing of Walter Rodney's book, *How Europe Underdeveloped Africa* (1972). These questions are part of that economic underdevelopment. How does one break free from that dynamic?

We went to the Bandjoun Palace, an incredible piece of architecture. It's a large house made with mud and bamboo. The temperature was over 35 or 40 degrees Celsius outside. The building is square-shaped, but when you get in, you have to go through concentric circles to get to the middle. By the time you get to the centre of the building, it is about 25 degrees. This is an architectural wonder. I asked the director of the palace, its caretaker and curator: 'Do architects come here? Do artists come here?' He said: 'no, no, no.' I told him it must be compulsory for university students studying art or architecture to visit this space – or students from any major, any faculty, for that matter. They have to come here and see this place and appreciate it. For me, this is part of the reparation process: finding value in this architecture, understanding that you don't have to build cities with glass or cement just because we were told to do so.

Architecture plays an important role in the colonial project; you see it everywhere. This is fundamental in the work of Hassan Fathy, the fantastic architect from Egypt, who wrote *Architecture for the Poor: An Experiment in Rural Egypt* (1973). In this book, he talks about the village of New Gourna, which he was invited to build in Upper Egypt, and all the resistance he faced. He said that you cannot just build erect buildings for architects, you have to build them for the people. You have to create architectural structures that consider their immediate environment. In a place like Egypt or Upper Egypt, for example, you cannot just build with glass and cement; you have to think of the materiality of the space, of the environment, of the trees that are indigenous to the area, of the surrounding landscape, and of the history of architecture within this particular space. This has yet to be done. Ron Eglash wrote a book titled *African Fractals: Modern Computing and Indigenous Design* (1999). In *African Fractals*, he writes about how spaces were built in fractal forms in many African countries. He gives the example of several sites in Cameroon: to visit the king, you have to go through circles, just like that house in Bandjoun that I described, and so and so forth. Because of the colonial enterprise, spaces have been structured in different ways. You have these lines from north to south, from east to west. People have lost their bearings. Rethinking space and spatiality is part of restitution. I think these projects are one step towards what we still need to do.

In Germany, after the country's reunification, the western part, which was larger and economically more robust, took over the East. A few scholars have written about that as a kind of colonial venture. One thing that happens with such colonial ventures is that they result in erasure. They erase the names of the streets, and so people grow up without any kind of bearings, and without any sense of navigation. This is how colonialism functions, and that is why they had to destroy the Palast der Republik. They said it had asbestos, and so on and so forth. Actually, interestingly, as a student, I worked in that building while it was being dismantled. I was helping to take down the asbestos to earn some money to pay my tuition fees. So, I have a particular relationship to that space. They demolished it, and in its stead, rebuilt something with the facade of a Prussian palace in the centre of Berlin. That is how they reinstated power.

AS

The points you're raising remind me of the urban history of Morocco. In Marrakesh, where we worked on the Marrakesh Biennale together back in 2014, the city is wavering between two hearts: the traditional city called the Medina, with its whole architectural ensemble and its winding streets and the Guéliz, the so-called modern city built during the French colonial rule, where streets and buildings have been completely aligned on vertical and horizontal lines. In the Guéliz, people tend to look and overstretch their neck and nose towards Europe, and speak mostly French. It's in the Medina that people feel connected to Marrakesh's African roots, more than any other place in the city, and where the most-spoken language is Darija, Morocco's vernacular language.

BSBN

When you see indigenous communities, say, in what is called Canada or Brazil, trying to relearn their languages, finding their indigenous knowledges or endemic knowledges – this is part of this respiratory work that we all have to do. Up until just a few years ago, indigenous people in Brazil were not allowed to give their children indigenous names. Imagine that kind of violence, having to fight for that right and possibility, which is part of that restitution and that reparation and that rehabilitation. I'm also thinking of Martinique, where people have come up with all kinds of ideas, including creole gardens, which rethink the colonial garden. They shift away from the monoculturality of the plantation system, planting in such a way so that different kinds of plants share space, and inform and support one another. These things are important. We need to see these small steps as active efforts towards rehabilitation. How do we learn to value the earth again? How do we learn to listen? How do we learn to shift from everything that is mono-, shift from these concepts of universalism and universality, and move towards multiplicities? These are the projects that we are faced with. Every step matters, and that is what we are trying to do with this project on restitution, and what we've been cultivating in different ways, through our many conversations and projects.

AS   Every step is important, not only exhibiting, writing, and talking about restitution and reparation. It is also about applying these concepts ourselves and taking daily actions. I will commit to that, and I will speak more often to my kids in Darija, and teach them the language of their ancestors. This is one of the things we can do; you've inspired me to re-engage in that.

As you said, this is only a starting point. One of the strong aspects of this debate is also who expresses it and where we express it from. These projects encompass laboratories in several parts of the world to de-centre the whole conversation about restitution. I'm smiling because, when I'm saying de-centred, it makes me think about the text you wrote years ago for the catalogue of the *Carrefour/Meeting Point* exhi-

bition at ifa-Gallery Berlin (2015): 'On the Construction of Liminality: Navigating the Heres and Elsewheres'. You argued that there is no de-centring, because there is no unique centre to begin with. From our position, we think that we're at the centre, but it's not the case. It's about opening up our eyes to something that is horizontally happening everywhere.

BSBN

Absolutely. In one edition of the *Chimurenga Chronic*, they wrote that the Sahara has never been a division; it's a crossroads. Thanks to you, we did the *Ultrasanity: On Madness, Sanitation, Antipsychiatry and Resistance* project at the Gnaoua Festival in Essaouira, in 2019. That festival is very important because it reveals those in-depth connections. On my way to Essaouira, I asked the driver to stop because I saw this incredible shop that was selling carpets. I went in there because I'm fascinated by these carpets, and I tell this story over and over again because I think it's just so beautiful. There were these Berber carpets. I asked the shop owner what they meant. He looked at me and said: 'Mon frère, please stop asking me these questions, because I don't know. If you really want to know, you have to meet the Berber women. They are our library; they are our dictionary.' I thought to myself, 'This is it.' In that effort to rethink where we find knowledge, in that effort to repair what has been destroyed, we need to find those women. We need to speak to them. They need to unlock – at least for some of us, though perhaps not all of us – what that carpet holds. Because that one carpet is a whole book, a philosophy book. The story is in there, the knowledge is in there, and we need to be able to encounter that, to unpack it. Just to value that, that is why we need to rehabilitate. We need to restitute our dignity to understand that, this is where we will find knowledge. This is our archive, to go back to your initial question. The core space of epistemes, of epistemologies, is in there.

AS   We have been overlooking it, but this is also a space of belonging, and we have to rethink the importance of that space. So here is our next adventure: going back to Morocco to meet these women, and listen to the stories they want to share with us.

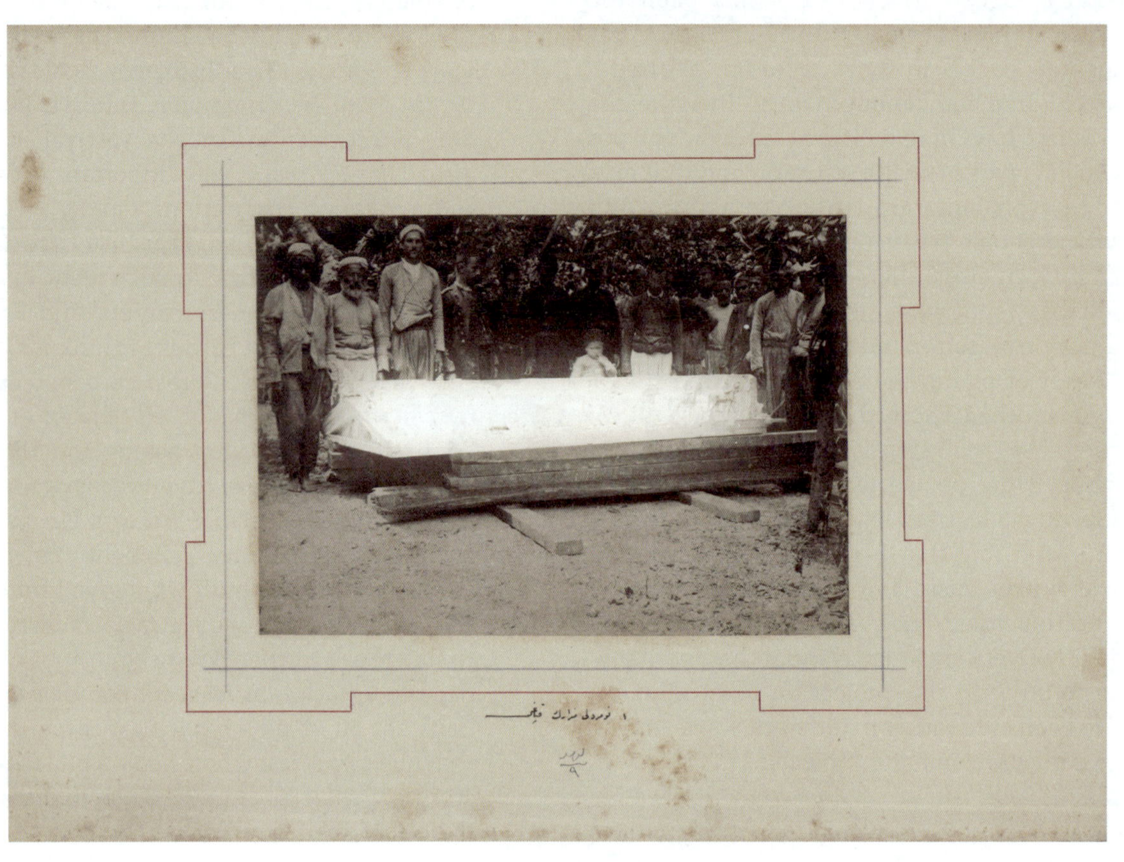

Akram Zaatari

A Second Reading

Osman Hamdi Bey's *A Royal Necropolis at Sidon*

This must have been some time in May 1887, in Bustan al Maghara, Saida.[1]

Archaeological finds have just been lifted up from ten metres below the earth. They are placed in a citrus grove, where they will remain for a few days before they are transported on a ship named *Asir* to Constantinople.

Until that moment in 1887, these finds have spent more time in darkness than in daylight. Here in this grove, they are being exposed to sunlight for the first time in more than 2,000 years. During those years, they were subjected to violence by looters looking for treasures. They have just been extracted from below the ground by men using ropes, pulling them and sliding them upwards on a wooden track. At this precise moment, these archaeological finds are posing for Osman Hamdi Bey's camera. The darkness of the burial chambers would not have been conducive for photography.

Many people have been invited to take a look at these objects before they were transported away from Saida. Most pictures taken in Bustan al Maghara from that time would typically show large ornamented stone pieces resting on wooden girders, surrounded by citrus trees. A few of them show people standing behind

This work was supported by the EUR Humanities, Creation, Heritage (PSGS HCH), Investissement d'Avenir ANR-17-EURE-0021.

All images: Akram Zaatari, *An Extraordinary Event*, 2018. 8 Inkjet prints, 30×43 cm each. Courtesy of the artist and Sfeir-Semler Gallery Beirut/Hamburg. Art Jameel Collection.

1   Sai'da, Saida and Sidon are different spellings of the same city.

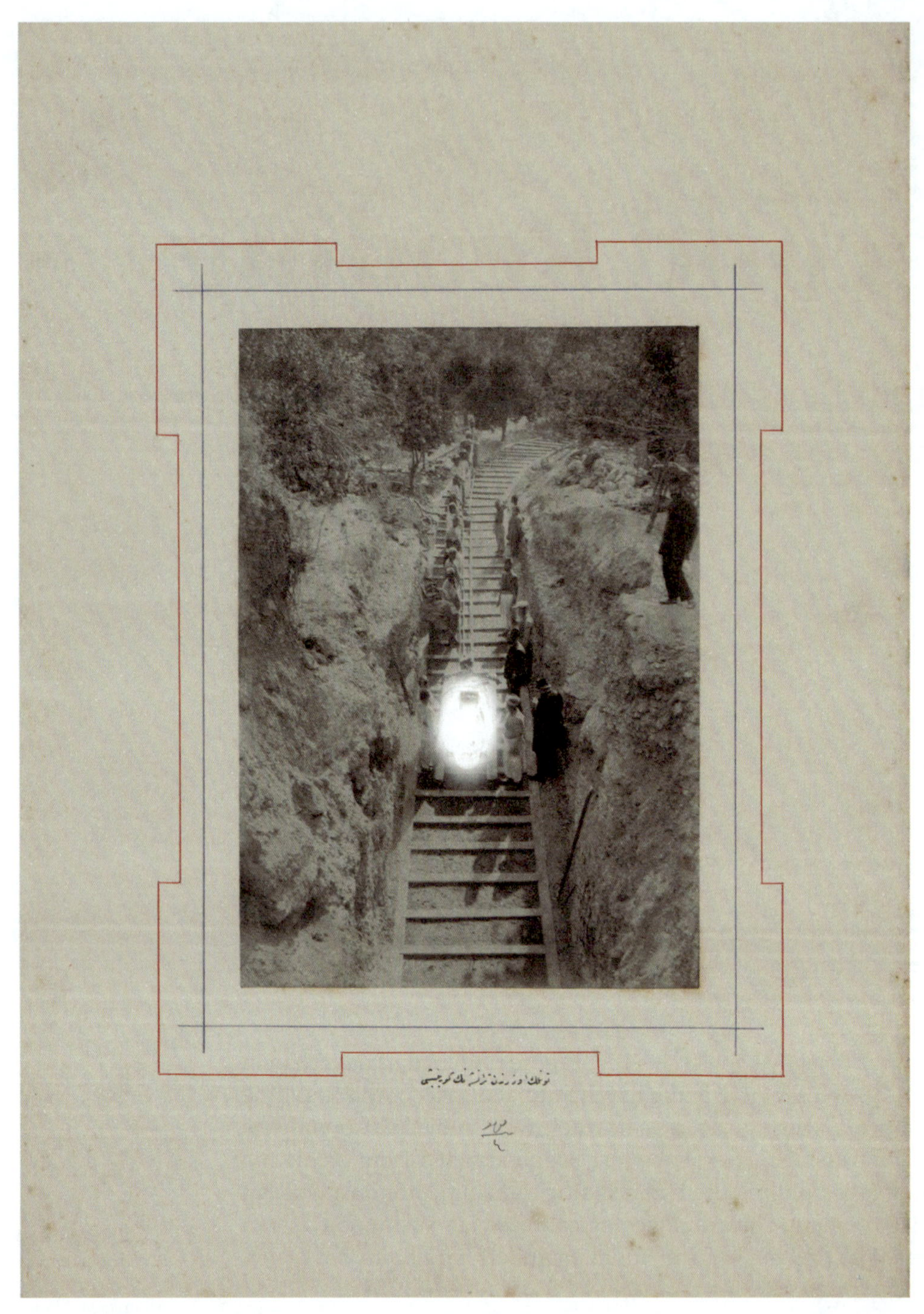

Akram Zaatari

the finds. However, the camera isn't there to record the presence of peasants or workers. Instead, it is there to capture an extraordinary event: Osman Hamdi Bey's extraction of important archaeological finds. Hamdi Bey had excavated Mount Nemrut a few years prior, but had never been as far south as Saida. It is not clear whether or not the people standing in the picture are happy, impressed, proud, or even excited about this discovery. Does anyone in the group regret the fact that these finds would soon leave the city? Does anyone in the group regret not having made any profit from selling them to European dealers?

It is not clear if they value the finds or not, but the presence of a camera on that occasion speaks volumes of the importance of the event. Given the times, they might even have come just to look at the camera.

Osman Hamdi Bey

On 30 April 1887, Ottoman artist and administrator Osman Hamdi Bey (1842–1910), founder of the Imperial Museum in Constantinople, embarked to Saida (in the south of modern-day Lebanon), certain he would unveil what would become one of the most important archaeological discoveries of the Ottoman Empire. Earlier that year, news had reached Constantinople that a landowner named Mehmet Sharif [2] had come across substantial archaeological finds on a dig in his land, northeast of Saida. Subterranean burial chambers were identified and subsequently examined by the local authorities before deciding that the scale of the discovery necessitated a high-ranking Ottoman presence on-site.

Three years earlier, Osman Hamdi Bey was the driving force behind the 1884 Ottoman Archaeology Law, which prohibited the trafficking or export of archaeological finds, and regulated their excavation on Ottoman territories. Amateur diggers and treasure hunters, who had been operating in the empire for decades, saw their operations punishable by law from this moment onwards. Hamdi Bey made it clear to everyone who had been digging and selling artefacts for years, that archaeology was the sole domain of the Sultan, under the administration of the Imperial Museum.

Hamdi Bey published a firsthand account of his excavations in Paris in 1892. [3] The story was recounted in many different ways within a decade of the events, reflecting cultural frictions within Saida and Lebanon at large, and the ongoing dispute over writing history.

Textual Registers

In March 1887, just over a month before Hamdi Bey arrived to Saida, Reverend William King Eddy, a second-generation American missionary born in Saida, published a letter [4] in *The American Journal of Archeology and of the History of the Fine Arts*, in which he first mentioned the discovery of sarcophagi in the Saida neighbourhood of Ayyaa. He writes:

> It has long been well known that the plain and the hills about ancient Sidon are full of interesting antiquities. The pots filled with 8,000 coins of Philip and Alexander, the sarcophagus of Ashmunazer [Eshmunazar] with its Phoenician inscription, and other finds, have aroused general interest in the

2   The way the story has been told by Hamdi Bey, including naming the informer, comes to confirm and promote, at the same time, the loyalty of an Ottoman citizen and the efficiency of the Ottoman laws. It brings to mind the story of the Abdel-Rasool brothers who revealed the location of the cache of Deir al-Bahary to the Egyptian authorities in 1881, as told by Gaston Maspero in his book *Les momies royales de Deir el-Bahari* (1889; 'The Royal Mummies of Deir al-Bahary').

3   Osman Hamdi Bey and Théodore Reinach, *Une nécropole royale à Sidon*, Paris, Leroux, 1892.

4   William King Eddy, 'Letter from Sidon Phoenicia', *The American Journal of Archeology and of the History of the Fine Arts*, vol. 3, no. 1-2, June 1887, pp. 97-101.

subject of hid treasure. At present all excavations are conducted by laborers who quarry for stones. The building stones that they sell nearly repay them for their work, while any antiquities found in the rubbish of ruined buildings or in unopened tombs make the work remunerative. No systematic exploration has been conducted since the French occupation of 1860, when the necropolis south of the city was excavated.

Eddy came from an American Protestant family that resided in Saida. Like many missionaries, he was active in the founding of distinguished educational institutions. He helped establish the Gerard Institute for Boys in 1881 and, according to his descendants, he translated the Bible from English to Arabic.[5] His father, Reverend William Woodbridge Eddy, founded the Sidon School for Girls in 1862. In his letter to *The American Journal of Archeology*, Reverend William King Eddy continues:

> Lately, some workmen, while they were digging in an open field about a mile to the north-east of Sidon, came upon a shaft, about twenty feet square, sunk in the sandstone. When this was cleared of earth to the depth of 30 feet, a doorway was found in each of the four perpendicular walls. These openings had been built up with stonework; and, by the removal of a few of these stones, access was obtained to the rooms. The floor, walls, and roofs of these rooms were of the natural rock without any traces of plaster... Entering first the south room, two large sarcophagi meet the eye: the one on the right, of black marble highly polished, but without any ornamentation; the other, of pure white marble...

> As the chamber is small, it was only with the greatest difficulty that I could squeeze between the sarcophagus and the walls. The opening was so small that there could be no good ventilation, and the two lighted candles which I had with me, if held near the ground, went out. My companion became dizzy and faint, so my stay was short. To add to the discomfort, water was dripping from the roof, making a thick mud upon the floor.

Eddy's text reminds us that 'burial' meant removing the bodies of the dead from the world of the living, sending them deep into the earth. Burial chambers are, in most cases, underground, away from light. These were times when Saida, like the rest of the world, did not have electricity, and sources of light were limited to candles and gas lanterns. He continues:

> After waiting a few hours for the workmen to clear the entrance to the east room, I descended again and found in it two sarcophagi, a large sculptured one on the right, and a plain one on the left: both of the finest white marble. The large sarcophagus is in the form of a Greek temple: the lid representing the roof, and the tomb (the body of the temple.)... The whole effect of this finely proportioned and richly ornamented temple, with the impressive row of statues, was one not easily forgotten. Unfortunately, a hole had been broken in the front, and at the same time part of the right entablature of the lid was broken off...

5   Lana Captan, 'American Missionary Family Returns Home', *The Daily Star*, Beirut, 15 March 1999.

Akram Zaatari

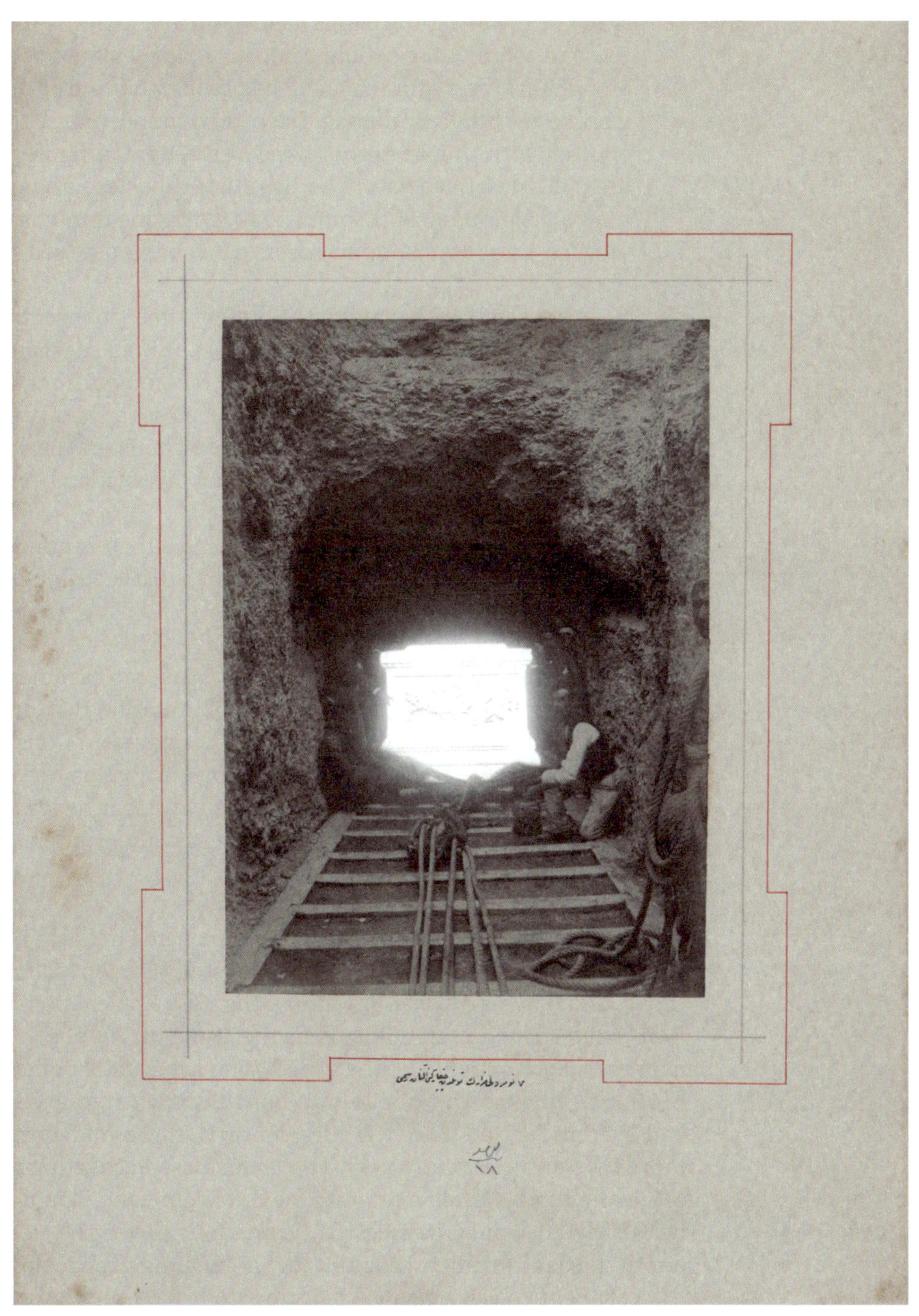

> As I walked about this sarcophagus, the surprises which met my eye rendered it difficult to make mental notes. That I was fortunate in seeing what I did, is evident, for from that hour no European has been allowed to enter the excavations. Anything like measurements, notes, or photographs, was wholly out of the question. If this jealous care were in the interest of preserving these treasures, there would be no objection: but a Moslem visitor has since brought away an arm which he had broken off one of the figures. Since my visit, seven other sarcophagi have been found: one sculptured on all sides, another with the lid in the shape of the human figure: the face and head-dress are described as of the Egyptian type, resembling the figure on the tomb of Ashmunazer [Eshmunazar]. Only one tomb has been found as yet unrifled, and that contained decayed wood or decayed mummy-remains…
>
> It is very singular that, up to the present time, no inscription of any sort has been found on either walls or sarcophagi… Either the material, or the finished work, of all these tombs must have been brought from some other country, as there is no such marble in Syria. At present, the place is guarded by soldiers, day and night, the doors to these chambers are fastened and sealed, and the local authorities are awaiting instructions from Constantinople.

Reverend William King Eddy mentions seeing a man running away with a piece of a sculpture, which he had taken from the site. He strikingly identifies him by his religion.

Hamdi Bey lived in Paris from 1860 to 1869. One can assume that he would have seen the sarcophagus of Phoenician King Eshmunazar II on display at the Louvre. Perhaps he asked himself why it was not displayed in Constantinople, instead. He had heard of Ernest Renan's excavations in Byblos and Tyre, and when he arrived to Saida in 1887, it was clear to everyone that he was responsible for the laws that protected cultural heritage from treasure hunters, who sought to sell what belonged to future generations.

The sarcophagus of Eshmunazar II was discovered in Saida in 1855 by Alphonse Durighello (1822 – 1896), who later assisted French scholar Ernest Renan (1823 – 1892) in his excavations during the 1860 French intervention in Lebanon. Durighello sold the sarcophagus to the Duke of Luynes[6] – a common and by no means illicit practice at the time – who eventually donated it to the Louvre in 1856. Alphonse Durighello was born in Saida into a Venetian family who had lived in Aleppo since the 18th century. In the mid-19th century, Alphonse moved to Saida to set up a new type of business: excavating and trading archaeological finds. He hired a team of local workers who would excavate sites that he suspected would house significant finds. Over the years, the Durighello family played an important role in unearthing archaeological objects along the Lebanese coast, securing their transfer to mainly European collectors. The Durighellos capitalised on the very loose Ottoman antiquity laws, conducting most of their early work within the rather lax confines of these regulations. Familiar with far stricter European antiquity laws, they knew how to take full advantage of the leniency of Ottoman laws, which were bound to become more restrictive. In the eyes of these adventurer-merchants, Hamdi Bey posed a real

6 Honoré Théodore Paul Joseph d'Albert, 8th Duke of Luynes (1802–1867).

Akram Zaatari

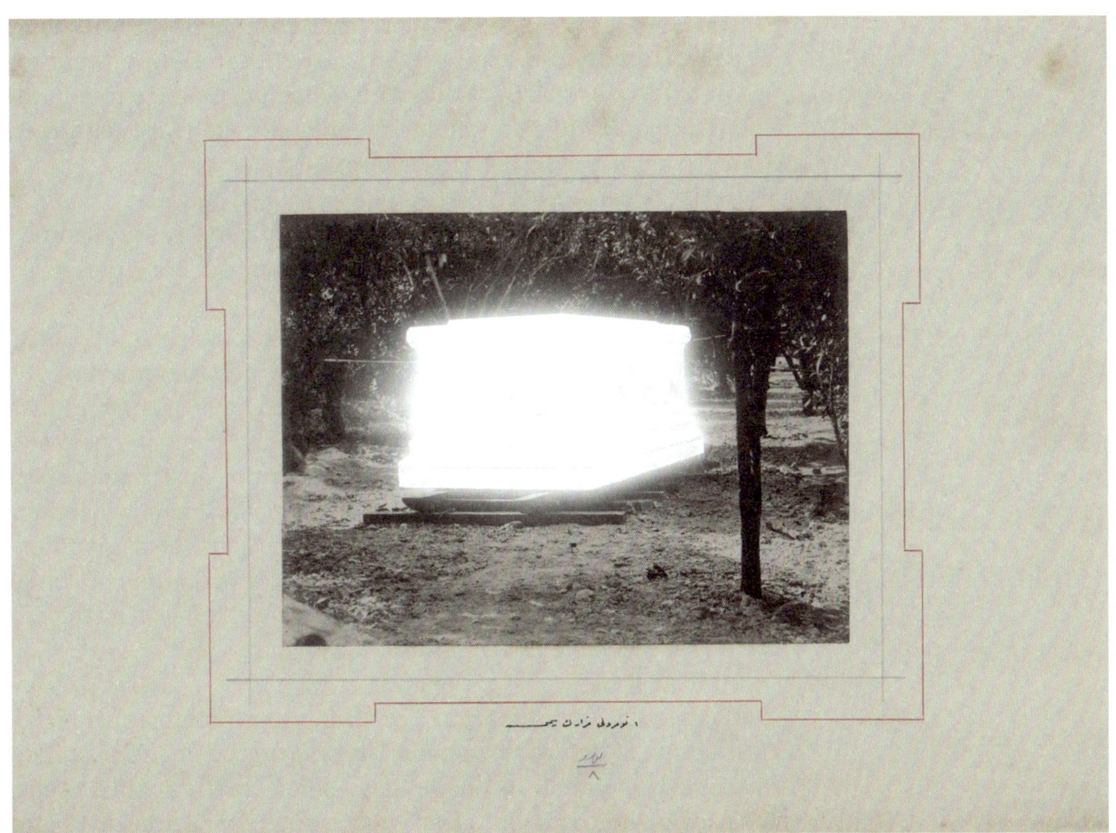

١ نومرولى مزارڭ يمكـ

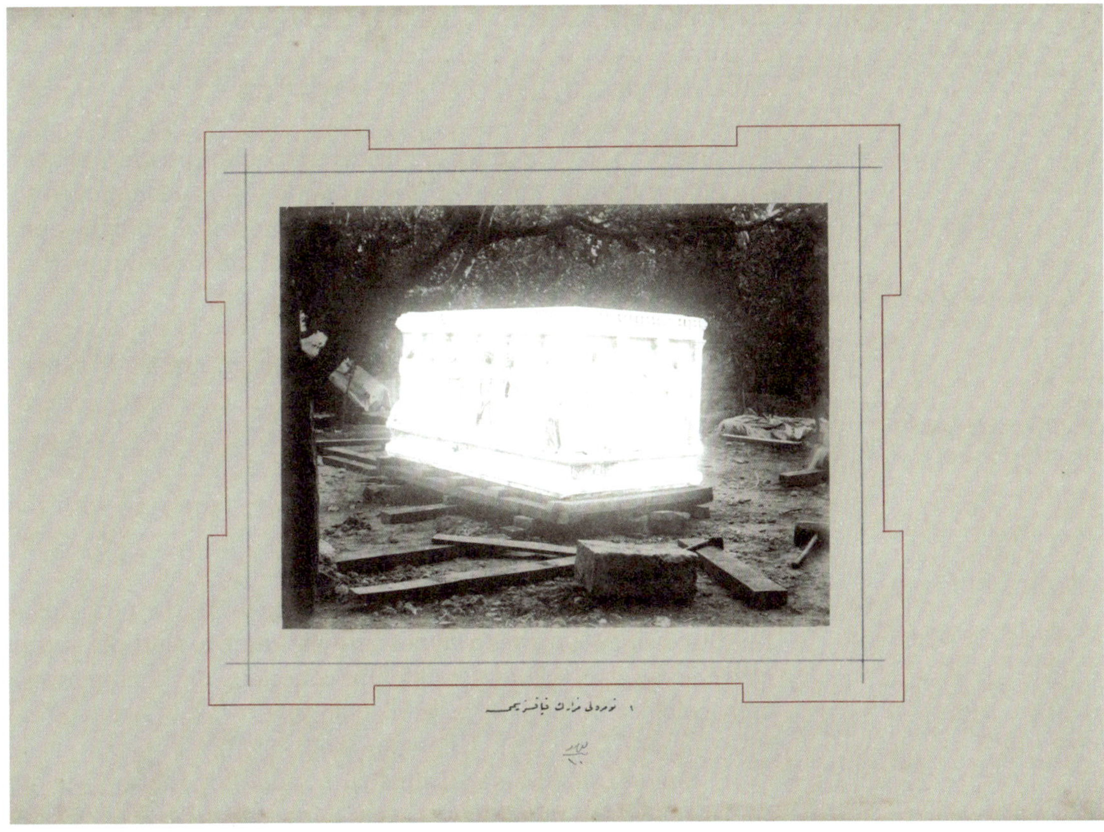

١ نومرولى مزارڭ خاصره يمكـ

threat. He was interested in the same archaeological finds they were after, only to collect, study, and exhibit them, rather than selling them for profit. Hamdi Bey looked to establish a solid archaeological practice rooted in and specific to the Ottoman Empire, and which would all take place within the institutional framework of the Imperial Museum.

Three years later, in 1890, the same journal published a very short letter by Edmond Durighello (1853–1922), Alphonse Durighello's son.[7] He writes:

> On my return to Sa'ida, I found that admirable necropolis, from which were taken those magnificent sarcophagi which the museum of Constantinople removed from Sa'ida three years ago, to have been annihilated! For the rock in which were these beautiful sepulchral vaults worthy of the archeologic marvels which they contained, the entire rock, had been brutally torn up and transformed into stupid masonry! And there, where reposed the ashes of King Tabnit, there is only an empty pit. That grandiose subterranean museum, which earthquakes and the devastations of conquerors and centuries of barbarism had respected, has been effaced by the criminal stupidity of a miserable gardener of Sa'ida.[8]

Durighello does not mention Hamdi Bey, but points at his responsibility in the destruction of Saida's necropolis. His take on the intrusive and destructive excavation led by Hamdi Bey could have been equally applied to most of Durighello's excavations. It is not clear what Durighello is accusing Hamdi Bey of. Is it the extraction of archaeological finds from their bedrock? He and his father have done the same in the past. Is it the lack of care or interest in the sepulchral structure itself? None of the Durighellos really cared for the sites from which they had extracted objects.

For more than 30 years, the Durighellos enjoyed the privilege of being Arabic-speaking Europeans and knew the Levant fairly well, which proved to be particularly beneficial when it comes to trading. Due to the Ottoman capitulation system, they had the advantage of being judged in a European court in the case of disputes with other Europeans in the Ottoman Empire.[9]

In 1890, Hamdi Bey wrote *Une nécropole royale à Sidon*, which would be published in Paris two years later. In the introduction, he states the following:[10]

> 2 March 1887, Mehmed Sharif Effendi, complying with the law regarding antiquities... (I)

With this opening line, Hamdi Bey gives credit to the newly established law for this discovery. He names a layperson, who came to alert the authorities of his discovery, now that the laws made him conscious of the importance of not selling archaeological finds.

> ...came to alert Saida's Qaimaqam, Sadik Bey, that he had discovered a deep shaft, which might have been a burial site. (I)

7   Michel G. Klat, 'The Durighello Family', *Archeology and History in Lebanon* 16, Autumn 2002, pp. 98-108.

8   Edmond Durighello, 'Letter from Sidon', *The American Journal of Archeology and of the History of the Fine Arts*, June 1890, p. 186.

9   'Litige entre Habib Abela et Alphonse Durighello à propos du sarcophage d'Eshmunazor II', *Archaeology and History in Lebanon* 16, Autumn 2002, pp. 109-114.

10 Hamdi Bey and Reinach, *Une nécropole royale à Sidon*. Translated from the French by the author.

Akram Zaatari

Here, Hamdi Bey praises an Ottoman citizen who obeyed the law that he himself had put in place, thus indirectly praising himself. He adds a footnote, saying:

> In Saida, everyone has excavated their gardens and no one ignores how such a shaft is configured or what it may contain. (I)

He adds:

> I can confidently say that the soil of Ancient Sidon still holds immense archaeological wealth despite the devastation that has been ongoing for centuries and until today. I am sorry to say that we're having difficulties putting an end to those practices. But it's a grave mistake to consider that such devastating practices are rooted, as it has been repeatedly claimed, in the fanaticism of Saida's citizens. One should seek the roots of the problem in the ignorance of the lower classes of the population, both Christian and Muslim, who have been encouraged by foreign individuals established in this country with no purpose other than trafficking antiquities. (IV)

Hamdi Bey illustrates his statement with a footnote including an excerpt from a letter that Edmond Durighello (without naming him) had addressed to Ernest Renan, saying:

> I enjoy spending most of my nights in the rubble with my loyal workers. It often happens during our 'clandestine' subterranean excavations that we run the risk of being crushed by landslides, but nothing deters our courage. (V)

In his text, Hamdi Bey admits that the vilayet engineer Beshara Dib had already started the works before his arrival, but nevertheless describes the unfolding process of discoveries, vault after vault, sarcophagus after sarcophagus.

The Stone Monolith

Hamdi Bey's discovery of King Tabnit's burial site was at the expense of the monolith that sealed the pit where Tabnit's sarcophagus had been placed. Because the pit was narrow, it was impossible to lift the monolith to the ground level. Hamdi Bey thus decided to break it into pieces. He writes:

> We can tell from the texture of the stone, inherently different from that of the rock where these shafts have been dug, that this monolith and those surrounding it were cut in another location far from this shaft, and carried all the way to be placed at the current site. I knew, then, that I was wrong to presume that I'd find other burial chambers here, and was convinced that he for whom this large shaft has been opened, and for whom so much effort has been put to conceal, in fact, lie underneath alone, in total solitude, away from any other deceased. (91)

Hamdi Bey adds:

> The following day, early in the morning, a dozen masons started attacking the monolith, which wasn't very difficult because the block of stone was soft.

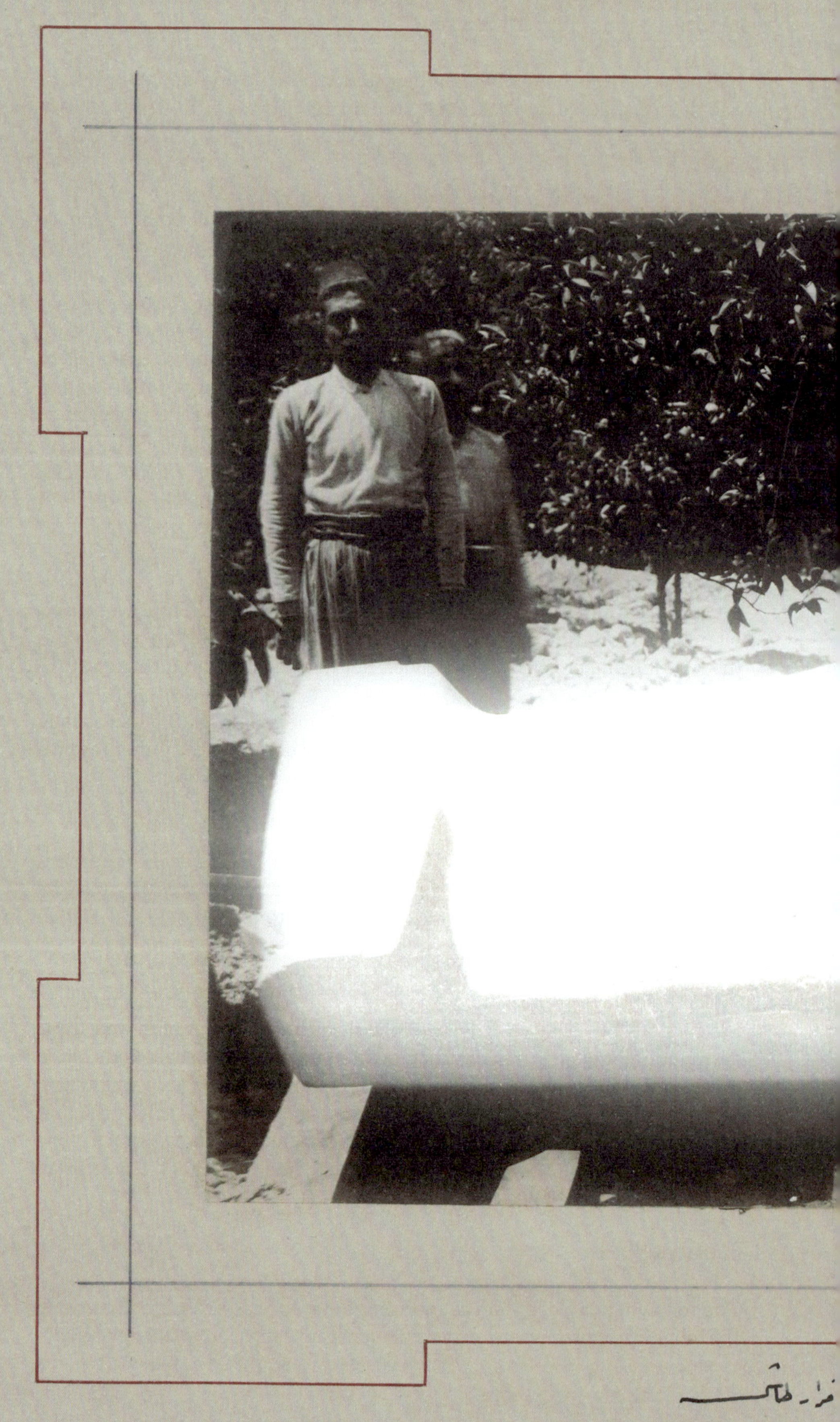

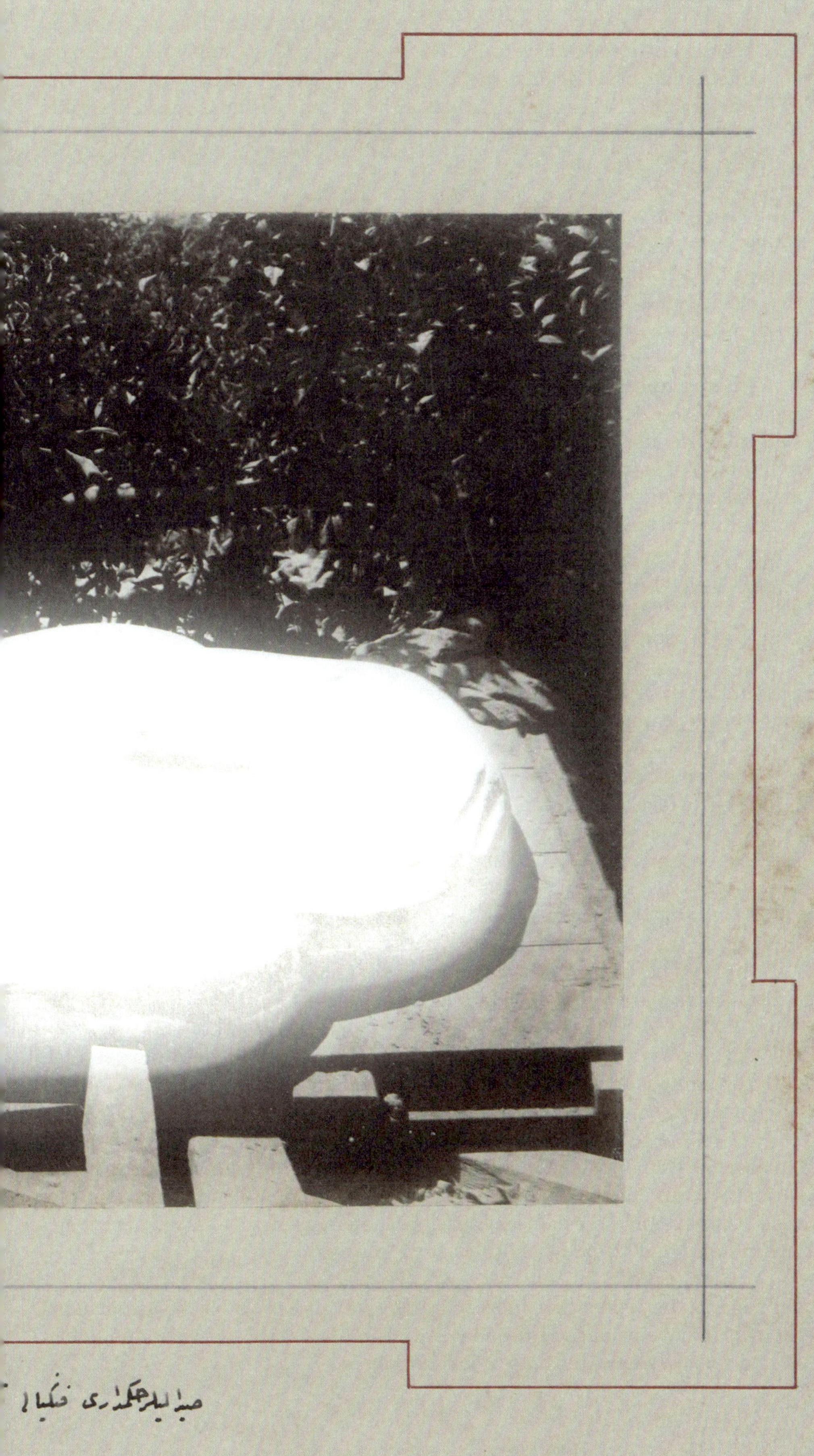

صبا ایله حکمدری شکیان

The work proceeded so well that by the afternoon, five-eighths of the block were gone, and what remained was 60 centimetres thick... The workers soon cut the last piece transversally into three parts. They simply needed to be lifted and turned against the side walls, which we did immediately. We lifted two of them against the wall to the left, and the third one to the right. The bottom of the monolith was as well polished as the top, and all the edges were even and sharp. (98)

The destruction of the monolith that sealed Tabnit's tomb was a common practice in 19th-century archaeology, which looked at extracting finds without preserving the setting in which they were found. Nevertheless, Hamdi Bey's description of the stone before its destruction and his detailed measurements speak to his appreciation of the knowledge that it carried.

Photography

In Saida, Osman Hamdi Bey takes photographs and paints a mosque by the seaside. He befriends Chibli Abela, the owner of the land next door, who allows him to display the archaeological finds on his grounds before everything is moved away. He returns to Constantinople with 17 sarcophagi that would become the pride of the future Imperial Museum, and form its nucleus collection.

In 1892, he publishes a manuscript that recounts his work in Saida, including the details of the destruction of the Sidon Necropolis, along with an archaeological study by Théodore Reinach. In this manuscript, he speaks of photography six times.

Osman Hamdi Bey first mentions it after the lid of the first sarcophagus made it to the nearby garden of Bustan al Maghara, in Saida. He writes:

It was noon. Workers needed to rest and have lunch. I took advantage of this break to take a photograph of this beautiful lid. (26)

He then writes:

Monday 23 May, sarcophagus 7 is finally brought to the ground, slowly climbing up the ramp. Given its weight, it moves by the centimetre... By noon, the most beautiful funerary monument of antiquity known to us today had taken its place behind its lid in the orange groves.

On this heart-warming morning which I will never forget, I took several photographs and spent the whole afternoon in the fields contemplating my conquests, moved beyond words. (60)

On page 68, Hamdi Bey mentions taking photographs of the sides of the grand sarcophagus and mentions that these images are the only existing record at the time of the extent of the damage caused by looters, given that broken parts were later restored and are now on display at the museum.

On page 84, he writes that following the excavation of a black sarcophagus thought to have belonged to Amoashtart, King Tabnit's sister-wife, and while sliding it slowly upwards on a wooden track:

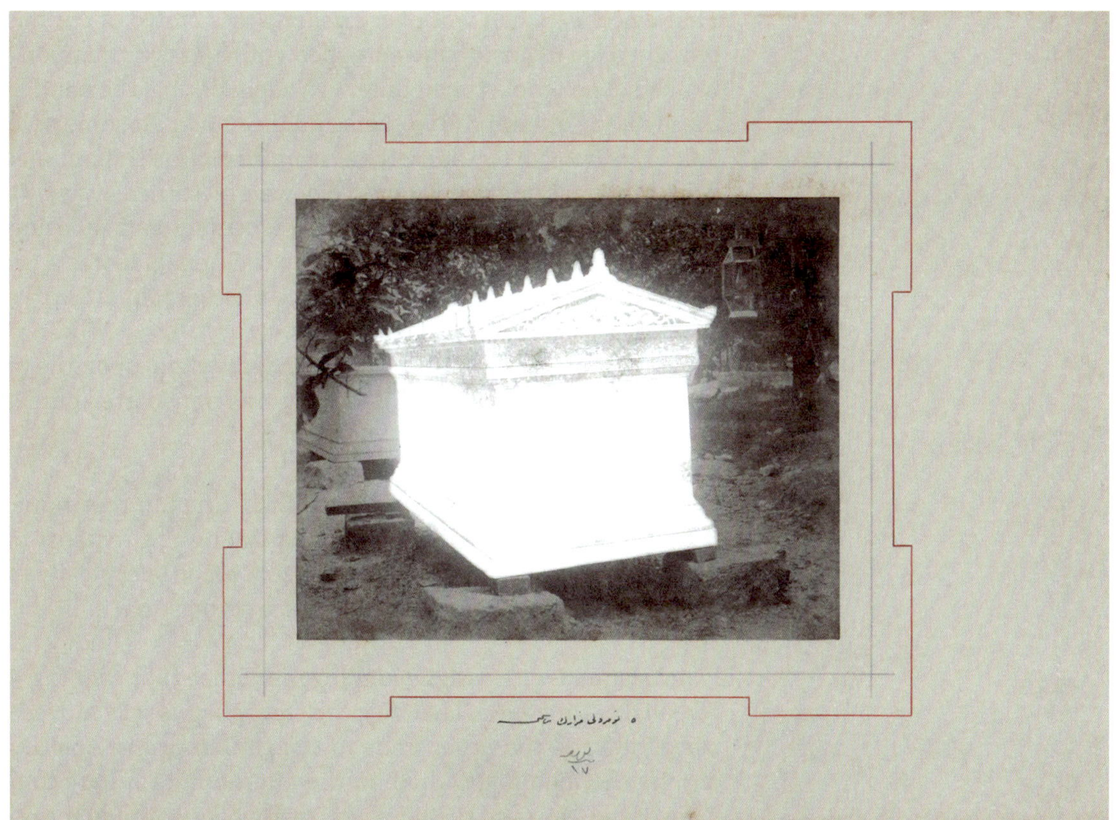

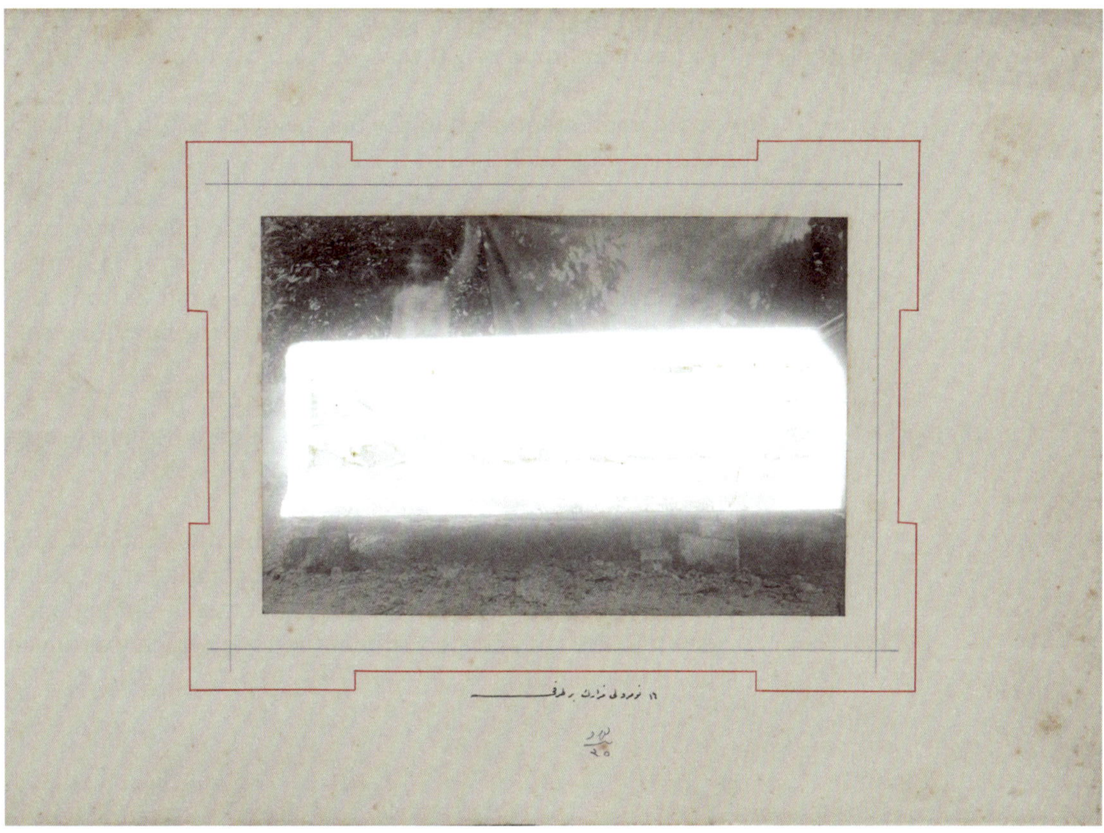

That day, the garden was overwhelmed by a crowd of curious visitors. I had brought a local music band equipped with a bass drum upon the wish of my workers. The whole time while we were working, the band played music to the great joy of both the workers and the crowd. At some point, the crowd of onlookers, moved by the workers' relentless efforts, spontaneously joined in, helping to pull the sarcophagus. They were all carried away by the music. Four hundred to five hundred people were cheering and shouting and, together, pulled the sarcophagus all the way up the trench. It was a curious spectacle that would have been worthy of being photographed. (84)

On page 108, Hamdi Bey describes the moment when, upon the opening of King Tabnit's sarcophagus, his mummified body was transported outside the funerary chamber and into the vestibule:

Outside, everything was packed. Murad Effendi, the municipal doctor of Saida, had just finished cleaning and drying the remains of the Sidonian king, who was laid in a box made of zinc made specifically for this purpose, and treated with a chemical substance to preserve it.

I was plagued with fatigue and feverish since that evening. I had to stay in bed all day on 3 June. That day, the sarcophagus was moved and its lid was placed next to the other finds in the garden of Mr. Abela, whom I visited despite the high fever I had on the afternoon of 4 June to photograph the body of the king and the lid of the sarcophagus, and to make rubbings of its inscriptions. It's only at that moment that we were able to read the name Tabnit, Priest of Astarte, King of Sidonians. It was, thus, the tomb of the father of Eshmunazar II that we had just uncovered. (108)

The photograph mentioned in the text below is not in the album, but an etched reproduction was published in the book.

That day, we put 14 crates aboard, and the following day, 20 June, we carried the grand sarcophagus, which weighed 15 tons, across the jetty. With a scaffold, the sarcophagus was placed on a raft in front of a large crowd of onlookers. The crowd was so large it filled the whole beach. I took a picture of the loading of the sarcophagus. (114)

The raft was then pulled towards the ship. Hamdi Bey was worried about lifting the sarcophagus from the raft onto the boat. He writes:

To reassure me, the brave Hassan Bey, the ship's captain, said: 'Do not worry. I am so confident of the success of the operation that I will stand under the crate, while you entertain yourself and take a photograph.' He then went down to the raft and stood under the crate, which was already a few metres up in the air. (110)

Epilogue

Men stand still, silently, for a few seconds only.

Everyone has been asked not to move, blink, or say a word.

They might have been told not even to smile.

Many of them have probably never seen a camera before.

They may not have seen other men in photographs before.

They will probably not even see this one.

This photograph will be developed and printed by agents of the Sébah & Joaillier studio, on-site in Saida, or possibly in their workshop in Constantinople.

This photograph will be mounted on off-white cardboard.

The cardboard will be bound to an album that will be named after this excavation, and which will carry the number 91533 and the title Sidon Lahdi ('Sidon Necropolis').

Album 91533 will be part of Sultan Abdülhamid II's favourite photographic collection indexed in 51 volumes that cover all aspects of modern life in the Ottoman Empire.

It will find its way, as a gift, to royal and presidential collections in European and American capitals, but not to southern provinces of the Ottoman Empire.

All album pages and the photographs mounted on them will age over 100 years and turn light yellow. There is no pure white in these photographs anymore.

Some of these men wear uniforms. They must have been vilayet officials, guards in charge of protecting the site against theft. Others must have been workers. Is Osman Hamdi Bey in the picture? Or is he behind the camera? Is the vilayet engineer Beshara Dib in it? Is Mehmet Assi the marine engineer in it? Is Mohammad al Sharif in it? None of the descendants of the Sharif and Assi families know what their great grandfathers looked like.

Who is Muslim? Who is Christian? Since William Eddy mentioned a 'Moslem' walking out of the site with a carved piece of stone, then people used to be able to tell who's who based on their physical appearance. Have we lost that ability today? I wonder. And if they were indeed able to tell who's who, did they care?

What do these men make of Osman Hamdi Bey? What do they think of the Ottoman authorities? Do they consider Ottoman rule an occupation, or is it simply an unchallenged fact of life?

The year is 1887. Twenty-seven years have passed since the killings between the Druze and Christians in Mount Lebanon, close to the same number of years that separate us from the end of Lebanon's many civil wars in 1990. Has anyone in the group lived through and suffered from the 1860 killings? Does any one of them remember? And if they do remember, would they have preferred that they hadn't?

Phantom Taste

The last time I remember seeing it at a family gathering must have been in the early 1980s, at my aunt's house in King's Point, New York: a large, white cloud on the sweets table. It was forbidden to tear a piece away until after dinner. So, my younger brother and I first ate our way through the *m'hasha* or *minhasha* (the Iraqi Jewish word for dolma or mashi) and *bamya* (stewed okra) that my mother had served us, until we were finally allowed to dig into the desserts. We had learned from past experience that Jordan almonds were more appealing to look at than to eat, their pastel colours betraying the promise of a chocolate M&M's centre with a thin layer of candied sugar encasing a stale almond. I do not recall if my brother went for the homemade *baklawa*; for me, it was the cartoonish white cloud that beckoned.

It was difficult to carefully tear away a piece, since the whole thing was covered in flour to keep the individual round balls from sticking to one another. When the piece I tugged at pulled along with it half of another, I felt like I'd received some kind of illicit bonus. The first contact with my tongue was tasteless flour, but as my teeth dug into the white nougat, cardamom was released. At nine years old, I found this flavour intoxicating, as if a window had been opened in my body and spiced air blown in. Chunks of properly roasted almonds mixed with pistachios and walnuts conjured up the mouthfeel of Snickers, my favourite candy bar. But even at my young age, I knew not to compare Halloween staples to the almost holy quality of this sweet called *manna*, which one of our relatives had somehow been able to get from Baghdad, even though none of them dared return to Iraq.

Manna, known in Iraqi Arabic as *mann al sama*, meaning 'manna from heaven', was first introduced to us as a kind of mythical food during our Passover Seders. According to our scripture, this white substance fell from heaven and fed the formerly enslaved Hebrews as they travelled for 40 years

in the Sinai before reaching Canaan. The word *manna* is believed to derive
from the Aramaic *man hu*, which means 'what is this?' – a word that is a question.
As a child, I had visions in my mind of a nutritious white cotton candy gently
falling from the sky like snow into the hands of my newly freed ancestors.
When I made a drawing of this as an activity in Ms Malin's class during my first
year of Hebrew school, I got props for my illustration. David Ettinger, an
Ashkenazi Jew and by far the best student in the class, drew roasted chicken,
broccoli, potatoes, and corn falling from the sky.

After my Iraqi grandmother Renée died in 1984, family gatherings became much
less frequent and *manna* was nowhere to be found. But we had other sweets to
nourish us, like the many jars of *silan* (date syrup) my grandfather Nissim had
hand-pressed and stocked in the freezer before he died in 1975. When we finished
those, we had to settle for substitutes: store-bought stuff made in California or
Israel. My mother complained that it was too filtered, with none of the depth and
texture of my grandfather's *silan*. 'It's almost as if they are trying to whiten us,'
she half-joked.

We entered our own desert, wandering. In those nine years after my grandfather's
passing, we still had an anchor connecting us to Iraq in my grandmother, who
happily told us stories of Baghdad. It felt quite normal for us to connect to
a place far away, and to love it, even though our family had been forced to
leave. Iraq was a footnote on the evening news, presented not as the place my
grandparents spoke lovingly about, but as a warzone, and only ever in the context of Iran. After Iraq invaded Kuwait, on the eve of the US-led Persian Gulf
War of 1991, something shifted. As my brothers and I sat at the dinner table
with the TV on watching the green-tinted, night-vision images of buildings in
our ancestral city being destroyed in real time, we collectively came to the realisation that the place our family had fled to was destroying the place we'd fled
from. My mother, looking to interrupt this violent episode, said, 'Do you know
there are no Iraqi restaurants in New York?'

Months later, our family took a spring break road trip to Washington, DC. Among
the usual car snacks was a surprise: a golden packet printed with lines of Farsi
script. The only English word on it said GAZ. I pressed on it and felt a round shape
about half the size of my palm. My mother smiled and said, 'Try it. See if it brings
back any memories.' When I opened it up, a burst of flour wafted into the air and
some gently fell on my jeans. I bit in and, like Proust with his madeleine, I was
transported back a decade to my aunt's sweets table. 'It's *manna*,' my mother said.
I felt like I was tasting a ghost. She explained that *gaz* was the closest thing she
could find to *manna*. The UN sanctions against Iraq, which would later claim millions of lives, were to blame, and so *gaz* was our substitute. I didn't know much
about what might distinguish one treat from the other, but to me, it made sense
territorially, Iraq and Iran being geographically intertwined, with so much shared
ecology, culture, and cuisine. Later, I would learn from an Iranian-Jewish friend
that the sweet takes its name from *gaz-angebin* or honey of *gaz*, in reference
to a species of tamarisk that grows in the Zagros Mountains, which extend from
Iran into Kurdistan in northern Iraq.

Michael Rakowitz

It turned out that in order to know more about the tamarisk, I would need to go through the date palm.[1] In 2007, I travelled to Jordan to meet Atheer, an Iraqi exporter with whom I had been working to import Iraqi dates to the US for the first time in decades as part of my project, *RETURN*, which I had begun in 2004. The narrative of the dates' ill-fated journey mirrored the plight of hundreds of thousands of Iraqi refugees waiting in a four-day-long line of cars at the Jordanian border; the dates ended up being sent back and forth to Baghdad, then finally on to Damascus, where it was determined they'd spoiled. Ten new boxes were finally airlifted out of Baghdad and into New York City in December 2006, but the overall transaction served as a surrogate for the larger human and ecological tragedy.

In the midst of our transaction, Atheer and his family had to flee the sectarian violence in Iraq and were now living in Amman. He would tell me about how beautiful Iraq was, how thick the trunks of the palms would get; he asked if he sounded like my grandparents yet.

On the last night of my visit, Atheer took me to an Iraqi sweets shop that had been displaced from Baghdad to Amman. He went up to the counter and pointed to a table behind the clerk, where white balls covered in flour were being cut from a larger loaf. *Manna.* The store owner spoke in Arabic and I needed no translation. *Min 'Iraq.* From Iraq. 'It arrived this morning,' explained Atheer, and he motioned to the owner to fill up a large round tin. He handed me the tin and said, 'For you, your mother, and your family.'

After I flew back to New York, I opened the tin with my parents. My mother tried it first, the flour falling on the kitchen counter. She rolled her eyes in pleasure, told my dad to taste it. It was like introducing an enzyme that catalysed a change in protein, the sweet taste coercing sweet memories of family gatherings to flow from their tongues. The *chagli*, an all-night party held in honour of my parents' engagement. A cousin's wedding. A visit from Uncle Niyazi and Auntie Tiffeh, who lived in London. The *manna* had witnessed it all.

Into my parents' freezer the *manna* went, to be cryogenically preserved for happy occasions in the future. It was too precious to be left to the elements to spoil, and G-d forbid we should eat it all in one sitting. It had to last, the way that our family did not last in Baghdad. It was not just a sweet, it was a taste of *thikra*, a memory, quite literally taken from the soil of our family's homeland.

Trabutina mannipara, also known as the *manna* scale, is a small insect that feeds on trees like tamarisks, which were once extensively found in places like the Sinai and what is now northern Iraq. The excess sap the bug ingests from the tree is secreted out the tip of its abdomen as honeydew. This collects in a kind of thick crystalline formation on branches and soil, which can be gathered and boiled down, making it easier to remove any remnants of twigs, leaves, and earth. To the *mann al sama* base is added cardamom, almonds, pistachios, walnuts, and rosewater, the honeydew acting as foundation and binder, pulling together multitudes – as Aram Nahrayn, or the land between two rivers, once did with Assyrians, Turkmen, Kurds, Yazidis,

1   There is an Akkadian text titled *Dispute Between the Tamarisk and the Date Palm*, wherein, according to the biblical scholar Dr. Alan Humm, 'the two trees argue about which one is more useful. The tamarisk bases its claim on the fact that its wood is used to make images of the deities, tools, and incense. The date palm points out that it is used to produce cloth and rope, and that it gives fruit, unlike its opponent.'

Jews, Mandeans, Chaldeans, Circassians, Shabaks, Kaka'i, Sunni, Shia, Marsh Arabs, Roma, Bedouin, Persians, etc. A sticky base that is a proposition for an inclusive and visionary future in the not-too-distant past, until it was interrupted by nationalist ideologies across West Asia.

After *RETURN* concluded, I saved a handful of Iraqi dates and, just as my mother had done with my grandfather's *silan* and the *manna*, I placed them in the freezer, awaiting a worthy celebration. When my daughter Renée was born in Chicago three years later, we placed one of those dates in her mouth, so her first taste of life would be sweet. Around the time her naming ceremony was to take place in Montreal, where my wife's family lives, my local Arabic grocery received a shipment of *manna*, not from Iraq, but made by an Iraqi confectioner in Mississauga, Ontario. They were individually wrapped in clear plastic and made from high fructose corn syrup. Knowing that I was settling for a mere substitute, I bought two dozen to serve at the sweets table after Renée was given her Hebrew name, Rina, meaning 'joyous song'. I sprinkled some flour on each piece, trying in vain to replicate the authenticity of the original: the taste was equivalent to what I imagine the experience of flying would be for a pilot playing Microsoft Flight Simulator. I wished I had asked my parents to bring the *manna* I gave them from Jordan, and which they surely still had preserved in their freezer. 'But we were driving up from New York, Michael, who knows if Canadian customs would have allowed it,' my father reasoned, trying to make me feel better. Still, for me, it was an insufficient substitute, but one that would have to be good enough to open up some kind of portal to Iraq in honour of my daughter, named for her Iraqi great-grandmother.

The word substitute is derived from the latin *substituere*, which comes from *statuere*, whose noun derivative is *statua* or statue. I have worked for much of the past two decades making statues that are substitutions for other statues that have disappeared or been destroyed. This echoes those generations of Iraqis making their traditional food in the diaspora, using ingredients that are often different from the ones available in Mesopotamia, substitutions for those things not readily available. A prosthesis, but also a kind of prayer to will what we have into what we have lost.

A year has passed since I agreed to write this essay, and in that time, several new Assyrian groceries have opened on Devon Avenue in Chicago. I recently visited one of them, and there on a shelf facing the entrance was a tin of *mann al sama*. The brand was Al Hamadan, made in the Rabieh neighbourhood of Amman, Jordan, where many displaced Iraqis live. The tin proudly illustrated a section of the Ishtar Gate, the central feature of Nebuchadnezzar's Babylon, taken by the Germans to Berlin in the early 20th century and still on display there, in the Pergamon Museum. My heart racing, I flipped the container over, anticipating that pure *mann al sama* would be listed as the first ingredient. But no. After ghee and flour came sugar. Another substitute, a placeholder, like the cheap wooden copy of the Ishtar Gate that has stood since the 1950s near the archaeological site of Babylon, commissioned by the Iraqi government to serve as an entrance to a museum but also as a reminder of what needed to be returned to Iraq.

I bought the tin, and into the freezer it went.

Michael Rakowitz

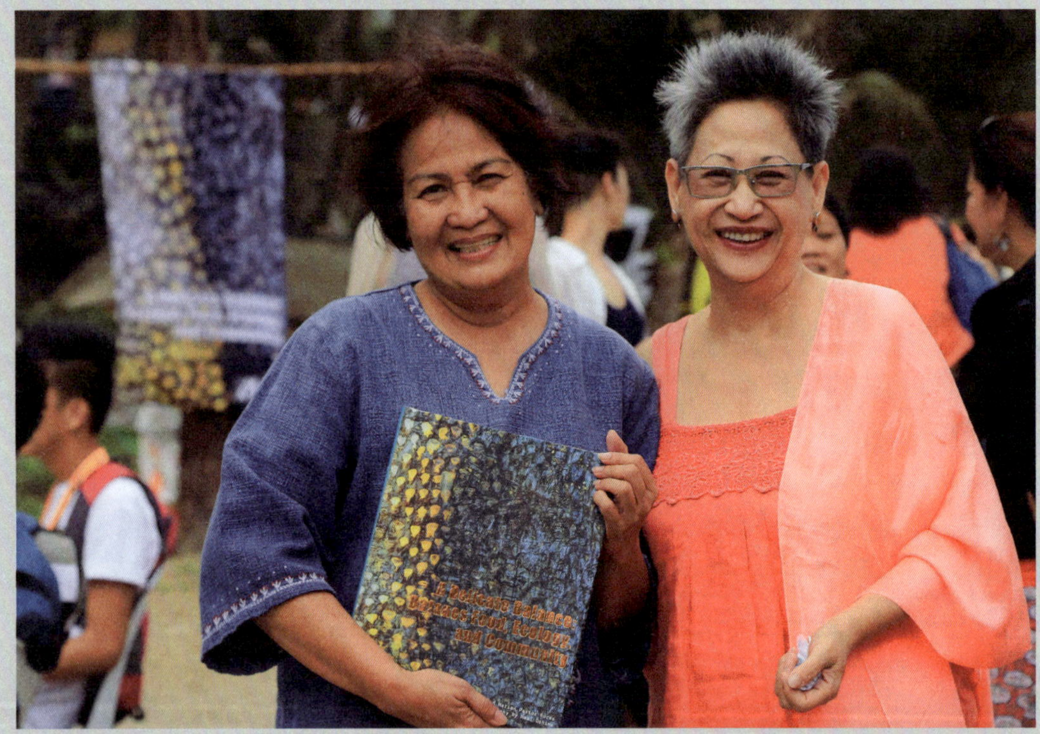

Dina Abad and Marian Pastor Roces at the booklaunch of *A Delicate Balance: Batanes Food, Ecology, and Community* in Yura, Batanes. Photo Courtesy of Pio Abad.

In Conversation Marian Pastor Roces and Pio Abad

PIO ABAD

I'd like to start with this photograph that I've only recently come across. It's a photo of you and my mother taken in Batanes during the launch of your book on Ivatan food[1] and community.[2]

For me, this photograph unravels so many interwoven personal and political threads. It was taken in March 2016, when we were still oblivious to the tsunami that would hit the country in the form of Rodrigo Duterte's presidency. My family and I weren't even aware of my mother's illness at the time. It is impossible for me to disengage her eventual passing from the anxiety and the difficulties caused by the challenges that she and my father faced politically.

I think about what I'm inheriting – both in terms of family, but also generationally – and the many layers of politics, exhaustion, bits of triumph, and devastating moments of despair that I struggled with, as I'm sure you did, too.

We have also had an ongoing conversation around our work questioning notions of heritage – both archaeologically proven and politically constructed – and Batanes is, in so many ways, the ideal place to unpack these projects. As much as our work has transcended many geographical boundaries, and is very much rooted in theory and art history, it is ultimately incredibly personal work and irrevocably bound with ideas of love and grief.

MARIAN PASTOR ROCES

And possibility and despair.

PA And triumph and failure.

MPR Massive failure. You are quite right, at once going for the personal. What possesses us to do what we do, other than to heed an unapologetically utopian, unrealised longing? Still, I no longer call it that, so it could simply be a bad habit.

I suppose when you get to my age – and your mother and I are the same age – it feels like endless years were irredeemably squandered in pursuit of hope. The power of that hope is in imagining resuscitating a country and a people who were thrown under the bus, as it were, by tyrants and their ilk. That is, the millions of Filipinos resigned to powerlessness, who can and should exit their lot; who are like me, as well, desirous of a kinder, more equitable order of things.

That desire and unreasonable hope, in any case, drive my curatorial practice. I have no illusions of success, but neither do I indulge in cynicism.

So here I am – alongside curatorial pursuits – in the middle of preparing to publish a book on the massacres that occurred in the late 1960s and early 1970s. These atrocities were perpetrated by Christian settlers in Mindanao, who expelled Muslims from their ancestral lands. Subterranean cultural flows from that time would produce a culture of violence which, among other outcomes, gave the Philippines its present sociopathic president.[3] Knowing all this in some detail makes me think of curation as limp, lifeless work.

And so, part of my hope is for curators to toughen up. Yes, artists and curators have long been engaged in the politics of memory everywhere, but we are mites to political-economic colossi. These forces are monumental in our country, where the scale of historical revisionism at play is transnational, nearly immeasurably networked, and supported by global standards, with staggering sums of money.[4] The campaigns work with public indifference in relation to how cultural memory is usurped by nefarious vested interest.

I had never had any intellectual or emotional investments in the notion of 'nation' – much less 'my nation' – so it is senseless to plunge repeatedly into the harshest politics of memory in the Philippines. But, for instance, I wrote that book on the Marcos-period killings to contribute, via additional data thrown into the air, to the creation of a new Bangsamoro Autonomous Region in Muslim Mindanao[5]. That curatorial practice can compete for space for the erased memories, which is why I indulge my stubbornness. That curatorial practice can do so without slipping into propaganda, and without losing any rigour – this is the sweet edge for me. Also, there is a generational spirit to be relished. My hope resides in a parallel and similar relation to the narrative of 'nation' that your parents fought hard to construct[6]. We engaged neo-colonial institutions that ultimately morphed into fascism.

PA   When I think about my parents' political struggle in relation to my work as an artist, I often think that their imagination – by which I mean the ability to hang on to possibility against all odds – is far greater than mine, and this unreasonable hope that you speak of has also been my greatest inheritance and burden.

So much of my thinking about 'nation' and their sense of nation is rooted in Batanes. One of my great-uncles

was beheaded by the Japanese for being part of the resistance.[7] My grandparents were very much a thorn on the side of the Marcos dictatorship[8] because they prevented the dictatorship from having a complete hold of the northern Philippines, Batanes being in constant opposition to the regime. There was an episode in the late 1960s where Ferdinand Marcos's goons sprayed the family home with machine guns. Everyone survived, but if that had gone any other way, I would not be here. From their early days as student organisers for the farmers and fisherfolk unions in the 1970s, to the difficulties they faced fighting for progressive policies and institutional change in government – an insurmountable and thankless task – my parents always found themselves at the crosshairs of asymmetric power. The sense of purpose and the trauma that comes with this lineage is now something that my siblings and I are internalising in different ways. In my case, it is through making art.

For me, Batanes really is about family, and how the family takes so much pride in being from this peripheral island. It's where we locate our place in the world and where my ancestors – my mother and my aunt Pacita among them – are buried. My mother was actually not originally from there, but my father's family traces a very long history on the island. Through that, it also became her home.

MPR   Peripheral doesn't begin to describe Batanes. Were your parents aware of what those of us who are in discursive fields, immersed in the postcolonial, call centre-periphery politics? Were they aware that Batanes was emblematic of the periphery?

PA   To a certain extent. Batanes is the collection of islands in the northernmost tip of the Philippines, and for the longest time, it was known as the place you couldn't reach. Remoteness is built into its fabric and mythology. Batanes was known primarily as the place where typhoons and hurricanes enter the Philippine Area of Responsibility (PAR). Its identity was based on these romanticised notions of isolation and resilience. It also helps that it looks nothing like the rest of the Philippines, and is closer to the crags of Scotland than this vision of a tropical beach.

MPR   The archaeology of the Philippines and the Pacific is contingent upon Batanes being the starting point of

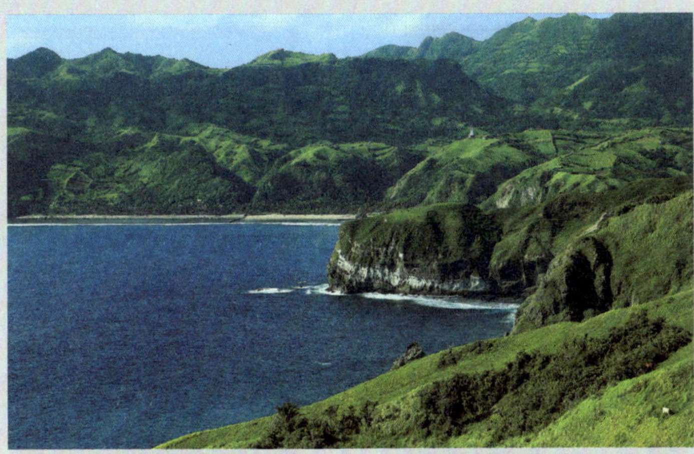

Batan Island, Batanes. Photo Courtesy of Opal Bala.

MPR Because Filipinos do not have a race discourse, it goes unnoticed that this origin story is racialised and outright racist.[15] It has a Social Darwinist frame that produced all the unfortunate consequences. In this construction, Indonesia is a metonym for civilisation. Kingdoms, empires can be cited, Srivijaya and Majapahit, even if these were curiously decentralised formations. Indonesians built Borobudur. In polite and educated circles, these words are uttered to hook onto greatness-by-association.

Up until today, Filipinos remain either indifferent or unknowing of how the north-to-south trajectory of language – and, therefore, culture – spread in the Philippine archipelago. This trajectory does not support fantasies of ancient aristocracies and urbanising settings. It appears to increase anxiety about a pre-colonial culture, which from all indications, consisted of naked creatures with bows, arrows, and spears, who were for the most part hunter-gatherers, swidden agriculturists, or small-plot cultivators. The shape of this pan-archipelagic foundational culture is discernible in the Batanes of your lifetime.

PA   When did the Batanes origin become the consensus in archaeology and linguistics?

MPR Thirty years ago, more or less.[16] But it was also the same moment in time that immediately followed the Marcos dictatorship, which muffled the desire to be regarded globally as civilised – a desire which, among other outcomes, made for the bizarre germination of a visual arts avant-garde at Imelda Marcos's Cultural Center of the Philippines. That avant-garde had already died a natural death when the dictatorship fell in 1986. But the heightened reinvestment in racial division and hierarchy during the dictatorship persisted as the tropes supported by the art and culture infrastructure.

On the other hand, outgrowing this desire to be civilised will put to shame many truisms about the Philippines: the 'racial' or 'blood' differences that we've fought decades-long wars over; the hyper-regionalism that glosses over the shared Austronesian language family that everyone speaks; the wrongly-construed antiquity of an aristocracy. The 50-year war of secession that Muslim Filipinos waged against the

the spread of the Austronesian languages southwards into the entirety of Southeast Asia. The date is firm: 4,000 years before the present.[10] The spread was to produce all 176 languages[11] spoken in the Philippines and many more in Indonesia. The same group of language speakers took off on boats with outriggers to Guam (Marianas), still during the Neolithic period, 3000–3500 years ago.[12] Austronesians populated the entire Pacific Ocean in the third epic movement of Homo sapiens – undertaken with small boats across oceanic waters. The Austronesian-speaking peoples also brought their language to Madagascar. Malagasy is Austronesian.[13] This current consensus in archaeology and linguistics has remained in place for some 30 years, although new reconstructions based on genetics may open up to multi-directional trajectories of arrivals, where and when. The general picture of the spread of this single language family is, unlikely to change, however.

It is deeply troubling to me that this is not widely known nor accepted as the Philippine genesis story. It shows the glacial pace of updating scientific information in education and public discourse. The slowness suggests an anti-science bias that should be unpacked. But most seriously, there have been great investments in the cultural field in the current and still colonial narrative of emergence. In that preferred narrative, today's Filipino is the outcome of 'waves of migration' culminating in an 'Indonesian type' that followed a 'Malay type'.[14] The Aboriginal population was the outcome of the earliest arrivals of black pygmies with tight curly hair, hence called Negritos.

Christian majority[17] was the outcome of violent marginalisation buttressed by an inaccurate picture of a cultural (and in the minds of many, racial) divide between Filipino Muslims and Christians. Extreme othering, hence, war, hence agonising social problems. Class anxiety (too poor) and race anxiety (too dark) produce many generations of bad art, violent social conflict, and inadequate policy.

PA There is a sense of how the Christian settlers in Mindanao have created this mythology for themselves. We are still dealing with this trauma and anxiety in the form of Duterte.

MPR Aside from perpetually inventing kings and queens in popular culture (the biggest project of which is Emperor Ferdinand and Empress Imelda), there are much more monstrous symptoms of this anxiety. The current president, Rodrigo Duterte, emerged from a Mindanao in which Christian settlers from the north armed themselves to the teeth to defend homesteads carved out of land that Muslim communities lived on for centuries. State-backed Christian militias attempted genocide, hoping to finally rid their hard-earned land from Muslim attempts to take it back. Horrors were committed. Duterte popped out of this sepsis to eradicate a century-old democratic project.

PA It is perhaps inevitable that one of the more bizarre pronouncements to come out of the Duterte presidency is the revival of Ferdinand Marcos's desire to rename the country as Maharlika,[18] the designation for a pre-colonial warrior class that Marcos co-opted to enforce his authoritarian worldview. He even had a film made titled *Maharlika* (1970/1987) about his exploits during the Second World War,[19] exploits that turned out to be pure fiction. Duterte's is a rehash of this performance of self-realisation through fraudulent means.

One of the more grandiose schemes of Imelda and Ferdinand was to appropriate the imagery of Malakas (the Strong One) and Maganda (the Beautiful One),[20] the primordial couple of Philippine mythology, distracting a traumatised public with the myth of pre-colonial royalty while robbing them blind. The origins of my ongoing artistic project, *The Collection of Jane Ryan and William Saunders* (2014–present), emerged from a desire to juxtapose this fraudulent 'pre-colonial' representation with an equally insidious one. Jane Ryan and

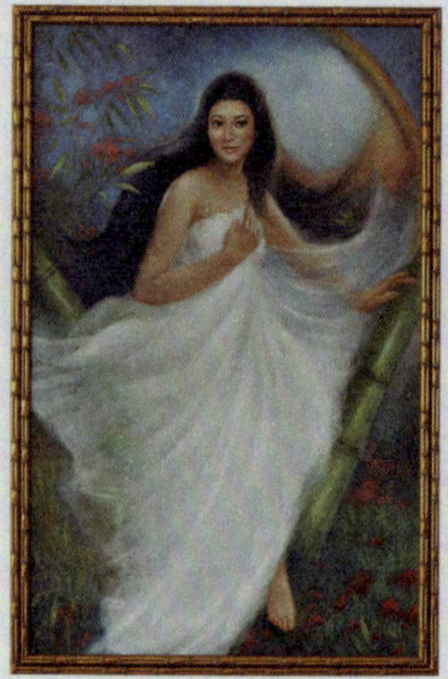
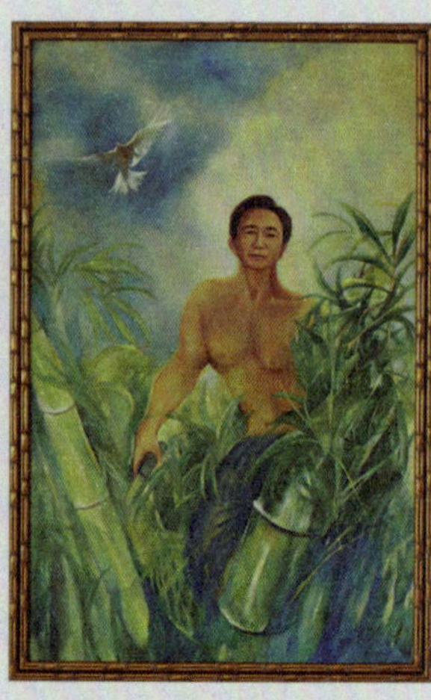

Pio Abad, *Imelda as Maganda, Ferdinand as Malakas*, 2014. Oil on canvas in faux gold bamboo frames. Image credit: by RJ Fernandez. Image courtesy of the artist.

William Saunders were another Marcos fabulation – the false identities they used to funnel sovereign wealth into their private Swiss bank accounts, grand larceny abetted by neo-colonial capitalist structures.

MPR In reality, there is no pre-colonial city to be found in the Philippine archipelago. The civilisational frame (and yearning) within which the Philippine art and culture field exists can only gloss over many vexations. The extraordinarily refined gold jewellery from archaeological sites in Surigao, Samar, and Batangas does not square with the assumption that such refinement could only have been created in court cultures. The special people who wore them are unlikely to have been the equivalent of civilisation's aristocracy. Who were they? I suppose that only a grasp of island Southeast Asian animism might assist in figuring out that sublime jewellery most likely was made for the ritualised shaping of states of being.

The heart-stopping beauty of the Philippine ancient and colonial period jewellery should be part of any discussion about the obvious fact that no monuments were ever built in the Philippines. No traditional cultural proclivity to monumentality, and no evidence otherwise: Filipino culturati have dreamt up retroactive make-believe kingdoms.

PA It's also worth talking about the lack of monumentality in our naming as a nation. The national consciousness comes from the name Philippine as a miniaturised designation – 'Little Philip'. I think so much of our trauma, so much of our national complex, comes from the historical fact that we were miniaturised from our colonial baptism, to begin with.

MPR That's true. It's strange that the small scale shifted from an exquisite phenomenology to a horrid one in our cultural history. Our best art was produced at the scale of the infinitesimally small. But when we were miniaturised by colonisers and their descendants in power – like the small, black men, the Negritos – it is classic othering. What do Filipino nativists pin longing on? On the fact that we had pre-colonial scripts, *baybayin*, for instance. But the historian William Henry Scott pointed out that that script was likely constituted only a few centuries before the Age of Encounter. Literacy, on the other hand, is the defining line between superior and inferior beings, as these things are formulated in imperia, hence the huge revivalism of *baybayin* in contemporary art, as a putative counter-narrative. But it is never a good strategy to claim to be a mirror image of the oppressor, especially because Filipinos still have to contend with the inconvenient truth that few of our ancestors wore clothes. And so, we're very big on clothing. The Philippine Congress gives itself many dress-up days, turning its precinct into a fashion show. And then you see wonderful tubular garments made of silk, produced in the last 400 years, by Filipino Muslims. So here are the royalty fantasies. This is a very serious problem for a nation as imagined through the fever of disease with signs of barbarity.

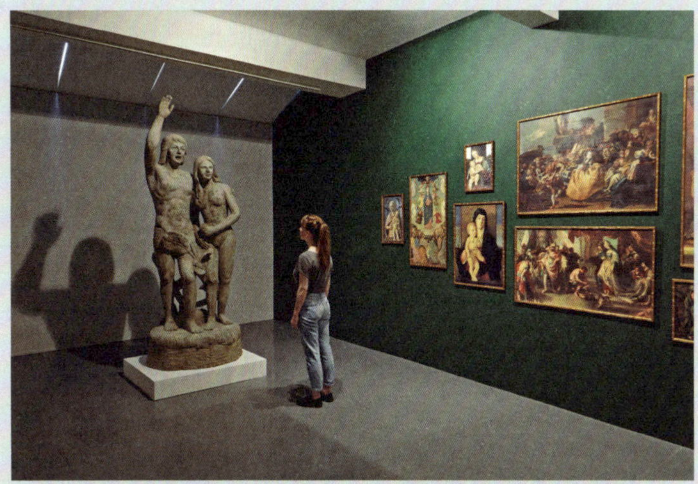

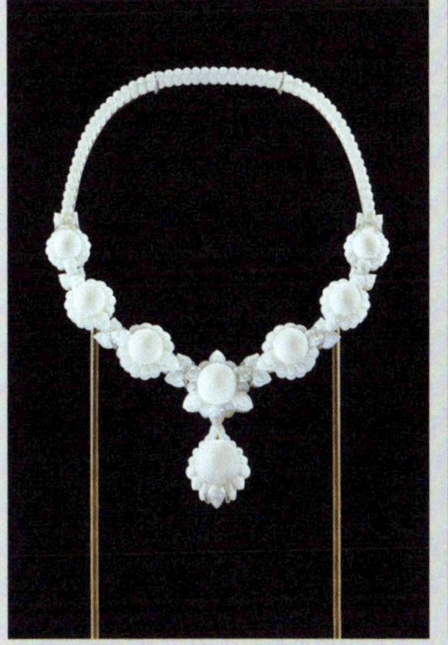 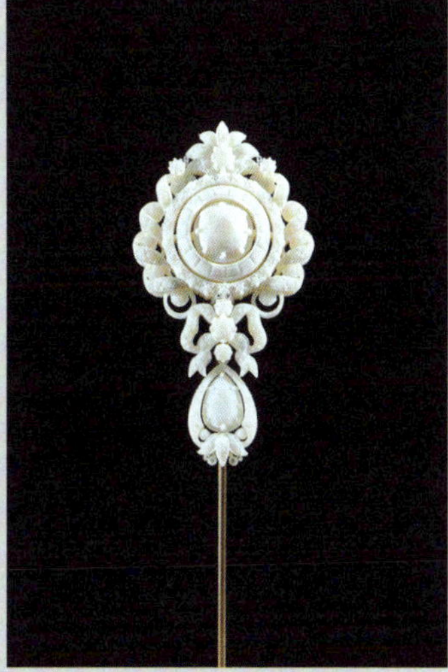

Top Installation view, Pio Abad, *Some Are Smarter Than Others*, Gasworks, 2014. Image Credit: by Matthew Booth. Courtesy of Gasworks and the artist.

Right Pio Abad and Frances Wadsworth Jones, *The Collection of Jane Ryan and William Saunders*, 2019 (detail). 3D printed plastic, brass stands and dry-transfer text. Courtesy of the artist.

Left Pio Abad and Frances Wadsworth Jones, *The Collection of Jane Ryan and William Saunders*, 2019 (detail). 3D printed plastic, brass stands and dry-transfer text. Courtesy of the artist.

PA The myth of an aristocracy.

MPR None more insidious, of course, than the Marcosian fabulation of a modern nation built on dressing up in the habiliments, so to speak, of modern progress. This meant, to them, surrounding themselves with art bought from both the most reputable and most shadowy dealers on earth, building the equivalent of palaces, and donning some of the most expensive jewellery on earth. It was agonising to see and to be projected upon.

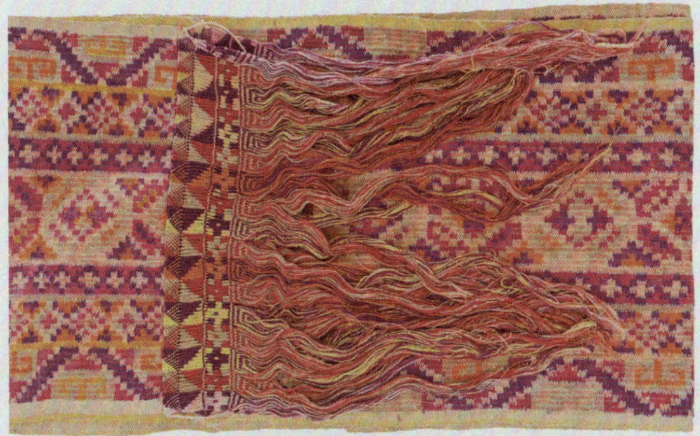

Waistcloth, kandit, tapestry-woven silk, Tausug people, Sulu Archipelago, late 19th century. Anak Mindanao Collection.

PA I have also been thinking about how my work can become a tool for unlearning this false narrative. *The Collection of Jane Ryan and William Saunders* started as fairly straightforward reproductions of the Marcos Collection – their statuary, Old Master paintings acquired through Armand Hammer and Knoedler Gallery, and Regency-era silverware. But then, over the past ten years, it has become part of a much larger network of objects and documents, whether it's annexed to things I have uncovered from the Reagan archives that invalidate the Marcos myth of selfhood, or the taxonomy determined by these new or not-so-new discoveries about Philippine archaeology. It explodes. It erupts into so many different segments.

The most recent iteration of this work is a collaboration with my wife and creative partner, Frances Wadsworth Jones, who is a jeweller by trade. The work consists of painstaking digital reconstructions of the collection of fine jewellery – tiaras, Van Cleef & Arpels necklaces, and diamonds – that Imelda Marcos amassed during her kleptocratic reign.

One of the decisions Frances and I made when creating this work was to not dwell on the outrageous aspects of the jewellery, but to read them as evidence of what continues to be denied to an already destitute nation. While still exquisitely rendered, these 3D printed versions of the jewels have all been stripped of colour to become spectral reconstructions. This project was initially developed in collaboration with the Presidential Commission on Good Government (PCGG)[21] during the last few months of the now late President Noynoy Aquino.[22] One of its last initiatives, which we incorporated into our work, was to calculate the equivalent value of Imelda's jewellery according to very specific aspects of national development. A pink diamond from the Indian mines in Golconda costs the same as entire domestic airports in Tawi-Tawi and Bicol, for instance. A set of diamond and sapphire bracelets and earrings could finance the full immunisation of 20,000 children. When viewed against these staggering equivalences, the work becomes a forensic counter-narrative to the story of progress that the Marcoses insist on foisting upon us.

Of course, talking about jewellery also becomes a segue into talking about the politics of beauty, and also, as you mentioned, the way that culture in the Philippines exists in miniature – in filigree rather than stone. Going back to Batanes, there is an incredible tradition of intricate gold jewellery that exists on the island, and research points to jade jewellery uncovered there as one of the main pieces of evidence that Batanes was the first Philippine landfall of Austronesian spread beyond Taiwan. These jade artefacts also echo traditional forms from the Maori culture, which emerged a few thousand years later.[23]

I can't help but view this jewellery as two facets of our complicated heritage: one crystallising the impunities and entitlements that continue to poison our sense of nation, and the other, based on archaeological fact which is potentially transformative, but largely uncelebrated.

MPR The difference between tiny and miniaturised is political. The tininess of the exquisitely made Philippine traditional art forms is a lesson in aesthetic refinement outside court systems. The miniaturised are humans and places reduced to the coloniser's possessions; like wild animals made into pets, lands claimed with title or bodies ravished for no reason other than self-entitlement. The Marcos jewellery that you are metaphorically redistributing across possibilities of criticality[24] is an embodiment of attempted monumentality: the accoutrements of a vast and revolting piece of social engineering. Imelda's jewels are artefacts of a period of wretched excess, of course, but more importantly, of an excessive desire to produce the king and queen we never had.

Martial Law imposed a dictatorial, centralised order on a people whose experience with central authority was edifying: having declared a democratic republic in 1898, Asia's first. It also made a spectacle of an idealised aesthetic – which should be called fascist – using fashion and jewellery as accoutrements of absolute control. This aesthetic is of an entirely different species from that which produced, for example, the traditional textiles of the Philippines, which were all articulated as exercises in subtlety.

PA These textiles were not meant to announce your arrival. They invite you to look closer.

MPR Or you're not sharing them. Or they're only yours because of ritual proscriptions against the willy-nilly sharing of knowledge. So, when did the ancestors start doing stuff for show? Surely, it began with the emergence of the bourgeoisie in the 19th century, the people we call *Ilustrado* today. The oil paintings, mostly portraits, invariably show Chinese and Spanish mestizos posed with their finery. These paintings are assiduously collected by a small nationalist circle and, instructively, for those like me who study institutions, entities such as the Central Bank of the Philippines. These are valued at millions of dollars each – prices that only the Filipino elite can pay for.

PA The bubble that speaks to itself.

MPR It speaks to itself, and it speaks to constructions of the nation. But the bubble, as you rightly describe it, sets itself up from a height above an entire people, as the beauty to emulate. Symbolically, the beauty had much to do, beginning with proposing a romanticised, civilised imaginary in the tropics. In the 20th century, these images shored up the cultural capital gained by this emergent class during the Philippine Revolution against Spain. As we know, members of that bourgeoisie, who engaged in reform politics as expatriates in Europe, form most of the pantheon of national heroes. A hierarchy of images was also constructed in the same 19th century. The *Ilustrado* portraits were one class of art. The others were images of various types of people in a marked space: the *Tipos del País* kind of artwork. The *Tipos* taxonomised denizens according to a touristic, quasi-anthropologic eye into a wild mishmash of labour, class, race, and other categories.

PA It's a delusion that was heavily propped up by other actors all over the world.

MPR Delusion is a good word to use for both the oils and watercolours (and photographs, eventually). The *Tipos del País* were embedded in the *Costumbrismo* visual and literary conversation with Neoclassicism and subsequently with modernising winds. The oils were sustained efforts to rise above the folklorism of the *Tipos*, deploying some academic training in European techniques. The creation of worlds through these art methods was not self-aware that worlds were being created in the image of their creators. The delusion was both happy and, in hindsight, noxious. It is a long but direct descent line from *Costumbrismo* to Disney World's 'It's a Small World (After All)'. And

of course, to the national and international beauty pageants.

PA 'It's a Small World (After All)' was one of the first songs I remember being taught in school. It's a very good analogy because the taxonomic eye that we've been forced to view ourselves through, particularly from the Marcos era, is an impoverished eye, a low-resolution version of national representation. The preoccupation was with the silhouette, not with the details.

MPR Indeed. Again, in hindsight, the Miss Universe beauty pageant of 1974 at the newly inaugurated Cultural Center of the Philippines Complex was inevitable as the first grand-scale project of Imelda Marcos. It was staged with the grandiloquent parade of thousands, *Kasaysayan ng Lahi* [History of the Race], culminating in the Folk Arts Theater built in 70 days. The Folk Arts Theater staged the folk – her version of *Tipos del País* using live examples. The long taproot leads to Europe. It is the German *Volk* that, idealised, produced a deadly form of nativism. And of course, it was *Costumbrismo* in Spain producing both typologies of its colonised subjects and literature focused on anthropological reality, with French and English versions. Dense terrains of imaginings overlap, interact, and metamorphose. The Philippine strand is fairly straightforward. The 20th-century beauty pageants channel the late 19th-century construction of nation as embodied in a racial-cum-class formulation sorting out body politic. The 'evolution' of the nation as a Darwinian ascent from primitive to glorious.

This brings us back to Batanes, specifically to Dr Maria Mangahas's research on two fishing communities:[25] one on the Badjao, in Tawi-Tawi; and the other, Batanes. The two ends of the Philippines. Great scholarship. It still blows my mind. Do you know the Matáw fishers?

PA Yes, they're the community of fisherfolk who live near our house in Batanes.

MPR Based on Mangahas's scholarship, the Matáw fishers live in relation to a concept and an actual geologic form, the *vanuá*. In Batanes, it refers to a channel underwater, through which the small outrigger-less boats can shoot out to the open water. Each existing Matáw group has exclusive use of a particular *vanuá*. A complex system of relations is maintained that moves from ritual to virtual to actual, seamlessly. But *vanuá* is an archaic Austronesian word that spread widely in the Austronesian-speaking world. Its physical and metaphoric use in Batanes is ritualised.

PA In Pampanga, where my mother is originally from, it means 'year'.

MPR Yes. In Ilonggo, it means *pueblo*, because that's how it was documented in the Spanish dictionaries for the vernacular languages. If you bring together *vanuá* or *banwá* entries in other dictionaries, it constellates archaic concepts of time and space. Scott, whom I cited earlier, summarises the 16th century Panay Island cluster of meanings encompassed by this word, which includes the sea from island to island, the place that you were born, and so forth. Here is a term from a local cosmology that was reduced into 'town'. Then I realised that, of course, I see it everywhere, there are the Tagbanwa of Palawan; the Mamanua of Mindanao; Vanuatu, on the other side of the Austronesian Pacific. And variations of the same word with what are clearly truncated meanings.

PA I think this idea of civilisational anxiety and the Marcoses' penchant for fictionalisation point to the reality that Filipinos don't quite know their place in the world. So much of the inferiority complex or the superiority complex, of these paradoxes that live within all of us, come from losing our *banwá*.

MPR Yes. We don't know our place in the world. We lost our *banwá*. The word came to mean 'town', and so much severed from the archaic concept without a stable construct in its stead.

PA You could say that *banwá* is our phantom limb.

MPR So, something about Marcos, perhaps not Imelda, though she had her own genius. Ferdinand Marcos had a particular intelligence. He was Ilocano, not an aristocrat. He was born to salt-of-the-earth parents; one was a public school teacher with a small house in Ilocos. So, Marcos, you can assume, grew up with the mythology of the Austronesian people. He knew the power of Malakas and Maganda, and to pick that myth as their representation backed into a very deep part of the past, which still exists. Imelda brought it in another direction, which I failed to understand. I think she's not part of any mythological world.

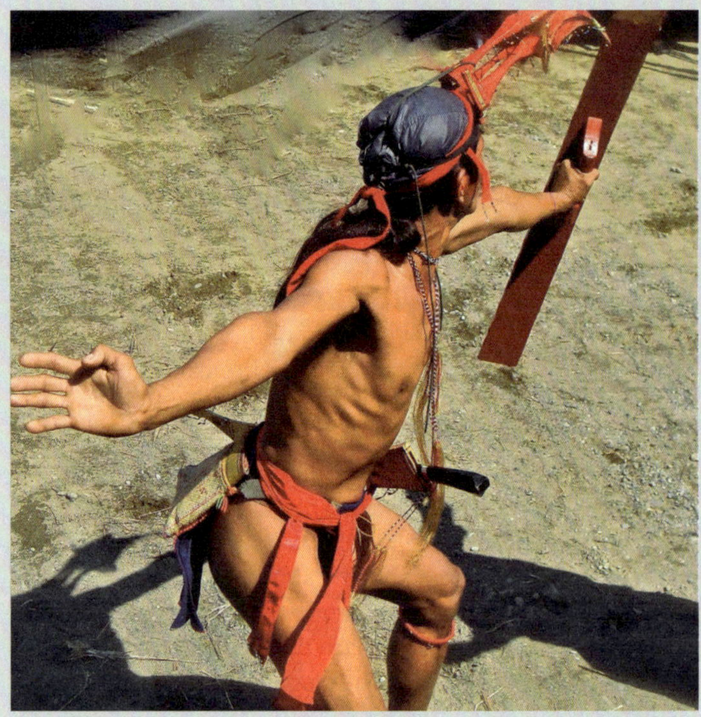

Image of an ancestor figure. Elder of the Bungkalot ethno-linguistic group. Image credit: Marian Pastor Roces.

I don't think she experienced it, though I think Marcos did. Imelda is closer to Miss Universe, so to speak.

PA Yes, the mongrelisation of all of these different fictions coming into one form.

Maybe it was Marcos's masterful manipulation of rooted myths and Imelda's incredible flights of fancy that created this sort of toxic mix that we're all still operating from…

MPR To this day. Seriously, I've had a strange practice. I've been commissioned to stage the Philippines in four world expos. The next one is in Dubai, and it's worth mentioning because I'm finally able to talk about these 4,000 years. We'll have Batanes in Dubai. When I speak about Austronesians, I always make the point that, if you think this is all history or archaeology, please remember that one out of every three sailors on earth right now is Filipino. You might consider that the Austronesian movement has not stopped.

I have a fantasy of going to Vanuatu and that I might find something there that allows for theorizing *banwá*; a concept of community in a water-filled cosmos that

In Conversation

may have been, for all we know, construed to be phantom-like.

Even if there have, indeed, been Austronesian kingdoms in Java, Bali, Sumatra, and Hawaii, you still have all the islands from Madagascar to Easter Island, on a vast stretch of earth, with peoples whose languages place them in precise relation to fluid particularities. In terms of numbers, aside from the 176 spoken in the Philippines, are some 350 Austronesian languages in Indonesia and more than 1,200 others across the globe. It is the fifth-largest language group in the world, spoken by more than 300 million people.

Pageant queens of fabulous kingdoms of beauty work to conceal the embarrassing memory of naked, tattooed, water-borne peoples. Even as a deep past, Filipinos are uncomfortable with this un-noble savage. Our leaders in politics, the intelligentsia, and the artists, too, have covered it with layers and layers of fraud, or exoticised it so fervently that no one realises that these are operations of othering.

What really irks me is that none of this informs political analysis. We have a hard time grasping the density of orality, even as we still swim in that density daily. And as a curator, and perhaps you as an artist, the jouissance in our practices can only be in archaeological performances that pry out the stuff buried under accretions of dirt and garbage, and deluded dreams. And then to recognise – calmly – that that buried stuff only suggests complexities that are irretrievable; or are truths far worse than we thought.

I can see that you're working with a particular part of recently buried ground; this is important because the 1970s were a massive site of cultural destruction.

PA I realised that your practice opened up mine in terms of the vastness of the history that needs to be addressed. The 1970s and 1980s have been my particular starting point because that era laid the foundations for my political self, from my parents' incarceration during the dictatorship to being born a few months before Ninoy Aquino was assassinated.[26] It is what shaped my political consciousness, and what continues to do so. But, as the artistic project evolved, it began to unmoor itself from that decade and to constellate further back or further forward.

But certainly, this period has been a preoccupation for the last ten years.

MPR What's it like to spend this much time on it?

PA I always think it's finished, and it never is, because it encompasses so many different things. I keep on finding it as part of a larger constellation of things, from Austronesian creationist myths and the history of the Romanovs to the Cold War alliances that connect the Marcoses with the Pahlavis and Pinochet.

Beyond that, it's also reckoning with the edges of the unreasonable hope that we mentioned earlier. I started putting together this project in 2011, just after the fall of Gaddafi in Libya, naively thinking that the worst aspects of fascism were behind us and that I was riding this wave of corrective history. I was wrong. Perhaps, we all need to grant ourselves that fantasy of hope from time to time, to be able to carry on doing what we do.

MPR I mentioned earlier about the 1970s avant-garde that was birthed at the Cultural Center. I've written of its misfortune;[27] that its slotting into the civilisational drive was, of course, unclear to the participants, including myself. It does take distance to recognise the unfortunate zeitgeist of one's own time. At that time, there was fun to be had, reading *Artforum* and, to use the appropriate period word, 'tripping' on Lynda Benglis, Tom Marioni, and Eva Hesse. All of it seemed utterly civilised, and we did not even think to connect that embrace of conceptualism and institutional criticism in one part of the CCP and the pageants and parades on the CCP grounds.

So, it bleeds into your world. But I am pleased – and grateful – that you grasp the interlocked contemporary art and folk-art programmes. We grant that no one conceptualised these and other activities as unified. Dictatorship, however, is an irreducible fact that over-determines – that wills to over-determine – everything and anything.

PA Once again, it is this misguided civilising impulse. In the end, you lose detail amidst the false grandeur of the institutions and the pageant noise. You lose the critical part that allows you to think for yourself.

MPR One loses the individual freedom to think and create, even without constricting rules imposed on anyone – Foucauldian panopticon stuff. You lose criticality, the ability to see the operations of power through the production of spurious narratives. And that inability drained conceptualism of its mojo. Because what's conceptualism about, except to analyse power?

PA I think it's important for me not to see myself through that lineage, and I guess there is the privilege of being diasporic that allows for distance and allows me to look at my place in the world through other prisms. It's been interesting to locate this research on the Marcoses, not through the lens of Philippine conceptualism or even a Southeast Asian perspective, but through the perspective of, say, artists coming out of Beirut from the 1990s, where the archive's role and the power of reconstruction meant something else. I think you and I share that need to constellate further in both our practices. That's how we get our *banwá*. You get your place in the world through these communities that you create that aren't necessarily the communities that you're immediately given.

As an artist, the mission is how to hold on to pockets of hope and imagine something else while grieving, not just for a specific family, but for what's happening in the country. In the case of *The Collection of Jane Ryan and William Saunders*, how do you imagine accountability, but also, how do you convince people to imagine accountability?

This is when the politics of beauty comes in.

MPR But we don't know if it works.

PA That's when the work of an artist is fundamentally a hopeful, some would say delusional, act. You cling on to the belief that the work will be transformative at some point.

MPR Most likely, it won't.

We don't know. You probably have to get shot for an artwork, like José Rizal, to commend something. Or you have to be a master of spectacle like Ai Weiwei. But the odds are against you if you're working with nuance, subtlety, smallness, and invisibility – as an aesthetic worthy of deep admiration and, possibly, the dreamlike counter-narrative to tyranny.

1   Ivatan is the name of the language and the people indigenous to the Batanes Islands, a group of small islands at the northernmost part of the Philippine archipelago. Pio Abad's paternal descent line is Ivatan.

2   Corazon S. Alvina and Marian Pastor Roces, *A Delicate Balance: Batanes Food, Ecology, and Community*, Manila, Museo ng Kaalamang Katutubo, 2018.

3   The president of the Philippines at the time of this conversation was Rodrigo R. Duterte, who explicitly and loudly ordered killings of 'drug addicts' in a so-called war on drugs. He walked back on these outrageous remarks by dismissing them as jokes. But the death toll from this rampage stands at an estimated 30,000 mostly underprivileged individuals.

4   For an anatomy of the disinformation campaigns, see Jonathan Corpus Ong and Jason Vincent A Cabañes, *Architects of Networked Disinformation: Behind the Scenes of Troll Accounts and Fake News Production in the Philippines*, University of Massachusetts Open Access, 2018.

5   The Bangsamoro Autonomous Region in Muslim Mindanao (BARMM) was created via legislation at the Philippine Congress: the passage of the Bangsamoro Organic Law (Republic Act no. 11054) and its subsequent ratification by popular vote in the areas concerned. The creation of BARMM in 2018 culminated more than 20 years of an often-derailed peace process; and ended 50 years of a war of secession.

6   The boomer generation of the Philippines came into early maturity while at university in the early 1970s, when President Ferdinand Marcos imposed Martial Law. This imposition over-determined their lives, as a substantial number spent their next decades in anti-dictatorship struggles – including Pio Abad's parents, Florencio and Dina Abad.

7   Japan attacked and occupied the Philippines from 1942 to 1945 during the Second World War. At that time, the Philippines was a colony of the United States and part of its territory.

8   Philippine President Ferdinand Marcos ruled with dictatorial power from 1972 to 1986.

9   The globally peripatetic artist Pacita Abad was the sister of Florencio Abad, Pio's father.

10 Peter Bellwood and Eusebio Dizon, ed., *4000 Years of Migration and Cultural Exchange: The Archaeology of the Batanes Islands, Northern Philippines*. Vol. 40, ANU Press, 2013.

11 *The Languages of the Philippines*, Ethnologue, Summer Institute of Linguistics, lists 186 Philippines languages, ten of which are immigrant or non-indigenous. All the rest are Austronesian languages. https://www.ehnologue.com/country/18-165

12 See, among others, the most recent work in genetics by Irina Pugach, Alexander Hübner, Hsiao-chun Hung, Matthias Meyer, Mike T. Carson, and Mark Stoneking 'Ancient DNA from Guam and the peopling of the Pacific,' *Proceedings of the National Academy of Sciences*, January 2021, 118 (1).

13 See, among others, Alexander Adelaar, 'Asian roots of the Malagasy: A Linguistic Perspective,' *Bijdragen tot de Taal-, Land- en Volkenkunde* 151, no. 3, 1995.

14 The 'waves of migration' reconstruction of 'peopling' of the Philippines from the south is typically associated with the early 20th-century American archaeologist working in the Philippines, Henry Otley Beyer. However, the basic framework predated Beyer's lifetime. Diffusion northwards from Indonesia was the standard trope by the 19th century.

15 Filomeno Aguilar Jr., 'Tracing Origins: *Ilustrado* Nationalism and the Racial Science of Migration Waves,' *The Journal of Asian Studies*, 64, no. 3, 2005, pp. 605–637.

16 The earliest major work formulating the linguistic family called Austronesian was Otto Dempwolff's, *Vergleichende Lautlehre des austronesischen Wortschatzes* [Comparative phonology of the Austronesian vocabularies], 3 volumes, (1934–1937). *Beihefte zur Zeitschrift für Eingeborenen-Sprachen* (Supplements to the Journal of Native Languages) 15; 17; 19 (in German). Berlin: Dietrich Reimer. The sub-groupings of the Austronesian languages that have been widely in use since was Robert Blust's *The Proto-Austronesian pronouns and Austronesian subgrouping: A preliminary report* (Honolulu, Department of Linguistics, University of Hawaii, 1977). A series of essays by the archaeologist Peter Bellwood consolidated the idea of Austronesian language expansion from Taiwan. See: Peter Bellwood, 'The Austronesian Dispersal and the Origin of Languages', *Scientific American* 265, no. 1, July 1991, pp. 88–93.
    Peter Bellwood, *Prehistory of the Indo-Malaysian Archipelago*, ANU Press, 1985.
    Peter Bellwood, 'Taiwan and the Prehistory of the Austronesians-speaking Peoples', *Review of Archaeology*, 18, 1998.
    Peter Bellwood, James Fox, and Darrell Tyron, *The Austronesians: Historical and Comparative Perspectives*, ANU Press, 1995. It was Bellwood's work of the 1990s and his subsequent work with Eusebio Dizon in the 2000s that cemented the Austronesian 'Out of Taiwan' consensus. Alternative views were held by the late Wilhelm Solheim and Stephen Oppenheimer.

17 The Moro National Liberation Front was formed in 1969 with a secessionist agenda. Its war with the Philippine Republic was paused with the signing of the Tripoli Agreement in 1974. Charges of non-compliance with the agreement precipitated renewed hostilities that were to last the next decades, under the leadership of the Moro Islamic Liberation Front. The peace process culminated in the creation of the Bangsamoro Autonomous Region of Muslim Mindanao in 2018.

18 *Maharlika* or *maharlikha* is a loan word from Sanskrit and its use was documented in friar accounts of the Philippines under Spanish rule. *Mahar* (big, large) and *likha* (penis) in the original became in Philippine usage a designation for a rank in pre-colonial society.

19 Ferdinand Marcos claimed that he received 32 war medals for his bravery and heroism during the Second World War, including the Distinguished Silver Cross, the second highest honour given by the US Military, and the Order of the Purple Heart, given to soldiers wounded in combat. These claims were immediately debunked by historical records.

20 In Philippine creationist mythology, Malakas (The Strong One) and Maganda (The Beautiful One) are the couple from which the entire Filipino race is said to originate. According to the most popular form of the story, they enter the world fully formed when a magical bird splits a single stalk of bamboo open, revealing them cradled inside. The cosmological figuration with a bilateral frame with male/female polarities was and remains typical for the islands of Southeast Asia and the rest of the Austronesian world.

21 The Presidential Commission on Good Government was established by the revolutionary government of Corazon Aquino in 1986 to uncover and liquidate the ill-gotten assets of the Marcos family, estimated at around $10 billion. When Rodrigo Duterte took over as president in June 2016, the PCGG was effectively placed under the office of the solicitor general, a known Marcos associate.

22 President Benigno Simeon C. Aquino III (2010-2016) went by the nickname Noynoy. To the general public, he was PNoy, President Noy.

23 Peter Bellwood, Hsiao-chun Hung, and Yoshiyuki Iizuka, 'Taiwan Jade
    in the Philippines: 3,000 Years of Trade and Long-distance Interaction',
    Paths of Origins: The Austronesian Heritage, ed. Purissima Benitez-Johannot,
    ArtPostAsia, 2011.

24 The most recent version projects the jewellery onto augmented reality,
    allowing the Filipino public to imagine possibilities of restitution through
    digital means.

25 Maria F. Mangahas, 'Seasonal Ritual and the Regulation of Fishing in
    Batanes Province, Philippines,' in *Managing Coastal and Inland Waters*,
    ed. Kenneth Ruddle and Arif Satria, New York, Springer, 2010.

26 Senator Benigno Aquino Jr., political nemesis of Ferdinand Marcos, was
    assassinated in 1983 as he exited the airplane that brought him to the
    Philippines from medical exile in the United States.

27 Marian Pastor Roces, 'Conceptual Art, Authoritarianism, 1970s, Asia',
    Gathering: Political Writing on Art and Culture, Museum of Contemporary
    Art and Design and Art Asia Pacific, Manila and Hong Kong, 2018.

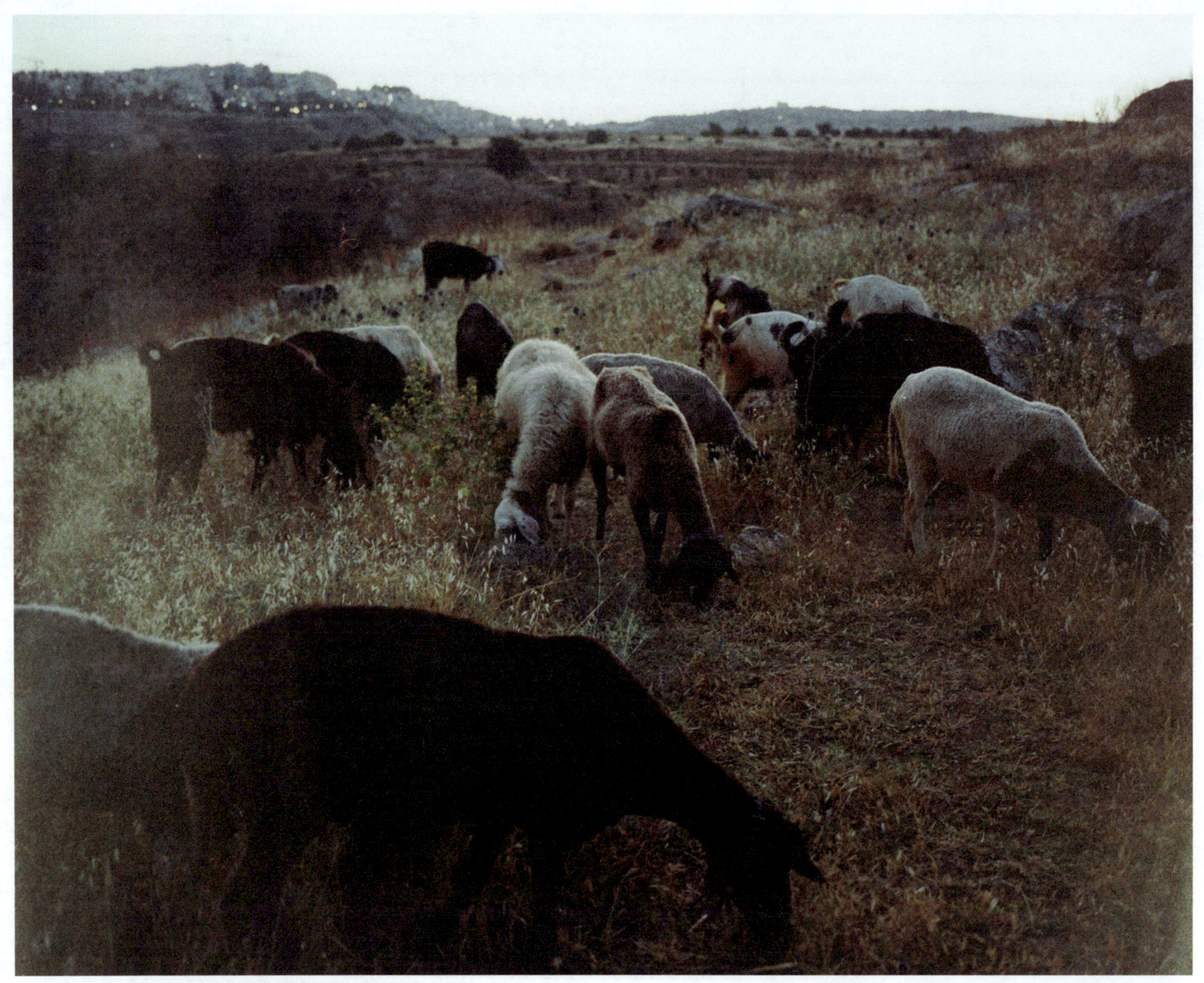

Goats and sheep in the valley. Shu'fat, East Jerusalem. Courtesy of the author.

Jumana Manna

Where Nature Ends and Settlements Begin

Lockdown

I came back home in spring to shoot a film about foraging wild food. At its heart, it is a chase film between the Israeli Nature Patrol and elderly Palestinians who gather plants listed as protected species, particularly the wild-growing, artichoke-like tumble thistle *'akkoub*, aka 'green gold'. Still in the making, *Foragers* is ultimately concerned with what is made extinct and what gets to live on; who gets to decide the fate of herb-picking cultures, and the options that remain for those who don't. Food manifests as a container for family and community histories tied to land – traditions that face suppression encoded into the legal dynamic of nature protection. The shoot has been cancelled due to the Covid-19 lockdown, and instead, I find myself quarantined with my parents in Shu'fat, East Jerusalem.

My daily activities are like that of a preteen or pensioner. They feature small adventures like foraging, collecting miscellaneous objects around the neighbourhood, home-improvement projects, reading, drawing, watching films, and writing. Having slowly accepted the serendipitous gifts offered by the virus, I begin enjoying my exilic nostalgia, a new-old way of being present in Jerusalem after having lived abroad for over a decade. In years past, I remember lamenting not spending enough time here, popping in for a few weeks at a time to shoot and gather my cultural

This essay was originally published in *e-flux journal* no. 113 (November 2020). Copyright the author and e-flux.

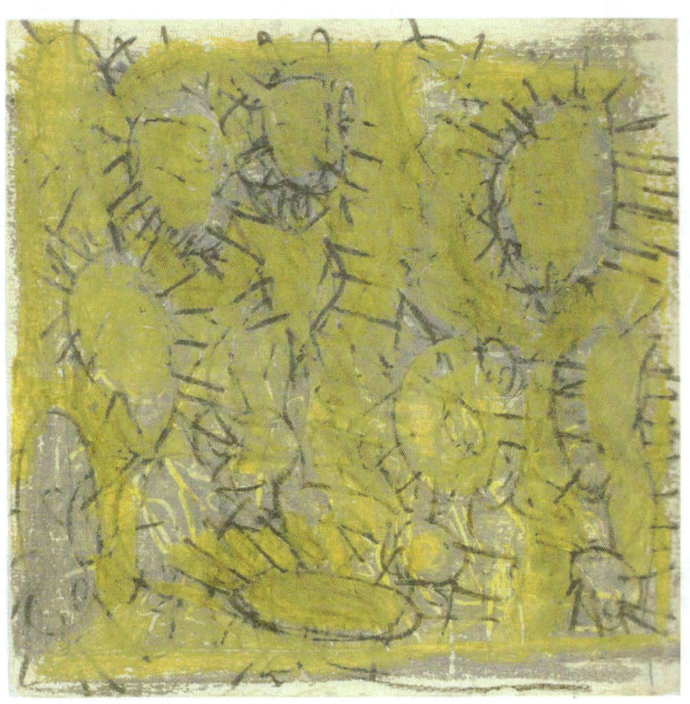

Asim Abu Shakra, *Cactus*, 1986. Gouache on paper. 15 × 15 cm.
Courtesy of Gallery One.

cachet, only to exit before the weight of this place could get to me. Lingering fears of having become a cultural tourist in my hometown are now, thankfully, relieved.

I go walking in the neighbourhood every day. I cross paths with animals, plants, and piles of scrap. I look at the neighbours looking at me, and get déjà vu of lethargic summer days, when school was out and there was time – lots of time. Helicopters watch us from above, and soundscapes from construction sites continue despite the strict curfew measures. As expected, Israel responds to the virus with a militarisation of medical discourse. It fills the streets with the army, police, and border control, and it bypasses a Knesset vote and authorises Shin Bet[1] tracking technologies to enforce social distancing. In one joint private-public effort, an Israeli tech company samples the voices of coronavirus patients, searching for clues about the illness in a person's voice and breathing patterns. A dataset of people gasping for breath.[2]

While picking wild edibles under quarantine, I've been thinking about the paradoxes inherent in the act of preservation – the politics behind the civilisational mask of a settler-colonial context. Red-listing nonhuman life to shield it from human damage on the one hand, and protecting populations from the nonhuman threat of an illness on the other, are not quite comparable activities. Yet the pandemic has highlighted varying governance structures and the intertwined politics of care all over the world. Within the immediate surroundings to which I have been confined, walking and writing have become the mediums through which to think about the militarisation of biological survival, as it gets pitted

1   Israel's domestic intelligence agency.

2   This sentence is paraphrased from a comment Amal Issa wrote on my Facebook wall, 25 March 2020.

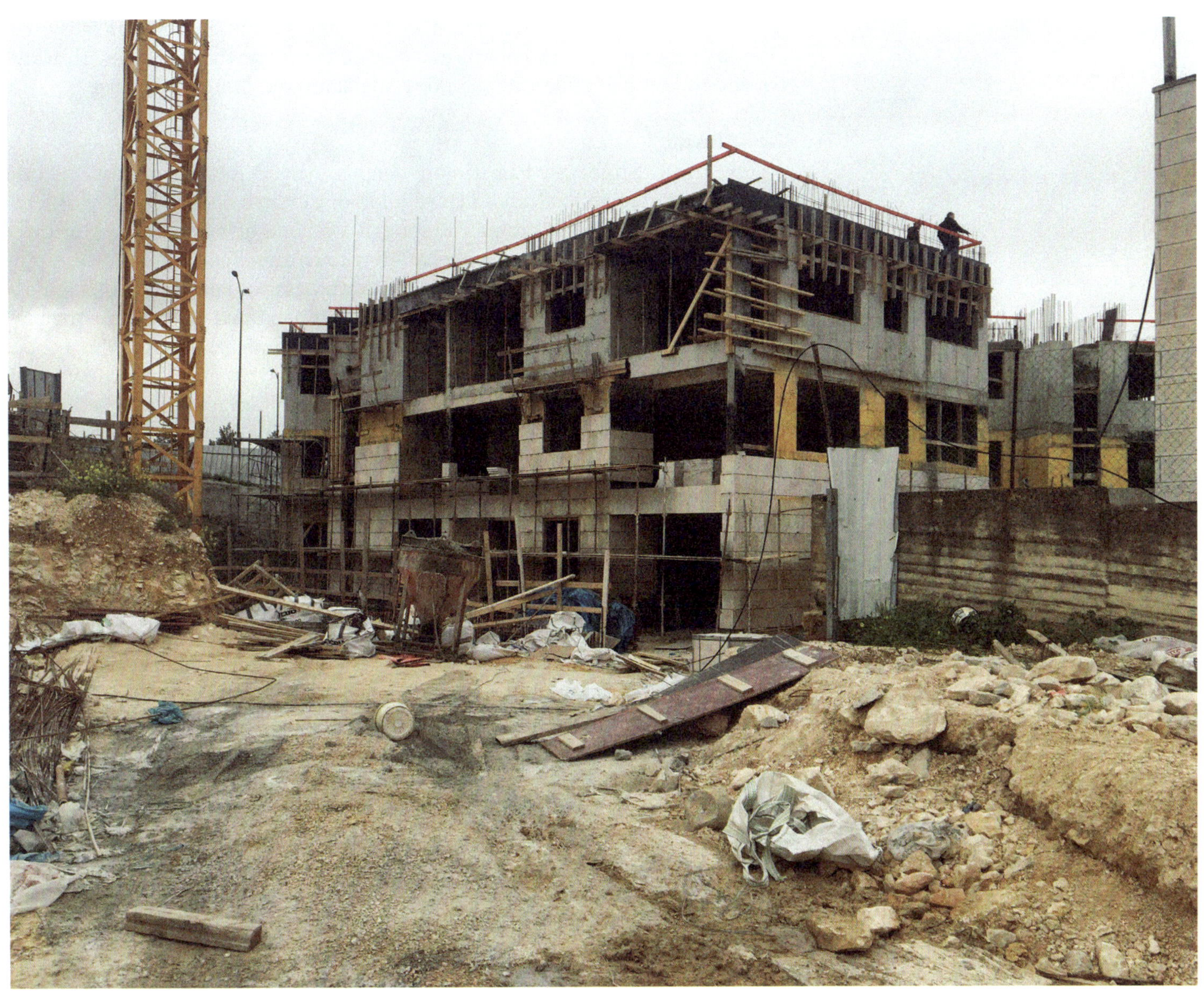

A construction site in Shu'fat. Courtesy of the author.

against other sociopolitical rights. This text, and eventually the film, are exercises in imagining alternative, affirmative care structures that remain, within and beyond the current reality, aligned towards plant and human life alike.

Shu'fat

I grew up in Shu'fat, a Palestinian neighbourhood located on the historic Jerusalem-Ramallah road, about three kilometres north of the Old City of Jerusalem. Throughout the Ottoman Empire, it was one of many villages in Liwa al-Quds (the district of Jerusalem) that grew to be an extension of the city from the first half of the 20th century onwards. At the time of East Jerusalem's annexation by Israel in 1967, Shu'fat had some 3,000 inhabitants. By the time my parents built a house there in the early 1990s, that number had grown to 15,000. Today, Shu'fat has about 35,000 residents.[3] In the 1970s and 1980s, few other Arab villages and neighbourhoods around Jerusalem, including Beit Hanina and Beit Safafa, still had available and affordable land. This availability and proximity weaved a new urban fabric made of growing Jerusalemite families, and early waves of Palestinian citizens of Israel arriving to the city from their villages for study and work.[4]

The heart of old Shu'fat maintains certain traditional architectural characteristics: domed roofs, thick one-to-two-story stone buildings, gardens with fruit trees, and *sanasel* – stone walls demarcating cultivated lands. These charming rural qualities did not always emerge out of the residing families' desire or choice, but rather out of a sustained strategy encoded into Israeli zoning laws. The strategy consisted of limiting the construction volume within a plot of land, in order to restrict Palestinian residents and manage the Arab 'demographic time bomb'. This racist phrase is often used to refer to the growing Arab population under Israeli jurisdiction, particularly in Jerusalem, where all means are deployed to maintain a Jewish majority.[5]

On the eastern side of the neighbourhood is Shu'fat refugee camp, the only Palestinian camp located inside Jerusalem's municipal borders. As a teenager, I spent a few summers training in the local pool there. It was a concrete hole with water so brown that it was impossible to see further than a metre through our Swedish goggles. Today my parents buy their fruits and vegetables there. The camp is frequently referenced in the media as a pocket of lawlessness, with high rates of hard drug use and trafficking. The Israeli settlements that surround our neighbourhood and the camp are many, and are all built on expropriated land to ensure that there is no territorial and social continuity between the Palestinian neighbourhoods of East Jerusalem. Instead, marginalised communities encircle the separation wall with unstable, rapidly built high-rises that house families desperately trying to hold onto their Jerusalem residence status.[6]

To the west of us is Shu'fat Ridge, a hillside that runs along the highway exiting the city. The hill used to be a planted pine forest, and up until the 1990s, it was marked as a public green space to improve the air and quality of life for nearby residents. My brothers and I used to play there as kids. But as former Jerusalem mayor Teddy Kollek confessed after this area was 'unfrozen' and earmarked for the construction of the Ramat Shlomo settlement in the early 1990s, the primary

3   This number does not include the refugee camp, which is inhabited by at least another 30,000 residents.

4   Primarily from towns and villages of the Galilee, also referred to as *a-shamaal*, or 'the north'.

5   After the occupation and annexation of East Jerusalem, the municipality passed a law limiting construction volume within a plot of land known as the 'floor area ratio' (FAR) to merely 25%. By comparison, Jewish neighbourhoods were built with high-rises, in order to exhaust the maximum capacity of the building area and to overlook the Arab neighbourhoods. As the decades passed, the FAR increased in East Jerusalem as the Israeli state realised that Arabs had run out of land. For further reading: Eyal Weizman, 'Jerusalem: Petrifying the Holy City,' chap. 1 in *Hollow Land: Israel's Architecture of Occupation*, Verso Books, 2007, pp. 25–57.

6   At the beginning of the Covid-19 outbreak, Israeli authorities threatened to shut the checkpoint and wall off the residents entirely, in a vague attempt to protect Jerusalemites from each other.

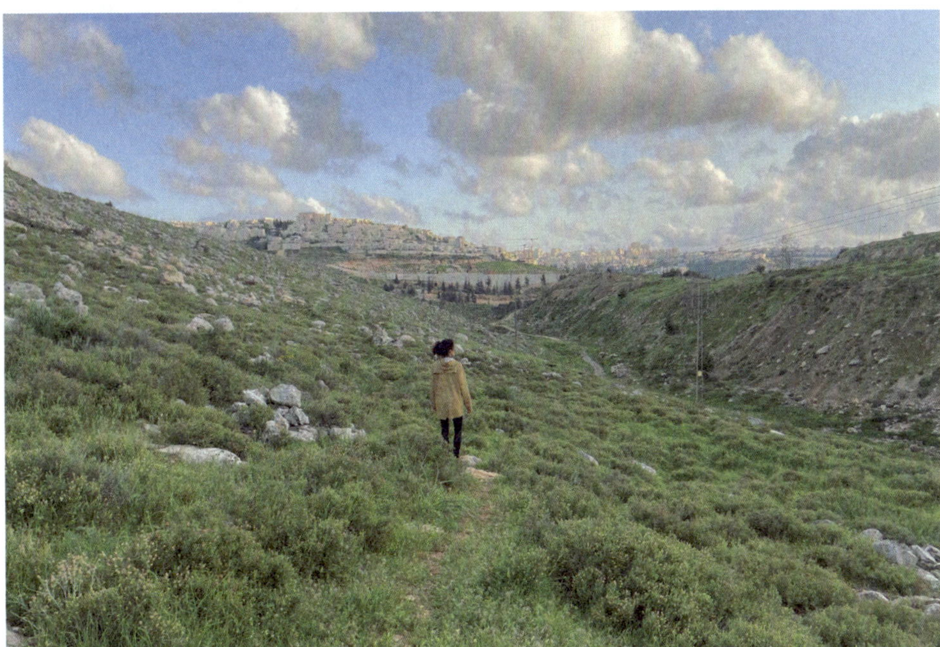

The valley, Shu'fat, and the Ramat Shlomo settlement are straight ahead.
Courtesy of Aline Khoury.

purpose of defining Shu'fat Ridge as a green area was in fact to prevent Arabs from building there, until it was time to build a new Jewish neighbourhood.[7]

Today all that separates Shu'fat from Ramat Shlomo is a two-lane road, beneath which our sewage flows in unison.

The Valley

I step outside my parents' house and walk westwards to the *sahel* (flat plane), through the old village, towards what remains of the olive groves that run beneath the bridges and alongside the highways exiting the city. Here, at the edges of the neighbourhood, I become acquainted with a valley that kept me close to the magic of spring and allowed me to live through what I could not film. I look at the limestone rocks peppered across the hills. They are inhabited by various growths, and marked by signs of former lives. Two palm-sized depressions are carved into a bed of limestone – ancient basins to collect rainwater for animals. There are rocks that indicate cave openings. Some contain signs of an oil or wine press, while others serve as habitats for plants, snails, the pods of microorganisms, and suntanning beds for lizards. To my surprise, gazelles regularly visit this valley, leaving little excretion pellets behind on their paths. We often meet and stop to exchange looks. I move closer; they run away.

A multitude of edible plants grow in this valley, as in much of the hilly landscape of Palestine/Israel. My parents, who forage frequently, both rave and complain about how quickly the fridge gets filled with greens that they have to wash, chop, and cook – before even going to the market. Between the months of February and May, they collect the following plants: *khubeizeh* (mallow), *shomar* (fennel), *za'atar* (thyme), *'elt* or *hindbeh* (dandelion), *hummeid* (bitter dock), *loof* (black

7   Sarah Kaminker, 'For Arabs Only: Building Restrictions in East Jerusalem', *Journal of Palestine Studies* 26, no. 4, 1997, p. 15.

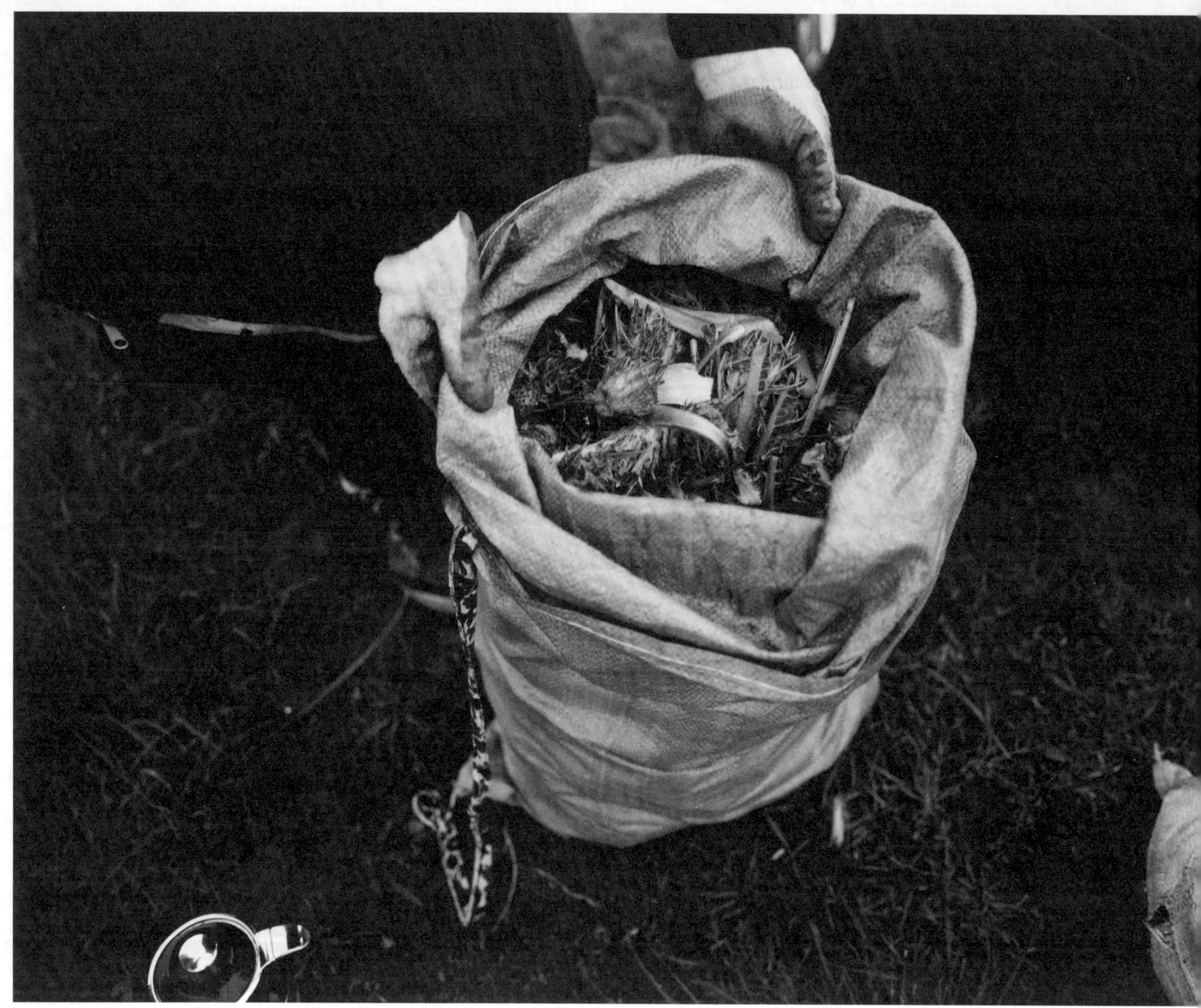

A sack full of foraged *'akkoub* in the Golan Heights. This quantity can take up to two hours for one person to collect. Once the thorns are cleaned, it will make a meal for a small family. Courtesy of the author.

Jumana Manna

calla), *wara' zquqiah* or *tutu* (ivy-leaved cyclamen), *halayoon* (wild asparagus), and the much-celebrated *'akkoub* (gundelia). It is indeed possible to live off of these wild leaves and vegetables in the springtime and only go to the grocer for a bag of onions, salt, olive oil, and perhaps some grains. This novelty is particularly poignant in times like these, where supermarket racks and trollies are not only potential virus transmitters, but also a symbol of the world's agricultural and ecological imbalance.

Many of the plants that grow in the region, once known as the Fertile Crescent, are wild relatives of the cultivated legumes that are sold in supermarkets today. The seasonal foraging practices here, as elsewhere, predate the rhythms of agricultural cultivation and state-imposed commercial and sovereign interests. Collecting wild-growing food was the backbone of human survival for millennia, and continued to be a daily practice alongside agriculture for just as long. In recent years, foraging has seen a resurgence of popularity across much of the world: for some, it's a leisurely weekend activity, a way of being close to nature, and for others, a means of survival – a safety net in precarious times. Inheriting knowledge about plants from my mother brought little moments of happiness, accompanied by the joy of witnessing the transformations of spring, the growths and disappearances of flowers, smells and changes in light quality from week to week. I felt so fortunate to experience this magic again. Throughout the quarantine, foraging became a hybrid performance of food sovereignty as well as culinary delight; it is for me an intimate practice that strengthened my sense of belonging and connection to the landscape.

Out of this plethora of forageable food growing in Palestine/Israel, the Israel Nature and Parks Authority (INPA) has listed three varieties as protected species: *'akkoub* (*Gundelia tournefortii*), *za'atar* (*Majorana syriaca*), and *miramiyyeh* (*Salvia tribola*). These are considered hard to find, as they grow in limited microclimates and are indeed often over-foraged. On my daily walks in the valley, I have made a new acquaintance, a shepherd named Abu Said. He has shared his knowledge of the area with me – a veritable embodied map of what edible food grows where. Most importantly, he's pointed me to where *'akkoub* grows in large quantities, and so my mother and I equip ourselves with thick gloves, knives, and bags, and get ready for our excursion.

'Akkoub tastes like a cross between asparagus and artichoke. It is a culinary obsession for many Palestinians, the utmost delicacy. For those who did not grow up eating it, however, it is simply an irrelevant thistle. Botanists have recorded the wide-ranging uses of this plant, and judging from its traces found at Neolithic sites in the region, its consumption dates back at least 10,000 years.[8] They say that *'akkoub* was mainly cooked like a vegetable, very much like how we eat it today.[9] It is very rarely cultivated and grows wildly on open limestone slopes and in reddish soil, from early February to early May, depending on elevation and rain patterns. It does not like turned-over soil, and wherever there are spills from construction sites or marks from screeching jeep tires, *'akkoub* is nowhere to be found. It is known for its wide range of health benefits: it can treat diabetes, liver diseases, chest pain, heart problems, stroke, gastric pain, diarrhoea, and bronchitis. It is antibacterial, anti-inflammatory, antioxidant, and anticarcinogenic. By

8 Nicholas Hind, 'Gundelia Tournefortii: Compositae,' *Curtis Botanical Magazine* 30, no. 2, July 2013, pp. 114–38.

9 A lone German man travelling through the Levant is the first known Westerner to have illustrated and described the *'akkoub*, scientifically known as *Gundelia tournefortii*. In November 1573, Leonhart Rauwolf (*lion heart, rough wolf*) left Bavaria to begin his search for herbal medicine supplies in Tripoli, modern-day Lebanon. He continued from there to the 'mighty city' of Aleppo, then to Baghdad and Mosul, before ending with a trip to Jerusalem. Rauwolf, relying on a description by the ancient Greek physician Discorides, mistook the *Gundelia* for milk thistle. A forgivable mistake really, as even locals today who eat *'akkoub* but aren't involved in its collection commonly confuse it with other similar-looking thistles. Prussian and other European botanists built on Rauwolf's *Aigentliche Beschribung der Reise in die Morgenländerin* (A true account of a voyage to the Levant). They noted how in the old Baghdad markets, the mature and hardened heads were eaten like nuts, and in some parts of Turkey and Iraq were used as a source of oil and gum.

the summer, the *'akkoub* dries and tumbles through the hills, spreading its seeds, and only goats are left chewing through its parched leaves.

On our *'akkoub* hunt, my mother and I clip the thistle at its base, slightly below soil level. We strip away the thorny leaves, and once we make it home, we meticulously shave off the remaining spikes before cooking. Our fingers turn black during this process of getting to the edible heart of the plant. The heart, along with the thicker stems, gets sautéed with onions and olive oil, or cooked with pieces of meat, sometimes covered with a yoghurt sauce. For me, *'akkoub* foraging and peeling is a Corona activity: a prickly passing of the time.

For as long as I can remember, we would get *'akkoub* from my aunts in the Upper Galilee. They would have already generously done the hard labour of cleaning the plant of its thorns, and we would prepare it for cooking. My aunts still live within the routines and time-space of rural life, wherein picking and peeling *'akkoub* is not considered time wasted. The plant also happens to be much more plentiful in the north, in Nablus, the Galilee, and most of all, in the occupied Syrian Golan Heights. Only as an adult did I understand that my aunts, now in their seventies and eighties, are perpetual scofflaws. Picking *'akkoub* has been deemed illegal by the Israeli authorities since 2005, and if you ask Palestinians why that is, many would say that it is 'because Arabs like it very much'.

The Law

Za'atar, the most widely used herb in any Palestinian (or Levantine) kitchen, was the first edible plant to be red-listed in Israeli law books. It was 1977 when Israel's then Minister of Agriculture, Ariel Sharon, declared it a protected species, effectively placing a total ban on the tradition of collection, punishable by hefty fines and up to three years in prison. There were no official scientific studies published to legitimise the ban; rather, it was presented as a 'gut' decision. Rumour has it that Sharon caught onto the symbolic value of *za'atar* after the 1976 siege of Tel al-Za'atar, Arabic for 'thyme hill'.[10] This Palestinian refugee camp, established north of Beirut in 1948, suffered one of the worst massacres of the Lebanese Civil War in a battle fought between the armed factions of the PLO and the Christian Lebanese Militia – the very same phalangist militia with whom Sharon would form an alliance in the 1982 massacre of Sabra and Shatila. Soon after the *za'atar* ban, a kibbutz in the Galilee started cultivating the herb and selling it en masse back to Palestinians, as well as exporting it to Arab countries, disguised by its packaging as a Palestinian product. The initiators of this project were the former Governor of Agriculture in the West Bank, Ze'ev Ben Herut, and his son, Yoram Ben Herut. Through extensive time spent with Palestinians, Ze'ev was able to gather the best recipes for *za'atar* mixes (various quantities of thyme, sumac, sesame seeds, and salt) from his Arab friends, catering to their tastes and market demands. This early example of food appropriation, a well-publicised and widespread strategy today (hummus, falafel, etc.), is one of many reminders of the occupation as an investment project, a military and technologically driven testing ground that services Israel's multilayered economies of extraction.

Nearly three decades after the *za'atar* ban, *miramiyyeh*, a sage variety primarily used for tea, and *'akkoub* were also added to the list of protected species.

10 Rabea Eghbarieh, *Limatha Takhsha Israeel al-za'atar w'al-'akkoub?* (Why does Israel fear *'akkoub* and *za'atar*?), *Fusha*, 8 May 2017

Jumana Manna

This law amendment was supported by 'science', in the form of a 1995 research paper by Didi Kaplan, Israeli botanist and employee of the INPA. Kaplan and his colleagues' research showed that over-foraging of *'akkoub* causes dwindling growth in the wild, as it has a negative effect on the flowering and rejuvenation of the plant. Kaplan, however, was against a total ban, recommending 'to restrict harvesting for domestic purposes only', and was adamant about preventing commercial exports to neighbouring countries.[11] Yet, due to the difficulty of enforcement and the slippage of scientific authority into the legal-political complex, the Ministry of Environment ended up passing a total ban instead of adopting a more nuanced approach. A common argument that INPA employees voiced to me during my field research was: 'How can we know whether these ten women in the valley all work for one man who goes to sell them in the market, or whether they are just picking a basket to feed their family?' Since Kaplan's paper, there has not been a single study following up on the impacts of the protection law on the plant's status in the wild.[12] And yet hundreds of people – exclusively Arabs – have been fined and gone to trial over the collection of *'akkoub* and *za'atar*.[13] These preservation laws constitute a thin ecological veil for racist legislation designed to further alienate Palestinians and Syrians in the occupied Golan Heights from their lands.[14] This is land that, in many cases, has been expropriated by the Israeli state and administered as Jewish towns, settlements, nature reserves, military training areas, and other forms of 'state land'.

Preservation under Zionism

Preservation measures have always been a double-edged sword. As our quarantine experience reminds us, every act of protection is accompanied by an erasure of another kind. The key question is often not whether to safeguard, but how and at what cost. In colonial contexts in particular, preservation laws have come as top-down decisions, imposed by the coloniser, armed with a claim to scientific expertise, and restricting the 'destructive tendencies' of the 'ignorant natives'. This dynamic has been particularly consistent in the national Zionist project, which has worked against the potential of a reciprocal exchange with the enemy other. Zionism has developed into an apartheid apparatus, a world cut in two, where the sovereign is in antagonism and vertical superiority vis-à-vis the Palestinian Arabs. Frantz Fanon likened master-subject relations in such colonial worlds to animal life where relations never lead to an affective community or common realm.[15] The master relegates his subjects to the category of lesser-than-human, thereby remaining forever untouched by their speech and subjecthood. In this symbolic structure, Palestinians are always on the receiving end, subjected to the law rather than subjects of its making. This sort of preservation impulse is particularly ironic in the case of the *'akkoub* ban, where a plant which is essential to northern Palestinian cuisine, and unheard of by most Israelis, is protected from the threat of Palestinians. Yet again, Israeli officials have forgotten to ask us what we think.

To restore a site or an object to its assumed and ultimately imagined original state often entails a preservation effort that severs the thing from its living environment. National Zionism constitutes a restoration event, a Judeo-Christian messianic effort to selectively 'return' what is believed to be the original, or 'natural', state of the land to Jewish hands, excluding others, through the idealised modern

11 Didi Kaplan, Dror Pevzner, Moshe Galilee, and Mario Gutman, 'Traditional Selective Harvesting Effects on Occurrence and Reproductive Growth of *Gundelia Tounfortii* in Israel Grasslands', *Israel Journal of Plant Sciences*, no. 43, 1995.

12 As Kaplan told me in an interview in March 2019.

13 Very few cases have been tried for the collecting of *miramiyyeh*, which is used mainly as an herb and not as food, and is, therefore, collected in lesser quantities.

14 *'Akkoub* is bountiful in many parts of the Golan Heights – Galileans forage most of their *'akkoub* from this region.

15 Achille Mbembe, 'Fanon's Pharmacy', chap. 5 in *Necropolitics* (Duke University Press, 2019), esp. p. 153.

configuration of being-in-common: the nation-state. In this ever-extending frontier – literally and conceptually, and along the lines of modernity at large – history-making has been a secularised version of messianic time.[16] Zionism did not stop at uncovering an archaeological site, locating the travelling sound waves of the music of the Second Temple, or speculating about the mentioning of *'akkoub* and *za'atar* in the Old Testament. This teleological construct of a state has historically used preservation and protection measures to further legitimise its claims to the land and reinforce its self-image by all means and in all fields, not least through conceptions of 'nature'.

The best-known example of a nationalised landscape – a reconfigured landscape designed to mirror the state's image – is the extensive monocultural planting of pine trees funded by the Jewish National Fund (JNF). This practice grew commonplace when Palestine/Israel gradually became the homeland of Ashkenazi Jews, and Europe the object of nostalgia. 'Making the desert bloom' was not a mere metaphor for the Zionist project; rather, by planting hundreds of man-made forests, Ashkenazis could imagine being back in Leipzig while living in Jerusalem.[17] The majority of afforestation projects were intended not only to make the 'primitive', semi-arid hills of Palestine look more 'civilised' according to European eyes, but also to erase the traces of the over 400 Palestinian villages that were destroyed during the Nakba of 1948, after their inhabitants were forced into exile.

With the rise of environmentalism in the 1990s, the JNF realised that it was not just the Palestinians who were erased; much of the flora and fauna of these lands were decimated along with them.[18] The intrusive acidity of the pine trees prevented other vegetation from growing back, and the over-prevalence of the pines increased the frequency and force of wildfires. This echoes disasters in Australia, North and South America, Portugal, and elsewhere. In California in particular, the erasure of indigenous American traditions of managed burning has caused an overgrowth of shrubbery, which, along with the spiking rates of global warming, has resulted in chronically uncontrollable fires. Today, Native American communities have partnered with the US Forest Service to steward land for traditional values and wildfire management.[19] In a similarly revisionist vein, environmentalists realised that draining the swamplands of Hula, in Galilee, in the 1950s damaged the migration routes of millions of birds flying between Europe and Africa. So in the mid-1990s, it was partially re-flooded in an effort to bring them back. The past century has seen many examples of this kind of 'misjudgement' and attempted repair: from desertification in the south – the Naqab/Negev – due to the depletion of groundwater resulting from the displacement of Bedouin populations, to grazing limitations that have affected Arab herders. Yet unlike other settler-colonial contexts such as the United States, Canada, or Australia, when the paradigmatic shift towards the politics of sustainability began to take root in Israel, it was not accompanied by an official apology or acknowledgement of historical crimes committed. As slim and ineffectual as these utterances have been in the West, Israel has not yet admitted that the displacement of a people went hand in hand with violence committed against the land. Instead, the new 'green' measures since the 1990s have been co-opted into the historical rhetoric of protection, where the binary relations of power continue to be reinforced to this day.

16 For more on the critique of techno-optimistic efforts enmeshed in Western end-time thinking, see Deborah Bird Rose, 'Reflections on the Zone of the Incomplete', in *Cryopreservation*, ed. Joanna Radin and Emma Kowal, MIT Press, 2017.

17 Paraphrased from Carol Bardenstein, 'Threads of Memory in Discourses of Rootedness: Of Trees, Oranges and Prickly-Pear Cactus in Palestine/Israel', *Edebiyat: A Journal of Middle Eastern Literatures* 8, no. 1 (1998). Bardenstein is quoted in Irus Braverman, 'Planting the Promised Landscape: Zionism, Nature, and Resistance in Israel/Palestine', *Natural Resources Journal* 49, no. 2, Spring 2009, p. 343.

18 Natalia Gutkowski, 'Governing through Timescape: Israeli Sustainable Agriculture Policy and the Palestinian-Arab Citizens', *International Journal of Middle East Studies* 50, no. 3, 2018.

19 Laren Sommer, 'To Manage Wildfire, California Looks To What Tribes Have Known All Along', *NPR*, 24 August 2020.

Despite the above-mentioned environmental 'mistakes', there is some ecological basis to the fear that *'akkoub, miramiyyeh,* and *za'atar* may be going extinct in the wild, well beyond the specifics of Israel/Palestine. Elderly people throughout the country and in neighbouring Jordan and Lebanon attest that these plants are much harder to find than they used to be. This new scarcity is also felt throughout Iran's Isfahani province, where it has already become common to intentionally plant *'akkoub* because the market demand is higher than what wild growth can provide.[20] Yet like most looming extinctions of biological life, the driving factors are damage to habitat, population growth, urbanisation, and climate change. When it comes to plant foraging, increased demand and unsustainable overharvesting are contributing factors, but are rarely primary causes. Professor Nativ Dudai, a botanist who has researched *za'atar*, confirms this in an interview:

> No one talks about the fact that we, the Jewish [Israelis], destroy much more *za'atar* than the Arabs pick. Do you know how many great *za'atar* populations were uprooted by bulldozers? In Har Adar or Elyaqim interchange – locations with beautiful amounts of *za'atar*, and all of it is now gone. But the Arab? He picks five kilograms and gets a fine.[21]

Negotiating the politics of plant extinction with an occupier is always complicated, especially in the context of Palestine, where over the past 70 years Palestinians themselves have been treated as an invasive species in urgent need of elimination and control. The protection of one form of life – nonhuman life – has been used as an extra tool to suffocate a people who have survived attempts at cultural erasure and ethnic cleansing.

This is an ontological paradox: the same state that creates security lists, kill lists, terrorist lists, and other databases to 'identify humans who risk to threaten' also establishes lists of nonhumans identified as threatened species, elevated to the political status of being in need of rescue.[22] The necropolitical state of Israel builds illusions of freedom and democracy through enmity and destruction, through a will to kill, while simultaneously adopting environmental rhetoric that claims to protect nature as virgin land, conveniently failing to recognise Palestinians' right to the land and self-determination. Instead, ancient Palestinian land practices are framed as an inherent threat to nature, and thus the right of Palestinians to access that nature is revoked. In the contested landscape of Palestine/Israel, then, the continued collection of *'akkoub* and *za'atar* in the wild, despite and in spite of the ban, is an act of both survival and anti-colonial resistance. Foraging these plants is part of a bid to hold on to forms of memory and know-how that are fast eroding.

Court Battles

An Israeli preservation law called the 'National Parks, Natural Reserves, and National and Memorial Sites Law of 1998' has been more like a pharmakon: a remedy and a poison at once. Many foragers claim that the law itself acts to propel commercial foraging. At times, in their haste and fear of being caught, foragers, especially those less familiar with the tradition, uproot the plant rather than cutting it at its base, thus depriving it of the possibility of regrowth. Others get a kick out of the illicit trade and enjoy putting up a defiant middle finger to Israel's unjust laws.

20 Habib Yazdansehnas, Ali Tavili, Hossein Arzani, and Hossein Azarnivand, 'Traditional Gundelia tournefortii Usage and its Habitat Destruction in Tiran va Karvan District in Iran's Isfahan Province', *Science Alert*, 15 June 2016.

21 Quoted in Rabea Eghabrieh, 'The Struggle for Za'atar and 'Akkoub: Israeli Nature Protection Laws and the Criminalization of Palestinian Herb-Picking culture', Oxford Food Symposium on Food and Cookery 2020, forthcoming.

22 Irus Braverman, 'The Regulatory Life of Threatened Species Lists', in *Animals, Biopolitics, Law: Lively Legalities*, ed. I. Braverman, Routledge, 2016, p. 20.

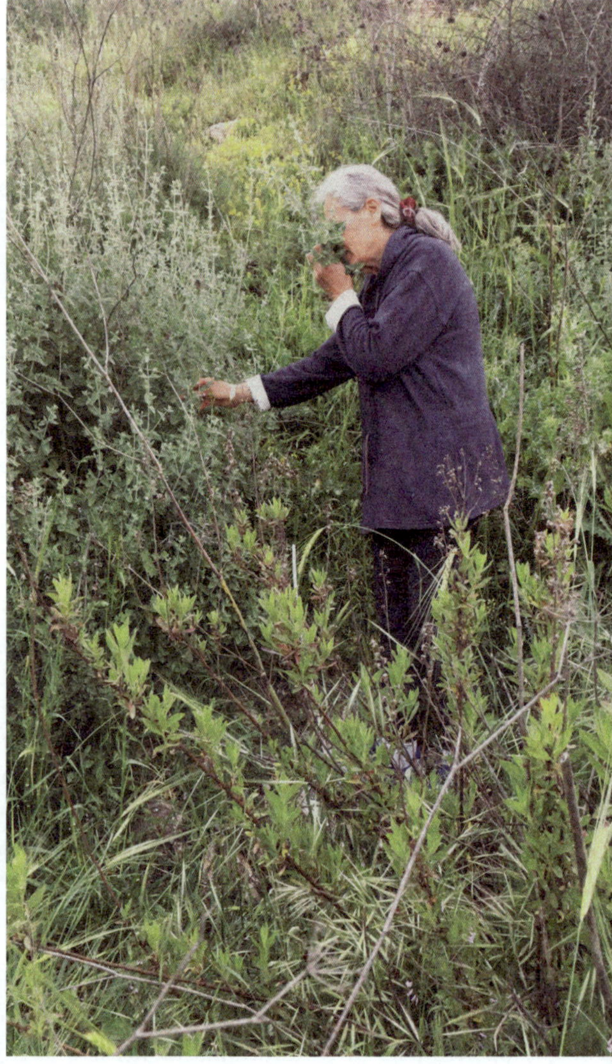

Aziza smelling Syrian catnip. Courtesy of the author.

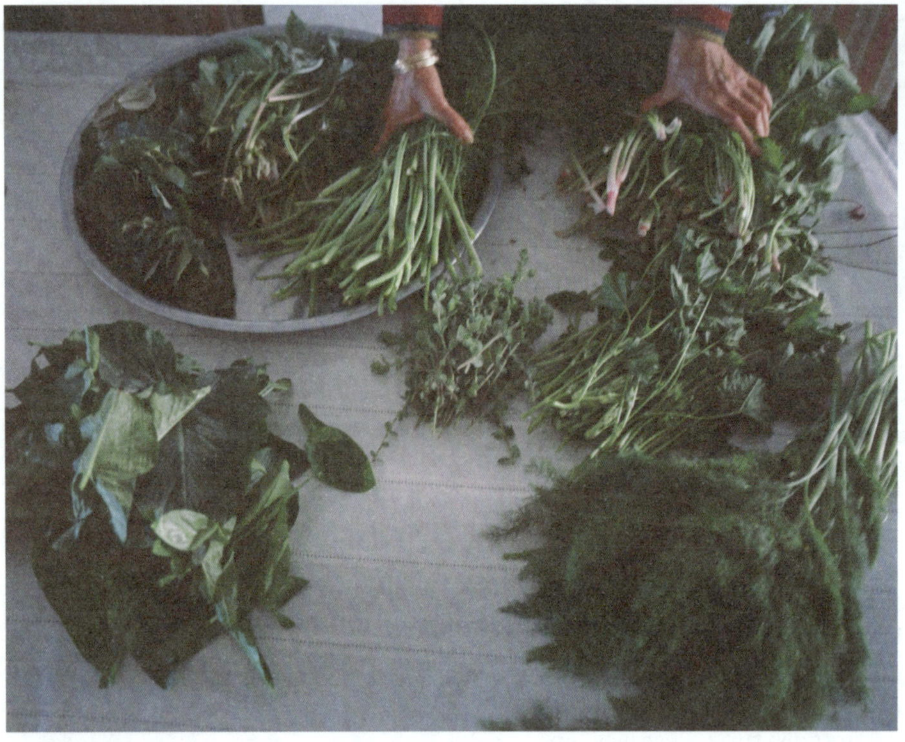

My mother, Aziza, sorting her foraged goods.
Courtesy of the author.

Over the past decade, Adalah, a legal centre for Arab rights in Israel, has demanded the decriminalisation of collecting *za'atar*, *'akkoub*, and *miramiyyeh*. The attorney and scholar Rabea Eghbarieh has been at the forefront of both Arab and Hebrew media campaigns, contributing to debates and publications on the topic. In a letter he wrote to Israel's State Attorney and Minister of Environmental Protection, Eghbarieh argued that 'the prohibition on gathering these herbal plants is not based on a reliable factual basis, does not serve the purpose of the law, and disproportionately harms the Arab population that has used these herbs for hundreds of years, particularly for cooking needs. Eghbarieh has often highlighted the gap in logic and rhetoric that arises during trials. The state representatives and judges perpetuate the expertise of the INPA and its scientific community, as well as the supposedly destructive tendencies of the Arabs. Meanwhile, the accused often state that they are simply out collecting food as they have done for generations. Moreover, indigenous knowledge and care around foraging practices are often dismissed: clipping the tops of *za'atar* and *miramiyyeh* stems, in fact, encourages fresh growth, and *'akkoub* will regrow the following year and sometimes within the same season, so long as it is clipped at its base. The judicial system wilfully ignores this expertise, the status of the plant as food, as well as the socioeconomic needs of those accused. Many who forage generally need to feed large families and can't always make ends meet. Instead, they are met with exorbitant fines, which, if not paid, result in jail sentences.

Adalah's persistence yielded results in late February 2020, when the INPA announced that enforcement measures would be softened. For a trial period of two years, everyone is now permitted to collect up to five kilograms of *'akkoub* for personal consumption. It is unclear whether the trial period is a commitment towards a lasting change of the law, or just a way to momentarily deflate what has become a topic of great sensitivity in the Arab sector inside Israel – and dodge Adalah's threat to petition the Higher Court.

Since February, nature patrollers have expressed their continued struggle to detect whether the collection is indeed only for personal consumption, or is rather for commercial sale in local markets. With a fast-growing, increasingly urbanised population, many want to eat *'akkoub* but few are willing to go out and put in the hard work. In response, the prevalent model has become so-called commercial foraging, where a small group picks between 30–100 kilograms a day to sell their harvest in the local market.

The real difficulty in enforcement clarifies the core of the problem: approaching conservation and preservation through criminalisation, supported by a bureaucratic system of law enforcement, is a strategy bound to fail. Criminalisation reinforces oppressive power relations, which, as with most societal challenges, rarely succeeds as a tool for structural and sustainable change. It is a monoculture and a mono-technology, a techno-fix – like pesticides, like antibacterial vaccines, like seeking a vaccine for Covid-19 while simultaneously leaving intact the faulty health structures, food industries, and globalised markets of the world. A new pandemic will only be a matter of time.

A Pause for Cat Orgasms

My mother and I walk eastwards this time, towards a wild hillside, hidden beneath a bridge that separates Shu'fat the neighbourhood and the camp from another settlement. On our way, a kid asks my mother and me if we're looking for someone. I say yes, the valley. This valley, too, is full of birds, stones, plants, and bushy trees. We assume it is expropriated land, given the massive concrete bridge that runs through it. But when we look below us, traces of plowing suggest that the original landowners seasonally come back to collect what is left of their fruit trees. The hill on the Shu'fat side is full of wild edibles and other kinds of native spring plants. The hill on the settlement side, however, is bland, covered mostly by grasses, with upturned soil to create a clean and orderly slope. Needless to say, there is nothing edible here. Back on our side of the hill, behind an old dilapidated metal fence, we find so many *za'atar* 'homes' that we can barely believe our eyes. By the look of it, no one has foraged here for years. So we do. Indulging in the process, we find another kind of thyme, one that is not illegal to pick: *za'atar al-bisas*, literally 'cat *za'atar*' (its Latin name is *Nepeta curviflora*). This type of thyme is also known as 'Syrian catnip' because of the pleasure cats get from licking it. Adorned with a substance that mimics their feline sexual pheromones, cats gets high and euphoric from *za'atar al-bisas*. In effect, it gives them an orgasm. The cat begins licking the plant and then leaps around in it and purrs loudly. This lasts for a few minutes before the cat loses interest, potentially to return two hours later for another go.[23]

Throughout the months of lockdown, my mother and I have returned frequently for new batches of *'akkoub* and *za'atar*, feeling like defiant mavericks, stealing moments of pleasure as we pick the plants that we love.

Decolonising Extinction Listings

When studying anthropogenic extinction, climate-justice researchers essentially seek to answer two central questions: Which forms of human life are driving processes of catastrophic loss? And what are the diverse ways in which humans and nonhumans have resisted this loss? The challenge is to move away from failed policing tactics to create a life-affirming culture of preservation and sustainability. What's sorely needed is an epistemological change that decolonises extinction and fundamentally reorients our relation towards each other and our surroundings. According to scholar Juno Salazar Parreñas, this decolonisation must be 'oriented towards process and experimentation and not toward foregone conclusion, except for the need to care enough about others, including and in particular, non-human others.'[24]

Unfortunately, most people today – and Palestinians are no exception – do not lead a life guided by cross-species care. Palestinian society at large is now detached from its historical intimacy with the land, which only two or three generations ago was a central part of Palestinian life. A seldom-discussed transformation caused by the Nakba of 1947–1949 – along with the massive expropriation of land that continued well afterwards – was the process of turning peasants (that is, historically speaking, the overwhelming majority of Palestinian society) into unskilled construction workers. This intentional and systemic transformation of an entire society is manifest today. One only has to drive through the West Bank to see the mutations of architecture and landscape brought about by

23 At the end of the spring, this plant blossoms with 'inverted' blue flowers. The leaves are heart-shaped and their scent is incredibly beautiful. Locally, it is traditionally used to calm nerves and as a pain relief for toothaches. It also repels cockroaches and mosquitoes.

24 Juno Salazar Parreñas, *Decolonizing Extinction: The Work of Care in Orangutan Rehabilitation*, Duke University Press, 2018.

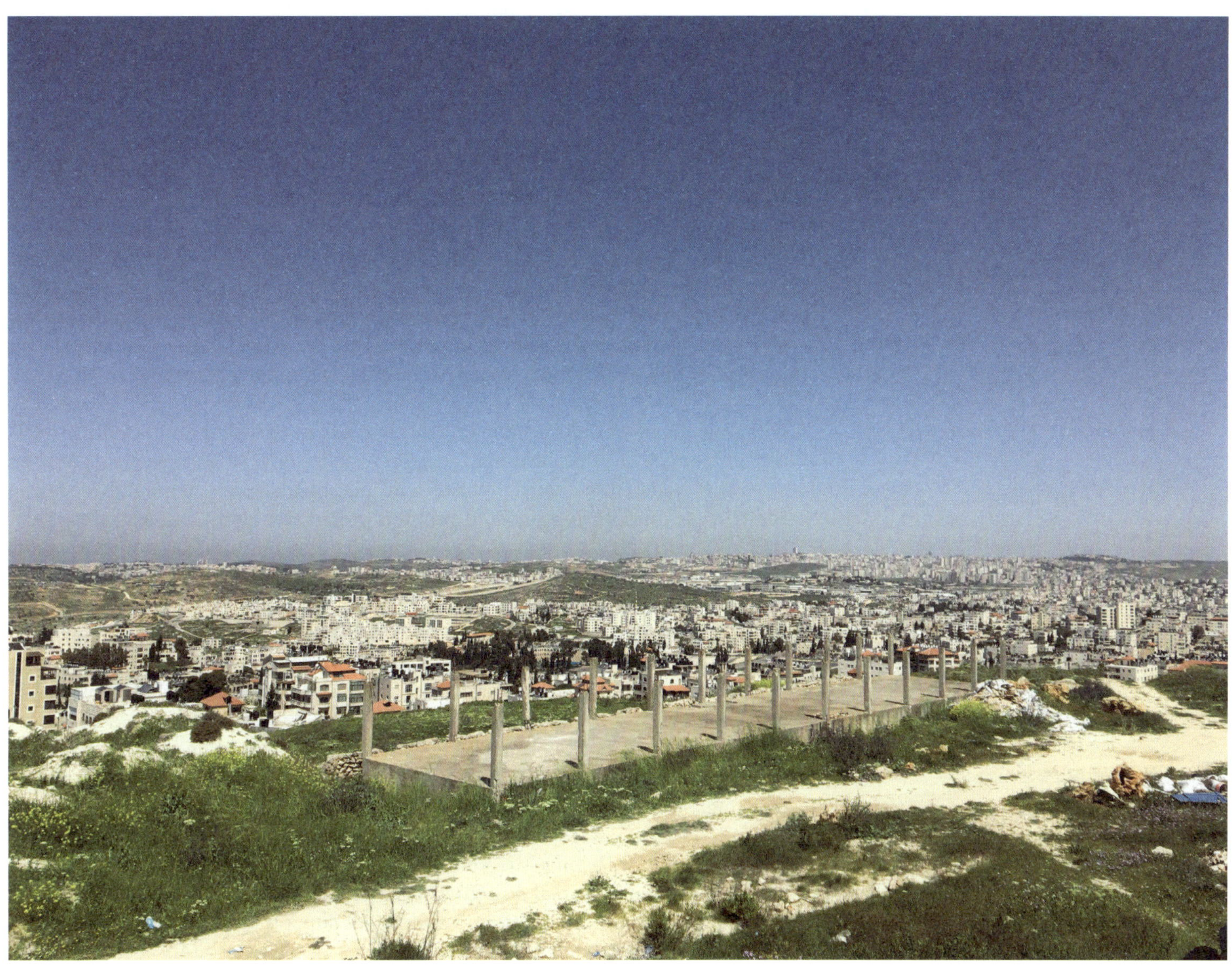

Tell el-Ful, overlooking East Jerusalem and the West Bank neighbourhoods of Shu'fat, Beit Hanina, Bir Nabal, Nabi Samuil, Al-Jib, and Qalandia, and the settlements of Ramot and Giva't Ze'ev. Courtesy of the author.

private owners and the Palestinian Authority alike. My grandfather, who was illiterate and who himself ended up a construction worker, learned lessons the hard way and repeatedly told my father to get a good education. 'They can take your land and house away from you, but knowledge is yours to keep.'

The disregard for agrarian life was underway well before 1948. It began in the final decades of the dying Ottoman Empire, and it continued to spread under the British Mandate and the implantation of capitalist ideals of modern life that we have come to call 'progress'. This 'progress' slowly transformed land from something embedded in the sociopolitical fabric of a community, into an extractable commodity. These ideals are still hard at work across an increasingly decaying planet.

Foraging, meanwhile, is an ancient method for recognising and learning about the abundance of one's surroundings. Since 9500–8000 BCE, farmers have been selecting seeds from their favourite wild plants, planting them, and repeating the process until both seeds and humans were thoroughly domesticated. Over millennia, this grooming gradually changed the genetic makeup of both partners into the tastes, shapes, and faces that are familiar to us today. The wild relatives, or 'weeds', that live near fields where their cultivated descendants grow play time-travel games. Genetically speaking, these relatives are many thousands of years apart. We need to foster an imagination that understands the depths of time embodied in these plants, an imagination that is outside the logic of origins and the oppressive boundaries of the state. This imagination would include a multitude of approaches to biodiversity: rewilding alongside 'zoning', with the aim of educating, building agency, and encouraging responsible – and joyful – foraging.[25]

We know that abolishing the police frees up massive amounts of public funding for implementing real structural change and building community strength through education, rehabilitation, and social support. In a similar vein, reallocating funds from law-enforcement bureaucracies and military forces towards education and biodiversity can support the changes necessary to disseminate plant-related knowledge and practices. This reallocation can also contribute to cross-border conservation strategies in regions where certain species are native. After all, seeds have always defied modern ideas of order, law, and borders.

This is one path towards a planetary democracy, or a democracy of the species – a possibility for freedom that breaks from slavery and colonialism in all their historical and contemporary forms. In this process, ecologies must be rebuilt and re-symbolised, so they are geared toward mutuality and affirmation, not exclusion. Only with this profound shift can preservation measures translate into a real attempt to protect life, rather than preserving the necropolitical regime already in place.

25 Restricting how much of certain plants can be foraged is both difficult to monitor and arbitrary, as the number of foragers visiting particular sites varies greatly. A more effective approach might be to designate certain areas for foraging for limited periods – say, one to five years – while closing off others to allow plants to rejuvenate and multiply. This is rewilding alongside zoning.

Jumana Manna

The A in Qaf

Heavy footsteps, two heads swaying. They can't take more than a couple of steps in the narrow space without knocking into one another. The creases in their thick skin yield and undulate, like waves, drawing fleeting patterns on their bodies. The great pinnae of their ears beat the air right and left. When they feel heavy, they shift their weight between their feet, move their heads from side to side, wag their slender tails. They remain like this all night long, until the inky darkness is broken by the dim crimson light that begins to emanate from their ivory tusks. Then the motion of their skin quietens and they lean on the wall, drained of energy, covered in sweat.

'The one laugh I heard today wasn't from the heart.'

'I heard a body crash, falling from up high. It only reminded me of the raucous of our feet running to escape the gas.'

'I hope we didn't get it wrong.'

'Don't lose heart. We have only just begun.'

Since they came into this world, all the sounds that reached Vastator's ears frustrated him: the jingling of keys, the creaking of doors, the bleating, wailing, and howling; sounds that in their colourlessness were no different from those of the world they had left behind.

Vastator and his friend Natator had come from another world on an urgent mission. Their world had been hit by catastrophe. A mysterious disease was claiming souls, leaving no species or breed unscathed. Humans and beasts were dropping dead in the street with no clear explanation. The cause had remained unknown until there were so many dead it was impossible to bury them all, and the bodies were left to decompose out in the open. It was then that the small stones had appeared. The hearts of the dead were full of smooth ink-black stones that stood out amidst the bones' whiteness. Everyone knew about kidney stones and bladder stones, but until then, no one had heard of heart stones. Fear and panic reigned. Despair closed down on the world.

When the mission had been assigned to them, the two friends had focused their hearing back through the years and applied themselves to remembering. They crossed dry lakes, and walked in the night with farmers who carried sharpened scythes that glimmered in the dark, for cutting through barbed wire fences and crawling underneath. They roamed green fields near a small village, where many had gathered around one of the houses, and military tanks growled as they tried to break in. They crossed wet marshes and reached the outskirts of an over-populated city, where bandits ruled the roads, barricades had been raised, and the people of the city cried out in the streets.

Vastator and Natator had walked and walked, through landscapes and times they didn't recognise, led by memories that weren't their own, when their tusks began to glow with a dazzling purple no elephant had ever seen before. They knew then they had received the sign. They didn't know what world they had reached but they figured they couldn't have gone very far – the hunger that gripped their guts was the same.

Many long years before the appearance of heart stones, the elephants' hyper-sensitive ears had picked up on a change in what they heard. Everything around them had suddenly paled. Life still went on as usual back then. Some went to work, others ran to escape the teargas. Forests burned, prices soared, and those expelled from their land put up tents. Then a day came when screams no longer sounded like screams, nor words like words. The sounds reached the elephants' ears as if a sheer curtain had been dropped over everything. A curtain that muffled the comings and goings of everyday life, so subtly that it wasn't discernible to other ears or measurable by machines, yet the implications were serious enough to throw the elephants into panic.

But they got used to the change over time. Fast forward a few years, and they could ignore what they heard or didn't hear, they who had lived by their ears. The elephants' own voices too had paled, and nothing called up their panic. They might have even forgotten that a change had occurred at all. Most significantly, they had forgotten what every elephant used to know, which is that vowels lived in the heart, and consonants lived in the head. Then, on the escape route, they remembered what they used to know, and the mystery of the smooth stones was solved. The stones that rose up in the hearts and damaged them were none other than the corpses of dead vowels. The elephants finally understood that the mysterious disease appeared when the enemies had killed all vowels, one letter at a time. No one had taken notice of the murders, or seen a connection between the cycles of increased hunger and destruction, and the vowels' death. When all vowels had died in all the hearts, catastrophe hit.

The ivory continued to glow a weak crimson in the night's darkness. Questions swirled in Vastator's mind: Had their tusks misjudged? Did they end up in the wrong world? Why didn't the glow reach that deep purple shade again since they'd got here? What was the meaning of that unrepeated sign? Without warning, they heard the sliding of the latch in the door, then the jailer entered the cell. A thick metal chain rattled in his hand, a small torch peeked out of his pocket. He went for Natator, chained his foot and pulled him to a spot near the door. He went out, came back with a massive pair of metal pincers, and walked towards Vastator. He held the torch between his teeth and gripped Vastator's left tusk with the pincers' jaws. The crimson glow reflected on the jailer's narrowing eyes. Vastator froze to the spot, didn't make the slightest move. Natator yelled at the jailer, who had begun to pull. But the pincers' jaws couldn't stay locked around the tusk. They slipped every time the jailer fixed them in place and pulled. The jailer flew into a rage, cursed the pincers and their mother, threw them down and walked out.

Vastator retreated into himself, while Natator yanked himself to the right and to the left, in an effort to break the chain. The jailer returned, this time with an electric drill, and when he pressed the button, the drill seemed to pierce the very air. He picked up the torch and put it back in his mouth, then, amidst Natator's screams, shot towards Vastator. He placed the head of the metal drill at the top of Vastator's left tusk, right under the flesh, and, with the drill on full power, pushed with all his strength. The metal drill head bore into the ivory, scattering its dust into the air with a burning smell. The jailer kept pushing until the tapered point pierced through to the other side. He pulled it out and tried to break off the tusk with his hands but failed. He went mad. He pushed the drill straight into the flesh and pulled the trigger. Blood and pieces of flesh scattered on the floor of the cell. Vastator's trunk trembled. The jailer kept pushing while shaking the tusk to loosen it, until it came off in his hand, leaving a small fragment hanging in Vastator's mouth. Intoxicated, his face smeared with flesh and blood, the jailer held the crimson ivory staff with both hands, then left.

Ivory is the essence of a bygone world, also known as 'prehistoric time'. Now it only comes up in solid form, tusks growing out of mouths like the alphabet of a lost language. But ivory has another form that is no longer known: as liquid inside the elephants' ears. Liquid ivory gives elephants their hypersensitive hearing. To sharpen it, they flap the pinnae of their ears, so that the capillaries stretch and expand, allowing the ivory to fill the inner cavities. No liquid on earth surpasses ivory in its sensitivity. The weakest of frequencies send ripples across its surface, and the filaments fused into it pick up on the subtlest vibrations and carry them to the auditory nerve. More importantly, though, the texture of liquid ivory allows the elephants' ears to detect what no other ears can: the hope hidden within sounds. Every sound carries within it the memory of a hope that stirs only when the time is right. The hope of hunger quelled, of the cycle broken. When elephants listened, they heard an entire history of hope. But it was that very hope, which accompanies each voice like a halo, that the elephants' ivory hadn't detected in years.

Nussa watched Natator and Vastator as they remembered, skins tightening and rippling with the rhythmic movements of their bodies. Like leather scrolls, the inscriptions slowly dissolved in the layer of sweat that gradually coated them. They listened so intently, the liquid ivory flowed over from their ears into the rest of their body, submerging internal organs, turning everything into a listening ear. The harder they listened in the darkness of the cell, the more abundantly they sweated. Nussa's eyes stayed fixed on the skin of the two elephants in their feverish movements, on the deep shine of their sweat. When the weak crimson light began to rise from their tusks, she abandoned herself to its visions, and forgot her hunger.

At the end of this fevered round of listening and remembering, Vastator leaned on the wall in silence, breathing unevenly, traces of blood still imprinted on his skin. Natator tried to soothe him by moving his ears right and left close to his face. Nussa approached Vastator and set to licking the skin of his trunk with her thin tongue. The liquid was viscid and transparent, its sharp bitterness intoxicating. When she was done, she sat still between the two elephants, and slowly faded away.

She saw herself in a house she hadn't seen before. But she wasn't just moving in the space of the house; she was also in all the objects within it. She melted into a sugarcane, then many hands came and clutched her. Rope wound around the hands, the hands around the sugarcane. Then the cane was squeezed, and Nussa left it as a droplet of juice and froze inside a sugar crystal. Then she was an atom of silver, and a vein of copper. She burned inside foundry rooms, moved through gears and chains, emerged in objects that were carried to the marketplace. Nussa multiplied in unending droplets, flowed in rivers of thick liquid, and lived imprisoned inside commodities. Then she was again in one of the rooms of the house, and a metal glint cut through the air above her – a thick tube ending in a blade ready to pierce. She was the blade, and she was the flesh. Then everything stopped, and a tongue was moving against her body, bringing her back.

Nussa paid nightly visits to the cells, always saving her favourite for last: the one that housed the two elephants from the future. They told her they had come in search of a vowel, because their enemies had killed all vowels, and since then, language had paled. A language without its vowels, they said, was a language with no memory of itself, a pile of consonants falling over one another forever. Those who live in a language with no memory soon forget who they are.

Beings in their world, they told her, having been driven from their land by the enemies, searched in vain for something to quell their hunger, and found only scraps. The search would exhaust them, hunger drain them, then they would accept the little they were given, and they would forget. Until the enemies drove them out again, and they would repeat the cycle, looking in vain for something to quell their hunger, finding only scraps, accepting the little they were given and forgetting. They raced like this in hollowed circles, no hunger quelled and no way out.

They told her of what happened on the escape route after the disease had spread. Hordes of all the species had jostled along a path that went around a mountain, where some fresh herbs still grew, then narrowed around a bend. In that bend in the path, amidst frightening waves of noise, Vastator had lost his hearing. For a while, he had heard nothing but a droning in his ears, a droning that seemed to come from the depth of the earth. He had shaken his head right and left, but the tormenting hum wouldn't leave him. When, a long while later, his hearing had returned, the hum had continued to shroud the noise of scurrying feet, and the rustle of beating wings. It had still obscured the screams and the sound of breaking bones. But underneath the pain, Vastator had clearly heard the crackle of the grass they were crushing under their feet, just as he used to hear it before the paling. It was a low crackle that had once carried the hope of hunger quelled. The full power of Vastator's hearing had returned abruptly, like a cut in the curtain that had been thrown over everything one cursed day. A minuscule rupture that was about to close over. Vastator had looked around him, bewildered, and found Natator beside him, having also stopped in his tracks, and knew that he too had heard. Both of them, and no one else, had heard the rupture.

The movement of the hordes around them had become chaotic that day, so the elephants withdrew into a gap in the mountain to confer. They understood that the mysterious disease was much more serious than they had thought. Vastator's and Natator's hearing was back to the way it was before the years of paling. The elephants understood that the murder of the vowels had dulled the world around them for years, and was now stopping hearts from beating. A few days later, they agreed that what was lost would not return, that the only hope for survival was to find new vowels, and to waste no time doing so. But vowels only existed in the past. Which past? Nobody knew. Only the elephants' tusks might be able to determine that. Natator and Vastator had set off on their rescue mission, listening and remembering across the years, in the hope that they might hear something that no one else had heard before. Then their tusks had glowed with that dazzling purple.

Every night Nussa half-listened to a new detail from the elephants' strange story, but what really drew her to their cell was the magic sweat that covered their skins when they remembered. The mouse licked the elephants' sweat every night, and every time she lost herself in dreams and hallucinations, waking only when most of the night had passed.

'Did you know that dinosaurs were silent?'

'What?'

'Their larynxes couldn't produce any sound. That's why they went extinct.'

'How's that?'

'They couldn't warn each other when danger threatened, not even scream. Winged reptiles were the only ones who could produce sound, so they survived and evolved into birds. They had huge bodies and high-pitched voices.'

'How do you know all that?'

'We mice study such things.'

'How come?'

'Do you really not know? For many long centuries, we have been fighting our eternal fear, searching for ways to defeat it. This fear has pervaded our species since time immemorial and caused us to be scared of everything, to run panic-stricken in the streets. Our struggle against the rule of fear has cost us dearly. And every generation has passed it to the next.

We did come up with some good plans. Once, we widened the entrance holes to our burrows, just enough to tempt the cats to try to enter when they chased a mouse. We thought they would get stuck, and we would attack from the outside and tear them apart with our sharp teeth. The trick worked. The cats did get stuck. But the mice that gathered outside were too scared to attack. Their courage failed them. Or rather, they were betrayed by the tyrant that ruled their bodies: fear. The mice stood frozen in place until the first cat got away and tore them into pieces. Then other cats did the same.

Grief-stricken, having lost many of our comrades, we retreated to our burrows. We had witnessed horrors, gathered our friends' remains, and those of us who had survived sat in the middle of the sea of blood thinking about this fear that inhabits our bodies. How could we change what we are? How can mice be free of their fear? We thought long and hard then came up with a new plan, tighter this time. Come dawn, we were out of our homes, crossing the city in groups and heading west. By the time the sun was out, we had reached the wilderness. Here we would live alone, and forget the fear that had ruined our lives, especially our fear of cats.

Year in and year out, we lived in the hot sands. But we failed to adapt to life in the wilderness. Many of us died of hunger and thirst. We reached a dead end and looked total extinction in the face, so we decided to return to the city. When we returned, we found that, in our absence, the cats had become unemployed and were driven out of human homes. The first mice entered the city, a small hope trembling within them, only to be ambushed by the herds of cats that now occupied the streets. As soon as the first cat intercepted them, the old terror struck and froze the mice to their place. The cats fell upon them and tore them to pieces.'

After he finished preparing the food on a small electric stove, Natator knocked on the iron door to signal lunch time. Minutes later, the warden entered the cell and sat down to eat, while Vastator and Natator watched. He swallowed the meat and vegetables in silence. After he was done, he complained about the quality of the food, lit a cigarette, looked from one elephant to the other and waited for an answer. Some time passed, without the elephants breaking their silence. So, he sighed, passed his hand over Natator's remaining tusk and smiled. No one stirred, until the jailer withdrew his hand.

'The Officer insists on transferring you to the residential wards.'

'…'

'Do you know, my dears, what that means? It means hard labour that would totally drain you. But don't you worry. I'll do my best to put off your transfer, even if it costs me the displeasure of the Officer.'

'…'

'Do you understand?'

'…'

'Where's my tea?'

Hard labour would drain Vastator, Natator thought as he looked over to his friend who stopped talking since the jailer broke his second tusk. His health was deteriorating rapidly. And although Natator's health was deteriorating too, since his right tusk was taken, he still had hope of getting out. He took care of his friend as well as he could, sharing with him whatever leaves his trunk could harvest from the tree outside the cell's small window. Even though Vastator remained drowned in his silence, he was still capable of remembering. He still paced up and down the cell with his friend every night, despite the pain and the hunger, straining to listen, until he was drenched in sweat. He remembered and remembered. Exhausted himself remembering everything that was hidden in the sounds of the present. Strained to remember any missed opportunity, forgotten word, or overlooked disruption. He wasn't remembering to reclaim his own story, but for language to remember itself, in the hope that out of the memory, a new vowel might emerge and restore to the dying hearts their pulse. The ivory that flowed in his ears still rippled and expanded in response to the subtlest resonance. But he no longer had tusks to pursue and seek out the vowels in the long nights. Natator's left tusk was their only remaining compass, their last hope to leave this world in which they were held captive without knowing why.

One day, the door of the cell was pushed wide open. The jailer, with three other men, shoved in a massive rock that made it through the door with great difficulty. They then dragged it by the ropes that were wrapped around it until it settled in the middle of the cell. Natator and Vastator huddled in a corner. When the men left and locked the door behind them, the two were pinned to their places, because the rock had taken up most of the space in the cell. It had a dusty surface of hewn stone, like it had been subjected to a strike or a fall, and was unevenly shaped, with one side bloated and the other caved in. It was difficult to tell its colour in the dark, but it was lighter than the elephants' skin. The rock remained silent.

'Do you have anything to eat?' asked Nussa.

'No. We can't move anymore because of the rock.'

'What are you going to do now?'

'We don't know.'

'Excellent planning from the people of the future! You're even worse than us! Did you really think they'd just let you walk around as you please? Did I not tell you it was dangerous here? They arrest rocks now, too. Do you under-stand what that means?'

'We must find a new vowel.'

'Vastator was right. Your tusks must have miscalculated. There are no vowels here. Nor consonants. How could there be when no one dares to speak? There's nothing here but fear. It emanates from every corner. Can't you smell it?'

Nussa circled the rock that night, then climbed it until she was settled on its back. The silence lingered among the three for a while. Then Nussa repeated what she had already told them, that the police had full control over this world, that they had ears and eyes everywhere, and that they considered anyone who speaks a suspect, as the speaker would most definitely be talking and plotting against them. That was why no non-humans spoke openly, out of fear the police would mistake them for humans in disguise and arrest them. But now the police were carrying out arbitrary arrests, of both humans and non-humans. And whenever one prison filled up, they built another.

The elephants spent that night in despair. Every time they shifted, they knocked into the rock. All their attempts to move it failed, so they resorted to shaking their heads, flapping their ears, and moving their feet in place. It was a heavy night. Out of its darkness, the elephants' sweat came out more bitter than usual. It dissolved slowly in Nussa's mouth. Once the elephants had calmed, Nussa lay between them and let herself relax while thinking up a new plan to defeat the fear.

'Who are those enemies of yours? Humans? The police?'

'Our enemies are those who drive us away from our homes and starve us. Those who drown us in harmful gasses every day. Those who kill the language that we speak. All speech relies on vowels, and we used to have so many. Vowels are the sites of weakness. They make our cries and our murmurs understood. If we don't find new ones, everyone will perish. The heart weakens when speech is deprived of its weakness.'

'But why did they kill the vowels?'

'Because vowels don't allow a word to stay unchanged. They are sounds of deviation, of weakness and vulnerability. They push things to become. Our speech is built on weakness. Without it, we have nothing to say to each other but empty talk. Our bodies have always endured hunger, withstood homelessness, but they die with the death of their speech.'

The three sat in silence in the depth of the night, chafed by hunger, the rock pressing on them and weighing on their hearts. Its weight fixed the cell in place. Then the door clattered and the jailer was standing in its frame, seething with rage, the electric drill in his hand. Cussing and cursing, he moved towards Natator, and stuck the running drill in his remaining tusk until the metal head pushed through and out the other side. Natator let out an awful scream that shook the walls of the cell and spread beyond them. Then everything stopped. The drill was switched off in the jailer's hand, the cell fell into a perfect silence. Vastator froze in his place, and Nussa hid behind him. The rock remained still, but a barely visible fissure cracked its surface. The jailer cursed the drill, the day, the inhabitants of the cell and, cursing electricity itself, left the machine stuck in Natator's tusk and went out. He found the electric socket in the corridor, secured the plug and returned to the cell. As soon as he got to the door, he let out the loudest scream: 'Aaaaa'.

Blinded by the light, they hurried along empty streets that were cut through every now and then by a speeding black car with opaque windows. Qaf rolled swiftly ahead of them, bolted suddenly in this or that direction, and knew to stand still when needed. Nussa was on Qaf's back, trying to keep her balance while watching the road from above. Vastator dragged his steps slowly with Natator's help. When the gap widened, Nussa gave Qaf a signal to stop and wait for the elephants. Whenever a black car appeared on the horizon, Nussa alerted the two elephants to hide behind Qaf. The whole way, Qaf did not utter one word. Nussa licked the cool surface now and again and her saliva mixed with sand grains and, beneath them, layers of unfamiliar flavours, which she estimated were as old as time. Qaf was leading them to the Mountain of Moqattam, where they could hide for the time being. They walked and walked until they arrived at the cemetery, and from there, with great difficulty, they climbed the Mountain.

The Pyramids were finally visible from a distance. Beyond them, the sand raged in the desert. Between the Mountain and the Pyramids, tick white smoke rose from various points in the city, and black cars roamed the empty streets at high speed. At the top of the Mountain, the sky was clear, and the surface of Ain el-Sira Lake shone as smooth as a mirror. The moment they arrived, Vastator collapsed on the ground. Natator, the drill still stuck in his tusk, set to fanning him with his ears. Qaf stood in silence next to the two elephants.

Nussa heard an urgent sharp voice and, looking around her, found another mouse furtively calling to her. She quickly climbed down from Qaf's back and followed him into one of the burrows. It troubled her to notice that his tail was amputated, a wound festering in its place.

'How are you all holding up?'

'We managed to stop their advances on this side, but the east side of the mountain is still under their control. I would advise you to avoid it.'

'You look tired. Did many fall?'

'Don't worry. We're doing fine. How did you escape?'

'Qaf made a sudden tumble towards the door and took the jailer by surprise. She rolled out and pulled us behind her and managed to break down the gates.'

'So …'

'I'm ready.'

The mountainside was fairly level and had a scattering of weeds. A few protrusions still towered over the city, but most of it had been paved for the asphalt roads that crisscrossed it. The Mountain of Moqattam had stood for thousands of years behind the cemeteries, as a border between two worlds. Those who climbed it had looked for the end of the physical world, hoping to transcend it. It had been a frontier where humans and beasts met. But since the Mountain had become just another residential neighbourhood, the dead no longer died, and the living no longer lived. The difference between life and death diminished over time, until the Mountain became a memory of the border that used to keep them separate. Those who inhabited the Mountain lived beyond death, and they also lived beyond life. They lived a life as frozen as death, a never-ending end of the world, which spread from there to the rest of the city. The Mountain loomed like a giant whale, concealing what it harboured. But its heart heaved, suppressing explosions that no one could see.

Nussa walked with the mouse Marzuk through a complex network of narrow tunnels. He led her to a storehouse where she would work alongside him, preparing food and provisions for the weekly prison visits. On their way there, he told her that mice numbers were in decline, but there were still some who went out to gather food, and others who secured cigarettes. They kept walking until they arrived to the place where the food was stored. Nussa circled piles of seeds, breadcrumbs, and tree leaves. She carried on alone until she reached a pile she couldn't identify. But when she looked closely, she was shocked. It was a pile of mouse tails. Marzuk stood quietly next to her, the two of them gazing at the pile.

Nussa gradually returned to the life of mice. Every day, those who went out returned to the storehouse with what they could gather, which Nussa and Marzuk, working in silence, sorted and organised into piles. Sometimes the harvest would be enough to grind, so they did that and mixed the flour with water. As the weekly visit got closer, they prepared the meagre meals. Nussa didn't quite recover from the shock of what she saw on the first day. Marzuk tried to reassure her, and dealt with the pile of tails himself. Still, Nussa was often distracted. She sat through the long working hours remembering everyone she knew who had fallen. But the memories slipped through her fingers. However hard she tried to remember, some things eluded her. And every time she thought she counted all those killed, she would discover new names that she forgot. One day, lost in thought, she saw museum vitrines housing rocks, bones, and mummified bodies. The display items told their stories and answered questions in a language that suited each visitor. The rocks spoke, the bodies sat up, the bones moved. Every vitrine was a complete theatre show that rose before its audience. She saw herself in one of the vitrines, standing in a body that wasn't her own, recounting the story of her death.

All of Nussa's and Marzuk's attempts to remove the electric drill from Natator's remaining tusk were met with failure. Vastator, who lay on the floor next to Qaf, wasn't improving. A whiteness began to spread over his legs, his tail, his head. Natator never stopped fanning him with his ears. Every night, Nussa continued to visit them and sit in her favourite spot on Qaf's back. Since coming to the Mountain, she no longer thought of new plans. Work in the storehouse ate up her days, but she climbed back to her friends as evening descended. Natator no longer spoke, and she was overtaken by the instinctive fear of speaking openly, so they all sat in silence and contemplated the city lights and the fires raging below. When the night's darkness intensified, Nussa

Haytham El Wardany

became gloomy and climbed down from her spot to lick Natator, but he wasn't sweating anymore.

One of those nights, just before dawn, Vastator's whitening was complete and he sank to his side. Nussa got up, left Natator and Qaf, and walked back to the burrows. On her way there, she noticed a gap that she hadn't seen before. She entered it, and it led her through narrow passageways, then to a few false rooms. She estimated that this burrow had taken many years to construct. She walked on, a chilling sound of inhalation and exhalation gradually rising through the walls, until she arrived to a crevice in the rocks and, overcoming her fear, looked through it.

What Nussa saw was a vast, high-roofed chamber in the heart of the Mountain. Thick tubes emerged from the stone and connected to strange-looking heaps placed around the floor. The space was divided into long compartments, and the heaps were distributed across them. Above each compartment hung an information board. Nussa looked closer and saw that the heaps were bodies, big bodies and small bodies. She saw that the tubes bore into them through openings in their chests. She froze when she recognised a face. It belonged to a friend she had lost in one of the battles against fear. The faces of the dead were cool, neutral, but their eyes were open and fear still lurked there. Each tube ended in a blade that pierced a chest. The air was filled with the rhythm of liquid flowing through the tubes. That was the sound of breathing that Nussa had heard through the walls in the tunnels.

The first word the elephants spoke was 'Aaaaaj', which came to mean 'ivory'. They uttered it after bitter struggles, after thousands of forcibly extracted tusks, and knew from that day on that every word was a wound, every sound a scar. They learned to speak despite the suffering, because it was the only way for the wounds to scab over. Speech melted words and wounds, and fused them with the words and wounds of others. The scars, carrying the story and hope of their own healing, used to touch the elephants' hearts and make their liquid ivory tremble.

But Natator's heart had become too heavy. Weighed down by the stones that had been slowly growing inside it, untouched by anything since the death of his friend. He was angry at himself for getting tricked by hope yet again. When they got to the Mountain, he thought he sensed something was moving within it. The ivory inside him responded to a sound that he didn't have the strength to follow. But he had a hope and he let it grow, a hope that rescue was closer than ever, that the enemies would never win, and that his friend would survive. And he was wrong. When he understood that, he hated hope forever. His friend wasn't killed by the stones, but by the false hope that *he* had stubbornly clung to.

'Even the dead can't get away.'

'We have come to the Mountain to find the place that no one outside knows about. They drag the bodies here so they don't decompose. We know from our research that there is a secret technology which makes it possible to access the knowledge of the dead. And that it's used to make profit. Speculations, gambling, buying and selling, risk assessment, you name it. You see, the dead are connected to what lies beyond the physical world. They have knowledge that can't be gleaned from regular computers. This place is a secret stock exchange of sorts. They inject the dead with data, then connect the tubes to their chests with a mysterious substance which occasionally causes explosions, but those are contained by the Mountain. That's all our research has brought up so far.'

'Even the dead can't get away, Marzuk.'

'We're barely managing to save ourselves, Nussa. How could we possibly save the dead?'

Nussa sat next to Qaf, as Natator lay dying by Vastator's body. She licked his trunk over and over. The wolves howled around them. He let out his last breath in the heart of the night. From under him, a purple liquid poured out and filled the darkness. It kept growing in density and volume. It flowed towards Qaf, seeped into her fissures, covered her surfaces, until she was shrouded in a purple light that radiated out of every inch of her. Nussa and Qaf were awestruck. Before dawn, Nussa was immersed in the purple ivory, licking it hungrily. Hot acidic fluids seeped out of Qaf's insides and immediately dissolved in the purple ivory. With that, she began to rasp out a jumble of words, murmurs, codes, and numbers. The thick fluids continued to splutter, and Qaf's dry croaks gradually filled the emptiness. She howled, hissed, screamed, then finally, spoke.

Nussa lifted her head, her tongue illuminated by the ivory, and heard Qaf say, 'I am Qaf, daughter of Nun. I am the U in Nun, the A in Qaf. I was dragged to the bottom of the Mountain, and for an eternity the Earth was closed on me. I lay in the ashes, injected with poison, not eating, not tasting. My tongue was petrified wood. Though frightened, I opened my eyes. No daylight yet. But the Mountain is shaking, and my tongue has moved.'

In the morning, Nussa had a plan. She would go to the river and climb the tree to speak to the Thirty Birds. Before she glided down towards the city, she went to the storehouse. She took some seeds, licked them thoroughly with her tongue, then set off. She climbed the tree and greeted the birds – she had briefly met them before, in prison – then took out the seeds that she had brought. The birds were very hungry and swooped on the offering. Then Nussa began to talk to them in whispers. She told them what she had seen in the heart of the Mountain. She told them about Vastator and Natator, and about the ivory that she had mixed in with the seeds. Then she made her request and stressed that no one but them can fulfil it. The Thirty Birds, back on their branches in the tree, looked at her.

Nussa's plan was to transfer the purple ivory to the dead: it would block the tubes and set them free. The only way for that to happen was if the birds traversed the seven valleys once more, crossing the border into the land of the dead, and recounting in their many tongues what they had just heard from her. The dead had to hear everything, in every voice. The birds looked at one another. Nussa repeated that they were the only ones capable of such a journey, and that this was the only hope that remained. The birds were silent. Nussa said that the dead must receive the ivory, because if they were not set free, nothing else would change. Then she stopped speaking, for there was nothing left for her to say. The silence went on for a long while, until the hoopoe finally broke it and said, 'What you're asking, sister, is a journey much more arduous than our first.' Then the birds began to discuss amongst themselves, and Nussa stayed in her place on a tree branch, looking down at the river, watching the reflection of the leaves in the water.

Visual Essays

Letters to Museum Directors

Gala Porras-Kim questions the skewed power dynamics at the heart of archaeological and museum practices. She pays particular attention to the way climate control is used within museum displays and storage spaces to preserve objects extracted from their original, often humid, contexts. The letters presented here – addressed to the National Museum of Brazil, Rio de Janeiro; the British Museum, London; and the Peabody Museum at Harvard University in Cambridge, Massachusetts – are part of a wider series of letters written to directors and curators of institutions holding artefacts, ritual objects, or human remains. Through these letters, she offers practical and poetic solutions for restoring dignity to the objects and subjects in their custody.

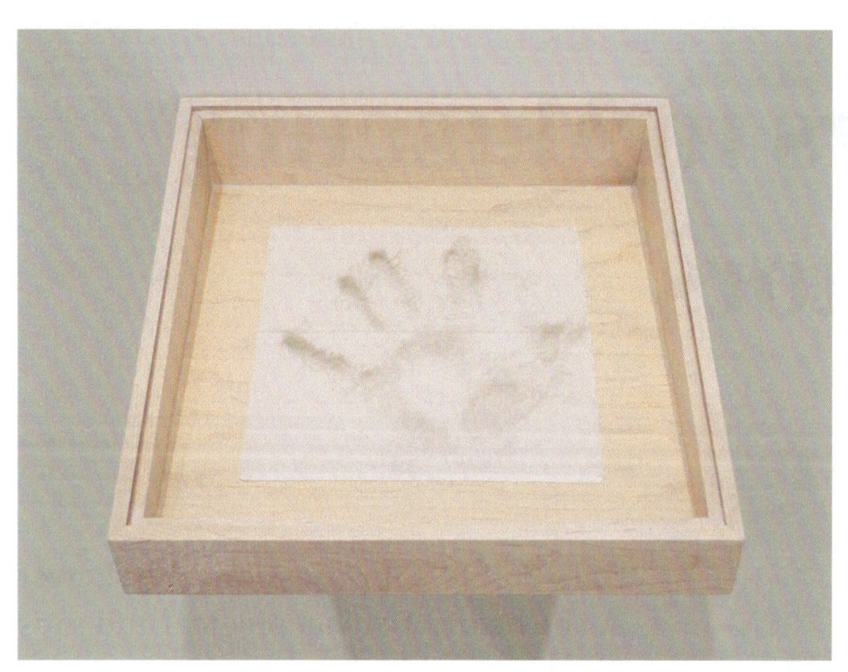

Gala Porras-Kim
4727 2nd Avenue
Los Angeles, CA 90043, USA

Los Angeles, July 31st, 2021

Mr. Alexander Kellner
Director
National Museum of Brazil
Quinta da Boa Vista – São Cristóvão,
Rio de Janeiro - RJ, 20940-040, Brazil

Re: Leaving the institution by cremation is easier than through a deaccession policy

Dear Mr. Kellner:

Thank you very much for allowing me to work with 'Luzia,' the oldest human fossil which is part of the National Museum of Brazil collection. In the past, I have had many conversations with various museum staff to understand the conditions of people being stored throughout institutions such as yours. Their remains, which are material parts of people who are unable to directly express and determine how they are kept, provoke several questions about their current existence in the museum -out of their final resting place- and a closer look at events surrounding their condition which might allude to their desired afterlife.

The 2018 fire that consumed your institution was a tragic event, and since many of these remains got burned, they are no longer able to exist primarily as historical objects as they have been doing since being unearthed, but now as ashes of cremated remains. This possibly can be seen as a way for such trapped people in the collection to escape their institutional life, since it is easier to leave the institution through cremation than as a result of a deaccession policy.

Significant effort has been made by the National Museum of Brazil to gather and preserve her left over remains in order to restore the collection to the extent possible, and 80 percent of her body is currently being reassembled. These efforts are done to prevent the current physical deterioration of 'Luzia' as an object and not prioritizing what her wishes for her afterlife might have been. This tissue with ash from the fire might be the closest thing to a cinerary urn to hold her cremains until you might try to see her personhood, and she stops being merely an object in the collection. Then, I would like to propose incinerating the rest of her remains, because when you let go of the shape you think she should be as an object, she will return to her life as a corpse once again.

Thank you again for your attention, consideration, and time.

Sincerely,

Gala Porras-Kim
4727 2nd Ave.
Los Angeles, CA 90043, USA

London, January 26th, 2022

Mr. Daniel Antoine
Acting Keeper
Cc: John H. Taylor
Department of Egypt and Sudan
The British Museum
Great Russell Street
London
WC1B 3DG

Re: Sights beyond the grave

Dear Mr. Antoine,

Thank you for your research and for making information available to the public regarding the plans for the afterlife of the ancient Egyptians in your collection. It is evident in the work your department undertakes that the British Museum is committed to the care and research of the people in your collection. The conservation efforts towards the material remains of ancient Egyptians in your department are remarkable and important, and seem to be aligned with their plans for their afterlife as evidenced by their careful planning, meticulous detail, and resource allocation to the preservation of the body and spirit. Since they have expressed and determined the way their material and spiritual parts were to be kept, this provokes several questions about their current existence in the museum -out of their final resting place- and a closer look at their condition in their current and ongoing afterlife.

Many of them likely have varying capabilities for reincarnation and presently exist in a myriad of shapes including mummies and statues intended as alternative bodies for their spirits. Some may have already reconstituted into the forms now in your galleries and storage so keeping them has turned the museum into their current accommodation. Since we cannot yet be certain of the mechanics of the afterlife, we could consider the perpetual plans of the persons under your charge as a guide for their care and, as such, in their display.

Since you 'hold the largest collection of Egyptian objects outside Egypt and tell the story of life and death in the ancient Nile Valley,' it could seem daunting to understand and accommodate so many peoples' eternal plans. Fortunately, many of the labels you have provided in your current display already outline the specific needs for their exposition. These guidelines might not interfere with the museography and the day to day activities at the museum and could be an opportunity for curating for that ancient audience to consider their positioning and views for sights beyond the grave. Such a small step to repairing the potential disruption caused by the relocation for the people who planned so well, can expand our knowledge of aspects of life which might be lost to us now.

Thank you again for your attention, consideration, and time.

    Sincerely,

Gala Porras-Kim
4727 2nd Avenue
Los Angeles, CA 90047

New York City, November 20, 2021

Ms. Jane Pickering
William and Muriel Seabury Howells Director
Peabody Museum of Archaeology & Ethnology
Harvard University
11 Divinity Ave, Cambridge, MA 02138

RE: Mediating with the rain

Dear Ms. Pickering,

Thanks very much to you and your staff for being so accommodating and helpful in providing records and information regarding the objects that were dredged from the Sacred Cenote at Chichén Itza currently located in your museum. As I mentioned in our last meeting, I am interested in objects suspended from their original function or purpose by being stored and displayed in institutions solely as historical objects. In this case, these votive offerings were submerged as tributes to the Mayan rain god Chaac, and probably never meant to leave the cenote. It is clear from the documents regarding the provenance of these objects that human laws were used to displace them from their intended place to their current location at the Peabody. Their owner, the rain, is still around.

Some of the objects had been preserved over centuries because they were submerged in water in the cenote. Their current state of dehydration, caused by their extraction and maintenance by conservators, permanently changed their composition so now they are just dust particles held together through conservation methods. The Peabody is, in fact, preserving this dust as a shell of its past shape. Your storage, being one of the driest environments in which they can exist, is in complete opposition to their submerged wet state, and their current condition as historical artifacts might make it difficult to realize their purpose with the rain.

The museum is tasked with caring for the object, but should not be limited only to the physical conservation of material form, by extending this care to the immaterial and the preservation of the ritual function—the dignitary interests—that may still exist within the object. Since we can only speculate on what the rain might want, we can, by extension, consider ways in which we can reinstitute the ritual life they continue to have within them as well.

For this purpose, I would like to thank you for collecting and providing the fallen dust that was available in the storage room, which is now being rehydrated through various means. Of course, there are many ways that these multiple functions can coexist and I've attached some initial ideas to brainstorm. I look forward to discussing with you future solutions to this arid landscape.

Thank you again for your attention, consideration, and time, and I await your reply with interest.

Sincerely,

غالا بوراس كيم

رسائل إلى مديري المتاحف

تطرح غالا بوراس كيم تساؤلاتٍ حول الديناميات الملتوية للسلطة في صميم العمل الآثاري والمتحفي. وتركز اهتمامها بشكل خاص على سبل استخدام التحكم بالمناخ داخل مخازن المقتنيات وفي قاعات العرض للحفاظ على قطعٍ سبق وأن انتُزعت من سياقها الأصلي الرطب على الأغلب. تأتي الرسائل المعروضة في هذا العمل والموجّهة إلى المتحف الوطني في البرازيل بمدينة ريو دي جانيرو والمتحف البريطاني بلندن ومتحف بيبودي في جامعة هارفرد بكامبريدج بماساشوستس، ضمن مجموعة أكبر من الرسائل إلى مديرين ومديرات وقيّمين وقيّمات في مؤسسات تحتفظ بالقطع الفنية الأثرية والأغراض الطقسية والرفات البشرية. وتتضمن الرسائل حلولًا عمليةً وأخرى حالمةً لسبل رد الاعتبار إلى الأغراض والرفات الموجودة في عهدتها.

Rand Abdul Jabbar

Tracing Origins

Artist and designer Rand Abdul Jabbar's visual essay is a paean to everyday domestic objects that inhabit a diasporic home. These domestic collections – tapestries, silverware, paintings and ceramics – carry stories of displacement, transforming into sites of memory that connect to places and people lost. Abdul Jabbar notes that traces of the past are not the exclusive domain of museums and that history can be drawn on a smaller scale, across generations, through language, and with everyday objects.

في ظل المعالم

توقعات حول المتاحف، الذاكرة الجمعية والتأريخ

كاف للنشر

فن جميل

في ظل المعالم
توقعات حول المتاحف، الذاكرة الجمعية والتأريخ

من منشورات دار كاف للنشر بالتعاون مع فن جميل

التحرير: نورا رازيان
إدارة التحرير: لوكاس مورين
تصميم المنشور: كلارا سانشو

الشكر موصول إلى كل من ساهم في هذا المنشور:
أرييلّا عائشة أزولاي، أكرم زعتري، أناهي ألفيسو مارينو، أنطونيا كارفر، أوزما ز. رضوي،
باسل عباس وروان أبو رحمة، بونافنتور سوه بيجينغ نديكونغ، بيو أباد، جمانة مناع،
ديما سروجي، رند عبد الجبار، عليا سبتي، عمر برّادة، غالا بوراس كيم، فوستان لنيكولا،
ماريان باستور رويس، مايكل راكوفيتز، نواه أنجيل، نورا البدري، نورا رازيان، هيثم الورداني

الترجمة من الإنجليزية إلى العربية: الأركيلوغ (جميع النصوص ما لم يذكر غير ذلك)
الترجمة من العربية إلى الإنجليزية: ناريمان يوسف ("الألف التي في القاف"، هيثم الورداني)
الترجمة من الفرنسية إلى العربية: الأركيلوغ ("إطلاق سراح التاريخ"،
فوستان لنيكولا وعمر برّادة)
الترجمة من الفرنسية إلى الإنجليزية: لارا فيرغنو ("إطلاق سراح التاريخ"،
فوستان لنيكولا وعمر برّادة)

المراجعة الأسلوبية باللغة العربية: أبوبكر العاني، بان قطان
التدقيق اللغوي باللغة العربية: محمد حمدان (دار كاف للنشر)
المراجعة الأسلوبية باللغة الإنجليزية: موريل قهوجي
التدقيق اللغوي باللغة الإنجليزية: زينة عساف (دار كاف للنشر)

تخطيطات إضافية: رومي بيطار ("صرح شمّي يومًا: 'المرأة الكويتية عطاء وفداء'" ،
أناهي ألفيسو مارينو، و"سبسطية: لمحة عن كثب حول الفصل العنصري"، ديما سروجي)

والشكر الجزيل لفادي جميل، وفريق فن جميل، ومعرض إيفا، ومعرض سافي للفن المعاصر،
والفنانين فاريوس وغولد

الحروفيات المستخدمة:
29Letters Type Foundry من 29LT Okaso، و29LT Zarid Display، 29LT Zarid Text

الورقيات المستخدمة: ورق Wibalin Natural Plum (غلاف)، وورق Wibalin Natural
Basalt (الورقة الأخيرة)، وورق Papyrus Rainbow Yellow and Fedrigoni Arena
(وزن 90 غ للمتر المربع).

طبعت في بلجيكا بدار دي كيورا للطباعة.

ردمك
978-614-8035-45-6

الطبعة الأولى، 2023
حقوق النشر محفوظة لدار كاف للنشر ومؤسسة فن جميل والمؤلفين

جميع الحقوق محفوظة. يحظر استنساخ هذا المنشور كلياً أو جزئياً، بأي شكل من الأشكال
وبأي وسيلة إلكترونية أو ميكانيكية أو غيرها، بما في ذلك التصوير أو التسجيل أو في أي نظام
لتخزين المعلومات أو استرجاعها، دون موافقة مسبقة من الناشر وفن جميل.

صدر هذا الكتاب على هامش معرض:

ذاكرة المبتور
بمشاركة
بيو أباد ووفرانسيس وادسوورث جونز، وأكرم زعتري، والعمارة الجنائية، وإنهاء الاستعمار، وبنجي
بويادجيان، وثيو مرسييه، وجمانة مناع، وخليل رباح، ورند عبد الجبار، وريان تابت، وعلي شرّي،
وقادر عطية.
قيمة: نورا رازيان

مركز جميل للفنون
و أكتوبر/تشرين الأول 2019 – 15 فبراير/شباط 2020

نشر وتوزيع:
كاف للنشر
شارع غورو، الجميزة
بناء رينو، الطابق 4
بيروت، لبنان
kaphbooks.com

فن جميل
مركز جميل للفنون
واجهة الجداف المائية
دبي، الإمارات العربية المتحدة
artjameel.org

متوفر أيضًا لدى
ديجون
Les presses du réel
lespressesdureel.com

أمستردام
Idea Books
ideabooks.nl

نيويورك
ARTBOOK LLC
D.A.P. | Distributed Art Publishers, Inc
artbook.com

بيروت ودبي
CIEL Book Distribution
ciel.me

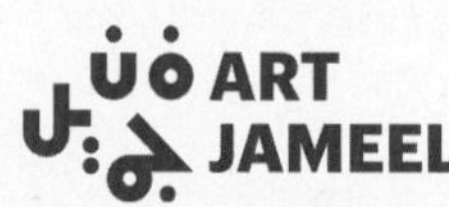

أنطونيا كارفر

تمهيد

"في ظل المعالم" هو ثمرة للاهتمام طويل الأمد لمؤسسة فن جميل في طرح قضايا التراث المادي والأفكار المتعلقة بصونه وهدمه وإعادة بنائه وإعادة إنتاجه. تطور هذا الاهتمام من التركيز على الحِرَفية والبيئة العمرانية - من خلال إدارة بيوت الفنون التراثية في جدة والقاهرة ودعم مشاريع توثيق التراث والعمران المحلية – ليصبح برنامجًا حافلًا يتضمن المعارض والمحاضرات والندوات على مدى السنوات الخمس الماضية. سعينا خلال هذه المسيرة إلى تحرّي وتفكيك مفهوم "التراث" عبر التفكير سويًّا وتبادل المعارف داخل أروقة المؤسسة و"أمام الجمهور" بالاشتراك مع فنانين/ات معاصرين/ات وغيرهم من الممارسين التشاركيين، معرّجين على مجالات العلوم المتحفية والآثار والذاكرة وعمليات صنع التواريخ وهدمها. وكان من بين المعارض والتكليفات التي انبثقت عن مشاريع مكتبة جميل البحثية معرض "ذاكرة المبتور" المُقام في مركز فن جميل بدبي عام 2019 الذي شكل نواةً لهذا المنشور الغني والمعرضان الفرديان لمايكل راكوفيتز وهيواك.

يأتي "في ظل المعالم" ضمن سياقٍ عالميٍّ بات الحديث فيه عن الممارسات المتحفية وصناعة التاريخ وأثر الصراعات وعمليات النهب على التراث المادي أكثر إلحاحًا من ذي قبل بحثًا عن سبل أخرى للمضي قدمًا نحو المستقبل. وقد شهد العقد الماضي تطوّرات بالغة الأهميّة من بينها صدور تقرير سار-سافوا 2018 والذي أسهم في تسريع عمليات الاسترداد من بعض المتاحف الغربية (وإن بوتيرة متفاوتة ومجتزأة وشبه استعراضية)، وصعود موجة الحركات الاحتجاجية عام 2020 والتي أدّت إلى تفكيك وإزالة بعض النُصب

التذكارية التي خلّدت شخصياتٍ تاريخيةٍ محل خلافية في أوروبا وأميركا الشمالية.

يُعتبر "في ظل المعالم" أول منشور من نوعه يركّز على المنطقة التي خرجت من رحمها مؤسسة "فن جميل،" وهي منطقة لا تزال تحمل ندوبًا من تواريخ بناء الأمة المستندة إلى عمليات التنقيب عن الآثار وحملات التدمير واسعة النطاق للقطع والمواقع الأثرية المهمة. وفي حين تدور معظم المساهمات في فلك الحديث عن منطقة غرب آسيا، وبالأخصّ العراق ولبنان وفلسطين ومنطقة الخليج، تقدّم المساهمات الأخرى مناظير مختلفةٍ من السياق العالمي لكيفية تصوّر الشعوب والمؤسسات والممارسات المتنوعة وممارستها لمفهوم امتلاك التراث.

يجمع "في ظل المعالم" حصيلة سنواتٍ من البحث والحوار حول ممارسات العرض وصناعة المعارض الفنية، ويضم أصواتًا متنوعةً وأشكالًا مختلفةً من النصوص الأكاديمية إلى المقالات البصرية والمقابلات والتأليف الأدبي. ويؤكّد هذا المنشور الصادر بالتعاون مع دار "كاف" للنشر في بيروت على التزام "فن جميل" بدعوة الكتاب إلى التأليف والنشر بالعربية والترجمة إليها بهدف إتاحة هذا المجال البحثي لشرائح جمهورنا كافة.

ساهمت مشاريع التعاون المؤسسية التي أطلقناها على مستوى العالم في إثراء هذه الحوارات، لا سيما تلك التي أطلقناها بالتعاون مع "سافي" للفن المعاصر وغاليري معهد العلاقات الخارجية ببرلين (ifa) ضمن البرنامج متعدد الاختصاصات "For the Phoenix"

to Find its Form in Us: On Restitution, Rehabilitation, and
Reparation" (كـي تتعـرف العنقـاء عـلى صورتهـا فينـا) عـام 2021.
ونخـصّ هنـا بالشـكر مديـري المؤسسـتين بونافنتـور سـوه بيجينـغ
نديكونـغ وعليـا سـبتي اللذيـن يتحدثـان عـن هـذا التعـاون ضمـن
هذه الصفحات.

كان فريـق عمـل فـن جميـل، ولا يـزال، مشـاركًا فاعـلًا في هـذا البحـث
المتواصـل في مسـائل التـراث والمـادة. أشـكر كل أعضـاء هـذا الفريـق
الرائـع وأخـص منهـم نـورا رازيـان التـي تولّـت بالتعـاون مـع راهـول
جودييـودي ولوكـاس موريـن تقييـم هـذا المبحـث وهـذا الكتاب ووضـع
تصورهمـا وإنتاجهمـا. كما نديـن بالامتنـان لكل الفنانيـن/ات والمؤلفيـن
والباحثيـن/ات والقيميـن/ات الذيـن رافقونا/ننا في هـذه المسـيرة وأنـاروا
دربنـا بآرائهـم/ن وملاحظاتهـم/ن الثاقبـة التـي أغنـت النقـاش حـول
هـذا المبحـث على امتـداد السـنوات الماضيـة. وقد تضمن هـذا الكتـاب
اسـتكمالًا لبعـض تلـك النقاشـات، في حيـن اتّخـذ بعضهـا الآخـر صيغًـا
متنوعـةً مـن مشـاريع وأعمـالٍ فنيـةٍ ومعـارض ونصـوصٍ ومحاضـراتٍ،
وينـدرج جميعهـا في إطـار التـزام فـن جميـل الكلـي بالتقصـي النقـدي
والمحايـث لمعنـى التـراث مـن منظـور الحاضـر.

أنطونيا كارفر

المديرة التنفيذية
فن جميل

نورا رازيان

مقدمة

فتح معرض "ذاكرة المبتور"[1] في مؤسسة فن جميل بدبي أبوابه في أكتوبر/تشرين الأول 2019. وجمع المعرض ثلاثة عشر فنانًا وفنانةً وجماعةً فنية من غرب آسيا وأماكن أخرى من العالم، لطرح أسئلةٍ ملحةٍ حول استخدام التراث كسلاح، ونشأة الأساطير المؤسّسة للعنف الاستعماري وموروثاته من خلال الهيمنة على التراث المادي وتقنينه. سعى المعرض إلى ممارسة "أركيولوجيا عكسية"، أي تتبّع آثار القطع الأثرية رجوعًا عبر الشبكة المتداخلة من الأيدي التي تداولتها والتشريعات والأطر الخطابية التي أدرجتها في حيّز "التراث" المحجوب.

لطالما شكل فضاء التراث المادي، والحقول البحثية المختصة به كعلم الآثار وعلم المتاحف بالتبعية، حيثيةً لترسيخ السرديات التاريخية التي توفر بدورها أدواتٍ للتدليل على الأحقية بالأرض من ناحيةٍ، ومسرحًا لاستعراض الهويات القومية والإثنية من ناحيةٍ ثانية. إلا أن تحولًا كبيرًا طرأ على النقاش العام في الفحوى والنبرة، فقد راحت النقاشات حول إعادة القطع الأثرية التراثية تتسلل خارج أروقة اليونسكو ومعتركات السياسة الوطنية وتطبع المزاج السياسي الراهن بمزيد من الإلحاح عن ذي قبل، وذلك بضغط من الحركات العالمية المطالِبة بتحقيق العدالة الاجتماعية والقضاء على التمييز العنصري وردّ الاعتبار. ترى تلك الحركات العالمية المتواصلة التماثيل والمعالم التذكارية والمواقع الأثرية كبؤر لترسيخ وإدامة تواريخ العنف والاضطهاد والتمييز المتصلة بالفرز العرقي وبنى الهيمنة الاستعمارية. ويدرك دعاة تفكيك هذه المواقع وإعادة تسميتها "تواريخ النسيان التي أُنشئت عليها ويرون بوضوح تام كيف تُستخدم المعالم الأثرية كأسلحة في الصراعات الدائرة حول العرق والأمة"[2]. وكما ينبهنا عالم الآثار يانيس

هاميلاكيس بحصافة؛ "لا تُعدّ الإطاحة بهذه المعالم والصروح 'قتلًا' رمزيًا للرجال الذين تمثلهم، وإنما محاولةً لتوظيف هذه الشخصيات في خدمة الاستعراض السياسي المؤثر". هذا الاستعراض الذي يسعى إلى جذب انتباهنا إلى التواريخ غير المنتهية التي ستعود لتلاحقنا جميعًا، ودعوتنا في الوقت عينه إلى اعتناق أنطولوجية للعيش تمليها علينا الأشباح"[3].

ينطلق هذا المنشور، وكذلك المعرض الذي سبقه، من الرغبة في التعاطي مع هذه "الأشباح". وتقدم المقالات والنصوص والمساهمات البصرية في هذا المنشور توسعةً لمحادثات كانت قد انطلقت أثناء معرض "ذاكرة المبتور" والذي ناقش الأسس التي يقوم عليها الفهم الحديث للتراث المادي. في هذا الإطار، طرح عمل جمعية دار للتخطيط المعماري والفني بعنوان "تراث اللاجئين" (2015 – 2021) إدراج مخيم الدهيشة للاجئين في بيت لحم على قائمة مواقع اليونسكو للتراث العالمي دافعًا في اتجاه احتمالية تعبئة خطاب التراث ليصبح عاملًا فاعلًا في مسار التحول السياسي. بالتوازي مع ذلك، يتحرّى فيلم "انعكاس الذاكرة" (2016) لقادر عطية مفهوم الترميم في سياق دولة ما بعد الاستعمار. ويسائل العديد من الأعمال الأخرى حقل الآثار برمته كمثال عمل ريان ثابت "أرثوستايتس" (2017 – متواصل) وصور أكرم زعتري المُقبِضة لحفريات عثمان حمدي بك في جنوب لبنان إبان العهد العثماني، وكلاهما يضيء على الضبابية القانونية التي أحاطت بعملية إزالة المكتشفات الأثرية والاستحواذ عليها.

يتضمن "في ظل المعالم" عددًا من المساهمات في الأدب والرقص والآثار وتاريخ الفن والفنون البصرية، يواصل من خلالها طرح تلك

الأسئلة الملحّة التي ذكرناها آنفًا، مقترحًا زوايا مختلفة للتعاطي مع الماضي ورواسبه. وكانت النية أن تتخلل المنشورَ مساهماتٌ متنوعة الأشكال، لكن نظرًا لصدوره بنسخةٍ واحدةٍ باللغتين العربية والإنكليزية، فقد قررنا وضع المقالات والمقابلات في الصدارة فيما تتوسطه المساهمات البصرية.

يبني **نواه أنجيل** نصه بعنوان "المتاحف تولّد الأشباح" على خلاصة محاوراته الممتدة لسنوات مع فريق التقييم الفني وفريق الحراسة الليلية في المتحف البريطاني الذي يضم أكثر من 8 ملايين قطعة، ما يجعله أكبر متحفٍ موسوعيٍ في العالم. يحتوي مبنى المتحف البريطاني على قاعات عرضٍ فسيحة ومخازن ضخمة للمكتشفات الأثرية من أغراضٍ وتحفٍ، بالإضافة إلى ما يزيد على 6 آلاف رفاتٍ بشرية. يجمع أنجيل شهاداتٍ عن أشباح ليلية وأغراض مضطربةٍ وأرواح متمردةٍ، ويسأل ماذا سيحدث لو تعاطى المتحف بجديةٍ مع هذه الظواهر والأحداث.

في سياق مشابه، تطالب **غالا بوراس كيم** في "رسائل إلى مديري المتاحف"، نيابةً عن الأغراض والرفات المتيبسة العطشى القابعة في قاعات التخزين، بعودتها إلى بيئاتها الرطبة والمفعمة بالحياة. وترى بوراس كيم أن المتاحف تساهم في الواقع بتدمير تلك المقتنيات بدلًا من الحفاظ عليها عن طريق سلخها عن سياقاتها الأصلية ومجتمعاتها التي أولتها الرعاية والعناية.

كيف يمكن لمجتمع الفن والتقييم والكتابة خلق منصاتٍ عامةٍ للذاكرة مع استحالة وصولهم إلى القطع والأرشيفات والمواقع الأثرية التي دُمّرت ونُهبت؟ كيف يستطيع الخيال أن يساهم في إعادة قراءة واسترجاع ما فُقد أو طُمس من التواريخ؟ يضيء الحوار بين **عمر بزّادة** والراقص والمصمم الحركي الشهير **فوستان لنيكولا** على عمل الأخير الأدائي بعنوان "باناتابا" (2017) في متحف المتروبوليتان للفن بنيويورك. يتطرّق الحوار إلى محاولة المرء استعادة تاريخه، وهي مهمةٌ شاقةٌ ومؤلمةٌ في أغلب الأحيان، من خلال التفاعل مع الأغراض التي انتُزعت من مجتمعاتها أملًا في لأم الجراح الكثيرة التي خلّفتها تواريخ الاستعمار والاستخراج المخضّبة بالعنف. تُنبهنا الكاتبة والناشطة **أرييلّا عائشة أزولاي** في كتابها المعنون "Potential History: Unlearning Imperialism" (تاريخ مُحتَمَل: التحرر من المعرفة الإمبريالية) الصادر عام 2020 والذي يورد هذا المنشور مقطعًا منه، إلى أنه "لا يمكن أن نسكت عن دور الاستعمار في اختزال صناعة الفن إلى مجرد إنتاج لأشياء ذات قيمةٍ متحفيةٍ وسوقيةٍ، والتي إن جُرّدت من سياقها، فقدت معناها، بحيث يصبح العمل الفني محض عمل فني. لابد أن نرى هذه القطع الفنية كآثارٍ

لعوالم محطمة تنطوي على حقوق يمكن أن تتحقق في وجود هؤلاء الذين انتفت عنهم تلك الحقوق، أو ورثتهم"[4]. تقدّم أزولاي في هذا الاقتباس مثالًا على كيفية البدء بالتفكير في العلاقة بين المقتنيات والأشخاص والمؤسسات التي تستحوذ عليهما من خلال مقاربتها النقدية للدعوى القضائية المرفوعة من تمارا لانيير ضد جامعة هارفرد للمطالبة بتسليم الأخيرة صورًا فوتوغرافيةً في عهدتها تعود إلى عصر العبودية وتخصّ أجداد لانيير.

يسعى العمل الفني للثنائي **باسل عباس وروان أبو رحمة** إلى تحويل "الخِربة" من مساحةٍ رومانسيةٍ متّصلةٍ تاريخيًا بالمفاهيم المؤسِسة للحداثة الأوروبية، إلى مساحةٍ لاستعادة الفاعلية والتمكين الجماعي. تنبثق مقالتهما البصرية بعنوان "ولكن قناعي منيع" عن مشروعٍ أعمّ يحمل الاسم عينه ويشتمل على طباعةٍ مجسّمةٍ لنسخٍ من أقنعةٍ نيوليثيةٍ عُثر عليها في حفرياتٍ أثريةٍ في الضفة الغربية بفلسطين، وتقبع حاليًا أسيرةً في خزائن مجموعاتٍ من المقتنيات الخاصة بالإضافة إلى مجموعة المتحف الإسرائيلي. يرتدي شبانٌ فلسطينيون هذه الأقنعة بينما يتجولون في قراهم المدمّرة، يأكلون ويرقصون ويغنون. يقول الفنانان إن العمل يُظهر "المواقع المدمرة لا كمساحات للخراب أو للندبات النفسية، بل كأماكن حرة مفعمة بالحيوية"[5]. تشكل هذه الطريقة المباشرة من التفاعل مع الخِرَب وعمليات التخريب بحسب آن ستولر وسيلةً "للحد من التعاطي مع الموجودات الأثرية لدى الإمبراطورية كمواد ميتةٍ أو كبقايا نظامٍ بائدٍ والتركيز على كيفية مصادرتها، وإهمالها، وموضعتها الاستراتيجية والفاعلة في سياسات الحاضر"[6].

يستشعر سكان غرب آسيا بشكل خاص تداعيات النقاش العالمي الملحّ والمحتدم حول تداول وعرض القطع الأثرية والتراث المادي. فقد شجعت التواريخ الطويلة من الاحتلال والصراعات في تلك المنطقة على استخراج الآثار وتبديدها بالتوازي مع نشأة سوق الآثار العالمية. فلا يزال أكثر من نصف القطع الأثرية التي نهبت من المتحف الوطني العراقي والبالغ عددها حوالي 15 ألف قطعةً مفقوداً حتى اللحظة، بينما يتعرض المئات من المواقع الأثرية والمتاحف والمعالم التاريخية في سوريا للدمار والنهب منذ بداية الحرب الأهلية عام 2011. تقدم لائحة الإنتربول للقطع الأثرية المسروقة، والتي يمكن اعتبارها مفتاحاً لخارطة الصراعات الماضية والراهنة، لمحةً عن إجمالي حجم تجارة الآثار غير المشروعة والتي تقدر بنحو 10 مليارات دولارٍ أميركيٍ سنويًا[7]. توظف **نورا البدري** مصطلح "التنكو- تراث" في مقالتها البصرية بعنوان "الرؤية البابلية: سلسلة تماثيل عصبونية قديمة" – وهو مصطلح يعبر عن التقاطع بين التكنولوجيا والتراث الثقافي- لطرح المزيد من

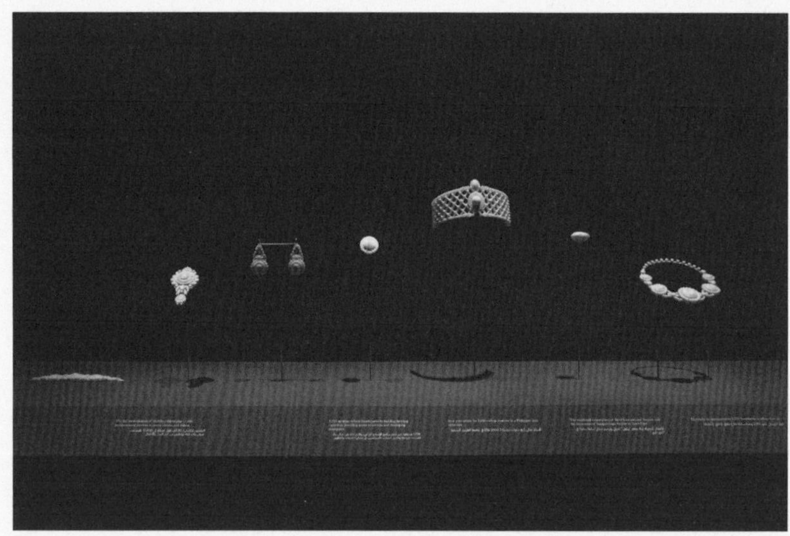

The Collection of Jane Ryan and William Saunders. بيو أباد وفرانسيس وادسوورث جونز.
("مجموعة جاين راين وليم ساندرز")، مركز جميل للفنون، 2019. مع التقدير لفن جميل. حقوق الصورة
لدانييلا بابتيستا.

الإشكاليات المرتبطة بمفاهيم الامتلاك وحقوق الملكية في سياق
الحديث عن المقتنيات المتحفية. جمعت البدري 10 آلاف صورة لآثارٍ
من حضارات ما بين النهرين وآثار نيو سومرية وأشورية موجودةٍ في
متحف المتروبوليتان للفن بنيويورك ومتحف كليفلند للفن وعرضتها
على الذكاء الاصطناعي بهدف تدريبه على تخليق وإنشاء قاعدة بياناتٍ
لقطعٍ أثريةٍ تخاطب الرغبة في إعادة إنتاج المفقود وتخيّل مستقبل
التراث المادي في العصر الرقمي.

اضطلع حقل الآثار المُسخَّر لخدمة المطامح الاستعمارية بدورٍ
مؤسّس في تشكيل الرغبات والتصورات الاستهلاكية حيال "الآخر"
من خلال إنتاج الصور الرومانسية عن الأطلال أو الخِرب وإسقاط
منطق إنقاذ وصيانة الآثار على الأرض وسكانها. تعاين **أوزما ز. رضوي**
في مقالتها الافتتاحية بعنوان "طبيعة صامتة" الآليات الاستعمارية
المحرّكة لحقل الآثار، كتقسيم الزمن الخطي وتصنيفه وتنظيمه
وقياس المسافة من الماضي كِسمةٍ للحداثة والتقدم، داعيةً في المقابل
إلى اكتشاف القوة التحررية في الصمت أو الجمود. تستدعي رضوي
مرجعياتٍ فنيةٍ حداثيةٍ ومعاصرةٍ إضافةً إلى صورٍ فوتوغرافيةٍ لمواقع

أثريةٍ من بدايات القرن العشرين لتدفع في اتجاه التفكير بالرفض
الذي يمثّله الصمت على سبيل "الاشتباك مع المنطلقات الجوهرية
للممارسات النظرية المناهضة للاستعمار".

يشكل صمت الصورة الفوتوغرافية، مقروناً بفعل الفرجة، منطلقاً
لنص **أكرم زعتري** "قراءة ثانية" الذي يقدم قراءةً متعمّقةً للصور
الفوتوغرافية التي التقطها عثمان حمدي بك والرسائل التي كتبها
في سياق الأحداث التي رافقت عملية تنقيب واستخراج سبعة عشر
ناووسًا أثريًا من صيدا في جنوب لبنان عام 1887. كان عثمان حمدي
بك فناناً وعالم آثارٍ ومؤسّسًا للمتحف الإمبراطوري في القسطنطينية،
أول متحف للآثار تحت سلطة الإمبراطورية العثمانية. ويعد عثمان
حمدي بك صاحب الفضل في إقرار قانون الآثار العثماني عام 1884
الذي نظّم عملية التنقيب عن الآثار داخل الأراضي التابعة للسلطنة
العثمانية وتصديرها إلى الخارج.

يظهر الارتباط بين المطامع الاستعمارية والأثرية جليًا في منطقة
بلاد الشام وفي فلسطين على وجه الخصوص، حيث كان التنقيب عن

الآثار ولا يزال، أداةً مسيّسةً لإنتاج "الحقائق" التاريخية التي تُوَظَّف بدورها كأدلّة لشرعنة الاحتلال والاستيطان المتواصلَين للأراضي الفلسطينية.[8]

تدخلنا مقالة **ديمة سروجي** البصرية بعنوان "سبسطية: لمحة عن كثب حول الفصل العنصري" في تفاصيل النضال اليومي لأهالي مدينة سبسطية التاريخية في فلسطين، أقدم مدينةٍ آهلةٍ في الضفة الغربية، وهم يحاولون التمسك بتراثها وأرضها وكرامتها. تحاور سروجي الخبير والناشط المحلي زياد أزهري في سياق تتبعها لتاريخ مقاومة البلدة لحملة تنقيب عن مواقعها الأثرية عام 1908على يد بعثة من جامعة هارفرد.

ليس الأرشيف مكاناً محايدًا، بل هو موقعٌ لإعادة إنتاج البنى السلطوية والاجتماعية السائدة. ما مغزى أن ننظر إلى الفضاء العام والمعالم والأسماء كأرشيفات موازية ومواقع لاكتساب المعارف أو لتفكيكها؟ يعرّج الحوار بين **بونافنتور سوه بيجينغ نديكونغ**، مؤسس "سافي" للفن المعاصر ومديره الفني، و**عليا سبتي** قيّمة ومديرة غالري معهد العلاقات الخارجية، على ممارسة كل منهما والتي تناقش بنى وأنماط الإنتاج المعرفي، ويبنيان على بعض الأسئلة التي طُرحت في معرض وندوة "For the Phoenix to Find its Form in Us: On Restitution, Rehabilitation, and Reparation"[9] (كي تتعرف العنقاء على صورتها فينا) الذي أقيم في برلين عام 2021 بالتعاون بين مؤسسة "فن جميل" ومؤسستيهما.

تتحرى الباحثة والأكاديمية **أناهي ألفيسو مارينو** بدورها النصب التذكاري كأرشيف من خلال مقالتها البصرية "المرأة الكويتية عطاءٌ وفداءٌ". تسبر مقالة أناهي ألفيسو مارينو البصرية التاريخ المضطرب الذي شهده هذا النصب من خلال أرشيف الفنان الكويتي خليفة القطان، بدءاً من تكليفه تخليدًا لذكرى الشهيدات والمدافعات إبان اجتياح العراق للكويت عام 1990، وتلقي الضوء على الفضاءات العامة والمعالم التذكارية المتنازع عليها في ظل السياقات السياسية المتغيرة.

يشترك مفهوما التراث والإرث في اللغة جذرًا ومعنىً، فهما يعبران عن موروث قيّم نتلقاه من الآخرين. يعبّر الاستخدام السياقي المعاصر لكلا اللفظين عن مراوحة مقياسية ما بين الصرحي والوطني من جهة والحميمي والعاطفي من جهةٍ ثانية. لكن تبقى الفضاءات الشخصية والحميمة، حيث يدور الحوار بين الأجيال، المكان الفعلي للسعي اليومي إلى تحديد كيفية نقل هذا الموروث سواء من خلال جمع التذكارات من أرضٍ مفقودةٍ أو إعداد الطعام أو التحلّق حول المائدة. تتراكم هذه الموروثات لتشكل خارطةً كبيرةً للصراعات الجيوسياسية والمنافي والحنين والرغبات كما الآمال وأفعال المقاومة الجماعية.

يتحدّث كل من **مايكل راكوفيتز ورند عبد الجبار** في مساهمتيهما عن كيفية تحول بيت المهجر بما يحتويه من أغراض ومأكولات وطقوس جماعية إلى بديل عن الوطن العراقي المفقود ويفتح الباب على مصراعيه نحو التأمل في الذاكرة والمعرفة المتناقَلين عبر الأجيال.

تصف **جمانة مناع** في مقالتها "حيث تنتهي الطبيعة وتبدأ المستوطنات" كيف ينطوي نشاطٌ بسيطٌ مثل تسليق النباتات البرية في محيط وادي شعفاط بالقدس الشرقية على فعل مقاومةٍ يمتد عبر الأجيال سعيًا للحفاظ على الروابط مع الأرض واستمرارية التراث المطبخي والزراعي الفلسطينيين. تطرح هذه الصورة تساؤلاتٍ حول الاستخدام التكتيكي للتشريع البيئي في السياق الفلسطيني/الإسرائيلي.

ويُعتبر تشويش أو تحوير التسلسل الوراثي من التكتيكات المتّبعة من قبل الطامعين بالسلطة لفرض هيمنتهم. في هذا الإطار، يناقش الفنان **بيو أباد** مع القيّمة الفنية والكاتبة **ماريان باستور روسيس** السياسة المتعلقة بالتراث الثقافي والإثني اللغوي في الفلبين والإرث المصادَر من قبل الدولة ما بعد الاستعمارية الفاسدة وموروث الأمل الذي لا يكف عن دفع ممارستيهما الملتزمتين سياسيًا.

أما النص الأخير في هذا المنشور فهو قصةٌ قصيرةٌ **لهيثم الورداني** بعنوان "الألف التي في القاف الـواو التي في النون" عن رحلة الفيلين الهدّام والعوّام القادمين من المستقبل حيث اختفت حروف العلّة من اللغة مخلّفةً اليأس والخراب في بلدهما. يقودهما الأمل في العثور على أحرف العلّة في مكانٍ آخر إلى بلدٍ تعِسٍ يُعاقب فيه الكلام أشدّ العقاب.

يدين عنوان هذا المنشور بالفضل إلى الثنائي الفني البرليني **فاريوس وغولد** في عمله المتواصل الـذي يتناول ظلال معالم الإمبريالية الألمانيا داخل ألمانيا وخارجها. كان الثنائي قـد أنتج بالتعاون مع مشروع "سافي" للفن المعاصـر المُعنوَن "Colonial Neighbours" (الجيران المستعمرون)، سلسلـةً من المشاريع في الفضاء العام، تعمد إلى "إنـزال" الشخصيات المخلّدة من العهود الاستعمارية من عليائها عـن طريق صنع قوالب ورقية لهذه الأنصاب التذكارية واستخدامها في عـروض أداءٍ تلقـي الضـوء على اتصالها التاريخـي مع القضايـا السياسية الراهنة.

يركز العديد من المساهمات في هذا المنشور على تواريخ الصراعات وآثارها، غير أنها تحتفي في الوقت عينه بالأغراض والأماكن والمواقع التذكارية المفعمة بالمعاني عبر الأزمنة. في المقابل، يطرح بعض هذه المساهمات مقارباتٍ أكثر شمولًا وأقل مركزيةً حيال صون "التراث" والتفاعل الهادف مع شبكة العلاقات التي يقع ضمنها كل موقعٍ أو غرض. وإن كان التفكير الجاد في مسألة نزع الاستعمار عن البنى المتحفية وإعادة تصورها والإبقاء على اتصالها مع الأجيال القادمة

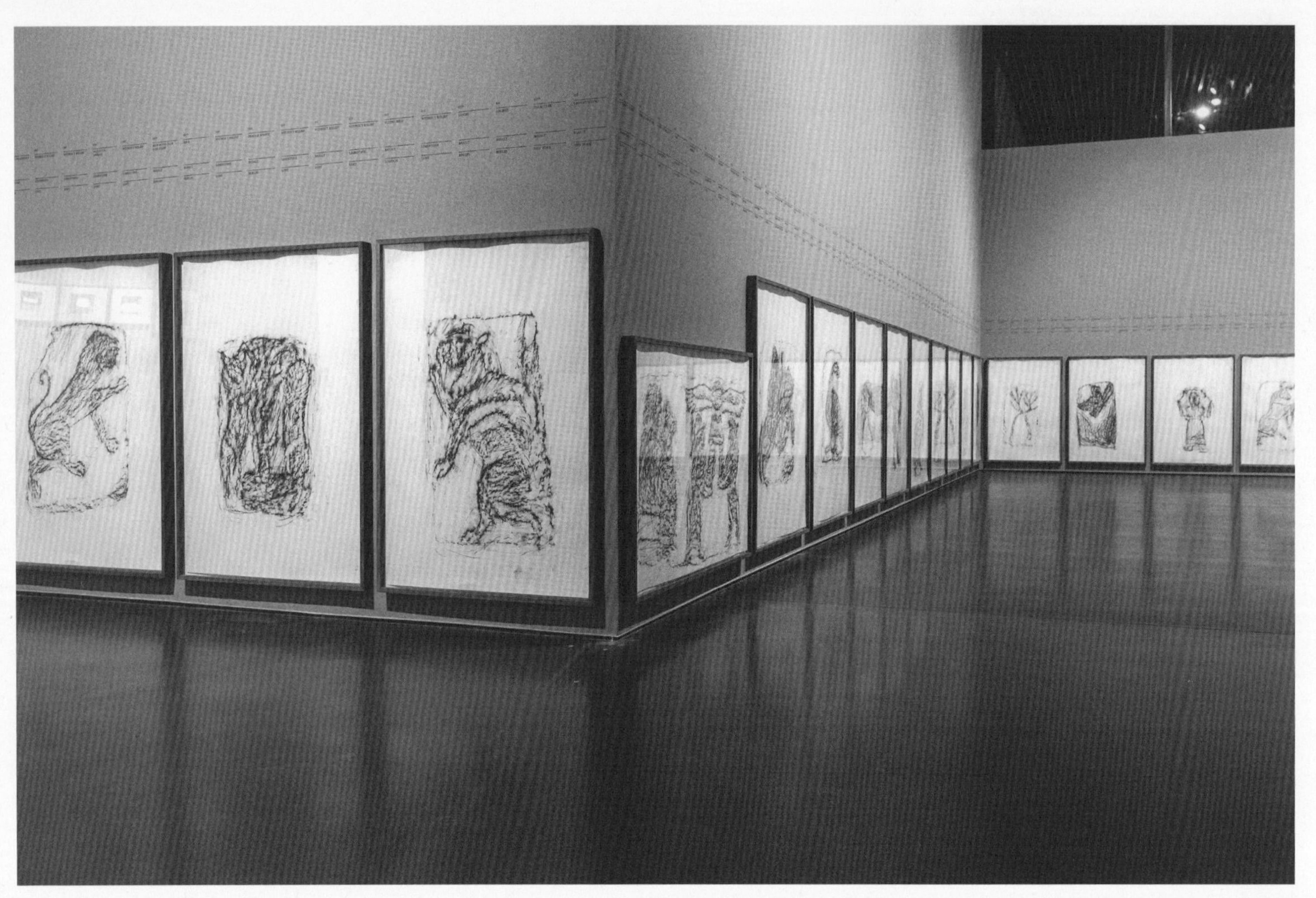

ريان ثابت. "أرثوستايتس"، 2017 – متواصل. مركز جميل للفنون، 2019. مع التقدير لفن جميل. حقوق الصورة لدانييلا بابتيستا.

ضرورةً، فـلا بد من طرح أسئلة جدية حول قضايا الملكية والرعاية والترميم والتعويـض المـادي أو غيره. نأمل أن تكون الأصـوات المجتمعة هنا مدخلاً لاستعراض السبل الممكنة لطرح الأسئلة الملحة عن الآفاق التي تفتحها متاحف المستقبل.

1   "ذاكرة المبتور"، مركز جميل للفنون"، دبي، 9 أكتوبر/تشرين الأول 2019 – 15
فبراير/شباط 2020. يتضمن أعمالاً لكل من رند عبد الجبار وبيو أباد وفرنسيس
وادسورث جونز وقادر عطية وبينجي بويدجيان وعلي شرّي ودار وفورينسِك
أركيتكتشر وجمانة مناع و تيو مارسيي وخليل رباح وريان ثابت وأكرم زعتري.
https://jameelartscentre.org/whats-on/phantom-limb

2   Raphael Greenberg and Yannis Hamilakis, *Archeology, Nation, and
Race* (Cambridge, Cambridge University Press, 2022), p. 152

3   Yannis Hamilakis, 'Learning from the "Vandals": Histories
of Forgetting', *LA Review of Books*, 26 June 2020
https://lareviewofbooks.org/short-takes/learning-vandals-histories-forgetting

4   Ariella Aïsha Azoulay, *Potential History: Unlearning
Imperialism* (London, Verso, 2019), p. 142

5   من موقع الفنانين. تاريخ الزيارة 10 نوفمبر/تشرين الثاني 2022.
https://baselandruanne.com/And-yet-my-mask-is-powerful-Part-2

6   *Imperial Debris: On Ruins and Ruination*, ed. Ann Laura
Stoler, Durham, Duke University Press, 2013, p. 11

7   Nada El Sawy, Sinan Mahmoud, and Mina Aldroubi, 'Stealing from history:
Inside the multimillion-dollar illegal trade in artefacts from the Middle East',
The National, accessed 20 May 2022
https://www.thenationalnews.com/weekend/2022/05/20/inside-the-
multimillion-dollar-illegal-trade-of-artefacts-from-the-middle

8   لدراسةٍ معمّقةٍ عن دور علم الآثار كأداةٍ للاحتلال يرجى الاطلاع على
Nadia Abu El-Haj, *Facts on the Ground: Archaeological Practice and Territorial
Self-fashioning in Israeli Society*
(Chicago, University of Chicago Press, 2001)
وقد استخدمت إسرائيل منذ عام 1967 التنقيب عن الآثار كذريعةٍ لتبرير الحق بالاستحواذ
على الأرض في الضفة الغربية وغزة. يرجى الاطلاع على المراجع الآتية:

https://www.thenational.ae/world/mena/palestinians-say-east-jerusalem
archaeology-project-inaugurated-by-us-is-fake-1.881837
https://www.msn.com/ar-eg/news/other/what-happened-to-gaza-s-apollo-
statue/ar-AA2sLM
https://www.theguardian.com/world/2010/may/26/
jerusalem-city-of-david-palestinians-archaeology

9   لمزيدٍ من المعلومات يرجى زيارة موقع :
https://savvy-contemporary.com/en/events/2021/phoenix-invocations

السير الذاتية

بيو أباد

من مواليد 1983. يقيم ويعمل في لندن، المملكة المتحدة.

تتقصى أعمال بيو أباد المتأثرة بتاريخ الفلبين الحديث دور الأسرة كفاعلٍ وكمادةٍ أرشيفية، موظفًا استراتيجيات الاستحواذ في التنقيب عن أحداث تاريخية بديلة أو مكتومة وتفكيك السرديات الرسمية وربط خيوط التشابك بين الوقائع والمفاهيم والأشخاص.

باسل عباس وروان أبو رحمة

من مواليد 1983. يقيمان ويعملان في نيويورك، الولايات المتحدة الأميركية.

يعمل الفنانان باسل عباس وروان أبو رحمة سويًا باستخدام مجموعة متنوعة من الوسائط كالصوت والصورة والنص والتركيب والأداء. تتمحور ممارستهما الفنية على العمل البحثي بشكل أساسي حول التقاطعات بين الأدائية والمتخيلات السياسية والجسد والحالة الافتراضية.

رند عبد الجبار

من مواليد 1990. تقيم وتعمل في أبو ظبي، الإمارات العربية المتحدة.

تحرص رند عبد الجبار في أعمالها على استعارة وإعادة بناء المكان والتاريخ والذاكرة كأشياء زائلة عبر توظيف التصميم والنحت والتركيب بوصفها الوسائط الغالبة على ممارستها الفنية. تتحرى عبد الجبار هشاشة الموروث المادي عبر استنطاق السرديات التاريخية والثقافية والأثرية والتفاعل معها سعيًا منها إلى صنع وتوليف أشكال مستوحاة من اللقى الأثرية والعمارة والأساطير.

نورا البدري

من مواليد 1984. تقيم وتعمل في برلين، ألمانيا.

نورا البدري هي فنانة وسائط مفاهيمية ألمانية عراقية متعددة التخصصات. تتعاطى أعمالها المستندة إلى البحث موضوعات شبه تخصصية وما بعد استعمارية وما بعد رقمية. وتركز ممارستها الفنية على سياسات التكنولوجيا الجديدة وإمكاناتها التحررية مثل الذكاء الاصطناعي أو نحت البيانات، والفاعلية والتفوق غير البشريين.

أناهي ألفيسو مارينو

تقيم وتعمل في باريس، فرنسا.

تتخصص الفنانة أناهي ألفيسو مارينو في العلوم السياسية وتهتم بالحياة المجتمعية للمنحوتات العامة لفنانين/ات من مدن مختلفة في شبه الجزيرة العربية. تجمع في مقاربتها المنهجية بين العلوم الاجتماعية والممارسات الفنية. سبق لها العمل الميداني في كل من اليمن والكويت وسلطنة عُمان والإمارات العربية المتحدة، لتركز على البحث الأرشيفي ودراسة الأعمال الفنية التذكارية العامة.

نواه أنجيل

من مواليد 1980. يقيم ويعمل في برلين، ألمانيا.

نواه أنجيل هو كاتب وفنان يعمل على موضوعات متعلقة بنقل التقاليد الشفهية التي تشمل القصص والأغاني. يعمل حاليًا على إنجاز كتابه الأول بعنوان: *Ghosts of the British Museum* (أشباح المتحف البريطاني). وكان قد بدأ عام 2016 بجمع شهادات موظفي المتحف البريطاني الحاليين والسابقين عن قطع أثرية غير ساكنة ورفاتٍ بشرية متمردة تتحدى ظروف تخزينها وعرضها.

أرييلّا عائشة أزولاي

من مواليد 1962. تقيم وتعمل في بروفيدنس، الولايات المتحدة الأميركية.

أرييلّا عائشة أزولاي هي قيّمة فنية ومخرجة أفلام وأستاذة في الثقافة والوسائط الحديثة في قسم الأدب المقارن في جامعة براون. تلقي أعمالها الضوء على العنف الذي تنطوي عليه عملية رسم الحدود الاستعمارية، مشيرة إلى علاقةٍ قلّما تلقى الاهتمام بين المقتنيات الأثرية الثقافية بالغة التوثيق والمهاجرين غير الشرعيين.

عمر برّادة

من مواليد 1980. يقيم ويعمل في نيويورك، الولايات المتحدة الأميركية.

عمر برّادة هو كاتب وقيّم فني ومدير دار المأمون، مكتبة ومركز للإقامات الفنية في مراكش. تركز أعماله على سياسات الترجمة والنقل العابر للأجيال. يدرّس حاليًا في معهد كوبر يونيون للفنون بنيويورك حيث يساهم في تنظيم سلسلة محاضرات الندوة متداخلة التخصصات.

هيثم الورداني

من مواليد 1972. يقيم ويعمل في برلين، ألمانيا.

هيثم الورداني هو كاتب ومترجم ومؤلف كتب "كيف تختفي" (2013) و"كتاب النوم" (2017). يجمع الورداني ما بين مقتطفات الشعر والتأملات الفلسفية والقَصص كوسيلة لزعزعة ثنائية الحاضر/الغائب التي يرتكز عليها مجمل تصورنا عن المقاومة السياسية، ليدور حول مواضيع محمّلة بالاستعارات.

فوستان لنيكولا

من مواليد 1974. يقيم ويعمل في كيسنغاني، جمهورية الكونغو الديموقراطية.

فوستان لنيكولا هو راقص ومصمم رقص ومدير مسرح. أسس عام 1997 "غارا" وهي أول فرقةٍ للرقص المعاصر في كينيا. وعام 2001، أسس ستوديوات كاباكو وهي منصةٌ للرقص والمسرح في كنشاسا تسعى إلى تعزيز الحوار الثقافي والبحث والإبداع الفني.

جمانة مناع

من مواليد 1987. تقيم وتعمل في برلين، ألمانيا.

جمانة مناع هي فنانةٌ بَصَرية ومخرجة أفلام. تتناول أعمالها سبل تعبير السلطة عن نفسها مع التركيز على الجسد والأرض والمادة بالعلاقة مع الموروثات الاستعمارية وتواريخ المكان. تستخدم مناع النحت والأفلام والكتابة لمواجهة المفارقات التي تشوب ممارسات الحفظ لا سيما في مجال الآثار والزراعة والقانون. نشأت مناع في القدس وتقيم حاليًا في برلين.

بونافنتور سوه بيجينغ نديكونغ

من مواليد 1977. يقيم ويعمل في برلين، ألمانيا.

البروفسـور بونافنتـور سوه بيجينـغ نديكونـغ هـو قيّم فني وكاتب ومتخصص في تكنولوجيا الأحياء وحاليًا يشغل منصب مدير مؤسسة بيت ثقافات العالم (HKW) ببرلين. أسس "سافي للفن المعاصر" وكان مديرًا فنيًا له ولسونسبيك 24-20 وهو معرض للفن المعاصر يُقام مرةً كل سنوات في آرنم بهولندا.

ماريان باستور رويس

تقيم وتعمل في مانيلا، الفلبين.

ماريـان باسـتور رويـس هي قيّمـة فنيـة فلبينيـة مسـتقلة ومؤرخـة للفن وناقـدة مؤسسـية. تتّسم كتاباتها المنشورة عالميًا بالالتزام تجاه قضايا العدالة الاجتماعية في مجالات العلـوم المتحفية والملبـس والمـدن والفن المعاصـر والتغييـر الثقافي.

غالا بوراس كيم

من مواليد 1984. تقيم وتعمل في لوس أنجلس، الولايات المتحدة الأميركية.

غـالا بـوراس كيم هي فنانة تعمل في إطار بحثي على مسـاءلة طـرق تمثيـل الأصـوات واللغـة والتاريـخ عبـر منهجيات الألسن والحفاظ التراثي.

مايكل راكوفيتز

من مواليد 1973. يقيم ويعمل في شيكاغو، الولايات المتحدة الأميركية.

مايكل راكوفيتـز فنـان عراقي أميركي تجمع أعماله بين إيجاد الحلـول وإثـارة المتاعب.

نورا رازيان

من مواليد 1980. تقيم وتعمل في دبي، الإمارات العربية المتحدة.

نـورا رازيـان هي مديرة المعارض في "فن جميل" حيـث تقيّم المعـارض الفنيـة وتشـرف علـى برنامج المعارض العالمـي للمؤسسة. تولّت رازيان منصب مديرة المعارض والبرامج في متحف سرسق ببيروت بين عامي 2015 و2017 حيث ترأست البرنامج الـذي واكب إعادة افتتاح المتحف بعد إقفال دام سبع سـنوات. وكانـت قيّمـة البرامـج العامـة في متحـف تايت بلندن بين عامـي 2009 و2015.

أوزما ز. رضوي

من مواليد 1973. تقيم وتعمل في بروكلين، الولايات المتحدة الأميركية.

أوزمـا ز. رضوي هي أستاذة مساعدة في علم الإنسان والدراسات الحضرية في معهد برات بنيويورك. تجمع أعمال رضوي بين علم الآثار والنقد الثقافي والفلسفة والنظرية النقدية والفن والتصميم.

عليا سبتي

من مواليد 1983. تقيم وتعمل في برلين، ألمانيا.

عليا سبتي هي مديرة غاليري إيفا (معهد العلاقات الثقافية الخارجيـة) ببرليـن. وهي كاتبـة ومحاضِـرة في الفن والفضـاء العام والبيناليات والممارسات الفنية العابرة للثقافات.

ديمة سروجي

تقيم وتعمل في رام الله، فلسطين.

ديمة سروجي هي معمارية وفنانة بَصَرية تتناول أعمالها الأرض كفضاء غائر ذي وزن ثقافي ومكان تتولد فيه إمكانية التحرر الخيالي. أسست ستوديو هولو فورمز عام 2016.

أكرم زعتري

من مواليد 1966. يقيم ويعمل في بيروت، لبنان.

أكرم زعتري هو فنان تتحرى أعماله مجموعة من الموضوعات والممارسات المتداخلة والمتصلة بالتنقيب والنضال السياسي وحيوات المقاتلين السابقين وإرث اليسار المستنزَف وانتشار الصور في أزمنة الحرب والرسائل الضائعة أو التي عُثر عليها أو المدفونة أو المكتَشفة أو تلك التي تأخرت عن بلوغ وجهتها.

نصوص و محادثات

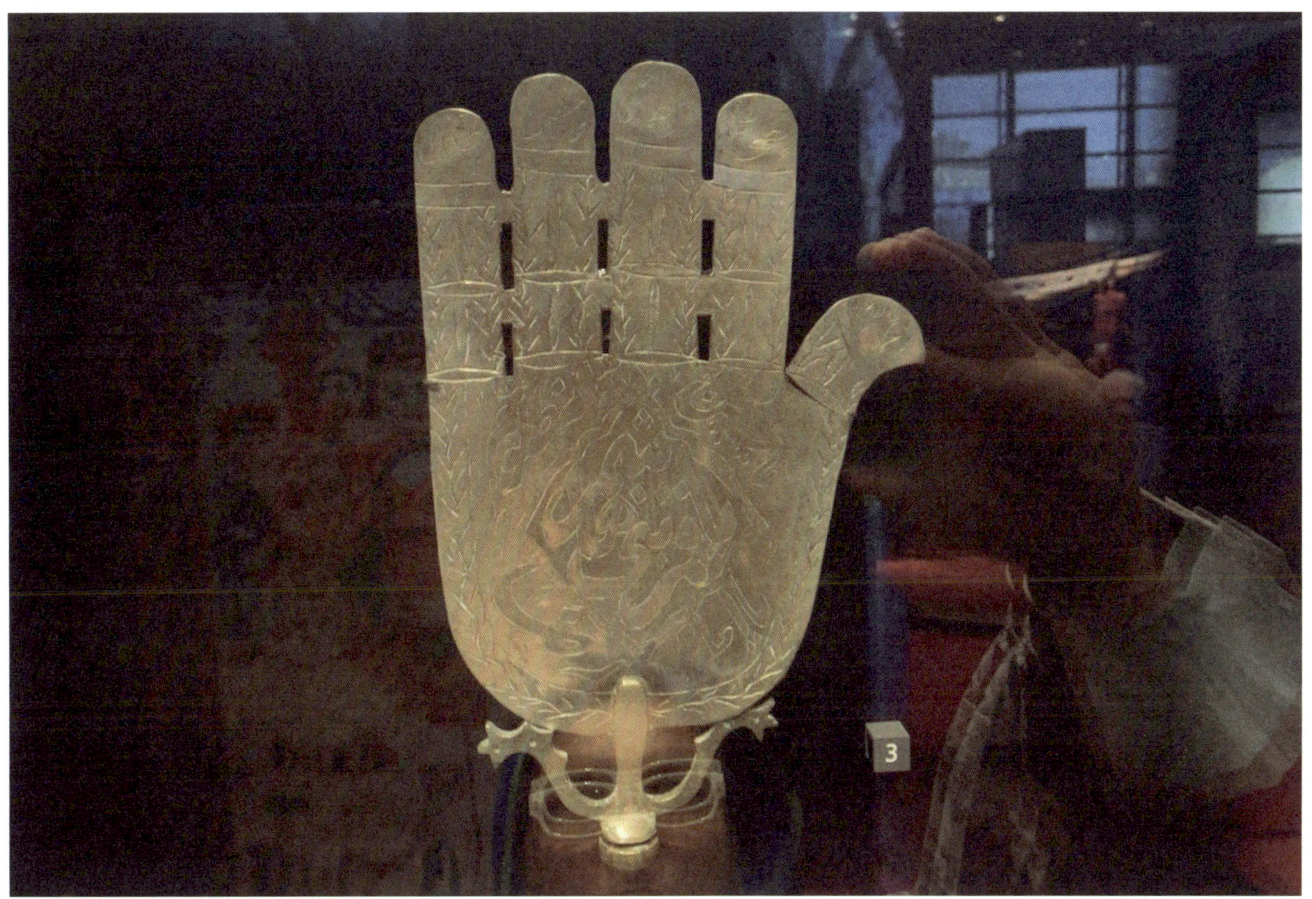

راية الموكب (العلم)، إيران، أوائل القرن العشرين. 71.1991.281.12. معدن أبيض.
29 × 2.5 × 18 سم. مجموعة متحف كاي برانلي. الصورة للمؤلفة، 2022.

أوزما ز. رضوي

طبيعة صامتة

تغمرني الدهشة والحيرة كلما دخلتُ متحفًا.

أرى ملامح من ذاتي في كل قطعةٍ قابعةٍ خلف زجاج العرض. يعكس الزجاج أوجه الحصار الذي يفرضه عليّ منطق الممارسة الأركيولوجيّة: منطق استعماري يحتجزني كعالمة آثار، ويحتجز التحفة الأثرية كمادةٍ للدراسة. الزجاج بيننا يكاد لا يقوى على احتواء الذعر الذي يكتنف التحف وشعوري بالخزي من مشاهدتها معروضةً مرةً أخرى.

تتبادر إلى ذهني فيما أنا أتنقل بين قاعات المتاحف أفلامٌ مثل "Les statues meurent aussi" (الأصنام أيضًا تموت) (1953)[1] و"Somniculus" (النوم الخفيف) (2017)[2]. تسكن نبضات قلبي كي تتعرف على الحيوات التي تلفت تلك الأفلام انتباهنا إليها داخل المتحف. تمتلئ تلك القاعات بالسكون، بإقرار صامت. أستكين أنا والتحف إلى درجة قد يُظنُّ منها أننا جماد – أو ربما نيام. أجد هذا البطء، هذا الهدوء، هذا السكون، عمديًّا ونازعًا للاستعمار.

يسمح البطء بتبني مقاربةٍ عمليةٍ إزاء التعاطي النقدي مع متطلبات "الحداثة الفائقة"[3]. وبدلًا من الإذعان لتسارعية التاريخ، تتيح الممارسة النظرية (البراكسيس) المتأنية مساحةً للعديد من التأويلات. ذلك أن فكرة "الطبيعة الصامتة" هي في حد ذاتها مفارقةٌ تخفي رغبتها الحداثية في التحكم عن طريق التمثيل. ينطلق تعريف الطبيعة الصامتة الوارد على صفحة الموقع الإلكتروني للمعرض الوطني بلندن من حالة الجماد في الأشياء:

يشكل الجماد كالفاكهة والأزهار والطعام وعناصر الحياة اليومية الموضوع الأساسي للوحات الطبيعة الصامتة. تعود هذه التسمية إلى كلمة "stilleven" الهولندية التي شاعت في التداول منذ عام 1650 للتعبير عن هذا النوع من الموضوعات. وقد راجت أعمال الطبيعة الصامتة بالأخص في هولندا في القرن السابع عشر حيث كانت تعبر في أغلب الأحيان عن التحلل المادي وفناء الحياة الدنيا[4].

1 ألان رينيه وكريس ماركر وغيزلان كلوكيه، "الأصنام أيضًا تموت". فرنسا: بريزانس أفريكان وتادي سينما، 1953

2 علي شرّي، "Somniculus" (النوم الخفيف). باريس: جو دو بوم والمؤسسة الوطنية للفنون الغرافيكية والتشكيلية وCAPC متحف بوردو للفن المعاصر، 2017، فيديو عالي الدقة، 14 دقيقة و40 ثانية.

3 Alfredo González Ruibal, "Time to Destroy: An Archaeology of Supermodernity," *Current Anthropology*, no. 49 (2008): 247-279

4 "Glossary: Still lives," National Gallery, accessed June 7, 2022. https://www.nationalgallery.org.uk/paintings/glossary/still-lives

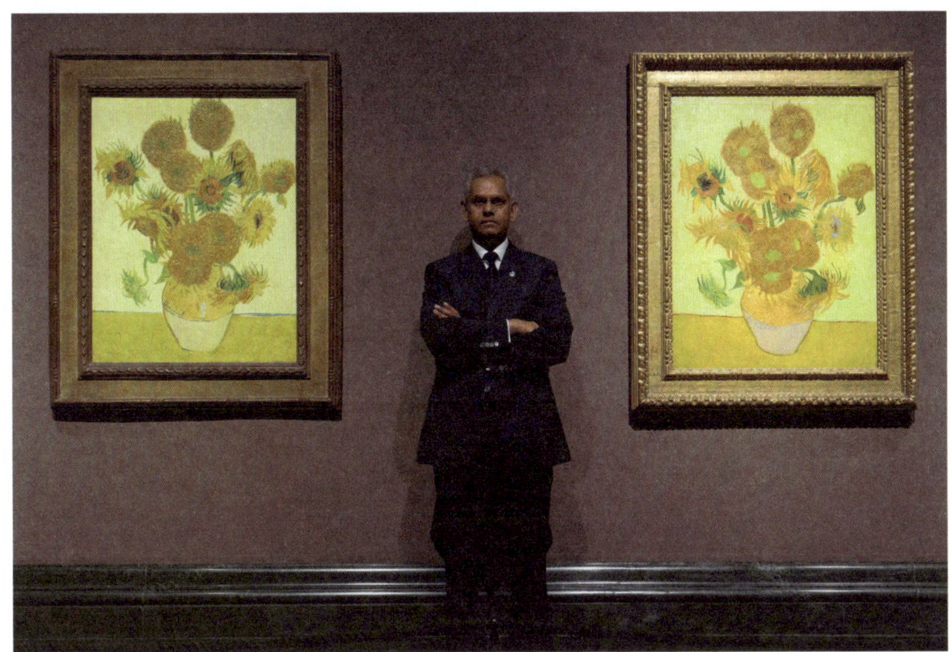

ليون نيل/وكالة الصحافة الفرنسية أ.ف.ب. مشرف غاليري يقف للصورة متوسطًا نسختين من سلسلة "عباد الشمس" للفنان الهولندي فنسنت فان خوخ في المعرض الوطني بلندن في 24 كانون الثاني/يناير 2014. للمرة الأولى منذ 65 عامًا ولغاية 27 نيسان/أبريل 2014، تجتمع لوحة "عباد الشمس" (1888) ضمن مجموعة المعرض الوطني بلوحة "عباد الشمس" (1889) من مجموعة متحف فان خوخ. صورة رقمية. بإذن من وكالة الصحافة الفرنسية أ.ف.ب. فوتو.

أتأمّل في فرضية الجماد وفي إلحاحه وواقعيته. في عام 2014، انتشرت صورة فوتوغرافية لنسختين من سلسلة "عباد الشمس" لفنسنت فان خوخ تعودان إلى عامي 1888 (يسار) و1889 (يمين)، وقد ضجت التقارير الصحافية بقصة التئام شملهما بعد 65 عامًا[5]. كانت الأجواء مفعمةً بمشاعر الحماس وكأن اللوحتين توأم فُرّق عند الولادة. أما أنا فأرى في الصورة الفوتوغرافية شكلين من التمثيل الذي يندرج تحت تعريف الطبيعة الصامتة: عباد الشمس والحارس الواقف بينهما.

يتقاطع مجالا الفن الأنثروبولوجيا مع دخول التصوير الفوتوغرافي، لا سيما التصوير العلمي، إلى مجالاتنا الخطابية. نشأ الداغيروتيب (Daguerreotype)[*]، وهو عملية شديدة البطء، كوسيلة للتعبير بدقة عن مفهوم الطبيعة الصامتة. هنالك على سبيل المثال الداغيروتيب الذي التقطه داغير نفسه بعنوان "Intérieur d'un cabinet de curiosité" (داخل حجرة العجائب) ويُعرف أيضًا بعنوان "L'Atelier de l'artiste" (ورشة الفنان) (1837) ليوثق ركنًا من عالمٍ ذي طابع خاص يبدو نابضًا بالحياة والسرد والمعنى. تحمل كل قطعة داخل الصورة الكثير من القصص. وكأن السكون يفيض من الكادر ليصب مباشرةً في مخيّلتنا. تخبّئ الصور داخل الصور، استدرار تلك التكنولوجيا الوليدة للأحاسيس والتعابير، في طياتها الرغبة الاستعمارية في التحكم والتمسك والاحتفاظ بالإحساس بذلك المكان الذي تتفتح فيه الأحلام وبذكراه. ومع هذه الصور المبكرة ترتسم مفارقة الطبيعة الصامتة.

استثنائية تلك الصور الفوتوغرافية الفريدة المطبوعة على ألواح نحاسيةٍ مفضضةٍ مصقولةٍ ومحسّسةٍ بأبخرة اليود يتم تعريضها للضوء داخل كاميرا ذات صندوق كبير ومن ثم تظهيرها بواسطة أبخرة الزئبق وتثبيتها بالماء والملح (ثيوكبريتات الصوديوم)، لم تكن تقتصر على قدرتها على التقاط المشهد فحسب. حوّلت هذه العملية التسجيل البصري إلى حقيقة وبالتحديد إلى وسيلةٍ لتوثيق المعلومات غير النصية. وبدأ علماء

The 10 Most Expensive Paintings" 5
On Public Display," *Business Insider*,
accessed June 7, 2022. https://www.
businessinsider.com/the-10-most-
expensive-paintings-on-public-
display-2014-2

* داغيروتيب تقنية من التصوير الفوتوغرافي ابتكرها لويس داغير وسميت باسمه. (المترجمة)

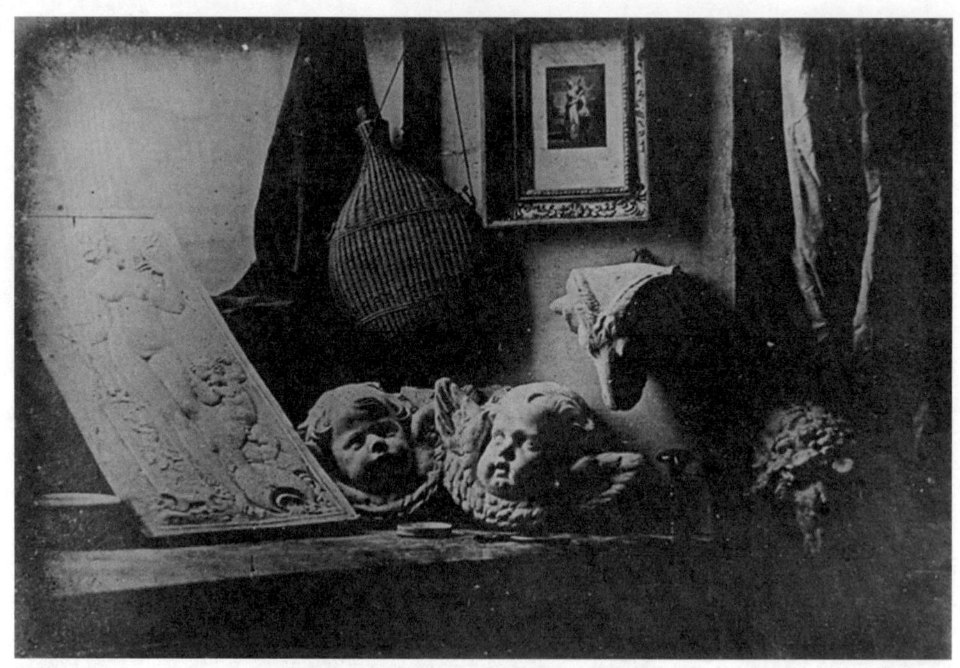

لويس داغير، " Intérieur d'un cabinet de curiosité" (داخل حجرة العجائب)، 1837، داغيروتيب
16.5 × 23 سم . مجموعة الجمعية الفرنسية للتصوير الفوتوغرافي.

الأنثروبولوجيا باستخدام هـذه التقنيـات لتقصّي "الآخـر" ورسـم صـورة لـه. تُلحـظ في هـذا الإطـار المجموعـات الفوتوغرافيـة مـن متحـف بيبـودي في هارفـرد والتـي تحتـوي عـلى بعـض الأمثلـة المبكرة عـلى عمليـات التوثيـق الإثنوغرافـي. ومـن أبـرز تلـك المجموعـات صـور داغيروتيـب تعـود إلى العـام 1850 كان عالـم الطبيعـة السويسـري لويـس أغاسيز قـد كلّـف لورينـزو ج. تشيس بالتقاطهـا، فجـاءت الصـورة الفوتوغرافيـة بالنتيجـة كشكل مـن أشكال التجميع الفني والتوثيق والتشييء. امتزج هذا التركيب البصري للآخر بسهولة مع الخيـارات التقنيـة والجماليـة التـي اتسـمت بها الطبيعـة الصامتـة.

تبين الفنانة كاري مـاي ويمز في عملها الفني بعنوان "From Here I Saw What Happened and I Cried" (مـن هنا رأيـت مـا حـدث وبكيت) (1995-1996) كيـف أراد أغاسيز الاستفادة مـن صـور الداغيروتيـب كأدلّـة بصريـة لدعم نظرياتـه عـن الدونيـة العرقيـة للأفارقـة وكدليل لتصنيـف الشعوب المستعبَدة وفق السمات الجسمانية. تعيد ويمز توجيـه استخدام تلـك الصور التي عثرت عليها في أرشيفات متحف بيبـودي وجامعة هارفـرد وتوظّفها نقديًّا عـن طريـق تحويلهـا إلى خلفيـة لمـرآة زجاجيـة حُفرت عليها بعـض الكتابة[6]. يجبرنـا هذا الفعل النقدي عـلى رؤيـة انعـكاس صورتنا في المـرآة وإدراك تواطئنا بينمـا نحـن نحـدق في العمل. مـا معنـى أن نتحـرك داخـل منظومـات العنف تلك؟ مـا معنـى أن نتواطـأ مـع الأشـكال البليدة والمنهجيـة من اللامسـاواة والحرمـان عـن طريـق المعرفة العلميـة وبذريعـة إنتاجهـا؟

يركـز عالـم الأنثروبولوجيـا أشيش تشـادا في كتابـه Visions of a discipline (رؤى مـن حقـل معرفي) عـلى التشـابهات الإبسـتمولوجية بيـن بنيـان المعرفة الأركيولوجيـة والدليل الأركيولوجـي وطبيعـة التمثيـل الأركيولوجـي، لا سـيما في أرشيف عالـم الآثار البريطانـي مـن القـرن العشـرين مورتيمـر ويلـر[7]. ببسـاطة، تُوظّـف الأجسـاد السـمراء في صـور ويلـر لمجرد القيـاس. ويقـول تشـادا إن ويلـر يجمع بحنكة الإيديولوجيـات العقابيـة للمشروع الاستعماري والعلمـي والعسكري مـن خـلال تلـك الصـور. والأهـم مـن ذلـك، والأقـرب إلى الطـرح الـذي أنا في

6 للاطلاع على تحليل ممتاز لهذا العمل يرجى مراجعة
Eunsong Kim, "Found, Found, Found, Lived, Lived, Lived," *Scapegoat*, no. 9, Eros (2016): 53-60.
وللمزيد من المعلومات حول السياق يرجى مراجعة
"Case Review: Lanier v. Harvard (2021)," Center for art law, accessed August 18, 2022.
https://itsartlaw.org/2021/07/27/case-review-lanier-v-harvard-2021/

7 Ashish Chadha. "Visions of a Discipline: Sir Mortimer Wheeler and the archaeological method in India (1944-1948)," *Journal of Social Archaeology*, no. 2 (2002): 378-401

طبيعة صامتة

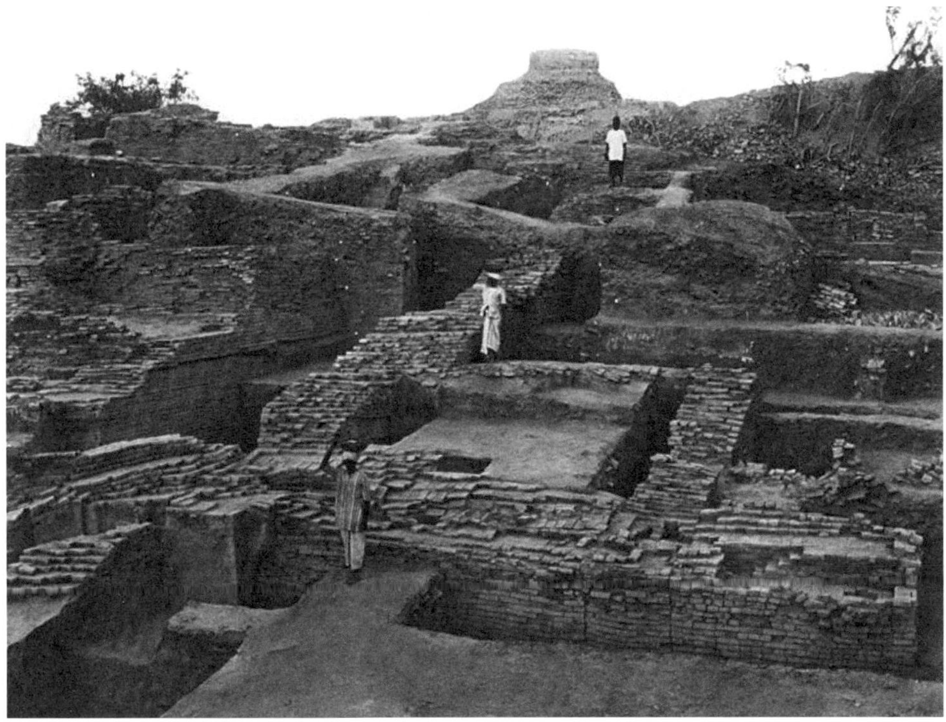

مورتيمر ويلر. صومعة الحبوب في منطقة REM (نسبة إلى روبرت إريك مورتيمر ويلر)، "الطرف الغربي من القلعة،
موهينجو دارو [122 أ]"، 1950. بإذن من موقع Harappa.com.

صدده، أن تشـادا يفسر كيف حدث ذلك مـن خـلال انتحـال فكـرة المحـدد المعرفي والمحـدد
الإثني كمجازيـن بصريـين. تسـفر هـذه المقاربـة للتوثيـق الأركيولوجي عـن تشـييء الأجسـاد
وسـلبها الحيـاة ووضعهـا تحـت سـطوة النظـرة الاستعماريـة.

تربـط أنمـاط الوسـم البصريـة تلـك الأشـكال الاستعماريـة مـن النظـر والتوثيـق بالمجـازات
البصريـة المعاصـرة الحاضـرة في التقاريـر الإعلاميـة – وهنـا أود أن أدعوكم/ن مجـدّدًا
إلى اسـتحضار صـورة لوحتي فـان خـوخ عـلى جانبـي الحـارس ذي البشـرة السـمراء[8]. وهنـا
أجدنـي أمعـن التفكـير في مـا توصـي بـه أريـلا عائشـة أزولاي في The Civil Contract of
Photography (العقد الاجتماعـي للصورة الفوتوغرافية) (2008) مـن ضـرورة عـدم الاكتفـاء
بالنظـر إلى الصـور الفوتوغرافيـة، بـل "مشـاهدتها"[9]. عندمـا نبـدأ بمشـاهدة تلـك الصـور
الفوتوغرافيـة يمتلـئ الفضـاء مـن حولنـا بالقصـص، ويصبـح في إمكانـي سـماع ويلـر وهـو
يوبـخ العمـال في الموقـع. وكان ويلـر قـد أسـهب في توثيـق أسـلوبه السـلطوي العسـكري في
عـدد عـام 1948 مـن Ancient Pakistan، حيـث يشـرح الطريقـة المثلى للتعاطي مـع العمـال،
"السكان المحليين الكسـالى" الذيـن يفضلـون نـوم القيلولـة تحـت القفف خلـف التلـة. يمكن
قـراءة مقالتـه كدليل إرشـادي لكيفيـة تأديب العمـال المتلكئيـن قليـلي الكلام باعتبـاره أسـلوبًا
للتنقيـب الأركيولوجـي. وتنتمـي هـذه الأسـاليب إلى عمليـة تحديـث المشـروع العلمـي.

في مصـر، اعتُبـر التحديـث نمطًـا مـن السـيطرة الاستعماريـة ونظامهـا البصـري. وقـد دعـت
احتجاجـات عـام 1919 ضـد الاستعمار البريطانـي مـن جملـة مطالبهـا إلى رفـض الإنـارة
الكهربائيـة المنجـزة حديثًـا مـن الشـوارع عـلى اعتبـار أنها تدبـير قمعـي يهدف إلى فرض النظـام
عـن طريـق إتاحـة الرؤيـة الليليـة. وفي عـام 1945، نشـر الكاتـب ألبير قصيري هجـاءً لاذعًـا
بعنـوان "كسـالى في الـوادي الخصيـب" يطرح فيـه تداعيـات التحديث في مصر عقـب إعلان

8   يحيل ذلك أيضًا إلى عملي الأخير عن تسجيلات
الأفلام التوثيقية الاستعمارية من دولة الإمارات
العربية المتحدة، جسد الحارس والعمل كمحددات
للسيطرة المعرفية والإثنية. يرجى مراجعة
"The Chowkidar: Epistemic Markers and
Transnational Labor Flows," in *Currency:
A Critical Reader*, ed. Oluremi C. Onabanjo
(Hatje Cantz, 2022), 8th edition of the
Triennial of Photography of Hamburg

9   Ariella Aïsha
Azoulay, *The Civil Contract of Photography*
(New York: Zone Books, 2008)

الاستقلال في عام 1922 الذي أدى إلى اعتراف المملكة المتحدة بمصر كدولة ذات سيادة[10]. تتصدى رواية قصيري للصورة النمطية للمواطن الكسول معيدةً تشكيلها خطابيًا وسياسيًا في إطار المقاومة والثورة. تتمحور الرواية حول فكرة أن الحداثة ليست تقدمية أو أخلاقية بالضرورة. بل وقد تكون في بعض الأحيان معادية للإنسانوية إلى حد بعيد بحسب قصيري. يحيلنا عمله إلى فكرة البطء كفعل مقاومة.

يقدم قصيري هذه الفكرة في مطلع الكتاب من خلال لقاء بين أحد الشخصيات واسمه سراج وبين ولد صغير:

نظر سراج إلى الطفل مرة أخرى. هذه المرة، شعر بخضّة في صدره. خارت ساقاه وكأنهما بُترتا. واصل الطفل بحثه المحموم. لم يعد بشريًا: كان أشبه بقوة شيطانية تنقضّ بضراوة على اللاشيء. نظر سراج إلى الصبي غير مصدق. اجتاحته حاجة ملحة إلى النوم. ولكن من أين يأتي النوم وسط هذه الرؤيا العبثية والمدمرة؟ كان أكثر ما أثار الرعب في أحشائه جراء ذلك المشهد الانفعالي الهائج هو اللغز الذي يقبع في ثناياه – لغز العالم الوحشي المليء برجال أهلكهم العمل وغلبهم الضنى. لا مجال للالتباس. رأى سراج في نوبة الجنون التي أصابت الطفل كل العلامات على الإجهاد والحصار اللذين تعيشهما الإنسانية.

يختار قصيري أن يجمّد الشخصية إزاء تلك الطاقة المحمومة والمجنونة والعبثية وحتى الشيطانية. يستشرف من خلال هذه الإشارة البلاغية الإطار النقدي الذي يجعل من السكون مساحة ما بين الجنون والنوم.

تخلص ريبيكا سولنيت في عملها Finding Time (إيجاد الوقت) الذي يعود إلى عام 2007 إلى ما مفاده: "في النهاية، أظن أن البطء هو فعل مقاومة، ليس لأن البطء محمودٌ بالمطلق، بل لأنه يفسح المجال لكل الأمور التي يستحيل قياسها أو شراؤها"[11]. في رأيي أن هذه الخلاصة تتفاعل مع ما يعدّ في صميم الممارسة النظرية اللااستعمارية. ففي ذلك الحيّز من الأشياء التي لا تُقاس ولا تُشترى، يمنح التمهل والإبطاء الأجساد السمراء العاملة في الصور القدرة على مقاومة التحول إلى محدد معرفي للقياس. وبالتالي، تصبح الأجساد التي يصفها ويلر بالكسولة النائمة خلف التلال أجسادًا مقاوِمة. فهي تطالب بحقها في أن تكون بشرًا. أن تصمت. أن تكون الحياة.

يفسح البطء المجال لإمكانية التزام الصمت ومشاهدة تلك الصور والإصغاء إلى صمتها المستكين. فكما تُنبهنا تينا كامبت في Listening to Images (الاستماع إلى الصور) (2017): "لا يعادل السكون غياب التعبير أو الكلام. السكون صيغة تغلف الصوت وتشرّبه بالتأثير والانفعال ما يغدق عليه إمكانية اكتساب المعنى"[12]. يسمح عمل كامبت بإيجاد المعنى في الصمت. يدعونا إلى الإصغاء إلى ما كنا قد درجنا على اعتباره صامتًا ساكنًا، ما يجعلنا نرى في سكون الأشياء مقاومةً وبالتالي فاعليةً من نوع مختلف. يمكن اعتبار أن التمثيل الخطابي والأركيولوجي يتواجد ضمن سياق معاصر من الصمت الذي يُعتبر بدوره بنية صوتيةً تستدعي منا "تعلُّم" كيفية الاستماع والبحث عما هو جدير بالاستماع إليه.

Albert Cossery, *Les fainéants dans la vallée fertile*, Éditions Gallimard, Paris, 2005 (Domat, Paris, 1948), 3   10

Rebecca Solnit, "Finding Time," *Orion Magazine*, accessed June 7, 2022. https://orionmagazine.org/article/a-fistful-of-time   11

Tina Campt, *Listening to Images* (Durham: Duke University Press, 2017)   12

إذًا فنحـن صامتون، وتواقون إلى التعلم وإلى التعـرف عـلى كيفية استعادة الحيـاة من غياهب الصمـت. ولكن طريقتنا في فهـم ورؤيـة مـا نسـمع متأثـرةٌ بمـن نحـن وبالمكـان الـذي جئنـا منـه. ومـع ذلـك، فهو أيضًا الفضـاء الـذي يشوّش فجأة كل السـياق المحيـط بنا. لا يتبقى سـوى سكون أجسادنا عندمـا تنوجد في أماكن معينة متصلـة بتواريخنا. ما إن توضع تلك التواريخ في المتحف حتى تصبح ناصعة وبليغـة، مع أننا نعرف جيـدًا أن الحياة فوضوية وصاخبـة وكويريـة وهمجيـة. نرى ظلـال المتحف ترشـح مـن جدرانـه لتتسـلل إلى صوابيـة المكعب الأبيض. تشهد الأجساد "الأخرى"، وأنا منهـا، كيـف تجد المحـددات الإثنوغرافية القادمـة من المتحف طريقها إلينا، بينما نحن نتنقل في عوالم الفن والأكاديميا. قد يفسر ذلـك ميلنا إلى الصمت.

كمـا يقول قصيـري، السكون هـو تلك المسـاحة بين النـوم والجنـون. هـو موقع التبصـر. وقد يجمّد المتحف أجسـادنا في تلك الحالـة مـن الصمت، خلف الزجاج، عـلى الرقّ، وربما فـوق منضـدة أو عـلى سـرير كمـا في البورتريـه الشـخصي لأوغسـتين باريديـس "How to Slouch When Sleeping" (كيـف تتراخـى أثناء النـوم)، 2018. بيـد أن النـوم ليس جمـودًا. بـل ثمة قوة تحرريـة كامنة في قلب هـذا السكون. نجد فيه لحظة التحرر من الاستعمار، لحظـة الكويريـة، عندمـا نتعـدد ونخرج عـلى المعياريـة. نحن التحـف خلف الزجاج، نحن آنيـة الخـزف، نحـن الخـرز المشـغول، نحـن الأجسـاد المخبـأة في الخزائـن والمخـازن. نحن الباحث/ة. نحـن القطع الأثريـة.

في الزيـارة المقبلة إلى المتحف أنظروا/ن جيـدًا وسترووننا/سـتريننا هناك، في حالة من الصمت. سـترووننا في مواطننا الجديدة نساكن "الآخريـة". وإن تمهلتم/ن بما يكفي فقد تألفون/تألفن أجسادنا وحيواتنا وأعمالنا لا كمحـددات أو مقاربات أو مقاييس للإثنية والعرق والجنوسة والطبقـة. لن تنتحلـوا/ن صورتنـا مـن أجل الحشـو الإبسـتيمي عـن الآخـر. بـل سـنوجد في بطئنا المعنى لمـا ترون/ترين. نقبـع في الانتظار داخـل هـذا الفضـاء، فوضويـيـن همجيـين. يفزعنا أننا محتجـزون في هـذا المكان، في هـذا الصمـت. هل تسـمعوننا ونحـن نسـأل متى ينتهي عنف الاكتنـاز؟ هل تشـعرون بفزعنا عندمـا تمرون مـن أمام الزجاج؟

ههنا حيث تروننا كطبيعة صامتة.

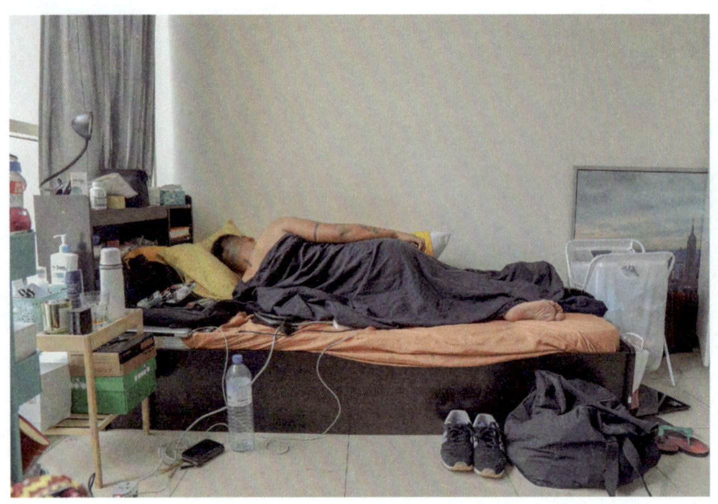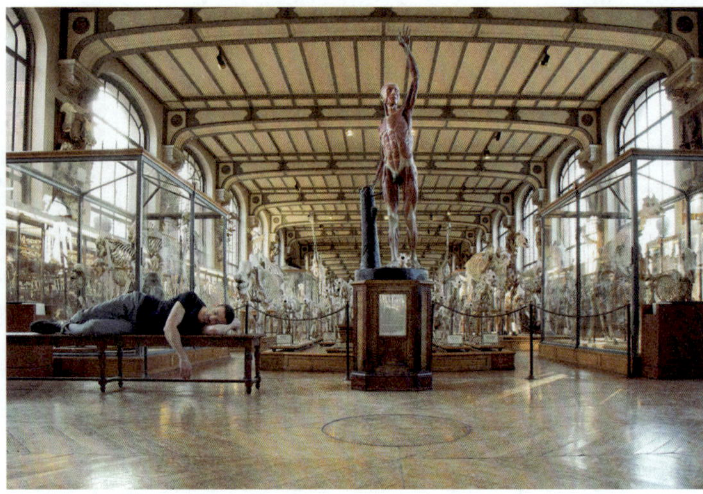

يسار: أوغستين باريديس. "How to Slouch When Sleeping" (كيف تتراخى أثناء النوم)، 2018. طباعة فوتوغرافية. بإذن من الفنان.
يمين: علي شرّي. "طبيعة صامتة"، 2017. صندوق ضوئي، طباعة دوراترانس فوتوغرافية، 95 × 150 سم. بإذن من الفنان وغاليري إيمان فارس.

محادثة بين فوستان لنيكولا وعمر برّادة

إطلاق سراح التاريخ

في عام 2017، عَرَضَ الراقص والمصمم الحركي فوستان لنيكولا عمله "باناتابا" للمرة الأولى في متحف المتروبوليتان للفن بمدينة نيويورك[1]. انبثق هذا العمل من زيارةٍ صادف فيها الفنان تمثالًا في مخازن المتحف ذاته، ما أخذه في رحلةٍ ماديةٍ وروحانيةٍ إلى قرية أسلافه في الكونغو، ودفعه إلى تأملٍ مستمر حول الماضي المنهوب والمستقبل المفتقِد إلى الإصلاح. وددتُ أن آخذ "باناتابا" كنقطة انطلاقٍ لحديثنا حول الاستعادة. وكما هي عادة فوستان الذي يفضّل تقديم نفسه بوصفه راوياً للحكايات، أخذ حديثنا الذي سجّلناه في أغسطس 2021 بالفرنسية عبر تطبيق "زووم" منعطفاتٍ عدّة. كنتُ حينها في الدار البيضاء أزور والديّ، بينما كان فوستان في دوسلدورف يعرض عمله "تمثال الفقد"، وهو عملٌ حركيٌّ آخر يتناول بقايا الاستعمار[2].

عمر برّادة

أودّ أن أستهل حديثنا بافتتاحية مقالٍ بعنوان Le gâchis (الإهدار) نشرَتْهُ مجلة "أنفاس" في المغرب في عام 1967، للشاعر عبد اللطيف اللعبي مؤسس المجلة، عندما كان في الخامسة والعشرين من عمره. فيه، كتَب اللعبي:

"بقي تاريخ الفن المغربي طوال ما يزيد عن نصف قرن اختصاصًا أوروبيًا وحكرًا على العلوم الغربية. ولا يهمنا هنا السجال الذي يعزو المحاولات الأخيرة للفنانين المغاربة باتجاه تصورٍ جديدٍ للفن المغربي، إلى محض فضولٍ مصطنع تمخضت عنه مطالعة الأعمال النقدية الأجنبية. إنّ اهتمامنا

بفننا، بغضّ النظر عن كونه أتى متأخرًا، لا يمكن ردّه إلى افتتانٍ ساذج بالفولكلور أو محاكاةٍ بورجوازيةٍ لانطباع الذائقة الأوروبية عنه. وإن كان للمختصين الأوروبيين أو لهواة جمع الفنون فضلٌ في جذب انتباهنا إلى الفن المغربي، فإن ذلك لا يعني بالضرورة أن فضولنا يجب أن يقتصر على جمع الأعمال الفنية أو التمجيد الشوفيني لتراثنا الفني. فمعرفة هذا التراث وتمجيده يقعان على طرفي نقيض إزاء الاستعادة الشاملة لهذا التراث والتي هي شرط إعادة بناء ذواتنا.[3]"

فوستان لنيكولا

يذكّرني هذا الاقتباس بمعرض "كونغو" (Kongo) الذي أقيم في متحف المتروبوليتان في عام 2015 وتناول المنحوتات الطوطمية المعروفة باسم "نكيسي"[4]. كنت أزور نيويورك حينها، وشعرت بالحزن عندما غادرت المتحف. فالأرشيفات المسجّلة المتاحة في جمهورية الكونغو تعود إلى 150 أو 200 عامٍ في أحسن الأحوال، وهي سجلاتٌ منحازةٌ لرواية المستعمِر المنتصر دون شك. بالمقابل، ابتكر أسلافنا طريقةً بديلةً للتدوين، وحاولوا نقل التاريخ من خلال منحوتاتٍ كتلك التي كانت معروضةً في متحف المتروبوليتان. وفي حين جَمَعَ المتحف منحوتاتٍ من أرجاء العالم كافة، إلا أنه ليس ثمّة طفل كونغولي بمقدوره الوصول إليها. فالأدوات التي يمكن من خلالها محاولة التعرف إلى بعضٍ من تاريخنا وثقافتنا أو نقلهما، هي أدواتٌ متاحةٌ فقط لقلةٍ ممّن يتمتعون بامتياز امتلاكها في الغرب. ومن هذا

يتحدث من داخله. كيف يمكن أن نطلق سراح هذا التاريخ، وأن نحرر أنفسنا من أسر تلك النظرة التي وُضعت لنا؟

تُنسِبُ مناهج التاريخ الرسمية في جمهورية الكونغو الديموقراطية اكتشاف مصب نهر الكونغو إلى المستكشف البرتغالي ديوغو كاو. وعندما تزور متحف إفريقيا الوسطى بمدينة تيرفورن البلجيكية، ستجد أن الحضارة وصلت إلى الكونغو مع مفوض الملك ليوبولد الثاني، وأنه ليس ثمّة شيءٌ قبلها سوى الفوضى، فقد أنقذنا البلجيكيون من تجارة الرق العربية وأدخلونا إلى رحاب التاريخ. كيف نُطلِقُ سراح هذا التاريخ أو نحرره؟ عندما أعلنت بلجيكا أخيرًا عن نيتها إعادة ما سلبته من آثار إلى الكونغو، قالوا لنا إن الكونغو ليست مستعدةً بعد، إذ لا متاحف لديها لاستقبال تلك الآثار.

هذه هي اللحظة التي أسأل فيها نفسي، "أليس ما نفعله هو إعادة كتابة التاريخ الأوروبي على أرض إفريقيا؟". قبل أربعة أعوام، عندما ذهبت إلى باناتابا، القرية التي وُلد فيها جدّي لأمي، أذهلني أن المنحوتات الموجودة هناك لا تلقى القدر ذاته من الاحترام والتعظيم في كل الأوقات. فالمنحوتة تبقى قطعة خشبٍ ملقاةً في ركن الغرفة، عُرضة لعوامل مختلفة كالرطوبة وبراثن الحيوانات الصغيرة وغيرها، ويمكن للكلاب التمرّغ بجانبها، إلى أن تحين مناسبةٌ معينة نُخرِجُ حينها الخَشَبة ونُفَعِّلُها فتُصبح لها قوة السحر. ليس ثمّة شيء سحري طوال الوقت، فالأشياء تكتسب سحرها فقط حين نقوم بتفعيلها. ما الذي يعنيه هذا عند الحديث عن استعادة هذه الآثار إلى المتاحف حيث تُتاح رؤيتها لقلةٍ من الناس مجدّدًا؟ إن كان هذا هو الأرشيف الذي يلزمنا لاستعادة تجربتنا التاريخية بشكلٍ كامل، كم من الأشخاص سيتمكنون من الوصول إليه عند عرضه في المتحف الوطني بكينشاسا؟ أنُطلق فعلًا سراح التاريخ إن كنّا بصدد مَثْحَفَتِهِ مرةً أخرى؟

انتابتنا ردود الأفعال نفسها في زمن التحرّر، عند استقلال غينيا على سبيل المثال. بالنسبة لسيكو توري، لم يكن الاستعمار هو العدو الألدّ للأمة المستقلة حديثًا بقدر ما كانت القَبَليّة. كان سؤاله الدائم هو: "كيف لنا أن نتغلب على النزعة القبلية؟ وكيف نعلّم الشعب ماهية أن يكون المرء غينيًّا؟". كان جوابه هو أن نطوّر لونًا من الباليه (ballet) الوطني. لكن ما عساه أن يكون الباليه الوطني؟ إنه المكان الذي تجتمع فيه ألوان الرقص والموسيقا من جميع أرجاء غينيا. وبموجب وضعها معًا في مكانٍ واحد، لا تعود هذه رقصة شعب البالوبا أو تلك رقصة

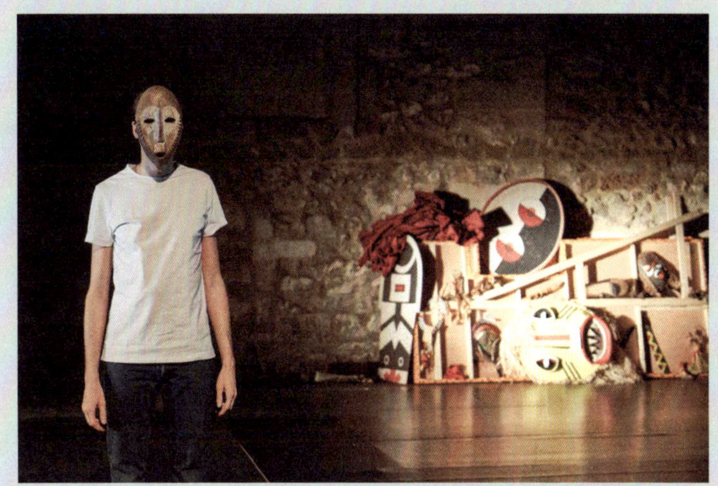

فوستان لنيكولا، ت(و)اريخ المسرح 2، 2019، الصورة بإذن من أجاثي بوبني.

المنطلق أعي كيف تصبح "الاستعادة الكاملة لهذا التراث شرط إعادة بناء ذواتنا"، كما يقول اللعبي.

كيف ننهض بأنفسنا إن لم يكن بمقدورنا الاطلاع على الأرشيف؟ في ظل هذه الظروف، كيف تتسنى لنا سُكنى أرض هي لنا؟ أتذكر هنا هذه الأبيات لأدونيس: "كيف أمشي نحو نفسي، نحو شعبي، ودمي نارٌ وتاريخي رُكام؟"[5]. أتساءل إن كان الوصول إلى الأرشيف هو الجواب عن ذلك التساؤل. هل يمكن للمعرفة الكاملة حول هذه الفنون أن تشفي التمزّق والضياع والخراب الذي حلّ بنا؟ لا يسعني الجواب بشكلٍ باتّ، لكن يمكننا المحاولة على الأقل.

ع.ب.

يقول اللعبي أيضًا إن هذه الاستعادة ما هي إلا خطوةٌ أولى على طريق النهوض. وحيث إنك عرّجت على ذكر الأرشيف، لزم أن أنوّه إلى أن المقطع الذي ذكرته في البداية يقع ضمن جزء من مقال يحمل عنوان Relâcher l'histoire (إطلاق سراح التاريخ)، وكأنها إشارةٌ إلى أن تاريخنا سجينٌ أو محتجزٌ.

ف.ل.

..أو مأخوذٌ كرهينة. في لحظةٍ معينةٍ، قَضَتْ أوروبا بأن لا تاريخ سوى تاريخها، وأن تاريخ الآخرين يُعرَف بدءًا من اللحظة التي وصل فيها الأوروبي إلى أراضيهم. نحن ننظر إلى أنفسنا حتى يومنا هذا من خلال أعين أوروبا، وهو ما يتضح بشكلٍ سافرٍ في الدوائر الأكاديمية لإفريقيا الفرنكفونية. فعندما يتحدث الإفريقي عن إفريقيا، غالبًا ما يراودني شعورٌ بأن هناك أوروبيًّا

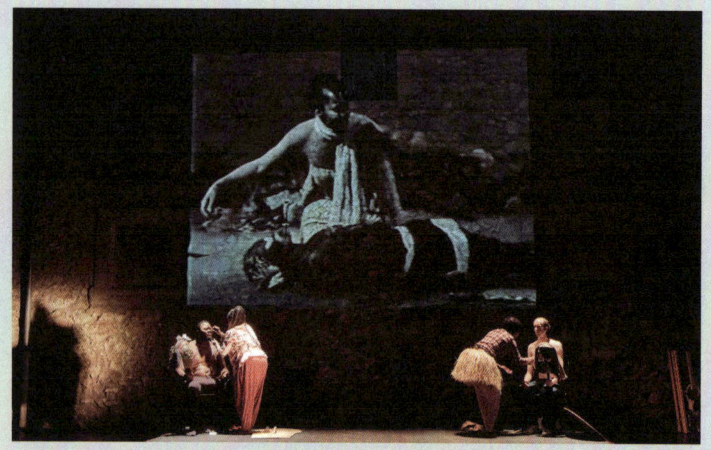

فوستان لنيكولا، ت(و)اريخ المسرح 2، 2019، الصورة بإذن من أجاثي بوبني.

شعب اللوكيلي على سبيل المثال، وإنما تصبح جميعها رقصاتٍ وطنية. وكراقصٍ، تُدهشُني رؤية سيكو توري للجسد كنقطة عبورٍ لمشروع بناء الأمة. وفي حين كان يمكن لذلك أن يكون حقلًا عظيمًا للتجارب، إلا أن غرض توري - كما أي سياسي - لم يكن مساءلة الجسد بقدر ما كان إملاء الأجوبة عنه. فلم يكن يعنيه التساؤل حول "معنى أن يكون المرء غينيًّا" وإنما الإقرار "بأنه هكذا يكون المرء غينيًّا". يدهشني أيضًا اختياره كلمة "باليه" لوصف المشروع، فما من فنٍ أكثر غربيةً من الباليه. والجدير بالذكر أن موبوتو فعل الشيء ذاته لاحقًا. كان البحث عمّن هو زائيريٌّ أصيل أو غينيٌّ أصيل، يتم دائمًا عبر أطرٍ تُعيد إنتاج التراث الاستعماري.

ع . ب .

هذا هو الجانب المظلم لاستعادة ما نهبه الاستعمار، إذ تتسابق العديد من الدول الإفريقية في إنشاء المتاحف لإقناع الأوروبيين بأحقيتهم في استعادة آثارهم كالتلاميذ المطيعين. كما ينطوي الأمر أيضًا - كما أشرتُ سابقًا - على شكلٍ من أشكال الازدراء الطبقي. إذ لم يتمخّض الاستقلال في واقع الأمر عمّا هو أكثر من أممٍ تشكّلت وفق حدودٍ رسمها الاستعمار لحماية البورجوازيات المحلية التي تخدم بدورها المصالح الأوروبية، وهو ما حذرنا منه فرانتز فانون سابقاً، وها نحن واقعون فيه الآن. فالنخب الإفريقية التي تُصِرُّ على امتلاك متاحفَ محليةٍ تمتلئ بالآثار، هي نفسها النخب القادرة على السفر والاطلاع على هذه الآثار في أوروبا أو الولايات المتحدة. يكمن الخطر هنا في أن هذه الرغبة في تقليد الأطر المتحفية المؤسساتية تنتهي في واقع الحال إلى عرقلة المشروع الأكبر "للاسترداد الكامل" لأنفسنا.

ف . ل .

يصحّ الأمر ذاته في حالة اللغة. على سبيل المثال، تُنَظَّم أنشطة الحياة العامة في جمهورية الكونغو الديموقراطية باللغة الفرنسية. وعادةً ما يُقال إن الكونغو هي أكبر بلدٍ فرنكفوني. إلا أن نسبة من يجيدون الفرنسية بين الكونغوليين قد لا تتجاوز 20 في المئة من عدد السكان. ما الذي يعنيه أن تنتظم الحياة العامة بلغةٍ تستثني غالبية الناس؟ إنها وسيلة النخبة الفرنكفونية الحاكمة لاستغلال البلاد لمصلحتهم. لنفترض مثلًا أن هناك نائباً برلمانياً لديه ما يود قوله. سيفشل النائب في شرح وجهة نظره بعد تكبّده عناء شرحها بلغةٍ لا يجيدها. بعدها سيسخر النواب الآخرون منه، تمامًا كما لو كنا في باحة

المدرسة، وستغرق كلماته في بحرٍ من اللغة. وعليه، فليس من المصادفة وجود تعبيرٍ شائع بلغة الينغالا المحلية يقول: "إن الفرنسية هي ما قتل هذا البلد". أسوأ ما في الأمر هو أنني جزءٌ من هذه النخبة وأنا أيضًا، بطريقةٍ ما، مستفيدٌ من ذلك.

ع . ب .

فلنتحدث عن عملك "باناتابا". بدأ الأمر كله نتيجة دعوةٍ للعمل على مجموعة متحف المتروبوليتان. إلا أن هذه الرحلة إلى نيويورك أعادتك إلى الكونغو وتحديدًا إلى ظروفٍ معينة. أود لو تخبرني قليلًا عن هذه الرحلة وعن العمل الذي تمخّضت عنه، لا سيما التمثال المركّب الذي ترقص معه.

ف . ل .

لكي أتمكن من الرد على سؤالك، لا بد لي من العودة إلى تلك الأطلال والخرائب التي ذكرتها سابقًا. أشعر وكأنني أبحث عن الكونغو أينما ذهبت، فما أكثر قطع الكونغو المتناثرة حول العالم. ولأنني أنتمي إلى تلك النخبة القادرة على السفر إلى أي مكان رغم تكاثر الحدود، فإنني أحاول البحث عن تلك القطع مرارًا. إلا أنني أجد نفسي في كل مرة في مراوحةٍ مزدوجة: فأنا أسافر بحثًا عن حياةٍ أفضل للكونغو، أملًا في حياةٍ أفضل في الكونغو. فالكونغو فضاءٌ ماديٌّ، وهي أيضًا مكانٌ ماثلٌ في المخيلة حاولت طيلة السنوات الماضية فهمه ولا أزال أحاول ذلك.

كنت قد عثرت على تمثالٍ خشبي في مخازن متحف المتروبوليتان، وُضِعَت عليه بطاقةٌ تعريفيةٌ مكتوبٌ عليها "شعب الينغولا"، وهي قبيلة أمي. ليس ثمّة شيء أقرب لما كنت أبحث عنه. كان ذلك التمثال الوحيد الذي يعود لشعب الينغولا في المتحف.

إطلاق سراح التاريخ

يُقال إن للتماثيل التي تُستعمل في طقوس الاحتفالات القبلية أرواحًا، فكيف تشعر هذه الروح وهي وحيدةٌ على بعد آلاف الأميال من الوطن؟

اتصلت بأمي من نيويورك وقلت لها، "وجدت لتوّي شيئًا رائعًا هنا، وأود أن أذهب في رحلةٍ إلى باناتابا التي لم أزرها من قبل". قالت لي: "بلى، لقد ذهبتَ إلى باناتابا سابقاً. اصطحبتُك إلى هناك وأنت في عامك الأول". كان ذلك في عام 1975. ولم أعد إلى هناك منذ ذلك الحين. فقلت لها: "أترغبين في الذهاب معي إلى هناك؟". وبذلك، قمنا بالرحلة معًا وأحضرتُ معي صورًا للتمثال الموجود في متحف المتروبوليتان. بالنسبة لي، كان همّي أن أرى إن كان هناك بين أهل القرية من لا يزال يتذكر هذا النوع من المنحوتات، وإن كانت تلك المنحوتات لا تزال حاضرةً في حياة الناس أم أنها اختفت تمامًا.

قلتُ لنفسي، إن وجدتُ في القرية من يهتم لأمر هذه التماثيل ويعرف كيفية صنعها، سأعود إلى نيويورك مع تمثالٍ من باناتابا كي لا يبقى تمثال المتروبوليتان وحيدًا. لم أتمكّن من فعل ذلك بالطبع، وجاء رد المتحف بالرفض على الفور. قالوا لي: "لا يمكننا اعتبار شيءٍ كهذا عملًا فنيًا. لكن إن اعتبرته جزءًا من ديكور العرض الأدائي، فيمكننا حينها القبول به في المتحف". هكذا بات بإمكاني أن أعزّي نفسي بأنني تمكّنتُ من إيجاد حضور آخر لشعب اللينغولا في إحدى قاعات متحف المتروبوليتان إلى جانب ذاك الذي هناك أقلّه أثناء فترة العرض... وربما أمكن لأحدهما، خلال وقت العرض على الأقل، التحدّث إلى الآخر.

غير أن هذا التمثال الذي أخذته معي من باناتابا لم يُستعمل في احتفالٍ قبليٍّ من قبل. ففي بلدنا، عندما يُنتج النحّات عملًا، يكون ذلك أحيانًا لاستعماله ضمن طقوس الاحتفالات القبلية. بعد الاحتفال، يكتسب التمثال قوةً وقد تسكنه روحٌ ما. عندما عُدت إلى باناتابا، كان هناك طقسٌ احتفالي استُخدِمَ فيه تمثالٌ كنت قد اشتريته من فنانٍ محلي. جلستُ مع كبار قريتي، وطرقتُ أقول لنفسي: "إن كان كلّ ذي قيمةٍ في بلادنا قد سُلب وهُرّب إلى الخارج على مدى قرون، ما الذي يعنيه إحضار تمثالٍ كهذا إلى المتروبوليتان أو غيره من المتاحف لعرضه وتداوله؟ أليس من الأفضل أن يبقى التمثال في باناتابا في عهدة خالي أندريه زعيم القبيلة؟".

وهكذا فعلت. ولكن لأنني أردت إحضار تمثالٍ لشعب اللينغولا إلى المتروبوليتان، طلبتُ صنع تمثال جديدٍ بدون استعماله في أيّ طقسٍ احتفالي. فكّرتُ أنّه إن كان خشب التمثال الجديد

يعود لشجرةٍ بالمنطقة ونحتته أيادي أهلها، فربما يكون قد سمع أصواتهم، وربما أمكنه إخبار ما سمع إلى التمثال الآخر في نيويورك. إذًا فلهذا التمثال قيمةٌ خاصة، إلا أنه في الوقت نفسه محض قطعةٍ من الخشب، إذ لم يسبق وأن استُخدِم في طقسٍ احتفاليٍ من قبل. بالإضافة إلى ذلك، كان التمثال مصنوعًا من أجزاءٍ يمكن فكّها وتركيبها، وكأننا خلال العرض نقوم بإعادة تركيب القصة أو نخلقها من جديد.

يذكرني ذلك بعملي السابق Histoire(s) du théâtre II ("ت(و) اريخ المسرح II") الذي تحدثت فيه إلى مشاركين سابقين في مؤسسة الباليه الوطني في زائير التي أنشأها موبوتو في عام 1974[6]. وقد أدركنا في نهاية الأمر أن ما يُساق لنا بوصفه صورة الشعب الأصيل، لم يكن سوى بناءٍ مُتَخَيّلٍ عن هويتنا، وأننا لا نزال نواصل بناء صورتنا عن أنفسنا مما نجده من العناصر المتناثرة هنا وهناك. كان أول ما عَرَضَته مؤسسة الباليه الوطني هو عملٌ بعنوان "ملحمة ليانجا". أخذ موبوتو قصة العمل عن أسطورة تأسيس قبيلة مونغو، وعمّمها كروايةٍ ملحميةٍ عن نشأة الشعب الزائيري ككل. بطريقةٍ ما، تُناظِرُ أسطورة ليانجا تَصَوُّرَ موبوتو عن نفسه كأبٍ للأمة الزائيرية. كما أخبرني الكبار بين المشاركين في العمل بأنهم أعادوا تأليف بعض الرقصات القبلية التي كانوا قد نسوا كيف كانت تُمارس في القرى. إلا أنه ليس ثمّة شيءٌ يصدر عن العدم، فالتأليف هنا ليس سوى إعادة توليفٍ لأجزاءٍ سابقة.

ع.ب.

هناك افتتانٌ استعماريٌّ بالأصالة، كما لو أن الظواهر الثقافية لا بدّ وأن تظل على حالها، وكأنها منذ الأزل لم تتطوّر أبدًا. يتجلّى ذلك في أنماط العرض المتحفي، لا سيّما في كيفية عرض المعروضات داخل الفترينات وكتابة أوصافها بحيث تُكرّس كقوالب جامدة. هذه هي فحوى "إطلاق سراح التاريخ" والمتمثّلة في ترك الأشياء لتحيا وإدراك أن الثقافات تتطور. عملتُ لفترةٍ وجيزةٍ على الحُليّ الأمازيغية في المغرب، ولاحظتُ امتعاض كثيرٍ من الأنثروبولوجيين الاستعماريين إزاء عادات أهل القرى في صَهر حُليّهم القديمة وصنع غيرها من المعدن المصهور. فهي تَصعّب العثور على بعض الحليّ التي كانوا يرغبون باستبقائها حبيسةً في متاحفهم.

ف.ل.

هناك دائمًا نفيٌ للموت يتم فرضه على دورة حياة هذه الأشياء. إلا أن من صَنعُوا تلك الأشياء كانوا يعلمون أنها ليست خالدة،

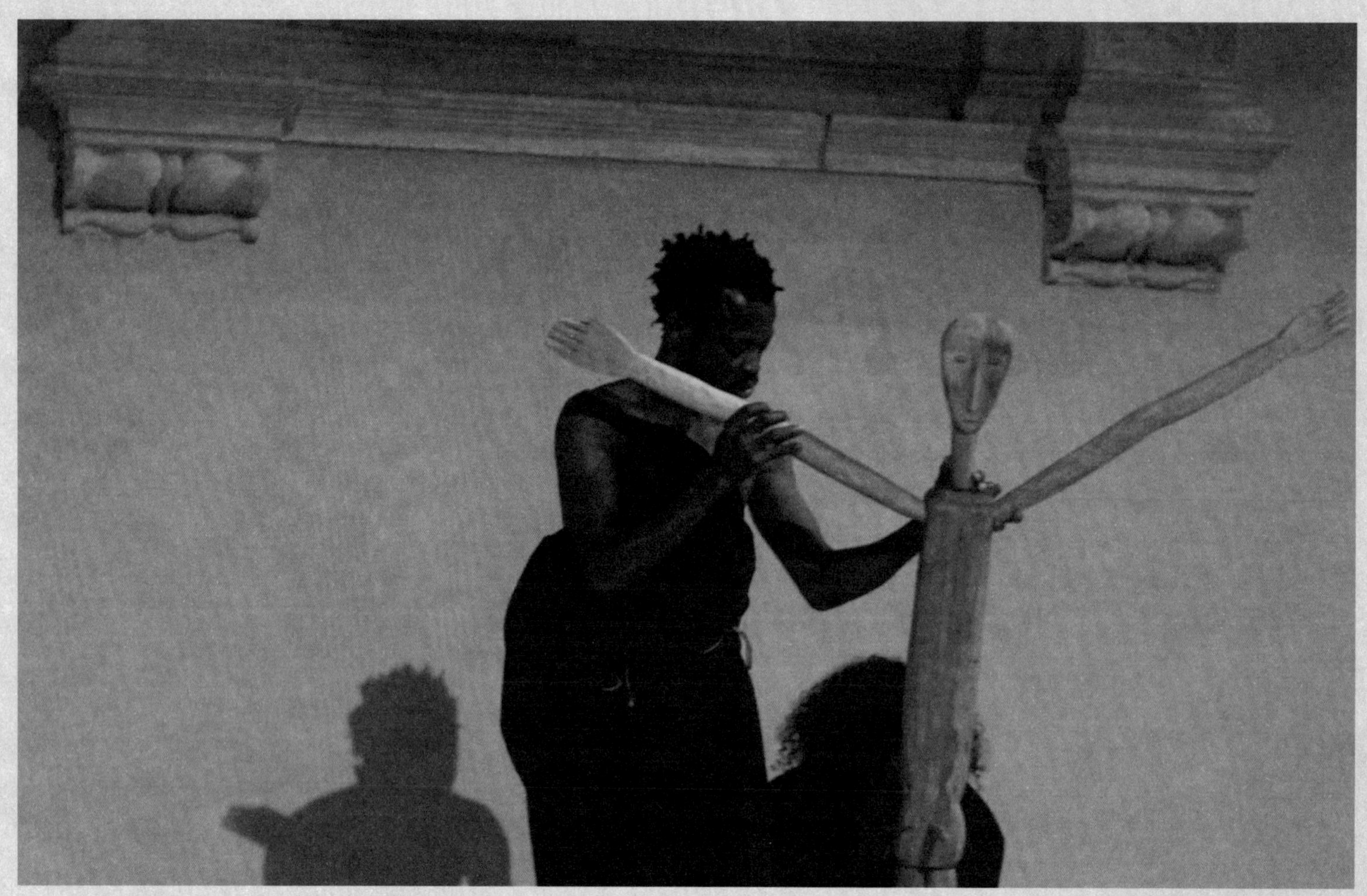

فوستان لنيكولا، باناتابا، 2017، الصورة بإذن من .إستوديو كاباكو

وأنها لا بد في لحظةٍ ما أن تموت أو تختفي ليحلّ محلها ما هو مصنوعٌ بطريقةٍ مغايرة. كلّ جيلٍ يعيد كتابة تاريخ هذه الأشياء ويضيف ما لديه. إنه إطلاق سراح التاريخ فعلًا.

ع.ب.

فلنكسر الفترينات! أفكر في كتاب دان هيكس الأخير The Brutish Museum ("المتاحف الوحشية")، الـذي سلّـط فيه الضوء عـلى قضية برونزيّات بنين وضرورة استعادتها[7]. أذهلني وصف هيكس لهذه المشغولات، وأظنـه سيخاطب فيك روح الراقص عبر "الأحداث غير المكتملة". بالعـودة إلى باناتابا، ما الـذي يختلف إن كان الشيء المعروض جزءًا من عرضٍ متحفي أم جزءًا مـن ديكور عـرضٍ أدائي، حتى وإن كان يُعرض داخل المتحف؟ هل يمكن للعـرض الأدائي أن يستحضر حياةً أخرى للمعروضات؟

ف.ل.

في حالـة باناتابا، كان التمثـال مُفَعَّلًا أثناء العرض فقط، ولا أقصد بذلك طـوال فترة العرض كلها، بل أقصد اللحظـات التي

كان يُستعمل فيها تحديـدًا. بعـد العرض وإلى أن يحين العرض التالي، يعـود التمثال إلى غرفة التخزين، وهي غرفةٌ غير مكيفة الهـواء، إذ يفقد الخشب رطوبته أكثر فأكثر مـع تغيّر درجات الحـرارة، وتفقد أجزاء العمل قدرتها عـلى التراكب معًا بإحكامٍ كسابق عهدها.

إن اللحظـة الوحيـدة التي يمكن اعتبار الشيء فيها مقدشا هي لحظـة تفعيلـه أثناء العرض. وفي مـا خـلا ذلك، فهو قطعةٌ مـن الخشب لها حياتها الخاصة وربما قـد لـن تعود صالحةً للاستخدام في لحظةٍ ما مستقبلًا. أعدنا عرض هذا العمل قبل شهرٍ ونصف في مارسيليا، كانت بعض أصابع التمثال قد تكسّرت بالفعل بحيث لم تعد قابلـة للإصلاح. بمرور الزمن، قد أُضظرُّ للعـودة إلى القرية لصنع تمثالٍ آخر. وبكل الأحوال، فإن انتفاء قدسية التمثال تُحرّرني من عبء قيمته. فالتمثال جزءٌ ضروريٌّ في العمل، أصنع منه ما أريد. وعـلى عكس مويا مايكل، الراقصة التي أشاركها فضاء العرض، هذا التمثال قابلٌ للاستبدال. إن تغيّب مويا عن العرض، أُقدّمه وحدي، لكن إن ينكسر التمثال أصنع غيره. لا أعلم إن كان ذلك يجيب عن سؤالك. أما بالنسبة

لتعبير "أحداث غير مكتملة"، فإنني ألمس فيه الحاجة إلى وضع الأشياء ضمن دورة حياتها، ما قد يعني أيضًا فناءها.

ع.ب.

أحب كثيرًا إصرارك على الإشارة إلى الموت كجزءٍ من الرواية، فالموت جزءٌ من الحياة أيضًا. لستُ متأكّدًا إن كان الأمر كذلك أيضًا عند النقّاد الأوروبيين، حتى الداعين إلى التحرّر من آثار الاستعمار.

ف.ل.

ربما تكون الحياة في الكونغو، ولو لبعض الوقت من كل عام، هي ما يذكّرني دائمًا بوجود الموت. ولا أعني هنا أنني لا أخشى الموت، بل بالأحرى أن نتعامل معه بشكلٍ أكثر هدوءًا. الموت لا يعني توقّف الأشياء ونهايتها. فهناك اليوم أماكن كثيرةٌ حول العالم تشبه الكونغو، حيث الموت هو جزءٌ من الحياة اليومية.

هناك كلمةٌ بلغة اللينغالا هي "لوبي" وتعني البارحة، لكنها تعني الغد أيضًا. فالزمن لا يسير بشكلٍ خطّي، بل يتعاقب في دوائر تسري خلالنا، فيصبح السَلَف هو الخَلَف والعكس. فنحن نعيش بضمائر من سبقنا من الأسلاف، ونعيش أيضًا في ضمائر من سيأتون من بعدنا. أو على الأقل، ينبغي أن نعيش معها، إذ ربما يساعدنا ذلك على الخروج من الحلقة المفرغة للدمار المستمر. أقول لنفسي إن أيقّنا بذلك الزمن الدائري الذي تعنيه كلمة "لوبي" — حيث أمس هو الغد وغدًا هو الأمس، لتوقّفنا عن الخوف من فناء الأشياء. فروح البارحة تتمثّل في صورة اليوم، والجوهرة التي ورثُها عن جدتي بالأمس، صنَعتُ منها اليوم شيئًا آخر، وأظن أنها كانت قد ورِثَتها سابقًا عن شخصٍ آخر. قبل أن يصل هذا الإثنوغرافي الأوروبي الذي يود تجميدها في الزمن، كانت تلك الجوهرة في دورةٍ مستمرة.

ع.ب.

لا يعني ذلك بالضرورة أيضًا انتفاء الفقد أو توقف الظلم والعدوان.

ف.ل.

هل من شفاء لجراح الماضي؟ ما مضى قد مضى، لقد وقع الأذى ودُمل الجرح، وحتى بعد قَطبِه تبقى الندوب. كيف ننظر إلى الندبة، وكيف نبني انطلاقًا منها؟ هذا هو السؤال الأهم بالنسبة لي.

ع.ب.

هل هذا ما عنيته عندما أشرتَ إلى بحثك عن الكونغو في قِطَعِها المتناثرة حول العالم؟ هل هو البحث عن الندبة أم اختلاقُها؟

ف.ل.

بل هو إعادة إنتاج الكونغو الخاصة بي من جديد. أتساءل، ما الذي يمكنني أن أصنعه بهذه الأجزاء؟ ربما تُمَكّنُني معرفة درجة انصهار هذا المعدن من توفير طاقتي والتركيز على إعادة إنتاج الكونغو الخاصة بي، وإعادة إنتاج ذاتي من داخلها. أفكّر أيضًا في أطفالي: ما الذي يمكنني أن أُورّثَهُم؟ كيف يمكنني أن أجعل من هذا الركام المتبقّي من الكونغو ملجأً آمنًا لهم؟ تكسّرت هذه المرآة إلى قطع صغيرة جدًا بحيث يستحيل على المرء جمع كل أجزائها، لكن ذلك لا يمنعني من جمع أكبر عددٍ من شظاياها لأقول لأبنائي "هذا هو ملجؤكم الصغير، أتمنى لو تصنعون منه شيئًا ما".

ع.ب.

لا أعلم إن تابعتَ ما سُمّي بـ"قافلة المهاجرين" في الولايات المتحدة قبل بضعة أعوام، حين خرج عددٌ من مواطني غواتيمالا وهندوراس وغيرهما من بلدان أميركا الوسطى سيرًا باتجاه الحدود الأميركية المكسيكية. كان ترامب حينها يشن حربًا من التصريحات الإعلامية ضدهم، محذّرًا من أنه سيواجههم بالقوة المسلحة عند الحدود. تزامن ذلك مع تقرير فلوين سار وبنيديكت سافوا عن استعادة التراث الإفريقي[8]، كما تصادف أيضًا مع بدء عرض فيلم "النمر الأسود" في عام 2018، حيث تظهر شخصية كيلمونغر في مشهدٍ بالمتحف البريطاني بعد مشادّةٍ مع مديرة المتحف، ليستعيد قطعة أثريةً كان البريطانيون قد سرقوها من أسلافه. تستدعي آرييلا أزولاي هذه الوقائع المتوازية في مقال تصِفُ فيه التناقض الرهيب بين أولئك المُهمَلين على الحدود الأميركية بلا وثائق دون أوراق ثبوتية من ناحية، وآثار بلادهم الأصلية التي تحظى بكل العناية والتوثيق في المتاحف من ناحيةٍ أخرى[9]. ترفض أزولاي هذا الفصل القسري بين الاثنين، وتدعو إلى اعتبار "قافلة المهاجرين" بمثابة حملةٍ مضادةٍ يستعيد فيها سكان أميركا اللاتينية، الذين حُرموا من تراثهم الثقافي طويلًا، قدرتهم على إعادة تخيّل العالم من خلال تلك الآثار التي سُلِبت منهم وأُبعِدَت عنهم. تُشير أزولاي إلى أن هذه الاستعادة هي أبعد ما تكون عن خرق القانون، بل وينبغي اعتبارها حقًّا ثابتًا. فضلًا عن استعادة الآثار، يمثّل ذلك دعوةً لإلغاء الحدود كافة.

ف.ل.

هناك مقابلةٌ مع ستوارت هول يقول فيها إنه لدى وصوله إلى بريطانيا في عام 1951، سأله أحدهم، "لماذا أنت هنا؟"، فردَّ عليه بما معناه: "لأستكمل الرحلة الاستعمارية التي بدأتموها في القرن الخامس عشر. الآن في القرن العشرين، أنا هنا لأُكمِلَ الخطوة الأخيرة. لقد شكَّلتُم حياتي، وأنا هنا لأواجهكم بالحقيقة". بالنسبة لي، لا يتعلق الأمر باستعادة الآثار بقدر ما يتعلّق باستعادة ذلك الذي أسهَم في تشكيل ذواتنا بشكلٍ جذري. في نهاية الأمر، لسنا غرباء هنا، لكن فكرة العودة إلى ذلك الذي أسهم في تشكيل ذواتنا، والحوار معه رغم صعوبته، هي فكرةٌ جميلةٌ للغاية. لن تمنع التصريحات العدائية وجدران الفصل الحدودي حركة الناس. فالناس تتحرك، وستستمر بذلك، وبالنسبة لكثيرٍ منهم، فلن يهمّ كثيرًا إن انتهى الحال بهم في البحر المتوسط أو في المحيط الأطلسي، في نهاية المطاف سيأتون ولا رادّ عن ذلك. لا يمكنني الحكم على هذا، ولا يمكنني القول إن كان ذلك أمرًا جيدًا أم لا، أنا أقول فقط إن هناك حركةً ما. لم يسبق لي أن ربطتُ تلك الحركة بعودة الناس إلى شيءٍ عميقٍ ومتجذّرٍ في تاريخهم، واستخلاصه من مَنطِق الاقتصاد. لكننا نجوب العوالم بحثًا عن أنفسنا دون أن نعلم، ولا شك أن أنفسنا هذه موجودةٌ في أوروبا أو أميركا أكثر مما هي موجودةٌ في البلاد التي نحمل جوازات سفرها.

ربما كانت جميع تلك الآثار القابعة في المتاحف جزءًا من تَوق تلك الأرواح الهائمة لإطلاق سراحها، تمامًا كما يتوق التاريخ لإطلاق سراحه. إنها صورةٌ بلاغيةٌ جميلة. أيمكنك تخيل هذا، جميع تلك الأرواح الهائمة تسير في رحلة من الشمال إلى الجنوب، ومن الجنوب إلى الشمال، وربما يتقاطع المساران في مكان ما. يومًا ما ربما سيجد جميع الذين يتحركون بين هذين العالمين ويمرّون بتلك الآثار طريقةً لتفعيلها وتحريرها. بالنسبة لباناتابا، أقول لنفسي: "إن عدتُ مع تمثالي إلى المتروبوليتان، وحيث إنني أعلم أن المنحوتات تتكلم، سأجلس لأستمع إلى حكايات التمثال الذي هناك. سأنصت إلى حكاياته عن حياةٍ سابقةٍ في أرض لينغولا، بينما يخبره التمثال الآخر عما أحدثته الحرب تلو الأزمة تلو الأزمة". لكن قبل ذلك، هناك تلك الحركة الدائبة. يمكن لذلك أن يكون رائعًا كفيلم. إنه فيلم رعب، لكن ليس ثمّة موتى أحياء يلتهمون الأطفال في هذا الفيلم. لا، بل فيه موتى أحياء يتعرف واحدهم إلى الآخر، ويجدون طريقةً لتحرير أنفسهم من القصة وإكمال هذه "الأحداث غير المكتملة".

ع.ب.

يعجبني أن إكمال "الأحداث غير المكتملة" هو مهمةٌ تقع على عاتق الموتى الأحياء الذين يتعرفون إلى بعضهم البعض. بعبارةٍ أخرى، ليس ثمّة نهاية هنا، ليس ثمّة شيءٌ ينتهي.

ف.ل.

على العكس، إنها بدايةٌ لاحتمالاتٍ جديدة. أتمنى لو يمكن لهذه الآثار المستعادة إلى أحضان القارة الإفريقية أن تكون بدايةً لاحتمالاتٍ جديدة. سيكون من المؤسف أن تعود تلك الأشياء لتُسجن من جديد كما كانت حبيسة المتاحف الأوروبية على مدى قرون.

Faustin Linyekula, *Banataba [new work]*, Crossing the Line Festival, 1
The Metropolitan Museum of Art, New York, September 9-12, 2017

Faustin Linyekula, *Statue of Loss*, tanzhaus nrw, 2
Düsseldorf, August 12-13, 2021

Abdellatif Laâbi, « Le gâchis », Souffles, numéro 7-8 3
Rabat, troisième et quatrième trimestres 1967, p. 1
https://archive.org/details/Souffles/Souffles%207-8%201967

Kongo: Power and Majesty. 18 Sep. 2015-5 Jan. 2016, 4
The Metropolitan Museum of Art, New York

"اللؤلؤة"، الآثار الكاملة، مجلد 2، دار العودة، بيروت، 1971، ص 573. 5

Faustin Linyekula, *Histoire(s) du théâtre II* 6
Festival d'Avignon, Avignon, 1822- juillet 2019

Dan Hicks, *The Brutish Museums* 7
(London: Pluto Press, 2020)

Felwine Sarr et Bénédicte Savoy, *Rapport sur la restitution du patrimoine* 8
culturel africain. Vers une nouvelle éthique relationnelle, novembre 2018,
n°2018-26. يمكن تحميل التقرير من الرابط: http://restitutionreport2018.com

Ariella Aïsha Azoulay, "Understanding the Migrant Caravan in the Context 9
of Imperial Plunder and Dispossession", in *Hyperallergic*, November 29,
2018. https://hyperallergic.com/473575/understanding-the-migrant-
/caravan-in-the-context-of-imperial-plunder-and-dispossession

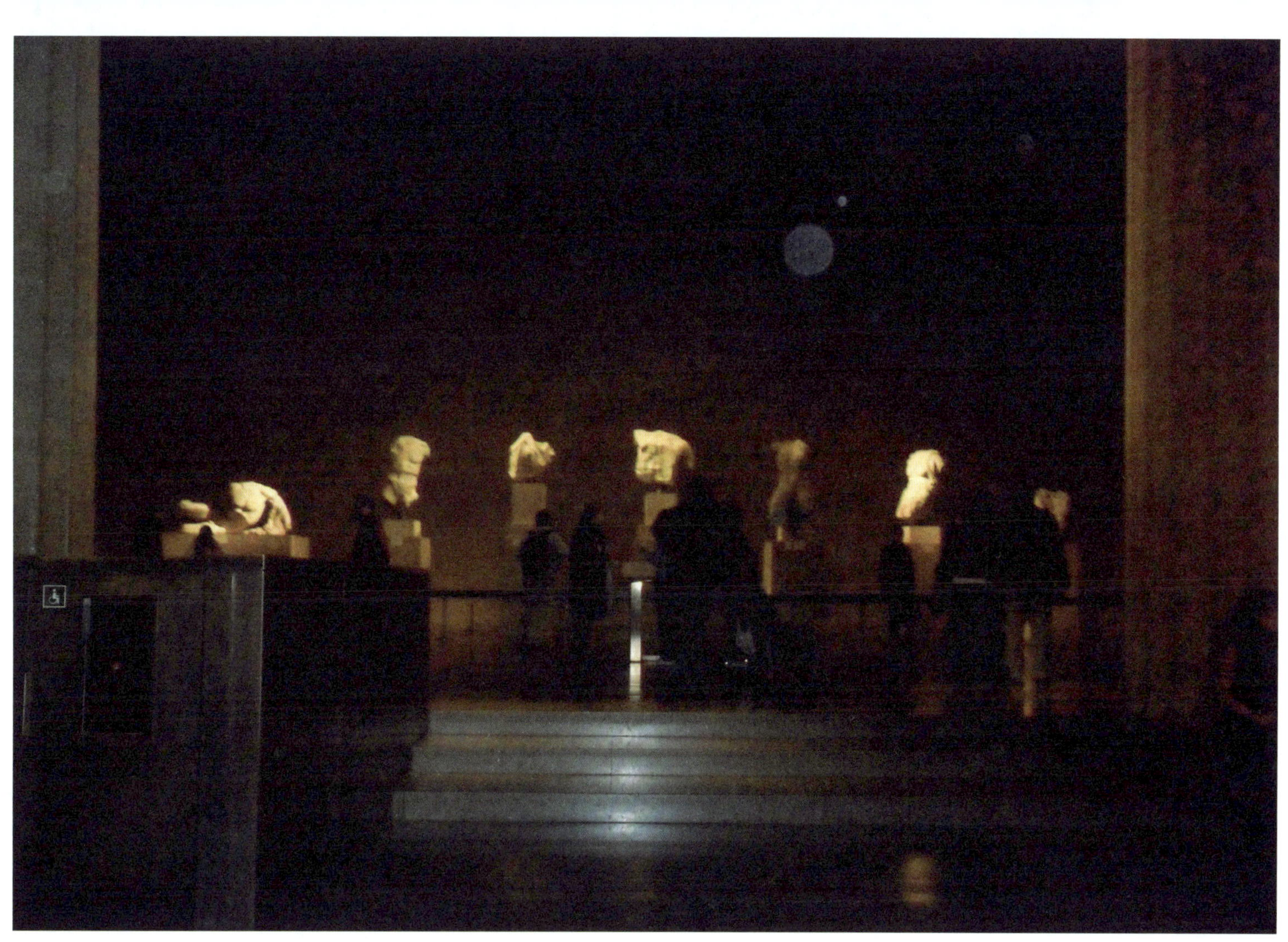

المتاحف تولّد الأشباح

"وعليه، خرجنا وأضرمنا النار في أنحاء المكان بعدما نهبناه. كالغوغاء دمّرنا من النفائس ما لا يمكن تعويضه بأربعة ملايين... لا يسعك حتى أن تتخيّل جمال وبهاء الأماكن التي أحرقناها. إن حَرقها ليُدمي القلب. لقد كانت تلك القصور ضخمةً جدًّا، وكنّا في عجلةٍ من أمرنا، فلم يتسنَّ لنا سرقة محتوياتها بروِيّة. أُضرِمَت النيران في كميّاتٍ من الحليّ المشغولة من الذهب، ظنًّا أنها من النحاس. لقد كان ذلك عملًا بائسًا محبطًا... كان الجميع متعطّشًا للنهب"[1].

المتاحف تولّد الأشباح. والمتاحف الاستعمارية والإثنولوجية تحديدًا مرشّحةٌ بشكلٍ خاص لأن تكون مسكونةً بالأشباح. من المتعارف عليه بين الثقافات أن الأشباح تزور الأماكن التي سبق وأن شهدت أحداثًا تكتمها الذاكرة، فتتقيّح كالجراح المفتوحة ويفاقمها الظلم الذي يسود عالم الأحياء تهتّكًا.

ولعلّ تكاثر الأشباح في المتاحف ناجمٌ عن أساليب الاستحواذ الشائعة فيها، حيث تقوم مجموعاتها بشكلٍ خاص على عمليّات الاستخراج والإبعاد بما يتضمّنه ذلك من عنفٍ ونهبٍ واحتيال.

وقد توصّلتُ إلى الربط بين المتاحف وبين مطاردات الأشباح بناءً على شهاداتٍ شفويةٍ حول قصص الأشباح التي جمعتها من العاملين/ات في المتحف البريطاني، ذلك المتحف الذي تأسّس في العام 1754 كأوّل متحف وطني، ولا يزال منتصبًا إلى اليوم كخزينةٍ مهيبة لغنائم النهب الاستعماري. فمنذ العام 2016، انصبّ اهتمامي على جمع شهادات حرّاس الأمن الليليين وموظّفي/ات خدمات الزوّار ومساعدي/ات المخازن ومديري/ات المجموعات والإداريين/ات والقيّمين/ات والباحثين/ات الزائرين/ات وغيرهم/ن من الموظّفين/ات في شتّى الأقسام الأخرى. وخلصتُ بشكلٍ قاطع إلى أن الإرث المادي يحتفظ ببصماتٍ ووظائف طقوسيّة تعود إلى مئات السنين، وأن الأغراض والرُفات المحفوظة في المتحف لا تجد الراحة والسكينة. كما أن الصراعات والأحداث التي أدّت إلى اقتلاع هذه

حقوق الصور للكاتب.

1   شهادة الميجور تشارلز غوردن الذي قام في 18 تشرين الأول/أكتوبر 1860 بنهب وإحراق القصر الصيفي في بكين إبّان حروب الأفيون ضمن حملة عسكرية إنكليزية ـ فرنسية مشتركة بقيادة الإيرل إلجين الثامن.
Demetrius Charles de Kavanagh Boulger, *The Life of Gordon* (London, 1896), 45-46

الأشياء وإحضارها إلى المتحف لا زالت تتردّد كالأصداء بين جدرانه بشكلٍ يثير الذعر بين الموظّفين/ات والزوّار، الأمر الـذي بـات يشكّل ظاهرةً تتداولها الألسنة همسًا في الأوساط المتحفيّة، فيما تتجاهلها السـلطات كجزءٍ مـن سياسـتها في التعامـل مـع الوضع القائم.

وقد عمدتُ إلى صياغـة كتابـي المُزمع نشـره قريبًا عـلى نسـق التاريخ الشـفوي اسـتنادًا إلى الشـهادات التي جمعتُها مـن العاملين/ات في المتحـف عـلى امتداد السـنوات، وذلـك إمعانًا في التأكيـد عـلى إظهار القلـق السـردي الـذي تنطـوي عليـه هـذه المـواد والشـهادات. يعمـل توثيق هذه الشهادات عـلى تكريس تجربة العاملين/ات المُعاشـة عـلى هلاميتها كجانبٍ مـن الفولكلـور الذاتـي المتناقَـل في أحاديـث الحانـة وأروقـة المتحـف. ويسـعى هـذا المشـروع إلى العـودة عـن تطبيـع المتحـف والحـث عـلى إعـادة التفكيـر فيـه بعيـدًا عـن كونـه بيئـةً معقّمـةً للأغراض الساكنة خلف الزجاج، وفي محاولةٍ لقراءة هـذه الأخيرة كحضورٍ فاعلٍ ومقلقٍ ومتداخـلٍ بأشـكالٍ يصعـب تفسـيرها.

لـو قلتُ لـك عزيزي/تي القارئ/ة أنني أخبّئ بعـض الجثـث البشرية في قبو منزلـي لظننتني مختـلًّا، ولـك كلّ الحـق في ذلـك. الآن لنتخيّـل ذلـك عـلى نطـاقٍ أوسـع: فجميعنـا نعلـم أن المتحـف البريطانـي يحتـوي عـلى آلاف الجثـث والرفـات البشرية، ابتـداءً مـن المومياوات المعـدّة بعنايـة والمدبّجـة بالزينة الطقسـيّة، ووصولًا إلى الجماجم وبقايا العظام المفكّكة. ويمكـن اعتبـار الرفـات البشـرية وغيرهـا مـن الأغـراض المتنازَع عليهـا ضمـن مجموعـات المتاحـف كسـجناء الحـرب. وليـس مسـتَهجنًا أن تُـدرَج الرفـات البشـرية ضمـن عمليّـات تبـادل الأسـرى بيـن الأمـم المحتربـة في أوقـات السـلم. ويرتبط الاحتفاظ بأجسـاد الآلاف من هـؤلاء الأسـرى وحرمانهم مـن الراحـة أو العـودة بتقليـدٍ مسـتمرٍ قائـمٍ عـلى اسـتعراض أجسـاد المغلوبيـن عـلى يـد القوة الإمبرياليـة كتجسـيدٍ لرفـض خسـارة الإمبراطوريّة أو عـدم القـدرة عـلى تقبّلها. مـن هنا، يمكننا فهم مقصد الرئيس اليوناني السـابق بروبوكيس بافلوبولـوس حين وصف المتحف البريطاني بأنـه "سـجنٌ حالك"[2]، تعليقًا عـلى الرفـض المتعنّت لإعـادة رخاميـات البارثينـون. إذ عبّر عـن واقـعٍ يألفـه العديد مـن موظفي/ات المتاحـف.

تروي بعـض الشهادات التي جمعتُها حادثة قذف عاملٍ ضخم الجثّة خارج قاعة ساتون بفعل قـوةٍ غير مرئية دفعته في الهواء ورمته خارجًا فسقط على ظهره. ويُقال إن موسيقى غامضة تصدح من قبّة نصب "نيريد" بعد انتهاء ساعات العمـل. وعـن إحدى حجرات قبو المتحف، يروي قيّمان أنّهما تعرّضا في حادثتين منفصلتين لضربةٍ عـلى الـرأس بحجرٍ طائـرٍ، بالرغم من عـدم وجـود غيرهما في المكان. وعـلى مدى ليالٍ، أظهرت شاشات كاميرات المراقبة كراتٍ من النـور تنطلق بسـرعة الصاروخ في محيـط مدخـل المعرض المتنقّل بعنوان "ألمانيا: ذكريات أمّة"، لتختفي مباشرةً بعـد إزالتـه. كمـا التقـط الـزوّار صورًا فوتوغرافيّة لشخصيّاتٍ غريبةٍ تظهر انعكاساتها عـلى زجاج خزائن العرض وهي تحـوم فـوق أرضيّة القاعة... بعـض الأشباح لا يظهـر سـوى في الصـور الفوتوغرافية، وبعضها عـلى شاشـات كاميرات المراقبة. وتستحضر هـذه الاختلافات دروسًا مـن الفيزيـاء الجزيئيّة حيث تُسـجِّل كثافة المـواد بشكلٍ مختلفٍ بحسـب اختلاف الأدوات المُستخدَمة لتصويرها، ما يستدعي التساؤل حـول طريقة فهمنا للأشـياء وصلابتها.

بعـض الأشـباح بـات مألوفًـا لدرجـة الحديـث عنـه كمـا لـو كان واحـدًا مـن زمـلاء العمـل. ويتّصل البعض الآخر بحوادث الإبادات الجماعيّة، فيما يرتبط غيرها بالرفات أو الأغراض

Nick Squires, "Greek president brands British Museum a 'murky prison' for Elgin Marbles," *The Telegraph*, April 15, 2019 https://www.telegraph.co.uk/news/2019/04/15/ greek-president-brands-british-museum- /murky-prison-elgin-marbles — 2

المُتنازَع عليها. وثمّة أشباح تحاكي أشكالًا أكثر غموضًا من التعلّق والتردّد، ولا يشي ظهورها بعلاقةٍ واضحةٍ مع صدمات الماضي.

ترجّح بعض الشهادات أن تكون لأشباح المتحف البريطاني صلةٌ لا بمقتنياته فحسب، بل بموقع المتحف ذاته أحيانًا. إذ شهد المبنى منذ لحظة تأسيسه قبل 250 عامًا على عددٍ من حوادث الموت سواء بين العاملين/ات أو الزوّار. كما شغله بصفةٍ مستمرّةٍ الكثير من المديرين/ات والقيّمين/ات والخدم وغيرهم ممّن أقاموا في الأجنحة الخلفيّة من المبنى، إضافةً إلى موظّفي/ات الأمن الذين واللواتي يقومون/ن بدوريّات الحراسة المتواصلة على مدار الساعة. كان الصرح الذي يشغله اليوم المتحف البريطاني يُعرف قبل ذلك بقصر مانتاغو، وهو منزلٌ أرستقراطيٌ فخمٌ يطل على ساحة هولبورن حيث المشنقة الشهيرة المخصصة لتنفيذ أحكام الإعدام العلنية. قبل بناء قصر مونتاغو، كان موقع المتحف أرضًا زراعيّة. وترجّح بعض السرديّات أن يكون المزارعون الذين شقّوا تربة تلك الأرض قد لاقوا حتفهم وهم ناقمون على تهجيرهم من مواطنهم، ما يضيف صدّى آخر إلى الأصداء التي تهجس بها أركان المتحف.

يختبر كل عامل/ة في المتحف هذه الخوارق في محيطه الوظيفي. فيتحدّث القيّمون/ات ومديرو/ات المقتنيات عن أغراضٍ مضطربةٍ داخل المخازن المحظورة على الزوّار. ويروي موظّفو/ات الأمن حوادث تتخلّل دوريّاتهم/ن الليلية مثل دوي أجهزة الإنذار وسطوع الأنوار من دون تفسير. بينما يفيد موظّفو الاستقبال وخدمات الزوّار عن حوادث تثير الذعر في قلوب الزوّار، إلى جانب بعض الظواهر الغريبة التي تترافق مع روتين ساعات الدوام والإقفال.

ويُلحظ الاختلاف الطبقي في أسلوب تفسير ورواية هذه الأحداث. فمعظم موظّفي/ات الأمن وخدمات الزوار هم/ن من الطبقة العاملة، ما ينعكس في مهاراتهم/ن السردية الفذّة وحضورهم/ن ودقّتهم/ن في رواية الأحداث وبلاغتهم/ن في التركيب الدرامي والترتيب الزمني لتلك الأحداث. وينحو القيّمون/ات إلى الاستفاضة في التنظير واستحضار السوابق التاريخية مع تجنّب الادّعاء أو الاعتراف بالمشاهدة العينية. ويغلب على هؤلاء شعورٌ بمتعة تخيّل أنهم ليسوا مجرّد حرّاس للأشياء بل وللأرواح الهائمة كذلك. ومع ذلك، كثيرًا ما يحرص هؤلاء على مصداقيّتهم/ن وعلى التزام الخط المؤسّسي بوضع هذه الأحداث والظواهر في إطار الظن والغرائبية. في المقابل، يأخذ موظّفو/ات الحراسة الليلية مهمّتهم/ن في صدّ الدخلاء وتأمين المبنى على محمل الجد. ثم إنهم/ن يجرون/ين دوريّاتهم/ن الليلية في مجموعاتٍ من اثنين، ما يدعّم شهاداتهم/ن حيال مشاهدات الأشباح.

أورَدَ فيل هيري، أحد الموظّفين السابقين الذين أمضوا أكثر من ثلاثين عامًا في قسم خدمات الزوّار، شرحًا مطوّلًا حول تأثير المجال الوظيفي للشخص على تشكّل علاقته/ا مع المتحف قائلًا:

"يتقوقع القيّمون/ات الفنيون/ات داخل بيئاتهم/ن الخاصة، فتغيب عنهم/ن أحيانًا مجريات الأحداث من حولهم/ن، أتفهمني؟ لا ينتقص ذلك من احترامهم/ن كأشخاصٍ على الإطلاق، فهم/ن شديدو/ات الذكاء والثقافة ولكنّهم/ن يفتقدون/ن للحنكة في الأمور الحياتية. بإمكانهم/ن أن يستفيضوا/ن في الحديث عن هذه الحجرة أو تلك

المنحوتة داخل قاعة المتحف، ولكنّهم/ن لا يمتلكون/ن أي دراية بالمجتمع الحديث أو بما يجري في العالم اليوم... لا يكترثون/ن مطلقًا لما يجري في قاعات العرض".

وعندما يشير هيري إلى التجربة الحياتية و"عدم الاكتراث لما يحدث في قاعات العرض"، فهو يقصد تحديدًا الأشباح موضوع بحثنا. إذ يمضي القيّمون/ات أيّامهم/ن منعزلين/ات في الأقسام الخلفيّة من المبنى حيث يجرون/يجرين الأبحاث ويهيّئون/يهيّئن المقتنيات للفهرسة أو العرض بينما يغيبون/ن عن معاينة سلوك الأغراض داخل قاعات المتحف أو الاستماع إلى انطباعات الزوّار حول هذه المعروضات.

ويؤيّده إيرفنغ فينكل، المشرف المساعد على المخطوطات واللغات والثقافات القديمة لبلاد ما بين النهرين في قسم الشرق الأوسط في المتحف البريطاني:

"خلال النهار، يكون المتحف مصطخبًا وكأننا في محطّة مترو هولبورن. كل إشارةٍ خافتةٍ تصدر عن المعروضات تتبدّد وسط هذا الضجيج. أما في الليل، عندما يفرغ المكان من الناس، فالأمر يتبدّل كليًا. يجول حرّاس الأمن في المبنى بعد حلول الظلام، فإذا المتحف مكتظّ بالأغراض الممسوسة. وقعُ أقدامك وأنت تخطو بين ظلال المنحوتات في القاعات عند الساعة الثانية بعد منتصف الليل يدفعك إلى التمعّن في الأشياء المعروضة داخل الخزائن الزجاجيّة والتفكير بها. فإن قُدّر للمرء أن يشهد على هذا النوع من الظواهر فتلك هي اللحظة المناسبة لحدوثها".

وفي حين ينفي أغلب عاملي/ات المتحف الذين واللواتي قابلتهم/ن الإيمان بوجود الأشباح، إلا أن الجميع متّفقون/ات على أن "الأشياء تختزن الطاقة"، وهو تعبيرٌ يتخطّى مسألة الإيمان بالأشباح. يصف أحد موظّفي خدمات الزوّار المسألة على النحو الآتي: "عندما تعزف الكمان فإنه يحتفظ بطاقتك أو بطاقة جميع الذين عزفوه من قبل". ويشير آخر إلى أن "العديد من هذه الأشياء مصمّمٌ ليصدر نوعًا من الرنين". وأعرب اثنان من العاملين عن إيمانهما "بنظريّة الشريط الحجري" في إشارة إلى المسلسل الدرامي الذي عُرض في العام 1972 على قناة بي بي سي بعنوان The Stone Tape (الشريط الحجري). وتقول هذه النظرية إن الأشياء بما فيها الأبنية — في هذه الحال المتحف البريطاني — تعمل كأجهزة تسجيل تمتصّ الأحداث التي تجري داخل جدرانها ولا سيّما الأليمة منها، وتبثّها لاحقًا أو تُعيد تمثيلها في لحظاتٍ غير متوقّعة.

لنفترض أننا سلّمنا جدلًا بمقولة أن "الأشياء تختزن الطاقة"، وأن كل غرضٍ هو بمثابة وعاءٍ يحتوي على آثارٍ للمكان الذي انتُزع منه وعلى الطاقة التي أودعها فيه مستخدموه أو المسؤولون عن العناية به، كما يتذكر وظيفته الأصلية وحالة الاضطراب التي أسفر عنها إحضاره إلى المتحف. عندئذٍ بإمكاننا رؤية المتحف كامتداد للعالم الخارجي لا كمساحةٍ منقطعةٍ عنه. فما إن يتبيّن لنا أن المتحف البريطاني ما هو إلّا نصبٌ تذكاريٌّ للإمبراطورية ولأنظمة التمييز والقهر التي ولّدتها المرحلة الاستعمارية وكرّستها، تكتسب المعارك والاضطرابات التي لا تزال تتردّد أصداؤها داخل المتحف حياةً جديدة.

عندما يتجاهل أمناء المتحف طلبات إعادة المقتنيات إلى مواطنها الأصليّة فيما يواصلون دعمهم لشركة "بريتيش بتروليوم" التي تمثّل الاستعمار الاستخراجي، فهم يفرضون على موظّفي الأمن في المتحف مهمّة ضبط الأشباح المحفوفة بالمخاطر. تواصل هذه

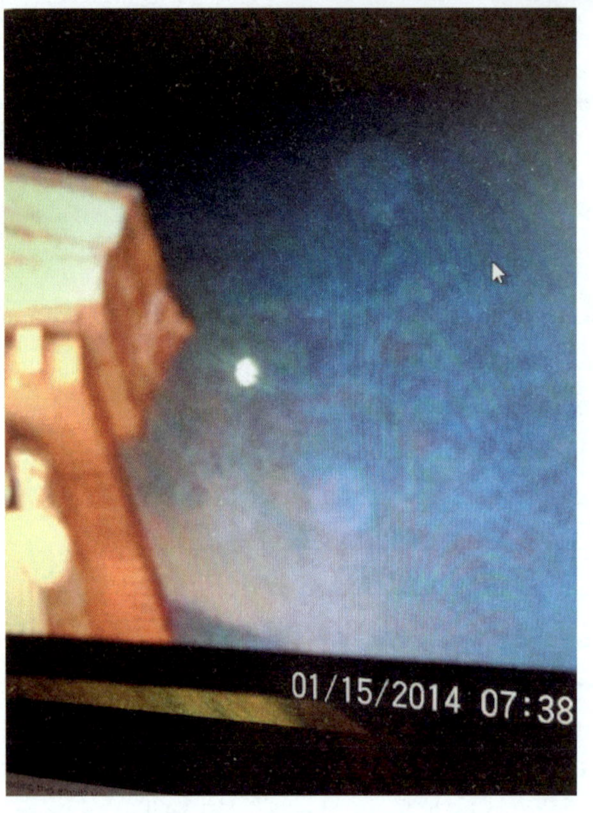

القصص استحضار البعد الاحتجازي للمتحف باعتباره سجنًا كبيرًا يضمّ بين نزلائه مجموعةً كبيرةً من الأشياء العاقلة المُهرَّبة من أنحاء العالم كافة، والمرصوصة جنبًا إلى جنب في ظروفٍ من الحصار والاستعراض اللارضائي. في المقابل، يميل عاملو/ات الأمن وخدمات الزوّار إلى التعاطف مع الأغراض الحبيسة في مكان عملهم/ن حالما يبدؤون/يبدأن بالتنبّه إلى هذه الديناميكيّة، ما يساهم في بعض الأحيان في تعميق إحساسهم/ن بالواجب حيالها كونهم/ن المؤتَمَنين/ات على رعايتها.

وقد أقرّ أحد الحرّاس ممّن شهدوا حوادث مثيرةً للفزع داخل قاعة مصر العليا باستنكاره لعمليات التنقيب عن الرفات واستخراجها وعرضها أمام الجمهور لكونها تشكّل انتهاكًا لحرمة الموتى وتؤدي إلى "اختلاط الأرواح". ورحّب آخر بالوافدين الجدد إلى المتحف قائلًا:

"في النهاية، يحتوي هذا المكان على مجموعةٍ هائلةٍ من الأشياء الآتية من أماكن مختلفة حول العالم. ولا أستغرب أن تأتي بعض هذه الأشياء بأصحابها المربوطين بها. بصراحة، لا ألومهم. لذا فأنا سعيدٌ باستقبالهم ومرحّبٌ بوجودهم هنا".

وهنالك بعض الحرّاس الذين يخاطبون الرفات أثناء دوريّاتهم الليليّة ويسألونها عن أحوالها. وقد سمعت مرّة أن بعضهم كان يعمد إلى تغطية إحدى المومياوات في ساعات الصباح الباكر:

"لم يكن الأمر يقتصر على الحديث فحسب، بل كان أشبه بوضع طفلٍ في فراشه. وكانوا يتمنّون له ليلة سعيدةٌ".

يأتي أصحاب الخبرة في الحراسة والأمن من وظائف سابقة في مكاتب الاستقبال في مجمّعات المكاتب أو ربّما في دور الموسيقى — بعدما كان موظّفو الأمن وخدمات الزوّار يُستقدَمون سابقًا من خلفيّاتٍ مهنيّة عسكريّة أو شُرَطيّة بشكلٍ أساسيّ حسبما علمتُ. أمّا موظّفو/ات قسم خدمات الزوّار فيأتون/ين غالبًا من خلفيّاتٍ وظيفيّةٍ في مجال خدمة العملاء. وكثيرًا ما يكون هؤلاء من طلّاب الفنون أو تاريخ الفن أو مجرّد أشخاص راغبين في تمضية المزيد من الوقت بين الأعمال الأثرية والفنية. لم يكن أيٌّ منهم يتوقّع أن تتضمّن مهمّاته الوظيفيّة مسؤوليّة حراسة عالم الأرواح الحاضرة أبدًا، سواء إلى جانب الأغراض المعروضة أو في أروقة المتحف وقاعاته — كما لم يحظ أيٌّ منهم بالتدريب اللازم لهذا النوع من المهام. وقد سمعت أيضًا أن بعض العاملين/ات في المتحف البريطاني

المتاحف تولّد الأشباح

تركـوا/ن وظائفهـم/ن بسـبب عـدم قدرتهـم/ن عـلى التغلّـب عـلى خوفهـم/ن إثـر حـوادث من هذا النوع.

إذًا فالأشياء تنطق: إذ وعلى بساطة التحوّل الجوهري الـذي تطرحـه هذه المجموعـة من الشهادات، إلا أنه يحمل تبعاتٍ متعدّدةٍ وبالغـة الأثـر.

يعمد الخطاب السائد حول موضوع الإعادة في الغالب إلى التعاطي مع مصنّفات التراث المادي كأحجارٍ عـلى رقعـة الصـراع بيـن الـدول الوطنيـة في ظل تاريخ شـديد الاضطراب. وكثيرًا مـا يتمّ استبعاد مطالب استعادة التراث المادي بحجّة أنها شكاوى تمُتّ إلى أوضاعٍ وظـروفٍ سـبق وأن حُسـمت منـذ زمـنٍ طويـلٍ، وأن الداعميـن لإعـادة إحيائهـا ليسـوا سـوى سياسـيين/ات وناشـطين/ات وصوليين/ات. فيُقال عـلى سبيل المثال: "ها هم اليونانيون ينوحـون عـلى رخاميـات إلغـن مجـدّدًا". ولكن مـاذا لـو كانـت رخاميّـات البارثينـون هي التي تنـوح؟ مـاذا لـو كانت المقتنيات التي يعجّ بها المتحف تتوق إلى السـكينة وتعبّـر عن احتجاجها عـلى ظـروف عرضهـا؟ مـاذا لـو أن الاحتجـاز يبعـث الحيـاة في الرفات ويحجب عنهـا الراحـة الأبديـة؟ ومـا الـذي يتوجّب علينـا فعلـه، نحـن الـزوّار والخبـراء المتحفيّيـن وأمنـاء المواقع الأثريـة، المقدّسـة والوثنيّـة عـلى حـدّ سـواء، حيال هذا المزيج من أصـوات الاحتجاج؟ وما الـذي يمكـن أن يتبـدّل في أسـلوب عمـل المتاحـف لـو أُخِذَت فاعليّـة المقتنيـات التـي تدّعـي الحفاظ عليها على محمل الجدّ؟

"كيـف لنـا أن نعيـد النظـر في تصـوّر المتحـف؟". هـو سـؤالٌ يتـردّد اليـوم في أوسـاط الخبـراء والمهنيين المتحفيين. يكثر اليـوم حديثٌ عـلى ألسنة العاملين/ات في المتاحف حول ضرورة التحـرّر مـن الاستعمار. غيـر أن المتاحـف قد تكون أشـدّ ارتباطًا بالمشروع الاستعماري من أي محاولةٍ لاجترار المعنى مـن هذا التحـرّر. "كيـف لنـا أن نعيـد النظـر في تصـوّر المتحـف؟". هـو الإطار اللغـوي الـذي يخطّ إمكانيّـة تفكيك المؤسّسات الإمبرياليّة[3]. إذًا لا بدّ لنـا مـن فهم هذا المسار الاستقصائي كمبحثٍ ثانوي مقابل السـؤال الأكثر إلحاحًا حـول كيفيّـة التوصّل جماعيًّا إلى صياغـة عالـمٍ أكثـر عدالـة والعيـش فيه. كمـا يمكـن أن نطـرح السـؤال الآتـي: "كيـف نسـتطيع تحريـر الأمـوات المُحتجَزيـن في مخازن المتحـف وتكريمهم بالدفن اللائـق في مواطنهم الأصليـة؟". ولعل الإجابة هنا تأتي في الدرجة الأولى مـن الإصغاء إلى الأغـراض بـدلًا مـن النظر إليها.

تقـوم النظـرة الإمبرياليـة التـي تحتـلّ صميـم المتاحـف الاستعماريـة كالمتحف البريطاني عـلى إنكار فاعليّـة الأغـراض ودور التـراث المـادي في تعزيـز اللُحمـة الاجتماعيـة للجماعـات عبـر صياغتهـا للـدلالات المشـتركة وارتباطها بالممارسـات الجمعية المتواصلـة والثابتة. هـذه النظـرة الإمبرياليـة تطاردنـا جميعًا وإن بدرجاتٍ متفاوتـةٍ كقوّةٍ غامضـةٍ لا تنفكّ تفـرّخ العنصريّـة والقوميـة وتَصِمُ بعضنـا بالتأخّـر والتخلّـف، وهي نـوعٌ مـن التعامـي المؤدلَـج والمدعَّـم مـن الممارسـات ذات المنظـور المركـزي الأوروبي في مجـالات علم الآثـار والأنثروبولوجيا وتاريـخ الفن وغيرهـا مـن الحقـول الأكاديمية. هذا فيما يـرى المتخصّصـون المعنيـون بفهم وسَلسَلـة تاريـخ المقتنيـات المتحفيـة العنف الإمبريالـي غيـر مفهومٍ أو مبـرّرٍ، بينمـا تسـتمرّ القـوى الاستعمارية التي لـم تكّف قـط عـن السـعي خلف مـوارد الآخريـن منـذ عهد الاستعمار وحتى هـذه اللحظة في ممارسـة استعراضها للقوة مـن خـلال الاستحواذ عـلى التـراث المـادي وعرضـه في المتاحف. إذ

Ariella Aïsha Azoulay, *Potential History: Unlearning Imperialism* (London: Verso Books, 2019)

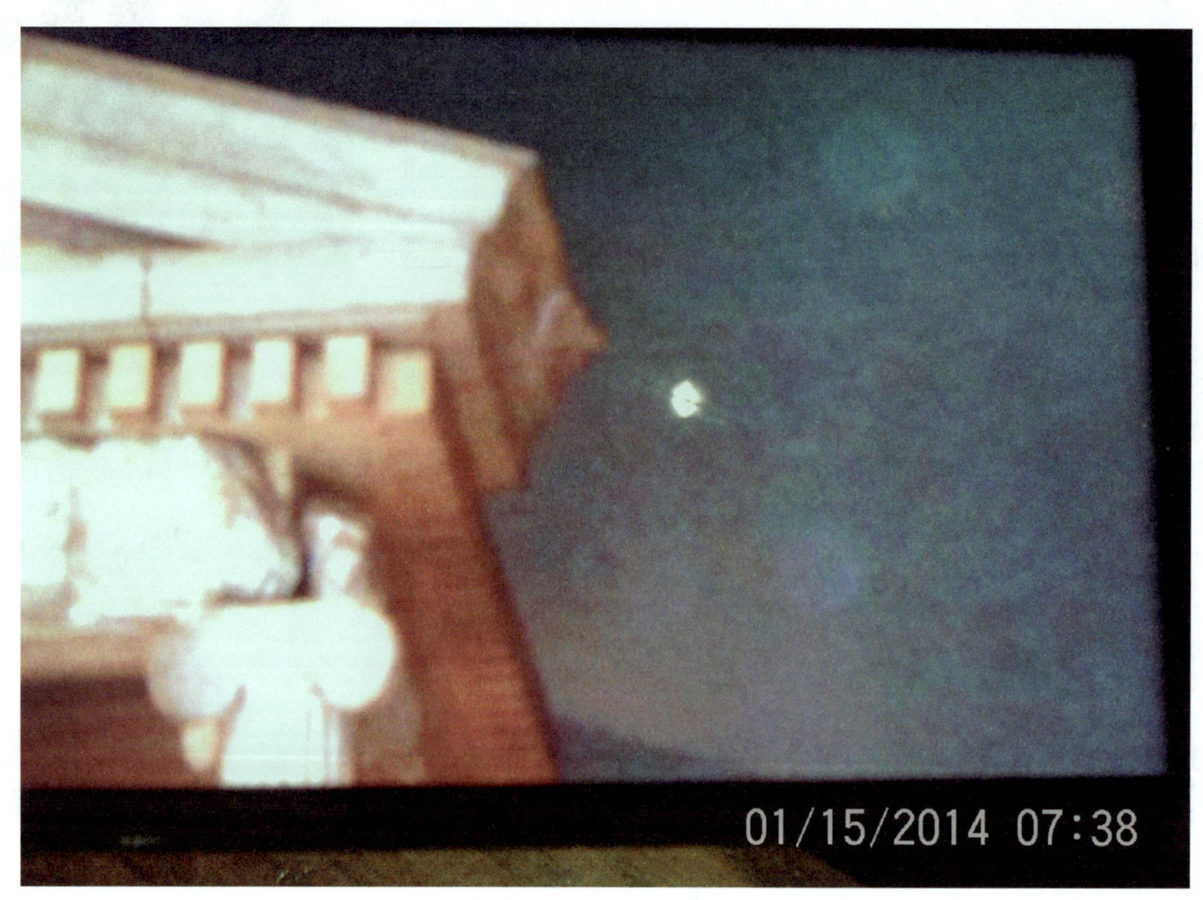

01/15/2014 07:38

يمثّل هـذا الفعـل بالنسـبة إليهـا وسيلة لإضعاف الشـعوب الأخـرى عبـر تجريدهـا مـن الأشـياء التـي تمدّهـا بالقـوّة في مواجهـة إمبرياليـة القهـر والاسـتخراج والعنف. فالعـرض في المتحـف الإثنوغرافي يُعـرّض التراث المـادي للتسـطيح؛ يحوّلـه إلى صورةٍ ويقدّمـه كشـذرةٍ مـن عالمٍ بالٍ مفقـود.

قـد يكـون إيـداع الأغـراض في المتحف مرادفًـا لجعلهـا أشـباحًا. وقد تكـون محاولـة اقتلاع مصنّف التراث المـادي (الفاشـلة) مـن موضعـه الأصلـي ووظيفته وكنف أصحابـه الموكلين برعايته، سـببًا في إيقاظ هذه الأشـباح. فالفولكلور يعجّ بالأيتام والأرامل والجنود والبحارة والمسـافرين والمضطهدين والمُبعَدين عـن أحبّتهـم والتائهيـن الذيـن يطـاردون الأحيـاء اليـوم. وبمـا أن المتاحـف الاسـتعمارية لا تقـوم إلا عـلى الإزاحـة الجماعيـة للتراث المـادي، فـإن الشـهادات الشـفوية التي جمعتُهـا تـؤدي إلى خلاصةٍ مفادهـا أن نهـج الانتـزاع والعرض الـذي يتّبعـه وكلاء الإمبراطوريـة هـو المسـؤول عـن اسـتحضار الأشـباح. ويبـدو أن محاولـة المتحـف الفاشـلة لتهجيـر الأغـراض عـن مواطنها الأصليـة، لـم تـأتِ سـوى بـردّ فعلٍ عكسـيّ، مُخلّفـة الكثير مـن النهايـات العصبيـة المتدلّيـة التي لـم تنقطع بشـكلٍ كاملٍ، وهـي الآن تسـعى للالتئام فتراها تهيم عـلى وجهها مثيرةً القلق والاضطراب في قاعـات المتحـف الـذي بـات مقـرًّا للأرواح الشـريدة.

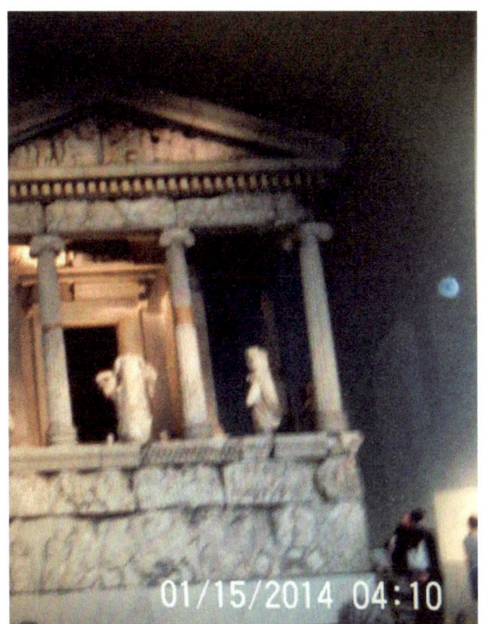

وإن كان الكثير من مصنّفات التراث المادي في المتحف يعـود إلى العصور القديمة، فالأشباح تمثّل أصواتًـا لا مـن ذلـك الماضـي بـل مـن صميم حاضرنا نحن. فالمؤكّـد أن الأغـراض الموجـودة في المتحـف البريطاني اليـوم سـتعمّر أطـول مـن النظرة الإمبرياليـة، مـا يجعلها أكثـر تكاملًـا مـع مسـتقبلنا الجماعـي مـن المبنـى الـذي يؤويهـا. ثـم إن المتحـف البريطاني عينـه سـرعان مـا سـيتحوّل إلى مفارقةٍ تاريخيّةٍ باعتبـاره أثـرًا للعهد الاسـتعماري ولعَظَمَـة بريطانيا البائدة. وما الشـهادات التي جمعتُها سـوى دليلٍ عـلى الاحتدام بين عددٍ لا يُحصى مـن الأغـراض المُبعـدَة عـن مواطنهـا الأصليّـة والمملـوءة بالطاقـة، وبيـن الزنازيـن الزائلـة التي تحتويها.

وقـد اكتشـفتُ في سـياق حواراتـي مـع العامليـن/ات في المتحـف البريطاني أن هذا الأخيـر يخشى سـماع مـا يمكن أن تقوله الأغـراض القابعة داخل جدرانه. وقد أسـرّ لي أحد العامليـن هناك بأنني لسـتُ الوحيد الذي سـعى إلى جمع هذه القصص:

"كنتُ قد تقدّمت من الإدارة (السـابقة) طلبًـا للمعلومات أو لتأكيد بعض المعلومات، فنهوني عـن ذلـك بلهجةٍ حاسمة. لم يُسمَح لي مطلقًـا بنشـر أي شـيء يتعلّق بالأشـباح في المتحف، لأن الإدارة لا ترغـب في أن يقترن اسـم المتحف بهذا النـوع مـن القصص. وكمـا تعلـم فقـد تضمّـن الأمـر بعـض الجوانـب المتعلّقـة بالأمـن، وقد منعوني مـن التحـدّث عنهـا بشـكلٍ قاطع. منعوني تمامًـا، وعلمت لاحقًـا من موظّفين آخرين أنه قد سـبق لاثنين من عاملي/ات المتحف أن حاولا وضع مؤلَّفَين عن الأشـباح في المتحف البريطاني وقد تلقّيا الرسـالة عينها".

وبالرغم من الحظر المفروض على الموظّفين/ات بخصوص نشـر أي معلومات عن الأشـباح في المتحـف البريطاني، فقـد خاطب هارتويغ فيشـر المدير الحالي للمتحف في العـام 2018 قاعةً مليئةً بالموظّفين/ات الجـدد خـلال احتفالٍ بنهاية الـدورة التأهيلية قائلًـا: "نحن هنا بسـبب الأشـباح". ومؤخّـرًا أدلى فيشـر باعترافٍ علنيٍ مثيرٍ للاهتمـام، فقال: "تلقّيـت زيارةً في إحدى

المرآت من أوني إيف، الحاكم الروحي لليوروبا. أتى إلى المتحف ووصفه بأنه منزلٌ للأرواح وأخبرني أنه تمكّن أثناء مكوثه هناك من التواصل مع الأرواح من كل العصور ومن كل الأماكن في العالم"[4].

بضع كلمات، أدّى اعتراف فيشر بوجود الأشباح في المتحف إلى توسيع مساحة الحوار الدائر حول المتاحف عمومًا بشكلٍ ملحوظ. فلم تعُد المسألة تقتصر على الأغراض المُحتجَزة في المتحف البريطاني وعلى ما يمثّله ذلك من انتهاكٍ لإرادة الشعوب الأصلية التي تعود إليها ملكيّة هذه الأغراض، بل وتشمل أرواح الأجداد الملازمة لها بحسب اعتراف فيشر. كما أن الحضور الكثيف لهذه الأرواح داخل قاعات المتحف ليس أثرًا جانبيًا لوجود هذه المقتنيات كما كنتُ أعتقد، بل هو جزءٌ من غاية المتحف وِفقَ ما أسرّ مديره للموظّفين/ات عشيّة استلامهم/ن وظائفهم/ن الجديدة. ولعلّ في هذه العبارة إشارةً إلى المتخَيّل الإمبريالي الذي يُعدّ القوّة الحقيقيّة لا في الاستحواذ على موروثات الآخرين فحسب، بل وعلى الفاعليّة الكامنة فيها. فما الاستحواذ على تلك الأغراض إلّا وسيلةً لإخضاع سلطة الآخرين الروحيّة. وعلى محملٍ آخر، يمكننا فهم عبارة فيشر حول أشباح المتحف من منظورٍ أبوي. فعندما يدّعي المتحف البريطاني أن هشاشة "برونزيّات بنين" لا تسمح بإعادتها إلى نيجيريا، فذلك يعني أن الجماعات التي قامت بصنع هذه البرونزيات تفتقر إلى الأدوات والمعرفة الكافية للعناية بها[5].

وينطوي الحظر المفروض على التداول العلني لمسألة الأشباح في المتحف، في وقتٍ يؤكّد المدير وجودها في الاحتفالات الخاصّة مع الموظّفين/ات، على رغبةٍ قلِقةٍ بالتملّك. وإن دلّ هذا الفصام على شيء فعلى الإقرار بأن الأغراض تنطق وأن المتحف يخشى مما قد تتفوّه به، ولا بدّ إذًا من لَجمِها عن البوح. فماذا لو أجمعت تلك الأغراض مع الناجين من الإمبراطورية البريطانية على المطالبة بأن تُودَع في عُهدَة مَن هُم خارج المتحف وأن تُعفى من المنطق المسيء للعرض والحفظ الأرشيفي؟ وحتى وإن كانت الإعادة لا تمثّل حلًّا ملائمًا في بعض الحالات، فهذا أسوأ ما تخشاه المتاحف لأنه سيؤدي لا إلى تصفية مجموعاتٍ كاملةٍ من مقتنياتها فحسب، بل إلى تفكيكِ آخِر متراسٍ من متاريس الإمبراطورية البريطانية.

إلى اليوم يرفض المتحف البريطاني إطلاق سراح هذه الأشباح. كما يمتنع عن الإقرار بالعنف الذي ارتكبه في سبيل مراكمة هذه المقتنيات على أنقاض قصورٍ لم تُخمد حرائقها بعد، ما يجعله سببًا في خرابٍ لا يُحصى مداه. على صعيدٍ آخر، يتواصل الصراع، لا على مستوى الأمناء والسياسيين/ات والنشطاء والأكاديميين/ات فحسب، بل وأيضًا بين بعض الأشباح وبعضهم الآخر وبين الحرّاس والزوّار/الزائرات الجاهلين/ات بما يحدث في أروقة المتاحف الاستعمارية حول العالم وداخل قاعاتها ومخازنها.

4   British Museum Events, "British Museum Youth Collective presents: Quizzing the British Museum's Director," YouTube, April 14, 2021. https://www.youtube.com/watch?v=0GApxVRsmLQ&t=746s&ab_channel=BritishMuseumEventsBritishMuseumEvents watch?v=0GApxVRsmLQ&t=746s&ab_channel=BritishMuseumEventsBritishMuseumEvents

5   "البريطانيون بارعون في ادّعاء الحجّة، يقولون لك: نحن نعتني بها، ولو كنتم أنتم من يتولّى رعايتها لكانت شرقت". الاقتباس من ديفيد أوموريغي في: Alex Marshall, "This Art Was Looted 123 Years Ago. Will It Ever Be Returned?", *The New York Times*, January 23, 2020. https://www.nytimes.com/2020/01/23/arts/design/benin-bronzes.htm

المتاحف تولّد الأشباح

محادثة بين بونافنتور سوه بيجينغ نديكونغ وعليا سبتي

عليا سبتي

كان لقاؤنا الأول محض مصادفة. التقينا عام 2012 أثناء إقامة معرض There is no wind on the moon (لا رياح على سطح القمر) حيث كنتَ أنت القيّم الفنيّ في "سافي" للفن المعاصر بمقره القديم بريتشاردبلاتز في نويكولن. كنتُ يومها مشاركةً بدورة صيفية في معهد غوته، وكان زميلاي ماريا إيوريو ورافاييل كومو من ضمن الفنانين/ات المشاركين/ات في المعرض. كانا يرددان اسم بونا بلا انقطاع. "بونا، بونا، بونا، بونا". وفي أحد الأيام زرتُ المعرض وتعرفتُ إلى "بونا" الشهير، هكذا تعارفنا. كان ذلك اللقاء فاتحةً جميلةً لمغامراتٍ كثيرةٍ لنا سويًّا. وما لبثنا أن بدأنا العمل على بينالي مراكش 2014. كان عنوان معرضك هناك ظريفًا لا ينسى: ,If You're So Smart Why Ain't You Rich? (إن كنت ذكيًّا فلمَ لست ثريًّا؟) مضت عشر سنوات من الحوار المتواصل بيننا، ويسعدني أن أواصل الحوار من حيث توقفنا آخر مرة.

كنتُ قد عاودتُ قراءة نص البيان التقييمي الذي كتبته لمعرض "لا رياح على سطح القمر"، ولاحظتُ كيف أثرتَ فيه موضوع مادية الأرشيف. كأنك أعدتَ إحياء الحديث عن الأرشيفات في أروقة برلين. منذ تلك اللحظة والجميع يتكلم عن الأرشيفات والأرشيفات والأرشيفات. دعني أستهل هذا الحوار بطرح السؤال: لماذا تعتبر الأرشيف على هذا القدر من الأهمية؟

بونافنتور سوه بيجينغ نديكونغ

في رأيي أن الأرشيف كان وما زال أحد أبرز ساحات النزاع. فالأرشيف هو مساحة لإنشاء بنى السلطة وصقلها وممارستها. إذًا فالأرشيف ليس فضاءً بريئًا محايدًا، بل هو مُعَدٌّ ليشمل أناسًا محددين وتواريخ بعينها، ويُقصي أناسًا آخرين وتواريخ أخرى. وقد كنا نسعى مع بداية عملنا في "سافي" إلى التفكير في فعل الأرشيف بدلًا من ماهيته – بعبارة أخرى، أردنا أن نتأمل في أدائية الأرشيف.

الحياة محض أرشيف. وقد أردنا النظر في الهرميات التي تنبثق عن البنى الأرشيفية. تساءلنا حول ما إذا كنا نحتاج بالفعل إلى السعي كي نكون جزءًا من أرشيفات قائمة، تقوم على أساس تغييبنا واستثنائنا وإقصائنا إذا جاز التعبير. أم نبحث عن نوع آخر من الأرشيف؟ وأين نذهب إن أردنا أن نبحث عن المعارف التي تخصّنا وتخبرُنا عن أنفسنا؟ دققنا في الجسد كمحل للخطاب، وتقصّينا المعرفة المتداولة في الشارع. نظرنا إلى الفضاء العام بوصفه أرشيفًا، نظرنا إلى الصروح كأرشيفات، إلى الأسماء، أسمائنا. مثلًا، ما معنى "عليا"؟ ما معنى "سبتي"؟ لماذا نطلق على أنفسنا هذه الأسماء؟ لا يتوقف السؤال هنا عند معرفة "لماذا أُطلقت علينا هذه الأسماء؟"، بل و"كيف تُشكلنا أسماؤنا؟"، وكيف لنا أن ننظر إلى الأمثال الشعبية أيضًا كمساحات أرشيفية؟

أسفرت هذه الأسئلة عن مشاريع كثيرة. ومن جملة المسائل التي شغلتنا حيال الأرشيف هي أنه وبالرغم من مِنعته وسلطانه وحجم تأثيره على وجودنا، فإن ثمة مساحات أرشيفية قد باتت بلا فائدة. وكان السؤال: كيف يمكننا أن نعيد إحياء مساحات أرشيفية بعينها، وأن نميت أخرى غيرها؟ وهذا جزءٌ أساسي من مشروعنا، وقد كان محورًا للمحاضرة التي ألقيتها في إسطنبول عام 2019 بعنوان Apoptotic Archive (الأرشيف المبرمج للموت)، أي الأرشيف القادر على التدمير الذاتي على غرار الخلايا الحية كي يفسح المجال لصعود أنماط أخرى من الأرشيف أو من المعرفة. وهذا هو مصدر اهتمامنا بالأرشيف، ولا أعتقد أننا أنهينا عملنا في هذا الصدد. بل سنواصل في السنوات المقبلة التفكير بهذه المفاهيم وبكيفية توسيعها والإحاطة بمعنى أن نفكر في أرشيفات المستقبل. لم تعد الشوارع مساحاتٍ للصراع، وإنما بات مكانها الأرشيف.

ع. س.

لطالما شجعتَني على الكتابة وأكّدتَ أهمية الكتابة وعدم ترك المجال للآخرين كي يرووا قصصنا. وأوليتَ الأهمية دومًا لمن يكتب تلك القصص، بل ولمن يمحوها أيضًا، ومن يملك أن يختار من تستحق قصته أن تُروى أو تُسمع (أو لا تُسمع) وكيفية استعادة مساحة الكتابة وترك بصمة لا تمحى. المعارض أحداث عابرة أما النصوص فتبقى. وأنتَ لا تتوانى في نصوصك عن الخوض في مسائل شائكة ومعقدة مع الإبقاء على بساطة اللغة وسهولتها. تشرّعها وتُسهب فيها وتقلّبها على جميع أوجهها، مع وعيكَ التام بأن هذه الوثائق تنتمي إلى أرشيف مستقبلي، وأنها ستبقى سواءٌ أكانت نصًّا مكتوبًا أم عنصرًا صوتيًّا أو أي شيء قابل للمشاركة والنشر المستقبلي.

ب. س. ب. ن.

وأنت تفعلين الشيء نفسه: هكذا أقرأ مشروعك Untie to Tie (الربط من أجل الحل). عندما تفكيكن الموروثات الاستعمارية ما الذي تجدينه في لبّها؟ وإذا كانت المسألة تدور حول الرابط فكيف السبيل إلى الحلّ والفكاك؟ أثناء عملك على هذا المشروع فكرتُ في نبذ ما تعلّمناه سابقًا على سبيل التعلّم. لا يمكننا أن نستمر هكذا ببساطة في البناء على أسس بعينها، بل لا بد لنا من هدمها كي نتمكن من إعادة بنائها من جديد، أي لا بد لنا من تفكيك السردية القائمة كي نكتب واحدة أخرى جديدة. ماذا هناك؟ كيف نحلّه، نفكّكه، ننسّله؟ عندها فقط يمكننا البدء بجمع الأجزاء وتركيبها. وأعتقد أن الأمر عينه ينطبق عليك وهو

ما أُجلّه فيكِ. وكان هذا تحديدًا محور ممارسات العرض التي طورناها على مدى السنوات القليلة الماضية: أقصد العمل مع الفنانين/ات كقصّاصين/ات يملكون/يملكن سرديات مختلفة. أجد هذه التعددية السردية والمنظورية التي أتيحت لنا في رواية قصصنا ضمن ممارستكِ أنتِ أيضًا.

ع. س.

شكرًا، تعلمت منك الكثير. بدأتُ العمل على برنامج "الربط من أجل الحل" في غاليري معهد العلاقات الخارجية (IFA) ببرلين، بعد أن أمضيت سنوات أتردد على "سافي" للفن المعاصر. هناك اكتسبتُ ثقتي في القدرة على العمل على موضوع من هذا القبيل ضمن مؤسسة ألمانية. أنتَ مهدتَ لي الطريق لتجاوز الإطار الخطابي التجميلي والتوجه نحو سبر مغزى الكلام عن موروثات الاستعمار اليوم وطرحه للمساءلة – من داخل المؤسسة الألمانية وعلى مدار سنوات عدة. فقد تمكنتَ من تحويل الأنظار إلى قلب المؤسسة في عزّ الحديث عن الاستعادة لتسأل: "ما معنى الحديث عن الاستعادة؟". هذا ما ركّزنا عليه معك في "سافي" ومع نورا رازيان وراهول جوديبودي في "فن جميل" For the Phoenix to Find its Form ضمن مشروعهما in Us (كي تتعرف العنقاء إلى صورتها فينا) الذي أقيم عام 2021. كان حديثك عن أن الاستعادة تتخطى الأغراض بحد ذاتها مؤثرًا جدًّا. ولن أقول "كان" في الماضي لأن المشروع ليس من الماضي، بل هو حوار متّصل.

أود أن نتوقف عند عنوان المشروع "كي تتعرف العنقاء إلى صورتها فينا: حول الاستعادة وإعادة التأهيل والترميم". لقد ذكرنا الاستعادة وإنما ليس في معرض الحصر. هلّا حدثتنا أكثر عن الكلمات الثلاث التي يتكون منها العنوان الفرعي؟

ب. س. ب. ن.

كان العنوان "الاستعادة وإعادة التأهيل والترميم" محاولةً لفتح هذا المجال. فمنذ أن بدأت موجة الحديث المحمومة عن الاستعادة – لا سيما إثر خطاب إمانويل ماكرون في واغادوغو في عام 2017 – جاءني الانطباع بأن الكل يريد أن يدلي بدلوه. لا شك في ضرورة التكلم عن هذه القضية، لكن ما الذي نعنيه حقًّا عندما نثير مسألة الاستعادة؟ شعرتُ بأن هذه المحادثات لا تخدم أهدافنا بالضرورة، بل غايات المؤسسات المُدَانة التي تتعرض للانتقادات، لا سيما بعد أن استحوذ العديد من المؤسسات على النقاش وركب الموجة إن جاز التعبير. وكنا في سياق مشروعنا في حاجة إلى جرد أو تقييم للوضع القائم. لذا

بدأثُ في التفكير بمعنى الاستعادة. هل نتحدث عن الأغراض فقط؟ الإجابة البديهية هي نعم، لكن الواقع أننا نتحدث عما هو أبعد من ذلك أي عن الذوات. نحن نتحدث عن كائنات اعتُبرت أغراضًا، بينما يتمتع الكثير منها بالذاتية. كيف السبيل إذًا إلى الاستعادة بالنظر إلى مدى التشابك بين هذه الذوات؟

ذُمّ الكثير من هذه الأغراض وشُيطنت وسميت بالطواطم وأطلقت عليها الصفات التحقيرية، ما أدى إلى حالات تدميرية في أماكن مثل الكاميرون ونيجيريا حيث أضرم كاهن مؤخرًا النار في مجموعة من الكائنات المقدسة بحجة أنها تخدم الشيطان. ولم يكتف الناس في الفرجة على هذا الطقس الهمجي فحسب، بل راحوا يشاركون الكاهن فعلته الشنعاء. كم يستلزم أن يكون المرء مستلبًا ومغسول الدماغ كي يشارك في فعلةٍ كهذه؟ علينا البدء بنزع الاستعمار من أذهان الناس. ويبقى السؤال عندئذٍ، كيف نفكر؟ يجب أن نكون قادرين على استعادة كرامة الناس كي يتمكنوا من إدراك القيمة الفعلية لما شُلب منهم.

إذًا لا تقتصر المسألة على ردّ "الأغراض" إلى أصحابها الأصليين، بل تستهدف إعادة كرامتهم إليهم. استمعثُ إلى متحدثين/ات في الكثير من الندوات التي شاركتُ فيها - ولم أعد أحضرها أو صرثُ أتجنبها قدر الإمكان حفاظًا على أعصابي - وهم/ن يقولون/ن: "إذا أرسلتم هذه الأغراض إلى آسيا أو إفريقيا أو الأميركتين فسوف لن يتمكن السكان الأصليون من إيلائها الرعاية اللازمة". كيف تقتحم منزلًا يعتني ساكنوه بأغراضهم منذ ألف أو ألفي عام فتسلبهم إياها لتودعها في صندوق زجاجي، ثم تزعم أنهم لا يجيدون الاهتمام بها؟ هذا مثالٌ على الاستطفال الذي يقع في صميم الممارسة الاستعمارية. وهو ما يسلب الناس كرامتهم.

ومن ثم فقد جرّبنا فكرة إعادة التأهيل. ما إن يتغير المكان والزمان تصبح العودة مستحيلة، لأننا بكل بساطة لا نستطيع أن نعيد عقارب الساعة إلى الوراء. علينا بالتفكير في إعادة التأهيل، أي العثور على مكان آخر لتأهيل تلك الأغراض وإيجاد وسيلة لإسكانها وإحلالها في سياقات محددة. أمامنا الكثير لنفعله في هذا الصدد.

يأتي فيما بعد السؤال المتعلق بترميم ما تهدّم ولأم الجراح المفتوحة - فالناس جراح متنقلة. يحمل الإنسان ما بعد الاستعماري الكثير من الجراح والندوب، وعلينا التفكير في كيفية التعافي من كل هذا. لا بد من نوع من التعويض، لكن كيف السبيل إلى احتساب قيمته؟ كما أن للتعويض جانبًا ماليًا

لا مجال للاستخفاف به أو تجاهله. ولكننا كثيرًا ما نغفل الوجه الاقتصادي لكل ذلك، وقد أشرثُ إلى هذه المسألة في مقالتي التي تحمل عنوان Ceux qui sont morts ne sont jamais partis (الأموات لم يغادرونا قطّ). عندما تجرّد الناس من كائنات معينة، فإنك تحرمهم من قدرتهم على الوجود في العالم. ولا مجال لإصلاح هذا الوضع من دون التعويض عنه، لا سيما إذا كان الاحتفاظ بهذه الأغراض في المتاحف يساهم في مراكمة القيمة الاقتصادية. يسافر الناس من بلد إلى آخر حول العالم كي يشاهدوا معروضات المتاحف كما هو الحال هنا في وسط برلين. ولا تقتصر تلك المراكمة على رسوم دخول الزوار إلى المتاحف، بل تشمل كامل القطاع الاقتصادي؛ من تذكرة السفر إلى حجز الإقامة في الفندق وإلى ما هنالك من المصاريف التي ينفقها الناس كي يتمكنوا من زيارة المتاحف. جمع المستعمِر ثروات طائلة من جراء كل هذا الاستغلال، هذا هو الاستخراج في أبرز تجلّياته. إذًا لا يمكننا أن نتحاور بشأن الترميم من دون الحديث عن التعويضات المالية.

ع. س.

أودّ العودة إلى النص الذي ذكرته "الأموات لم يغادرونا قطّ" الذي نُشر في مجلة South as a State of Mind. كتبتُ حينها عن العمارة كأداة لمحو التاريخ وعن الإنشاءات كممحاة عمرانية، وكان ذلك في سياق الحديث عن متحف منتدى هومبولدت ببرلين الذي أنشئ مكان ما عرف باسم "قصر الجمهورية" في عهد ألمانيا الشرقية. إذًا لا بد من تقصّي البعد العمراني في سياق الحديث عن الاستعادة وعن محو المعرفة العمرانية، بل ومحو مدن بأكملها وإعادة بنائها بأشكال ساهمت في التعدي على كرامة المجتمعات المحلية. كيف نتحدث عن الاستعادة؟ وما الذي نسعى إلى استعادته؟

ب. س. ب. ن.

عدنا مؤخرًا من رحلةٍ إلى باندجون في الكاميرون. تعيش الكاميرون محنةً قاسيةً هذه الأيام ويشهد الجزء الذي أتحدّر منه حروبًا مستمرة منذ نحو خمس سنوات. دعونا هناك نحو 40 شخصًا من تلك المنطقة ومن مناطق أخرى في أنحاء الكاميرون من فنانين/ات وباحثين/ات إلى فضاء "محطة باندجون" للفنان برتيليمي توغو من أجل إحياء الذكرى الخمسين لنشر كتاب والتر رودني How Europe Underdeveloped Africa (كيف أخرت أوروبا نمو إفريقيا) في عام 1972. تأتي الأسئلة التي نطرحها في سياق تأخر النمو الاقتصادي. كيف السبيل إلى

التحرر من هذه الديناميكية؟

زرنا هناك قصر باندجون. إنه تحفة معمارية تتمثل في بيت ضخم مصنوع من الخيزران والطين. كانت حرارة الطقس يومها ما بين 35 و40 درجة مئوية. المبنى مربع من الخارج، أما من الداخل فهو عبارة عن حلقات متمركزة عليكِ أن تجتازيها كي تبلغي نقطة المركز، حيث تنخفض درجة الحرارة إلى 25 درجة مئوية. آيةٌ مدهشة من العمران. سألتُ مدير القصر ومتوليه وقيّمه: "هل يأتي المعماريون/ات لزيارة المكان؟ هل يزوره الفنانون/ات؟ قال: كلا، كلا، كلا. قلتُ له يجب أن تكون زيارة هذا المكان إلزامية لطلاب العمارة والفن في الجامعات، بل لجميع الطلاب. يجب أن يأتوا/ين إلى هنا لرؤية هذا المكان ومعرفة أهميته. وهذا في نظري جزءٌ من عملية الترميم: أن نفهم أهمية العمارة، وأن ندرك أننا لسنا مضطرين لبناء مدنٍ من الإسمنت والزجاج لمجرد أن ذلك مفروض علينا.

أدّت العمارة دورًا مهمًا في المشروع الاستعماري، فهي موجودة في كل مكان. هذا هو محور عمل المعماري المصري البارز حسن فتحي الذي كتب "عمارة الفقراء: تجربة في ريف مصر" (1973). يروي فتحي في هذا الكتاب قصة قرية القرنة الجديدة التي كُلف بنائها في صعيد مصر والمقاومة التي شهدها. يقول فتحي إنه لا يمكن إنشاء المباني للمعماريين، بل يجب أن تبنى للناس. لذا يجب بناء منشآت عمرانية تأخذ بيئتهم المباشرة في الاعتبار. على سبيل المثال، لا يمكننا البناء بالزجاج والإسمنت في أماكن مثل مصر أو الصعيد، بل يجب التفكير في الخصائص المادية للموقع وبيئته والأشجار المتوطنة فيه ومحيطه الطبيعي وتاريخه المعماري. وها نحن لا نزال في انتظار أن يحصل ذلك. كتب رون إيغلاش كتابًا في عام 1999 بعنوان :African Fractals (الجزيئيات Modern Computing and Indigenous Design الإفريقية: الحوسبة الحديثة والتصميم المحلي)، تحدث فيه عن كيفية اعتماد بعض البلدان الإفريقية عمارة ذات تشكيلات جزيئية. ويعطي أمثلة على ذلك من مواقع عمرانية عدة في الكاميرون: مثلًا، تتطلب مقابلة الملك اجتياز قاعات دائرية على نسق تلك التي سبق أن وصفتها وما إلى هنالك. وفي المقابل، أسهم المشروع الاستعماري في تشكيل الفضاءات المعمارية على نحو مغاير. باتت لدينا تلك الخطوط الممتدة من الشمال إلى الجنوب ومن الشرق إلى الغرب. أضاع الناس وجهتهم. من هنا تصبح إعادة التفكير في الفضاء وماهيته جزءًا من عملية الاستعادة. تمثل هذه المشاريع في رأيي خطوةً إلى الأمام في مسار طويل نحو هدفنا.

في ألمانيا، أسفر التوحيد عن إحكام سيطرة الجزء الغربي الأكبر حجمًا والأقوى اقتصاديًا على الجزء الشرقي. قلة من الباحثين/ات كتبوا/ن عن هذا التحول من منظور كونه مشروعًا استعماريًا، حيث يتمظهر المحو كإحدى تبعات هذا النوع من المشاريع الاستعمارية. فهي تمحو أسماء الشوارع فينشأ الناس بلا اتجاهاتٍ وبلا قدرة على تحديدها أو الاستدلال عليها. تلك هي وظيفة الاستعمار، ولهذا السبب كان هدم قصر الجمهورية. زعموا أن المبنى يحتوي على الأسبستوس وإلى ما هنالك. في الواقع كنت قد عملتُ في ذلك المبنى أثناء سنوات دراستي بالتزامن مع البدء بإزالته. كنت أساعد في إزالة الأسبستوس مقابل أجر يغطي تكاليف دراستي. لهذا السبب لدي علاقة خاصة مع ذلك المبنى. هدموه وشيّدوا مكانه بناءً بواجهة قصر بروسي في وسط برلين. هذه هي الطريقة التي أعادوا بها تكريس تلك السلطة.

ع. س.

تستحضر النقاط التي تثيرها في ذهني التاريخ المديني للمغرب. فمراكش التي عملنا فيها معًا على بينالي مراكش عام 2014 هي مدينة تتأرجح بين مركزين: الأول هو المدينة القديمة ونطلق عليها المدينة بكامل طرازها المعماري وبأحيائها الملتفّة، والثاني هو الجليز ويُعدّ القسم الحديث من المدينة بأبنيته وشوارعه المتعامدة، وقد بُني إبان الاستعمار الفرنسي. يرطن رواد الجليز بالفرنسية مشرئبين بأعناقهم وأنوفهم نحو أوروبا. أما في المدينة فيستشعر الناس تماشيهم مع جذور مراكش الإفريقية أكثر من أي مكان آخر ويتحدثون باللهجة الدارجة.

ب. س. ب. ن.

نجد في محاولات جماعات السكان الأصليين استرجاع لغاتهم واستعادة معارفهم الأهلية أو المتوطنة في البلدان التي باتت تسمى كندا أو البرازيل على سبيل المثال، نموذجًا للمهمة التي تنتظرنا جميعًا. وكان سكان البرازيل الأصليون حتى بضع سنوات خلت ممنوعين من تسمية أبنائهم بالأسماء التقليدية. لكِ أن تخيلي نوع العنف والحاجة إلى الدفاع عن ذلك الحق، وهو ما يندرج في إطار الاستعادة والترميم والتأهيل. أفكر أيضًا بشعب المارتينيك الذي ابتدع شتى الأفكار لإعادة النظر في النمط الاستعماري للحديقة، بما في ذلك ابتكار الحديقة الكريول التي تنبذ نظام المزرعة الأحادي وتستبدله بزراعة أنواع مختلفة من النباتات في مكان واحد كي يساعد ويقوّي بعضها البعض الآخر. تلك أمورٌ مهمة. وعلينا وضع هذه الخطوات الصغيرة في سياق الجهود الفاعلة نحو إعادة التأهيل. كيف نتعلم مجددًا احترام

الكوكب؟ كيف نتعلم الاستماع؟ كيف نتعلم التحول من كل ما هو أحادي ومن مفاهيم الكونية والشمولية إلى التعددية؟ هذه هي المشاريع التي تقابلنا. كل خطوة مهمة، وهذا ما نحاول تحقيقه من خلال مشروع الاستعادة، وما نحاول تنميته بشتى الطرق وبسائر الأحاديث والمشاريع.

ع. س.

كل خطوة مهمة. لا يقتصر الأمر على العرض والكتابة والحديث عن الاستعادة والترميم، بل يرتبط بالدرجة الأولى بتطبيق هذه المفاهيم على أفعالنا ونواحي حياتنا اليومية. سأتعهد بذلك وسأكثر من الكلام باللهجة الدارجة مع أطفالي حتى أعلّمهم لغة أجدادهم. هذا أحد الأمور التي يمكننا القيام بها، ها أنت تشجعني على العودة إلى الانخراط في هذا المشروع.

وكما أشرتَ، إنها ليست سوى نقطة البداية. كما أن من أبرز أوجه هذا السجال سؤال من يعبّر عنه ومن أي موقع. تشتمل هذه المشاريع على مختبرات موزعة في شتى أنحاء العالم تهدف إلى لامركزة الحديث حول الاستعادة. أبتسمُ إذ تحضُرني كلمة "لامركزة" في نص كنت قد نشرتَه قبل عدة سنوات في كتالوغ معرض Carrefour/Meeting Point (تقاطع/ملتقى) في غاليري معهد العلاقات الخارجية (IFA) ببرلين عام 2015 بعنوان On the Construction of Liminality: Navigating the Heres and Elsewheres (حول إنشاء الحدّية: التنقل بين الهُنا والهُناك). وكانت وجهة نظرك في ذاك النص أن ما من لامركزة، على اعتبار أن لا وجود لمركز واحد من الأساس. يخيل إلينا من موقعنا أننا في المركز، ولكننا لسنا كذلك. وما المطلوب منا سوى أن نفتح أعيننا لرؤية ما يحدث بالتوازي في كل مكان.

ب. س. ب. ن.

بلا شك. كتبت مجلة Chimurenga Chronic في أحد أعدادها أن الصحراء الكبرى ليست حاجزًا بل تقاطع طرق. وقد أنجزنا بفضلكِ مشروع Ultrasanity: On Madness, Sanitation, Antipsychiatry and Resistance (فرط الصواب: عن الجنون والتدابير الصحية ومعارضة الطب النفسي والمقاومة) ضمن مهرجان كناوة في الصويرة عام 2019. يمثل ذاك المهرجان محطة مهمة، لأنه يُظهر تلك الروابط العميقة. أذكر أنني بينما كنت في طريقي إلى الصويرة طلبت من السائق أن يتوقف أمام محل مذهل يبيع السجاد. دخلتُ إلى المحل لأنني كنث معجبًا بالسجاد المعروض، وهذه قصة أردّدها دائمًا لروعتها. كانت السجاجيد المعروضة على الطراز البربري. سألتُ صاحب المحل

عن معانيها فقال: "يا أخي، أرجوك أن تتوقف عن سؤالي لأنني لا أعرف. إن كنت حقًا ترغب في المعرفة فعليك الذهاب للقاء النساء البربر. هن مكتبتنا وقاموسنا". قلتُ في نفسي: "وجدتُها". علينا أن نجد أولئك النساء إن كنا نسعى إلى إعادة التفكير في كيفية إيجاد المعرفة وفي ترميم ما تهدم منها أو فُقد. علينا أن نخاطبهن. وعليهن أن يطلعننا – البعض منا على الأقل - على الأسرار التي تكتنزها تلك السجاجيد. فالسجادة الواحدة كتابٌ كامل، كتابٌ فلسفي. هنالك تكمن القصة وتُختزن المعرفة ويجب أن نكون قادرين على تلقّي تلك المعرفة وتفكيكها. ونحن في أشدّ الحاجة إلى إدراك قيمة هذا الفعل، ومن أجل ذلك نحتاج إلى إعادة التأهيل. نحتاج إلى استرداد كرامتنا كي نفهم. هكذا نجد المعرفة. ذاك هو أرشيفنا إجابةً عن سؤالك الأول. هنالك تتمركز الإبستيمات والإبيستمولوجيات.

ع. س.

أهملنا هذا الجانب طويلًا، ولكنه مساحةٌ للانتماء، وعلينا أن نعيد التفكير في أهمية هذه المساحة. إذًا فهنالك مغامرةٌ جديدةٌ تنتظرنا: أن نرجع إلى المغرب للقاء أولئك النساء والاستماع إلى قصصهن التي يرغبن في مشاركتها معنا.

حقوق دنيوية

ينبغي أن نفهم الفن كمجموعةٍ من الأنشطة التي تنشد بناء العوالم والتي لا يجب أن تقتصر على الخلق المحض للقطع الفنية. فتلك الأنشطة هي ما يحدد موقع البشر في عالم مشترك، وهي ما يكرس حقوقهم في هذا العالم. في هذه الحالات الثلاث – الإنتاج الفني المناهض للاستعمار عبر استخدام الأشكال المنحوتة كطريقةٍ لحماية النسيج الاجتماعي العابر للأجيال ممّا يتهدده؛ والفوتوغرافيا، لا كعلاقةٍ خاصةٍ بين المصوِر وموضوع الصورة، بل كممارسةٍ مشتركةٍ بين عوامّ الناس؛ وفن إظهار البعض وإخفاء البعض الآخر من التفاصيل – حاولت تبيان أن النهب الاستعماري لـ"أفضل العيّنات المختارة" من فنون الشعوب الأصلية لا ينفصل عن تدمير الأطر السياسية والثقافية لهذه الشعوب من خلال دمجهم قسريًا في أنظمة سياسية تحكمهم استنادًا إلى تمايزهم، كما أنه لا ينفصل عن مأسسة الفن كمجالٍ خاصٍ من النشاط الإنساني متاحٍ للبعض وممنوعٍ على البعض الآخر.

كان تمزيق القوى الاستعمارية للعوالم المختلفة أساسيًّا لتمدد رأس المال. فالترابط الداخلي للعوالم التي أتت منها هذه القطع الفنية، كان عائقًا في وجه الحركة الدائبة لتحويل كل شيء إلى سلعٍ تُباع وتُشترى بثمن. في مجتمعات الصنّاع (-fabri communi ties)، حل الآن التبادل العالمي للسلع والفن العالمي محل المعارف التي امتلكها أفراد المجتمع المحلي سابقًا دون الحاجة إلى وساطة الخبراء الذين كان ظهورهم في واقع الحال مؤذنًا بتحويل الصنّاع إلى عمال وتحويل عالمهم إلى احتياطي من المواد الخام. يتشكل عمل هؤلاء الخبراء من درجاتٍ مختلفة من معالجة البيانات المبنية على التغافل البنيوي لمكان العمل ولمجتمعات العمال وللبيئة التي تُستخرج منها المواد الخام. بعبارةٍ أخرى، كلما كان لزامًا على المرء إثبات خبرته، كان لزامًا عليه الانفصال أكثر عن العالم الذي يعيش فيه. لا يمكن اختزال هذه الخسارة الفادحة للمعرفة عن العالم وللمهارات

دار فيرسو للنشر. جميع الحقوق محفوظة 2019.

مُقتطف من أزولاي، أرييلّا عائشة،
Potential History: Unlearning Imperialism
(تاريخ مُحتَمل: التحرر من المعرفة الإمبريالية)،
الفصل 2، فيرسو 2019.

اللازمة لحمايته في بيانات تخضع للجمع والدراسة والقياس باستخدام أدوات ومعايير وتدابير وضعتها الإمبريالية. ففي ظل الإمبريالية لا فرق بين تدمير العالم والتغافل عنه.

على مر الزمن، تمرّس مرتادو المتاحف، والذين يُحتفى بهم كأشخاص على درجةٍ من الثقافة والوعي، على تعريف أنفسهم بثقافات الغير واستهلاكها بنهمٍ لطيف؛ نهمٍ يلطّف من جرح العدوان المسلّح الذي "فتح" ثقافات متنوعة وسلب منها ما تملكه من قطع فنية. يجب أن يظل العنف المتواصل المبذول لتأمين هذه القطع الفنية محصورًا بالهوامش، بحيث لا يمكن لأفعال كتلك التي قامت بها شخصية كيلمونغر في فيلم "نمر الأسود" أن تتخطى حدود الخيال السينمائي. تحويل واجهة العرض وقاعدة التمثال والحوائط البيضاء السميكة وأنظمة الإنذار والحراس المسلحين كمساحةٍ طبيعيةٍ لعرض الحيوات المنهوبة هي مسألةٌ متوقفةٌ على القيمة السوقية المجردة لهذه القطع الفنية. كمرتادين للمتاحف، يُتوقع منا إدراك القيمة الفريدة لتلك القطع المنهوبة والمشاركة بالتبعية في استدارها، وكأن صانعها الأصلي غير قادر على الإتيان بالمزيد منها، أو كأن كل ما يصنعه الآن هو محض تذكارات ليس لها قيمة تُذكر بجانب هذه القطعة الأصلية.

ضمن هذا الإطار، لا يمكن رد العنف الإمبريالي والواقع الذي خلّفه، إلا من خلال استعادة هذه القطع "القيّمة". فلا يمكن رؤية استعادة هذه القطع، وإن كانت بعشرات الآلاف، كغايةٍ لإصلاح ما أتلفه النهب الاستعماري للعالم. ولا يمكن للتفاوض بشأن هذه الاستعادة أن يُعهد لمدراء المتاحف الذين دأبوا تاريخيًّا على تمثيل الدولة ورأس المال عوضًا عن تمثيل المجتمعات التي وقفت في وجه سلطة الاثنين[1]. وصف أخيل مبيمي المبادرة التي أطلقتها المتاحف الفرنسية لإعادة القطع الفنية المنهوبة لمَواطنها الأصلية بأنها أبويةٌ ومنصبةٌ على الجانب القانوني. أولًا، جاءت المبادرة من دون تفسيرٍ واضح؛ ثانيًا، لم يكن امتعاض الجانب الإفريقي ورفضه الصفقة المقترحة احتمالًا واردًا من وجهة نظر الجانب الفرنسي. هذا الفقد، كما يصر مبيمي، لا يتعلق بالقطع الفنية المنهوبة نفسها بقدر ما يتعلق بالعوالم التي كانت هذه القطع تسكنها. عوضًا عن السعي إلى العدالة والإقرار بالحقيقة وإصلاح ما خربه الاستعمار، يسعى الغرب، كما يوضح مبيمي، إلى "التخلص منا نحن الأجانب وإعادة قطعنا الفنية إلينا هكذا دون تفسير. وكأن الغرب يودّ لو يقول أخيرًا "الآن وقد أصلحنا الضرر، ليس هناك ما ندين به لكم". يسأل مبيمي، ما الذي سيحدث إن "تجرأ الأفارقة ورفضوا العرض؟"[2]. هناك أسباب توجب رفض الشروط المفروضة أحاديًّا من الغرب، إلا أن هذه الأسباب لا ترمي بالضرورة إلى نفس النتائج التي يتوقع مبيمي أن تترتب على هذا الرفض – أي أنها لا ترمي إلى تحول القطع الفنية نفسها:

إلى إثباتاتٍ دامغة على الجريمة التي ارتكبها الغرب، والتي يرفض الاعتراف بمسؤوليته عنها. هل سنطلب منهم العيش إلى الأبد مع ما أخذوه وتقمّص وتقمّص صورة قايين إلى النهاية[3]؟

لا تُعد هذه الإثباتات نتيجةً مترتبةً على رفضٍ محتملٍ في المستقبل للعرض الفرنسي، بل هي جزءٌ من أنطولوجيا النهب الاستعماري عمومًا. فهذه القطع الفنية هي إثباتات أبدية على الجريمة، وصورة قايين هي قدر القاتل بغض النظر عن هذا الرفض. إن كان لهؤلاء أن يلعبوا دورًا في عملية إصلاح العالم، لا بد لجمهور هذه المتاحف أن يتوقف عن اعتبار هذه الأعمال الفنية ملكًا لتلك المتاحف والتوقف عن اعتبار مدراء ومجالس أمناء تلك المتاحف كممثلين عنهم في هذا التحول من النهب الاستعماري إلى مآلات ما بعده.

1 ترى مجموعة (إم تي إل) الأعمال المناهضة لمعارض وقرارات المتاحف من جملة ما تعتبره "أزمة تعصف بالمؤسسات الثقافية الكبرى وتهدد شرعيتها بين الجماهير التي تدّعي تلك المؤسسات العمل من أجلها، وبين العمال الثقافيين الذين تعتمد تلك المؤسسات على عملهم". إم تي إل، 2018، ص 193.

2 Achille Mbembe, "À propos de la restitution des artefacts africains conservés dans les musées d'Occident," AOC, May 10, 2018, 9, aoc.media

3 المرجع نفسه.

لا بد أن تسبق معارضة الشعوب المحلية لاستخراج ثرواتها المادية أي دعوات لاستعادة الأعمال الفنية المنهوبة. كمرتادين للمتاحف لا يمكننا تجاهل الدعوات التي تنادي: لا تطلق النـار؛ لا تدمـر، أو ربمـا، اقتلنـي إن شـئت. لا يمكننـا السـكوت عـن دور الاسـتعمار في اختـزال صناعة الفن إلى مجرد إنتاج أشياء ذات قيمة متحفية وسوقية، والتي إن جُرّدت من سياقها، فقدت معناهـا، بحيـث يصبـح العمـل الفنـي محـض عمـل فنـي. لا بـد أن نـرى هـذه القطع الفنيـة كآثـارٍ لعوالـم محطمـة لهـا حقـوق يمكـن تحقيقهـا في وجـود هـؤلاء الذيـن انتفـت عنهـم تلك الحقـوق أو ورثتهم.

بعد معركة ووترلو، تعهد دوق ويلنغتون بما وصفته عالمة الآثار مرغريت م. مايلـز "بأول عمليةٍ حربيةٍ لاستعادة أعمالٍ فنيةٍ على نطاقٍ واسع، وهي حدثٌ لا مثيل لـه في أي مكان في العالـم"[4]. في خطاب مفتوح إلـى لـورد كاسـلراي، شـرح دوق ويلنغتـون "ضـرورة اسـتعادة الأعمـال الفنيـة التـي نهبتهـا جيـوش نابليـون مـن الـدول الأوروبيـة"[5]. وفي مواجهـة موقف القـوى المنتصـرة التي رأت في التحـف المنهوبة غنيمة حرب، كان ويلنغتـون مـن أنصار إعـادة تلك الأعمـال إلى "مهدهـا القديـم". ورغـم مـا تبـدو عليـه الفكـرة مـن وجاهـة، إلا أن تطبيقهـا اقتصـر على أوروبا دون غيرها: "جاوبت [على عرض المندوب الفرنسي] بأنني أقـف إلى جانـب كل شـعوب أوروبـا، وسـأطالب بحصـول الشـعوب الأوروبيـة كافة على مـا حصلـت عليـه بروسـيا"[6]. يمكـن ربـط مسـاعي ويلنغتـون بصعـود مفهـوم "الملكيـة الثقافيـة" قبـل بضعـة عقـود مـن هـذه الواقعـة، وهـو المفهـوم الـذي حـلّ محـل مفهـوم آخـر عـن "الفـن كغنيمـة حـرب" بحسـب مايلـز. ارتبـط صعـود الملكيـة الثقافيـة "كماهيـةٍ خاصـةٍ تجب حمايتها في حالتـي الحـرب والسـلم"، بالتغيـر في "الذهنيـة القانونيـة والشـعور العـام حيـال مفهـوم الجرم الأخلاقـي"[7]. مـا يغيـب بشـكلٍ كامـلٍ عـن حديـث مايلـز لا يقتصـر على المركزيـة الأوروبيـة لهـذا الخطـاب، بـل يتخطـاه إلى الارتبـاط الوثيـق بيـن نشـأة هـذا المفهـوم والنهـب المُمَأسِس للثقافـة والثـروات الماديـة الـذي مارسـه الأوروبيـون ضـد غيرهم من الشـعوب. فبمـوازاة هـذا الخطـاب الأخلاقـي لحمايـة الملكيـة الثقافيـة، امتهـن الأوروبيـون سـرقة ونهـب وخصخصـة الثقافـات الماديـة للشـعوب الأخـرى. وللمفارقـة، توصـف اليـوم المؤسسـات القائمـة على رعايـة هـذه الثقافـات التـي تمـت خصخصتهـا في الماضـي بالمؤسسـات "العامـة" كالمتاحف والمكتبـات والأرشـيفات التـي تتألـف محتوياتهـا ممـا نُهب وجُلب مـن حـول العالـم ومـن ثم عولج وأتيح (مجدّدًا) للعمـوم.

عندمـا يكون العنف هـو السـمة التي يتشـارك بها الناس عيشـهم، يصبح العنف سـمة كل مشـترك. بوسـعنا إنكار ذلـك أو إسـكاته أو احتـواؤه لبعـض الوقـت، ولكـن لا يمكننـا طمسـه إلى الأبد تحت غطاء خطابٍ ظاهره تقدمي وباطنه داعم للإمبريالية. يتوقف تحـوّل تلك المؤسسـات وإصلاحهـا بشـكل أساسـي على ضـرورة الإقرار بالنهب الاسـتعماري كبنيـةٍ تحتيةٍ لهـا وكمصـدرٍ لأشـكال الفن المختلفـة التي تنتجها. لـذا يجب ألا تقتصـر إعـادة المنهوبات على القطـع الفنيـة وحسـب، بـل يجـب أيضًـا أن تشـمل الممارسـات المرتبطـة بهـذه القطـع؛ الممارسـات التـي يجـب أن تُعـاد إلى كنـف أولئـك الذيـن شُـلبت هـذه القطـع مـن بيـن أيديهم، والذيـن مُنعوا لاحقًـا مـن الوصـول إليهـا.

بحلـول أواخـر القـرن الثامـن عشـر كان الاسـتعمار قـد قضـى على آلافٍ مـن أشـكال العيـش المشـاعية التـي تمحـورت حـول تقاليـد متنوعـة تطـورت على مـر القـرون. أصبـح الدمـار

Margaret M. Miles, *Art as Plunder:* *The Ancient Origins of Debate about* *Cultural Property*, Cambridge: Cambridge University Press, 2008, 11 — 4

المرجع نفسه، ص. 370. — 5

الخطابات ملحقة بالمرجع نفسه، ص. 373. — 6

المرجع نفسه، ص. 286-285. — 7

الآن جزءًا من المشاع العالمي؛ جزءًا مما يتشارك فيه الناس فعليًا حول العالم. يمكن للكثيرين إنكار هذا العنف بقدر ما يؤشر تنوع معاني الدمار على الاختلاف بين ما يظنه الناس مشاعًا وما يتشاركونه بالفعل.

وعليه، في اللحظة نفسها التي أصبح فيها تدمير ثقافات الغير أمرًا واقعًا، كان مفهوم حماية المشاعات، والتي أصبحت "الملكية الثقافية" جزءًا رئيسيًا منها، قد تبلور كجزءٍ لا يتجزأ من "قانون الأمم". في كتابه قانون الأمم The Law of Nations والمنشور عام 1758، يميز إمير دي فاتيل بين "ما تمتلكه الأمة من أشياء داخل الدولة" ويؤكد أن "هنالك من الأشياء ما لا يمكن اقتناؤه بالطبيعة، ومنها ما لا يطالب أحد بملكيته، وهذه هي المشاعات"[8]. إذا ما قرأنا هذه الكلمات بعيدًا عن سياق الدمار الإمبريالي، لتصورنا أن استثناء بعض الأمور من نطاق الملكية الفردية ربما كان نابعًا من كبح التوسع الإمبريالي والدفاع عن المشاعات – والتي هي كل مشترك لا يمكن امتلاكه. إلا أنه وفي ضوء الدمار الرهيب الذي جلبه قانون الأمم الاستعمارية، يبدو حديث دي فاتيل العقيم وحياديته الكاذبة كناطق بلسان الاستحواذ الإمبريالي على الأرض، وكأنها بلا شعب – وكأنها تلك الأرض التي "لا يطالب بملكيتها أحد،" وهو ما "يسوّغ للأمم استملاك الأرض"[9]. لا يأتي حديث دي فاتيل بمعرض السجال ولا يمثل صرخةً للثورة على الإمبريالية أو نقدًا لوضع المشاعات أو مطالبةً بإعادة المشاعات إلى ما كانت عليه أو ما يجب أن تكون عليه. إن ترويج القوى الاستعمارية لهذا الخطاب الحيادي هو في واقع الحال ضربٌ للمشاعات وعرضٌ من أعراض السقم الإمبريالي. هذا الشكل من الإنكار هو تحديدًا ما يُطلب من الجمهور إعادة إنتاجه في علاقتهم مع آثار الماضي المحفوظة في مؤسسات تتعهد بحمايتها كالأرشيفات والمتاحف. يأتي حديث دي فاتيل عن المشاعات باللسان المؤسسي المحايد للإمبريالية: بلهجةٍ تُعلي النزعة العالمية المتسامية. ازدهر الحديث بهذه اللهجة أواخر القرن الثامن عشر بالتزامن مع الانتشار العالمي لعددٍ من المشاريع الإمبريالية الفجّة التي قامت تارةً على استحواذ قلةٍ من الشعوب وتارةً أخرى على مصادرتها لثروات كل من عداها. استعمل هذه اللغة ونقحها فلاسفةٌ عملوا كرجال دولة ودبلوماسيين، كما استعملها رجال دولة عملوا كفلاسفة وخبراء في القانون الدولي، بغرض مفهمة ومأسسة هذا العنف. ربما يفسر ذلك جزئيًا كيف يمكن لاتفاقيةٍ تستهدف حماية المشاعات بالأساس أن تقرن دوافع تدمير التراث الإنساني بعملية إنقاذه: "إذا كان لا بد أن يشمل الدمار بلدًا ما لأي سببٍ كان، ينبغي تجنيب هذه البنايات التي هي شرفٌ للجنس البشري والتي ليس من شأنها أن تسهم في منعة العدو، كدور العبادة والمقابر والبنايات العامة وكل الصروح ذات القيمة الجمالية المميزة"[10]. بين كتاب دي فاتيل واليوم، أمثلة لا حصر لها على الاستخدام الحرفي لهذا المنطق معكوسًا، أي من قِبل القوى الإمبريالية التي دمرت جانبًا واسعًا من الأطر الاجتماعية والثقافية والمادية للمجتمعات المحلية في مسعاها لإنقاذ القطع الفنية "العظيمة" التي كانت جزءًا من نسيج هذه المجتمعات.

يستعيض الخطاب السائد حول الملكية الثقافية، من جهة تركيزه على الروائع الفنية الفريدة، عن كفّ الضرر ورأب ما أنتجه من مآسٍ بإعادة القطع الفنية فحسب. في العام 2004 أصدر ثمانية عشر من مدراء المتاحف الهامة في الولايات المتحدة وأوروبا بيانًا لا يشجب إعادة القطع الفنية فحسب، بل يسعى لغلق باب النقاش حول إعادتها من الأساس:

8   Emer de Vattel, *The Law of Nations—Or, Principles of the Law of Nature, Applied to the Conduct and Affairs of Nations and Sovereigns, with Three Early Essays on the Origin and Nature of Natural Law and on Luxury*, Indianapolis: Liberty Fund, 2008, 228

9   المرجع نفسه.

10   المرجع نفسه، ص. 293.

11   "Declaration on the Importance and Values of Universal Museums," 2002, Archives, archives.icom.museum

بمرور الوقت، أصبحت القطع الفنية التي تم الاستحواذ عليها – سواء عبر الشراء أو التبرع أو الاجتزاء – جزءًا من مجموعات المتاحف التي اعتنت بها وبالتبعية جزءًا من تراث الأمم التي تحتضنها[11].

لا عجب في أن هذه المتاحف ومدراءها ومجالس أمنائها يستعملون مصطلح "الاستبقاء" في مقابل المطالبات الرامية لاستعادة القطع الفنية. ولا نغفل هنا الغاية غير البريئة من استعمال صيغة الاستفعال والتي تود لو تفرض شكلًا من التماثل مع الطرف الآخر المطالب بـ"الاستعادة". عوضًا عن التجاوب بجدية مع مطالبات الاستعادة، يمثل هذا الرد السطحي محاولةً لطمس هذه المطالبات سريعًا ومعاودة العمل المعتاد، وكأن كل أسباب المطالبة باستعادة القطع الفنية لا ينبغي أن تؤثر على العمل المتحفي. في الحالتين، تشير صيغة الاستفعال إلى لحظةٍ سابقة وتثبت موقفًا فيها: تطلب المتاحف استبقاء القطع الفنية، التي هي بالفعل في حوزتها، بينما يحاول المطالبون باستعادة هذه القطع انتزاع اعتراف بملكيتهم المسبقة لهذه القطع.

لا تختلف مساعي الفريقين من حيث الغاية النهائية وحسب – أحقية امتلاك القطع الفنية – بل أيضًا من حيث علاقة كل منهما مع العنف. فأنصار الاستبقاء يفصلون القطع الفنية عن العنف الذي سمح بالاستحواذ عليها وعن الآثار المستمرة للعنف الناتج عن استبقائها، بينما يناهض أنصار الاستعادة الأوضاع التي أنتجها العنف الإمبريالي سعيًا وراء إعادة القطع إلى ملكيتهم. يتم تأطير النزاع إذًا كنزاعٍ بين فريقين يطالبان بأحقية امتلاك شيءٍ ما. إلا أن النقاش حول ما ينبغي فعله بعد قرون من العنف الإمبريالي لا يمكن أن يتم اختصاره بإعادة بعض الروائع الفنية لأصحابها الأصليين، أو بموجب تقسيم عمل لا يزال يرمي مسؤولية إصلاح مظالم العنف الاستعماري وآثاره طويلة الأمد على عاتق ضحاياه المباشرين. يقول روبنسون "ليس من مجتمع آخر يمكن أن يكون أكثر اهتمامًا بحل مشاكلنا أكثر منا"[12].

حرروا رينتي – قلب الأساس الإمبريالي للفوتوغرافيا

ينبغي أن تكون الدعوى القضائية التي قدمتها تمارا لانير ضد جامعة هارفرد ومتحف بيبودي جديرة باهتمامنا جميعًا. فالفوتوغرافيا هي صنوّ الإمبريالية، ومنذ البداية كان تشكّلها ومأسستها جوهريًا لتكريس وتسهيل إعادة إنتاج الحقوق الإمبريالية المنتزعة والمحازة عبر تقنيات الاستخراج، والتي جعلت عبر عملها على نطاق واسع الموافقة الرضائية والتفاهم المتبادل بين المصور وموضوع الصورة أمرًا فائضًا على وظيفة التقنية نفسها. بعبارةٍ أخرى، لكي تنتشر الفوتوغرافيا حول العالم، كان لا بد من استبقاء تدخل الناس في عملها – هؤلاء الناس الذين لا يمكن للفوتوغرافيا أن تعمل دون وجودهم وعملهم وموافقتهم – عند الحد الأدنى. هذا النفي لحق الأفراد في المشاركة الفعالة في كونهم موضوعًا للتصوير (ناهيك عن الموافقة الرضائية على ذلك) ليس جزءًا من أنطولوجيا التصوير الفوتوغرافي، ولكنه نتاج المبدأ الاستخراجي نفسه والذي هو أساسي لمأسسة الفوتوغرافيا.

قد يقول البعض إن عملية تصوير الأشخاص عمومًا – لا الأشخاص المستعبدين كما في حالة رينتي تايلور على وجه الخصوص – لا تنطوي دائمًا على الحصول المسبق على موافقتهم. وهذا صحيح إذا اقتصرت نظرتنا على لحظة التقاط الصورة. لكن إذا

Randall Robinson, *The Debt: What America Owes to Blacks*, New York: Penguin, 2001, 205   12

ما تركنا ستوديو التصوير ونظرنا إلى الفوتوغرافيا كممارسةٍ إمبريالية لاستخراج موارد العالم منذ منتصف القرن التاسع عشر، سنلحظ بوضوح دور الفوتوغرافيا في التقسيم العنصري للعمل ومراكمة الثروة البصرية من أجل الربح. استنزفت الفوتوغرافيا، شأنها شأن التقنيات الإمبريالة الأخرى، المجتمعات الأصلية من ثرواتها البصرية دون أن تدفع لهم شيئًا بالمقابل. بالمقابل احتفظ أفراد المجتمعات الإمبريالية بإمكانية التعبير عن موافقتهم أو رفضهم كما احتفظوا بحقهم في الدفاع عن ذلك في كثير من مجالات الحياة العامة، وكذلك بحقهم في تشكيل العالم الذي يصوِّرون فيه، حيث يصوِّرون الآخرين من دون موافقتهم بالضرورة. فضلًا عن ذلك، تمتع هؤلاء بسلطة تجريد الآخرين من حقوقهم، وهو تجريد لم تكن الفوتوغرافيا مساحة لإظهاره وحسب، بل وتكريسه أيضًا. التمتع بهذه الصلاحيات هو أحد الأوجه التي أعرّف بها الحقوق الإمبريالية.

لنتذكر أن الفوتوغرافيا هي الوسيط الذي يرسخ صورة الشعوب الأكثر عرضة للتصوير كشعوب مستلبة، كما أنها الوسيط الذي يسمح للمستعمر بالنظر إلى آلام هذه الشعوب من موقع الاستمتاع أو التعاطف. إن تقسيم العمل على هذه الشاكلة والأوضاع التي تسمح بإعادة إنتاجه، هي تحديدًا ما تحاول دعوى لانير القضائية دحضه وتغييره، تقول: "أُلغيت العبودية قبل 156 عامًا، لكن رينتي وديليا بقيا عبدَين في كامبردج، ماساشوستس. ظلت صورهما كما جسماها خاضعةً لتحكم واستغلال الأقوى، وسُلبت منهما هويتاهما العائليتان".

عندما يتحدث من سُلبوا حقهم في التعبير عن رأيهم في أي من مسائل الحياة (ليس فقط في تصويرهم)، تفقد الفوتوغرافيا شرعيتها كممارسة مؤسسية تقوم بشكل أساسي على استعبادهم. منعُ هؤلاء من حقهم في التعبير – سواءً هم شخصيًا أو ذووهم – هو كما تقول لانير، تعدٍّ على المادة الثالثة عشرة من الدستور الأميركي التي "تمنع، وتحضّ على تعويض، حالات العبودية وما اتصل بها من ممارسات". تقع مذكرة الدعوى القضائية على ذكر عددٍ من هذه الحالات التي منها "حق عقد وإنفاذ التعاقدات". يمكن للفوتوغرافيا لعب دور أساسيٍ في إلغاء العبودية من زاوية الإصلاح والترميم. ولكي يحدث ذلك، يجدر بنا ألا ننظر فقط بعين اللهفة – أو الأمل – إلى النظام القانوني، بل أن نستلهم دعوى لانير في تقويض الأسس الإمبريالية التي قامت عليها الفوتوغرافيا. يجب أن ننكر (أو نتبرأ من كوننا مصورين أو نتخلى عن أي دور مؤسسي) الحقوق الحصرية التي لم تكن لتنشأ إلا على حساب الآخرين. يجب أن نتيح هذه الثروات المنهوبة للمجتمعات التي حُرمت منها وأن نتعلم كيف يتعامل أفرادها مع كل حالة على حدة كأساس للإصلاح والترميم.

عن المشاعات العنيفة

العنف الإمبريالي هو مشاعنا المشترك، هو شكل تواجدنا معًا. صار العنف في صورته المؤسسية موجودًا في كل مكان بحيث أصبح هو المورد الأكثر تشاركًا بيننا. على عكس الأرض والماء والهواء التي يُعدّ تبديدها ضررًا فاجعًا، ليس من ضرورة للحفاظ على العنف أو العناية بأسبابه، لكن هناك ضرورة بالمقابل للإقرار باشتراكنا جميعًا فيه وبكونه مشكلتنا المشتركة التي يجب أن نعمل على كبحها وإصلاحها. بعد قرون من الإمبريالية، أصبح هذا العنف شكل مشاعنا المشترك. عوضًا عن تصورنا للمشاع كمقابل حصري للفضاءات المخصخصة أو كمساحة أتت عليها الرأسمالية والإمبريالية ويجب استعادتها[13]، أزعم أن

13 "إن التضامن الإنساني كما يعبر عنه شعار 'الكل من أجل الفرد والفرد من أجل الكل' هو أساس المشاعية": Peter Linebaugh, *Stop, Thief!: The Commons, Enclosures, and Resistance*, Oakland, CA: PM Press, 2014, 13

المشاعات ليست طريقة بين طرق عدّة لتشارك الحياة، بل هي الوضع المادي الأوضح لذلك. المشاع هو نتاج لتشارك الناس حتى وإن كانوا خصومًا.

ربما يكون سؤال إصلاح آثار العنف أكثر إلحاحًا بالنسبة لضحاياه المباشرين. ولمّا كان هذا العنف هو ما يتشارك فيه الجناة والضحايا، لا يسع أيًّا منهم إعفاء نفسه من مسؤولية إصلاح آثاره. فليس من عالم منفصل يعيش فيه الضحايا وحدهم، وما وقع بحقهم هو جزء من مشاعنا جميعًا. لا يُفترض في العنف أن يعكس مقاصد مرتكبيه. بل إن أثر العنف دائمًا ما يمتد إلى ما هو أكثر من الأجسام والأشياء التي يستهدفها. لذلك، عوضًا عن الحركة إلى الأمام، يتطلب إصلاح آثار العنف العودة إلى الوراء؛ إلى منطلقات العنف ومقاصده وإعادة تخيّلها مع يقين بأننا لا نزال نعيش تبعات ذلك العنف.

لا يمكن لقوام خطاب الاستعادة أن يكون هو لغة القانون وعمل المحامين وحدهم. فعل اختلاف تفاصيل الخطاب القانوني بين الدول التي استفادت تاريخيًّا من العبودية، لم يتحول خطاب الاستعادة إلى مشروع مركزي لإعادة تشكيل النظام السياسي والاجتماعي في أي من تلك الدول. يميز القانون البريطاني، على سبيل المثال، بين قانون الاستعادة الذي يتناول حالات "استرجاع المكاسب" وقانون التعويض الذي يتناول حالات "تعويض الخسائر"[14]. المكسب والخسارة بحسب القانون البريطاني ينتميان إلى عالمَين مختلفَين، وكأن تلازم هذين العالمَين ليس أمرًا واقعًا في أغلب الأحيان[15]. في محاولة للإجابة عن عدم صلاحية خطاب الاستعادة في المطالبة بإصلاح الآثار المترتبة على العبودية وما شاكلها من المظالم التاريخية الكبرى، تشرح الباحثة القانونية إميلي شيروين:

تسعى دعوى الإثراء غير المشروع إلى إصلاح الضرر لا عبر إصلاح ما ترتب على الضحية من تبعات، بل عبر تحجيم ثروة الجاني. بعبارةٍ أخرى، يستدعي مفهوم الإثراء غير المشروع قياسًا يلتمس مشاعر الاستياء والرغبة في الثأر لا الرغبة في إحقاق الحق وجبر خواطر أصحابه[16].

وعليه فالقول بإمكانية إصلاح العنف الإمبريالي دون تغيير جذري للعالم الذي صنعته الإمبريالية، ودون إحلال الامتيازات الاستعمارية بطرق أكثر عدلًا لتشارك العالم، هو قول يقوم على افتراض أن هذا العنف لا يطال سوى هامش العالم، وبالتالي يمكن اجتثاثه دون التأثير على العالم نفسه. حتى ضمن حدود الخيال القانوني، إذا قبلنا بالاستعادة كحق يعود لطرف الدفاع في القضية، لا يزال بإمكاننا تفسير هذا الحق بشكل يتجاوز مفاهيم الثأر بين طرفين، كما تفصل شيروين، بحيث يصبح حقًّا في تشارك المشاع.

الاستعادة لا تقتصر بالضرورة على الحق في ملكية الأشياء، بل هي الحق في نصيب من عالم مشترك. سأعود إلى هذه النقطة لاحقًا في الكتاب، لكن سأكتفي الآن بالقول إن امتلاك نصيب من العالم هو ما يضمن للناس (ماديًّا) "الحق في أن يكون لديهم حقوق". فهذا النصيب هو ما دمره الاستعمار، وهو أيضًا ما يلزم استعادته. وقع هذا الدمار مرتين: مرة أولى مع دمار العوالم التي عاش فيها الناس والتي آمنوا فيها على حقهم في أن يكون لديهم حقوق، ومرة ثانية عندما سُلبوا ثمرة عملهم في بناء "العالم الجديد"، فحُرموا من مكان آمن ونصيب فيه، ومُنعوا من حقهم في أن يكون لديهم حقوق[17]. بالإضافة إلى كل ما تعنيه العبودية، فهي أيضًا "400 سنة من الاستثمار من الكدح والدم لمراكمة ما

[14] Peter Birks, *Unjust Enrichment*, Oxford: Oxford University Press, 2005, part 1

[15] مصطلح "استعادة" restitution كما يشير بيركس، "لا يستقيم بشكلٍ تام مع مفهوم التعويض". (المرجع ذاته، ص. 3-4).
عوضًا عن ذلك يقترح بيركس اصطلاحين آخرين هما: الإثراء غير العادل unjust enrichment، والذي هو أحد أبرز دوافع استعادة القطع الفنية، والإعادة الجبرية disgorgement و"الذي رغم افتقاده للتأصيل القانوني إلا أنه يمكن أن يكون أكثر ملاءمة ويسرًا".

[16] Emily Sherwin, "Reparations and Unjust Enrichment," Cornell Law Faculty Publications. Paper 6, 2004, 1,444, scholarship.law.cornell.edu

[17] يصف ستيفن ج. هول إسهام الأميركيين من أصول إفريقية في هذه "اللحظة الواعدة والمفعمة بالأمل من التاريخ الأميركي عقب هزيمة البريطانيين عام 1812 وما راح سدًى من بحثهم عن التقدير والعرفان لإسهامهم في هذا العمل الوطني"؛ Stephen G. Hall, *Faithful Account of the Race: African American Historical Writing in Nineteenth-Century America*, Chapel Hill: The University of North Carolina Press, 2009, 17

تملكه [الولايات المتحدة] من ثروة هائلة"[18] لم يُعترف بها إلى الآن. ما جرى انتزاعه من المستعبَدين من أموال وحقوق تمت مأسسته عبر تجنيس أولئك الذين أُعثرف بنصيبهم من العالم. لذا فالحق في امتلاك نصيب من العالم وحق الجنسية هما حقان يعزز ويبرر أحدهما الآخر. اللغة القانونية الحالية مناسبة لتأطير القانون كأداة محايدة يمكن لأيٍّ كان استعمالها، لذا ليس غريبًا أن يجري استخدامها وإساءة استخدامها المرة تلو الأخرى على يد أولئك الأكثر تمتعًا بالامتيازات.

في هذا الإطار، لا عجب في أن أكبر ما دُفع من تعويضات إلى اليوم كان من نصيب المستفيدين من الاستعمار لا ضحاياه[19]. وأشير هنا بشكل أساسي إلى القضية الشهيرة لـ"ديون الاستقلال" التي أُجبرت هايتي على دفعها لفرنسا بين أعوام 1825 و1947[20]، إلا أنها ليست المثال الوحيد في هذا الشأن. هناك أيضًا قضية ضرائب القطن عام 1915 التي ادّعى فيها المحامي كورنيليوس ج. جونز على الحكومة الفيدرالية للولايات المتحدة لتعويضه عن الضرائب التي حصلتها تلك الأخيرة عن إنتاج القطن بطريق السخرة وهي القضية التي رُدت دفوعها وأُسقطت لأن "محاكم الاستئناف الأميركية لا يُمكن مقاضاتها دون موافقتها"[21]. عجز القانون في هذه الحالات وغيرها عن تحقيق أبسط ما يمكن اعتباره عادلًا – التعويض عن سنوات الاستعباد والسخرة – هو ما بات معروفًا من الضرورة[22]. إلا أنه من المهم أن نؤكد أن هذا العجز لا يتوقف عند حدود القانون. ففي المخيلة الديموقراطية عادةً ما يُنتظر صدور التغيير الجذري عن النظام القانوني. فشل هذا النظام في تحقيق التغيير المنشود لا يتأتى إلا على حساب قدرة الناس على تخيّل ما يمكنهم تحقيقه في ما عداه من دوائر الفعل.

إعلان مدراء المتاحف هو أحد أعراض ذلك، فهو مكتوب بلغة شبه قانونية تعيد تدوير اصطلاحات الملكية والتملك والسلطة التي تشكلت تاريخيًّا بسلاح القوى الإمبريالية وصولًا إلى تقعيدها لاحقًا كلغة قانونية "نظيفة" تجري بشكل اعتيادي على ألسنة الناس. إن التفكير المتعمق في العمل المتحفي ومنهجياته هو تفكير تأخر كثيرًا عن حينه. بل إن أغلب المراجعات التي تتعلق بطرق وضع وشرح وعرض القطع الفنية تظل مراجعات ناقصة إن عجزت عن إصلاح العنف الإمبريالي الذي أتى على أنماط تعددية عديدة لصنع الفن سعيًا نحو فنٍّ متحفيٍّ متسامٍ[23].

على عكس الفرضية الإمبريالية لمدراء المتاحف والتي تقول إن "كل الأعمال الفنية العظيمة هي ميراث مشترك للإنسانية"، أقترح أن "كل الجرائم الإمبريالية هي دون شك ميراث مشترك للإنسانية"[24]. فضلًا عن ذلك، فإن الأعمال الفنية التي تحمل بصمة هذه الجرائم (بطرق أخرى غير التمثيل) إلى جوار عددٍ آخر مع الذكريات (التي يمكن للناس العاديين – غير المتخصصين المتحدرين من المجتمعات التي سُلبت منها هذه القطع الفنية، إعادة إحيائها) يمكنها أن تلعب دورًا محوريًا في تغيير تصورنا عن التغيير وما يمكن أن يبدو عليه. يتطلب ذلك وقفة لكف الحركة الدائبة لعالم الفن وسعيه النهم لاكتشاف ما لم يُعرف أو يُكتشف أو يُسمى أو يُعرض أو يُخلق بعد في صورة كل جديد واستعراضي ومبالغ فيه. إن المواجهة الجادة مع الجرائم الإمبريالية في كل المجالات هي أساسية لهذه الحركة.

Chancellor Williams, *The Destruction of Black Civilization: Great Issues of a Race From 4500 B.C. to 2000 A.D.*, Chicago: Third World Press, 1987, 342 [18]

كان إجبار المهزوم على رد نفقات الحرب أمرًا شائعًا بين القوى الإمبريالية. على سبيل المثال، بعد غزوها مدغشقر عام 1883، أجبرت الحكومة الفرنسية سكان الجزيرة على دفع 10 ملايين فرنك فرنسي لرد كلفة الاحتلال. [19]

للمزيد حول هذه "الإصلاحات" التي اضطرت هايتي إلى تحملها، انظر Hilary McD. Beckles, *Britain's Black Debt—Reparations for Caribbean Slavery and Native Genocide*, Jamaica: University of the West Indies Press, 2013 [20]

للمزيد انظر Robinson, *The Debt*, 207 Mary Frances Berry, *My Face Is Black Is True: Callie House and the Struggle for Ex-Slave Reparations*, New York: Vintage, 2006 [21]

تذكر غرينفيلد أن بيرو مع عدد آخر من دول الكاريبي وأميركا الوسطى كانت قد تقدمت عام 1979 بطلب لدراسة "إمكانية تقديم تعويضات بديلة على شكل مقايضة بقطع أخرى بقيمة مناظرة في الحالات التي يستحيل فيها رد القطع الفنية الأصلية". إلا أن لجنة اليونسكو المختصة خلصت إلى أن هذه الفكرة تنطوي على عدد من المخاطر، وأن التركيز يجب أن يظل على الاتفاقات الثنائية"؛ Jeannette Greenfield, *The Return of Cultural Treasures*, Cambridge: Cambridge University Press, 1989, 226 [22]

يتمحور نقد ثنائية المشغولة الفنية artifact في مواجهة القطعة الفنية object حول الرغبة في إعادة تصنيف بعض القطع ورفعها إلى مصاف الأعمال الفنية عوضًا عن مساءلة الكيفية التي تحول بها نمط معين لإنتاج الفن إلى قانون لتقييم ومعالجة أنماط الإنتاج الفني الأخرى: "في الوقت الذي حظيت فيه الجوانب الزخرفية للمشغولات الكونغولية بالتقدير العام، لم تكن هناك نية لرفع أي من القطع الفنية الإفريقية إلى مصاف الأعمال الفنية في متحف سميثونيان"؛ M. J. Arnoldi, "Where Art and Ethnology Met: The Ward Collection at the Smithsonian," *The Scramble for Art in Central Africa*, eds. Enid Schildkraut and Curtis A. Keim, Cambridge: Cambridge University Press, 1998, 214 [23]

الاقتباس الأول من Neil MacGregor, "Oi, Hands Off Our Marbles," *The Sunday Times*, January 18, 2004, 7 [24]

إصلاح أثر العنف الإمبريالي يعني أيضًا إصلاحًا لأثر الزمان والمكان وسياسات الجسد كأشكال للتجربة المعاشة وكأوضاعٍ مجردةٍ للفهم والإدراك والفعل والحكم. عندما كتب كانط نقدياته الثلاث، كانت عجلة التقدم قد أخذت بالفعل في التحرك ولم يعد من الممكن – بـل وكمـا رأى كانط وكثيـرٌ غيره لـم يعـد من المستحسن أيضًا – إيقافها. كان لا بد أن يتحول إدراك الزمان والمكان إلى متصلية لانهائية وشكل بديهي من الحدس يسبق ويشكل تجربتنا المعاشة حتى يصبح التقدم قابلًا للقياس. لـم يستطع كانط رؤية مـا قضت عليه الإمبريالية من أشكال متنوعة من إدراك الزمن والتنظيم المكاني وسياسات الجسد – أو ربما لـم يكن مهتمًّا برؤية ذلك، أو ربما رآه ولم يرغب بالإقرار به – وهو ما جعل الإمبريالية في نظره وضعًا مفارقًا لكل ما سبقه. لذا لـن نجد في حديثه عن "ما هـو التنوير؟" و"القصور العقلي المفروض ذاتيًّا" و"التجابن" و"التكاسل" أي ذكر للدمـار الـذي طال التقاليد والثقافات المتنوعـة في أوروبا، ناهيك عن خارج أوروبا ("البشر ككل"). يصف كانط الناس كأشخاص تنقصهم الجرأة "لاستخدام ذكائهم الذاتي دون الاتكال على بعضهم البعـض". بنهاية القرن الثامـن عشر كانت مقولات كانط بالفعل تحمل بصمـة العنف الإمبريالـي الـذي صنّف الشعوب حسب مواقعهـم مـن المقيـاس الزمني للتقدم. غير أن دمـار ثقافات كاملة وإفقار وقهر الشعوب عبر تصنيف ثقافاتهم كثقافات متأخرة أو متخلفة لـم يكن يُعدّ مصدرًا ومسبّبًا "للقصور الفكري". يعرض كانط هذه النقيصة بوصفها تعبيرًا عن طبيعة أولئك الذين يمكن للتنوير أن يجعلهم أفضل". لكننا نملك دلائل واضحة على أن الطريـق بات ممهّدًا لكي يسلكه البشـر إلى هذه الوجهة بملء إرادتهم، وأن العقبات في سبيل التنوير الشامل – الـذي يحرّرهم مـن القصور العقلي المفروض ذاتيًّا – لا تنفك تتضاءل"[25].

بعبارة أخرى، وعوضًا عن الإشـارة إلى تدمير الثقافات والتقاليد كجرائم، يعكس كانط الآية ويحـذّر من تناقل العادات والتقاليد عبر الأجيـال والاعتداد بها:

لا يمكن لجيل أن يفرض على الـذي يليه وضعًا يمنعه مـن توسيع مداركه أو تصحيح معارفه، لاسيما في الشـؤون الهامة، أو مـن تحقيـق أي نـوع من التقدّم في سبيل التنوير. فتلك جريمة ضد الطبيعة البشرية التي يرتبط مصيرها تحديدًا بهذا التقدم[26].

شكلّت كتابات كانط العقيدة الفلسفية لتدمير كل مـا كان يعتبَر بدائيًّا وقاصرًا وتقليديًّا، الأمر الـذي أحدث تطورًا نوعيًّا في النظرية الإمبريالية النقدية.

تخفي الروايات الزائفة التي تعمد إلى إظهار المتاحف كوسائل لدمقرطة الفنِ وقائعَ نشأتها كأدوات لممارسة العنف – فضاءاتٌ حديثةٌ تستعرض الثقافات المادية للشعوب الأخرى وتصوّر تخلّف تلك الثقافات على أنه حقيقة. وما كانت تلك الادعاءات لتجد أرضًا خصبة لـولا أن سُلخت القطع عن مناشئها وتداولتها أيـدي الغرباء وأبعدتها عمّن يستطيعون نقض المعاني التي فرضتها الطقسنوميات[*] الإمبريالية. وقد تعيّن على فضاءات عرض الفنون أن تكفل مقروئية سرديات التطور وأن تظهر كتجسيد لأعلى مراحل هذا التطور. بالتالي، فإن المكعّب الأبيض الشهير ليس فضاءً محايدًا لعرض الفنون، بل هو مكانٌ مصمَّمٌ خصيصًا ليبدو وكأنه في قمة التطور، الأمر الـذي يجعله قابلًا لتقديم رواية محايدة عمّا هو قائم. وقد كانـت مسألة إيجـاد "المكان الصحيح" للقطع بمثابة أولوية قصوى، يمكن تناولها

25 Immanuel Kant, "An Answer to the Question: 'What Is Enlightenment?,'" in *Kant: Political Writings*, ed. Hans Reiss, Cambridge: Cambridge University Press, 1991

26 المرجع نفسه، ص. 57.

* ارتأينا استحداث مفردة "طقسنومية" وفاءً لنحت المفردة الأصلية باليونانية والذي يدمج لفظتي τάξις (بمعنى الطقس أو النظام أو الترتيب) وνόμος (بمعنى الناموس أو القانون) في إشارة إلى الناموس الذي تنتظم وفقه الأشياء ضمن ترتيب عام. تجدر الإشارة أيضًا إلى كون النقل الحرفي عن اليونانية تقليد معهود في الترجمات العربية. [المترجم]

حقوق دنيوية

على بسـاط البحـث في إطار مـن الحريـة الأكاديميـة والنقـاش الديموقراطي طالمـا أن مبدأ إيجاد المكان الصحيح لها محفوظ. مثلًا، يمكن ربط التجريد مع "الفن البدائي" في لحظة معيّنة – بحسـب وصـف هنـري هولمـز لفن الأشـكال الهندسـية أو الفـن اللاإيديوغرامـي – وتصويـره كمرحلـة متقدمـة مـن عمليـة التخفـف التدريجيـة مـن السـرد وبلـوغ شـكل فني محـض في لحظـة أخـرى[27].

لا يـزال الخبـراء يهيمنـون عـلى عالـم الفـن الإمبريالي. ففـي غيـاب هـؤلاء الخبـراء وهـذه المؤسسـات، ينتفـي وجـود الأعمـال الفنيـة الملحقـة بمجالات خبراتهم، ويخـرج الكثيـرون ممن يسـاهمون في بنـاء العالـم مـن خلـف الكواليس، وتحظـى مجتمعات الصنّاع المتعددة بالاعتراف بفضل مهاراتها ومسـاهماتها ونصيبها في المشاع بدلًا مـن العمالـة التي تمثلها. وهنالـك العديد من التدابير المهنيـة التي تضمن إبقاء هذه القطع الفنية عـلى قيد الحيـاة كدلائل حيّة عـلى أن حفظها بما هو مهمةٌ حضاريـة لم ينطوِ عـلى العنف. إلا أن السر البيّن للعنف الإمبريالي موجـود في الأشياء كلها، وعـلى نحو أكبر في مـا تعمّد الخبراء إحلاله مـن معـارف وخبـرات شـعوب كانـت هـذه الأشياء جزءًا مـن حياتها يومًا مـا.

قطعٌ متمرّدةٌ

بيـن الحيـن والآخـر، ثمّـة حـوادث قـد تقـع جـرّاء نقـل القطـع الفنيـة مـن مكان إلى آخـر، كأن تتمـرّد تلـك القطـع فتأتـي بأمـور غريبـة وتملأ قاعـات المتاحف بأصوات غير مألوفة. وقد عمدت المتاحـف إلى وضـع المزيـد مـن البروتوكولات المختصّـة بكيفيـة التعامـل مـع هذه القطـع بهدف السـيطرة عـلى سـلوكها وعـلى اللغة التي تتكلّم بها وعـلى مدى إفصاحها عـن العنف الـذي وقـع عليها في سياق اسـتخراجها. هكذا يعيد الفنان وليد رعد النظر في الرواية المتعلّقـة بمصيـر 300 قطعة فنية لـدى ورودها مـن قسـم الفنـون الإسـلامية في متحف اللوفر بباريـس إلى فـرع المتحف في أبـو ظبي. يقـول رعـد إن الأشـخاص الذيـن تولّـوا فتح الصناديـق صُعقوا عندما اكتشـفوا أن "القطع التي وصلت لم تكن هي ذاتها التي أرسلت". يقـول، في البـدء "قيـل إن القيّميـن قـد أصيبـوا بالهـلاوس كونهـم غير معتاديـن عـلى طقس الإمارات الحـار". ثمّ وصل خبراء فرنسـيون أكثـر قـدرة عـلى التأقلم مع ارتفاع درجات الحرارة، فعاينوا الأغـراض عـن كثب برفقـة الخبـراء المحليين. بعدها حـاول الجميع التعتيم عـلى المشـكلة والتخفيـف مـن وطأتهـا واحتوائهـا في أيدي الخبـراء، لعلمهم بالمدلـولات الفادحـة لما رأوه هناك. قالـوا إن القطع تعرّضت "لضرر كيميائي" نتيجة لفتح الصناديق المُكيّفة ودقيقة الصنع في مناخ الصحـراء العربية". لـم يقتنع رعد بتقرير الخبراء نظرًا لمعرفتـه بالنزعة التمرّديـة لـدى الأعمـال الفنيـة الإسـلامية، فعكف عـلى تجاربه الخاصة النابعة، عـلى حـدّ ظني، مـن قناعته بـأن تلـك ليسـت أعمالًا فنية وإنما صحبة حية. وقد أفضت تجاربه إلى خلاصـة مغايـرة: "لقـد تبادلـت الأغـراض جلودها في مـا بينها فصـارت بـلا ظلال"[28]. قـد تُسـتَبعد روايـة رعد عـلى اعتبارها خرافة، إلّا أن تخفّي القطع كالحرباء في لحظة تمرّدها قـد أتاح للقيّميـن تجاهـل مجمل تلـك الأحـداث وارتباطهـا ببعضها البعض والتصـرّف وكأن شـيئًا لـم يكن.

وهنالـك السـردية الأخـرى التـي تتكشّـف تفاصيلهـا عكسـيًّا؛ سـردية اسـتعراض الحنكـة الإمبرياليـة المُسـتنفَرة لكشـف الخـداع الـذي كان قـد بـدأ فعليًـا مـن الأماكن غير المنضبطة قبـل تعبئة الصناديـق بالقطع الفنية، أي داخـل الأسـوار الحصينة للمؤسسـات والدولة الأمة. تبدأ

27 للمزيد حول وليام هنري هولمز، انظر
Hinsley Curtis, *Savages and Scientists: The Smithsonian Institution and the Development of American Anthropology 1846–1910*, Washington, DC: Smithsonian Institution Press, 1981

28 اقتباس من نص رعد المصاحب لـ"جولته التعريفية" في التركيب الفني بعنوان "خدش في أشياء يمكنني التنصل منها" (Scratching on things I could disavow) الذي عُرض في متحف الفن الحديث بنيويورك، كانون الأول/ديسمبر 2015.

هذه القصّة من لحظة ملء صناديق كهذه بآلاف القطع المُعدّة لتُنقَل من الكونغو إلى المتاحف في الخارج. يكشف جامع التحف فريدريك ستار الذي عمل في الكونغو في مطلع القرن العشرين الآتي:

كنا قد بدأنا نتوجّس من تلك القطع الجديدة المصنوعة بلا غرض، كالقِرب الصغيرة المملوءة بالعقاقير العلاجية الطازجة والأصداف التي تعلوها. كان علينا أن نضع حدًّا لكل هذا وأن نردّ معظمها [..] أمضينا النهار كلّه نردّ الأصنام البديعة جديدة الصنع [..] رددنا كلّ ما أحضروه إلينا تقريبًا[29].

من لحظة مغادرتها، خرجت القطع الفنية عن السيطرة – راحت تسعى إلى أن تكون غير ما هي عليه بعدما عجزت عن البقاء على ما هي عليه. وقد تصرّف كل من الأشخاص المعنيين وكأنه المتحكّم بما يجري من وراء الكواليس والمسؤول عن تحديد السمات الفاصلة بين القطع الإفريقية الأصيلة المنزّهة عن أي اتّصال بالأوروبيين وتلك التي صنعها السكان المحليون خصيصًا لعرضها على المتاحف الغربية بغرض جمعها. للأسف، سرعان ما اكتشف اللصوص زيف تلك الأخيرة.

وليست القطع الفنية المحفوظة في المتاحف الأوروبية مجرّد تحف نموذجية، بل هي مجاز مرسل يعبّر عن العنف الإمبريالي الذي يتوجّب علينا تفكيكه. فعندما نرى كيف تمّ ترحيل هذه القطع من مواطنها الأصلية إلى المتاحف الغربية، نكاد لا نميّز حالتها عن حالة اللجوء. أتت هذه القطع وحيدة دون أي شيء واحتُجزت لعقود داخل مخيّماتٍ مقفرةٍ مفتقِدةً حياتها السابقة وكل من خلّفتهم أو ضيّعتهم بعدما رُحّلوا إلى وجهة أخرى. ولعل انتهاء الحرب العالمية الثانية وما رافق ذلك من إبرام معاهدات دولية تضمن حرية التبادل الثقافي وتداول المقتنيات والتحف الفنية، كان سيمنحها فرصتها الذهبية – فرصتها لمغادرة مخيّمات الاعتقال المتمثّلة في هيئة مكعّبات بيضاء والعودة إلى كنف المجتمعات التي سُلبت منها – أو ربّما كانت سياسة البوابات المفتوحة التي أقرّتها تلك المعاهدات إزاء القطع الفنية لتشمل أفراد تلك المجتمعات أو أبناءهم. ولكن حركة الأفراد – لا سيّما الذين خرجت من عندهم تلك القطع الفنية التي باتت اليوم من المقتنيات القيّمة – لا تزال محظورة رغم إجازة التصاريح والتأشيرات (للدخول والعمل والإقامة) لفئات أوسع من الناس بين الحين والآخر.

أطلقت الحملات الإمبريالية عملية واسعة من التهجير طالت الأشياء والأشخاص والنباتات والميكروبات والحيوانات، بدافع من الرغبة الجشعة في وضع كل شيء في مكانه الصحيح الذي تبيّن أنه المكان الخطأ لمعظمها. بخلاف ذلك، لا يمكن إطلاق النداء بأن: ها أنا ذا اقتلني إن شئت، تلك الصرخة النابعة من وجدان شعوب سُلبت الحق بممارسة أحقّيّتها في القطع التي صنعتها. إذًا ولكي نبطل مفعول العنف الإمبريالي، لا بد لنا أن نرفض الوضعية الضمنية لتلك القطع كأصل وكمخزن للقيمة قابل "للادّخار والاسترداد والمبادلة اللاحقة وتحقيق الاستفادة المتوقعة منه عند استرداده" والتي تساهم في إبقاء الغالبية من شعوب العالم في حالة من الإقصاء[30]. يجب أن نلتفت إلى النسيج الممزق لعوالم ومجتمعات الصنّاع التي جاءت منها تلك القطع الفنية. يتعيّن علينا أن نرفض التعرّف إليها كقطع فنية متحفية، بل أن نتعامل معها كمرجع للحقوق اللاإمبريالية التي لا يمكن لعالمهم – وعالمنا – أن يلتئم من دونها.

29 مذكّرات ستار، 11 شباط/فبراير 1906، واردة في اقتباس من Enid Schildkrout, "Personal Styles and Disciplinary Paradigms: Frederick Starr and Herbert Lang," in *The Scramble for Art in Central Africa*, eds. Enid Schildkrout and Curtis A. Keim, Cambridge: Cambridge University Press, 1998, 182–183
تقول شيلدكراوت في معرض الحديث عن بعض التحف "المزيّفة" في المتحف: "اليوم، تبدو هذه الأقنعة القابعة في مخازن المتحف اليوم وكأنها صُنعت بالأمس بالرغم من أنها تُعدّ من أقدم الأمثلة الموثّقة على الفن في الكونغو. فهي أقنعة قيد التصنيع، لم يبلِها الاستخدام ولم يعتّقها الصانع. ومع ذلك فهي مهمّة بالنسبة إلى الباحثين لما فيها من تفاصيل أيقونوغرافية تشير إلى الصورة التي اختار الأفارقة تقديم أنفسهم بها إلى الغربيين ما بين العام 1905 و1906"، المصدر نفسه، ص. 189.

30 "Store of Value"، تعريف ويكيبيديا الإنكليزية، en.wikipedia.org

حقوق دنيوية

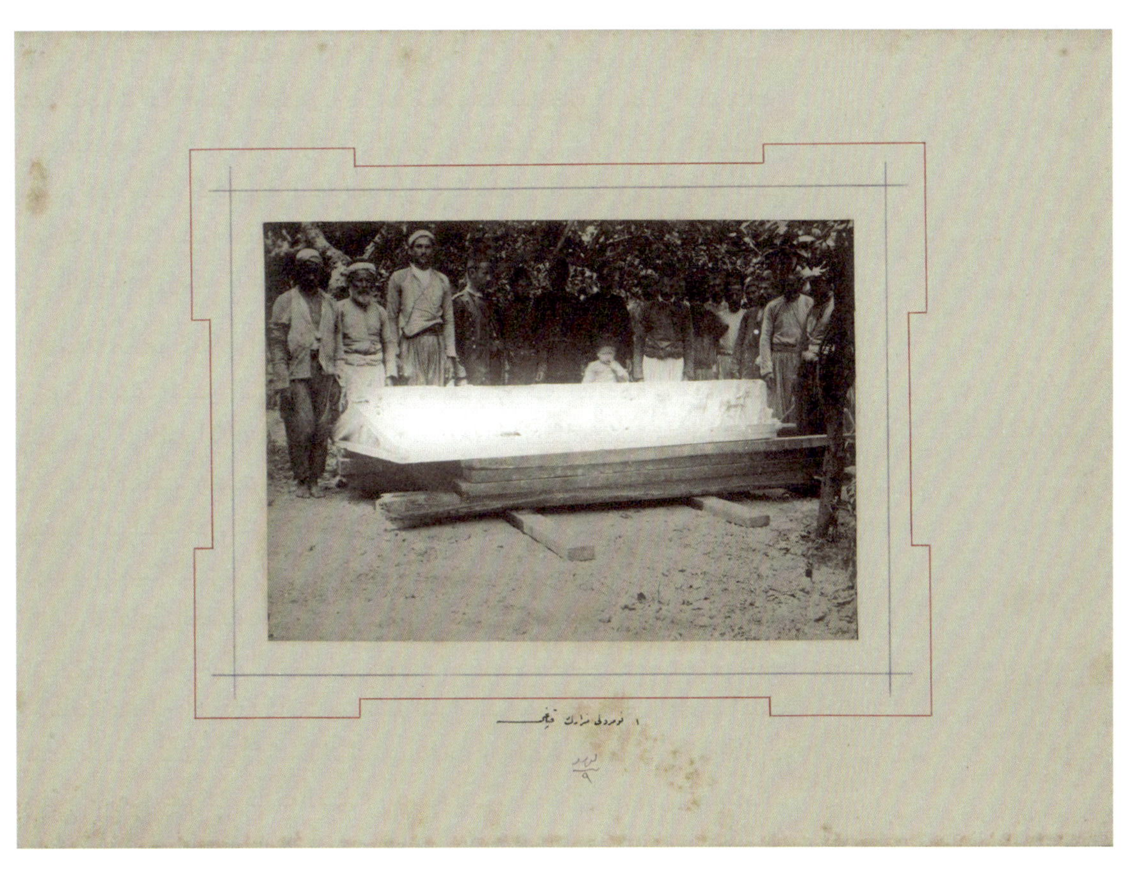

أكرم زعتري

قراءة ثانية

عثمان حمدي بك: "مجمع جنائزي ملكي في صيدا"

حدث ذلك على الأغلب في شهر أيار/مايو 1887 في بستان المغارة بمدينة صيدا.

فقد تـم رفـع المكتشـفات الأثريـة للتـو مـن عمـق 10 أمتـار تحـت الأرض ووضعهـا في بستان للحمضيـات بانتظـار نقلها إلى القسطنطينية عـلى متـن سفينة تحمـل اسـم "عسـير".

مكثت تلك المكتشفات زمنًا في العتمة سبق لحظة استخراجها عام 1887 وهو أكثر مما أمضته في ضـوء النهـار. وهـا هـي اليـوم تبصر نـور الشـمس للمرة الأولى منذ أكثـر مـن ألفي عـام، تعرضت خلالهـا للنهـب عـلى أيـدي اللصـوص وصائـدي الكنـوز. أخرجهـا الرجـال مـن باطن الأرض عـن طريـق رفعهـا بالحبـال وسـحلها عـلى سكك خشـبية. هنا ، تَمثُـل المكتشـفات الأثريـة أمام عدسة عثمان حمدي بك، لأن عتمـة حجرات الدفن غير مؤاتية لعملية التصوير.

دُعي أناسٌ كثرٌ لإلقـاء نظرةٍ عـلى القطـع الأثريـة قبيـل نقلهـا مـن صيـدا. تبيـن معظـم الصـور الفوتوغرافيـة التـي التقطـت في بستان المغـارة يومهـا مجموعـةً كبيرةً مـن الحجـارة المزخرفة الموضوعـة (المائلة) عـلى عـوارض خشـبية وسـط أشـجار الحمضيات. بعـضٌ منهـا يظهر أناسًا واقفين خلف القطـع الأثريـة المكتشـفة. لم تحضر الكاميرا لتصوير الفلاحين والعمال المتواجدين في المكان. بـل أتت لتغطيـة حدثٍ استثنائي: اكتشاف حمدي بك لآثار

أنجز هذا العمل بدعم من المعهد الجامعي للبحوث في مجال الإنسانيات والإبداع والتراث - باري سين للدراسات العليا EUR Humanities, Creation, Heritage PSGS (HCH)، برنامج Investissement d'Avenir ANR-17-EURE-002

كلام الصورة
أكرم زعتري، "An Extraordinary Event حدث استثنائي"، 2018. 8 طبعات بالطابعة نفاثة الحبر، قياس كل طبعة 30 × 43 سم. بإذن من الفنان وغاليري صفير زملر بيروت/هامبورغ. مجموعة فن جميل.

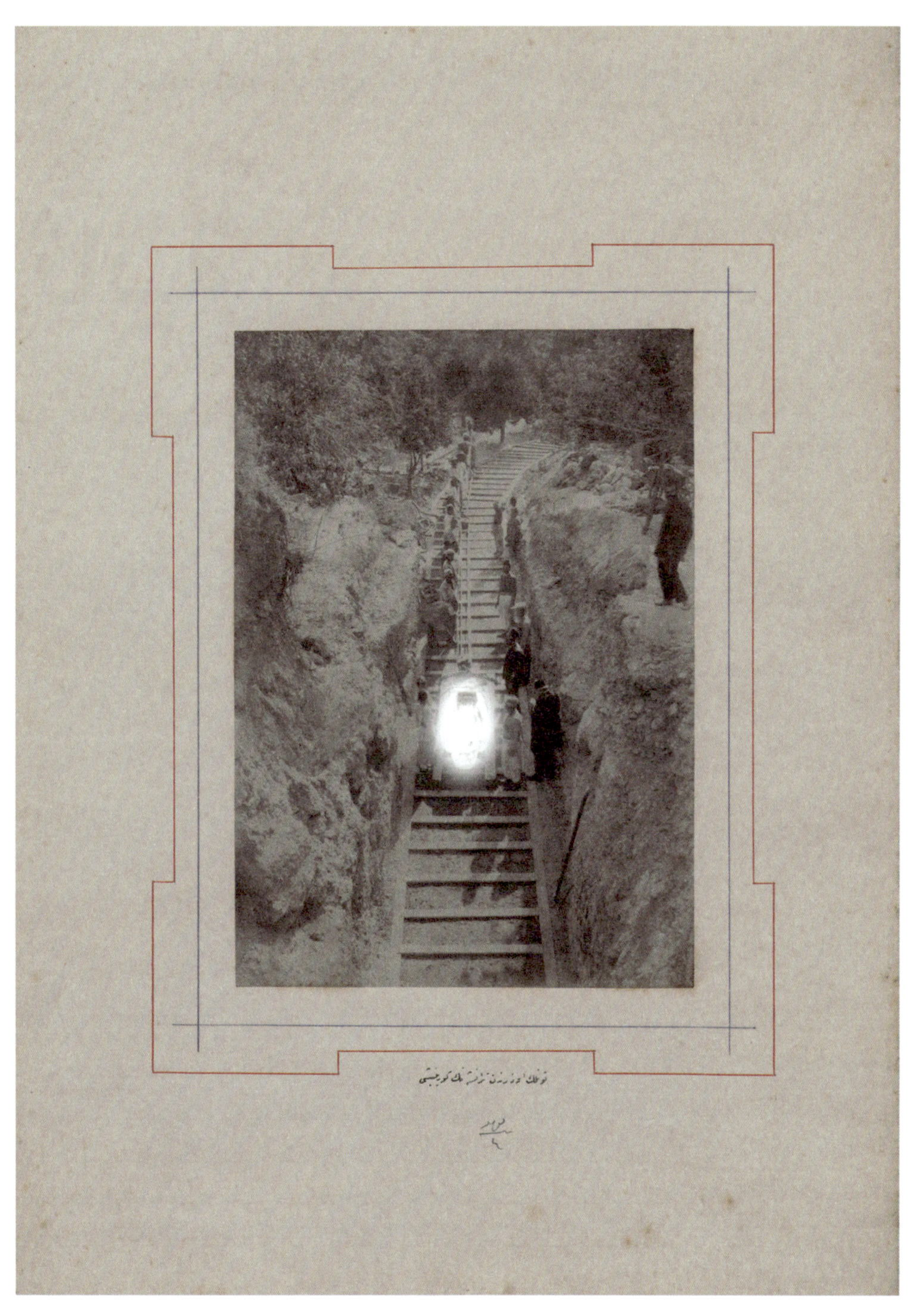

فائقة الأهمية. قبل ذلك ببضع سنوات، كانت لحمدي بك اكتشافات مهمة في جبل نمرود، لكن أسفاره لم تحمله أبعد من ذلك جنوبًا نحو صيدا. ليس واضحًا ما إذا كان الماثلون في الصور مبتهجين أو مشدوهين أو فخورين أو حتى متحمسين للاكتشاف العظيم. هل يتحسّر بعضهم على القطع الموشكة على مغادرة المدينة؟ هل يأسف أي منهم لضياع فرصة لجني الربح عبر بيع تلك الآثار لتاجر أوروبي؟

لا نعرف إن كان الحاضرون يدركون قيمة تلك المكتشفات، لكن وجود الكاميرا لتسجيل اللحظة هو أبلغ دليلٍ على أهمية الحدث. وبالنظر للفترة الزمنية، لعل الكاميرا أشد إثارة في أعينهم من الكشف الأثري.

يوم 30 نيسان/أبريل 1887، توجه الفنان والمسؤول الحكومي العثماني ومؤسس المتحف الإمبراطوري في القسطنطينية عثمان حمدي بك (1842 – 1910) إلى مدينة صيدا (جنوب ما أصبح لاحقًا لبنان الحديث)، وكله ثقةٌ أن ما سيجده هناك سيكون من أهم الاكتشافات الأثرية في الإمبراطورية العثمانية. كانت أنباءٌ قد وصلت ذلك العام إلى القسطنطينية تفيد بأن أحد مالكي الأراضي هناك واسمه محمد شريف[1] قد عثر على عددٍ كبيرٍ من القطع الأثرية أثناء حفر أرضه في شمال شرق مدينة صيدا. قيل إنها حجرات دفن موجودة تحت الأرض، فاستُدعيت السلطات المحلية لمعاينتها وأصدرت توصيةً بضرورة حضور مسؤول عثماني رفيع إلى الموقع نظرًا لحجم المكتشفات.

قبل ثلاثة أعوام من ذلك الحدث، كان عثمان حمدي بك المحرك الأساسي لإقرار قانون الآثار العثماني عام 1884 الذي حظر الإتجار بالآثار أو تصديرها إلى الخارج ونظّم عملية التنقيب عنها داخل الأراضي التابعة للسلطنة العثمانية. جرّم القانون الجديد عمل المنقّبين الهواة وصائدي الكنوز الذين شاع فعلهم على مدى عقود. بذلك أعلم حمدي بك الجميع من منقّبين وتجار على مدى سنوات بأن الآثار شأن السلطنة حصرًا وأنها تخضع لإدارة المتحف الإمبراطوري.

نشر حمدي بك تفاصيل أعمال التنقيب تلك باللغة الفرنسية في باريس عام 1892. وقد انتشرت خلال العقد الذي تلا الاكتشاف الأثري عدة روايات حول تلك الأحداث. تعكس الحزازيات الثقافية التي تحكم العلاقات داخل مدينة صيدا وفي لبنان بشكل عام، وكذلك الخلافات المستمرة حول كتابة التاريخ[2].

السجلات المكتوبة

في شهر آذار/نيسان من عام 1887، أي قبل شهر من وصول حمدي بك إلى صيدا، نشر التبشيري الأميركي القسيس ويليام كينغ إيدي المولود في صيدا رسالةً[3] في "المجلة الأميركية لعلم الآثار وتاريخ الفنون الجميلة" (The American Journal of Archaeology and of the History of the Fine Arts) تتحدث عن اكتشاف نواويس في حي القيّاعة بصيدا. تقول:

نعرف منذ زمنٍ طويلٍ أن السهول والتلال المحيطة بمدينة صيدا الأثرية مليئة بالآثار المهمة. وقد أثارت الخوابي المليئة بثمانية آلاف قطعة نقدية من مسكوكات فيليب والإسكندر وناووس عازر أشمون المنقوش بكتابات فينيقية وغيرها، اهتمامًا عامًا بموضوع الكنز الدفين. يتولى التنقيب عنه حاليًا عمال المحاجر. لا تكاد حجارة

1 تأتي رواية حمدي بك والتي تتضمن اسم المخبر للتأكيد على إخلاص المواطن العثماني والترويج لصواب القوانين العثمانية. وتذكّر بقصة الأخوين عبد الرسول اللذين كشفا للسلطات المصرية عن موقع دير البحري عام 1881 وفق ما روى غاستون ماسبيرو في كتابه *Les momies royales de Deir el-Bahari* (1889)

2 Osman Hamdi Bey et Théodore Reinach, *Une nécropole royale à Sidon*, Leroux, Paris, 1892

3 William King Eddy, "Letter from Sidon Phoenicia," *The American Journal of Archeology and of the History of the Fine Arts*, vol. 3, no. 1-2 (June 1887): 97 - 101

البناء التي يبيعونها تكفي أجرة عملهم، في حين يجنون الكثير من المال مقابل الآثار التي يعثرون عليها بين حطام الأبنية الأثرية أو في القبور غير المنبوشة. لم تتم أي عملية استكشاف نظامية لتلك النواحي منذ الاحتلال الفرنسي عام 1860 عندما جرى التنقيب عن المجمعات الجنائزية في جنوب المدينة.

انحدر إيدي من أسرة أميركية بروتستانية سكنت صيدا. كان ناشطًا في إنشاء المؤسسات التعليمية في المدينة شأنه في ذلك شأن سائر التبشيريين. ساهم في تأسيس مدرسة جيرارد للبنين في عام 1881. ويقول أحفاده إنه ترجم الإنجيل من الإنكليزية إلى العربية [4]. والده القسيس ويليام وودبريدج إيدي أسس مدرسة صيدا للبنات في عام 1862. يضيف القسيس ويليام كينغ إيدي في رسالته إلى المجلة ذاتها:

مؤخرًا، عثر بعض العمال على بئرٍ غائرةٍ في الحجر الرملي أثناء حفرهم في حقل مفتوح يبعد مسافة ميلٍ واحدٍ شمال شرق صيدا، مساحتها نحو 20 قدمًا مربعًا. عندما فرّغوا منها التراب وجدوا أربعة أبوابٍ على عمق 30 قدمًا، موزّعةً على الجدران الأربعة. كانت تلك الفتحات مبنيةً من الحجارة، وقد أزالوا بعضها ليتمكنوا من دخول الحجرات الموصدة خلفها. كانت جميع الأرضيات والجدران والأسقف من الصخر الطبيعي من دون أي أثر للملاط... دخلنا أولًا إلى الحجرة الجنوبية فوجدنا فيها ناووسين كبيرين: إلى اليمين ناووس من الرخام الأسود المصقول بعناية شديدة وإنما بلا زخرف، أما الآخر فمن الرخام الأبيض الناصع...

عبرتُ بين الناووس والجدران بمشقة بالغة نظرًا لضيق الحجرة. كانت الفتحة صغيرةً جدًا لا تسمح بالتهوئة الجيدة، وقد انطفأت الشمعتان اللتان حملتُهما معي بمجرد أن أدنيتهما من الأرض. أصيب مرافقي بالدوار والإغماء لذا لم أطِل المكوث. وزاد الطين بلة أن السقف كان يرشح ماءً فيحوّل الأرضية إلى طين لزج.

يذكرنا وصف إيدي بأن معنى الدفن هو استبعاد أجساد الموتى من عالم الأحياء ونفيها إلى باطن الأرض. غالبًا ما تكون حجرات المدافن تحت الأرض بعيدًا عن النور. لم تكن صيدا تعرف الكهرباء في ذلك الزمن، وكانت مصادر الإنارة تقتصر على الشموع وقناديل الزيت. يتابع:

بعد انتظار بضع ساعات ريثما يفرغ العمال من فتح المدخل إلى الحجرة الشرقية، هبطتُ مجددًا لأجد فيها ناووسين، واحدًا كبيرًا ومنحوتًا إلى الجهة اليمنى، وآخر أملسَ إلى اليسرى. كلاهما من الرخام الأبيض الناصع. الناووس الكبير منحوتٌ على شكل معبدٍ إغريقي، غطاؤه سطح المعبد والتابوت بدنُه.. لهذا المعبد المترف بالتفاصيل الدقيقة والزخارف والمزدان بصف من التماثيل البديعة أثر لا يُنسى على الناظر. لسوء الحظ، كان الناووس مكسورًا من الجهة الأمامية وقد بانت فيه فجوةٌ، وكذلك هو حال جزء من الإفريز الأيمن...

طفتُ حول الناووس فألفيتُ من المفاجآت ما فاق قدرتي الذهنية على تسجيلها. لا شك أنني كنت محظوظًا بما رأيت، فقد حُظِر الأوروبيون منذ تلك اللحظة من الدخول إلى موقع التنقيب. ومُنع الجميع من أخذ أي مقاسات أو ملاحظات أو صور فوتوغرافية. لا اعتراض أن تلك الحماية الغيورة فعلًا في مصلحة الحفاظ

Lana Captan, "American Missionary 4
Family Returns Home," *The Daily
Star* (Beirut, March 15, 1999)

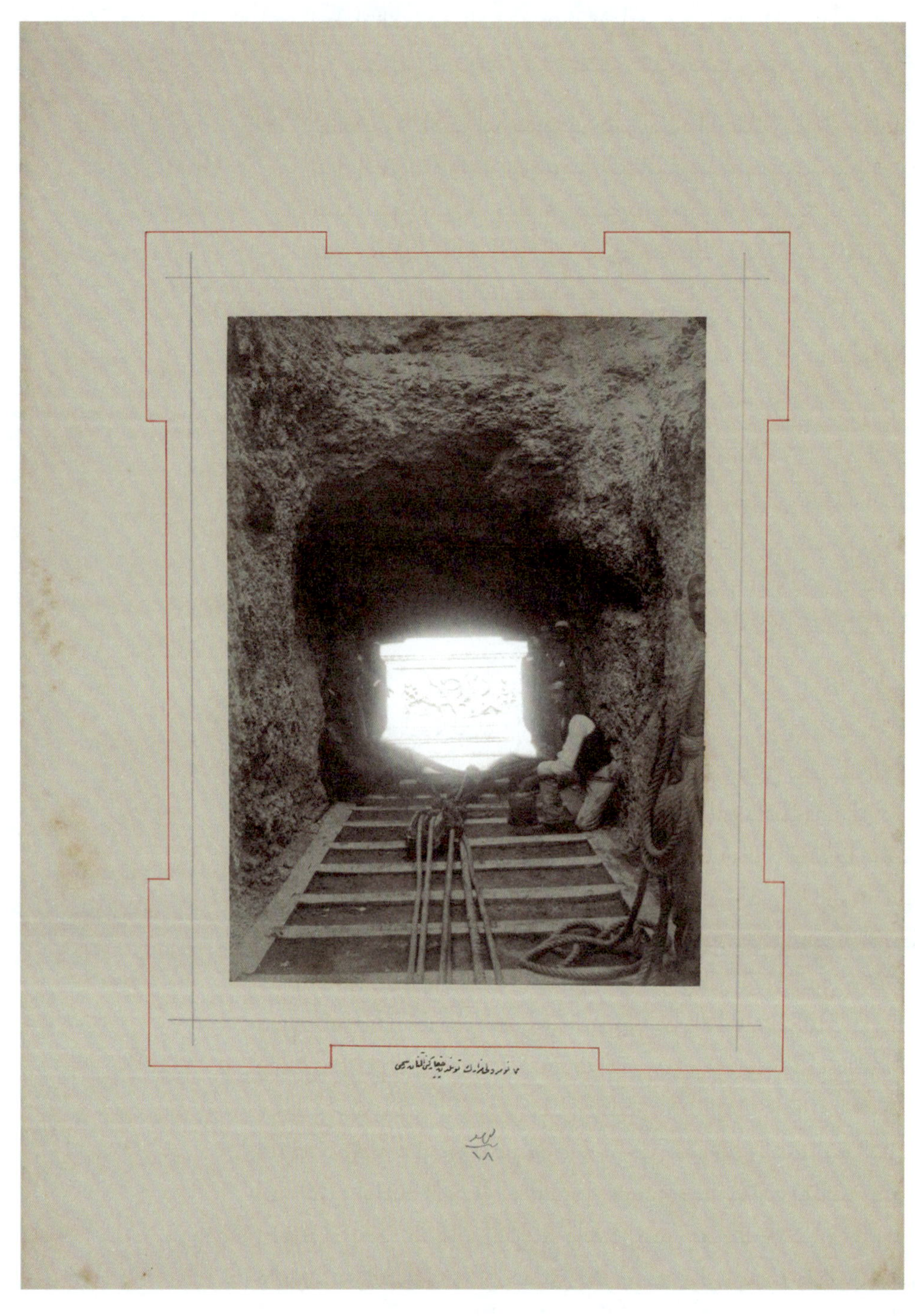

على الكنوز، لكن زائرًا مسلمًا غادر المكان حاملًا ذراعًا اقتطعها من أحد التماثيل. اكتُشفت سبعة نواويس أخرى منذ أن زرتُ الموقع: أحدها مزين بالمنحوتات من جميع جوانبه وآخر ذو غطاء على هيئة بشرية، ويُقال إن الوجه وغطاء الرأس من الطراز المصري الشبيه بالشكل المنحوت على تابوت أشمون عازر. واحدٌ فقط منها لم يتعرض للسرقة وقد احتوى على خشب متحلّل أو بقايا مومياء متحلّلة.

...اللافت في الأمر أنه لم يُعثر حتى هذه اللحظة على أي كتابة على جدران الناووس... لعل المواد الأولية أو الأعمال النهائية قد استُقدمت من بلدٍ آخر. إذ لا وجود لمثل هذا النوع من الرخام في سوريا. وحاليًا، يخضع المكان للحراسة العسكرية في الليل والنهار والمداخل إلى هذه الحجرات مسدودة بينما تنتظر السلطات المحلية التعليمات من القسطنطينية.

يذكر القسيس وليام كينغ إيدي أنه شاهد رجلًا يفرّ ومعه قطعة من تمثال التقطها من موقع الحفريات. من اللافت أنه أشار إلى الرجل بديانته.

أقام حمدي بك في باريس بين عامي 1860 و1869. يُفترض أنه شاهد ناووس الملك الفينيقي أشمون عازر الثاني معروضًا في متحف اللوفر. ولعله سأل نفسه لماذا لا يُعرض بدلًا من ذلك في القسطنطينية. كان قد سمع بالحفريات التي قام بها إرنست رينان في جبيل وصور. ولدى وصوله إلى صيدا كان الجميع على علمٍ بمسؤوليته عن قوانين حماية التراث الثقافي من صائدي الكنوز الذين كانوا يتاجرون بممتلكات الأجيال القادمة.

اكتُشف ناووس أشمون عازر الثاني في صيدا في عام 1855 على يد ألفونس دوريغيلو (1822–1896) الذي عاون إرنست رينان (1823 – 1892) لاحقًا في حفرياته إبان التدخل الفرنسي في لبنان عام 1860. باع دوريغيلو الناووس بحسب الممارسات الشائعة وغير المحظورة في ذلك الزمن، إلى دوق لوين[5] الذي أهداه لاحقًا إلى متحف اللوفر عام 1856. وكان ألفونس دوريغيلو من مواليد صيدا لعائلة من البندقية عاشت في حلب منذ القرن الثامن عشر.[6] انتقل ألفونس إلى صيدا في منتصف القرن التاسع عشر ليؤسس نوعًا جديدًا من التجارة: التنقيب عن الآثار وبيعها. وقد جمع لهذه المهمة فريقًا من العمال المحليين الذين كانوا يقومون بحفر المواقع التي كان يظن أنها تحوي مكتشفات ثمينة. لعبت أسرة دوريغيلو لسنوات دورًا مهمًّا في التنقيب عن الآثار على الساحل اللبناني وتأمين بيعها إلى جامعي الآثار الأوروبيين. استفادت الأسرة من قوانين الآثار العثمانية الفضفاضة ونفذت معظم حفرياتها الأولى في ظل الفلتان التنظيمي. أعانتها خبرتها بالقوانين الأوروبية الأشد صرامة على اقتناص فرصة تراخي القوانين العثمانية التي لم تكن لتدوم طويلًا. لذا، اعتبر أولئك التجار المغامرون حمدي بك بمثابة تهديدٍ حقيقي لهم، فقد شاركهم الاهتمام بالمكتشفات الأثرية وإنما ليس بهدف التجارة والربح بل لأغراض الجمع والدراسة والعرض. وكان حمدي بك يسعى إلى إرساء وتطوير علوم التنقيب عن الآثار داخل الإمبراطورية العثمانية وضمن الإطار المؤسسي للمتحف الإمبراطوري.

بعد ثلاث سنوات من الكشف عن حفريات القيّاعه، نشرت المجلة عينها عام 1890 رسالةً قصيرةً جدًا لإدموند دوريغيلو (1853 – 1922)، ابن ألفونس دوريغيلو، كتب فيها ما يأتي:

لدى عودتي إلى صيدا، وجدتُ أن المجمع الجنائزي البديع الذي استُخرجت منه تلك النواويس المهيبة لينقلها متحف القسطنطينية بعيدًا عن المدينة قد دُمّر! اقتُلعت

5   أونوريه تيودور بول جوزيف دالبير دوق
لوين الثامن (1802 - 1867)

6   Michel G. Klat, "The Durighello Family,"
Archeology and History in Lebanon
16 (Autumn 2002): 98-108

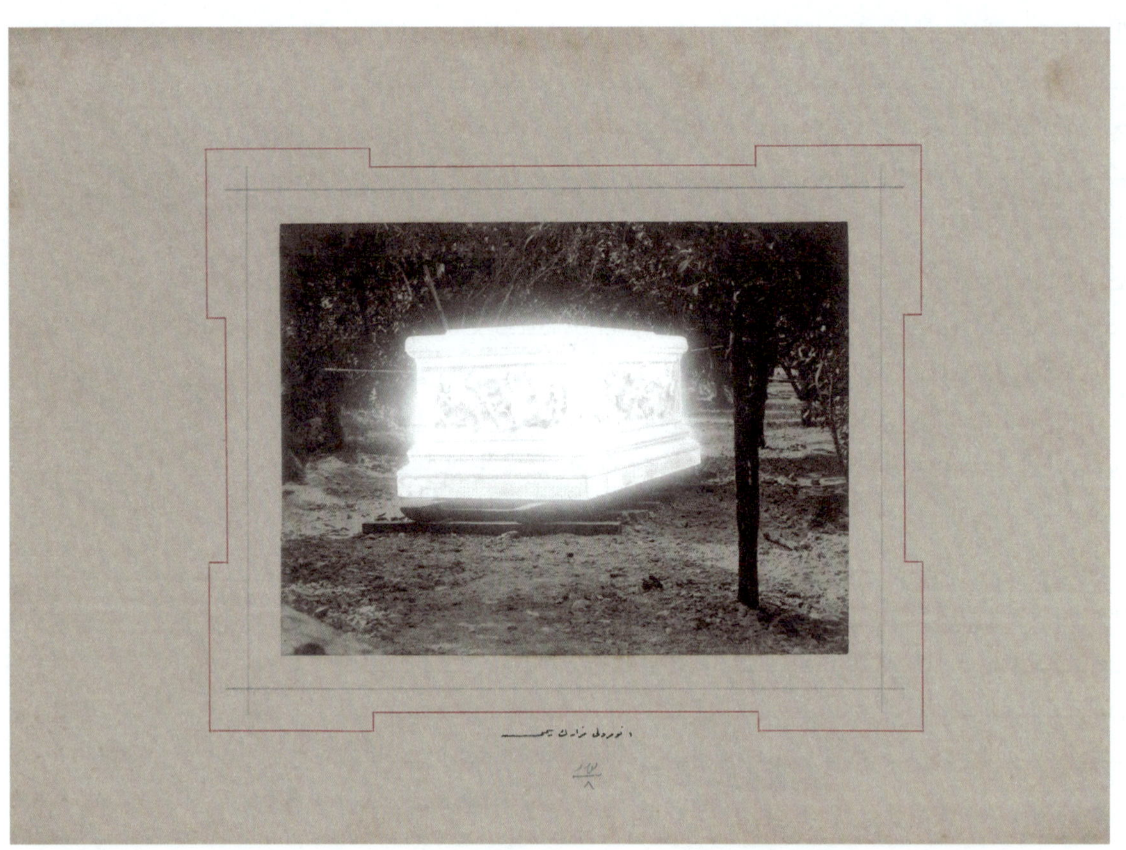

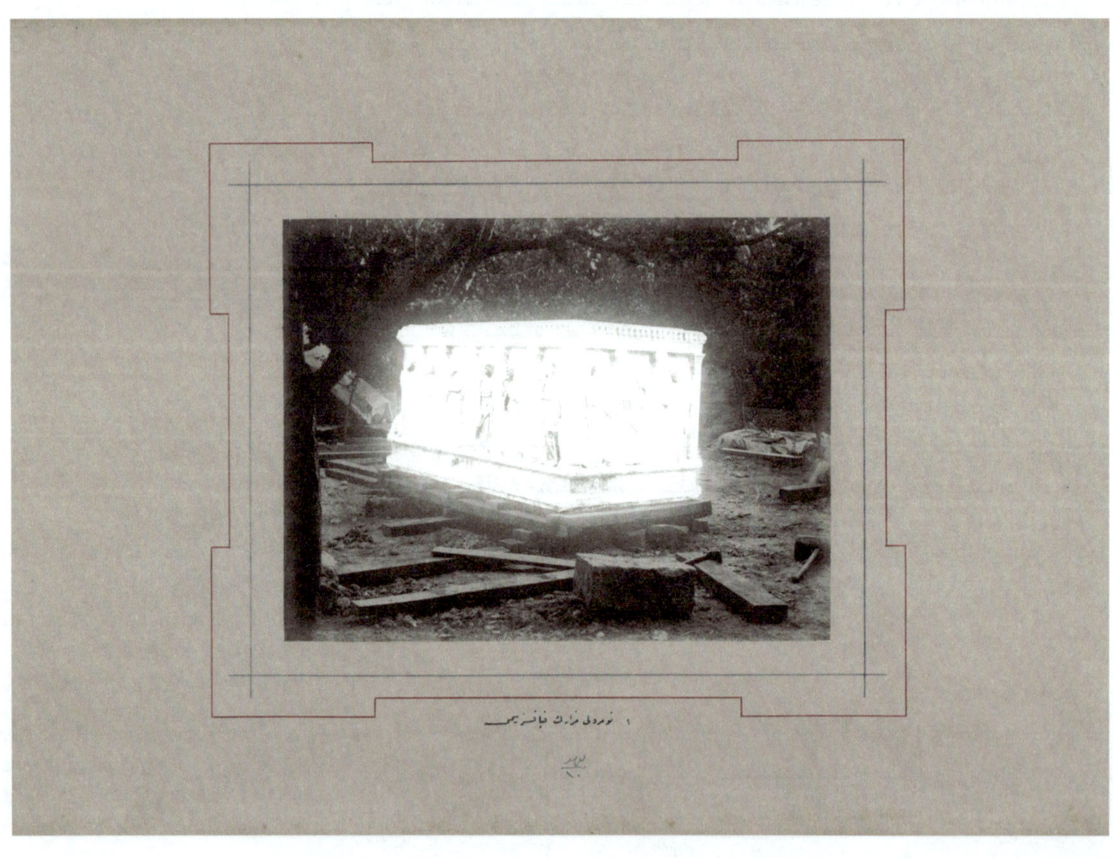

قراءة ثانية

الصخرة التي حُفرت فيها تلك المدافن البديعة حيث خُبِّئت كل تلك الروائع الأثرية، اقتُلعت بالكامل وقُصّبت أحجارَ بناءٍ حقيرة! ولم يبقَ من المكان الـذي وُجدت فيه رفـات الملـك تبنيـت سـوى حفرة خاويـة. لقد صمد ذلك المتحـف الجوفي العظيم أمـام الـزلازل وحـروب الفاتحيـن وقـرون مـن الهمجيـة حتـى أتـى بسـتانيٌ بائـسٌ مـن صيدا ليهدمها بحماقته الإجرامية[7].

لا يذكر دوريغيلو حمدي بك بالاسم ولكنه يشير إليه بإصبع الاتهام ويحمّله مسؤولية تدميـر مجمـع صيـدا الجنائـزي. يمكـن القـول إن مآخـذ دوريغيلـو عـلى عمليـة التنقيـب المقحمة والمدمرة التي قادها حمدي بك تنطبق بحذافيرها على معظم أعماله الحفرية. بماذا يتهم دوريغيلو حمدي بك، لا نعلم بالتحديد. هل يقصد اقتلاع المكتشفات الأثريـة مـن الطبقات الصخريـة؟ لـم يتوانَ هو ووالـده عـن فعلـة مماثلـة في السـابق. أم يشكو من الإهمـال الـذي لحـق صرح الدفن؟ لـم يكترث أبنـاء أسـرة دوريغيلـو بـأيٍّ مـن المواقـع التي نقبـوا فيها عن الآثار.

تمتعـت أسـرة دوريغيلو لأكثـر مـن ثلاثيـن عامًـا بامتيـاز كونهـم أوروبييـن ناطقيـن باللغـة العربيـة وعـلى درايـة جيـدة بمنطقـة الشـام، الأمـر الـذي كان في صالحهم وصالح تجارتهـم. كما انتفعت الأسـرة مـن نظام الامتيازات الأجنبية في السـلطنة العثمانيـة الـذي كان يخولهم التقاضـي أمـام المحاكـم الأوروبيـة في حـال النـزاع مـع مواطنيـن أوروبييـن آخريـن عـلى أراضي السلطنة[8].

في عـام 1890، أنجـز حمـدي بـك كتابـه "Une nécropole royale à Sidon" (مجمع جنائزي ملكي في صيدا) الـذي نُشـر في باريس بعدها بعاميـن. كتب في مقدمته ما يأتي:*

2 آذار/مارس 1887، قام محمد شريف أفندي، التزامًا منه بقانون الآثار. (ص. I)

ينسب حمـدي بـك الفضـل بهـذا الاكتشـاف في مسـتهل كتابـه إلى القانـون الجديـد. يسـمّي مواطنًا كان قد أبلغ السـلطات بما وجده بعدما عرّفته القوانين بأهمية الامتنـاع عـن بيـع الآثار.

بإبلاغ قائمقام صيدا صادق بك بأنه قد عثر على بئرٍ عميقةٍ يُحتَمل أن تحتوي على نواويس. (ص. I)

هنا، يثني حمـدي بـك عـلى المواطن العثمانـي الـذي امتثل للقانـون الـذي سـاهم هـو في اسـتصداره وكأنـه يمـدح ذاتـه بطريقـة غيـر مباشـرة. ويضيـف حاشـيةً يكتـب فيهـا:

لـم يبقَ أحد في صيدا إلا ونقّب بسـتانه، ولا يخفـى عـلى أي منهـم مـا قـد تعنيـه تلك البئـر ومـاذا في داخلها. (ص. I)

ويتابع:

أستطيع أن أجـزم أن تـراب صيـدا الأثريـة لا يـزال يحتـوي عـلى كميـات ضخمـة مـن الكنوز الأثريـة بالرغم من التخريب المتواصل منذ قرون. ويؤسفني القول إننا نواجه المصاعب في محاولاتنا لوضع حدٍّ لتلك الممارسـات المسـتمرة إلى اليـوم. لكنْ مخطِّئٌ جدًا من يظن أن هذه الممارسـات التخريبية نابعة من تزمّت أهالي صيدا كما يُشاع دائمًـا. يرجـع السـبب الحقيقـي إلى الجهـل والفسـاد لـدى الطبقـات الدنيـا، سـواء كانـوا

Edmond Durighello, "Letter from Sidon," 7
*The American Journal of Archeology and of
the History of the Fine Arts* (June 1890): 186

"Litige entre Habib Abela et Alphonse 8
Durighello à propos du sarcophage
d'Eshmunazor II," *Archaeology & History
in Lebanon* 16 (Autumn 2002): 109-114

* الاقتباسات مترجمة من اللغة الفرنسية الأصلية ومن ترجمة المؤلف الإنكليزية

مسلمين أو مسيحيين، بتحريض ودعم بعض الأجانب المقيمين في هذا البلد بغية تحقيق هدف أوحد، ألا وهو تهريب الآثار. (ص. IV)

يذيّل حمدي بك مقولته هذه بحاشية تتضمن مقتطفًا من رسالة بعثها إدمون دوريغيلو (من دون ذكر اسمه) إلى أرنست رينان يقول فيها:

"أسعد بتمضية معظم أمسياتي وسط الحفريات بصحبة عمالي المخلصين. لا تخلو حفرياتنا الجوفية السرية من مخاطر الانزلاقات الترابية ولكن لا شيء يحبط عزيمتنا". (ص. V)

يقرّ حمدي بك في كتابه بأن مهندس الولاية بشارة ديب كان قد بدأ أعمال الحفر قبل وصوله إلى صيدا، ورغم ذلك يشرح بالتفصيل تطور عملية التنقيب وتوالي الاكتشافات، قاعةً تلو الأخرى وناووسًا تلو الآخر.

الكتلة الصخرية

أدى كشف حمدي بك عن مدفن الملك تبنيت إلى تدمير الكتلة الصخرية التي كانت تسدّ مدخل التجويف الذي وُضع فيه ناووس تبنيت. لم يكن ممكنًا رفع الكتلة إلى مستوى سطح الأرض بسبب ضيق الفتحة. لذا قرر حمدي بك تكسيرها إلى قطع صغيرة. يقول:

يُستدَّل من خامة الحجر المختلفة في طبيعتها عن الصخر الذي حُفرت فيه البئر على أن هذا الحجر والحجارة التي تحيط به وتغطيه قد استُقدمت من مكان آخر بعيدٍ عن البئر ونُقلت كل تلك المسافة إلى موقعها الحالي. عندها أدركت أنني كنت مخطئًا في ظني بأنني سأعثر على المزيد من حجرات الدفن، وتيقّنتُ من أن صاحب هذا المدفن الذي حُفرت من أجله تلك البئر وبُذل ما بُذل من الجهد لإخفاء معالمه يرقد في جوفه وحيدًا معزولًا تمامًا عن الأموات الآخرين. (ص. 91)

يضيف حمدي بك:

في الصباح الباكر من اليوم التالي، بدأ عدد من البنائين بتفتيت الكتلة الصخرية، ولم يكن ذلك عسيرًا لأن الحجر كان طريًا. استمر العمل على قدم وساق، ومع حلول العصر كان العمال قد أتوا على خمسة أثمان منه، وما تبقى منه كان بسماكة 60 سنتيمترًا.

وأخيرًا كسّر العمال القطعة الأخيرة المتبقية بقطعها عرضيًّا إلى ثلاثة أجزاء. ولم يتبقَّ لنا سوى أن نرفعها ونسندها إلى الجدار.

لم يكن تكسير الكتلة الصخرية التي سدّت قبر تبنيت غريبًا عن الممارسات الشائعة في التنقيب عن الآثار خلال القرن التاسع عشر والتي كانت تبتغي استخراج المكتشفات الأثرية من دون الاكتراث للحفاظ على الموقع الذي وجدت فيه. إلا أن وصف حمدي بك الدقيق وقياساته المفصلة للحجر قبل تفتيته تدل على أن الرجل كان مدركًا لأهمية المعارف التي يحتويها.

التصوير الفوتوغرافي

سيلتقط حمدي بك الصور الفوتوغرافية في صيدا وسيرسم مسجدًا بالقرب من شاطئ البحر، ويصادق شبلي أبيلا مالك الأرض المحاذية حيث سيسمح له هذا الأخير بعرض

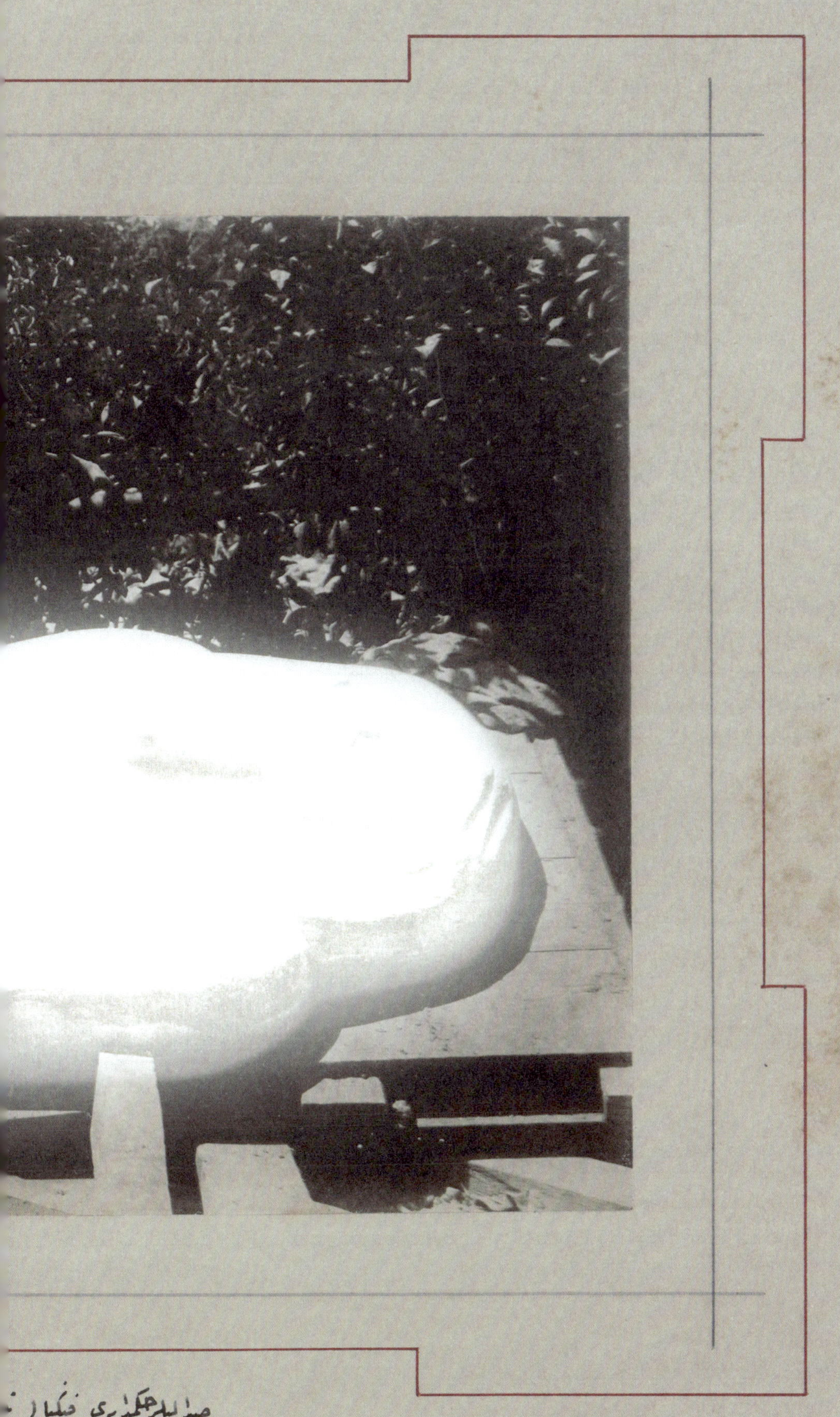

صبا ایلدرحكذری فنكیا ن

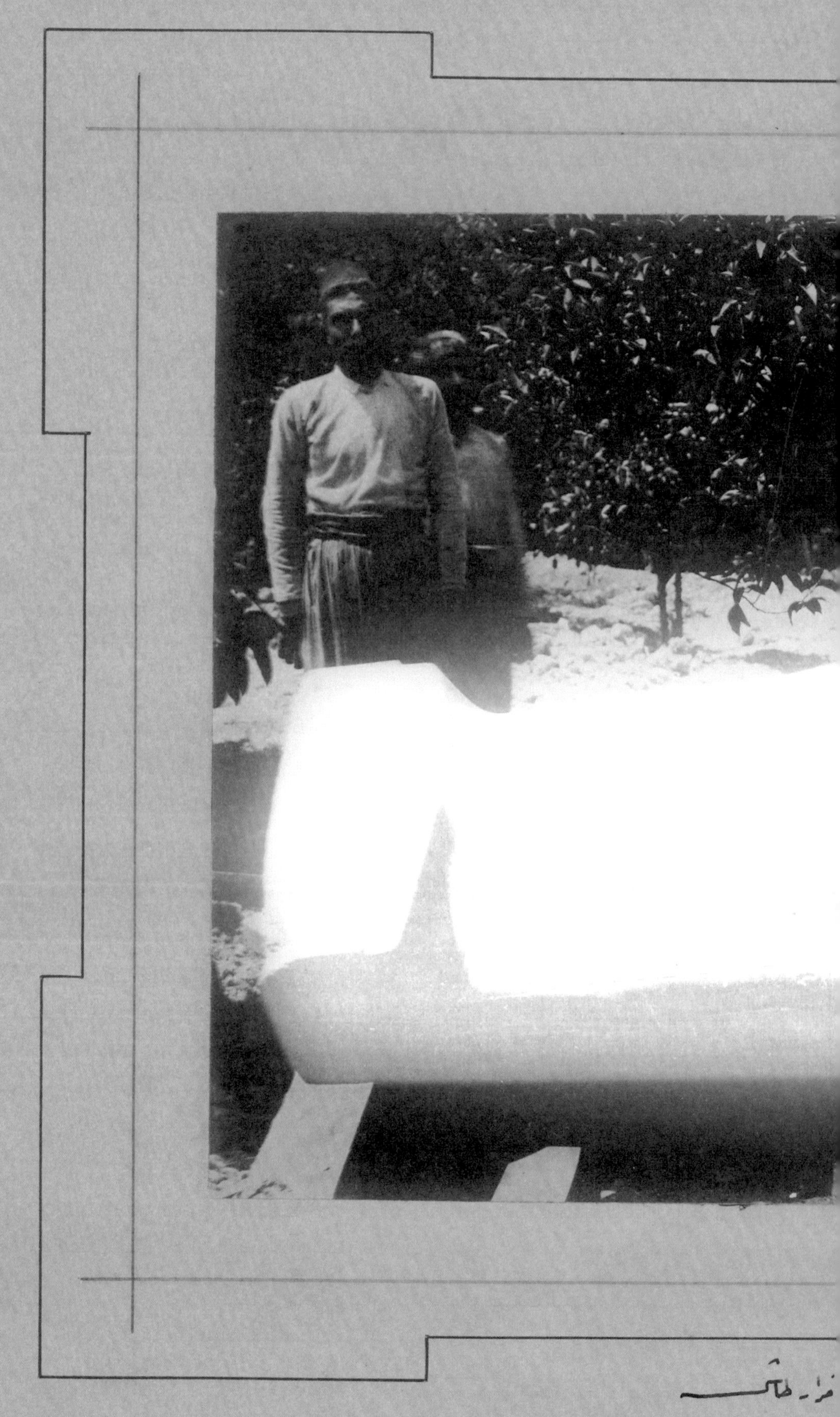

المكتشفات الأثرية على أرضه قبل نقلها إلى خارج المدينة. سيعود بعدها إلى القسطنطينية برفقة سبعة عشر ناووسًا ستصبح في المستقبل مفخرة المتحف الإمبراطوري العتيد ونواةً لمجموعة مقتنياته.

في عام 1892، سينشر حمدي بك مخطوطًا يستعرض عمله في صيدا ويتضمن تفاصيل تدمير مجمع صيدا الجنائزي إلى جانب دراسة أثرية لتيودور ريناك. يشير حمدي بك إلى التصوير الفوتوغرافي في نصه ست مرات.

يذكر عثمان حمدي بك التصوير أول مرة بعد وصول غطاء الناووس الأول إلى بستان المغارة المجاور، حيث يقول:

كان الوقت ظهرًا. كان العمال بحاجة إلى الاستراحة وتناول وجبة الغداء. اغتنمت الفرصة لألتقط صورة فوتوغرافية لذلك الغطاء البديع. (ص. 26)

ثم يضيف:

الاثنين 23 أيار/مايو، وصل الناووس رقم 7 إلى السطح أخيرًا متسلّقًا المنحدر ببطء شديد من ثقل وزنه... عند الظهيرة، كان هذا الصرح الجنائزي الأثري الأجمل من كل ما عرفناه إلى جانب غطائه في بساتين الليمون.

كان صباحًا مفعمًا بالمشاعر لن أنساه ما حييت، التقطت فيه العديد من الصور الفوتوغرافية وأمضيت طيلة فترة بعد الظهر في الحقول أتأمل غنيمتي بتأثرٍ غامر. (ص. 60)

يذكر حمدي بك في الصفحة 68 أنه التقط صورًا فوتوغرافية لجوانب الناووس الأكبر لافتًا إلى أنها الوحيدة التي توثق الأضرار التي ألحقها به اللصوص، علمًا أن الأجزاء المتضررة خضعت لاحقًا للترميم وهي معروضة حاليًا في المتحف.

وفي الصفحة 84، يقول إنه بعد استخراج الناووس الأسود الذي يُعتقد أنه يخص أم عشترت زوجة وأخت الملك تبنيت وبينما كان ينزلق ببطء صعودًا على السكك الخشبية:

اكتظ البستان في ذلك اليوم بحشود من الزوار الفضوليين. كنت قد أحضرتُ فرقةً موسيقية مع طبلٍ كبيرٍ نزولًا عند رغبة العمال. رافقتنا الفرقة الموسيقية طيلة فترة العمل، ما أدخل السرور إلى قلوب العمال وجميع الحاضرين. ثم ما لبث جمع المتفرجين أن انضم بعفوية إلى العمال بعدما ألهم دأبهم حماسة الموجودين وراحوا يتعاونون جميعًا على رفع الناووس. كان الجميع منتشيًا بالموسيقى. كانوا حوالي أربعمائة شخص أو ربما خمسمائة يصرخون ويهلّلون وهم يجذبون الناووس إلى الأعلى عبر الخندق. كان مشهدًا فريدًا يستحق التصوير. (ص. 84)

يصف حمدي بك في الصفحة 108 لحظة نقل مومياء الملك تبنيت إلى الممر خارج القاعة الجنائزية بعد فتح ناووسه:

كان كل شيء موضبًا في الخارج. كان مراد أفندي طبيب البلدية قد أنهى للتو تنظيف وتجفيف رفات الملك الصيدوني التي وُضعت في صندوق من الزنك صُنع خصيصًا لهذا الغرض وعولجت بمادة كيميائية لحفظها.

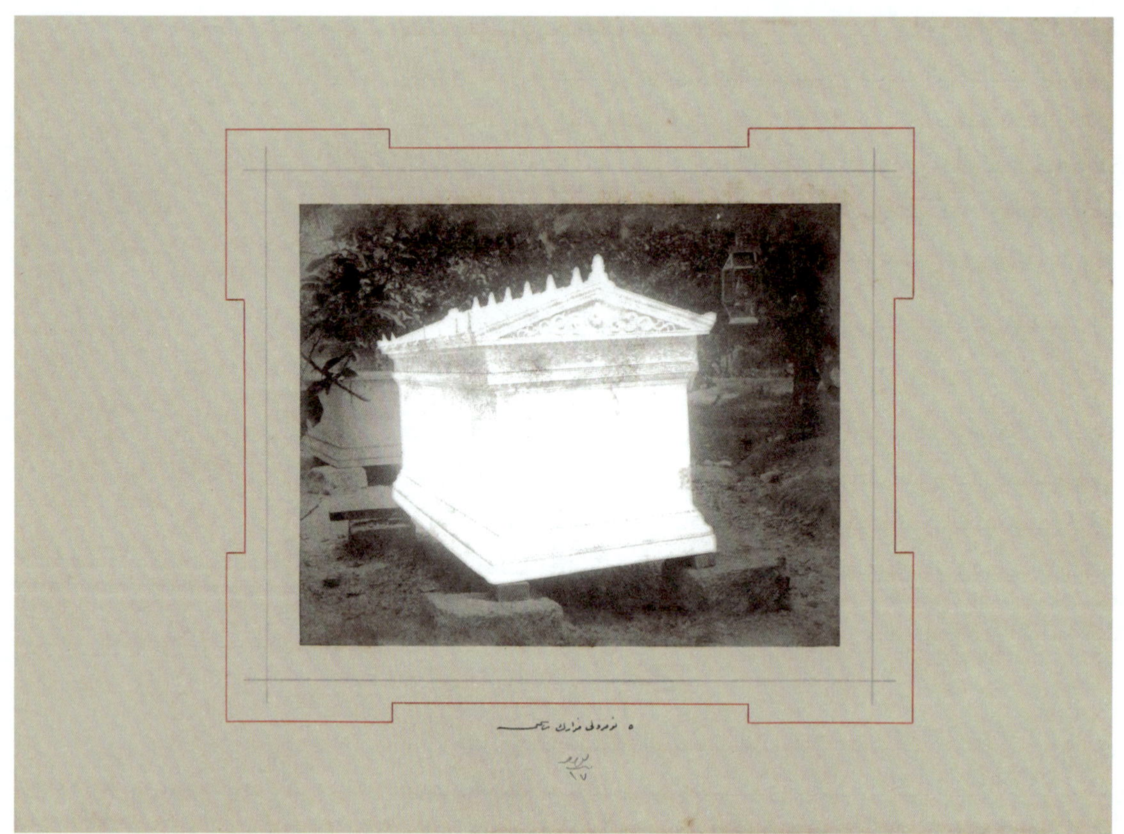

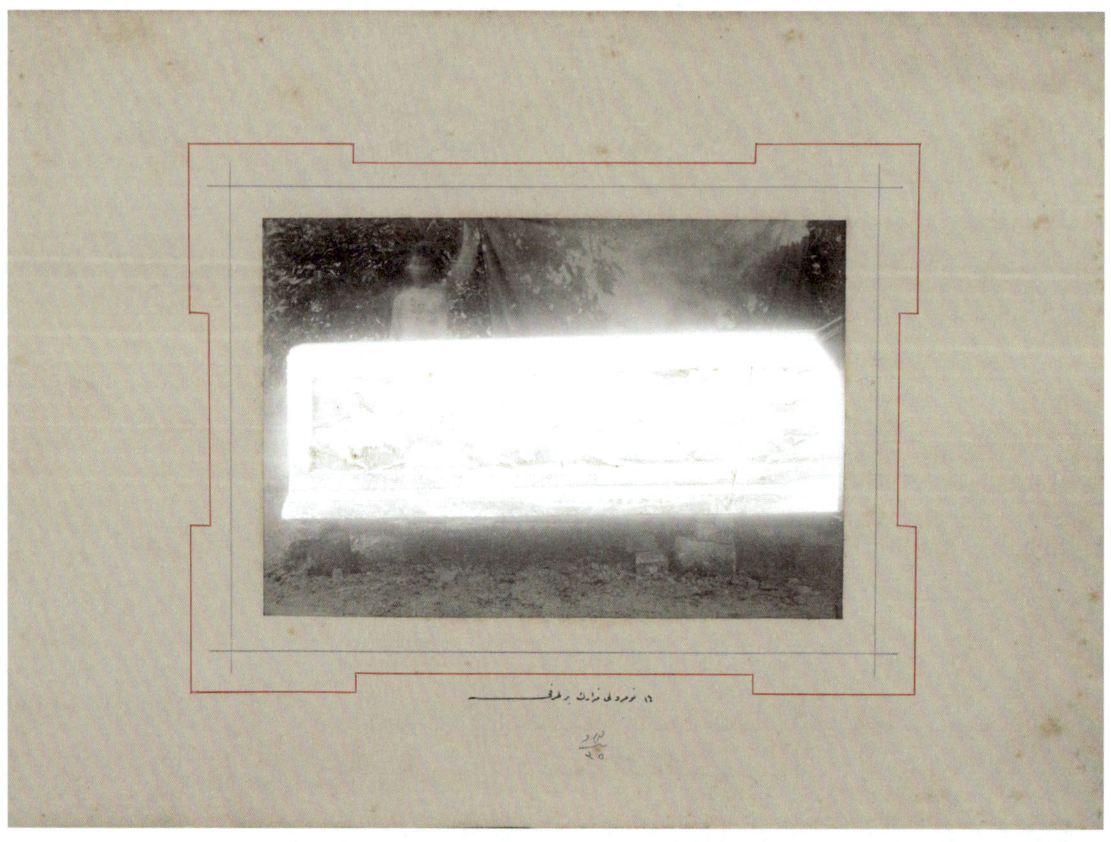

كنت منهكًا ومحمومًا منذ المساء. أُجبرت على ملازمة السرير طيلة يوم 3 حزيران/
يونيو. نُقل الناووس يومها ووُضع مع غطائه إلى جانب المكتشفات الأخرى في
حديقة السيد أبيلا التي زرتها عصر يوم 4 حزيران/يونيو متغلّبًا على الحمى لألتقط
الصور الفوتوغرافية لجسد الملك وغطاء الناووس وأشقّ الكتابة المنقوشة. عندها
تمكّنا لأول مرة من قراءة اسم تبنيت كاهن عشترت وملك الصيدونيين. إنه إذاً
ضريح والد إشمون عازر الثاني الذي كشفنا عنه. (ص. 108)

الصورة الفوتوغرافية الواردة في هذا النص غير موجودة في الألبوم إلا أن ثمة نسخةً
منقوشةً منها منشورة في الكتاب.

حمّلنا 14 صندوقًا على متن السفينة ذلك اليوم. وفي اليوم التالي 20 حزيران/يونيو
حملنا الناووس الذي بلغ وزنه 15 طنًا إلى المرسى. من هناك وُضع الناووس على
طوف بواسطة سقالة أمام أعين حشد كبير من المتفرجين. كان الحشد ضخمًا
يغطي الشاطئ بأكمله. التقطت صورة لتحميل الناووس. (ص. 144)

بعدها سُحب الطوف نحو السفينة. وكان حمدي بك قلقًا من عملية نقل الناووس من
الطوف إلى متن السفينة. يقول:

قال حسن بك قبطان السفينة الشجاع مطمئنًا: "لا تقلق. أنا واثق جدًّا من نجاح
العملية، لذا سأقف تحت الصندوق بينما تأخذ أنت الصورة الفوتوغرافية". ثم
نزل إلى الطوف ووقف تحت الصندوق الذي كان قد ارتفع بضعة أمتار في الهواء.
(ص. 110)

خاتمة

تسمّر الرجال لبضع ثوانٍ في أماكنهم صامتين.

طُلب إلى الجميع أن يتوقفوا عن الحركة وألا يرف لهم جفنٌ أو ينطقوا بكلمة.

وربما طلب منهم الامتناع عن الابتسام.

العديد منهم لم يرَ كاميرا في حياته قط.

ربما لم يروا أناساً في صور فوتوغرافية من قبل.

وعلى الأرجح لن يطلعوا حتى على هذه الصورة.

سيعمل مبعوثون من استوديو سبح وجواييه (Sébah & Joaillier) على تظهير هذه
الصورة الفوتوغرافية وطباعتها في صيدا، أو ربما في معملهم في القسطنطينية.

ستُثبّت الصورة على ورق مقوّى ذي لونٍ مائلٍ إلى الأبيض.

ستُضبّر في ألبوم سيحمل اسم الحملة التنقيبية التي ستحمل بدورها الرقم 91533
والعنوان "صيدون لحدي" (نواويس صيدا).

سيصبح الألبوم 91533 جزءًا من المجموعة الفوتوغرافية المفضلة لدى السلطان
عبد الحميد الثاني المفهرسة في 51 مجلّدًا تغطي كافة مناحي الحياة العصرية في
السلطنة العثمانية.

ستجد طريقها كهديةٍ إلى المجموعات الملكية والرئاسية في العواصم الأوروبية والأميركية، ولكنها لن تصل إلى الولايات الجنوبية من الإمبراطورية العثمانية.

ستبلغ جميع صفحات الألبوم والصور المثبتة عليها عمر المائة عام وسيميل لونها إلى الاصفرار. لن يعود هناك لون أبيض ناصع في تلك الصور بعد الآن.

بعض هؤلاء الرجال يرتدي زيًا عسكريًا. لا بد أنهم من عساكر الولاية، حراشٌ موكلون بتأمين موقع التنقيب ضد اللصوص. وهنالك آخرون، ربما عمال. هل يظهر عثمان حمدي بك في الصورة؟ أم أنه خلف الكاميرا؟ هل يظهر مهندس الولاية بشارة ديب فيها؟ هل يظهر المهندس البحري محمد عاصي؟ محمد شريف؟ لا أحد من أبناء سلالة عاصي أو شريف يعرف هيئة جده الأكبر؟

من منهم المسلم؟ من المسيحي؟ ذكر القسيس ويليام إيدي أنه رأى "رجلًا مسلمًا" يخرج من الموقع حاملًا قطعة من الحجر المنحوت، إذًا لا بد أن الناس كانوا قادرين على تمييز المسلم من المسيحي من هيئته؟ هل فقدنا تلك القدرة اليوم؟ لا أدري. وإن كانوا فعلًا قادرين على التمييز فهل كانوا يكترثون؟

كيف ينظر هؤلاء الرجال إلى عثمان حمدي بك؟ ما موقفهم من السلطات العثمانية؟ هل يعتبرون الحكم العثماني احتلالًا أم واقعًا لا يستدعي التفكير أو المساءلة؟

كان ذلك عام 1887. سبعة وعشرون عامًا مرّت على الاقتتال بين دروز جبل لبنان ومسيحييه – أي ما يقارب المدة التي تفصلنا عن عام 1990 لحظة وضعت الحروب الأهلية الكثيرة في لبنان أوزارها. هل شهد أحد من الواقفين في الصورة أحداث القتل في عام 1860؟ هل يتذكرونها؟ وإن كانوا يتذكرونها فهل يفضّلون نسيانها؟

مذاق شبحي

أذكر أنني رأيته آخر مرة في اجتماعٍ عائليٍ مطلع الثمانينيات عند خالتي في كينغز بوينت بنيويورك: غمامةٌ بيضاء كبيرة تطفو فوق مائدة الحلويات. لم يأذنوا لنا بتناول قطعة منها حتى ننهي طعام العشاء. فرُحتُ أنا وأخي الأصغر نلتهم ما سكبته أمي في طبقينا من المحشّى أو المنحشى (التسمية اليهودية العراقية لطبق المحشي) والبامية أولًا، حتى سمحت لنا أخيرًا بالانقضاض على الحلوى. كنا نعلم من سابق تجربةٍ أن الملبّس منظرٌ بلا طعم، طبقةٌ رقيقةٌ خادعةٌ من السكر الملون تغلّف حبّة لوز بائتةً بدلًا من شوكولاتة أم أند الشهية. لا أذكر إن كان شقيقي قد اختار البقلاوة البيتية، أما أنا فقد كانت تلك الغمامة البيضاء شبه الكرتونية تناديني.

كان من الصعب انتزاع قطعةٍ منها، فقد كان الطبق كله مغمّسًا بالطحين ليمنع الكريّات الصغيرة من الالتصاق ببعضها البعض. لذا عندما خرجت القطعة التي كنت أحاول انتزاعها ملتصقةً بنصف حبةٍ أخرى شعرت بأنني قد نلتُ نصيبًا محرّمًا فوق نصيبي. حطّ مذاق الطحين على لساني أولًا قبل أن تنغرس أسناني في اللدينة البيضاء فيتدفق منها الهال. كانت نكهةً مسكِرةً بالنسبة لابن السنوات التسع، وكأن نافذةً قد شُرعت في جسدي وهبّت منها نسمةٌ فوّاحةٌ بالتوابل. وكان لقطع اللوز المحمّص الممزوجة بالفستق والجوز في فمي قوام قضمة من شوكولاتة سنيكرز المفضلة عندي. مع ذلك، كنت أدرك في سني الصغيرة تلك خطيئة المقارنة بين سكاكر الهالووين وتلك الحلوى المجاورة من مرتبة القداسة والتي كان أحد أقربائنا قد تمكن من جلبها من العراق رغم أن أحدًا من أسرتي لم يجرؤ على العودة إلى هناك قط.

كان أول عهدنا بالمنّ أو "منّ السما" كما يقال له باللهجة العراقية كنوع من الطعام الأسطوري في سدر الفصح. يقول النص المقدس إن هذه المادة قد انهمرت من السماء ليقتات منها العبرانيون الهائمون أربعين سنةً في التيه ما بين سيناء وأرض كنعان. ويُعتقَد أن أصل كلمة "منّ" يعود إلى الآرامية "من هو" ومعناها "ما هذا؟" وهي كلمةٌ في صيغة

سـؤال. وكنـت فـي طفولتـي أتخيـل ندفًـا مـن هـذه الحلـوى البيضـاء المغذيـة وهـي تتسـاقط كالثلج مـن السـماء لتتلقفهـا راحـات أجـدادي المحرريـن مـن نيـر العبوديـة. أذكـر أننـي رسمتُها في صـف الآنسـة ماليـن خـلال سـنتي الأولـى فـي المدرسـة العبريـة فأثنـت عليّ، بينمـا رسـم التلميـذ الأكثـر تفوقًـا دايفيـد إيتنغـر، وهـو يهـود أشـكينازي، سـماءً تمطـر دجاجًـا محمّـرًا وقرنبيطًـا أخضـر وبطاطـا وذرة.

تباعدت اللقاءات العائلية بعد وفاة جدتي العراقية رينيه عام 1984 واختفى المنّ مـن عـلى موائدها. لكن كانت هناك حلويات أخرى كالسيلان (دبس التمر) الذي كان جدي نِسيم قد عصره بيديه وخزّنه في المجمدة قبل وفاته عـام 1975. وبعدما أنهينا تلك صرنـا نبحث عـن بدائل: منتجاتٍ نشـتريها مـن السـوق مصنوعةٍ فـي كاليفورنيـا أو إسـرائيل. وكانـت أمـي تشـكو كثـرة تكريرهـا وافتقادهـا إلـى الكثافـة والقـوام اللذيـن يمتـاز بهمـا سـيلان جـدي. كانـت تقـول شبه مازحةٍ: "كأنهم يحاولون جعلنا بيضًا".

تهنـا وهمنـا عـلى وجوهنـا فـي صحرائنـا الخاصة. بعد وفاة جـدي حافظنـا عـلى صلتنـا بالعراق لتسـع سـنوات مـن خـلال القصـص السـعيدة التـي كانـت ترويهـا جدتـي عـن بغـداد. اعتدنـا أن نشـعر بالتعلّـق بذلـك المكـان البعيـد وأن نحبـه بالرغـم مـن مغادرتنـا لـه مكرَهيـن. كان العراق حينهـا مجـرد حـدثٍ هامشـيٍ فـي نشـرة أخبـار المسـاء، لا بصفتـه المكـان الـذي حدّثنـا عنـه جـدّاي بكثيـر مـن الحـب، بـل كسـاحة حـربٍ متصلـةٍ بالسـياق الإيرانـي. ثـم حـدث تغيـر مـا بعـد أن اجتـاح العـراق الكويـت عشـيّة حـرب الخليـج التـي قادتهـا الولايـات المتحـدة الأميركيـة عـام 1991. فبينمـا كنـا نتحلـق حـول مائـدة العشـاء ونتابـع كاميـرات الرؤيـة الليليـة ذات الصـور المخضـرّة فـي نقلهـا المباشـر لعمليـة تدميـر المبانـي فـي مدينـة أجدادنـا، أدركنـا أن البلـد الـذي لجـأت إليـه عائلتنـا يَقصـف فـي تلـك اللحظـات البلـد الـذي فررنـا منـه. تدخلـت أمـي مقاطعـةً مشـهد العنـف قائلـةً: "هـل تعلمـون أن ليـس مـن ثمـة مطعـمٍ عراقـي فـي نيويـورك؟"

بعد بضعـة أشـهر، ذهبـت العائلـة فـي رحلـةٍ بالسـيارة إلـى واشـنطن بمناسـبة عطلـة الربيـع. كانت تنتظرني بيـن الوجبـات الخفيفـة المعـدّة للرحلـة مفاجـأةٌ: لفافـةٌ ذهبيـةٌ كُتـب عليهـا بالأحـرف الفارسـية. كانـت GAZ (غـز) هـي الكلمـة الوحيـدة المكتوبـة عليهـا باللغـة الإنكليزيـة. ضغطتُ عليهـا فـإذا بهـا شـيءٌ مسـتديرٌ بنصـف حجـم كفّـي. ابتسـمت أمـي وقالـت: "تذوّقـه. لعلّه يعيد إليـك بعـض الذكريـات". مـا إن فتحـت اللفافـة حتـى تناثـرت ذرات الطحيـن فـي الهـواء وتساقطت برفـق عـلى بنطلـون الجينـز. أخـذتُ قضمـةً فـإذا بـي أُنقـل مثـل بروسـت والماديـن إلـى مائـدة الحلويـات عنـد خالتـي قبـل عقـدٍ مـن الزمـن. "إنـه المنّ"، هتفـت أمـي. شـعرتُ وكأنـي أتذوّق شبحًا. قالـت إنهـا لـم تعثـر عـلى مـا هـو أقـرب إلـى المنّ مـن الغـز. أدت عقوبـات الأمـم المتحـدة عـلى العـراق إلـى سـقوط ملاييـن الضحايـا كمـا انقطـع بسـببها وجـود تلـك الحلـوى، فـكان علينـا أن نرتضـي بالغـز بديـلًا عنهـا. لـم أكـن وقتهـا عـلى درايـة كافيـة تمكننـي مـن تمييـز الاختلافـات بيـن هذيـن الصنفيـن مـن الحلـوى، لكـن التشـابه بينهمـا بـدا لـي منطقيًـا بسـبب التداخـل الجغرافـي والتشـارك فـي البيئـة والثقافـة والمطبـخ. علمـتُ لاحقًـا مـن أحـد الأصدقـاء، وهو إيرانـي يهـودي، أن اسـم الحلـوى الإيرانيـة مأخـوذ عـن كلمـة "انگبيـن گـز" أي شـهد الگـز وهـو فصيلـةٌ مـن الأثـل تنمـو فـي جبـال زاغـروس الممتـدة مـن إيـران إلـى كردسـتان شـمال العـراق.

ولكـي أعـرف المزيـد عـن الأثـل، كان لا بـد لـي مـن أن أعـرّج عـلى نخيـل التمـر.[1] سـافرت فـي عـام 2007 إلـى الأردن للقـاء أثيـر، المصـدّر العراقـي الـذي كنـت أتعامـل معـه بهـدف اسـتيراد التمـر

1 ثمة نص أكادي بعنوان "خصومة الأثل ونخيل التمر" تتبارى فيه كلا الشجرتين بحسب الباحث التوراتي الدكتور ألان هام "في إثبات أنها أكثر نفعًا. تستند شجرة الأثل في حجّتها إلى كون خشبها يُستخدم لنحت تماثيل الآلهة وصنع الأدوات والبخور. تشير النخلة بدورها إلى أنها تُستخدم في صناعة القماش والحبال كما تنتج الثمر على عكس غريمتها".

العراقي إلى الولايات المتحدة لأول مرة منذ عقود ضمن مشروع كنت قد بدأته عام 2004 بعنوان "عودة" (RETURN). لا تختلف قصة شحنة التمر المشؤومة تلك عن محنة مئات الآلاف من اللاجئين العراقيين الذين جلسوا لأربعة أيام في سياراتهم بطابور الانتظار الطويل عند الحدود الأردنية. أُرسلت الشحنة أخيرًا إلى بغداد ومنها إلى دمشق وكانت قد فسدت وباتت غير صالحةٍ للأكل. لاحقًا، وصلت عشرة صناديق من التمر إلى نيويورك عام 2006 عن طريق الشحن الجوي وباتت العملية بمجملها رمزًا لمأساة إنسانية وبيئية أعم.

اضطر أثير إلى الفرار من أحداث العنف الطائفي في العراق في منتصف المشروع وبات مقيمًا في عمّان. كان يحدّثني عن جمال العراق وعن ضخامة جذوع النخيل هناك؛ سألني مرةً عما إذا أصبح يشبه جدّي.

في آخر أمسية لي في عمّان، اصطحبني أثير إلى متجر لبيع الحلويات العراقية كان أصحابه قد تهجروا من بغداد. توجه إلى البائع مباشرةً وأشار إلى منضدةٍ خلفه تُقطّع عليها كريات بيضاء مغلّفة بالطحين من عجينة كبيرة. المنّ. تكلّم صاحب المحل بعربية مفهومة. "من العراق". "وصلت صباحًا"، أردف أثير طالبًا من البائع أن يضع بعضًا منها في علبة معدنية مستديرة. ثم أعطاني إياها قائلًا: "إنها لك ولوالدتك ولعائلتك".

بعد عودتي إلى نيويورك فتحت العلبة مع والديّ. تذوقتها أمي أولًا والطحين يتساقط على منضدة المطبخ. رفعت عينيها متلذذةً ودعت أبي لتذوقها. كما تحفّز الخمائر تغير البروتين، أسال مذاق الحلوى الذكريات العذبة على طرفي لسانيهما. حفل خطبتهما؛ زفاف أحد الأقرباء؛ زيارة الخال نيازي والخالة تيفي المقيمين في لندن؛ أحداثٌ كان المنّ شاهدًا عليها.

غابت العلبة في أعماق المجمدة لتتجمد في انتظار مناسبةٍ سعيدةٍ ستأتي. كانت أثمن من يفرّط بها أو أن تُترك لتفسد، كما لم يكن جائزًا أن نأكلها دفعةً واحدة. لا بد أن تدوم لأطول وقتٍ ممكن بخلاف أسرتي التي لم تدم حياتها في بغداد. لم تكن مجرّد حلوى، بل كانت طعم الذكرى من نبات أرض أجدادي.

ترابوتينا مانيبارا (Trabutina mannipara) أو المنّ هو اسم الحشرة التي تتغذى على أشجار الأثل التي كانت تنمو بكثافة في السابق في مناطق مثل سيناء وما بات اليوم شمال العراق. تفرز هذه الحشرة الفائض من العصارة التي تمتصها من الشجرة في شكل عسل المن. يتجمع عسل المنّ في تشكّلات بلورية كثيفة على الأغصان والتربة، فيُجمَع ويُغلى كي تسهل تنقيته من الشوائب كالأغصان الصغيرة والأوراق والتراب. يُضاف بعدها الهال واللوز والفستق والجوز وماء الورد إلى "منّ السما"، فيعمل عسل المنّ كخامةٍ ومادةٍ مكثّفة تربط المكونات ببعضها البعض، تمامًا كما جمعت أرام النهرين أو بلاد ما بين النهرين فيما مضى الأشوريين والتركمان والكورد والإيزيديين واليهود والمندائيين والكلدانيين والشركس والشبك والكاكائيين والسنة والشيعة وعرب الأهوار والغجر والبدو والفرس وغيرهم. في ماض غير بعيد، أحال هذا العجين الدبق إلى تصورٍ جامعٍ ورؤيويٍ لمستقبل ما لبث أن طوته الإيديولوجيات القومية التي اجتاحت غرب آسيا.

بعد اختتام مشروع "عودة" احتفظتُ بحفنةٍ من التمر العراقي وأودعتُها في الثلاجة، كما فعلت أمي بسيلان جدي ومنّ السما، في انتظار مناسبةٍ احتفالية. عندما وُلدت ابنتي

رينيه في شيكاغو بعدها بثلاثة أعوام وضعنا في فمها حبةً من ذلك التمر كي يكون أول مذاق هذا العالم حلوًا. وتصادف الاحتفال بتسميتها والذي سيقام في مونتريال حيث تقيم أسرة زوجتي، مع وصول شحنةٍ من حلوى المنّ إلى البقالة العربية في حيّنا. لم تكن آتيةً من العراق، بل من مصنع حلويات عراقي في ميسيساغا بأونتاريو. كانت كل حبّة ملفوفةً بغلاف من البلاستيك الشفاف ومصنوعةً من مركّز الذرة عالي الفركتوز. اشتريت دزينتين منها رغم علمي بأنها ليست الأصلية لكي أقدّمها على مائدة الحلويات احتفالًا بمنح رينيه اسمها اليهودي رينا ومعناه الأنشودة الجذلى. ذررتُ بعض الطحين عليها في محاولةٍ فاشلةٍ لتقليد الأصل، ولكن المذاق كان أشبه بتجربة الطيران بالنسبة إلى طيّار محترف يلعب لعبة لمحاكاة الطيران. تمنيتُ لو أنني طلبتُ من والدي أن يحضرا بعضًا من المنّ الذي كنتُ قد جلبتُه معي من الأردن. كنتُ متأكدًا من أنهما لا يزالان يحتفظان ببعض منه في ثلاجتهما. وكانت حجة أبي للتخفيف عني أن "جئنا بالسيارة من نيويورك، ماذا لو لم تسمح لنا السلطات الكندية بإدخاله عبر الحدود؟". بالطبع لم أكن راضيًا بالبديل، ولكنني كنت آمل لو أنه كان من الجودة بمقدار يمكّنه من أن يشق نافذةً على العراق على شرف ابنتي التي تحمل اسم والدة جدّتها العراقية.

يشتق لفظ substitute الإنكليزي ومعناه البديل من الفعل *substituere* باللاتينية الذي يشتق بدوره من *statuere* والاسم *statua* أو *statue* أي تمثال. ولقد انصب معظم اهتمامي خلال العقدين الماضيين على صناعة بدائل لتماثيل أخرى فُقدت أو دُمرت. تحاكي هذه المسيرة أجيالًا من العراقيين في المهاجر يصنعون المأكولات التقليدية من مكوّنات لا تشبه تلك الموجودة في العراق، بل تنوب عما فُقد منها. طرفٌ اصطناعي وشيءٌ من الرجاء بأن يحضر ما كنا فقدناه بين أيدينا.

مرّ عامٌ على قبولي الدعوة لكتابة هذا النص. شهد شارع ديفونشير أفنيو في شيكاغو خلال هذا العام افتتاح بقالات شامية عدّة. قصدتُ واحدةً منها مؤخرًا فإذ بي أفاجأ برؤية علبة منّ السما على الرف قبالة المدخل. كانت الحلوى تحمل اسم العلامة التجارية "الحمدان"، وقد صُنعت في منطقة الرابية في عمان حيث يقطن الكثير من النازحين العراقيين. رُسم على العلبة جانب من بوابة عشتار التي تمثل المعلم الأساسي لبابل في عهد نبوخذ نصّر والتي حملها الألمان إلى برلين في مطلع القرن العشرين ولا تزال معروضة إلى اليوم في متحف بيرغامون. تسارعت نبضات قلبي وأنا أقلب العلبة لأقرأ "منّ السما" في رأس قائمة المكونات. لكن لا. سمنٌ وطحينٌ وسكر. بديل آخر لا أكثر، شاغل رمزي، تمامًا مثل النسخة الخشبية الرديئة المقلّدة من بوابة عشتار التي شُيّدت في الخمسينيات بتكليف من الحكومة العراقية بالقرب من موقع مدينة بابل الأثرية والتي تمثل حاليًا مدخلًا إلى أحد المتاحف كما لا تزال ينتظر أن يعود إلى العراق.

اشتريت العلبة وحملتها إلى المجمدة مباشرةً.

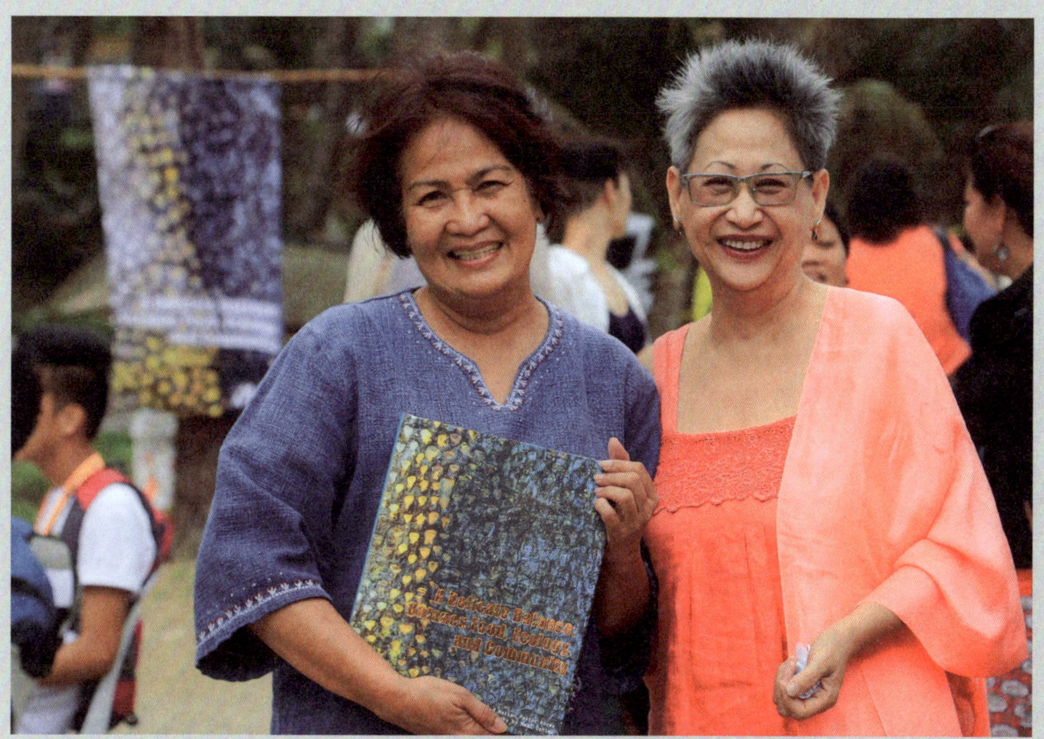

دينا أباد وماريان باستور رويس في حفل إطلاق كتاب *A Delicate Balance: Batanes Food, Ecology, and Community* (2016) في يورا، باتانس.

محادثة بين بيو أباد وماريان باستور رويس

بيو أباد

أودّ أن أبدأ بهذه الصورة الفوتوغرافية التي عثرتُ عليها مؤخّرًا. الصورةُ لـك ولوالدتي في باتانِس أثناء حفل إطلاق كتابك عـن جماعة إيفاتان[1] ومأكولاتها[2].

تكشف هذه الصورة في نظري عن الكثير من الخيوط المتداخلة على الصعيدين الشخصي والسياسي. كانت قد الْتُقِطَت في آذار/ مارس من العام 2016 حين كنّا لا نزال غافلين عن التسونامي الـذي يوشك أن يعصف بالبلاد مـع حلـول رئـاسة رودريغـو دوتيرتي. ولـم نكن أنـا وعائلتي نعلم آنذاك بعدُ بمرض والدتي. يصعب عليّ الآن تحييد وفاتها عن القلق والصعوبات المتلازمة مع التحدّيات السياسية التي واجهَتها مع والدي.

أفكّر في ما ورثتُه – بالمعنى العائلي وإنّما أيضًا بالمعنى الجيلي – وفي تراكمات السياسـة والإرهـاق وبعض النصر ولحظات اليأس المدمّرة التي عانيتُ منها والتي لا شك قد عانيتِ منها كذلك.

ثمّ كان لنا حديثٌ جارٍ حول عَمَلِنا ودورِه في مُساءلة مفاهيم التراث – سواء المُثْبَت أركيولوجيًّا أو المختَلق سياسيًّا – وباتانِس هي المكان المثالي لإفراد هذه المشاريع والحديث عنها لأسبابٍ عدّة. وعلى قدر تجاوُز عملنا الحدود الجغرافية وتجذّره العميق في مجالَي التنظير وتاريخ الفن، فهو في النهاية شديد الخصوصية ومطلقٌ في تماشِه مع مفهومَي الحب والحزن.

ماريان باستور رويس

والإمكانية واليأس.

ب. أ.

والنصر والإخفاق.

م.ب.ر.

إخفاقٌ هائل. أنت محقّ في الخوض مباشرةً في الجانب الشخصي. مـا الـذي يعترينا كي نندفع لنفعل ما نفعله غير السعي بلا وجلٍ وراء رغبةٍ طوباويةٍ لم تتحقّق؟ ومع ذلك، فقد أقلعتُ عـن هذا الوصف، قـد تكون مجرّد عادةٍ سيّئة.

أظن أنك عندما تبلغ سنّي هذا – ووالدتك وأنا من السنّ نفسه – تشعُر وكأنـكَ قـد بـدّدتَ سنواتٍ لا عـدّ لـها هباءً في سعيك وراء الأمـل. ذلـك الأمـل الـذي تكمُـن قوّتـه في إتاحته تصوّر إنعـاش بلـدٍ وشعبٍ خانهما الطغاة وأعوانُهُم، أي إنقاذ الملايين مـن الفلبينيين الذين استسلموا لليأس وقلّـة الحيلـة، والذين ينتظرون الخروج مـن هذا المصير مثلي أنـا ومثل غيري من التوّاقين للعيش في كنف نظامٍ أكثر عدالة ورحمة.

تلك الرغبة والأمل اللاعقلانيّان هما في مُجمَل الأحوال الدافع وراء ممارستي كقيّمة فنية. لا أوهام لدي بالنجاح، ولكنني في الوقت عينه لا أتمادى في التشاؤم.

إذًا ها أنا – إلى جانب مشاريعي في مجال التقييم الفني – بصدد التحضيـر لنشر كتـاب عـن المجـازر التي ارتكبها المستوطنون

المسيحيون في ميندانـاو بيـن أواخـر السـتينيات وأوائـل
السـبعينيات، والتـي أسـفرت عـن تهجيـر المسـلمين مـن أرض
أجدادهم. وقد صعدت تيـاراتٌ ثقافيـة سـرّية منذ ذلـك الحين،
أسـهَمَت في إنتاج ثقافـةٍ عُنفيّـةٍ كان مـن تَبِعاتِها الكارثية وصول
شخصٍ مختـلّ اجتماعيًّـا إلى سـدّة الرئاسـة الحالية في الفلبين[3].
وإزاء معرفتي بهذه التفاصيل أجد التقييم الفني عملًا واهيًا لا
حياة فيه.

لـذا بعـض أملـي في أن يكتسـب القيّمون/ات المزيد مـن الصلابة
في معتـرك العمـل. نعـم، لقـد تمـرّس الفنانـون/ات والقيّمـون/
ات طويـلًا في سياسـات الذاكـرة في كل مـكان، ولكننا لسـنا سـوى
حشـراتٍ صغيـرةٍ في مواجهـة عمالقـة السياسـة والاقتصاد. إن
حجم هـذه القوى في بلدنا هائـلٌ حيث تبلغ المُراجعة التاريخية
مسـتوياتٍ عابـرةً للحـدود، وتَعتَـدّ بشـبكاتٍ لا حصـر لهـا تَتّبـع
بدورهـا معاييـرَ عالميـةً وتبتلـع أمـوالًا طائلـة[4]. وتمـارس هـذه
الحمـلات اللامبـالاة العلنية حيال اغتصاب الذاكرة الجماعية من
قبـل فئـةٍ مـن أصحـاب المصالـح الخبيثة.

لـم أكتـرث قـط لا فكريًـا ولا عاطفيًـا لمفهوم الأمّـة – ولا حتى
لمفهـوم أمّتـي أو انتمائـي – لـذا لا جـدوى مـن الخـوض مجدّدًا في
سياسـات الذاكـرة في الفلبين. ولكنني وضعـتُ كتابًـا على سـبيل
المثـال عـن الاغتيـالات في فتـرة ماركـوس كي أدعـم بالمزيد مـن
المعلومات قضية إقامة منطقة الحكم الذاتي في بانغ سـامورو
لمسـلمي ميندانـاو[5]. بإمـكان ممارسـة التقييـم الفنـي أن تسـعى
لإفـراد مسـاحةٍ لهـا للحديـث عـن الذاكـرة المحذوفـة، وهـذا هـو
السـبب في تمسّـكي وعنـادي. إذ لا تـزال إمكانيـة ممارسـة التقييم
الفنـي مـن دون التخلّـي عن الانضبـاط المهني وبعيـدًا عن الانزلاق
إلى الدعائيـة موجـودةً في نظـري. ثم هنـاك الـروح الجيليّـة التي
يجـب أن نحتفـي بهـا. وأمَلـي في أن تنشـأ علاقـةٌ جديـدةٌ مع سَـردية
الأمّـة تكـون متشـابهة ومتماثلـةً مـع تلـك التـي ناضَـلَ والـداك
لبنائهـا[6]. لقـد انخرطنا في مؤسّسـاتٍ اسـتعماريةٍ جديدةٍ مـا لبثت
أن تحوّلـت إلى الفاشـيّة.

ب. أ.

عندمـا أتأمّـل في نضال والـدي السياسي مقارنـةً بعملي كفنّـان،
يبـدو لي في كثيـرٍ من الأحيان أن مخيّلتهمـا – أعني قدرتهمـا على
التمسّـك بالممكـن في وجـه كل الصعـاب – تفـوق مخيّلتـي، كما
أن هـذا الأمـل اللاعقلاني الـذي تتحدّثيـن عنـه قـد بـات الميـراث
والعـبء الأكبـر بالنسـبة إلـيّ. يجـد الجانب الأكبـر مـن تصوّراتـي
ومفاهيمهما عـن الأمّـة جذوره في باتانِـس. هنـاك، أعدَمَ اليابانيون

أحـد أعمـام أبي بقطـع الـرأس عقابًـا على انضمامه إلى المقاومة[7].
كان جـدّاي شـوكةً في خاصـرة حكم ماركوس الديكتاتـوري[8] لأنّهما
حـالا دون إحكامـه السـيطرة الكاملـة علـى شـمال الفلبين، حيث
وقفت باتانِـس في معارضـةٍ مسـتمرّةٍ للنظام. وقد وقَعَـت حادثةٌ
في السـتينيات عندمـا قامت عصابـات فرديناند ماركوس بَرشـق
منزل العائلـة بالأسـلحة الآليّـة. نجا الجميـع، إذ لو حدث مكروةٌ
لأي منهـم لمـا كنـت هنـا الآن. هكذا عـاش والـداي باسـتمرار في
مرمـى السـلطة اللامتكافئـة بدءًا مـن مقاعـد الدراسـة الجامعية
حيـن نشـطا كمنظّمين في صفوف نقابـات المزارعين والصيّاديـن
في السـبعينيات، ووصولًـا إلى المصاعـب التي تعرّضـا لها كمناضِلَين
تقدّميَّيـن مؤمنَيـن بضـرورة التغييـر المؤسسـي الحكومـي، وهي
مهمّـةٌ شـاقة وغير مجزية. ذلك الإحسـاس بالانتمـاء إلى القضيّة
مـع مـا رافقـه مـن صدمـاتٍ وآلام هـو إرث عائلتنا الـذي يعشّش
الآن في صميـم وجداننـا أنا وإخوتي وإن بأوجـهٍ مختلفة. بالنسبة
لـي، أعبّـر عـن هـذا مـن خـلال الفـن.

تُذَكّرني باتانِـس بالعائلـة وباعتزازهـا بالانتمـاء إلى هـذه الجزيرة
الطرفيـة. إنّهـا مكانـي في هذا العالـم وحيـث يرقـد أجـدادي ومن
بينهم عمّتـي باسـيتا[9] وأمـي. أصـول أمـي ليسـت من هنـاك، وإنّما
لعائلـة أبي أصـولٌ تاريخيـةٌ في الجزيرة، فبـاتَت بذلـك موطنها
هـي أيضًـا.

م. ب. ر.

لا يكفي مصطلح "طرفي" لوصف مكانة باتانِس. هل كان والـداك
علـى اطّـلاع علـى مـا كنّـا نقولـه عـن سياسـات المركز/الأطراف في
مجالاتنا الأكاديميـة المنخرطـة في بحوث ما بعد الاسـتعمار؟ هل
كانـا يدركان رمزيّـة باتانِس بالنسـبة إلى الأطراف؟

ب. أ.

إلى حـدّ مـا، نعـم. باتانِس هي مجموعـةٌ من الجزر في أقصى شمال
الفلبين، عُرفَت لوقـتٍ طويـلٍ باعتبارها المكان الذي يصعب الوصول
إليه. وقد تداخَـل مفهـوم البُعد في نسـيج الجزيرة وأسـاطيرها.
وبشـكلٍ أساسـي، كانت باتانِـس تُعـرَّف كنقطـة دخـول الأعاصير
المداريّـة إلى منطقـة مراقبة التغيّـرات المناخية التابعة للفلبين
(Philippine Area of Responsibility - PAR). واكتسَـبَت
هويّتها بنـاءً علـى رمَنَسَـة مفاهيـم العُزلـة والمرونة. وقد سـاهم
في ذلـك أن الجزيـرة لم تكُن تُشـبه باقي أنحـاء الفلبين في شـيء،
بـل كانت أقـرب إلى شـواطئ اسـكتلندا الصخرية منهـا إلى الصورة
الذهنيـة الشـائعة عـن الشـواطئ الاسـتوائية.

"موجاتٍ من الهجرات" التي أدّت إلى ظهور "النوع الإندونيسي" على نسق "النوع المالايو"[14]. وكذلك نشأت الشعوب الأصلية من الوافدين الأوائل من محدودي الطول ذوي البشرة الداكنة والشعر الأجعد والذين أُطلقت عليهم تسمية "نغريتو".

ب. أ.

هذا ما تعلّمناه في المدرسة الابتدائية.

م. ب. ر.

في غياب أي خطابٍ عرقيٍ في الفلبين، يكاد يغيب عن الأذهان الجانب العرقي من هذه السردية ومدى عنصريّتها[15]. فهي تقوم في إطارٍ من الداروينية الاجتماعية التي أسفرت عن عواقب مشؤومة. استنادًا إلى هذه السردية، تمثّل إندونيسيا الجانب المتحضّر. ويمكن تعداد الممالك والإمبراطوريات الإندونيسية أمثال سريفيجايا وماجاباهيت وإن كان وجودها طرفيًا. كما أن الإندونيسيين هم من بنوا بوروبودور. تُثار هذه السرديات في الأوساط الراقية والمثقّفة كنوعٍ من الاعتزاز بالعراقة بالمَعيّة.

إلى اليوم، لا يزال الفلبينيون غير مُطّلعين أو غير مُبالين بمسارات انتشار اللغة – وبالتالي الثقافة – من الشمال إلى الجنوب عبر أرخبيل الفلبين. فهذه السرديّة لا تتّفق مع أوهام الأرستقراطية القديمة ومواقع التَّمدين. كما يبدو أنها تُفاقم القلق حيال ثقافة ما قبل الاستعمار والتي تشير كل الدلائل إلى تكوّنها من أفكارٍ حول مخلوقاتٍ عاريةٍ تتسلّح بالأقواس والنشاشيب والرماح تعمل على الصيد والالتقاط وحصاد الوقيد أو الزراعة على نطاقٍ ضيّق. ويمكن الاستدلال على هذه الثقافة المؤسّسة العابرة للأرخبيل في باتانِس التي عاصرتها.

ب. أ.

متى حدث الإجماع على منشأ باتانِس في علم الآثار والألسنيات؟

م. ب. ر.

تم ذلك منذ نحو 30 عامًا[16]، ولكنه تزامَن مع اللحظة التي تَلَت سقوط ديكتاتورية ماركوس مباشرةً والتي ظَغَت عليها الرغبة في الظهور بوجهٍ حضاريٍ أمام العالم، تلك الرغبة التي بزّرَت من جُملة نتائجها الصعود الغريب لطليعة الفنون البصرية في مركز الفلبين الثقافي التابع لإيملدا ماركوس. وكانت تلك الطليعة قد لاقَت نهايتها الطبيعية مع سقوط الديكتاتورية في العام 1985. غير أن إعادة التوظيف المُطردة في التقسيمات والأفضليات العرقية التي اعتمدها النظام الديكتاتوري تواصلَت

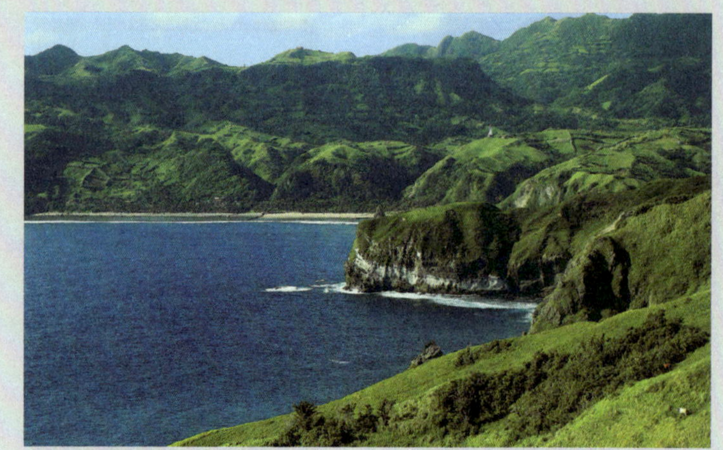

جزيرة باتان، باتانِس. الصورة بإذن من أوبال بالا.

م. ب. ر.

تُرجّح الآثار الفلبينية ومناطق المحيط الهادئ أن تكون باتانِس نقطة البداية لانتشار اللغات الأسترونيزية جنوبًا نحو أنحاء جنوب شرق آسيا كافة. التاريخ حاسم: 4000 سنة إلى الوراء[10]. وقد أسفر هذا الانتشار عن ولادة 176 لغةٍ[11] محكيّةٍ في الفلبين إضافة إلى المزيد في إندونيسيا. ثمّ ركّب المتحدّثون بهذه اللغات البحر وصولًا إلى غوام (مارياناس) خلال العصر النيوليثي، أي قبل 3000 إلى 3500 سنة[12]. وقد توزّعت الشعوب الأسترونيزيّة في مُجمل مناطق المحيط الهادئ إبّان المرحلة الثالثة من هجرات الإنسان الأوّل (هومو سابينس) بواسطة مراكب صغيرة عَبَرَت مياه المحيط. كما أحضرَت الشعوب المتحدّثة بالأسترونيزية لغتها إلى مدغشقر. والمالاغاسي هي من اللغات الأسترونيزية أيضًا[13]. وقد استمرّ هذا الإجماع في علم الآثار والألسنيات طيلة 30 عامًا، علمًا أن عمليّات إعادة التشكيل المبنية على الوراثيّات قد تُفسح المجال لاكتشاف مساراتٍ متعدّدة الاتجاهات لكيفية وصول هذه الشعوب ومتى وأين، لكن من غير المرجّح أن يؤدّي ذلك إلى تغيير صورة انتشار عائلة اللغات هذه.

إن عدم انتشار هذه الرواية أو الاعتراف بها في سياق سردية نشأة الفلبين يشعرني بالضيق الشديد. إذ يدلّ ذلك على البطء الشديد في تحديث المعلومات العلميّة في المناهج التربوية وفي الخطاب العام على السواء، ما يشير إلى انحيازٍ ضد العلوم يستدعي التمعّن والتحليل. ولكن الأخطر هو حجم التوظيفات الثقافية في السردية الاستعمارية لنشأة الفلبين والتي لا تزال سائدةً حتى اليوم. إذ تقول هذه السردية التي تحظى بالتفضيل بأن الشعب الفلبيني قد تشكّل نتيجة

     بيو أباد وماريان باستور روسِس

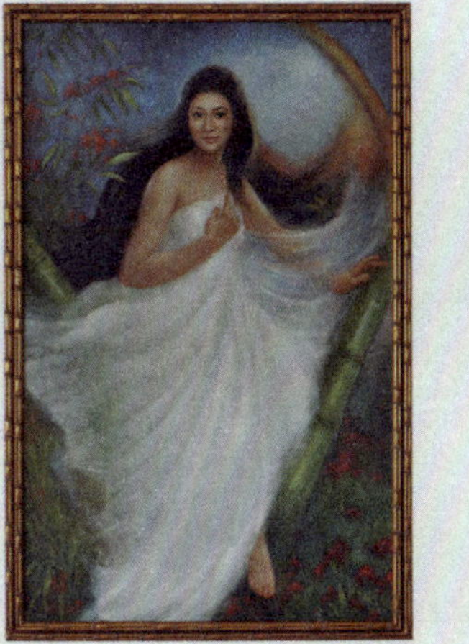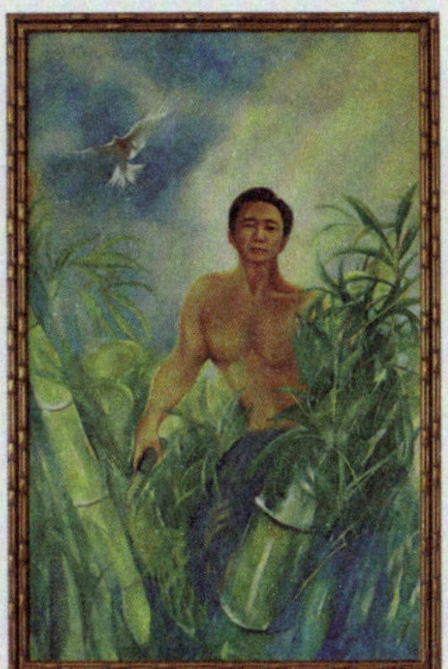

بيو أباد، "إيملدا في هيئة ماغاندا وفرديناند في هيئة مالاكاس"، 2014. زيت على قماش في إطار من الخيزران المطلي بالذهب الزائف. الصورة الفوتوغرافية لـ ر.ج. فرنانديز . الصورة بإذن من الفنان.

بعـد رحيلهـا في صِيَـغٍ تعبيريـةٍ عزّزَتها القواعد الفنية والثقافية.

من ناحيةٍ أخرى، سيؤدّي التخلّـص مـن هـذه الرغبـة في التحضّـر إلى فضـح الكثيـر من الحقائـق عن الفلبين: الاختلافات "العرقية" و"العصبية" التي اقتُئتِلًا حولها لعقـودٍ طويلةٍ، والنزعـات الإقليمية المفرطة التي طَغَت على الوحدة اللغوية الأسترونيزية، والتفسيرات الخاطئة لتاريخ الأرستقراطية. لقد كانـت الحـرب الانفصاليـة التي خاضهـا الفلبينيـون المسلمون ضد الأكثرية المسيحية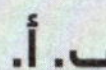[17] على امتداد 50 عامًا نتيجةً للتهميش العنيـف علـى خلفيـة التصـوّر الخاطـئ للفروقـات الثقافيـة (والعرقيـة مـن وجهـة نظر البعـض) بين الفلبينيين المسلمين والمسيحيين، والإمعـان في تصنيفهـم كأغيارٍ وبالتالـي الاقتتـال معهم وخلق أوضاع اجتماعيـةٍ مأسوية بذلك. وفي المُحصّلـة، يـؤدّي القلق الطبقـي (الفقر المدقع) والقلق العرقي (السمرة الداكنـة) إلـى إنتـاج أجيـالٍ عديـدة مـن الفـن الـرديء والصراع الاجتماعـي الحـادّ والسياسـات العاجـزة.

ب. أ.

هناك تصوّر معيّنٌ عن كيفية اختلاق المستوطنين المسيحيين في مينداناو هذه الأسطورة عـن أنفسهم. ونحن لا نـزال حتى الآن في مواجهة الصدمة والقلق في صورة الحكم الدوتيرتي.

م.ب.ر.

هنـاك عـوارض أشـدّ بشاعةً لهذا القلق تتمثّل في المحاولات المستمـرّة لاختـلاق الملـوك والملكات في الثقافة الشعبية (أكبَرُها مشروع الإمبراطور فرديناند والإمبراطورة إيملدا). فالرئيس الحالي رودريغو دوتيرتي متحـدّر من مينداناو حيث دجّج المستوطنون المسيحيون من الشمال أنفسهم بالسلاح للدفاع عن ملكيّاتهم المقتطعة من أراضي الجماعات المسلمة التي عاشت هناك لقرون. وقد سعت الميليشيات المسيحية المدعومة من النظام إلى ارتكاب المجازر أملًا في التخلّص من محاولات المسلمين استرجاع أراضيهم، ما أوقع الأهوال. خرج دوتيرتي من هذا الواقع الآسن ليُطّيح بمائة عامٍ من التجربة الديمقراطية.

ب. أ.

لعـلّ مـن أغرب الأحكام التي جـاءت نتيجة رئاسة دوتيرتي إعادةُ إحياء رغبة فرديناند ماركوس بتغييـر اسم البـلاد إلى ماهارليكا (Maharlika)[18]، وهـو اسمٌ كان يُطلَـق علـى طبقـة المحاربين في فترة مـا قبـل الاستعمار، واتّخذه ماركوس

كقاعـدةٍ لرؤيته الاستبدادية حتى وَصَـل بـه الأمـر إلى إنتاج فيلم بعنوان "ماهارليكا" (1987/1970) حول مآثره في الحرب العالمية الثانية[19] (والتي اتّضح لاحقًا أنّها مجرّد اختلاقٍ كاذب). وما قام به دوتيرتي هو مجرّد إعادة تمثيل لهذه الصورة من التحقق الذاتـي لكن من خـلال التلفيـق.

كذلك، كان من المشاريع الأكثر طموحًا لـدى إيملدا وماركوس هو تقمّصهمـا صورة الزوجين مـالاكاس (القوي) وماغانـدا (الجميلة)[20] في الأساطير الفلبينية بغية صرف انتباه الجمهور المُرَوّع عن عمليّات النهب المستمرّة من خلال نسجِهما أسطورة مَلَكيّة ما قبل الاستعمارية. وقد انبثق مشروعي الفني الجاري The Collection of Jane Ryan and William Saunders (مجموعـة جاين راين ووليَم ساندرز) (2014 – إلى الآن) مـن الرغبة بوضع هذه السردية المضللة مما قبل الاستعمار جنبًا إلى جنب مع سرديّةٍ أخرى لا تقلّ عنها مكرًا وخداعًا. جاين راين ووليَم ساندرز هما أكذوبة أخرى من أكاذيب الثنائي ماركوس، وهما الهويّتان الزائفتان اللتان استخدماهما لتغطية عملية الاختلاس الضخمة التي تضمّنت تحويل ثرواتٍ سياديةٍ إلى حساباتٍ سرية في مصارف سويسريّة، مُستفيدَين من نُظُم الرأسمالية النيو-استعمارية.

م.ب.ر.

في الواقع، ما مـن مدينةٍ في أرخبيل الفلبين تعود إلى فترة مـا قبـل الاستعمار. ولا يَسَع المنظور الحضاري (والتعطّش للتحضّر) الـذي يؤطّر المشهد الفني والثقافي في الفلبين أن يتجاهل بعض الحقائق المُنغّصة. فالحلي الذهبية متقنةُ الصنع التي وُجدت في المواقع الأثرية في سوريغاو وسامار

وباتانغـاس لا تتماشـى مـع الفَرَضِيّـة التـي تَقصِـر دقّـة الإتقـان على ثقافـات البـلاط. ولا يُرَجَّـح أن يكون الأشخاص الاستثنائيون الذيـن ارتـدوا هذه الحلـيّ مـن طبقـاتٍ مماثلـةٍ للأرسـتقراطية في المجتمعـات الحضريـة، فمـن كانـوا إذًا؟ فـي اعتقـادي أن فهم الممارسـات الإحيائيـة في جزر جنوب شـرق آسـيا قد يُظهـر لنا اسـتخدامات هذه المجوهرات البديعـة في طقـوس تجسـيد المخلوقـات.

ولا بُـدّ مـن إدراج الحديـث عـن جمال وبراعـة الحلـيّ الأثريـة والاسـتعمارية في الفلبين كجـزءٍ مـن أي نقـاشٍ يتنـاول مسـألة الغيـاب التـام لممارسـات بنـاء الصـروح في الفلبيـن. فـلا نَزعَـةً ثقافيـةً تقليديـةً نحـو الصَّرحيّـة، ولا دلائـلَ تُشـير إلى عكـس ذلك. لا شـيءَ سـوى قصّـةٍ مُلَفَّقـةٍ عن مَمالـكَ مُتخيَّلـةٍ يَتداولُها المثقفون الفلبينيـون بأثـرٍ رجعي.

كمـا يجـدُر الحديـث عـن غيـاب الصرحيـة في تسـميتنا كشـعبٍ وكأمّـة. فوَعيُنـا القومـي مرتبِـط بصيغـة التصغـير في تسـمية الفلبيـن - "فيليـب الصغيـر". أُفكِّـر كثيـرًا في الصدمـة التي نعانـي منهـا كشـعب، وفـي عُقدتنـا القوميـة النابعـة بالدرجـة الأولى مـن الحقيقـة التاريخيـة المتمثلـة في أننـا قد أصبحنـا نسـخةً مصغَّـرةً عن أنفسـنا منـذ لحظـة عِمادَتِنـا الاسـتعمارية.

ذلـك صحيـح. كـم غريـبٌ أن يتحـوّل صِغَـرُ المقيـاس مـن ظاهـرةٍ بديعـةٍ إلى أخـرى مَقيتـةٍ في سـياق تاريخنـا الثقافـي. فقـد أنتجنـا أبـرَع الفنـونِ في مقاييـس متناهيـة الصغـر. ولكـن

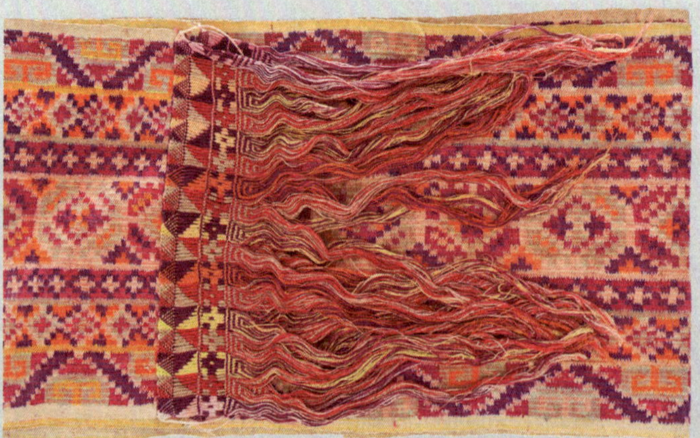

مئزر، كائيت، حرير منسوج على النول، شعب التاوسوغ، أرخبيل سولو، أواخر القرن التاسع عشر. مجموعة آناك مينداناو.

المسـتعمرين وخلفاءهم في السـلطة عمدوا إلى تصغيرنا – علـى غرار النغريتـوس، أولئك "الأقـزام" ذوي البشـرة "السـوداء" – لاسـتبعادنا كأغيـار. علامَ يُعلِّـق القوميون الفلبينيون حنينهم إلى الماضـي؟ هـم يقومـون بذلك بنـاءً على وجـود نُظُم كتابـةٍ تعـود إلى مـا قبل الاسـتعمار مثل نظام البايبيين (baybayin) مثـالًا. ولكـن المـؤرّخ وليـم هنري سـكوت رجّح أن تكـون هذه النُّظُـم قد طُـوِّرت قبل بضعة قرون فقط مـن عصر الاسـتكشاف. ولكن الحـدّ الفاصـل بيـن الرفعـة والانحطـاط يَتَحـدّد بالقدرة علـى الكتابـة والقـراءة. ومـن هنا يأتـي هذا الاهتمـام البالغ بإعـادة إحيـاء البايبييـن في الفن المعاصر بوصفـه سـرديةً مضادّةً تحظـى بالإجمـاع. إلا أن اسـتراتيجية التماهـي مـع الطاغيـة قـد لا تنفـع بـأي حـالٍ مـن الأحـوال، لا سـيّما وأن على الفلبينيين التعامـل مـع الحقيقـة المزعجـة وهـي أن أغلب أجدادنـا كانـوا عُـراة، لذا فنحـن مولَعـون بالأزيـاء. فهـا هو الكونغرس الفلبيني يحتفـل بارتـداء الأزيـاء الرسـمية عند كل مناسـبةٍ مُحوِّلًا باحَتَـهُ إلى صالـةٍ لعـروض الأزيـاء. ثم هنـاك تلك الأثـواب الأسـطوانية الحريريـة البديعـة التي يحِيكُها مسـلمو الفلبين منذ 400 عام. هـا هـي إذًا أوهـام المَلَكيّـة. هـذه هـي المشـكلةُ العويصـة لأمّةٍ يتم تخيّلُها عبـر حمّى المرض ودلائـل الهمجية.

إنها أسطورة الأرستقراطية.

لا أشَـدّ خُبثًـا مـن كذبـة الثنائي ماركوس حول أمةٍ حديثةٍ قائمةٍ علـى التأنُّـق والتباهـي بأزيـاء التقدم والحداثـة إن جاز التعبير، مـا اسـتدعى بالنسـبة لهمـا إحاطـة نفسـيهما بالأعمـال الفنية التي اقتنياهـا مـن أفضل وأسـوأ التجار سُـمعة في العالم، وبنـاء القصـور وارتـداء المجوهـرات الأغـلى في العالم. لقـد كان ذلك مشـهدًا معذِّبًا.

أنا منشغِـلٌ كذلك بالتفكير بكيفية تحويـل عملي الفني إلى أداةٍ للتخلّـص مـن هذه السـردية المُضَلِّلـة. بـدأ مشـروع "مجموعـة جايـن رايـن وويليـم سـاندرز" كعمليّـة لإنتاج نُسَـخ عن أعمـالٍ مـن مجموعـة ماركـوس منهـا التماثيل ولوحات الأسـاتذة الكبار التي اقتُنيـت عـن طريـق أرمان هامر وغاليـري كنودلر، وكذلك عـددٍ مـن الفضيّـات العائـدة إلى عهـد الوصايـة البريطانية. ولكـن خلا عـن السـنوات العشـر الماضيـة، فقـد تحـوّل هـذا المشـروع إلى جـزءٍ مـن شـبكةٍ أوسـع مـن الأغـراض والوثائـق، سـواء تلك التي

والتـي تضـمّ تيجانًـا وقلائـد وقطعًـا مـن الألمـاس مـن فـان كليـف فـون أربيـل.

أثنـاء عملنـا علـى هـذا الجـزء مـن المشـروع، ارتأينـا أنـا وفرانسـيس ألّا نتوقّـف عنـد القيمـة الفاحشـة لتلـك المجوهـرات، بـل أن نتعامـل معهـا كأدلّـةٍ علـى مـا سُـلِبَ مـن هـذا البلـد الفقيـر ولا يـزال. وبالرغـم مـن تقديمهـا الأنيـق، فقـد جُـرّدَت نُسـخ المجوهـرات المطبوعـة بتقنيـة الأبعـاد الثلاثيـة مـن الألـوان كـي تكـون أشـبه بالأشـباح. وقـد تـمّ تطويـر هـذا المشـروع فـي البدايـة بالتعـاون مـع المفوّضيـة الرئاسـية للحكـم الرشـيد [21] (Presidential Commission on Good Government - PCGG)خـلال الأشـهر الأخيـرة مـن ولايـة الرئيـس الراحـل نوينـوي أكوينـو [22]. وكان مـن المبـادرات الأخيـرة لهـذه المفوّضيـة والتـي أدرجناهـا فـي عملنـا عمليـةُ احتسـاب قيمـة مجوهـرات إيملـدا نسـبةً إلـى بعـض جوانـب التنميـة القوميـة. فعلـى سـبيل المثـال، تمتلـك إيملـدا ماركـوس خاتمًـا مـن الألمـاس الـوردي المُسـتخرَج مـن مناجـم غولكونـدا فـي الهنـد تـوازي قيمتـه مُجمَـل تكلفـة بنـاء المطـارات الداخليـة فـي كل مـن تـاوي تـاوي وبيكـول. كمـا أن لديهـا طقمـاً يتضمّـن سـوارًا وأقراطًـا مـن الألمـاس والزفيـر تغطّـي قيمتـه تكلفـة التطعيـم الكامـل لنحـو 20,000 طفـل. ومـن شـأن هـذه المقارنـات المذهلـة أن تقـدّم أدلّـةً جنائيـةً تدعّـم السـردية المضـادة لروايـة التقـدّم والنمـو التـي ملأت عائلـة ماركـوس بهـا رؤوسـنا.

وبالتأكيـد، يقودنـا الحديـث عـن المجوهـرات إلـى طـرح مسـألة سياسـات الجمـال وأيضًـا، كمـا ذكـرت، كيفيـة تجسـّد ثقافـة الفلبيـن فـي صيغـةٍ منمنمـةٍ، فـي الزخـرف بـدلًا مـن الحجـر. وبالعـودة إلـى باتانـس، فـإن هـذه الجزيـرة تمتـاز بتـراثٍ مدهـشٍ مـن المصوغـات الذهبيـة المزخرفـة، كمـا تـدلّ المجوهـرات المصنوعـة مـن أحجـار اليشـم الكريمـة وفـق الأبحـاث علـى كـون باتانـس قـد شـكّلَت موطـن الأقـدام الأوّل للتوسـّع الأسـترونيزي خـارج تايـوان نحـو الفلبيـن. كمـا تُحاكـي هـذه الأثريـات اليشـميّة الأنمـاط التقليديـة لصناعـة الحلـي لـدى شـعوب المـاوري التـي ظهـرت بعدهـا ببضعـة آلاف مـن السـنين [23].

ولا تَسَعُنـي رؤيـة هـذه المجوهـرات سـوى كوَجهيـن لثُرائنـا المعقّـد: الأول يُبَلـوِر الحصانـات والامتيـازات التـي تُواصـل تَسـميم جِسـنا بالانتمـاء الوطنـي، والثانـي يسـتند إلـى الحقيقـة الأركيولوجيـة ويحمـل إمكانيـة التغييـر ولكنـه غيـر معـروفٍ علـى نطـاقٍ واسـع.

م.ب.ر.

إن الفـارق بيـن المُثَمَّـم والمُستصغَـر هـو أمـرٌ سياسـي. فالأنماط

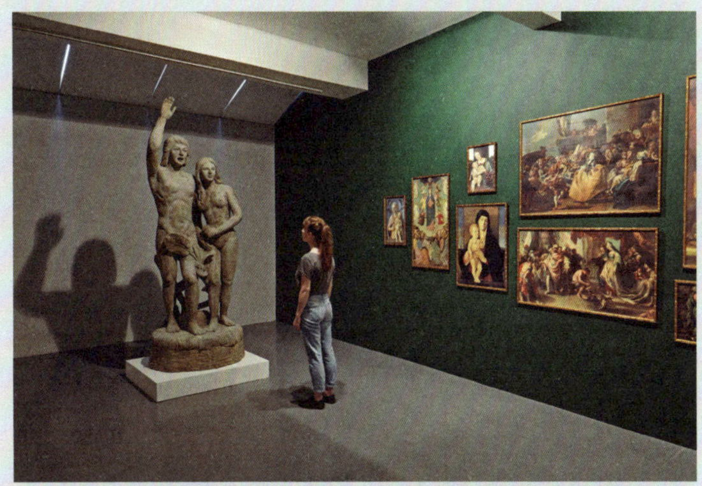

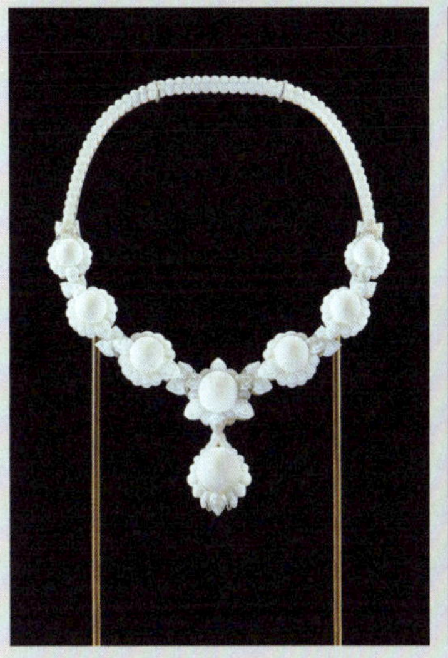

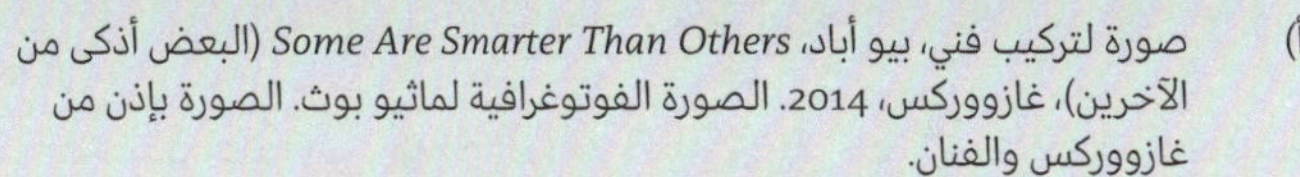

أ) صورة لتركيب فني، بيو أباد، (Some Are Smarter Than Others) (البعض أذكى من الآخرين)، غازوووركس، 2014. الصورة الفوتوغرافية لماثيو بوث. الصورة بإذن من غازوووركس والفنان.

ب) بيو أباد وفرانيس وادسوورث جونز، The Collection of Jane Ryan and William Saunders (مجموعة جاين راين وويلم ساندرز)، 2019 (تفصيل). بلاستيك مطبوع بتقنية ثلاثية الأبعاد، منضدة نحاسية، نص بتقنية النقل الجاف. الصورة بإذن من الفنان.

ت) بيو أباد وفرانيس وادسوورث جونز، The Collection of Jane Ryan and William Saunders (مجموعة جاين راين وويلم ساندرز)، 2019 (تفصيل). بلاستيك مطبوع بتقنية ثلاثية الأبعاد، منضدة نحاسية، نص بتقنية النقل الجاف. الصورة بإذن من الفنان.

ارتبَطَت بأشـياء عُثِـرَ عليهـا فـي أرشـيفات ريغـان وتدحـض أسـطورة ماركـوس الشـخصية، أو بالتصنيفـات التـي حدّدتهـا الاكتشـافات الجديـدة وغيـر الجديـدة عـن آثـار الفلبيـن. وهـا هـو المشـروع يتمـدّد ويتفـرع إلـى أجـزاءٍ كثيـرةٍ مختلفـة.

النسـخة الأخيـرة مـن هـذا العمـل هـي نتـاج تعـاونٍ بينـي وبيـن زوجتـي وشـريكتي الإبداعيـة فرانسـيس وادسـوورث جونـز التـي تحتـرف صياغـة المجوهـرات. يتضمّـن العمـل إعـادة تشـكيلٍ رقميـةٍ بالغـة الدقـة لمجموعـة المجوهـرات التـي اكتنزتهـا إيملـدا ماركـوس علـى امتـداد حكمهـا القائـم علـى النهـب والسـرقة،

الفنية الفلبينية التقليدية المنمنمة مثالٌ على حُسن الصَنعة خارجَ مَنظومات البلاط. أما المُستصغَرون فَهُم البشر والحجر الذين تحوّلوا بوَضع اليدِ إلى مِلكيّاتٍ تحت سيطرة المُستَعمِر، كالحيوانات البرية المدجّنة أو الإقطاعيّات أو الأجساد المنتهَكة لا لشيء سوى الاستحقاق الشخصي. وتُجسّدُ مجوهرات ماركوس، التي تُعيدُ توزيعها مجازيًّا على أوجهٍ مختلفةٍ للنقد[24] محاولةً لإرساء صرحيّةٍ ما، هي عتادُ حملةٍ واسعةٍ ومُقزّزة من الهندسة الاجتماعية. ومما لا شك فيه أن مجوهرات إيملدا هي تحفٌ تُعبّرُ عن مرحلةٍ بائسةٍ من الغلوّ والإسراف، ولكنّ الأهمّ هو تعبيرها عن الرغبة المفرطة في إنتاج صورتهما بمثابة الملك والملكة اللذين لم يقوما بحُكمنا قظ.

فَرَضَت الأحكام العسكرية نظامًا ديكتاتوريًّا مركزيًّا على شعبٍ جُلّ علاقته بالسلطة المركزيّة هو التهذيب: إذ كان هو الذي أعلن النظام الجمهوري الديموقراطي الأول في آسيا في العام 1898. كما صَنَعَت هذه الأحكام مَشهديّةً ذات جماليّة مُعَظّمة – يجدُر وصفُها بالفاشيّة – تستخدم الأزياء والمجوهرات كعُدّةٍ لفَرضُ سلطتها المُطلَقة. وهذه جماليّةٌ من صنفٍ مغايرٍ تمامًا لتلك التي تتّسم بها على سبيل المثال المنسوجات الفلبينية التقليدية المُمعنة في الدقة.

ب. أ.

لم تكن تلك المنسوجات مُعدَّةً للتباهي والاستعراض، بل هي تدعو الناظر إلى التمعّن فيها عن كثب.

م. ب. ر.

أو قد لا يكون الهدف منها المشاركة، أو قد تكون قد وَصلَت إلى عُهدَتكَ بمُوجب نهي طقسي عن مشاركة المعرفة اعتباطيًّا. إذًا، متى بدأ الأجداد بالقيام بأفعالٍ تستهدف الظهور؟ بدأ ذلك مع نشأة البرجوازية التي نطلق عليها اليوم Ilustrado* (إلوسترادو أو المتنوّرون) في القرن التاسع عشر. تُظهر اللوحات الزيتية، وهي بورتريهاتٌ شخصية في معظمها، أشخاصًا من

الـ mestizos (المستيزو هم أبناءٌ لأخلاطٍ عرقيةٍ بين الإسبان وسكان المستعمَرات) الإسبان والصينيين يستعرضون كامل زينتهم. وقد دَأَبت على جمع هذه اللوحات مجموعةٌ صغيرةٌ من الوطنيين، فضلًا عن عددٍ من المؤسسات (وهو الأمر المهم بالنسبة لمن يدرسون المؤسسات من أمثالي) كالمصرف المركزي الفلبيني. تُناهز قيمة كلٍ من هذه اللوحات ملايين الدولارات، وهو سعرٌ يمكن لقلةٍ فقط من الصفوة الفلبينية دفعه.

ب. أ.

الفقاعة مُخاطبةٌ ذاتها.

م. ب. ر.

تُخاطبُ ذاتها وتُخاطبُ في الوقت عينه السرديات المُركّبة عن الأمّة. ولكن الفقاعة، بحسب وصفك الدقيق لها، تَضَعُ نفسها فوق بقيّة الناس باعتبارها الجمال الواجب الاحتذاء به. فمن الناحية الرمزية، ارتبط هذا الجمال بدايةً بالخيال المُرَمنَس عن التمدّن في الأقاليم المداريّة. وقد شكّلت تلك الصور دعامة رأس المال الثقافي الذي راكَمَتهُ تلك الطبقة الصاعدة خلال الثورة الفلبينية ضدّ إسبانيا في القرن العشرين. وكما نعلم، فقد تشكّلَ محفَلُ الأبطال الوطنيين من أبناء الطبقة البرجوازية الذين انخرطوا في النهج الإصلاحي من مواقِعِهم في المهجر الأوروبي. وشَهِدَ القرن التاسع عشر بناء تراثُبيّةٍ لتلك الصور. فكانت بورتريهات الإلوسترادو فئة مستقلّة من الأعمال الفنية. أما البقية فكانت عبارة عن تصاوير لأصنافٍ متنوّعة من الناس ضمن فضاءٍ محدّد وعلى غرار أسلوب Tipos del País ** ("تيبوس ديل باييس" أي طُرَز أهل البلد) في الأعمال الفنية. فأفرَزَت رسوم "الطُرَز" هذه تصنيفًا للسكان وفقَ منظورٍ سياحيٍ شِبه أنثروبولوجي قائمٍ على الخلط العشوائي بين الانتماءات المهنية والطبقية والعرقية وإلى ما هنالك.

ب. أ.

وقد غذّى هذا النوعُ من الإيهام إلى حدٍ كبيرٍ عددًا من الفاعلين الآخرين على الساحة العالمية.

م. ب. ر.

يُعدّ الإيهام كلمةً مُعبّرةً في وصف اللوحات الزيتية والمائية على السواء (وصولًا إلى الصور الفوتوغرافية). ثمّ إن التيبوس ديل باييس كانت ماثلةً في صميم الحوار الأدبي والبصري بين Costumbrismo*** (الكوستومبريسمو) والنيوكلاسيكية وإرهاصات الحداثة. كما جاءت اللوحات الزيتية تحديدًا في سياق جهودٍ حثيثةٍ للترفُّع عن فولكلورية التيبوس عن طريق التدريب الأكاديمي على التقنيات الأوروبية. ولم يكن تكوين هذه العوالم عن طريق تلك الأساليب الفنية عمليةً تَعِي مِن ذاتها أنّ ما تعكِسهُ هو صورةٌ لصانعيها، فقد كان الإيهام مُبهجًا بقدر ما نراه بغيضًا الآن. وهناك صلةٌ مباشرةٌ - مهما بدت بعيدة - بين الكوستومبريسيمو وأغنية عالم ديزني It's a Small World After All† وطبعًا مسابقات ملكات الجمال المحلية والعالمية.

ب. أ.

كانت It's a Small World After All مـن أولى الأغنيـات التي أذكر أننا تعلّمناها في المدرسة. وهذا تشبيهٌ ممتاز، لأن المنظار التصنيفي الـذي أُرغِمنا علـى رؤيـة ذواتِنا مـن خلالـه ولا سـيّما مـن قِبَل نظام ماركوس، لا يقدّم سوى صورةٍ مفقَّرةٍ، ونسخةٍ متدنيّة الدقـة عـن التمثيـل الوطنـي. لقـد كان الانشغال الأكبر بالظِـلّ لا بالتفاصيـل.

م. ب. ر.

بلا شك. ثمّ، هل هناك أجدَرُ من مسابقة ملكة جمال الكون التي استُضِيفَت في مُجَمَّع مركز الفلبين الثقافي في العام 1974 كي تكون مستهلًّا لسلسلة مشاريع إيملدا ماركوس الضخمة؟ استعرَضَت تلك المسابقة الموكب الطنّان الـذي شـارك فيـه الآلاف والـذي حمـل عنـوان Kasaysayan ng Lahi (تاريخ الجنس البشري) وانتهى إلى مسرح الفنون الشعبية الذي أُنجِزَ بناؤه في سبعين يومًا. وقد عَرَضَ مسرح الفنون الشعبية ما هو شعبيّ – أي نسخة إيملدا الحيّة من التيبوس ديل بابيس والتي تعود جذورها إلى أوروبا. إنّها الـ Volk الألماني عينه الذي أسفَرَ تمجيدُه عن نشأة نموذج قاتِل مِن الأهلَويّة. ولا ننسى أن الكوستومبريسمو في إسبانيا هي ما أنتج هذين النموذجين مـن الرعايا المستعمَرين والأدب الاستعماري المتمحوِرَين إلى الواقع الأنثروبولوجي بنسختيهما الفرنسية والإنكليزية. هنا، تتقاطع مساحاتٌ كثيفةٌ من التخيُّلات وتتفاعل وتتحوّر. وفي الجزئيّة المتعلّقة بالفلبين، فإن المسألة واضحةٌ ومباشرة. هنا، تُمرَّرُ مسابقات الجمال في القرن العشرين سرديّات أواخر القرن التاسع عشر حول الأمّة المتجسّدة ككيانٍ سياسي قائم على استحضار العرق - الطبقة. فيتجلّى "تطوّر" الأمّة كارتقاءٍ داروينيّ من البدائية إلى المجد.

وهـذا يُحيلُنـا ثانيةً إلى باتانِس ولا سـيّما إلى بحـث الدكتـورة ماريا منغاهاس حول جماعتين من الصيّادين[25]. الأولى منهم في باجاو في تـاوي تـاوي والثانية في باتانِس عند أقصى طرفي الفلبين، وهو بحـثٌ مهـمٌ جـدًّا لا ينفـك في إبهاري. هل تعرف صيّادي الماتاو؟

ب. أ.

نعـم، إنهـم مجموعـة مـن الصيّاديـن الذيـن يعيشـون بالقرب مـن منزلنـا في باتانِس.

م. ب. ر.

تقـول منغاهـاس في بحثهـا أن حيـاة صيـادي الماتـاو تتصل

ب. أ.

يمكنك القول أن banwá هي طَرَفُنا الشبحي.

م. ب. ر.

في هذا الإطار، لدي ملاحظةٌ أخرى حول ماركوس، بعيدًا عن إيملدا وإن كانت تتمتّع هي بعبقريةٍ خاصة، فقد كان فرديناند ماركوس يمتلك ذكاءً من نوعٍ خاص. كان متحدّرًا من إيلوكوس ولم يكن أرستقراطيًا. كان والداه نزيهين، أحدهما مدرّس في المدرسة الحكومية ويمتلك منزلًا في إيلوكوس. إذًا نستطيع أن نفترض أن ماركوس قد شبّ على درايةٍ بأساطير الأسترونيزيين، وكان يعرف مدى تأثير أسطورة مالاكاس وماغاندا، ما يعني أن اختياره لتَمَثُّلِه هو وإيملدا يرجع إلى ماضٍ سحيقٍ لا يزال ماثلًا إلى اليوم. أما إيملدا فقد ساقت هذه الأسطورة في اتجاهٍ آخر لم أفهمه قطّ. أظن أنّها لم تكن تنتمي إلى أي من العوالم الأسطورية. لا أعتقد أنها اختبَرَت ذلك على عكس ماركوس. فقد كانت إيملدا أقرب منها إلى ملكة جمال الكون، إن صحّ القول.

ب. أ.

بالفعل. إنّه المزج بين مختلف تلك الروايات في قالبٍ واحد. لعلّ براعة ماركوس في الاحتيال والتلاعب بالأساطير المتجذّرة في الأذهان قد اجتمعت مع شطحات أهواء إيملدا لتكوّن ذلك المزيج السامّ الذي لا زلنا نتعامل من خلاله...

م. ب. ر.

إلى اليوم.. كانت ممارستي عجيبة بحق. كُلِّفتُ بتقديم الفلبين في أربعة معارض عالمية كان المعرض الأخير منها هو دبي إكسبو 2020، وهو جديرٌ بالذكر لأنه سمح لي أخيرًا بفرصة الحديث عن 4000 عام. سَتَكُونُ باتانِس معنا في دبي. كلّما وجدتُ مناسَبةً للحديث عن الأسترونزيين، أشدّدُ على أنه إن كان البعض يعتقد أنها مسألةٌ تقتصر على التاريخ أو الأركيولوجيا، فعلينا أن نتذكّر حينها أن هنالك فلبينيًّا من بين كلّ ثلاثة بحّارة في العالم اليوم. وبذلك يمكننا القول إن الحركة الأسترونيزية لم تتوقّف قطّ.

أحلُمُ بالذهاب إلى فاناواتو، ويُخيّل إليّ أنني سأعثُر هناك على ما يُمَكّنُني من التنظير لمفهوم banwá كمفهومٍ للجماعة في عالمٍ مائي مَبلَغُ علمنا عنه أنه أشبه بِعالَمٍ شبحي.

وحتّى وإن وُجِدَت ممالِكُ أسترونيزية في جاوا وبالي وسومطرة وهاواي، فليس في وسعنا أن نَغفَلَ عن تلك الجزر الممتدّة

على مُسَطّحاتٍ شاسعةٍ من الكرة الأرضية بين مدغشقر وجزيرة القيامة والتي يتحدّث أهلها بلُغاتٍ ذات صلاتٍ مباشرةٍ بخاصيّاتٍ مائية. ومن الناحية العَدَدِيّة، فثمّة 350 لغةٍ أسترونيزيةٍ محكيّةٍ في إندونيسيا، وأكثر من 1200 لغةٍ في باقي أنحاء العالم، هذا إلى جانب 176 لغة محكيّةٍ في الفلبين. فالأسترونيزية هي خامس أكبر عائلةٍ لغويةٍ في العالم ويتحدّث بها أكثر من 300 مليون نسمة.

تسعى ملكات الجمال في ممالك الجمال الأسطورية إلى طمس الذاكرة المخجلة حول الشعوب المائية ذات الأجساد الموشومة العارية. إذ يشعر الفلبينيون بالارتباك حيال أصولهم البدائية غير النبيلة مهما ابتَعَدَت في الماضي السحيق. كما عَمِدَ قادَتُنا ومثقَّفُونا وفنّانُونا إلى إخفاء هذه الحقيقة تحت طبقاتٍ وطبقاتٍ من الزيف والتضليل، أو جعلوها تبدو غرائبيّةً إلى حدّ التعامي الكامل عن گون تلك الممارسة تنطوي على استبعاد هؤلاء الأجداد كأغيارٍ عنّا.

ما يؤرّقني فعلًا هو غياب هذه الحقائق عن التحليل السياسي. فنحن نواجه صعوبةً حقيقيةً في إدراك مدى كثافة الثقافة الشفاهية فيما نحن نسبح فيها بلا انقطاع وبصورةٍ يومية. وكقيمةٍ فنيةٍ، وربّما بالنسبة إليك كفنّان، فإن المُتعة التي نستقيها من ممارساتنا تكمُنُ فقط في الأداء التنقيبي الذي يَنبِش كُلَّ ما هو مدفونٌ تحت تراكُمات الغُبار والنفايات والأحلام الواهية. ومن ثَمّ، يتبيّنُ لنا على مهلٍ أنّ الدفائن لا تقدّم سوى ألغازٍ لا مجال لاسترجاع معانيها ومدلولاتها، أو حقائق أسوأ مما توقّعناه.

أراك تعملُ على مساحةٍ محدّدةٍ وحديثةٍ نسبيًا من الأشياء الدفينة، وهذا في حدّ ذاته أمرٌ بالغ الأهميّة لا سيّما وأنّ مرحلة السبعينيات شهدت حملة تدميرٍ ثقافي هائلة.

ب. أ.

أدركتُ مدى مساهمة ممارستكِ في توسيع آفاق ممارستي الفنية لجهَة اتّساع مساحة التاريخ التي تنتظر منّا الخوض فيها. وقد اخترتُ أن أنطلِقَ من عَقْدَي السبعينيات والثمانينيات لكونِهُما قد شَكّلا المرحلة التي كوَّنتُ فيها شخصيّتي السياسية، بدءًا باعتقال والدي خلال فترة الديكتاتورية وحتى تاريخ ولادتي قبل أشهرٍ قليلةٍ من اغتيال نينوي أكوينو[26]. تلك هي الوقائع التي شَكّلَت وعيي السياسي ولا تزالُ حتى هذه اللحظة. ومع تطوُّر المشروع الفني، راح يندفعُ بعيدًا عن ذاك العَقدِ في اتّجاه حُقَبٍ أبعدَ أو أقرب. ولكن لا شكّ

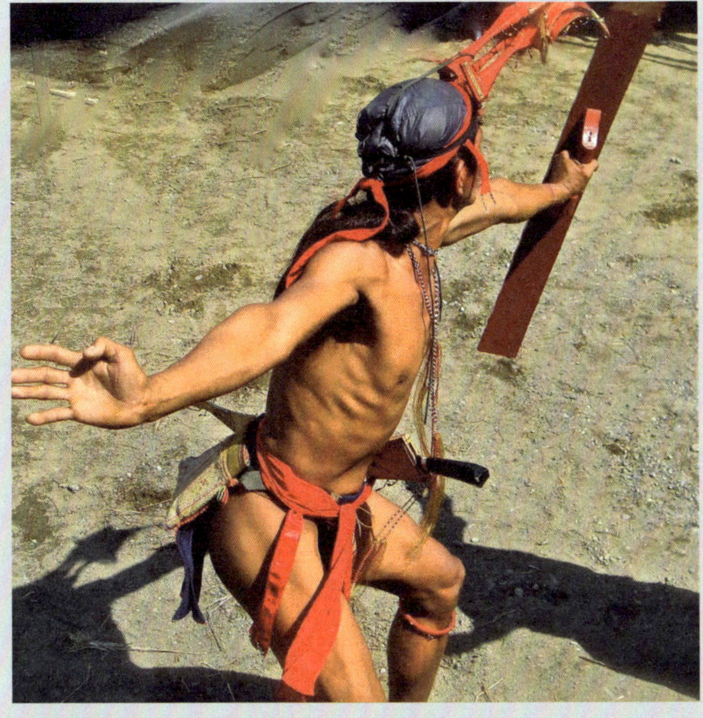

تصوير دقيق لهيئة أحد الأجداد. زعيم جماعة بونغكالوت الإثنو - لغوِيّة. التصوير الفوتوغرافي لماريان باستور رويس.

إرادته، في تحديد كل شيء وأي شيء.

ب.أ.

إنها - مرةً أخرى - نزعة التحضّر المضلّلة. وفي النهاية، تضيع التفاصيل وسط الأبّهة الزائفة التي تكتنف المؤسسات. ووسط صخب مسابقات الجمال، يضيع الجانب النقدي الذي يتيح لكِ المجال للتفكير المستقلّ.

م.ب.ر.

يفقد الفرد منّا حريّة التفكير والإبداع حتى في غياب القوانين القمعية - كما في البانوبتيكون عند فوكو. يضيع حسّك النقدي وقدرتك على رؤية مفاعيل السلطة القائمة على إنتاج السرديات الباطلة. وقد أُفرِغَت المفاهيمية تحت تأثير هذا العَجز من سحرها وتأثيرها. فما المغزى من المفاهيمية إن لم يكن تشريح السلطة؟

ب.أ.

يهمّني كثيرًا ألّا أنظُر إلى ذاتي من خلال هذا النَسَب، وأعتقدُ أن امتياز انتمائي إلى الشِّتات يمنحُني هذه المسافة لأعاين موقعي في هذا العالم من خلال مناظير أخرى. المثير للاهتمام هو مقاربة هذا البحث عن آل ماركوس لا من منظور المفاهيمية الفلبينية ولا حتى الجنوب آسيوية وإنما من منظور الفنانين

أن تلك المرحلة قد استحوَذَت على اهتمامي خلال السنوات العشر الماضية.

م.ب.ر.

كيف تشعر وقد أمضيت كل هذا الوقت على دراسة تلك المرحلة؟

ب.أ.

يراودني دائمًا الشعور بأنها قد انتَهَت وانقَضَت، ولكنها لا تنتهي أبدًا لأنها تنطوي على الكثير من الأمور المختلفة. وأجدها في كلّ مرّة جزءًا من مجموعةٍ أكبر من الأشياء، بدءًا من أساطير الخلق الأسترونيزية وتاريخ آل رومانوف ووصولًا إلى تحالفات الحرب الباردة التي تمثَّلَت في علاقات آل ماركوس بآل بهلوي وبينوشيه.

كما أنها محاولة للتعاطي مع حواف الأمل اللاعقلاني الذي كنتُ قد ذكرتُه في السابق. فقد بدأتُ العمل على هذا المشروع في العام 2011 إثر سقوط القذّافي في ليبيا مباشرةً. وكنتُ من السذاجة بأن اعتقدتُ أنّ الفاشية قد بائَت وأنني قد بثُّ على مَتن الموجة التصحيحية من التاريخ. وقد كنتُ مخطئًا. ربما علينا جميعًا أن نمنح أنفسنا هذه الأحلام بين الحين والآخر كي نتمكّن من مواصلة ما نفعله.

م.ب.ر.

كنتَ قد أشرتَ سابقًا إلى طليعة السبعينيات التي أبصَرَت النور في المركز الثقافي. وقد كتبتُ عن نَكَباتِها[27]، لا سيّما أن تواطؤها مع النزعة الحضارية لم يكن واضحًا للمشاركين فيها وأنا من بينهم. لا شكّ في أنّ علينا أخذ مسافةٍ كي نفهم روح العصر البائس الذي عايشناه. أمّا ونحن في خضمّ تلك المرحلة، فقد كنّا نستمتع بمطالعة أعداد "آرت فوروم" واستخدام المفردات الملائمة لتلك الحقبة، مُنتَشين بكتابات ليندا بنغليس وتوم ماريوني وإيفا هسه. بدا كلّ شيء غايةً في التحضّر، ولم يطرأ على بالنا تقييم الربط بين الاحتفاء بالمفاهيمية والنقد المؤسسي في جانبٍ من أروقة مركز الفلبين الثقافي من ناحية، وبين حفلات مسابقات الجمال والمواكب الاستعراضية التي كانت تُقام داخل حَرَمِهِ من ناحيةٍ ثانية.

وها هي تتسرّبُ إلى عالمك. ولكنني مسرورةٌ، بل ممتنّةٌ لكونك تدرك التشابُك بين برامج الفن المعاصر والفنون الشعبية. نُقرُّ بأن أحدًا لم يتصوّرهما أو أي أنشطةٍ أخرى في إطار برنامجٍ موحّد. ولكن الديكتاتورية هي واقعٌ مُطلقٌ يُفرِط، بل ويفرِضُ

الذيـن خرجـوا مـن بيـروت في التسـعينيات عـلى سـبيل المثـال، حيـث ينطـوي دور الأرشـيف وسـلطة إعـادة الإعمار عـلى معانٍ أخـرى. أعتقـد أننـا نشـترك في حاجتنـا إلى تجميـع المزيـد مـن المقاربـات في ممارسـتينا الفنيّتيـن. هكـذا نُـدرك مفهـوم banwá الـذي نَنشُـدُه. نَجِـدُ موقعنا في العالم مـن خـلال هذه الجماعـات التـي نُوجِدُهـا والتـي ليسـت بالضـرورة أمـرًا معطـى.

ومهمّتي كفنّـان تتمثّـل في كيفيّـة الاسـتمرار في التمسّـك بمسـاحات الأمـل الصغيـرة وتصـوُّر احتمـالاتٍ أخـرى، وفي الوقت عينه الحُزن لا عـلى عائلـةٍ بعينهـا، بـل عـلى كل مـا يجـري في البـلاد. مـن هنـا، يطرح عمل "مجموعـة جايـن رايـن ووليـم سـاندرز" السـؤال حـول كيفية تصـوُّر قضية المسـاءلة وأيضًا كيفية إقنـاع الآخرين ببنـاء تصوّرهم الخاص عن المحاسبة.

وهنا تدخل مسألة سياسات الجمال.

م. ب. ر.

لكننا لا نعرف إن كانت ستنجح.

ب. أ.

هـذا ما يجعـل عمل الفنّـان من الناحيـة الجوهرية عمـلًا مفعمًا بالتفـاؤل، أو الهنيـان كما قـد يقول البعـض. تتمسكين بالإيمان بـأن العمل سـيحدث التغيير عند نقطـةٍ معيّنة.

م. ب. ر.

الأرجح أنه لن يحدث هذا التغيير.

لا نعلـم. ربّمـا عليـك أن تُقتَـل رميًـا بالرصاص مثـل خوسـيه ريـزال من أجـل عملٍ فنيٍّ كي تكـون مسـموعًا. أو أن تكـون بارعًا في الاسـتعراض مثـل أي وَي وَي. ولكـن الحـظ لـن يحالفـكَ عند وقوفـكَ عـلى التفاصيـل الدقيقـة وسـبر المعاني الغامضة، والتعامـل مـع الخفـاء كخيـارٍ جمالـيٍّ يسـتحقّ التقديـر البالـغ، وربّمـا كسـرديةٍ مرتجـاةٍ ضـد القهـر في حـدّ ذاتـه.

1 إيفاتان هو الاسم الذي يُطلق على شعب جزر باتانِس الأصلي ولغته. وباتانِس هي مجموعة من الجزر الصغيرة إلى أقصى الشمال من أرخبيل الفلبين. يتحدّر بيو أباد من الإيفاتان من ناحية الأب.

2 Corazon S. Alvina and Marian Pastor Roces, *A Delicate Balance: Batanes Food, Ecology, and Community* (Manila: Museo ng Kaalamang Katutubo, 2018)

3 كان روديغو ر. دوتيرتي رئيس الفلبين لحظة إجراء هذا اللقاء، وهو الذي أصدر أوامر علنية واضحة بقتل "مدمني المخدّرات" في سياق حربه المزعومة على المخدّرات. وقد تراجع لاحقًا عن هذه التعليقات متحجّجًا بأنها كانت في إطار المزاح. غير أن عدد ضحايا هذه الحملة الهائجة كان قد وصل إلى ما يقدّر بنحو 30 ألفًا من القتلى معظمهم من الفقراء والمحرومين.

4 للمزيد من تحليل حملات التضليل يرجى مراجعة Jonathan Corpus Ong and Jason Vincent A. Cabañes, *Architects of Networked Disinformation: Behind the Scenes of Troll Accounts and Fake News Production in the Philippines* (University of Massachusetts Open Access, 2018)

5 تأسّست منطقة بانغ سامورو ذاتيّة الحكم لمسلمي مينداناو (BARMM) بواسطة تشريع أُقرّ في البرلمان الفلبيني: المصادقة على قانون بانغ سامورو الدستوري (المرسوم الجمهوري رقم 11054) وإبرامه لاحقًا من خلال استفتاء شعبي أجري على سكّان المناطق المشمولة بالقانون. وقد تُوّج هذا القانون المُبرَم في العام 2018 عمليّة سلام مُتعثّرة دامت أكثر من 20 عامًا، واضعًا نهاية لنحو 20 عامًا من الحرب الانفصالية.

6 شهد جيل ما بعد الحرب في الفلبين حالة نُضج مبكّرة بين طلّاب الجامعات في السبعينيات من القرن الماضي بالتزامن مع فرض الرئيس فرديناند ماركوس الأحكام العسكرية. وقد أدّى فرض هذه الأحكام إلى تقرير مصير أبناء ذلك الجيل، حيث أمضى العديد منهم العقود اللاحقة في النضال ضد الديكتاتورية – ومن بينهم فلورنسيو ودينا أباد، والدا بيو.

7 شنّ اليابانيون هجومًا على الفلبين واحتلّوها بين العامين 1942 و1945 خلال الحرب العالمية الثانية. وكانت الفلبين آنذاك مستعمرةً أميركيةً وجزءًا من أراضي الولايات المتّحدة الأميركية.

8 حكَمَ الرئيس فرديناند ماركوس الفلبين حكمًا ديكتاتوريًّا بين العامين 1972 و1986.

9 باسيتا أباد الفنانة التشكيلية المعروفة عالميًّا هي شقيقة فلورنسيو أباد والد بيو.

10 Peter Bellwood and Eusebio Dizon, ed., *4000 Years of Migration and Cultural Exchange: The Archaeology of the Batanes Islands, Northern Philippines*. Vol. 40 (ANU Press, 2013)

11 يُعَدّد معهد الإثنولوج The Languages of the Philippines, *Ethnologue*, Summer Institute of Linguistics نحو 186 لغة فلبينية من بينها عشر لُغات مهاجرة أو غير أصيلة. أما البقيّة فمن اللغات الأسترونيزية. https://www.ethnologue.com/country/18-165

12 يرجى مراجعة العمل الأخير في مجال الوراثيّات Irina Pugach, Alexander Hübner, Hsiao-chun Hung, Matthias Meyer, Mike T. Carson, and Mark Stoneking "Ancient DNA from Guam and the peopling of the Pacific," *Proceedings of the National Academy of Sciences*, January 2021, 118 (1)

13 يرجى مراجعة Alexander Adelaar, "Asian Roots of the Malagasy: A Linguistic Perspective," *Bijdragen tot de Taal-, Land- en Volkenkunde* 151, no. 3 (1995).

14 تُنسَب رواية "موجات الهجرة" التي "أعمَرَت" الفلبين من الجنوب بشكلٍ أساسي إلى عالم الآثار الأميركي هنري أوتلي باير الذي عمل في الفلبين في مطلع القرن العشرين، علمًا أن الإطار العام لهذه النظرية سابقٌ لحياة باير. وقد سادت سرديّة الهجرات من إندونيسيا شمالًا خلال القرن التاسع عشر.

15 Filomeno Aguilar Jr., "Tracing Origins: Ilustrado Nationalism and the Racial Science of Migration Waves," *The Journal of Asian Studies* 64 no. 3 (2005): 605-637

16 أوّل المؤلَّفات حول العائلة اللغوية المعروفة بالأسترونيزية Otto Dempwolff's, *Vergleichende Lautlehre des austronesischen Wortschatzes* [Comparative phonology of the Austronesian vocabularies], 3 volumes, (1934-37)

Beihefte zur Zeitschrift für Eingeborenen-Sprachen (Supplements to the Journal of Native Languages) 15;17;19 (in German). Berlin: Dietrich Reimer. The sub-groupings of the Austronesian languages that have been widely in use since was Robert Blust's *The Proto-Austronesian pronouns and Austronesian subgrouping: A preliminary report* (Honolulu: Department of Linguistics, University of Hawaii, 1977)

كما دعّمت مجموعة من المقالات لعالم الآثار بيتر بلوود فكرة توسّع اللغة الأسترونيزية قدومًا من تايوان. يرجى مراجعة Peter Bellwood, "The Austronesian Dispersal and the Origin of Languages," *Scientific American* 265 no. 1(July 1991): 88-93

Peter Bellwood, *Prehistory of the Indo-Malaysian archipelago* (ANU Press, 1985)

Peter Bellwood, "Taiwan and the Prehistory of the Austronesians-speaking Peoples," *Review of Archaeology* 18 (1998)

Peter Bellwood, James Fox, and Darrell Tyron, *The Austronesians: Historical and Comparative Perspectives* (ANU Press, 1995). It was Bellwood's work of the 1990s and his subsequent work with Eusebio Dizon in the 2000s that cemented the Austronesian "Out of Taiwan" consensus. Alternative views were held by the late Wilhelm Solheim and Stephen Oppenheimer.

17 تأسّست الجبهة الوطنية لتحرير مورو في العام 1969 كحركةٍ انفصالية. قَضَت اتفاقية طرابلس الموقَّعة في العام 1974 بوقف القتال بين الجبهة وجمهورية الفلبين، إلّا أن الاعتداءات تجدّدت على خلفيّة اتّهامات بعدم الامتثال لشروط الاتفاقيّة، ما أدّى إلى عودة الحرب واستمرار القتال لعقودٍ لاحقة بقيادة الجبهة الإسلامية لتحرير مورو. أسفرت عمليّة السلام عن تأسيس منطقة بانغ سامورو ذاتية الحكم لمسلمي مينداناو في العام 2018.

18 Maharlika أو maharlikha هي كلمة مأخوذة عن السنسكريتية وقد وُثّق استخدامها في مدوّنات الرهبان تحت الحكم الإسباني عن الفلبين. ومن كلمتَي Mahar (بمعنى كبير أو ضخم) وlikha (بمعنى القضيب) في اللغة الأصلية، تمّ نحت هذا التعبير للإشارة إلى طبقة مُجتمع ما قبل الاستعمار في الفلبين.

19 زعَمَ فرديناند ماركوس أنه حاز على 32 وسام حرب لشجاعته وبطولته خلال الحرب العالمية الثانية، من بينها صليب الاستحقاق، ثاني أعلى وسامَ شَرف في العسكرية الأميركية، ووسام القلب الأرجواني الممنوح لجرحى الحرب العسكريين. وسرعان ما دَحَضَت الوثائق التاريخية تلك المزاعم.

20 مالاكاس (القوي) وماغاندا (الجميلة) هما والدا العرق الفلبيني في أسطورة الخلق الفلبينية. وتقول النسخة الشعبية من هذه الأسطورة أنهما ظهرا على العالم في أكمل صورة بعد أن قام طائرٌ سحري بشَطرِ ساق خيزرانٍ كانا في داخلها.

21 تأسّست المفوّضية الرئاسية للحكم الرشيد (Presidential Commission on Good Government - PCGG) بمبادرة من حكومة كورازون أكوينو الثورية في العام 1986 بهدف الكشف عن الأصول والأموال التي اختلستها عائلة ماركوس والتي قُدِّرت قيمتها بنحو 10 مليارات دولار أميركي وتسييلها. وعندما تولّى رودريغو دوتيرتي الرئاسة في العام 2016، وُضعت المفوّضية تحت إشراف مكتب النائب العام المعروف باتّصاله بماركوس.

22 عُرف الرئيس بينينيو سيميون س. أكوينو الثالث (2010 – 2016) بلقب نوينوي. كما أطلق عليه العامة اسم بينوي أو الرئيس نوي.

23 Peter Bellwood, Hsiao-Chun Hung and Yoshiyuki Iizuka, "Taiwan Jade in the Philippines: 3,000 Years of Trade and Long-distance Interaction," in *Paths of Origins: The Austronesian Heritage*, ed. Purissima Benitez-Johannot (ArtPostAsia, 2011)

24 تعمد النسخة الأحدث من العمل إلى إعادة إنتاج المجوهرات ضمن وسائط الواقع المعزّز، ما يتيح للفلبينيين تصوّر احتمالات استردادها عبر الوسائل الرقمية.

* *Ilustrado* كلمة تعني حرفيًّا "المتعلّمين" أو "المستنيرين" وكانت تُطلَق على طبقة من المثقّفين الفلبينيين من أبناء الإقطاعيين الأغنياء الذين ساهموا في صياغة المشروع القومي في الفلبين إبّان الاستعمار الإسباني في أواخر القرن التاسع عشر (المترجمة).

** *Tipos del País* ومعناها "طُرُز أهل البلد" هو أسلوبٌ في الرسم المائي انتشر في الفلبين في مرحلة الاستعمار، ويصوّر فئات مختلفة من الناس في أزيائهم التقليدية التي تعكس أيضًا مِهَنَهُم ومستوياتهم الاجتماعية (المترجمة).

*** *Costumbrismo* (كوستومبريسمو) تيارٌ أدبي وتصويري يمثّل السلوكيات والعادات ومختلف مناحي الحياة اليومية المحليّة في إسبانيا والمستعمَرات الإسبانية خلال القرن التاسع عشر بشكل خاص. يتّصل هذا التيار بالواقعية والرومانسية مع التركيز على الوصف الدقيق للشخصيات المحلية والسلوكيات الاجتماعية النمطية مع تفاصيل فولكلورية تدخُل في إطار السخرية أو حتى الرومانسية (المترجمة).

† الأنشودة الثيمية لأحد معالم ملاهي ديزني باركس الذي يحمل نفس الاسم. ألّفها الأخوان روبرت وريتشارد شيرمن في العام 1963 بناءً على رغبة والت ديزني بوضع أغنية تعبّر عن الوحدة العالمية تكون قابلة للترجمة إلى أكبر قدرٍ من اللغات والعزف في أكبر عددٍ من الأماكن. وقد تزامن إطلاق هذه الأغنية مع نشوء أزمة الصواريخ الكوبية (المترجمة).

25 Maria F. Mangahas, "Seasonal Ritual and the Regulation of Fishing in Batanes Province, Philippines," in *Managing Coastal and Inland Waters*, ed. Kenneth Ruddle and Arif Satria (New York: Springer, 2010)

26 اغتيل بينينيو أكوينو جونيور، الخصم السياسي لفرديناند ماركوس، في العام 1983 فيما كان يهمّ بمغادرة الطائرة التي حملته عائدًا إلى الفلبين من منفاه العلاجي في الولايات المتحدة الأميركية.

27 Marian Pastor Roces, "Conceptual Art, Authoritarianism, 1970s Asia" in *Gathering Political Writing on Art and Culture* (Manila and Hongkong: Museum of Contemporary Art and Design and Art Asia Pacific, 2018)

بيو أباد وماريان باستور روسيس

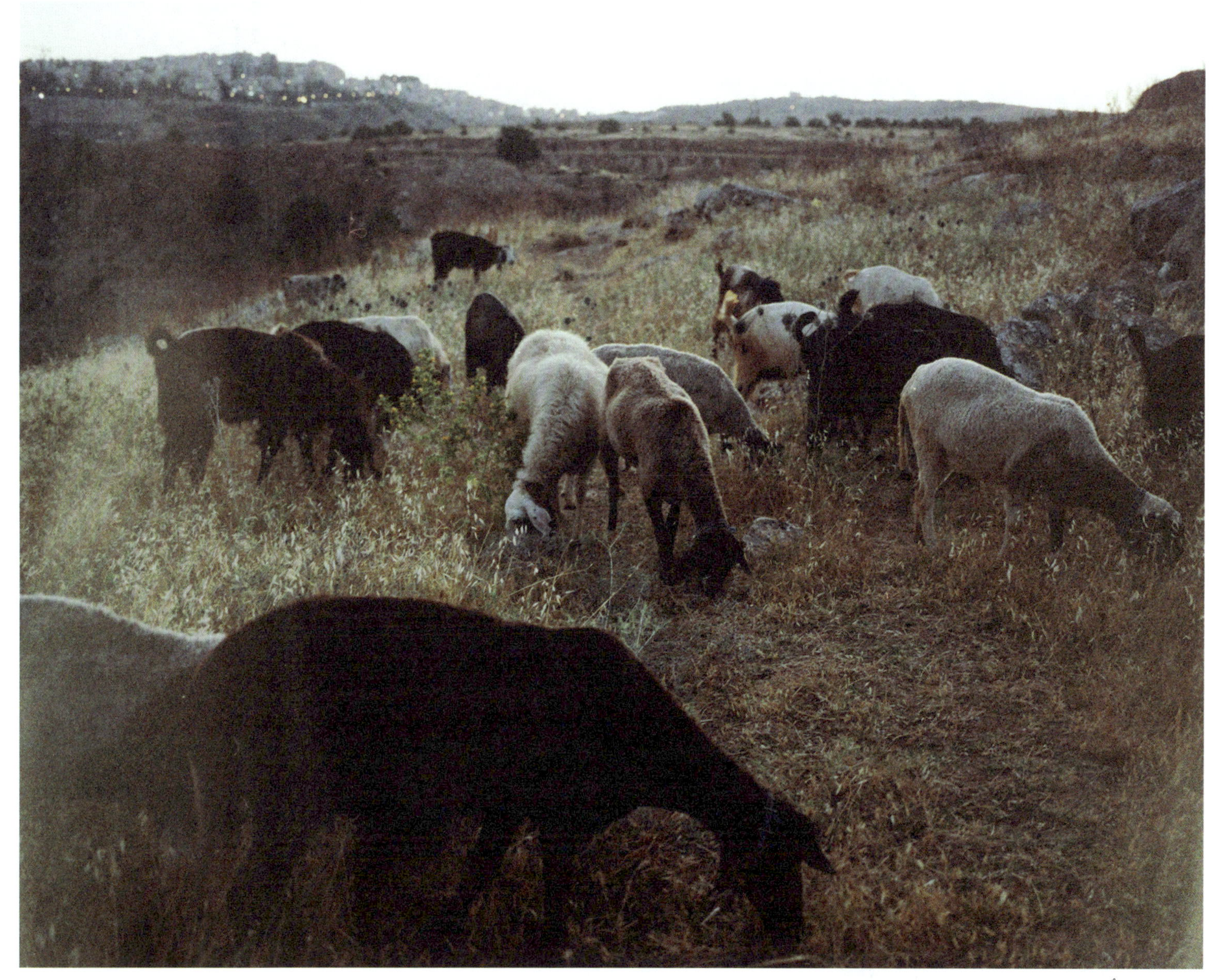

ماعزٌ وخرافٌ ترعى في الوادي. شعفاط، القدس الشرقية. بإذنٍ من المؤلفة.

حيث تنتهي الطبيعة وتبدأ المستوطنات

الإغلاق العام

عدت إلى الوطن في الربيع لأصوّر فيلمًا عن "التسليق"*. في الواقع، هو فيلم مطاردة بين حراس البيئة الإسرائيليين وفلسطينيين مسنين يحاولون جمع نباتات مصنّفة كأجناس محمية، ولاسيما البري منها كنبات العكّوب الشبيه بالخرشوف والذي يُقال عنه "الذهب الأخضر". يُعنى الفيلم "اليد الخضراء" (Foragers) الذي لا يزال في طور الإعداد بشكل أساسي بما يقرر انقراض أجناس معينة ونجاة أجناس أخرى، أو بمعنى أصحّ بمن في وسعه تقرير مصير الثقافات القائمة على جمع الأعشاب البرية وما يتبقى لأولئك الذين لا يملكون هذا القرار. يمثل الطعام مستوعبًا للتواريخ العائلية والجمعية المرتبطة بالأرض، وللعادات التي تجابه القمع بصيغته القانونية تحت مسمى حماية البيئة. أُلغي التصوير بسبب الإغلاق العام إبان جائحة كوفيد-19، فإذا بي أمضي أيامي في الحجر الصحي مع أهلي في شعفاط بالقدس الشرقية.

كانت أنشطتي اليومية أشبه بيوميات مراهقة أو متقاعدة. تتخللها مغامرات صغيرة كالتسليق وتجميع أغراض متنوعة أعثر عليها في الحي، بالإضافة إلى بعض مشاريع التجديد المنزلي والمطالعة والرسم ومشاهدة الأفلام والكتابة. مع الوقت، بدأت أتقبل

نُشر نص جمانة مناع، "حيث تنتهي الطبيعة وتبدأ المستوطنات"، أوّل مرّة في مجلّة إي-فلَكس العدد 113 (نوفمبر/تشرين الثاني 2020). حقوق النشر محفوظة للمؤلفة ولمجلة إي-فلَكس.

* "التسليق" أو "التجميع" أو "تلقيط "تعابير عامية يستخدمها الفلاحون وأهل القرى في بلاد الشام ليدلّوا على جمع نبتة السلق البرية ولكنه لا يقتصر عليها بالضرورة، بل يشمل سائر الأعشاب والنباتات البرية الصالحة للأكل. [المترجمة]

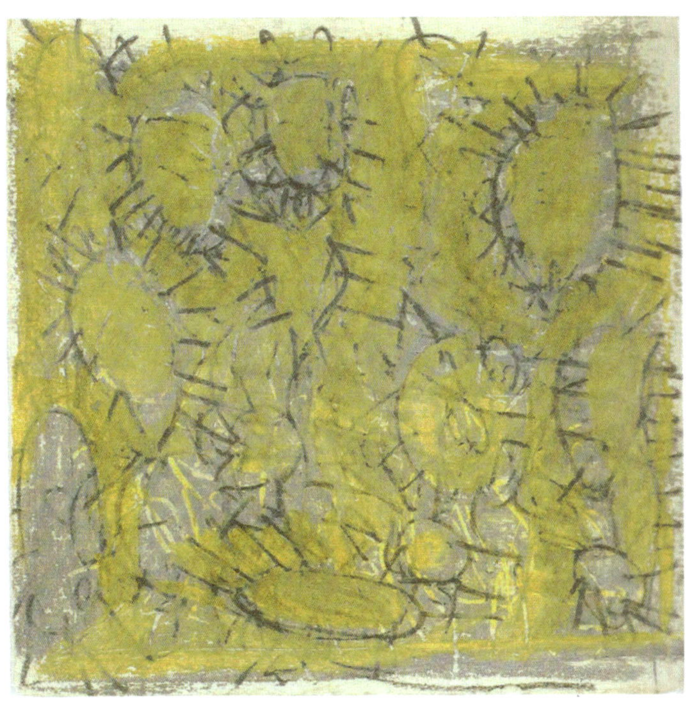

عاصم أبو شقرا، "صبار"، 1986. غواش على ورق 15 × 15 سم. بإذنٍ من غاليري وان.

المصادفات التي أهداني إياها الفيروس، ورحت أستمتع بنوستالجيا المنفى وهي طريقتي المتجددة للتعامل مع وجودي في القدس بعد مضيّ أكثر من عقد على مغادرتي لها. أذكر أنني كنت دائمة التحشّر على عدم تمضيتي الوقت الكافي هنا، زيارات قصيرة لا تتعدى بضعة أسابيع أخصصها للتصوير أو لجمع بعضٍ من المخزون الثقافي، أسارع بعدها إلى المغادرة قبل أن يدركني ثقل المكان. أما الآن، فأنا ممتنّة لهذا الظرف الذي بدد هواجسي من التحول إلى سائحة ثقافية في مدينتي.

أتنزه في الحي يومياً. أصادف حيواناتٍ ونباتاتٍ وأكوامًا من النفايات. أتأمل الجيران وهم يتأملونني، فيذكّرني المشهد بالصيفيات الناعسة أيام العطلة المدرسية حين كان في الوقت متّسع. المروحيات تراقبنا من السماء، بينما تستمرّ جلبة ورش البناء المحيطة متحدية التدابير المشدَّدة لحظر التجول. كالعادة، تتمثل استجابة إسرائيل للفيروس في عسكرة الخطاب المتعلق بالرعاية الصحية. الحكومة تزرع الشوارع بعناصر الجيش والشرطة وحرس الحدود وتتحدى تصويت الكنيست لتجيز لجهاز الشاباك[1] استخدام تكنولوجيات التتبّع من أجل فرض التباعد الاجتماعي. شركة تكنولوجيا إسرائيلية تنتقي عيّنات من أصوات مرضى بفيروس كورونا في مسعىً مشترك بين القطاعين العام والخاص للبحث عن وسيلة للاستدلال على المرض من أصوات المصابين ووتيرة تنفّسهم. إنها قاعدة بيانات لأشخاص مقطّعي الأنفاس[2].

فكرت كثيرًا في التناقضات التي ينطوي عليها فعل الحماية وأنا أجمع النباتات البرية الصالحة للأكل خلال فترة الحجر الصحي – والسياسات المستترة وراء القناع التحضري

1   وكالة الاستخبارات الداخلية الإسرائيلية.

2   هذه العبارة مقتبَسة بتصرّف عن تعليق لأمل عيسى على حائطي الفيسبوكي في 25 آذار/مارس 2020.

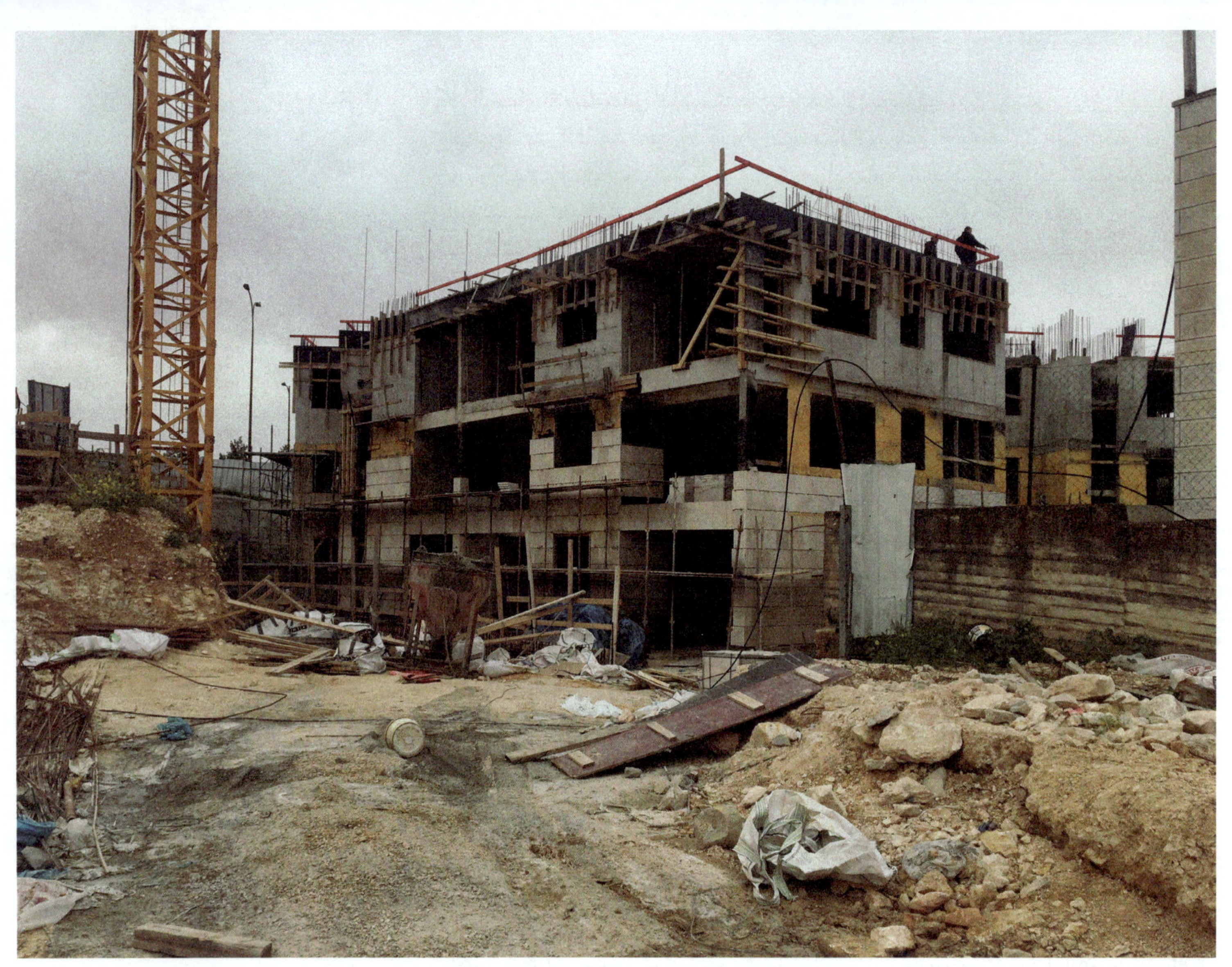

موقع بناءٍ في شعفاط. بإذن من المؤلفة.

في السـياق الاسـتيطاني – الاسـتعماري. لا مجـال للمقارنـة بيـن وضع أشـكال الحيـاة غيـر البشرية على القائمة الحمراء للأنواع المهددة بالانقراض لحمايتها مـن أذى البشر مـن جهة وبيـن حمايـة التجمعـات السـكانية مـن خطـر الإصابـة بالوبـاء. غيـر أنّ الجائحـة قـد سـلطت الضـوء عـلى هيكليـات الإدارة وسياسـات الرعايـة المتداخلـة في مختلـف أنحـاء العالـم. وقـد بـات التجـوال والكتابـة في محيطـي المباشر الـذي احتجـزت فيـه وسيطين للتفكيـر مليًا بعسـكرة السـلامة البيولوجيـة مـن خـلال مفاضلتها مـع مـا تبقى مـن الحقـوق الاجتماعيـة السياسـية. هـذا النـص، والفيلـم بنهايـة المطـاف، همـا بمثابـة تمريـن عـلى تخيّـل هيكليـات بديلـة وإيجابيـة للرعايـة – في إطـار الوضـع الراهـن ومـا بعـده – تنحـاز إلى تعزيـز بقـاء النبـات والبشـر عـلى حـدٍّ سـواء.

شعفاط

نشـأتُ في شـعفاط، وهو حـي فلسـطيني عـلى طريـق القـدس - رام الله التاريخي، تبعد نحو ثلاثـة كيلومتـرات شـمالًا مـن البلـدة القديمـة. كانـت في عهد الإمبراطوريـة العثمانيـة واحـدة مـن القـرى التابعـة للـواء القـدس التي تحولـت إلى امتـدادٍ للمدينـة بدءًا مـن منتصـف القـرن العشـرين. عندمـا احتلـت إسـرائيل القـدس الشـرقية عـام 1967، كان تعـداد سـكان شـعفاط لا يتجـاوز ثلاثـة آلاف نسمة[3]. وعندمـا بنى والـداي منزلهمـا هنـاك في أوائل التسـعينيات، كان هذا العـدد قـد ارتفـع إلى خمسـة عشر ألفًا. أمـا اليـوم، فيبلـغ عـدد السـكان نحـو خمسـة وثلاثيـن ألـف نسمة.[3] وحتـى فتـرة السـبعينيات والثمانينيـات، كان لا يـزال في الإمـكان إيجـاد قطعـة أرض معقولـةٍ بسـعر مقبـول في بعـض القـرى والأحيـاء العربيـة الأخـرى المحيطـة بالقـدس أمثـال بيـت حنينـا وبيـت صفافـا. وقـد سـمحت هـذه الوفـرة، بالإضافـة إلى قـرب المسـافة، بتكويـن نسـيج حضـري جديـد مـن العائـلات المقدسـية وفلسـطيني الداخـل الوافديـن مـن قراهم للدراسـة والعمل في القـدس[4].

لا تـزال شـعفاط القديمـة تحتفّـظ ببعـض السـمات المعماريـة التقليديـة: أسـطح مقبّبـة ومبانٍ حجريـة سـميكة مؤلفـة مـن طبقـة أو اثنتيـن وبسـاتين مـن الأشـجار المثمـرة وسناسـل حجريـة تسـوّر الأراضي الزراعيـة. ولـم تبـرز تلـك السـمات الريفيـة البديعـة دائمًا بنـاءً عـلى اختيـار السـكان أو رغبتهـم، بـل نتيجـة الاسـتراتيجية المتّبعـة والمتمثلـة في قوانيـن فـرز المناطـق العمرانيـة الإسـرائيلية. وقـد تمثلـت الاسـتراتيجية في الحـد مـن حجم البنـاء عـلى الأراضـي العقاريـة بهـدف التضييـق عـلى السـكان الفلسـطينيين والسـيطرة عـلى مـا تسـميه إسـرائيل "القنبلـة الديموغرافية الموقوتة". غالبًا مـا يُستخدم هذا التعبيـر العنصري للإشـارة إلى ارتفـاع تعـداد السـكان العـرب ضمـن مناطـق النفـوذ الإسـرائيلي ولا سـيما القـدس حيـث تُسـخّر جميـع الوسـائل الممكنـة للحفـاظ عـلى الأكثريـة اليهوديـة للمدينـة[5].

إلى الشـرق مـن هـذا الحـي، يقـع مخيـم شـعفاط للاجئيـن، وهو المخيـم الوحيـد الموجـود ضمـن الحـدود البلديـة لمدينـة القـدس. أمضيـت بضـع صيفيـات خـلال مراهقتـي أتـدرب في المسـبح هنـاك. كان عبـارة عـن حفـرة إسـمنتية تحتـوي عـلى ميـاه شـديدة العكـارة إلى حـدّ تتعـذر معـه الرؤيـة بنظـارات السـباحة السـويدية أبعـد مـن متـر واحـد تحـت المـاء. اليـوم، يقصـد والـداي المخيـم لشـراء الخضـر والفاكهـة. وكثيـرًا مـا يشـار إلى المخيّـم في الإعـلام عـلى أنّـه بـؤرة خارجـة عـن القانـون حيـث يكثر تعاطـي المخـدرات الثقيلـة والإتجـار بهـا. تكثـر

3 لا يشمل هذا التعداد سكّان المخيّم الذي يقطنه نحو ثلاثين ألف نسمة على الأقل.

4 تحديدًا من بلدات وقرى الجليل والتي يشار إليها ببلدات وقرى الشمال.

5 بعد احتلال القدس الشرقية وضمّها إلى دولة إسرائيل، أصدرت البلدية قانونًا يحدّد حجم البناء على العقار أو ما يُعرَف بنسبة الاستثمار بـ25% فقط. في المقابل، اكتظّت الأحياء اليهودية بالأبراج المصمّمة لتشغل المساحة القصوى المسموح بها للبناء ولتطلّ على الأحياء العربية. وبعد مرور عقود، زيدت نسبة الاستثمار في القدس الشرقية بعد أن أدركت الدولة الإسرائيلية أنّ العرب قد استنفدوا مساحات البناء المتاحة لهم. لقراءة المزيد Eyal Weizman, "Jerusalem: Petrifying the Holy City," chap. 1 in *Hollow Land: Israel's Architecture of Occupation* (Verso Books, 2007), 25–57

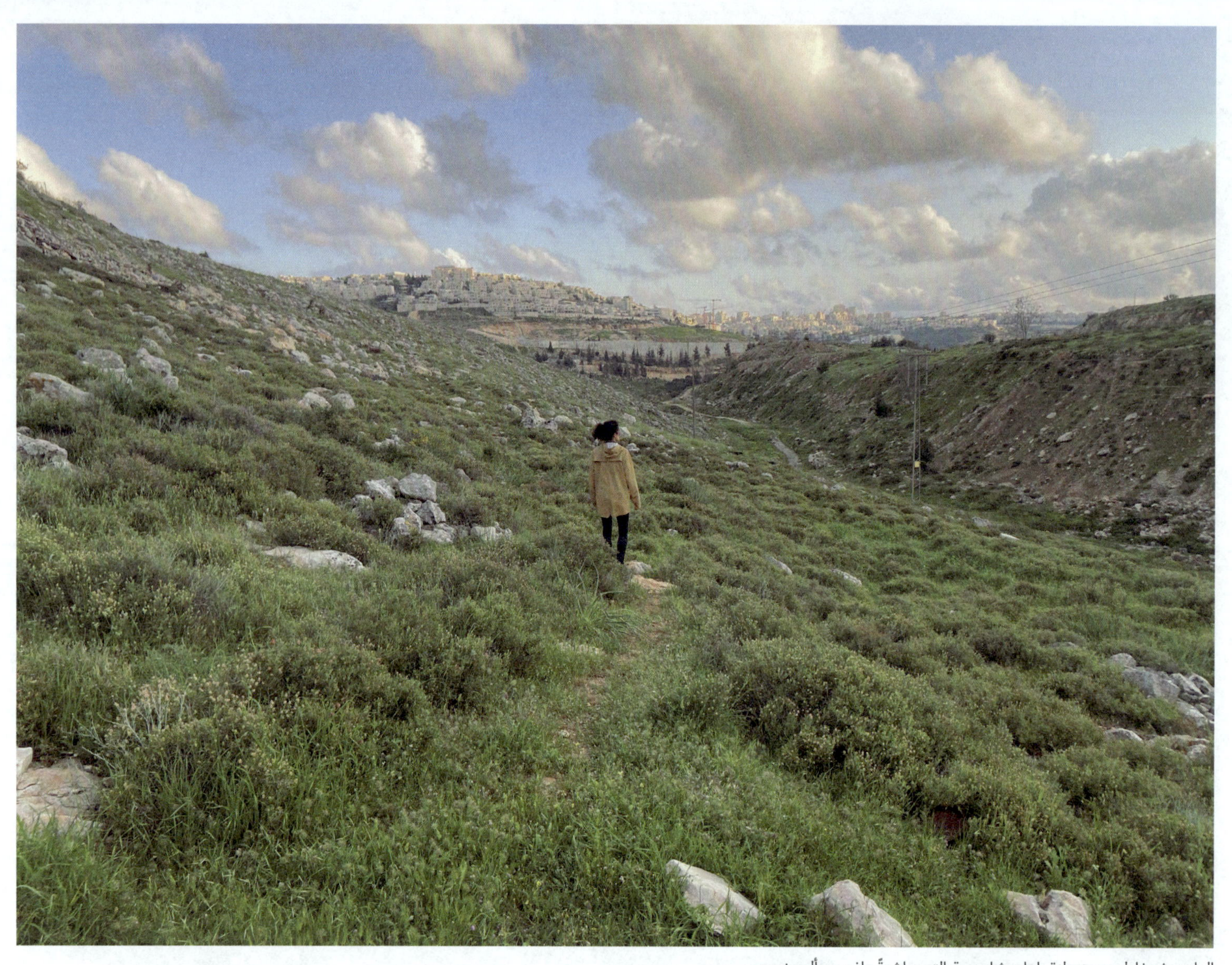

الوادي، شعفاط، ومستوطنة رامات شلومو قبالته مباشرةً. بإذن من ألين خوري.

حيث تنتهي الطبيعة وتبدأ المستوطنات

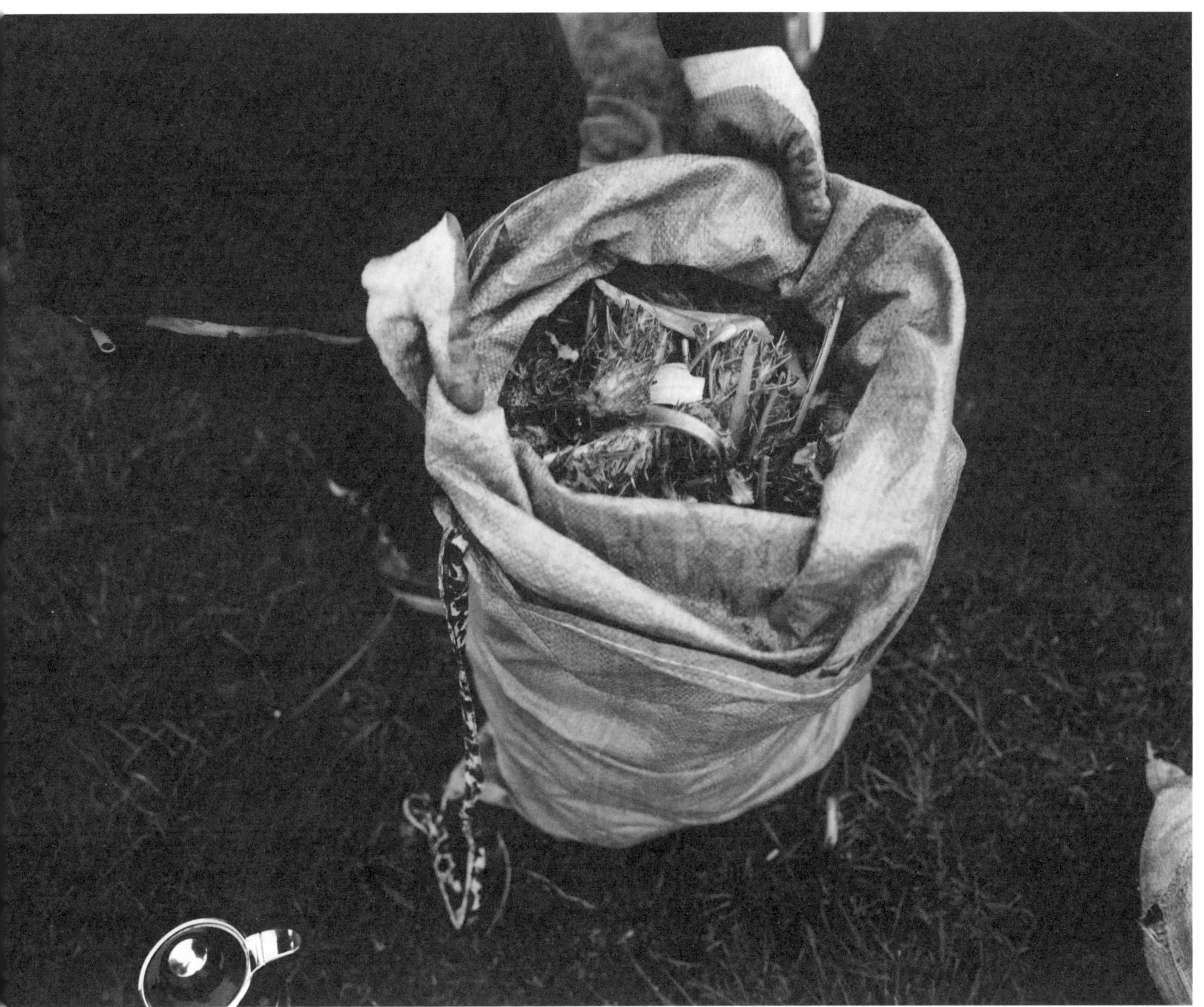

جرابٌ مليءٌ بالعكّوب من مرتفعات الجولان. يحتاج الشخص الواحد إلى ساعتين لجمع هذه الكمّية. وهي تكفي وجبةً لأسرةٍ صغيرةٍ بعد تنظيفها من الأشواك. بإذنٍ من المؤلّفة.

المستوطنات الإسرائيلية في محيط حيّنا والمخيم، شيّد جميعها على أراضٍ مُصادَرة بهدف ضمان تقطيع أوصال الأحياء الفلسطينية في القدس الشرقية مناطقيًا واجتماعيًا. في المقابل، تلتفّ التجمعات السكانية المهمّشة حول منطقة جدار الفصل العنصري ضمن مناطق عمرانية مكتظة بالمباني الشاهقة التي شُيّدت سريعًا وعلى أسس غير مستقرة والتي تؤوي عائلاتٍ تحاول جاهدة أن تتمسّك بإقامتها داخل نطاق القدس[6].

وإلى الغرب منا، تمتد سفوح تلال شعفاط على طول الطريق السريع الذي يغادر المدينة. في الماضي، كانت غابات الصنوبر المزروعة تغطي التل، وقد بقي مصنفًا حتى التسعينيات من القرن الماضي كمساحة خضراء عامة لتنقية الهواء وتحسين جودة معيشة السكان. كنت وإخوتي نلعب هناك في طفولتنا. ولكن الهدف الحقيقي لتصنيف تلال شعفاط كمساحة خضراء كان، بحسب رئيس بلدية القدس الأسبق تيدي كوليك الذي اعترف بعد إزالة "التجميد" عن الأرض ورصدها لبناء مستوطنة "رامات شلومو" في مطلع التسعينيات، منع العرب من التوسع العمراني في تلك المنطقة في انتظار بناء حي يهودي جديد[7].

لا يفصل بين شعفاط ورامات شلومو اليوم سوى طريق من مسارَيْن تقع فوق تمديدات الصرف الصحي حيث تتحد نفاياتنا البشرية.

الوادي

أخرج من بيت أهلي وأمشي غربًا نحو السهل عبر القرية القديمة في اتجاه ما تبقى من أحراج الزيتون تحت الجسور في محاذاة الطريق السريع الذي يغادر المدينة. هنا، على تخوم الحي، أجيل النظر في الوادي الذي أتاني بسحر الربيع وغمرني بمشاعر لا تلتقطها الكاميرات. أتأمل الصخور الكلسية المتناثرة فوق التلال. تنمو فيها النباتات البرية من كل نوع وتطبع الحيوات السابقة عليها آثارها. هنا تجويفان بحجم الكف محفوران في الصخر الكلسي – حوضان قديمان تتجمع فيهما مياه الأمطار لتروي الحيوانات. وهنالك صخور تشير إلى مداخل كهوف، بعضها يحتوي على بقايا لمعصرة زيت أو نبيذ، فيما يشكل البعض الآخر موطنًا للنباتات والحلزونات وقواقع الكائنات الدقيقة، ومرتعًا تتشمّس فيه السحالي. ولكم أدهشتني رؤية الغزلان تتردد إلى الوادي من وقت لآخر، مخلّفة في طريقها حبيبات البراز. ألقاها أحيانًا فنقف لنتبادل النظرات. أقترب منها، فتبتعد عني.

يعج الوادي بالنباتات الصالحة للأكل، شأنه كسائر المناطق الجبلية في فلسطين/إسرائيل. كثيرًا ما يقصده والداي للتسليق، فتجدهما يتباهيان ويشكوان في الوقت عينه من سرعة امتلاء الثلاجة بالخضروات التي يتعين عليهما غسلها وتقطيعها وطهوها، حتى قبل أن يتسنى لهما أن يقصدا السوق. يمتد الموسم من شهر شباط/فبراير إلى أيار/مايو، يجمعان فيه الخبّيزة والشومر والزعتر والعلت أو الهندباء والحمّيض واللوف وورق زقوقيا أو الطوطو والهليون والعكّوب الشهير. تكفي هذه النباتات والخضروات للاستهلاك طيلة فصل الربيع، فتقتصر زيارة البقّال على شراء البصل والملح وزيت الزيتون وربما بعض الحبوب. وليس أحوج إلى هذا النظام من هذه الأيام، بينما يتربص بنا خطر العدوى بالفيروس فوق رفوف وعربات السوبرماركت التي باتت رمزًا لانعدام التوازن البيئي والزراعي الذي يعيشه العالم اليوم.

---

6 في بداية جائحة كوفيد-19، هدّدت السلطات الإسرائيلية بإقفال المعابر وعزل السكان كليًا في محاولة ملتبسة لحماية المقدسيين من بعضهم البعض.

7 Sarah Kaminker, "For Arabs Only: Building Restrictions in East Jerusalem," *Journal of Palestine Studies* 26, no. 4 (1997): 15

يعد العديد من أجناس النباتات البرية التي تنمو في هذه المنطقة التي عُرفت فيما مضى بمنطقة الهلال الخصيب، من عائلة الخضروات المزروعة التي تُباع في السوبرماركت. وكما في أي مكان آخر، تعود ممارسات التسليق هنا إلى عهد ما قبل دورات الإنتاج الزراعي والمصالح التجارية والسيادية التي تفرضها الدول. فقد شكل نشاط جمع النباتات البرية العمود الفقري للحياة البشرية على امتداد آلاف السنين كما استمر آلافًا أخرى من السنين بموازاة النشاط الزراعي. وقد عاد التسليق إلى الشيوع من جديد في السنوات الأخيرة وفي مختلف أنحاء العالم: فبات بالنسبة إلى البعض نوعًا من الأنشطة الترفيهية يمضون بها عطلات نهاية الأسبوع ووسيلة للتقرب من الطبيعة، فيما أصبح بالنسبة إلى البعض الآخر مصدرًا للقوت وطوق نجاة في زمن الهشاشة وانعدام الاستقرار. نعمثُ بلحظاتي الصغيرة من السعادة بفضل معرفتي بالنباتات التي أورثتني إياها أمي، تصاحبها متعة مشاهدة التحولات الربيعية، أزهار تتفتح ثم تذبل وروائح وتغيرات في نوعية الضوء بين الأسبوع والآخر. كم كنتُ محظوظةَ بأن عشتُ ذاك السحر مجدّدًا. وقد بات التسليق في فترة الحجر المنزلي فعلًا متمازجًا ما بين الاستقلالية الغذائية والمتعة المطبخية وجدثُ فيه حميمية عززت شعوري بالانتماء والاتصال بالطبيعة المحيطة بي.

ومن بين هذه الأجناس الوفيرة من النباتات البرية الصالحة المنتشرة في فلسطين/إسرائيل، انتقت هيئة الطبيعة والمحميات في إسرائيل (INPA) ثلاثة لتُدرجها على قائمة الأجناس المحمية من الانقراض، هي العكّوب والزعتر والمريمية. وتعتبر هذه النباتات نادرة لأنّها تنمو في جيوب مناخية محدودة بينما تُجمَع بكثرة. تعرّفت خلال نزهاتي في الوادي إلى راعٍ اسمه أبو سعيد. وقد أخبرني بما يعرفه عن المنطقة كما لو أنّه خريطة متجسدة لكلٍ ما ينبت في تلك الأنحاء من أعشاب صالحة للأكل. والأهم أنّه أرشدني إلى أماكن تنمو فيها نباتات العكّوب بوفرة. وبناءً عليه، تسلحنا أنا وأمي بالقفازات السميكة والسكاكين والأكياس وأتممنا استعدادنا لرحلتنا.

للعكّوب طعم هو مزيجٌ بين الهليون والخرشوف. يعشقه الكثير من الفلسطينيين ويعتبرونه من الأكلات المفضلة. أما الذين لم يتذوّقوه في الصغر فيعتبرونه مجرد عشبة شوكية عادية. وقد لحظ علماء النبات الاستخدامات المتعددة لهذه النبتة، وقد وُجدت آثارها في مواقع أثرية نيوليثية، ما يرجّح أن يعود استخدامها إلى نحو عشرة آلاف سنة على أقل تقدير[8]. ويقال إنّ العكّوب كان يُطهى كالخضروات بذات الطريقة التي نعرفها اليوم[9]. وهو ينمو على المنحدرات الكلسية المفتوحة وفي التربة المحمرّة من أوائل شباط/فبراير إلى أوائل أيار/مايو بحسب الارتفاع عن سطح البحر وكثافة الأمطار، ونادرًا ما يُستزرع. لا يحب العكّوب التربة المفلوحة كما لا يقترب من المواضع التي تتناثر فيها مخلفات ورش البناء أو مواطئ إطارات السيارات الكبيرة. ويُعرف بفوائده الصحية الجمّة: فهو علاج لأمراض السكري والكبد وآلام الصدر ومشاكل القلب والجلطات والآلام المعوية والإسهال والالتهاب الرئوي. وهو أيضًا مضاد للبكتيريا والالتهابات والأكسدة والمسرطنات. في الصيف، ييبس العكّوب وينثر بذوره على السفوح ولا يبقى منه سوى الأوراق الجافّة التي تقتات بها الماعز.

8 Nicholas Hind, "Gundelia Tournefortii: Compositae," *Curtis Botanical Magazine* 30, no. 2 (July 2013): 114–38

9 كان ليونهارت راوولف (قلب الأسد، الذئب الضاري)، الرحالة الألماني الذي سافر وحيدًا في بلاد الشام، أول رجل غربي يصوّر العكّوب المعروف باسمه العلمي *Gundelia tournefortii* ويوصّفه. غادر ليونهارت راوولف بافاريا ليبدأ رحلة البحث عن مكونات للعلاجات العشبية في طرابلس، لبنان اليوم. ومن هناك أكمل نحو مدينة حلب الشهباء ومنها إلى بغداد والموصل قبل أن يختتم رحلته في القدس. اعتمد راوولف على وصف الطبيب الإغريقي القديم ديسكوريدس فظن خطأً أنّ نبتة *Gundelia* هي الخرفيش أو شوكة الحليب. وهذا الخطأ مفهوم، فكثيرًا ما يختلط أمر هذه النبتة حتى على السكان المحليين الذين لا يحترفون التسليق. وقد اعتمد علماء النباتات البروسيون والأوروبيون على مؤلَّف راوولف *Aigentliche Beschribung der Reise in die Morgenländerin* (رواية حقيقية عن رحلة إلى بلاد الشام). وقد لحظوا كيف كانت رؤوس النبات اليابسة تؤكَّل كالمُكسّرات في أسواق بغداد القديمة، كما كانت تستخدم كمصدر للزيت والصمغ في أجزاء من تركيا والعراق.

نعثر على العكّوب أنا وأمي فنجزّه من الأسفل تحت مستوى التربة بقليل. نجرده من الأوراق الشائكة ومن ثم نزيل الأشواك الباقية بعناية عند عودتنا إلى المنزل وقبل طهيه. تسودّ أصابعنا ونحن نحاول الوصول إلى قلب النبتة الصالح للأكل. ومن ثم نقلي القلب والجذوع السميكة مع البصل وزيت الزيتون أو نطبخه بقطع اللحم وأحيانًا نغمره بمرق من اللبن الرائب. وقد بات تعكيب العكّوب وتقشيره بالنسبة لي من الأنشطة المرتبطة بجائحة كورونا: تسلية شائكة بمعنى الكلمة.

أذكر أنّ العكّوب كان يأتينا دائمًا من خالاتي في الجليل الأعلى. كنّ يتولّين مهمة تنظيفه الشاقة من الأشواك برحابة صدر وكنا نحن نعدّه للطهي. عماتي يعشن إلى الآن روتين الحياة الريفية وحيزها الزمكاني حيث لا يعتبر جمع العكّوب وتقشيره مضيعة للوقت. كما أن نبتة العكّوب أكثر وفرة في مناطق الشمال، في نابلس والجليل ومعظم أنحاء مرتفعات الجولان السورية المحتلة. خالاتي اليوم في السبعين والثمانين من العمر، لم أعلم أنّهن كنّ خارجات عن القانون حتى كبرت. وكانت السلطات الإسرائيلية قد جعلت في العام 2005 جمع العكّوب عملًا غير قانوني، وإن تسأل عن السبب يخبرك الفلسطينيون بأنّ "السبب هو أنّ العرب يحبونه كثيرًا".

القانون

كان الزعتر، وهو العشبة الأكثر استخدامًا في المطبخ الفلسطيني (أو الشامي)، أول الأعشاب الصالحة التي أدرجت على قائمة الأجناس المهددة بالانقراض في التشريعات الإسرائيلية. حدث ذلك عام 1977 عندما فرض وزير الزراعة آنذاك أريئيل شارون حظرًا شاملًا على جمع الزعتر تحت طائلة الغرامة المالية الباهظة والسجن لمدة ثلاث سنوات كحد أقصى. ولم يكن هذا الحظر مستندًا إلى أي دراسة علمية رسمية بل كان قرارًا مبنيًا على "الحدس". وتقول الرواية إنّ شارون أدرك القيمة الرمزية للزعتر إثر حصار تل الزعتر[10] عام 1976. وقد شهد هذا المخيم الفلسطيني الذي أقيم في شمال بيروت عام 1948 أبشع مجازر الحرب الأهلية اللبنانية أثناء معركة بين الفصائل المسلحة لمنظمة التحرير الفلسطينية وميليشيا اليمين المسيحي بقيادة حزب الكتائب اللبنانية التي سيتحالف معها شارون لاحقًا في مجزرة صبرا وشاتيلا عام 1982. وما إن فُرض الحظر حتى باشر أحد الكيبوتزات في الجليل بزراعة الزعتر وبيعه جملةً إلى الفلسطينيين وتصديره إلى البلدان العربية مموهًا في توضيب يوحي بأنّه منتجٌ فلسطيني. وقد أطلق المشروعَ الحاكم الزراعي الأسبق في الضفة الغربية زئيف بن هيروت وابنه يورام بن هيروت. وكان زئيف قد أمضى وقتًا طويلًا مع الفلسطينيين، فعرّفه أصدقاؤه العرب على أفضل وصفات خليط الزعتر (بمقادير مختلفة من الزعتر والسماق والسمسم والملح) التي تناسب ذائقتهم وتلبي الطلب في السوق. ينبّهنا هذا المثال المبكر من انتحال الهوية المطبخية التي تعدّ اليوم من الاستراتيجيات المعروفة والشائعة (الحمص والفلافل، إلخ.) إلى الاحتلال كمشروع استثماري، كحقل تجارب ميسرٍ عسكريًا وتكنولوجيًا للاقتصاديات الاستخراجية الإسرائيلية متعددة الأوجه.

بعد نحو ثلاثة عقود من الحظر المفروض على الزعتر، أضيف كل من المريمية التي تستخدم كمشروب ساخن والعكّوب إلى قائمة الأجناس المحمية. وقد تحجّج التعديل

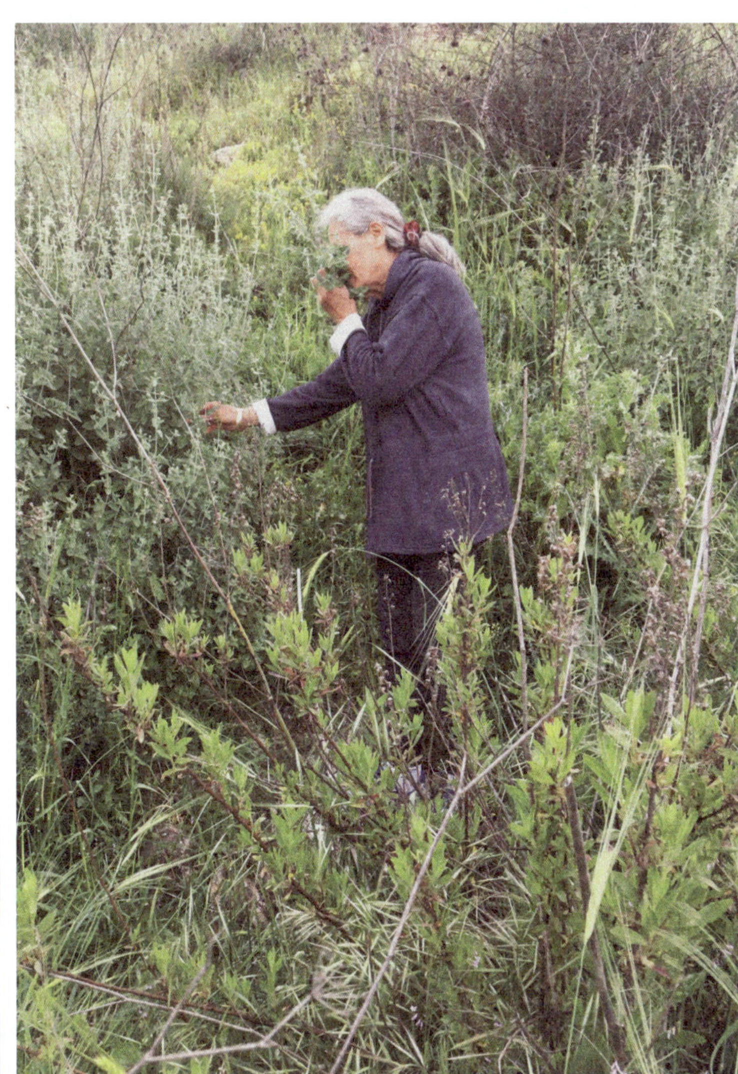

عزيزة وهي تستنشق زعتر البسَس. بإذنٍ من المؤلفة.

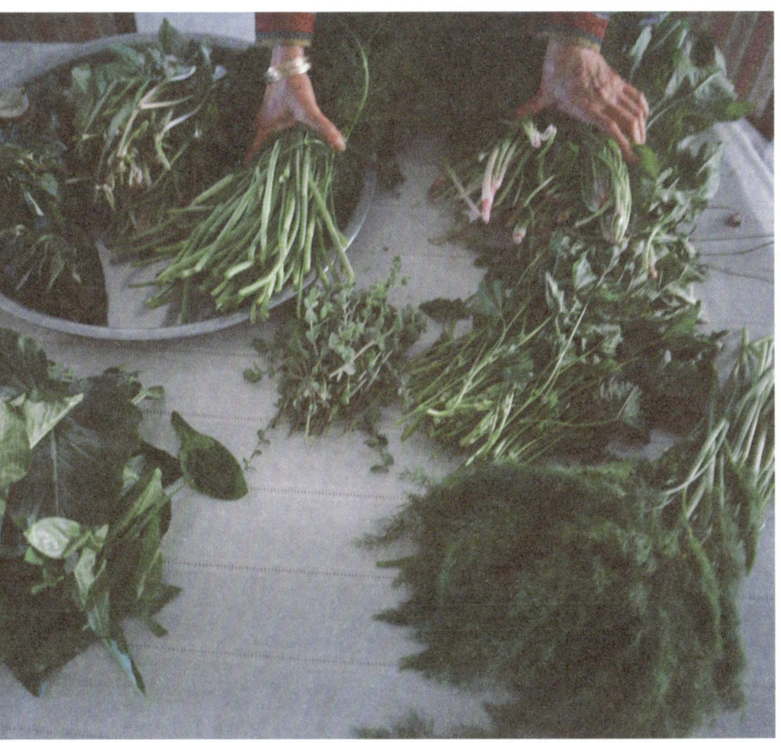

والدتي عزيزة وهي تفرز النباتات المسلَّقة. بإذنٍ من المؤلفة.

القانوني بالعلم مستندًا إلى ورقة بحثية لعالم النباتات الإسرائيلي وموظف هيئة الطبيعة والمحميات في إسرائيل (INPA) ديدي كابلن تعود إلى العام 1995. وقد أظهر بحث كابلن وزملائه أنّ كثرة التعكيب تتسبب في الحد من نمو العكّوب في البرية كونه يحمل أثرًا سلبيًا على إزهار النبتة وتجددها. غير أنّ كابلن كان معارضًا لفرض الحظر التام وأوصى بأن "يُحصر التسليق بالاستخدام المنزلي فقط" وأن يمنع تصديره تجاريًا إلى البلدان المجاورة[11]. ومع ذلك، عمدت وزارة البيئة إلى إقرار الحظر الشامل بدلًا من انتهاج مقاربة أكثر استيعابًا بسبب صعوبة الرقابة على التطبيق وغلبة المجمع القانوني السياسي على السلطة العلمية. وكانت الحجة الدارجة التي رددها أمامي موظفو هيئة الطبيعة والمحميات في إسرائيل خلال بحثي الميداني أن: "كيف لنا أن نجزم أنّ تلك النساء العشر في الوادي يجمعن الأعشاب ليطعمن عائلاتهن لا ليسلمنها إلى من يشغّلهن كي يبيعها في السوق؟". وفيما عدا ورقة كابلن، لم تصدر أي دراسة علمية لاحقة لتقف على آثار قانون الحماية على حال هذه النبتة في الأحراج البرية[12]. ومع ذلك فقد غُرّم المئات من الأشخاص من العرب حصرًا وحوكموا بسبب جمع الزعتر والعكّوب[13]. إذًا، تضفي هذه القوانين الحمائية غطاءً بيئيًا هزيلًا على تشريعات عنصرية هدفها إقصاء للفلسطينيين والسوريين في هضبة الجولان المحتلة أكثر فأكثر عن أراضيهم[14]. تلك الأراضي التي استولت عليها الدولة الإسرائيلية غالبًا لتقيم عليها البلدات اليهودية والمستوطنات والمحميات الطبيعية ومناطق التدريب العسكري وإلى ما هنالك من استخدامات لما يعرف "بأراضي الدولة".

المحميّات في ظل الصهيونية

لطالما كانت تدابير الحماية سيفًا ذا حدين. تذكرنا تجربتنا في الحجر الصحي بأنّ أي تدبير للحماية لا بد وأن يترافق مع شكل من أشكال المحو. ولا يعود السؤال الرئيسي هنا عما إذا كنا نريد الحماية أم لا، بل كيف وبأي كلفة. ففي ظل الاستعمار خصوصًا، تأتي قوانين الحماية كقرارات فوقية تُفرض على الشعوب المستعمَرة بحجة الخبرة العلمية للحد من "النزعات التدميرية" لدى "السكان المحليين الجهلاء". ولقد اتّسقت هذه الدينامية دومًا وبشكل خاص مع المشروع القومي الصهيوني الذي عمل باستمرار على إقصاء أي احتمالية تبادلية مع الآخر العدو. فتحولت الصهيونية إلى جهاز للفصل العنصري، عالمٍ مقسومٍ إلى قسمين حيث تستعدي السلطة السيادية الفلسطينيين العرب وتستعلي عليهم. شبّه فرانتز فانون علاقة الأسياد والرعية في هذه العوالم الاستعمارية بحياة الحيوانات حيث لا تنتج هذه العلاقات أي شكل من أشكال روحية الجماعة أو الفضاء المشترك[15]. إذ يتجاهل السيد في هذه الحال الرعية ويضعها في خانة دون البشر فيتجنب إلى الأبد أي نوع من التماس أو الحوار معها. وفي هذه المنظومة الرمزية، يبقى الفلسطينيون في خانة المتلقّين الخاضعين للقانون بدلًا من المساهمين في صياغته. أما في حالة الحظر على جمع العكّوب، تأتي هذه النزعة للحماية البيئية مفارقةً، إذ يُعتبر العكّوب مكوّنًا أساسيًا من مكوّنات المطبخ في شمال فلسطين في حين يجهله معظم الإسرائيليين، ومع ذلك فهو خاضع للحماية من تهديد الفلسطينيين. وكما في كل مرة، ينسى المسؤولون الإسرائيليون أن يأخذوا رأينا في المسألة.

11 Didi Kaplan, Dror Pevzner, Moshe Galilee, and Mario Gutman, "Traditional Selective Harvesting Effects on Occurrence and Reproductive Growth of Gundelia Tounfortii in Israel Grasslands," *Israel Journal of Plant Sciences*, no. 43 (1995)

12 بحسب ما أخبرني كابلن في مقابلة في آذار/مارس 2019.

13 حالات قليلة من المحاكمات استهدفت جامعي المريمية التي تُستخدم كعشبة لا كطعام، لذا تُجمع بكميات أقل.

14 يتواجد العكّوب بكميات وافرة في أنحاء عدّة من مرتفعات الجولان حيث يجمع معظم الجليليين حاجتهم منه.

15 Achille Mbembe, "Fanon's Pharmacy," chap. 5 in *Necropolitics* (Duke University Press, 2019), esp. 153

تستلزم مسألة إعادة موقع أو غرض ما إلى حالته الأصلية المفترضة وبالتالي المتخيلة مسعىً للحماية من شأنه أن ينتزع الشيء من بيئته الحية. تشكل القومية الصهيونية حدثًا استعاديًّا ينطوي على سعي مسيحاني يهودي -مسيحي لإعادة ما يعتقد أنّه الأرض في حالتها الأصلية أو "الطبيعية" بشكل انتقائي إلى اليهود دون غيرهم من خلال البنية الحداثية النموذجية للتعايش: أي الدولة الأمة. عند هذه الجبهة دائمة التوسع – بالمعنيين الحرفي والمفاهيمي وبشكل متسق مع الحداثة بشكل عام – باتت صناعة التاريخ مجرد نسخة معلمنة من "نهاية الأيام"[16]. فالصهيونية لم تكتفِ بالكشف على موقع أثري أو التقاط موجات صوتية صادرة عن موسيقى المعبد الثاني أو الزعم بشأن ورود العكّوب والزعتر في نص العهد القديم. بل اتسمت هذه التركيبة الغائية للدولة تاريخيًّا باعتماد تدابير الحماية والوقاية لإضفاء المزيد من الشرعية على زعمها بأحقّيتها بالأرض وترسيخ صورتها عن ذاتها في مختلف المحافل ومن بينها مفاهيم "الطبيعة".

ومن أشهر الأمثلة على هذه الطبيعة الخاضعة للمفهوم القومي – أي المصممة لتعكس صورة الدولة – هو الاستزراع الأحادي لأشجار الصنوبر بتمويل من الصندوق القومي اليهودي (JNF). وقد شاعت هذه الممارسة تحديدًا مع التوطّن التدريجي لليهود الأشكينازيين في فلسطين/إسرائيل وتحول أوروبا إلى باعث على النوستالجيا. ولم يكن "جعل الصحراء تزهر" مجرد مجاز يعبر عن المشروع الصهيوني، بل تمثل في استنبات المئات من الغابات لكي يتخيل الأشكينازيون أنفسهم في لايبتسغ بينما هم في القدس[17]. وقد هدفت معظم مشاريع التحريج لا إلى إضفاء منظر من "التحضّر" على التلال الفلسطينية "البدائية" شبه القاحلة فحسب، بل من أجل إخفاء معالم وآثار أكثر من أربعمائة قرية فلسطينية دُمرت إبان نكبة 1948 بعدما نُفي ساكنوها منها.

ومع صعود حركات المناصرة البيئية في تسعينيات القرن الماضي، أدرك الصندوق القومي اليهودي أنّ عمليات المحو هذه لم تقتصر على الفلسطينيين بل دمرت معهم معظم الغطاء النباتي والحيواني لتلك الأراضي[18]. فقد حالت الحموضة المرتفعة لأشجار الصنوبر دون عودة الغطاء الخضري إلى النمو كما ساهمت في ارتفاع وتيرة اندلاع حرائق الغابات وشدتها. يحاكي هذا الوضع الكوارث التي طالت أستراليا وأميركا الشمالية والجنوبية والبرتغال وغيرها من الأماكن. فقد أدى القضاء على عادات التحريق المحصور لدى السكان الأصليين في كاليفورنيا بالأخص إلى ازدياد كثافة الأشجار والنباتات البرية التي تساهم مع ارتفاع معدلات الاحتباس الحراري في التسبب المزمن بالحرائق الضخمة الخارجة عن السيطرة. أما اليوم، فقد توصلت مجتمعات السكان الأصليين الأميركيين إلى شراكة مع مصلحة الغابات في الولايات المتحدة تدير بموجبها الأراضي بهدف الحفاظ على العادات والتقاليد والسيطرة على حرائق الغابات[19]. وبنفس هذه الروحية الإصلاحية، أدرك المناصرون البيئيون أنّ تجفيف مستنقعات سهل الحولة في الجليل في الخمسينيات قد أضر بمسار هجرة الملايين من الطيور بين أوروبا وإفريقيا. وبناءً على ذلك، أعيد غمر هذه المنطقة جزئيًا في منتصف التسعينيات على أمل إعادة الطيور المهاجرة إليها. وقد شهد القرن الماضي الكثير من الأمثلة على هذا النوع من "سوء التقدير" والمراجعة: من التصحير في النقب جنوبًا بسبب استنفاد موارد المياه الجوفية الناجم عن تهجير مجتمعات البدو، إلى القيود المفروضة على المراعي والتي تأثر بها الرعاة العرب. غير أنّه وعلى عكس السياقات الأخرى للاستعمار الاستيطاني كأمثلة الولايات المتحدة الأميركية

16 للمزيد حول الجهود المتفائلة تقنيًا والمتداخلة مع التصور الغربي عن "نهاية الزمان" يرجى الاطلاع على
Deborah Bird Rose, "Reflections on the Zone of the Incomplete," in *Cryopreservation*, ed. Joanna Radin and Emma Kowal (MIT Press, 2017)

17 بتصرّف عن
Carol Bardenstein, "Threads of Memory in Discourses of Rootedness: Of Trees, Oranges and Prickly-Pear Cactus in Palestine/Israel," *Edebiyat: A Journal of Middle Eastern Literatures 8*, no. 1 (1998)
ورد الاقتباس عن باردنستين في
Irus Braverman, "Planting the Promised Landscape: Zionism, Nature, and Resistance in Israel/Palestine," *Natural Resources Journal* 49, no. 2 (Spring 2009): 343

18 Natalia Gutkowski, "Governing through Timescape: Israeli Sustainable Agriculture Policy and the Palestinian-Arab Citizens," *International Journal of Middle East Studies 50*(2018) no. 3

19 Laren Sommer, "To Manage Wildfire, California Looks To What Tribes Have Known All Along," *NPR*, August 24, 2020

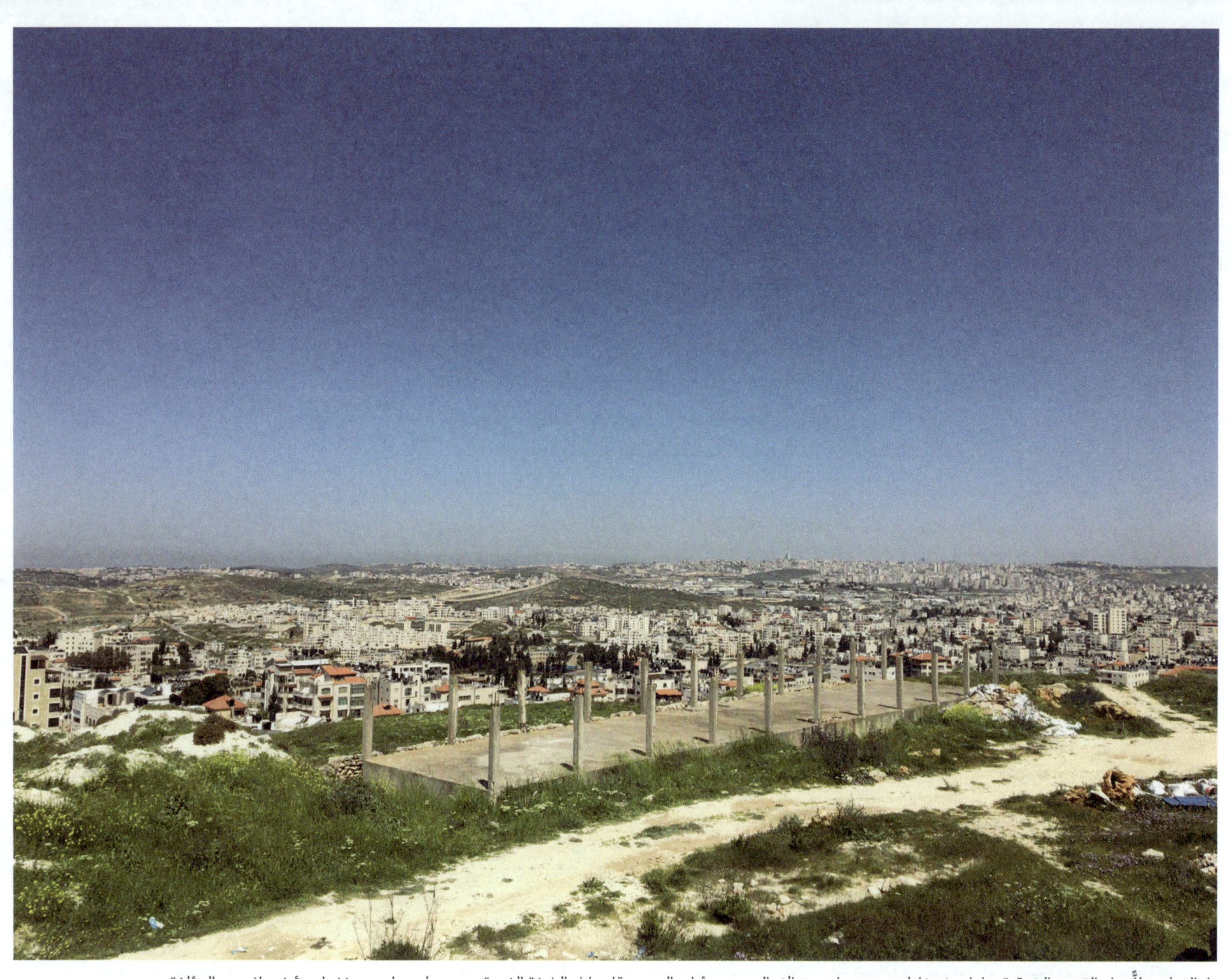

تل الفول مطلًّا على القدس الشرقية وبلدات شعفاط وبيت حنينا وبير نبالا والنبي صموئيل والجيب وقلنديا في الضفة الغربية ومستوطنتي راموت وغفعات زئيف. بإذنٍ من المؤلفة.

وكندا وأستراليا، لم يترافق التحول الجذري نحو السياسات المستدامة في إسرائيل مع أي اعتذار رسمي أو اعتراف بالجرائم التي ارتكبت على مر التاريخ. وكذلك لم تعترف إسرائيل بعد، على غرار الاعترافات الغربية رغم هزالها وانعدام جدواها، بترافق عمليات تهجير السكان مع العنف المرتكب ضد الأرض. بل على العكس من ذلك، حيث أُدرجت التدابير "الخضراء" المعتمدة منذ التسعينيات في إطار خطاب الحماية التاريخي ليتواصل إرساء وتدعيم الثنائيات السلطوية حتى اليوم.

على الرغم من "الأخطاء" البيئية التي ذكرتها آنفًا، ثمة ما يستدعي الخوف على أعشاب العكّوب والمريمية والزعتر البرية من الانقراض على نطاق أوسع من إسرائيل/فلسطين. إذ يؤكد كبار السن في الداخل كما في الأردن ولبنان المجاورَين على ازدياد صعوبة العثور على هذه الأعشاب. كما يستشعر هذه الندرة المستجدة أهل ولاية أصفهان في إيران حيث شاعت زراعة العكّوب من أجل تلبية الطلب المتزايد والذي يتجاوز الكميات المتوافرة من جني الأعشاب البرية[20]. وكما في معظم حالات الحياة البيولوجية المعرّضة لخطر الانقراض، تشمل العوامل الدافعة في هذا الاتجاه الإضرار بالبيئة الطبيعية والنمو السكاني والتمدّين والتغير المناخي. أما في ما يتعلق بالتسليق، فقد يكون لازدياد الطلب والجني المفرط غير المستدام للأعشاب البرية دورٌ مساهمٌ في تعزيز مخاطر الانقراض، ولكنها نادرًا ما تكون من مسبباته الأساسية. يؤكد البروفسور ناتيف دوداي عالم النباتات الذي خصص بحثه للزعتر في مقابلة أنّ:

لا أحد يتكلم عن دورنا نحن اليهود (الإسرائيليون) في القضاء على كميات من الزعتر تفوق بكثير ما يقطفه العرب. أتعلمون كم اقتلعت الجرافات من جَمم الزعتر؟ في هار أدار وتقاطع إلياكيم حيث كان الزعتر ينمو بكثرة ولم يعد له أثرٌ الآن. أما العربي؟ يقطف خمسة كيلوغرامات منه فيُغرّم[21].

إنّ التفاوض مع المحتل بشأن السياسات المتعلقة بانقراض النباتات هو أمرٌ معقد، لا سيما بالنسبة إلى الفلسطينيين الذين أمعن الاحتلال على امتداد سبعين سنة ماضية في التعامل معهم كجنسٍ دخيلٍ يحتاج إلى ضبط وإزالة عاجلَين. وقد استخدم حماية كائناتٍ بذاتها – كائناتٍ غير بشريةٍ – كوسيلةٍ إضافيةٍ من وسائل التضييق على شعب قاسى الأمرّين للنجاة والتغلّب على محاولات الطمس الثقافي والتطهير العرقي.

وهذه مفارقة أنطولوجية: فالدولة التي تضع القوائم الأمنية وقوائم القتل وقوائم الإرهابيين وغيرها من قواعد البيانات التي تفيد في "التعرف إلى الأشخاص الذين يشكلون تهديدًا"، هي نفسها التي تضع قوائم لتحديد الأجناس غير البشرية المهدَّدة وتضعها في المرتبة السياسية لمن هم بحاجة إلى الإنقاذ[22]. تنشئ دولة إسرائيل ذات السياسة النكروية (السياسة الإماتية)* أوهامًا عن الحرية والديموقراطية من خلال الاستعداء والتدمير ومشيئة القتل، فيما تتبنى خطابًا بيئيًّا يدّعي حماية الطبيعة كأرض بِكر على حساب الاعتراف بأحقية الفلسطينيين بالأرض وحريتهم في تقرير المصير. لا بل وتعمد هذه الدولة إلى تصوير ممارسات الفلسطينيين المتعلقة بالأرض كما لو أنّها تشكل تهديدًا للطبيعة، ما يسوّغ حرمانهم من الوصول إليها. عندئذٍ يصبح جمع العكّوب والزعتر البري في أحراج فلسطين/إسرائيل المتنازع عليها بالرغم من الحظر بمثابة صراعٍ من أجل البقاء

[20] Habib Yazdansehnas, Ali Tavili, Hossein Arzani, and Hossein Azarnivand, "Traditional Gundelia tournefortii Usage and its Habitat Destruction in Tiran va Karvan District in Iran's Isfahan Province," *Science Alert*, June 15, 2016

[21] مقتبَس من ربيع إغبارية،
Rabea Eghabrieh, "The Struggle for Za'atar and 'Akkoub: Israeli Nature Protection Laws and the Criminalization of Palestinian Herb-Picking culture," Oxford Food Symposium on Food and Cookery 2020. سيُنشَر لاحقًا.

[22] Irus Braverman, "The Regulatory Life of Threatened Species Lists," in *Animals, Biopolitics, Law: Lively Legalities*, ed. I. Braverman (Routledge, 2016), 20

* السياسة النكروية أو الإماتية (من أمات يميت إماتةً) (بالإنكليزية Necropolitics) هو اصطلاح نحته المؤرخ والمنظر السياسي الكاميروني أخيل مبيمبي للإشارة إلى "الأنماط المعاصرة في إخضاع الأحياء لسلطة الموت." يقول مبيمبي إنّ مفهوم "سلطة الحياة" (Biopower) الذي تحدث عنه ميشال فوكو لا يفي لتفسير هذه الأنماط، ولا سيما لجهة مركزية الحرب كناظم للعلاقات ولما يسميه "عوالم الموت" حيث الناس أموات أحياء، وكموقع يتقرّر منه من يستحق الحياة ومن يمكن الاستغناء عنه. [المترجمة]

وضربًا من مقاومة المستعمِر. ويصبح تسليق هذه النباتات جزءًا من محاولةٍ للتمسك بالذاكرة والمعرفة الآخذتين بالتآكل السريع.

معارك قضائية

يعتبر قانون حماية البيئة الإسرائيلي الذي يحمل اسم National Parks, Natural Reserves, and National and Memorial Sites Law of 1998 (قانون المنتزهات الوطنية والمحميات الطبيعية والمواقع الوطنية والتذكارية للعام 1998) أشبه بفارماكون: دواءٌ وسُمٌّ في آن واحد. يعتقد العديد من المسلّقين أنّ القانون يستحثّ على التسليق لأغراض تجارية. أحيانًا، يسارع بعض المسلّقين، ولا سيما قليلي الخبرة منهم، باقتلاع النباتات في عجالتهم خوفًا من الضبط بدلًا من قصّها من أسفل الساق، ما يعيق احتمالية تفريخه من جديد. ويجد البعض الآخر متعة في تحدي القوانين الإسرائيلية الجائرة عن طريق الانخراط في تلك التجارة غير المشروعة.

سعى مركز "عدالة" القانوني لحماية حقوق العرب في إسرائيل إلى المطالبة بالتراجع عن تجريم قطف العكّوب والزعتر والمريمية طيلة العقد الماضي. وقد تصدّر المحامي والباحث ربيع إغبارية حملات المطالبة الإعلامية العربية والعبرية مساهمًا في النقاشات والمنشورات التي تناولت الموضوع. وقد أرسل إغبارية رسالة إلى المدعي العام الإسرائيلي ووزير الحماية البيئية يقول فيها إنّ "حظر قطف تلك النباتات العشبية لا يستند إلى حقائق مثبتة كما لا يخدم أهداف القانون، بل ويضرّ بشكل غير متكافئ بالمجتمعات العربية التي عرفت استخدامها في مطبخها لمئات من السنين". وقد دأب إغبارية على إظهار الخلل في المنطق واللغة المتّبعين أثناء المحاكمات، حيث يكرر ممثلو الحكومة والقضاة خطاب هيئة الطبيعة والمحميات في إسرائيل ومجتمعها العلمي ويؤيدون فكرة أنّ للعرب نزعات تخريبية، في حين يفيد أغلب المتهمين بأنّهم ضبطوا أثناء جمعهم الطعام تمامًا كما فعل أجدادهم على مر الأجيال. كما يتجاهل هؤلاء المعرفة المحلية وأساليب العناية المتّبعة في التسليق: إذ يساهم جزّ أطراف سيقان الزعتر والمريمية في تحفيز نموّها وتجددها، بينما يعاود العكّوب التفريخ في العام التالي وأحيانًا في الموسم ذاته إذا ما قُصّ من أسفل الساق. يمعن النظام القضائي في تجاهل هذا النوع من الدراية، كما يغفل الأهمية الغذائية لهذا النوع من النبات والاحتياجات الاقتصادية والاجتماعية التي تدفع المتهمين إلى جمعها من البرية ومعظمهم من أرباب الأسر الكبيرة الذين يكادون لا يؤمّنون ما يسدّ رمقها. في المقابل، يجد هؤلاء أنفسهم مرغمين على دفع غرامات باهظة أو قضاء مدة في السجن في حال عجزوا عن السداد.

أثمر إلحاح "عدالة" في أواخر شهر شباط/فبراير 2020، عندما أعلنت هيئة الطبيعة والمحميات في إسرائيل أنّها ستتراخى في تطبيق التدابير الجزائية. وسمحت للجميع بجمع خمسة كيلوغرامات كحد أقصى من العكّوب للاستخدام الفردي، لفترة تجريبية مدتها سنتان. ولا يمكن الجزم بما إذا كانت هذه الفترة التجريبية تمهيدًا لتعديل دائم في القانون أم أنّها مجرد خطوة هدفها التخفيف اللحظي من وطأة تحول هذه المسألة إلى مثار للحساسية لدى القطاع العربي داخل إسرائيل وتفادي تهديدات "عدالة" بالتماس المحكمة العليا.

في شهر شباط/فبراير، بدأ حراس الأحراج يتكلمون عن الصعوبات التي يواجهونها في تحديد ما إذا كان التسليق للاستخدام الفردي أم للتجارة في الأسواق المحلية. فمع التنامي المطّرد للكثافة السكانية المدينية، كثر مستهلكو العكّوب وقلّ الراغبون في تكبد عناء تسليقه. لذا وتلبيةً للطلب المتزايد انتشر نموذج التسليق التجاري حيث تجمع مجموعة صغيرة ما بين ثلاثين ومائة كيلوغرام يوميًا ومن ثم تبيع هذه المحاصيل في السوق المحلية.

تشير الصعوبة البالغة في فرض تطبيق القانون إلى عمق المشكلة: إنّ مقاربة مسألة الحفاظ على البيئة وحمايتها عن طريق التجريم وفي ظل منظومة ضبطية قانونية بيروقراطية هي استراتيجية حتمية الفشل. فالتجريم يعزز العلاقات السلطوية القمعية التي نادرًا ما تنجح في إحراز أي تغيير هيكلي مستدام. وهو ليس إلا ثقافةً أحاديةً، تكنولوجيا أحاديةً، ترقيعًا تكنولوجيًا – كالمبيدات الحشرية واللقاحات المضادة للبكتيريا، وكالسعي لإيجاد لقاح لكوفيد-19- من دون الإخلال بالمنظومة الصحية والصناعات الغذائية والأسواق العالمية. الأمر الذي يجعل احتمالية حدوث جائحة أخرى مسألة وقت لا أكثر.

وقفة مع رعشات القط

نتوجه أنا وأمي هذه المرة شرقًا نحو سفح تلة حرجية بعيدًا عن الأعين تحت جسر يفصل بين حي ومخيم شعفاط ومستوطنة أخرى. نصادف ولدًا في طريقنا فيسألنا إن كنا نبحث عن أحد ما. نجيبه نعم، الوادي. هذا الوادي أيضًا مليء بالعصافير والحجارة والنباتات والأشجار الكثيفة. نحسب أنّ الأرض مصادَرةٌ، نظرًا إلى الجسر الإسمنتي الضخم الذي يمر فيها. ولكن عندما ننظر إلى الأسفل، نلمح آثار حراثة في الأرض وكأن ملّاكها الأصليين يزورونها موسميًا لقطاف ما تبقى من أشجارهم المثمرة. التل ناحية شعفاط مليء بالنباتات البرية الصالحة للطعام وغيرها من الأعشاب الربيعية المتوطنة. أما ناحية المستوطنة فخالٍ تمامًا، يعلوه بساط من العشب الأخضر في تراب محروث مسوّى كي يعطي المنحدر منظرًا نظيفًا ومرتبًا. لا شيء يؤكل هناك. عند جانبنا من التل، عثرنا على الكثير من "مَواطِن" الزعتر خلف سور حديدي قديم، لم نصدق أعيننا. بدت وكأن أحدًا لم يسلّق هنا منذ سنوات. فرُحنا نسلّق. وفيما نحن هناك، عثرنا على نوع آخر من الزعتر لا يشمله الحظر: زعتر البلاط واسمه العلمي Nepeta curviflora. يُعرَف هذا النوع من الزعتر أيضًا باسم "زعتر البِسَس" لأن القطط تجد لذّة في لعقه. تحتوي هذه النبتة على مادة تحاكي الفيرومونات التناسلية السنّورية فتمنح القطط النشوة والرعشة. تبدأ القطة بلعق النبتة فتروح تقفز وتموء بصوتٍ عالٍ. تستمر هذه الحالة لبضع دقائق تغادر القطة من بعدها لتعود مجددًا بعد ساعتين طلبًا لجرعة أخرى[23].

عدنا أنا وأمي إلى هذه البقعة مرارًا خلال أشهر الحجر الصحي نجمع العكّوب والزعتر كمتمرّدتين نسرق لحظات المتعة من جمع النباتات التي نحب.

نزع الاستعمار عن قوائم الأجناس المهددة بالانقراض

عند البحث في حالات الانقراض ذات المسبّب البشري، يسعى باحثو العدالة المناخية إلى الإجابة عن سؤالين جوهريين: ما هي أنماط العيش البشرية الدافعة نحو هذه الخسارة الكارثية؟ وما هي الأساليب المتنوعة التي اتبعها البشر وغير البشر في مقاومة هذه الخسارة؟ يكمن التحدي في نبذ تكتيكات الخفارة غير المجدية لمصلحة خلق ثقافة حمايةٍ

23 تزهر العشبة في أواخر الربيع زهرة زرقاء "مقلوبة". أوراقها على شكل قلب وعطرها آخّاذ. تُستخدم محليًا لتهدئة الأعصاب وتسكين آلام الأسنان. كما تطرد الصراصير والبعوض.

واستدامةٍ محبةٍ للحياة. يتطلّب ذلك تغيّرًا إبستمولوجيًّا ينزع الاستعمار عن مفهوم الانقراض ويعيد توجيه علاقتنا ببعضنا البعض وبمحيطنا. يقول الباحث جونو سالازار بارينياس إنّ هذه المقاربة في نزع الاستعمار يجب أن "تستهدف الصيرورة والتجربة لا النتائج الماضية إلا في ما يتعلق بالحاجة إلى مراعاة الآخرين وبالأخص إذا كانوا من غير البشر"[24].

للأسف، يمارس أغلب الناس، ومنهم الفلسطينيون، حياتهم بلا اكتراث للأجناس الأخرى. ويعيش المجتمع الفلسطيني اليوم قطيعة عن الأرض التي ارتبط بها ارتباطًا حميمًا على مدى التاريخ، وكانت جزءًا أساسيًا من الحياة الفلسطينية حتى جيلين أو ثلاثة أجيال خلت. تُعدّ عملية تحول الفلاحين الفلسطينيين الذين كانوا يشكلون الغالبية العظمى من المجتمع الفلسطيني إلى عمال بناء غير مهرة من التحوّلات التي يندر التطرّق إليها في إثر النكبة بين عامَي 1947 و1949، والتي ترافقت مع عمليات مصادرة الأراضي واستمرّت بعدها. تظهر اليوم بوضوح آثار هذا التحول العمدي والنظامي الذي خضع له المجتمع الفلسطيني بأكمله. جولة قصيرة بالسيارة في الضفة الغربية كفيلة بإظهار مدى التحولات العمرانية والطبيعية التي أحدثها كل من أصحاب الملكيات الخاصة والسلطة الفلسطينية على حد سواء. تلقّن جدي الأمّي الذي انتهى به الحال عامل بناء العبرة بعدما عانى الأمرّين، وكان يردد دائمًا على مسمع أبي أنّ عليه أن يحصّل تعليمًا عاليًا. "بإمكانهم أن يأخذوا أرضك ومنزلك، أما العلم فهو لك".

بدأ الفلسطينيون بهجر الحياة الزراعية قبل العام 1948 بزمن طويل، في العقود الأخيرة من عهد الإمبراطورية العثمانية المتهالكة، واستمرت هذه الظاهرة بالتوسع في ظل الاستعمار البريطاني وصعود المفاهيم الرأسمالية عن الحياة الحديثة والتي صرنا نطلق عليها صفة "التطور". وقد أدى هذا "التطور" تدريجيًا إلى تحويل الأرض من عنصر مكوّن للنسيج الاجتماعي السياسي إلى سلعة قابلة للتنقيب والاستخراج. ولا تزال هذه المفاهيم سائدة اليوم بينما الكوكب آخذ في الاضمحلال بوتيرة متسارعة.

أما التسليق فهو من الأساليب القديمة لاستكشاف الطبيعة المحيطة الوافرة بالخيرات والتعلم منها. وقد درج الفلاحون منذ 9500 - 8000 سنة قبل الميلاد على انتخاب بذور النباتات البرية التي يفضّلونها ليزرعوها، ومن ثم يعيدون الكرّة مرة بعد مرة إلى أن تدجّنت البذور وتدجّن البشر بصورة تامة. وقد ساهم هذا الصقل التدريجي على امتداد آلاف السنين في تغيير التكوين الجيني لكليهما والذي تجلى في النكهات والأشكال والوجوه التي نعرفها اليوم. تدور لعبة السفر عبر الزمن بين النباتات البرية أو "الحشائش" التي تنبت على أطراف الأراضي الزراعية وبين نسبائها المتحدّرين منها من الأجناس المستنبتة هناك. فمن الناحية الجينية، تفصل بينهما آلافٌ من السنين. ونحن بحاجة إلى بناء مخيلةٍ قادرةٍ على فهم عمق البعد الزمني الذي تجسده هذه النباتات ومتحررةٍ من منطق الأصول والحدود السياسية الاستبدادية. تتضمن هذه المخيلة ابتداع مجموعة من المقاربات إزاء التنوع الحيوي تشمل إعادة إحياء الطبيعة البرية مع "التصنيف المناطقي" بهدف نشر المعرفة وتعزيز الفاعلية والحث على التحلي بالمسؤولية – والاستمتاع – أثناء التسليق[25].

يمكن لإلغاء الشرطة أن يحرر مبالغ ضخمة من التمويل الحكومي يمكن تخصيصها لإنفاذ تغييراتٍ هيكليةٍ حقيقيةٍ وبناء المجتمع وتمكينه من خلال التعليم وإعادة التأهيل والدعم الاجتماعي. كذلك، يمكن أن يساهم تحويل الموارد المالية من البيروقراطيات

24 Juno Salazar Parreñas, *Decolonizing Extinction: The Work of Care in Orangutan Rehabilitation* (Duke University Press, 2018)

25 يواجه الحد من كميات النباتات المُسلّقة مشكلتين هما صعوبة الرقابة والكيفية في التطبيق، إذ يتفاوت عدد المسلّقين الذين يرتادون بقعًا بعينها. والأجدى تحديد مناطق معينة يسمح بالتسليق فيها لفترات محدودة – لنقل من سنة إلى خمس سنوات – ومنع التسليق في مناطق أخرى حيث يُسمح للنبات بالتجدد والتكاثر. وهذا هو مفهوم إحياء الطبيعة البرية مع "التصنيف المناطقي".

الشـرطية والقـوى العسـكرية نحـو دعـم التعليـم والتنـوع الأحيائـي في تحقيـق التغييـرات اللازمـة لنشـر المعـارف والممارسـات المتعلقـة بالنباتـات. كمـا يمكـن الاسـتفادة مـن هـذه المـوارد في تعزيـز اسـتراتيجيات الحفـاظ عـلى البيئـة العابـرة للحـدود ولا سـيما في المناطـق التـي تتوطـن فيهـا بعـض الأجنـاس المحـددة. فالبـذور لا تتقيّـد بالتصـورات الحداثيـة عـن النظـام والقانـون والحـدود.

هـذا واحـد مـن السـبل نحـو تحقيـق الديموقراطيـة عـلى المسـتوى الكوكبـي أو ديموقراطيـة الأجنـاس كباعـثٍ عـلى التحـرر مـن العبوديـة والاسـتعمار في جميـع أشـكالهما التاريخيـة والمعاصـرة. وهـو مـا يسـتدعي إعـادة بنـاء وترميـز الإيكولوجيـات عـلى أسـس التعاضـد والإيجاب عوضًا عـن الإقصاء. وحدها هذه النقلة النوعية قادرةٌ على ترجمة تدابير الحماية إلى محاولةٍ جديةٍ لصـون الحيـاة بـدلًا مـن إدامـة النظـام النكـروي القائـم.

هيثم الورداني

الألف التي في القاف الواو التي في النون

خطواتهما ثقيلة، ورأساهما يتأرجحان. لا يكادان يسيران بضع خطواتٍ في المساحة الضيقة، حتى يصطدما ببعضهما البعض. تغضُّناتُ جلدَيهما السميك تَلِينُ وتتماوج بطء، صاعدة وهابطة، فترتسم عليها نقوشٌ عابرة. ترفرف في الهواء صِيواناتُ آذانهما الهائلةُ يميناً ويساراً. وعندما يزيد الحمل عليهما ينقلان ثِقَلَ جسديهما من قَدَمٍ لأخرى، ورأسَيهما من جانبٍ لآخر، ويهزّان ذيليهما الرفيعين. يظلّان هكذا طيلة الليل حتى ينبعث في الظلام الحالك ضوءٌ قرمزيٌّ خافتٌ من الأنياب العاجية. عندها تهدأ حركة جلديهما، ويميلان مستندين إلى الحائط خائرَي القوى، وهما ينضحان عرقاً.

-الضحكة الوحيدة التي سمعتها اليوم لم تكن نابعةً من القلب.

-سمعتُ ارتطام جسمٍ هَوَى من عَلٍ. لكنه لم يذكّرني سوى بجلبة أقدامنا ونحن نركض هرباً من الغاز.

-أتمنى أن لا نكون قد أخطأنا التقدير.

-لا تيأس، فنحن ما زلنا في البداية.

منذ أن وصلا إلى هذا العالم والأصوات التي كانت تتناهى إلى مسامع الهدّام تثير قُنُوطَه. صَلصَلةُ المفاتيح، صرير الأبواب الثقيلة، الثُغاء، العَويل، العُواء، كل تلك الأصوات لم تختلف في شحوبها عن أصوات العالم الـذي أتيا منه. جاء الهـدّام مع صديقه العوّام إلى هذا العالم قادمَين من عالم آخر في مهمّة عاجلة. فعالمهما ضربته كارثة. مرضٌ غامضٌ حَصَدَ الأرواح حصداً، ولم يترك فصيلة ولا جنساً في سلام. تَساقَط الموتى في الطرقات من دون سببٍ ظاهر، فحار الجميع في أمرهم. ولم يُعرف السبب إلا بعد أن كَثُرَ الموتى، ولم يَعُد بالإمكان دفنهم جميعاً، فتُركت الجثث مكشوفة، إلى أن تَحَلَّلَت فظَهَرت الحصوات. قلوب الموتى كانت مليئة بحصواتٍ صغيرةٍ ملساء حالكة السواد، تطلّ بوضوح وسط بياض العظم. ولم يكن أحدٌ قد سمع من قَبْل بظهور حصواتٍ في القلب، فعمّ الخوف والفزع، وأطبَقَ اليأس على العالم.

وعندما أوكِلَت إليهما المهمة، أصابـا السمع عائدين عبر السنين، وأخذا يمعنان التذكُّر. عَبَرا بحيراتٍ جافة، وسارا في الليل مع فلاحين يحملون مناجل مسنونة، تلمع في الظلام، ويقطعون بها سياجاً شائكاً، يعبرون من تحته زاحفين. هامَا على وجهيهما في حقولٍ خضراء بالقرب من قريةٍ صغيرةٍ تَحَلَّقَ كثيرون حول أحد بيوتها، بينما زَمْجَرَت الدبابات محاولةً اقتحام القرية. اخترقا مستنقعاتٍ رطبة، ووصلا إلى تخوم مدينةٍ مزدحمة، قُطعت فيها الطُرُق، وأُقيمت المتاريس، وسار أهلها في شوارعها يصيحون بصوتٍ عال. ظلا يسيران ويسيران عبر تضاريسَ وأزمنةٍ لا يعرفانها، تقودهما ذكرياتٌ لا تخصُّهُما، إلى أن تَوَهَّجَت أنيابهما باللون الأرجواني الباهر الذي لم يره فيلٌ من قبل، فعرفا أنهما قد استقبلا الإشارة. لم يعرفا إلى أي عالَمٍ قد وَصَلا، لكنهما قدّرا أنهما لم يبتعدا كثيراً. فالجوع الـذي يقرص الأمعاء واحدٌ لم يتغيّر.

قبل سنواتٍ طويلة مـن ظهور حصوات القلوب، كانت آذان الأفيال الرهيفة قد التقطت تغيُّراً في مـا تسمعه، إذ شَحَبَ فجأةً كلُّ ما حولها. كانت الحياة تسير آنذاك كالمعتاد، البعض يذهب إلى العمـل، بينما يجري البعض الآخر هربـاً مـن الغاز المسيل للدمـوع. الغابات تحترق، والأسعار تزداد، ومن طُردوا من أرضهم ينصبون الخيام. إلى أن حدث ذات يـوم أن الصراخ لـم يعد صراخـاً، والكلام لـم يعد كلاماً. وتناهت الأصوات إلى أسماع الأفيال كمـا لـو أن أحدهم ألقى بستارةٍ شفافة فـوق كل شـيء. كَتَمَـث الستارةُ تصاريف الحيـاة اليوميـة كتمـاً طفيفـاً لا تدركه أذنٌ أخرى، ولا يستطيع جهازُ قياسٍ تسجيله، غيـر أن لـه تَبِعاتٍ كبيرةً فَزَعَت لها الأفيـال.

لكنها اعتادت التغيّر بمرور الوقت. وبعد عشر سنوات أصبَحَت تتجاهلُ ما تسمعُه، بعد أن كانت تعيش بآذانها. شَحِبَ صوتها هي أيضاً، ولم يَعُد هناك مـا يثير فَزَعَها. بل إنها

نَسَتْ أنّ تغيُّراً قد حدث أصلاً. والأهم أن الأفيال نَسَتْ ما عرِفَتهُ دوماً. فكلُّ فيلٍ كان يعرف أن حروف العلّة مكانها القلب، والحروف الساكنة مكانها العقل. وما إن تَذَكَّرْت ما كانت تعرِفُهُ بالفعل، وهي على طريق الهرب، حتى انجلى سرُّ الحصوات الملساء. فالكارثة ضَرَبَتْ العالم لأن حروف العلّة قد ماتت في القلوب. والحصوات التي أصبحت تطفر من القلوب وتعظُّبها ما هي إلا جُثَّتها. أدرك الأفيال فجأةً أن المرض الغامض قد ظهر بعد أن قَتَلَ الأعداء حروف العلّة حرفاً وراء الآخر، من دون أن يلحظ أحدٌ ذلك. لم يربُط أحدٌ دورات اشتداد الجوع وخراب الأرض بموت حروف العلّة. حتى غابت حروف العلّة جميعاً فوقعت الكارثة.

واصل العاج توهّجَهُ القرمزيَّ الخافتَ في ظلام الليل. وظلت الأسئلة تدور في بال الهدّام: هل أخطأت أنيابهما التقدير؟ هل أوصلتهما إلى العالم الخطأ؟ ولماذا لم يصل الوهج القرمزي إلى الدرجة الأرجوانية مرة أخرى منذ أن جاءا؟ ثم ماذا تعني هذه الإشارة الأرجوانية التي لم تتكرر؟ وفجأة، سمعا قفل الباب يُفتَح، ومزلاجه يُسحَب، ثم دخل السجّان إلى الزنزانة. في يده سلسلةٌ معدنيّةٌ غليظةٌ تُصَلْصِل، ويبـرُزُ من جَيْبِهِ مصباحٌ يدوي. اتّجه من فوره نحو العوّام وقيّد قَدَمَهُ بطَرَفِ السلسلة الثَقيلَةِ وسَحَبَهُ إلى جانب الباب. ثم خرج وأحضَرَ كَمّاشةً معدنيةً كبيرة، وسار نحو الهدّام. وَضَعَ المصباح الأسطواني الصغير في فمه، وأمسك بالناب الأيسر للهدّام بين فكي الكَمّاشة، وانعَكَسَ الضوء القرمزي على عينَي السجّان الضَيّقَتَيْن. تَجَمَّدَ الهدّام في مكانه، ولم تصدُر عنه أيُّ حركة، وأخَذَ العوّام يصيح في السجّان الـذي كان قد بدأ بقَلْع الناب. لكن فَكَّي الكَمّاشة لـم يستطيعا إحكام الإمساك بالناب وانزلقت المرة تلو المرة. وفي كل مرة كان السجّان يُعيدُ تثبيتها، ويسحبُ بعَزْم، فتنزلق مرة أخرى. انفعل السجّان وأخذ يسبُّ أمَّ الكَمّاشة، ثم ألقاها على الأرض، وخرج من الزنزانة.

انكمش الهدّام على نفسه، فيما أخذ العوّام يُحَرّكُ رأسه يمنة ويسرة محاولاً تحرير نفسه من السلسلة. حتى دخل السجّان مرة أخرى وفي يده "شـنيورٌ" موصول بالكهرباء هذه المرة، وضغط على زرّه فثَقَب الهواء. ثم التقط المصباح ووضعه في فمه ثانية، وانطلق نحو الهدّام وسط صراخ العوّام. ثبّت السجّان رأس الشنيور المعدني في قمّة الناب، تحت اللحم مباشرة، وضغط بكل قوته وقد أدار الشنيور، فانغرز رأس الخابور المعدني في العاج، وتطاير النُثار مع رائحة احتراق. أكمل السجّان الضغط حتى مرّ الرأس المُدَبب إلى الناحية الأخـرى. فأخرجه، وحـاول كسـر الناب بقـوّة قبْضَـتِه، لكنه لـم يَقدِر. جُنَّ جُنُونُه، وغَـرَزَ الشنيور في اللحم مباشرة، وضَغَـط على الزناد، فتنـاثر الـدم والأشلاء على أرضية الزنزانة. وأخذت زَلّومَةُ الهدّام ترتعش. استمرَّ السجّان في الضغط مع لَخْلَخَة الناب، حتى انخلع في يده، وبَقِيَ جزءٌ صغيرٌ منه عالقاً في فم الهدّام. أمسَكَ السجّان بين يديه قضيب العاج القرمزي وهو مُنْتَشٍ، ووجهه مُلَطَّخٌ بنثار اللحم وخيوط الـدم، ثم غادَر.

العـاج هـو روحُ عالـمٍ آفِـلٍ يُدعـى "عالـمَ مـا قبـل التاريـخ"، لـم يعـد يظهـر في عالـم اليـوم سـوى في صـورة صلبـة. إذ ينمـو مـن الأفـواه، وتبـرز أنيابـه وكأنهـا حـروف لغـةٍ قديمـةٍ لـم تعـد مفهومـة. لكـنّ هنـاك صـورةً أخـرى للعـاج، لـم يَعُـدْ أحـدٌ يعـرف عنهـا شيئـاً، وهـي الصـورة السـائلة التـي يوجـد عليهـا في آذان الأفيـال. فالعـاج السـائل هـو مـا يجعـل حاسـة السـمع لديهـا مرهفـة. وعندمـا تَـوَدُّ أن تزيـد مـن رهافـة حاسـتها، فإنهـا تُرَفْـرِفُ بصيـوانِ أُذُنِهـا، فتتمـدد الأوعيـة وتتَّسِـعُ، لِيَتَدَفَّـق العـاجُ مالئـاً تجاويـف الأذن الداخليـة. ولا يوجـد سـائل علـى الأرض أكثـر حساسـية منـه، فسـطحُهُ يلتقـط أشـدَّ التـرددُداتِ خفوتـاً، ليتمـوّج علـى إثرهـا حتـى تلتقـط الشـعيراتُ الذائبـة فيـه حركتـه الرهيفـة، وتنقلهـا إلى العصـب. ليـس هذا فحسـب، بـل هنـاك مـا هـو أهـم مـن ذلـك. فقَـوامُ العـاج السـائل يجعـل آذان الأفيـال تسـتطيع أن تلتقـط مـا لا يمكـن لأيِّ أُذُنٍ أخـرى التقاطـه. يجعلهـا تلتقـط الأمـل الـذي تنطـوي عليـه الأصـوات. فكلُّ صـوتٍ يحمـلُ معـه ذكـرى أمـلٍ لا يتضـوّع إلا في اللحظـة المناسـبة. أَمَـلٍ في أن يَتَسَـكَّنَ الجـوع، أَمَـلٍ في أن تنكسـرَ الدائـرة. عندمـا تُصغِـي الأفيـالُ، فإنّهـا تسـمعُ تاريخـاً كامـلاً مـن الأمـل تحمِلُـهُ الأصـوات معهـا. وهذا الأمـلُ المصاحِـبُ للصـوتِ كَهْالَتِـهِ هـو بالضبط مـا لـم يَعُـدْ عـاجُ الأفيـالِ يلتقطـهُ منـذ سـنوات.

تأمَّلَـتْ نوسـة العـوّام والهـدّام وهمـا يتذكّـران. كان جلدُهُمـا يضطـربُ ويتمـاوَجُ مـع حركـة جَسَـديهِما الإيقاعيـة. كأنـه رُقْعَـة، كلُّ مـا نُقِـشَ عليهـا يـذوبُ ببطءٍ في طبقـة العَـرَق التـي أخـذت تكسـو الجلـد شـيئاً فشـيئاً. مـن شـدة إرهافهمـا السـمع، كان العـاج السـائل يتدفّـق مـن الأذن إلى باقـي الجسـم، فيغمـر كل أعضائهمـا الداخليـة، لتصبـح كلهـا آذانـاً صاغيـة. وكلمـا زاد إصغاؤهمـا في ظُلمـة الزنزانـة اشـتدَّ تعرّقهمـا. ظلّـت عينا نوسـة مُرَكَّزَتَيـن علـى جِلـد الفِيلَيـن في غمـرة حركاتهمـا المحمومـة، تُراقـبُ اللّمعَـةَ الداكنـةَ لطَبقـة العَـرَق. حتـى بـدأ الضـوء القرمـزي الخافـت في الانبعـاث مـن الأنيـاب، فتَرَكَـتْ نفسـها لخيالاتـه، ونسـيت جوعهـا.

بعـد دورة الاسـتماع والتذكّـر المحمومـة، مـالَ الهـدّام إلى الحائـط صامتـاً يتنفـس باضطراب، ولا تـزال آثـار الدمـاء مُنْطَبِعَـةً علـى جِلـده منـذ أن اقتلـع السـجّان نابـه. فيمـا حـرّك العـوّام صيـوان أُذُنِـه يمينـاً ويسـاراً قريبـاً مـن وجـه الهـدّام لِيُخَفِّـفَ عنـه. اقتربَـت نوسـة مـن الهـدّام ولَعَقَـتْ جِلْـدَ زَلُّومَتِـه بلسـانها الرفيـع لَعقـاتٍ متتاليـة. كان السـائل دبقـاً وشـفافاً للغايـة. مَرارَتُـهُ اللاذعـة مُسـكِرَةٌ. ثـم جَلَسَـتْ بيـن الفِيليـن سـاكنة، قبـل أن تغيـب ببطء. رأت نفسـها في بيـت لـم تدخلـه مـن قبـل. لـم تكـن فقط تتحـرك في فضـاء البيـت، ولكنهـا كانـت أيضـاً في كل شـيء مـن أشـيائه. رأت نفسـها ذائبـة في قَصَبَـةِ سُـكّر، ثـم جـاءت أيـدٍ كثيـرة والتَصَقَـتْ بهـا. جِبـالٌ تلتَـفُّ علـى الأيـدي، والأيـدي تلتَـفُّ علـى القَصَبَـة. ثـم عُصِـرَت القَصَبَـة، فخَرجَـتْ هي كقطـرة، ثـم تجمّـدت في حبّـة سُـكّر. لكنهـا أصبحـت أيضـاً ذرّةَ فِضّـة، وعِرْقَ نُحـاس. احتَرَقَـت في غُـرَفٍ حراريـة، وتحـرَّكَـتْ عبـر تُـرُوسٍ وسُـيور، حتـى خَرَجَـتْ أشـياءَ وحُمِلَـتْ إلى الأسـواق. تكاثـرت نوسـة كقطـراتٍ لا تنتهـي، تسـري في أنهـارٍ مـن السـوائل الكثيفـة، وتعيـش محبوسـة في

الأشياء التي تتجمّد في الأسواق. ثم رَأَت لَمْعَةً معدنيةً تشُقُّ الهواء فوق رأسها في إحدى غرف البيت. خرطومٌ صغيرٌ ينتهي بنَصْلٍ قاطعٍ مُعدٍّ للغَرز. هي النَصْل، وهي اللحم. ثم توقَّفَ كلُّ شيء، وتَحَرَّكَ لسانٌ فوقها وأخذ يلعقها.

اعتادت نوسة القيام بجولةٍ ليليةٍ على الزنازين، تُنهيها بزيارة زنزانتها المفضلة: زنزانة الفيلين القادمين من المستقبل. رَوَى لها الفيلان أنهما جاءا بحثاً عن حرفِ علّةٍ، لأن الأعداء قتلوا حروف العلّة، فأضْحَت اللغة من بعد ذلك شاحبة عليلة. لغةٌ فَقَدَت حروف علتها هي لغةٌ نسيت نفسها، وأصبحت كومةً من حروفٍ ساكنةٍ تعيد تكرار ما يُقال فيها إلى الأبد. ومن يَعِش في لغةٍ نسيت نفسها يَنْسَ نفسه أيضاً، قالا لها. فعَبَثاً كانت الكائنات في عالمهما تبحث عمّا يُسْكِن جوعها بعد أن طردها الأعداء من أرضها، فلا تجدُ سوى أقلّ الفُتات. ينهِكُهُم البحثُ المضني، ويعتصِرُهُم الجوع، إلى أن يَقنَعوا بما سُمح لهم به، ويَنسَون. ثم يطردهم الأعداء مرة أخرى، فيعيدون الكرّة، ويبحثون عبثاً عما يُسكِنُ جوعهم، فلا يجدون سوى الفُتات. ويظلون هكذا يَجرُون في دوائر مفرغة. لا جوعهم سكن، ولا هم وجدوا مخرجاً.

رَوَيَا لها ما حدث على طريق الهرب بعد أن استشرى المرض. فقد تدافعت حشودٌ هائلةٌ من كل الفصائل، وساروا في طريقٍ دارَت حول جبلٍ لا تزال تنمو حوله بعض الأعشاب النَضِرَة، ثم ضَاقَت في إحدى المنعطفات. في هذا المنعطف انقطع سَمْعُ الهدّام لوهلة وسط موجات الصخب المخيفة. لم يعد يسمَعُ شيئاً سوى الطنين الذي ملأ أذنيه. طنينٌ قادمٌ من باطن الأرض. ظلَّ يُحَرِّكُ رأسه يميناً ويساراً، لكن الطنين القاتل لم يبارحه. وعندما عاد إليه سمعه بعد وقتٍ طويل، ظَلَّ الطنينُ يُغَلّفُ دبيب الأقدام التي تُهَرْوِل، ورفيف الأجنحة التي تضرب. يُغَلّفُ الحناجر التي تصيح حوله، والعظام التي تتكسر بجواره. لكنه وسط هذه الآلام سَمِعَ بوضوح خشخشة الأعشاب التي يدكّونها بأقدامهم، كما كان يسمعها من قبل. خشخشةٌ خافتة، لكنها كانت تحمل معها ذات يوم أمَلاً في تسكين الجوع. عادت لسَمْع الهدّام قوّته فجأة، وكأن ثقباً قد حدث في الستارة الغامضة التي ألقاها أحدهم ذات يومٍ مشؤوم. ثقبٌ دقيقٌ على وَشَكِ أن يَنْسَدّ. فنَظَرَ الهدّامُ حوله مدهوشاً. وَجَدَ بجواره العوّام وقد توقّف عن الجري هو أيضاً. فعَرَفَ أنه سَمِعَ أيضاً ما سَمِع. كلاهما سَمِعَ الثقب، ولم يسمعه غيرهما.

اضطرَبَتْ حركة الحشود حولهما ذلك اليوم، وانسحَبَتْ الأفيال إلى فجوةٍ في الجبل للمداولة، بعد أن أدرَكَتْ أن أمر المرض الغامض هو أخطر بكثيرٍ مما كانت تعتقد. عاد سمع العوّام والهدّام إلى ما كان عليه قبل سنوات الشحوب، فأدرَكَتِ الأفيال أنّ قَتْلَ حروف العلّة هو ما جَعَلَ العالم حولها يَشْحَبُ منذ سنين، وجعل القلوب تهمَد الآن. وبعد أيامٍ اتّفَقَتْ على أنّ ما ذهب لن يعود، وأنّ الأمل الوحيد في النجاة هو العثور سريعاً على حروف علّةٍ جديدة. لكن حروف العلّة لا توجد سوى في الماضي. أيُّ ماضٍ؟ لا أحد

يعرف. وحدها أنياب الأفيال تستطيع تحديده. فانطلق العوّام والهدّام في مهمتهما لإنقاذ القلوب. يصغيان ويتذكران عبر السنين، لعلهما يسمعان في ما حدث فيها ما لم يسمعه أحد من قبل، حتى أضاءت أنيابهما باللون الأرجواني. كانت نوسة تسمع بنصف أُذنٍ كلَّ ليلةٍ تفاصيلَ جديدةً لقصة الفيلين الغريبة، إذ ما كان يجذبها حقاً إلى زنزانتيهما هو العرق السحري الذي يغطي جلديهما عندما يتذكران، الفأرة نوسة تلعق عرق الفيلين كل ليلة، وما إن تلعقه حتى تغيب (عن وعيها)، تغيب في أحلامها وهلاوسها، ولا تفيق إلا بعد أن يمر معظم الليل.

-هل تعرفان أن الديناصورات كانت صامتة؟

-ماذا؟

-لم يكن باستطاعة حناجرها إخراج أي صوت. ولذلك انقرضت.

-كيف ذلك؟

-لأنه لم يكن باستطاعتها تنبيه بعضها البعض عندما يُحِيقُ بها الخطر، ولا حتى الصراخ. الديناصوراتُ المُجَنَّحةُ هي الوحيدة التي استطاعت إخراج صوتٍ من حنجرتها، فحافَظَتْ على بقائها، وانحَدَرَتْ الطيورُ من سُلالَتِها. كانت أجسامها ضخمةً وتُصْدِرُ أصواتاً رفيعة.

-كيف عَرِفتِ ذلك؟

-نحن الفئران ندرُسُ مثل هذه الأشياء.

-لماذا؟

-ألا تعرف حقاً؟ منذ قرونٍ طويلةٍ ونحن نقاومُ خوفنا الأبَدِيّ، ونبحثُ عن طريقةٍ للتخلُّصِ منه. إنّه خوفٌ يسري في سُلالتنا منذ قديم الأزَل، ويجعلنا نخافُ كل شيء، ونَفِرُّ مذعورينَ في الطُّرُقات. معركتنا مع قانون الخوف كَلَّفَتْنا كلَّ شيء، كلُّ جيلٍ ينقُلُها إلى الذي يليه. تَوَصَّلْنا ذات مرةٍ إلى خطّة مُحْكَمَة وهي توسيعُ جُحُورنا قليلاً لإغراء القطط لدخولها، عندها ستنحشر، فيتكاثر عليها باقي الفئران من الخارج ويمزقونها بأسنانهم الحادة. وانظَلَتْ الخدعةُ على القطط، فانحشَرَ أوّلُ قِطٍّ في مدخل الجُحْر وهو يجري وراء فأر، لكن الفئران التي تجَمَّعَتْ في الخارج خافَتْ أن تتكالب عليه، وخانتها الشجاعة، بل خانتها أجسادها بفِعْلِ قانونها المُسْتَبِد ... الخوف. وبَقِيَتْ الفئران جامدةً من الذعر إلى أن أفْلَتَ أوّلُ قِطٍّ من الفتحة الضيقة ومزَّقَهُم تمزيقاً في الخارج. وهكذا فعلت بقية القطط.

عدنا مفجوعين إلى جُحُورنا بعد أن فقدنا الكثير من رفاقنا. رأينا أهوالاً، وجمعنا أشلاءً، وجلسنا نحن الباقين على قيد الحياة وسط بحار الدماء، نُفَكِّرُ في ذلك

الخـوف الـذي يسكنُ أجسـادنا. كيف يمكننا أن نغيّر ما جُبِلْنا عليـه؟ كيـف يمكن أن تتحـرّر الفئرانُ مـن خوفها؟ فكَّرْنا مليًّا، ثم خرجنـا بخطـةٍ جديـدة، هـذه المرة أكثـر إحكاماً. فغادرنا في الفجر جُحورَنا، وقطعنا المدينة مُتَّجِهينَ إلى غَزْوِها جماعات. ولم تَكَدْ الشمسُ تطلع حتى كنا قد وصلنا إلى البرّية. هنا سـوف نعيش وحدنا، وننسى الخـوف الـذي أرّق حياتنا، لا سيما الخوف من القطط. عاماً وراء عامٍ عشـنا بين الرمال الساخنة، لكننا فشلنا في التأقلم مع الحيـاة في البرية، ومات الكثير منا بسبب الجوع والعطـش. ولمـا غُلبنـا عـلى أمرنـا، ورأينا الهـلاك قادمـاً لا محالـة، قرّرنـا العـودة إلى المدينة. عدنا فوجدنا القطط قد تبَطّلَت بسبب غياب الفئران، ولم يَعُدْ لها عمل، فطردها أصحاب البيوت، وباتـت تعيش في الشوارع. وعندما دخلت الفئران المدينة، وأمـلٌ صغيـرٌ يرتعش داخلها، فوجِئَـت حينها بأسرابٍ لا حصر لها من القطط تشغَلُ الطرقات. ومـا إن قَطَعَ أوّلُ قـطٍّ الطريـق عليهم حتى صَعَقَ الرعبُ القديمُ أعصاب الفئرانِ مـرة أخرى، فانهالَـت عليها القطط، ومزَّقَتْهُا إرباً إرباً.

بعـد أن أتَـمَّ إعـداد الطعـام عـلى الموقـد الكهربائـي الصغيـر، طَـرَقَ العـوّامُ البـابَ الحديـدَّ
مُؤذِناً بوقـت الغـداء. وبعدها بدقائـق، فتـح الحـارس بـاب الزنزانـة وجلـس يـأكل، بينمـا بَقِـيَ
العـوّامُ والهـدّامُ ينظـران إليـه. ازدَرَدَ في صمـتٍ الخضـارَ باللحـم. وبعـد أن فَـرَغَ تأفَّـفَ مـن رداءة
الطَعْـم وأشعل سـيجارة، وأخـذ يُجيـلُ ناظـره بينهما منتظـراً إجابـة. مـرّت فتـرةٌ، ولـم يخرج
الفيـلان عـن صمتهمـا. عندهـا زَفَـرَ، ثـم مـرَّرَ يـده عـلى نـاب العـوّام الأيسـر المتبقـي مبتسـماً.
بقيـت الأعيـن مُعَلَّقـةً، ثـم سـحب السـجّان يـده.

-الضابط مُصرٌّ على نقلكما إلى عنابر الإقامة.

-...

-هـل تعرفان يـا أحبائـي مـاذا تعنـي عنابـر الإقامـة؟ تعنـي عمـلاً شـاقّاً سـيُرهِقُكُما كثيـراً،
لكنـي أبـذل مـا في وسـعي لكـي أؤجـل نقلكمـا، مُعَرِّضـاً نفسـي لتوبيـخ الضابـط.

-...

-طيّـب، سـتُحضِران لـي علبتـي سـجائر إضافيتيـن أسـبوعياً بـدءاً مـن اليـوم، وإذا لـم
تأتيانـي سـأترك الضابـط ينقلكمـا إلى عنابـر الإقامـة كمـا يريـد.

-...

-هل فهمتما؟

-...

-أين الشاي؟

العمـل الشـاقّ سـيُرهِق الهـدّام بالتأكيـد، فَكَّـرَ العـوّام وهـو ينظـر إلى صديقـه الـذي سـاءت
أحوالـه كثيـراً بعـد أن انتـزع السـجان كلا نابيـه، ولـم يعـد يتكلـم. وبالرغـم مـن صحـة العـوّام
قـد سـاءت هـي الأخـرى بعـد انتـزاع نابـه الأيمـن، إلا أنـه لـم يفقـد الأمـل في الخـروج، واعتنـى
بصديقـه قـدر اسـتطاعته. فـكان يقتسـم معـه مـا تحصّلـه زلّومتـه مـن أوراق الشـجر، عندمـا
يمدهـا مـن كـوّة الزنزانـة. لكـن الهـدّام بقـي غارقـاً في صمتـه، وإن كان لا يـزال قـادراً عـلى التذكُّـر.
يـذرع هـو وصديقـه الزنزانـة كل ليلـة صامتـاً رغـم الألـم والجـوع، مُرهِفـاً السـمع حتـى يتصبـب
عرقـاً. يتذكـر ويتذكـر. يُرهِـقُ نفسـه في تذكُّـرِ مـا تنطـوي عليـه أصـواتُ الحاضـر. يسـعى لتذكُّـر
فرصـة سَـنَحَتْ لكنهـا أهدِرَتْ، أو كلمـةٍ نُسِيَتْ، أو خللٍ طـارئ لـم يلتفت إليـه أحـد. لا يتذكَّـر
لكـي يسـترجع سـيرته، وإنمـا لكي تتذكّـر اللغـةُ نفسَـهَا، عـلى أمَـلِ أن يخـرُجَ منهـا حـرفُ عِلـةٍ
جديـدٌ يُعيـدُ النبـضَ إلى القلـوب. العـاج الـذي يسـري في أذنـه لا يـزال يتمـدّد ويتمـوّج مسـتجيباً
لأدَقِّ نأمـة، لكـن لـم يعـد لديـه أنيـابٌ تحـدو حـروف العِلـةِ في الليالـي الطويلـة. نـابُ العـوّام
الأيسـر هـو البوصلـة الوحيـدة المتبقيـة، والأمـل الأخيـر لهمـا مـن أجـل الخـروج مـن هـذا

العالم الـذي قُيِّدا إليه ولا يعرفان لماذا.

وذات يوم، فُتِحَ باب الزنزانة على مِصراعيه، ودَفَعَ السجّانُ ومعه ثلاثةُ رجالٍ صخرةً كبيرةً مَرَّتْ بصعوبةٍ بالغةٍ عبر الباب، ثم جرّوها بالحبال التي أحاطت بها حتى استقرّتْ وَسَط الزنزانـة. انزوى العـوّام والهـدّام في رُكْـنٍ مفزوعَين. وبعـد أن خـرج الرجال وأوصـدوا البـاب مـن ورائهم، انحشر الاثنان في مكانهما، لأن الصخـرة كانت قد شَغَلَتْ معظم حَيْـز الزنزانة. كان سطحها مشـطوفاً ومُتَـربـاً، كأنها تعرَّضَتْ لضربةٍ فوقـه أو سَـقَطتْ عليه. كُتَلَتُها غير منتظمة. يكْتَنِزُ أحد جوانبها، ويَنْبَعِجُ الجانب الآخر. كان من الصعب تمييز لونها في الظلام، لكنـه كان أفتح مـن لـون جلد الفيلَين. وبَقِيَت الصخرة صامتة.

-هل لديكما أي شيءٍ يؤكل؟

-لا. لم يعد بإمكاننا الحركة بسبب الصخرة.

-وماذا ستفعلان الآن؟

-لا ندري.

-يا لها مـن خطة محكمة يا أهل المستقبل! إنكم أسوأ مـنا بكثير في التخطيط. هل كنتم تعتقدون حقًّا أنهم سيتركونكما تسيران على هواكما في الشوارع؟! ألم أقل لكما إن الوضع هنا خطير؟ لقد أصبحـوا يلقون القبـض عـلى الحَجَر أيضاً. أتفهمان ماذا يعني ذلك؟

-يجب أن نعثر على حرف علّةٍ جديد.

-الهـدّام على حق، لقد أخطأَتْ أنيابكما التقدير بالتأكيد. لا توجد هنا لا حروف علّةٍ ولا حـروفٌ سـاكنة. كيف يمكن أن توجد حروف علّةٍ ولم يعد أحد يتكلم أساساً؟ لا يوجد هنا سـوى الخوف. يخرج من كل ركن. ألا تستطيعون شم رائحته؟

أكمَلَتْ نوسـة دورتها حول الصخـرة في تلك الليلـة، وتسلَّقتهَا حتى جَلَسَتْ على سطحها الأملس. امتد الصمت بين الثلاثة لفترة. ثم كرَّرَت عليهما ما سبق وأخبرتهما به، من أن الشرطة قد أحكَمَتْ سيطرتها على هذا العالم، وزَرَعَتْ آذانها في كلّ مكان، واعتَبَرَتْ أن كل من يتكلّم هو مشتبهٌ به، لأنه بالتأكيد يتكلم عنها أو ضدها، ويخطط لضربها. لذلك فإن لا أحد من غير البشر يتكلّم عَلَناً، خوفاً مـن أن تظنّه الشرطة بَشَراً مُتَنَكِّراً فتُلقي القبض عليه. فأصبحت الشرطة تُمسِكُ عشوائياً بمن تَجِدُهُ أمامها، ولا يهمُّها إذا كان بَشَراً أم لا. وكُلّما اكتظّتْ السجون، بَثَّتْ أخرى جديدة.

أنفَقَ الفيلان الليلَ في حركاتٍ يائسة، إذ كلّما تحرّكا اصطدما بالصخرة، وعادا للوقوف في مكانيهما. فشلت كل محاولاتهما لزحزحتها، واكتفيا بهز رأسيهما ورفرفة آذانهما، وتحريك

أقدامهما في مواضعها. كانت ليلةً ثقيلة، خَرَجَ عَرَقُ الفِيلَين من عتمتها بمذاقٍ أشدَّ مرارة، ذابَ ببُطءٍ في فم نوسة التي تمَدَّدَت وسط الفِيلَين بعد أن هدآ. تركت نفسها تسترخي ببطء، بعد أن لَعَقَتْ جُرعةً كبيرة، وانشَغَلَت في التفكير بخطةٍ جديدةٍ للتغلُّب على الخوف، ثم انتَبَهَت لرؤيةِ نجومٍ تلمَعُ في أرض الزنزانة. وعندما دقَّقَت النظر رأَت مساميرَ مُنبَعِجَة. كانت المسامير المعدنية تبدو كخطوطٍ ضامِرةٍ مكسورة، تلمعُ في الضوء القرمزي الضعيف لِنابِ العوّام. لا يتشابه أيُّ مسمارَين منها في طريقةِ تَلَفِه تحت ضربات المطرقة الواحدة. تهوي كلُّ ضربةٍ كالقَدَرِ على مسمارٍ فتُثْلِمُهُ. أينما نظرت نوسة كانت ترى مساميرَ لامعةً حولها، وأينما سارَت كانت المسامير المُنبَعِجَة تُحيطُ بها.

-من هم أعداؤكم هؤلاء؟ البَشَر؟ الشرطة؟

-أعداؤنا هم من يطردوننا من مساكننا، ويجوّعوننا. من يُغرِقونَنا بالغازات كل صباح. من يقتلون اللغة التي نتكلّمها جميعاً. كلُّ كلامنا يعتمد على حروف العلّة، وكان لدينا الكثير منها، فهي ما يجعل صرخاتنا وهمهماتنا مفهومة. علينا أن نجد حروف علّةٍ جديدة وإلا هلكنا جميعاً. فالقلبُ يَغْتَلُّ إذا حُرِمَ الكلامُ مَواضِعَ عِلّتِهِ.

-ولماذا قَتَلُوا حروفَ العلّة؟

-حروفُ العلّة هي مَوضِعُ الضعف، لأنها لا تترك الكلمة على حالها. الكلمة الضعيفة هي كلمَثُنا، ومن دونها لم يَعُدْ لدينا ما نقوله لبعضنا البعض غير الكلام الخاوي. أجسادُنا التي طالما تَحَمَّلَت الجوع، وصَبَرَت على التشَرُّد، تمُوتُ إذا ماتَ كلامُها.

جَلَسَ الثلاثةُ صامِتِينَ في قَلْبِ الليل. الجوعُ يعتَصِرُهُم، والصخرةُ تحشِرُهُم وتُثْقِلُ على صُدورهم. تُثَبِّتُ بوَزْنِها الزنزانةَ في مكانها حتى لا تَميلَ ذات اليمينِ أو ذات الشِمال. ثم صَلْصَلَ الباب ووَقَفَ السجّانُ في حَلْقِهِ. كان يتميَّزُ غضباً، ويحمل في يده "الشنيور"، واتجه نحو العوّام وهو يسِبُّ الدين. ثم غَرَزَ الشنيور الدائرَ في نابِ العوّام الأخير، حتى مَرَّ الخابُورُ المعدني إلى الجهة الأخرى. فصَرَخَ العوّامُ صرخةً مُريعةً ارْتَجَّت لها حيطان الزنزانة، وخَرَجَت من الكُوّةِ الصغيرة، ثمّ توقّف كلُّ شيءٍ بعدها. انطفأ الشنيور في يد السجّان، وسقَطَت الزنزانة في صمتٍ مُطبق. تجمّد الهدّام في مكانه، واختبأت نوسة خلفه. الصخرة بقيت في مكانها، لكن شرخاً صغيراً لا يكاد يُرى شقّ سطحها. سَبَّ السجّان الشنيورَ واليومَ والجالسينَ في الزنزانة، وغادرها وهو يسِبُّ الدينَ للكهرباء، تاركاً الآلة مغروزة في الناب، وسار في الممر نحو مقبس الكهرباء، وعندما تأكد أن السلك مُثَبَّت في مكانه عاد إلى الزنزانة. لكنه ما إن دَخَلَها حتى صرخ بأعلى صوته: عععااااا.

أعشاهُم النور، وساروا على عَجَلٍ في شوارعَ خَلَت من المارّين، تقطَعُها من حينٍ لآخر سيّاراتٌ سوداء مُسرعةٌ بزُجاجٍ مُعتِم. كانت قاف تتدحرج أمامهم بسرعة، تندفع بُغتَةً في هذا الاتجاه أو ذاك، لكنها تَثبَت في مكانها فوراً إذا تطلّب الأمر. وفوقها نوسة تحاول أن تحافظ على توازُنِها، وتُراقِبُ الطريقَ من أعلى. أما الهدّام فيَجُرُّ الخطى وَئِيداً بمساعدة العوّام. تَزيدُ المسافة، فتُعطي نوسة إشارةً لِقاف حتى تَسكُنَ وتنتظرَ الفيلَين. وتظهَرُ سيارةٌ سوداء في الأفق، فتُنَبِّهُ نوسة الفِيلَين أن يختبئا خلف قاف. وطوال الطريق لم تنطق قاف بكلمة، فكانت نوسة تلعق سطحها البارد من آن لآخر. وفي كل مرة كان لُعابُها يختلطُ بحبيبات رملٍ تحتها طبقاتٌ من طعومٍ لا تعرفها، لكنها قَدَّرَت أنّها موغلةٌ في القِدَم. قادَتْهُم قاف إلى جبل المُقَطَّم، حيث بإمكانهم الاختباء هناك إلى حين. وساروا طويلاً حتى وصلوا إلى المقابر، ومن هناك صعدوا بِمَشَقّةٍ بالغةٍ إلى الجَبَل.

بانَت الأهرامات أخيراً من بعيد. وثارَت الرمال من خلفِها في الصحراء. وبين الجبل والأهرامات انبَعَثَ الدُخان من مناطق شتى في المدينة. دُخانٌ أبيضُ كثيف. وجابت سيّاراتٌ سوداء الطرق الخالية مسرعة. من فوق سطح المُقَطَّمِ ظَهَرَت السماءُ صافية، وانجلى سطحُ بُركةِ "عين الصِيرة" كالمرآة. ما إن وصلوا حتى تهاوى الهدّام على الأرض من فوره. وانهَمَكَ العوّامُ في الرفرفةِ عليه بأُذُنَيه، والشنيور لا يزال مغروزاً في نابه. فيما ظلَّت قاف بجوار الفِيلَين صامتة. ثم سَمِعَت نوسة صوتاً حاداً سريعاً، فالتفَتَت حولَها، لترى فأراً يناديها بصوتٍ خافت. نَزَلَت بسرعة من فوق قاف، وتَبِعَتْهُ. ثم انحرفا داخل أحد الجُحور. لاحَظَت أن ذيله مبتور، ومكانَه مُتَقَيِّح، فاضطَرَبَت.

-كيف أحوالكم؟

-استطعنا صدَّهُم في هذه الناحية، لكن الجانب الشرقي من الجبل لا يزال تحت سيطرتهم. ولا أنصحكم بالذهاب هناك.

-تبدو متعباً، هل سقط الكثير منا؟

-لا تقلقي، نحن بخير. كيف هربتم؟

-تَدَحرَجَت قاف بسرعة وجَرَّتْنَا خلفَها. باغَتَت حركتها الحَرَسَ، واستطاعت تحطيم البوابة، فتبعناها وفررنا.

-...

-أنا جاهزة.

سَفحُ الجَبَلِ مُنبَسِطٌ، تنمو فيه أعشابٌ قليلةٌ مُتَفَرِّقَة. لا تزال تظهر منه نُتوءاتٌ حجريّةٌ تُطِلُّ على المدينة، رغم تشذيبِهِ وتسويَتِهِ بفضل الشوارع الإسفلتية التي تقطَعُه. وَقَفَ

جبـل المُقَطّمِ منـذ آلاف السـنين خلـف المقابـر كحَـدٍّ بيـن عالَمَين. يرتقيـهِ مَنْ يبحـثُ عـن نهاية العالم المحسوس، لعَلَّهُ يستطيع تجاوُزَهُ. حَدٌّ يلئَقي فيـه البشرُ والوحوش. ومنذ أن أصبـح الجَبَلُ مُجَـرَّدَ حيٍّ سَكَنِيٍّ تقليديٍّ في المدينة، لـم يَعُدْ الموتى يموتون، ولم يَعُدْ الأحيـاء يعيشـون أيضـاً. تَضـاءَلَ الفـارقُ بيـن الحيـاةِ والمـوتِ مـع الوقـت، ليُصبِحَ الجَبَلُ ذكرى لِحَدٍّ كان موجوداً بينهما وامّحى. مَنْ يسكن الجَبَلَ يعِش بَعْدَ الموت، وبَعْدَ الحيـاةِ أيضـاً. يعِشْ حياةً تُشبه الموتَ في تَجَمُّدِها. يعش نهاية العالم التي لا تُريدُ أن تنتهي. هذه النهايـة الأبديـة خَيَّمَـتْ من هنـاك علـى كُلِّ المدينة. وكَحُوتٍ ضَخْم، يَقِفُ الجَبَلُ ويُخْفي ما انطوى عليه. أما قَلْبُهُ فَيَمُوْر. يَكْتُمُ انفجاراتٍ لا يراها أحَد.

سـارَتْ نوسـة ومعهـا الفـأر "مـرزوق" في شـبكةٍ مُعَقّـدةٍ مـن الأنفـاق الضيقـة. قادهـا إلى المخازن لكي تعمل معـه على تأمين الطعام والتحضير لزيارة المساجين الأسبوعية، ريثَمَا تسـتعيـدُ عافيَتَهـا. في الطريـق أخبَرَهـا أنَّ أعـداد الفئـران في تَنَاقُـص، بعضُهـا يخـرُجُ لِيَجْمَـعَ الطعـام، والبعض الآخـر يعمـلُ علـى تأميـن السـجائر. ظلّـا يسـيران حتى وصـلا إلى المكان الـذي خُـزِّنَ فيـه الطعـام. دارَتْ نوسـة حـول كَوْمَـاتِ الحبـوبِ وفُتـاتِ الخُبْـز وأوراق الشـجر، ثُـمَّ سـارَتْ وحْدَهـا حتى وَصَلَـتْ إلى كومةٍ لَم تُمَيِّـزْ ما فيها. تَطَلّعَتْ جيداً، وصُعِقَتْ، فتَسَـمَّرَتْ في مكانها. كانت كومَـةً مـن ذيـول الفئـران. وَقَفَ مـرزوق بجوارهـا، وظَلّ كلاهما يتطلّع إلى الكَومةِ في صمت.

عـادت نوسـة تدريجيـاً إلى حيـاة الفئـران. كلُّ يـومٍ يَعـوُدُ مَنْ خـرج مـن الفئـران بمـا اسـتطاعوا جَمْعَـهُ إلى مكان التخزين، فتقـوم نوسـة مع مرزوق بِفَـرْزِهِ وتخزينـه في كَوْمَـاتٍ صامِتين. في بعـض الأحيـان كانـت الغِلّـةُ تكفي لِطَحْنِهـا، فيقومـان بذلـك، ثـم يخلُطـانِ الطحيـن بالمـاء. وعندما يقتربُ موعدُ الزيارة الأسبوعي، يُجَهّزانِ الوجبات الهزيلة. لكن نوسة لم تَفُقْ من هَـوْلِ مـا رأَتْ في المَخْـزَنِ رغـم مـرور الأيـام. حـاوَلَ مـرزوق أن يُهَـوِّنَ عليهـا، وأن يقوم هـو بالتعامـل مـع كومـة ذيـول الفئـران، وتجهيزهـا مـع الوجبـات، غيـر أن نوسـة بَقِيَـت شـاردة، تجلـسُ في سـاعات العمـل الطويلـة تتذكـر مـن عَرَفَتْهُـم وقَضَـوا. لكـنّ الذكـرى كانـت تَتَبَخَّـرُ دومـاً مـن بيـن أصابعهـا، والراحلـونَ لا يبقَـونَ في الذاكـرة مهمـا جاهَـدَتْ لتَذَكُّرِهِـم. إذْ كانـت هنـاك دائمـاً أسـماءٌ جديـدةٌ تكتَشِـفُ أنّها نَسِـتْها، بعـد أن ظَنّـتْ أنها أحْصَـتْ كُلَّ مَـنْ قُتِـلَ. شَـرَدَتْ ورأَتْ أحجـاراً وعِظامـاً وأجسـاداً مُحَنّطَـةً في "فاترينة". الفاترينـةُ في مُتْحَـفٍ. مـا إنْ يَقِـفَ زائـرٌ أمـام أحَدِهَـا، حتى تبـدأ مَعْروضـاتُ الفاترينـة في شَـرْح نَفْسِـها بِصـوتٍ مُناسِـبٍ للزائر، والإجابـة عـن أسـئِلته أيضـاً. الأحجـارُ تَتَحَـدَّثُ، والأجسـادُ تَنْهَـضُ، والعِظامُ تَتَحَـرّك. كلُّ فاترينة هي عرضٌ مسرحيٌّ مُتَكامِلٌ يَنْتَصِبُ أمـام زائرِها. رأَتْ نفسَها في إحدى الفاترينات، تَقِـفُ في جِسْـمٍ لا يخُصُّـها، وتَـرْوِي قصّـةَ مَوْتِها.

فَشِـلَتْ كُلُّ محاولات نوسـة ومـرزوق لانتـزاع الشنـيور المرشـوق في نـاب العوّام الأخيـر. ولم تتحسّـن حالـة الهـدّام المُلقـى علـى الأرض بجـوار قاف، إذ بدأ البيـاض يَعْلو سـيقانه وذيله

ورأسه، رغم رفرفة العوّام المستمرة فوقه بأذنيه. في الليالي كانت نوسة تزورهم وحدها في المكان الذي تركتهم فيه، وتجلسُ في مكانها المفضل فوق قاف. منذ أن وصلت إلى الجبل لم تعد تُفَكِّر في خُطَطٍ جديدة. يبتَلِعُها العملُ في الجُحْر طوال اليوم، ثُمَّ تَصْعَدُ إلى مكان أصدقائها إذا حَلَّ الليل. العوّام لم يَعُدْ يتكلّم، وهي يسيطر عليها الخوف الطبيعي من الكلام في العَلَن، فكانوا يجلسون جميعاً صامتين، يتطلّعون إلى أضواء المدينة وحرائقها المشتعلة في الأسفل. وعندما تتضاعف ظُلمةُ الليل تَغْتَمُّ نوسة، وتنزِلُ من مكانها وتلعَقُ العوّام، لكنه لم يَعُدْ يتصبّبُ عَرَقاً.

في إحدى الليالي اكتَمَلَ بياضُ الهدّام قبل الفجر، ومال إلى جانبه. نَهَضَتْ نوسة وتَرَكَتِ العوّام وقاف، وسارَت عائدةً إلى الجُحْر. لكنها لاحظت في الطريق فتحةً أخرى لم تَرَها من قبل. دخلَتْها، فقادَتها الفتحة إلى ممراتٍ ضيّقة، ثم مجموعةٍ من غُرَفِ التمويه. قَدَّرَتْ أنّ ذلك الجُحْر تَمّ حَفْرُهُ على مدى سنواتٍ طويلة. ظلّت تسيرُ وصوت شهيق وزفير مُخيفٍ يَعلُو تدريجياً في جنبات الجُحْر، حتى وَصَلَتْ إلى موضعٍ ظَهَرَ فيه شَقٌّ في أحد الصخور، فَنَظَرَتْ من خلاله بفضول. رأَت نوسة قاعة واسعةً ومرتفعة السقف في قلب الجَبَل. تخرجُ من الصخور خراطيمُ رفيعة، تتّصلُ بأكوامٍ غريبة موضوعة فوق أرضية القاعة. كانت القاعة مُقَسَّمةً إلى ممرّات، وفوق كُلِّ ممرٍّ لافتة، والكومات موزعة على الممرات. أمعَنَتْ نوسة النظر فَرَأَتْ أن الكوماتِ هي أجساد، أجسادٌ كبيرة وأخرى صغيرة. ورأَت أنّ الخراطيم تختَرِقُها عبر فتحةٍ في صدرها. تجمَّدَت نوسة في مكانها عندما مَيَّزَت أحد الوجوه، وكان لأَحَدِ أصدقائها، فَقَدَتْهُ في إحدى محاولات التخلص من الخوف. وجوه الموتى كانت باردة، مُحايِدَة، وعيونهم مفتوحة، لا يزال الخوف يُطِلُّ منها. صَدْرُ كُلٍّ منهم يخترقُه نَصْلُ خرطوم، وحركةٌ تسري في الخراطيم. ملأ المكان إيقاع تحرّك السوائل في الخراطيم، وصدَر عنها صوت التنفس الذي سَمِعَتْهُ يتضخّم في جنبات الممر.

أول كلمةٍ نَطَقَتْ بها الأفيال كانت كلمة "عاج"، وذلك بعد صراع مرير، وآلاف الأنياب المُنتَزَعَة. ومن يومها عرَفَتْ أنّ أيّ كلمةٍ هي جُرح، وأيُّ صوتٍ هو ندبة. وتعلَّمَتِ الكلام رغم العناء الشديد، لأنه كان الطريقة الوحيدة لِدَمْلِ هذه الجراح. فالكلام يُذيبُ الكلمات، ومعها الجراح، لتَدخُل في كلام الآخرين. هذه الندوب تمَسُّ قلوبَ الأفيال مباشرةً، ويهتَزُّ لها عاجُها السائل، وتحمِلُ معها أمل اندمالها. لكن قلب العوام أصبح ثقيلاً. تُثقِلُهُ الحَصوات التي تكبَرُ في قلبه شيئاً فشيئاً. ولَمْ يَعُدْ يَمُسُّه شيءٌ منذ أن مات صديقه. وبَقِيَ حانقاً على نفسِهِ لأنَّ الأمَلَ خَدَعَهُ للمرة الثانية. فمنذ أن وَصَلا إلى الجَبَل وهو يَظُنُّ أن شيئاً يتحرّك داخله. العاج الذي يسري داخله يستجيبُ لصوتٍ لم يَعُدْ هو يقوَى على الإصغاء إليه. منذ أن وَصَلا إلى الجبل وقناعته تزدادُ أنَّ إنقاذَ صديقه قد أصبحَ قريباً أكثر من أيّ وقتٍ مضى، وأن الأعداء لن ينتصروا أبداً. لكنه كان مُخطئاً. وعندما أدرك ذلك كرِهَ الأمَلَ إلى الأبد. صديقه لم تقتله الحَصوات، بل قَتَلَهُ الأمَل الزائف الذي أصرّ على التمسُّك به.

-حتى الموتى لم يَنْجُوا!

-عندما وصلنا الجَبَلَ عَثَرْنا مصادفة على هذا المكان الذي لا يعرف عنه أحدٌ في الخارج شيئاً. يسحبون إليه الجثث فلا تتحلّل. ما توصلنا إليه من بحثنا هو أن هناك تقنيةً سريةً تُمَكِّنُ من يستخدمُها من الوصول إلى معرفة الموتى، ومن ثم توظيفها في قرارات المُضارباتِ والرهاناتِ والبيع والشراء وتحديدِ المخاطر لجَني أرباحٍ طائلة. فالموتى يَتَّصِلونَ بعالمٍ يَلي العالمَ المحسوس، ولديهم معرفةٌ أخرى غير معرفة الحواسب الموجودة في البورصات التقليدية. هذا المكان هو نوعٌ من البورصات السريّة. يحقنون الموتى بالمعلومـات، ثـم يسـري في الخراطيـم المُتّصلـةِ بصُدورِهِم شـيءٌ غريـبٌ لا نعرف ما هو، ويتسبب من حينٍ لآخر في انفجاراتٍ يكتِمُها الجَبَل. هذا كُلُّ ما توصّلنا إليه من بَحْثِنا.

-حتى الموتى لم ينْجُوا.

-نحن لا نكادُ نُنْقِذُ أنفُسَنَا، فكيف نُنْقِذُ الموتى؟!

جَلَسَت نوسـة بجوار قـاف، والعـوّام يحتضر بجوار جثّـة الهـدّام. لَعَقَتْ زِلُّومَتَهُ مـرّةً بَعْدَ أُخرى. وعَوَت الذئابُ مِنْ حولِهم. لَفَظَ أنفاسه الأخيرة في قَلْب الليل. ومن تحتِهِ أخَذَ سائلٌ أرجوانيٌّ يتدفّق ويملأ ظُلمة الليلة. ظلَّ يزدادُ كثافةً وحجماً. ثم سَالَ ناحيةَ قاف، ونَفَذَ من شُقوقِها، وغطّى سطوحها حتى اكْتَسَتْ بضوءٍ أرجوانيٍّ يشعُّ من كُلِّ جوانِبِها. بَقِيَت نوسة وقاف مبهوتَيَـن، وقبل أن يلُوحَ الفجر، غَرِقَتْ نوسـة في العاج الأرجواني وأخَذَت تلعَقُهُ بِنَهَمٍ، بينما تدافَعَتْ من جوف قاف سوائلُ حمضيةٌ ساخنة، سُرعانَ ما ذابَتْ في العاج الأرجواني، ومعها تَحَشْـرجَ صوتُها بِكَلِماتٍ مُتَداخِلَةٍ وهَمْهَماتٍ وشفراتٍ وأرقـام. تناثَرَت لُطَخُ السوائل الكثيفة، وعَلَت حَشْرجَةُ قاف الجافة حتى مَلأَت الفراغَ حولَهُما. كانـت تَعوي ثمّ تَخُورُ ثمّ تصرُخ، وأخيراً نَطَقَت للمرة الأولى. رَفَعَت نوسـة رأسها وقد أضاء لسانُها بالعاج، وسَمِعَت قـاف وهي تقول: أنا قـافُ بنتُ نون. أنا الـواو التي في النون. الألِفُ التي في القاف. سُجِبْتُ إلى أسفل الجبل. أُغْلِقَتْ عليَّ الأرضُ إلى الأبَد. جلَسْتُ على الرماد. حُقِنْتُ بالسَمّ النافِع. لا أمْضِغُ، ولا أُطْعَم. لسـاني تَخَشَّب. خِفْتُ، لكنّي فَتَحْتُ عينَيَّ. لم أرَ النهارَ بَعْد. وإذا بالجبل يَهْتَز، ولساني يَتَحَرَّك.

في الصباح كان لـدى نوسة خِطّة. سـتَذهَبُ إلى النهر وتَصعَدُ الشجرة لتُكَلِّمَ الثلاثين طيراً. وقبـل أن تَنْحَدِرَ مُتَّجهةً نحو المدينة ذَهَبَت إلى المخـزَن وأحْضَرَت بعض الحَبّ، ولَعَقَتْهُ جيّداً بِلِسانِها، ثم انْطَلَقَت. عندما صَعَدَت إلى الشجرة سَلَّمَت على الطير، وكانت قد الْتَقَتْهُم سابقاً في السجن، ثم أخْرَجَت الحَبّ. كانَت الطيرُ جائعةً بشدّةٍ فأقْبَلَت تلْتَقِطُ ما أحْضَرَتْهُ نوسـة. ثـمّ هَمَسَت لهـم حتى لا يلاحظ أحَدٌ حولَهُم حديثَهُم، ورَوَت لهم ما رَأَتْـهُ في قَلْب الجَبَل، وأخبَرَتْهُم بأمر الهدّام والعوّام، والعاج الذي خَلَطَتْهُ مع الحَبّ. بعدها طَلَبَت منهم

طلباً، قالَت إنَّ أَحَداً غيرَهم لن يستطيع تَلْبِيَتَهُ. فَتَطَلَّعَت إليها الطير، كُلٌّ مِنْ على غُصْنِهِ. خِطّةُ نوسة كانت أن ينتقل العاج الأرجواني إلى الموتى، حتى يسدّ الخراطيم عندما يَشْرِي فيها، وسَاعَتَها سيستطيعون أن ينهَضُوا. والطريقة الوحيدة لكي ينتقل العاج هي أن تَعْبُرَ الطيرُ الحدود، وتقطع الأوديةَ مرّةً أخرى، وتطير إلى بلاد الموتى لكي تروي هناك بألسِنَتِها ما سَمِعَتْهُ الآن منها، تُسْمِعُهُم كُلَّ شيء، وبكُلِّ صوت. فَتَطَلَّعَت الطيرُ إلى بَعْضِها البعض مَلِيّاً. قالَت نوسة إنّهم وَحْدَهُم مَن يستطيع الذهاب إلى هناك، وإنّ ذلك هو الأَمَلُ الوحيدُ المُتَبَقّي. لكنّ الطيرَ بَقِيَت صامتة، فأَرْدَفَت نوسة أنّه يجب أن يَحْصُلَ الموتى على العاج لأنّهم إذا لم يتحرّروا ممّا هُم فيه فسيبقى كُلُّ شيءٍ على حاله. ثمّ سَكَتَت، إذ لم يَتَبَقَّ لديها ما تقُولُه. وظَالَ الصمت، إلى أن قَطَعَهُ الهُدْهدُ أخيراً قائلاً: ما تطلبينهُ يا أختي هو رحلةٌ أشقُّ بكثيرٍ من رحلَتِنا الأولى. ثمّ أَخَذَت الطيرُ في التشاوُر، بينما ظَلَّت نوسة في مكانها على غُصْنِ الشجرة، تَتَطَلَّعُ إلى النهر، وتُشاهِدُ انعكاس الأغصانِ على صفحةِ المياه.

مقال بصري

أناهي ألفيسو مارينو

صرح سُمّي يومًا:

"المرأة الكويتية عطاء وفداء"

تستلهم مقالة أناهي ألفيسو مارينو البَصَرية مادة الأرشيف الشخصي للفنان الكويتي خليفة القطان (1943 – 2003). صمم القطان نصبًا تذكاريًا على أعقاب حرب الخليج التي أشعلها اجتياح العراق للكويت عام 1990، ليخلّد تحرير الكويت ويحيي ذكرى شهيداتها من النساء. شهد هذا النصب تاريخًا حافلًا ومضطربًا: مع الوقت، أُزيل كل ذكر للنساء وتغير اسم النصب ونُقل من مكانه مراتٍ عدة. تحاكي هذه التحولات السياق السياسي المتغير في الكويت وفي منطقة الخليج عمومًا، وتلقي الضوء على الفضاءات العامة التي تشكل ساحات للنزاع ومواقع للذاكرة.

تستعين ألفيسو مارينو بأرشيف القطان لتقتفي آثار الحيوات المتعددة التي عاشها النصب التذكاري. وتعود إلى مجموعة من الدفاتر الممتلئة بملصقات من الصور الفوتوغرافية والبطاقات البريدية كان القطان قد جمعها وأفردها على صفحاته بعنايةٍ، من بينها عددٌ من الأنصاب التذكارية والمدن من حول العالم أسهمت في تشكيل مخياله البصري.

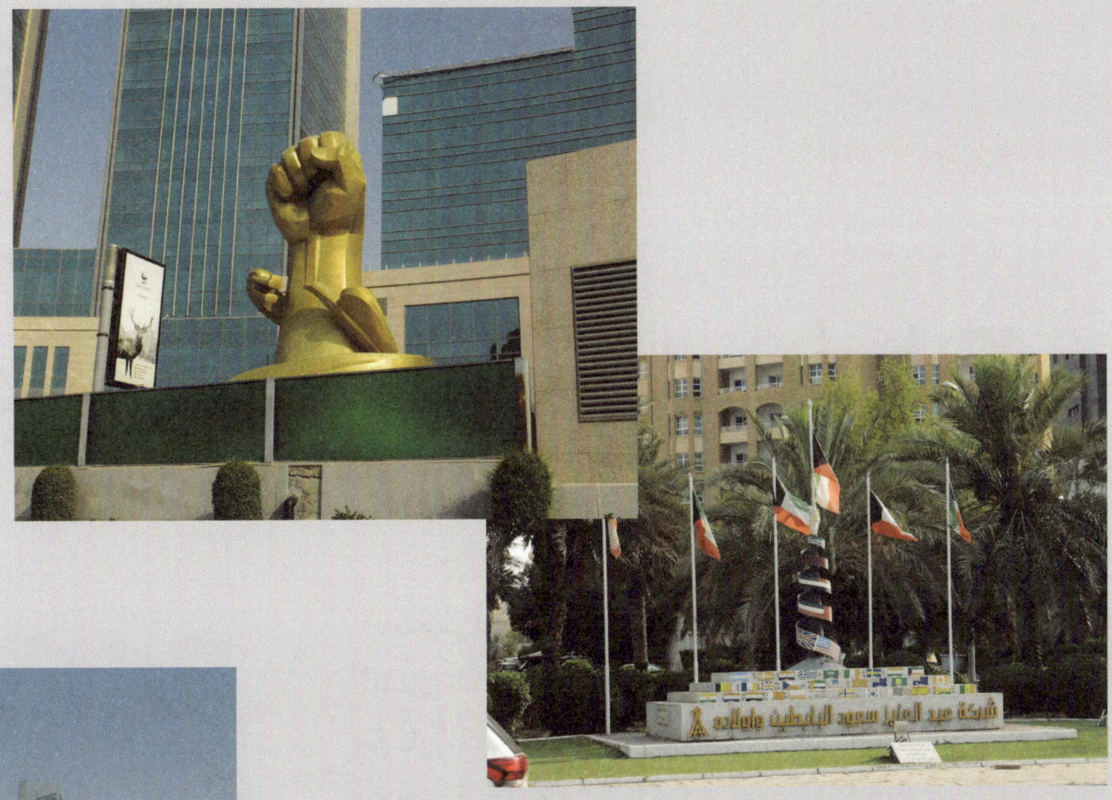

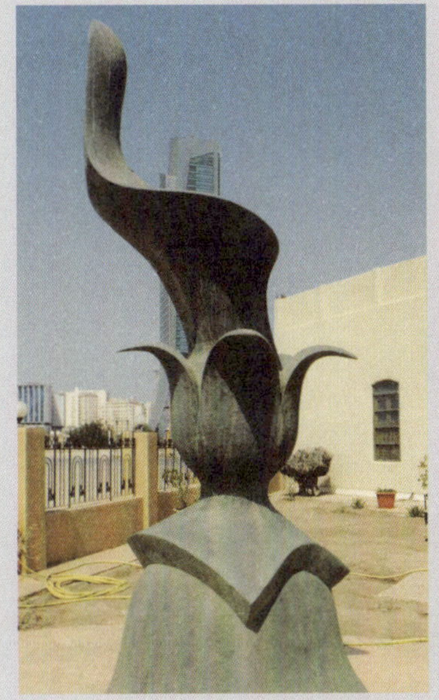

The artwork moves in different ways around the city and around the homes of the prize recipients.

The memorial statue once named *Kuwaiti Women, Giving and Sacrifice* is still looking for its place in the country's urban landscape and its history, if only symbolically.

Kuwait is home to other monuments and memorials commemorating the lives that were lost in 1990-1991. To date, Qattan's monument is the only one dedicated to women.

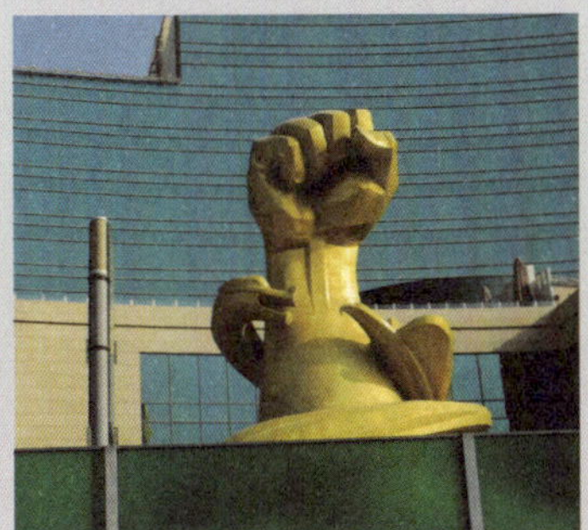

In 2020

A biographic account of this monumental sculpture was first published:
Anahi Alviso-Marino and Deema al-Ghunaim, "Un monument pour les femmes martyres: itinérances urbaines du travail artistique de Khalifa Qattan dans la ville de Koweït," *Les cahiers d'EMAM (Études sur le Monde Arabe et la Méditerranée)*, n°33 (2020).
https://journals.openedition.org/emam/3307

In 2021

Anahi Alviso-Marino and artist Neïl Beloufa performed an experimental research protocol in which they activated archives that retrace the story of this monument as well as others. The protocol was presented at the seminar series "The stories we tell. Engaging archives otherwise" organised by the Observatory of the Arab and Muslim Worlds at ULB/MSH, 2021-2022.
https://msh.ulb.ac.be/fr/video/omam-smmac-stories-we-tell-session-3-2

The current location of the monument remains contested and several actors are involved in this shifting biography.

Some wish the memorial statue to be moved to Al Shaheed Park (Martyrs' Park), which was created in 2015 by the Diwan Al-Amiri and hosts large sculptures and memorial projects. Others envision it in the main courtyard of the Museum of Modern Art. Since 2008, small replicas of the monument even served as artists' prizes given by the Plastic Arts Association.

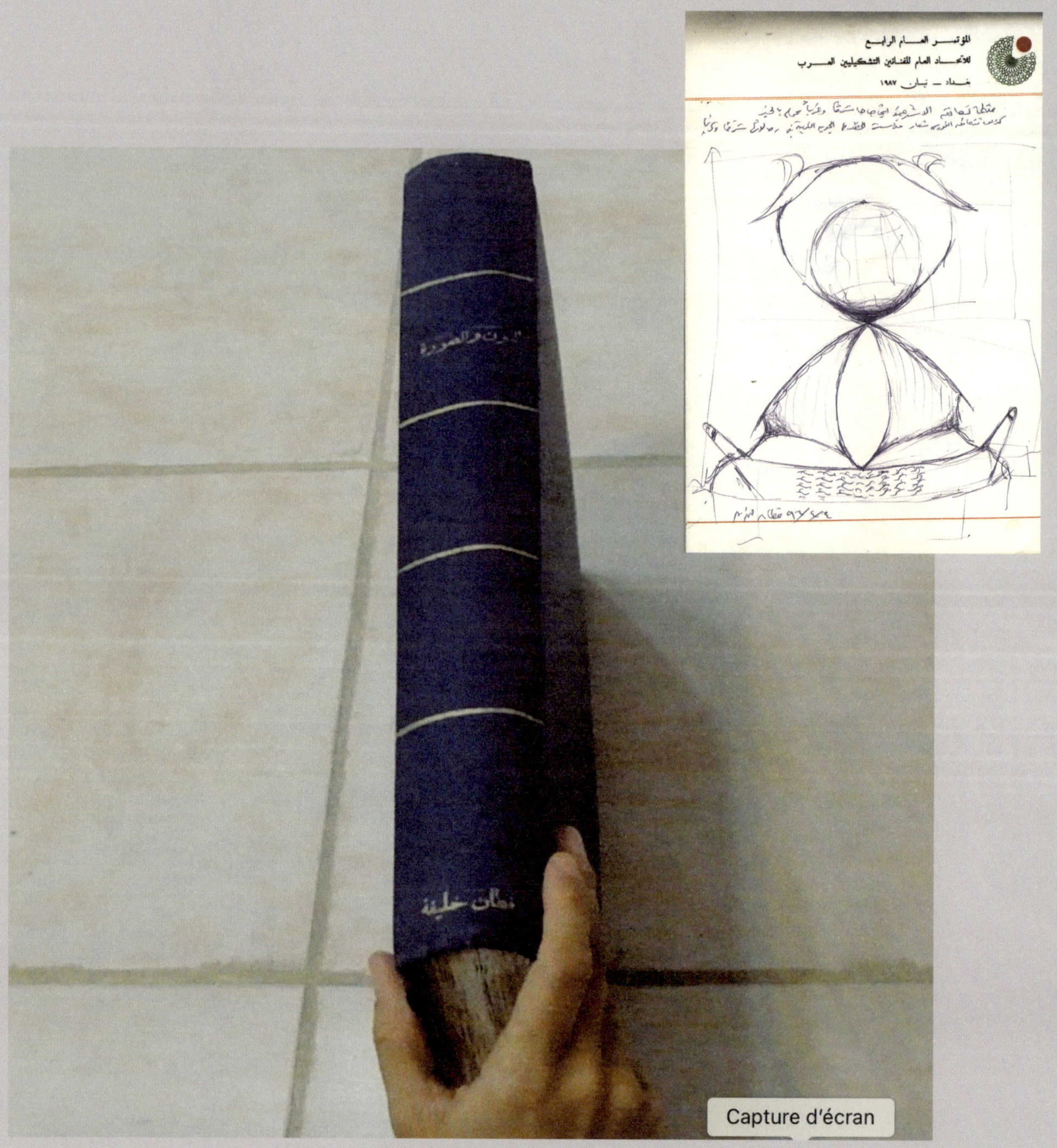

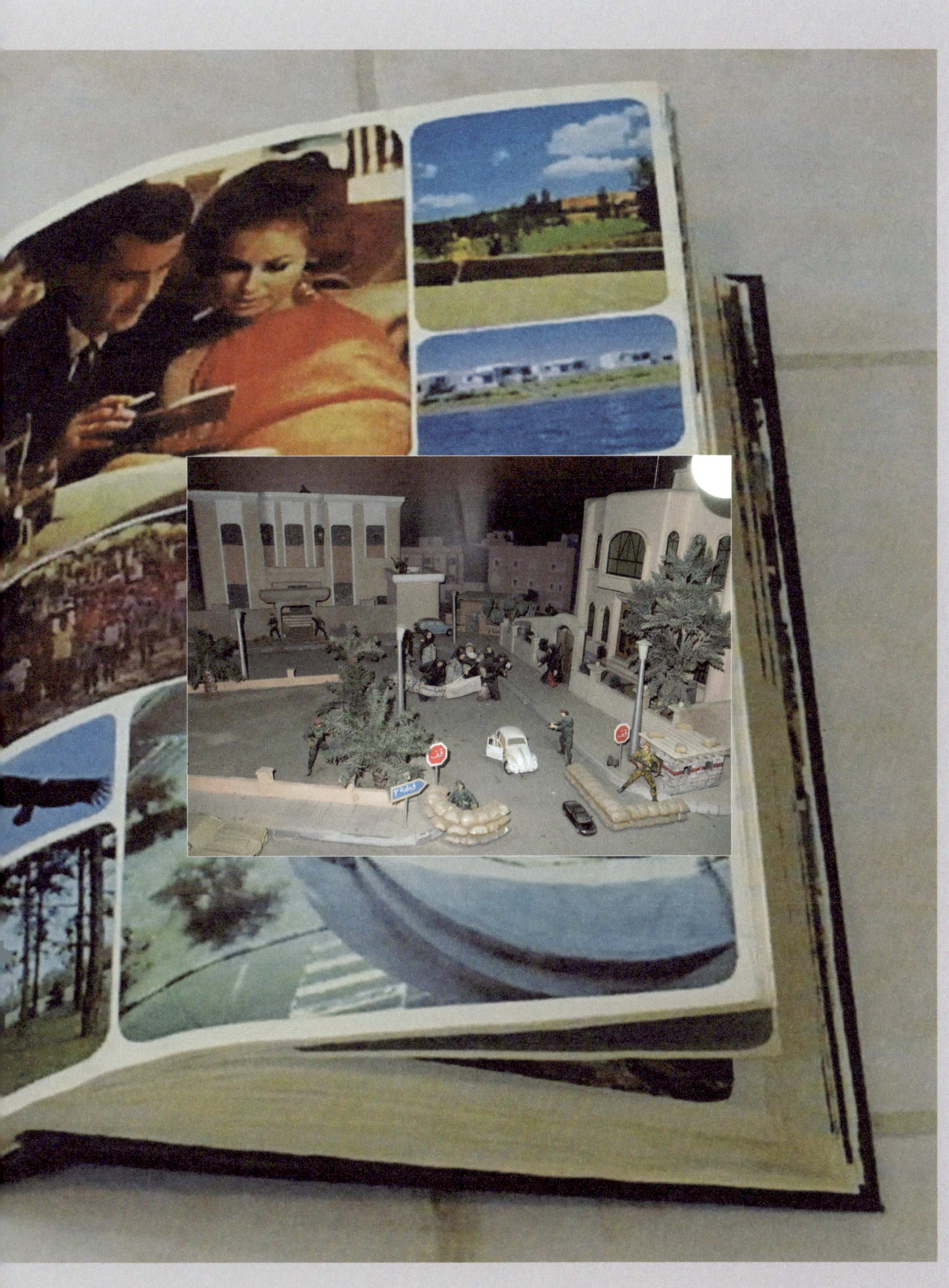

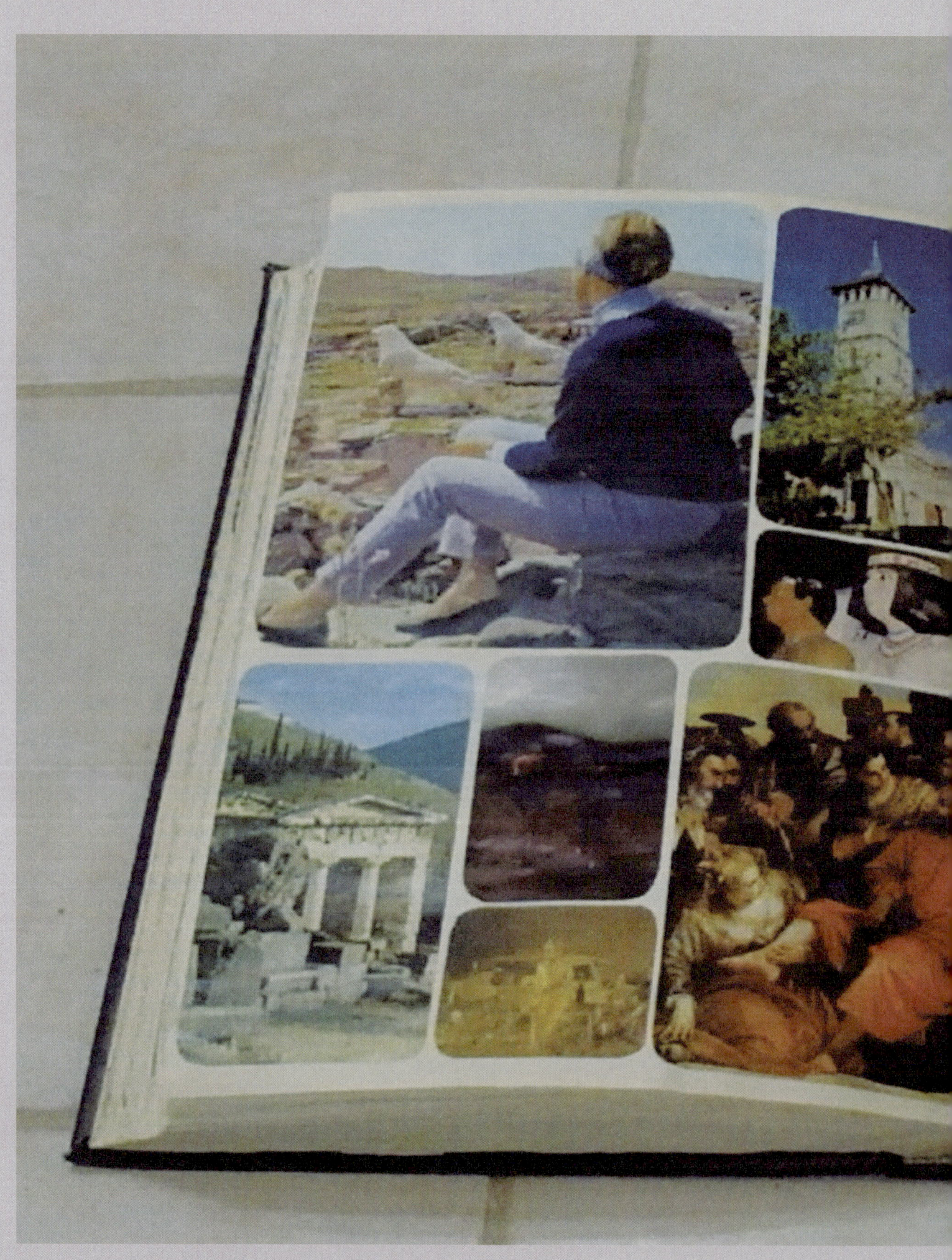

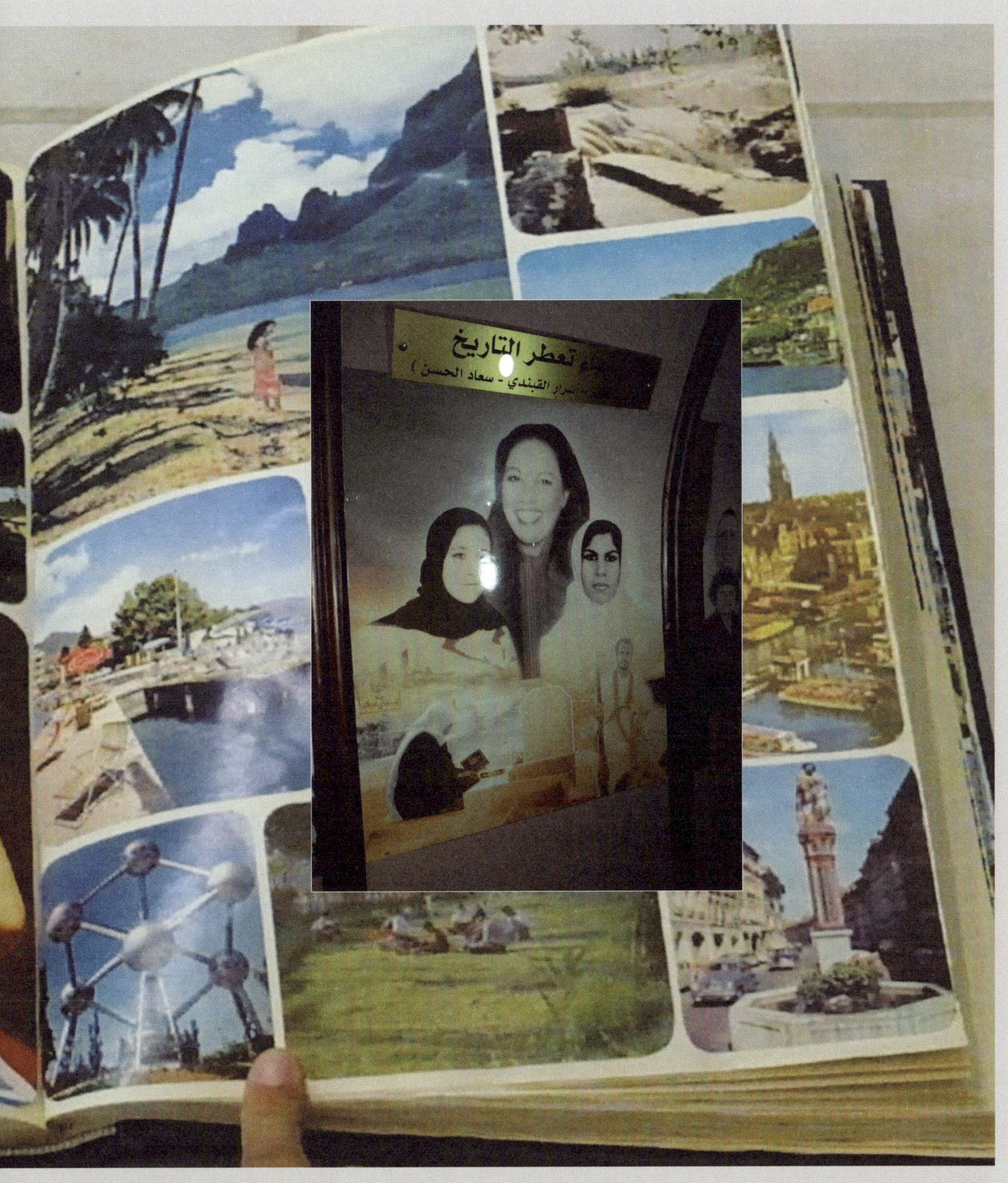

Although their names are no longer part of the statue, the five women, along with many other Kuwaiti martyrs, have become the "Symbol of Giving" in documents disseminated by the Martyrs' Bureau and in images produced by the Kuwait House for National Works – Not-to-Forget Museum [of] Saddam Hussein Regime Crimes.

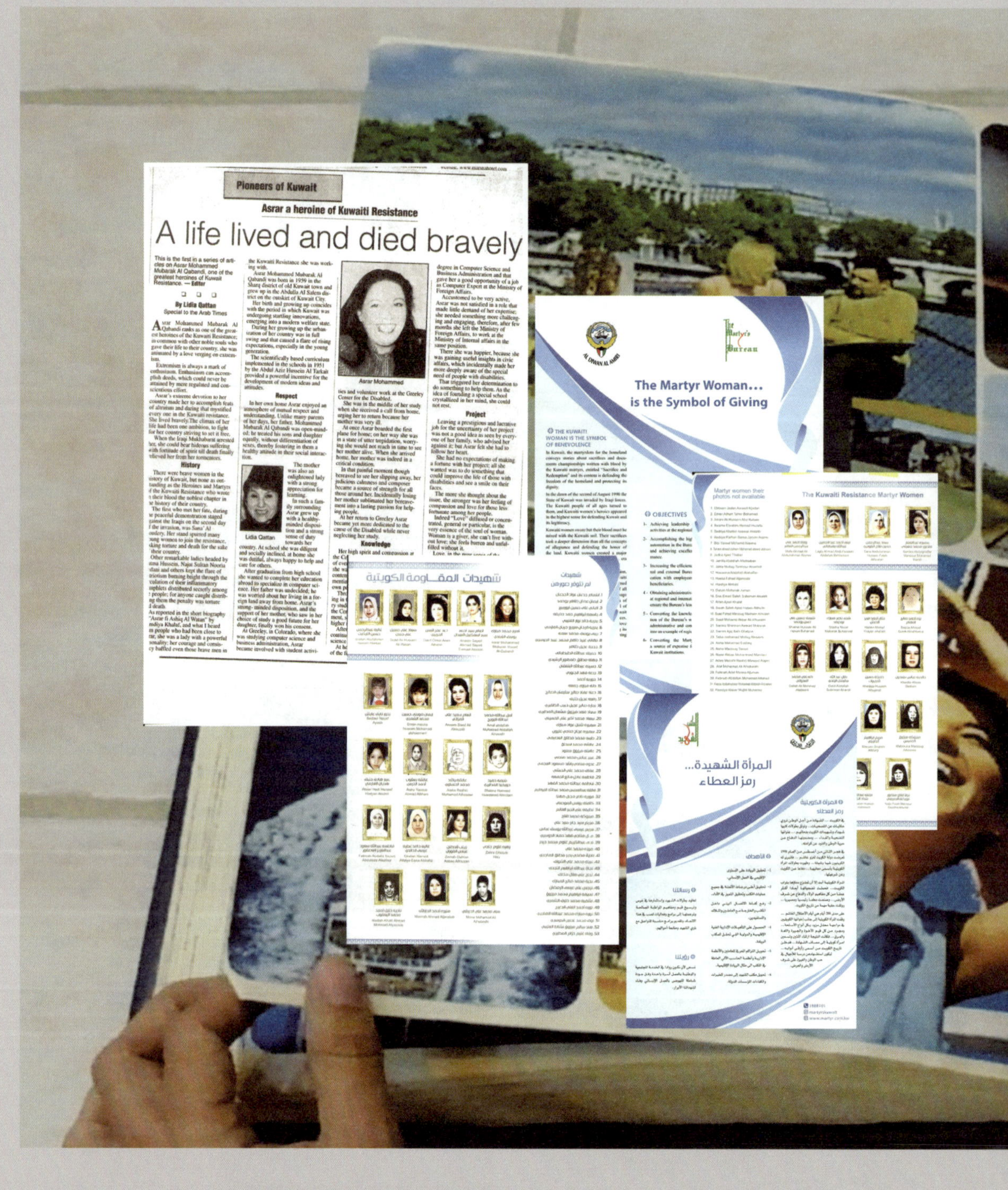

Pioneers of Kuwait
Asrar a heroine of Kuwaiti Resistance
A life lived and died bravely
By Lidia Qattan
Special to the Arab Times
Asrar Mohammed
Lidia Qattan
The Martyr's Bureau
The Martyr Woman...
is the Symbol of Giving
OBJECTIVES
THE KUWAITI WOMAN IS THE SYMBOL OF BENEVOLENCE
Martyr women their photos not available
The Kuwaiti Resistance Martyr Women
شهيدات المقاومة الكويتية
المرأة الشهيدة...
رمز العطاء

Narjes al-Shatti visited the memorial between 2001 and 2003. During one of her visits, she discovered that the monument had been taken down, wrapped in a blue nylon tarp, and abandoned on-site. Workers at the site explained to her that the <u>Touristic Enterprises Company</u>, a government body, had it removed. Al-Shatti paid for the monument to be placed in the al-Zahra neighbourhood where she had opened a daycare centre.

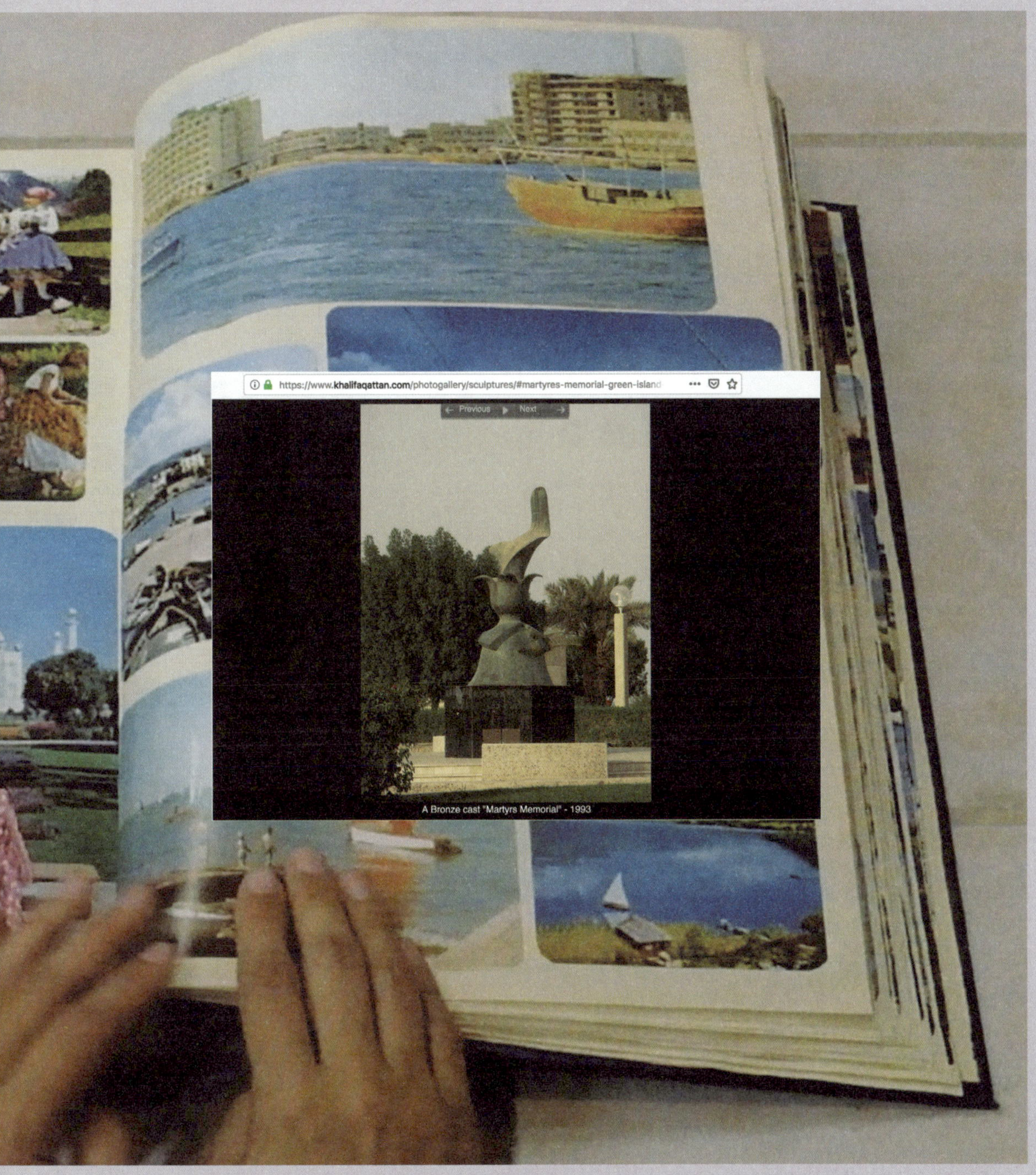

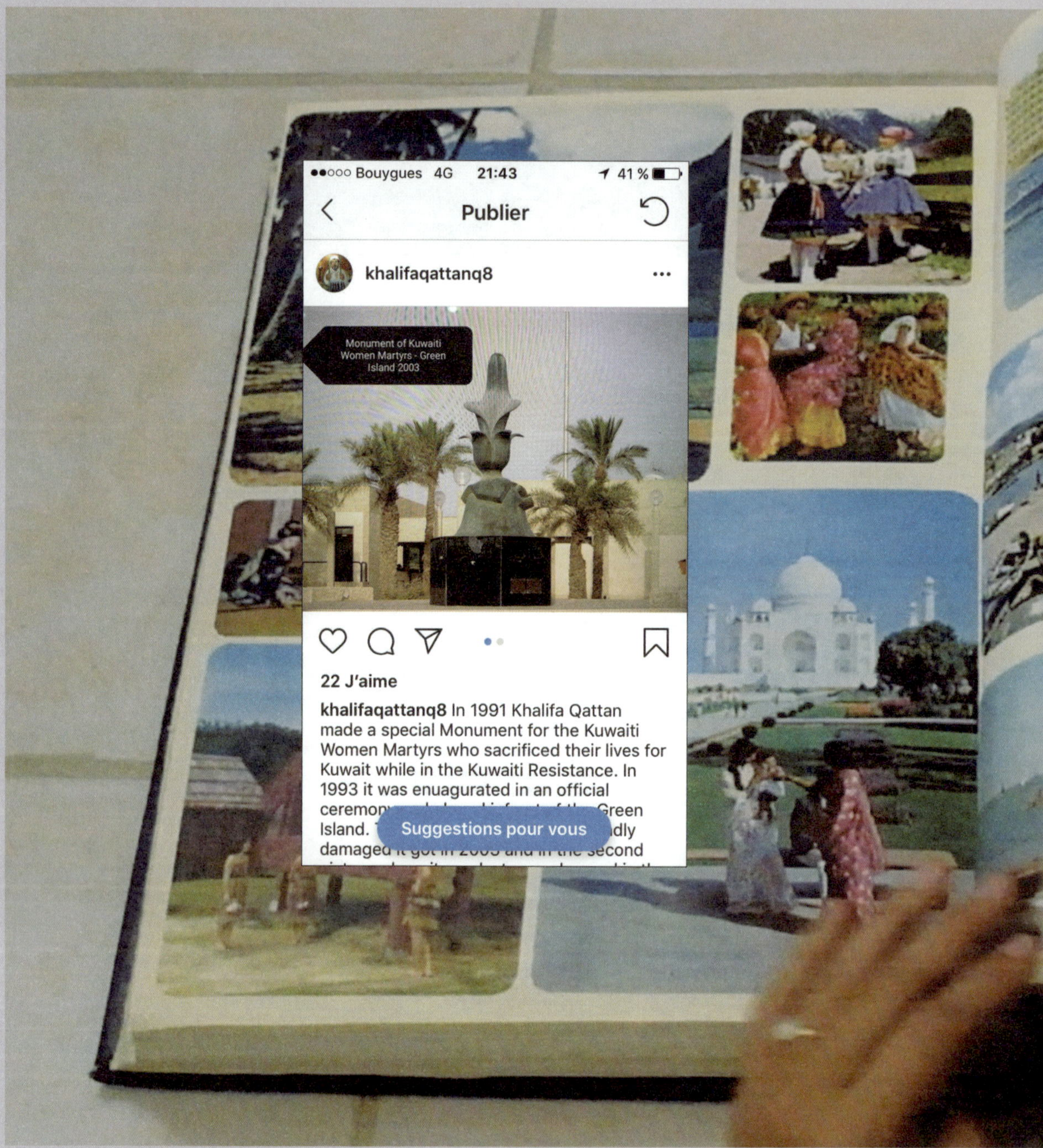

At the 1993 inauguration ceremony, Qattan, al-Shatti and al-Ghanim were not formally acknowledged.

No further records of Qattan's involvement in the later life of the monument are found in his personal archives.

In the years that followed, the memorial statue was vandalised and restored, then gradually forgotten by passersby and authorities alike.

Khalifa Qattan passed away in 2003.

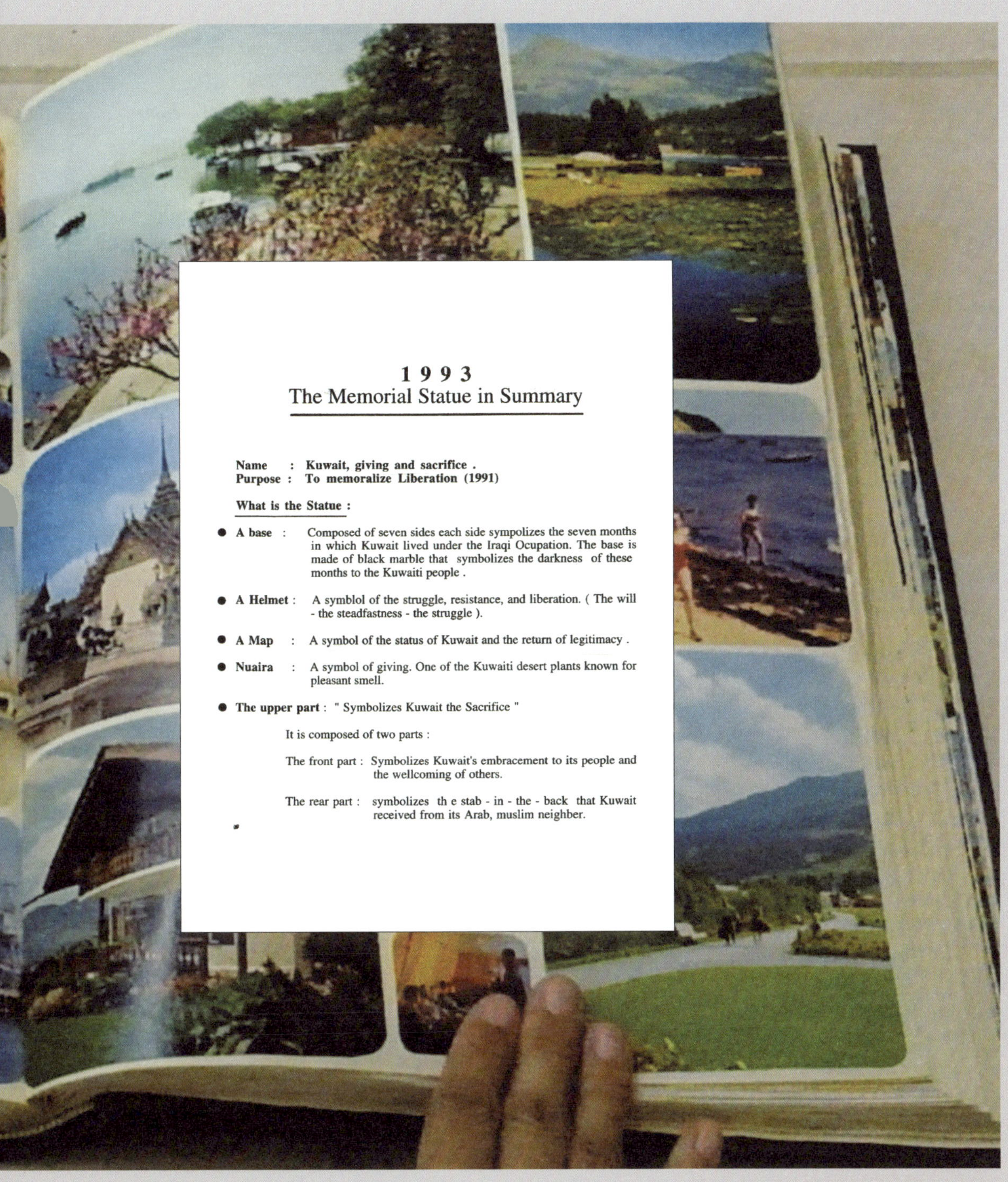

1 9 9 3
The Memorial Statue in Summary

Name   : **Kuwait, giving and sacrifice .**
Purpose : **To memoralize Liberation (1991)**

What is the Statue :

- **A base** : Composed of seven sides each side sympolizes the seven months in which Kuwait lived under the Iraqi Ocupation. The base is made of black marble that symbolizes the darkness of these months to the Kuwaiti people .

- **A Helmet** : A symblol of the struggle, resistance, and liberation. (The will - the steadfastness - the struggle).

- **A Map**   : A symbol of the status of Kuwait and the return of legitimacy .

- **Nuaira**   : A symbol of giving. One of the Kuwaiti desert plants known for pleasant smell.

- **The upper part** : " Symbolizes Kuwait the Sacrifice "

     It is composed of two parts :

     The front part : Symbolizes Kuwait's embracement to its people and the wellcoming of others.

     The rear part :   symbolizes th e stab - in - the - back that Kuwait received from its Arab, muslim neighber.

A document titled "1993 Summary of the Memorial Statue," found among Khalifa Qattan's personal archives, relates these changes.

The title of the monument was changed to *Kuwait, Giving and Sacrifice*, and its purpose became the "commemoration of the liberation (1991)." The symbolic elements were described in a way that omitted any reference to women and women martyrs.

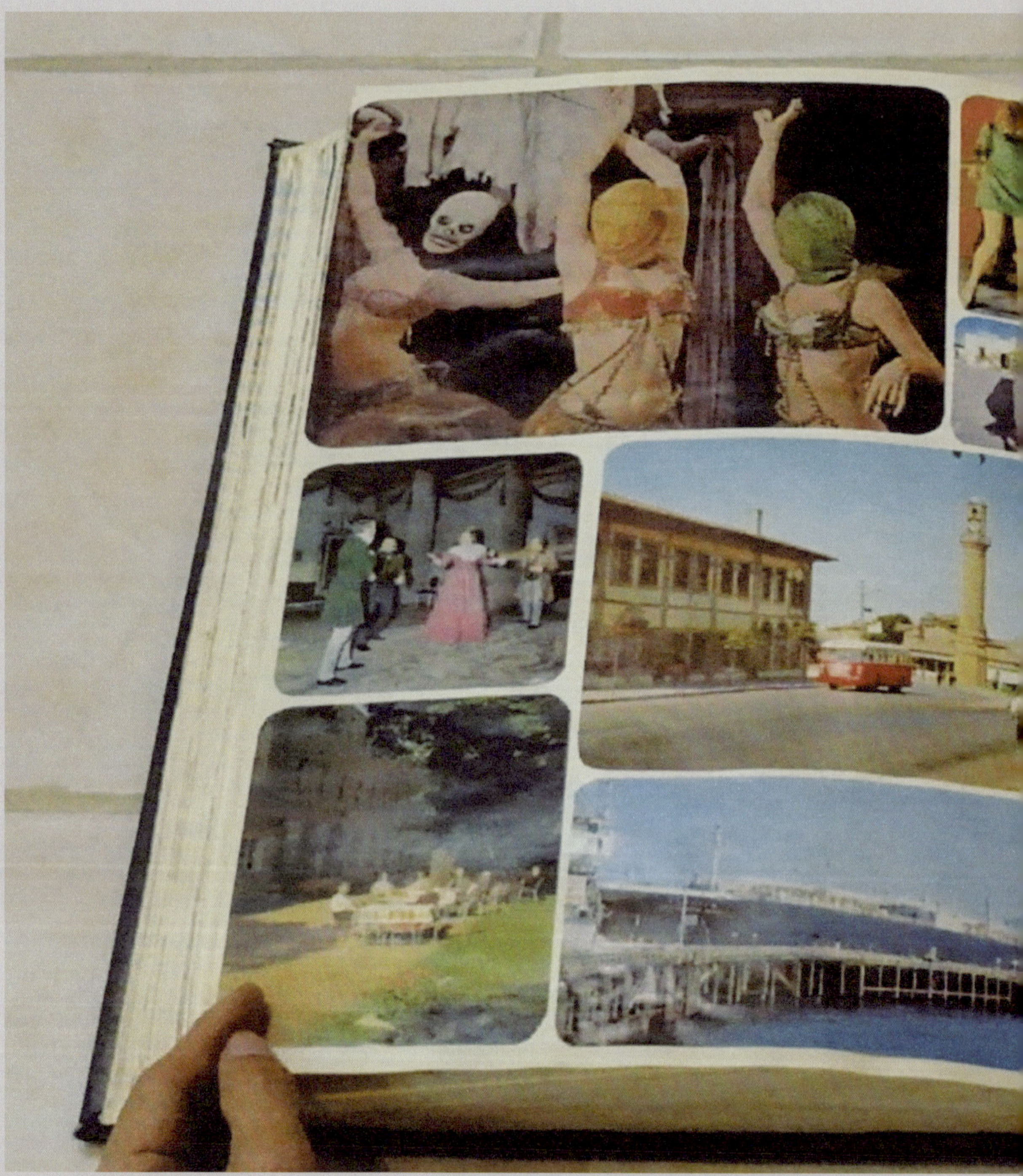

In 1993, it was decided that the monument would be put up in the Green Island waterside park, and an unveiling date was set. At the time, Narjes Al-Shatti and Layla al-Ghanim were volunteering with Desert Peace, an organisation hosting people who lost a family member during the military operation Desert Storm.

They offered to set up the monument before a delegation of American families arrived. At this point, the Council of Ministers authorising the installation of the monument requested that all references to women be removed. The names of the five women martyrs were not engraved onto the monument.

When the monumental bronze statue made it to Kuwait from
Italy, it still had not been assigned a site to be put up.

The inauguration did not take place as planned, and the monument was
confined to its crate and stored in an alley by the Ministry of Information.

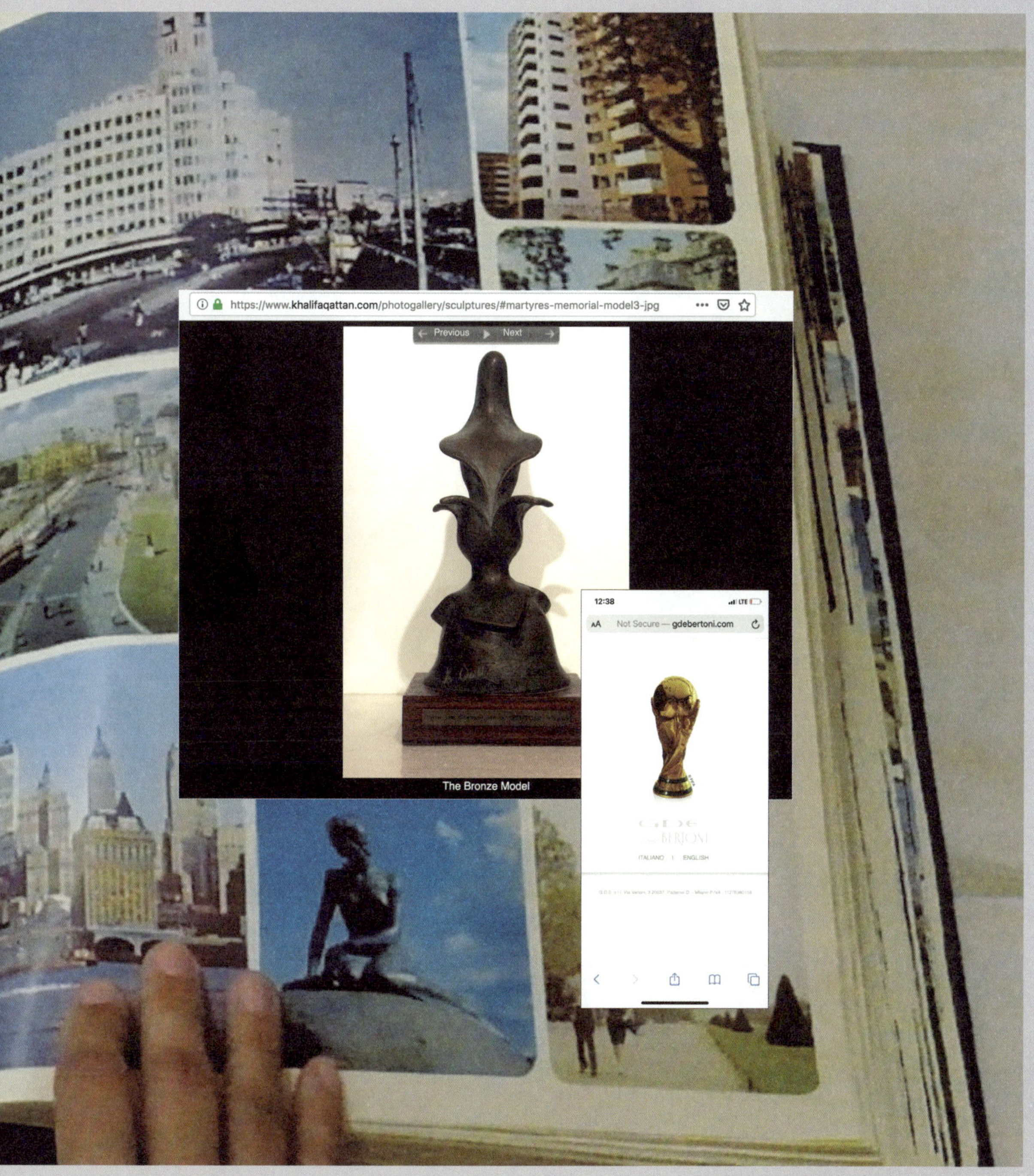

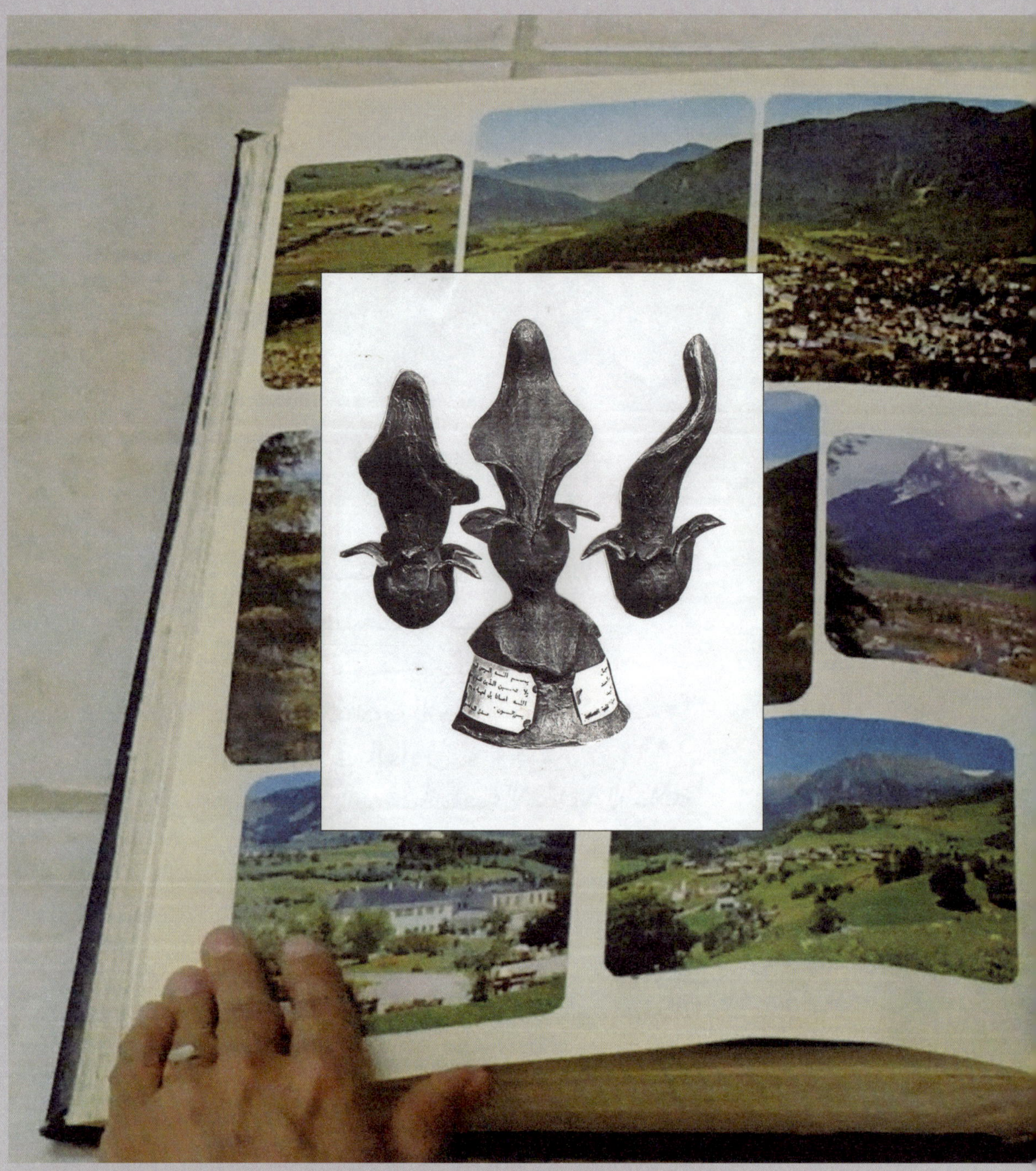

The project took shape between November 1991 and February 1992, precipitated by exchanges between Khalifa Qattan, the <u>Consorzio Societa Italiane per il Kuwait</u> – in charge of producing and shipping the bronze monument in Italy, and the <u>Ministry of Information of Kuwait</u>, which funded the project for a sum of USD 80,000.

Qattan produced clay models, and Bertoni Milano, a company specialised in the manufacture of trophies and medals, including the FIFA World Cup Trophy, sent him a miniature bronze maquette.

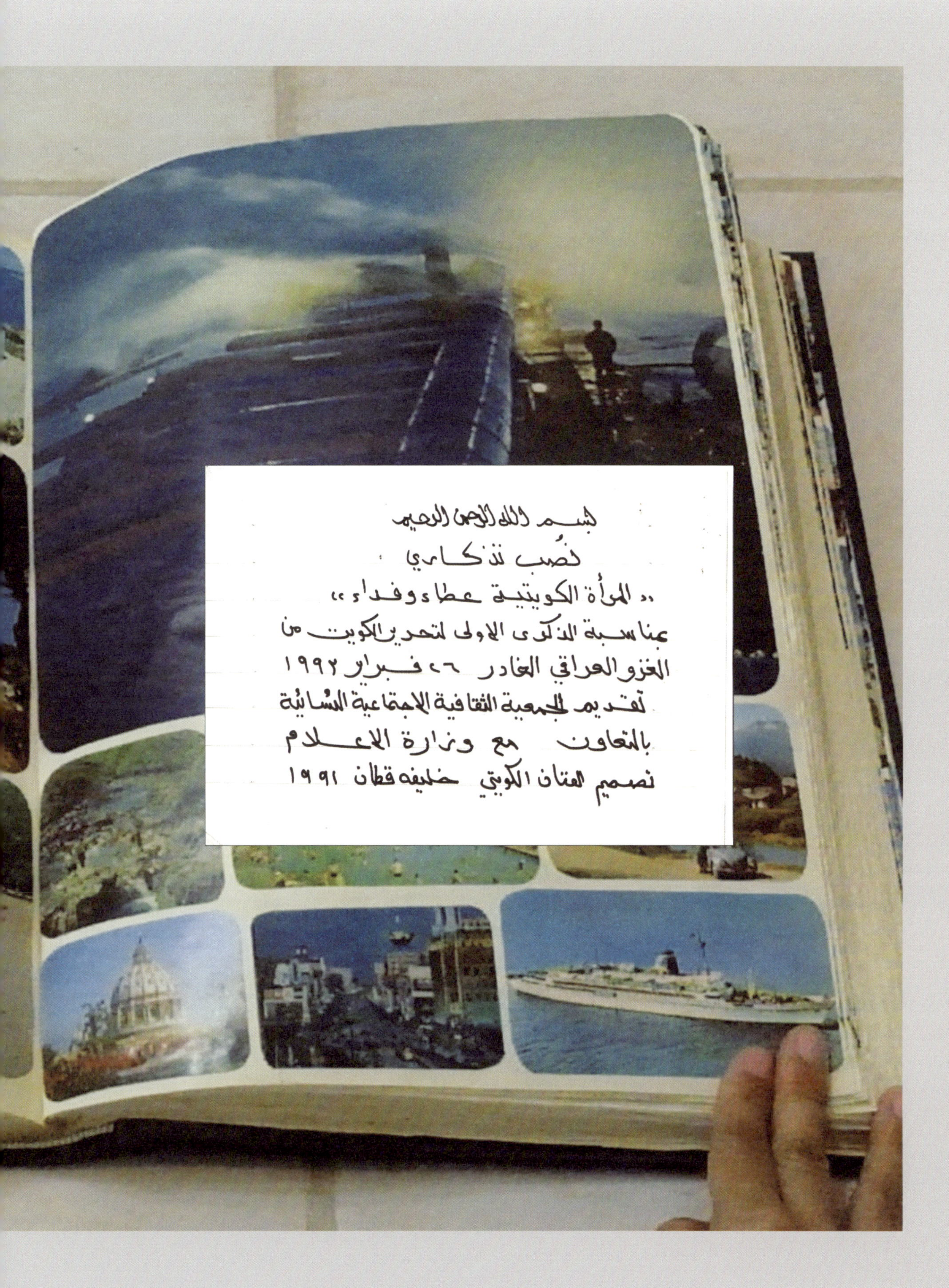

بسم الله الرحمن الرحيم
نصب تذكاري
«المرأة الكويتية عطاء وفداء»
بمناسبة الذكرى الاولى لتحرير الكويت من
الغزو العراقي الغادر ٢٦ فبراير ١٩٩٢
تقديم للجمعية الثقافية الاجتماعية النسائية
بالتعاون   مع وزارة الاعلام
تصميم الفنان الكويتي   خليفه قطان ١٩٩١

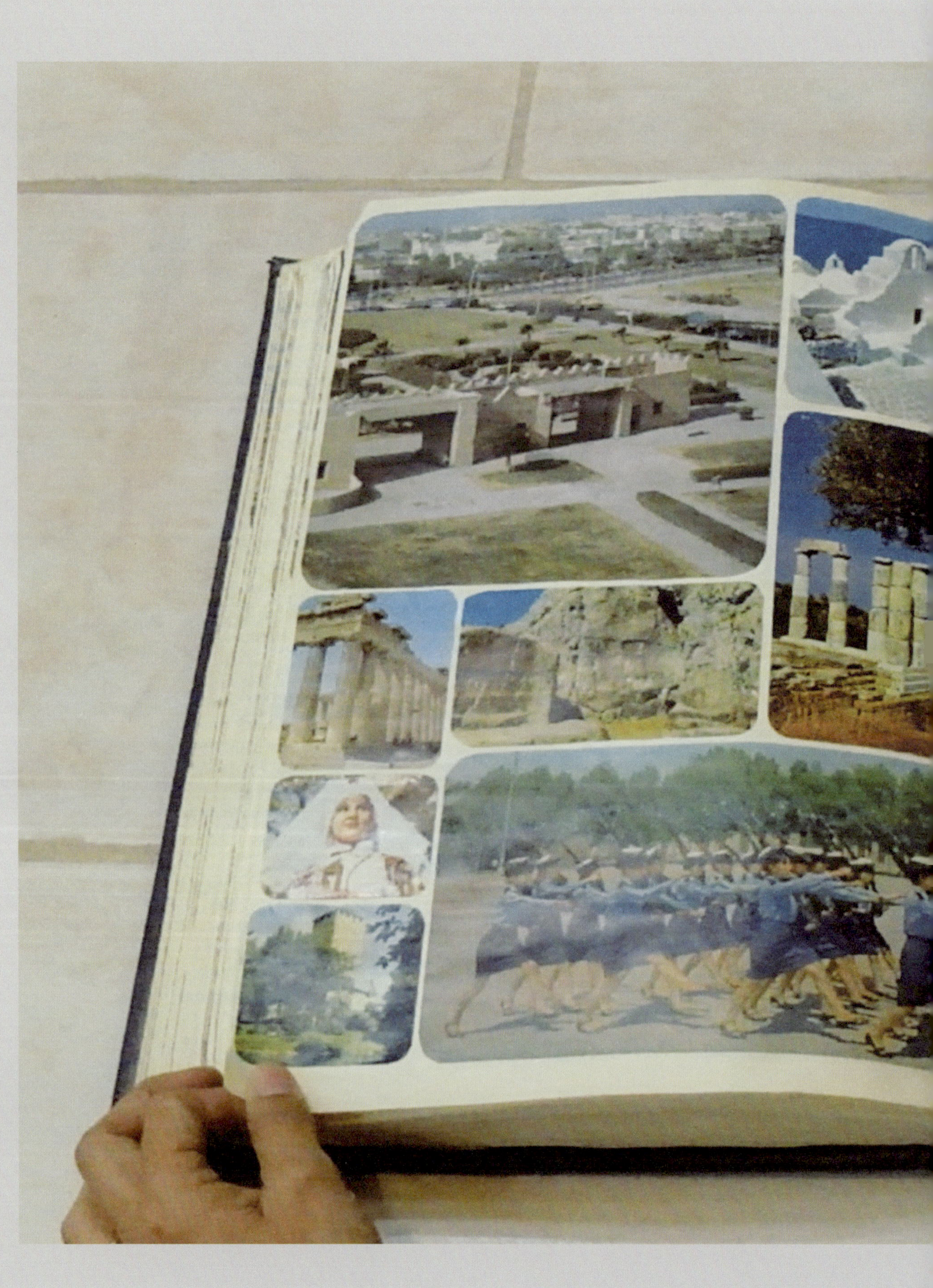

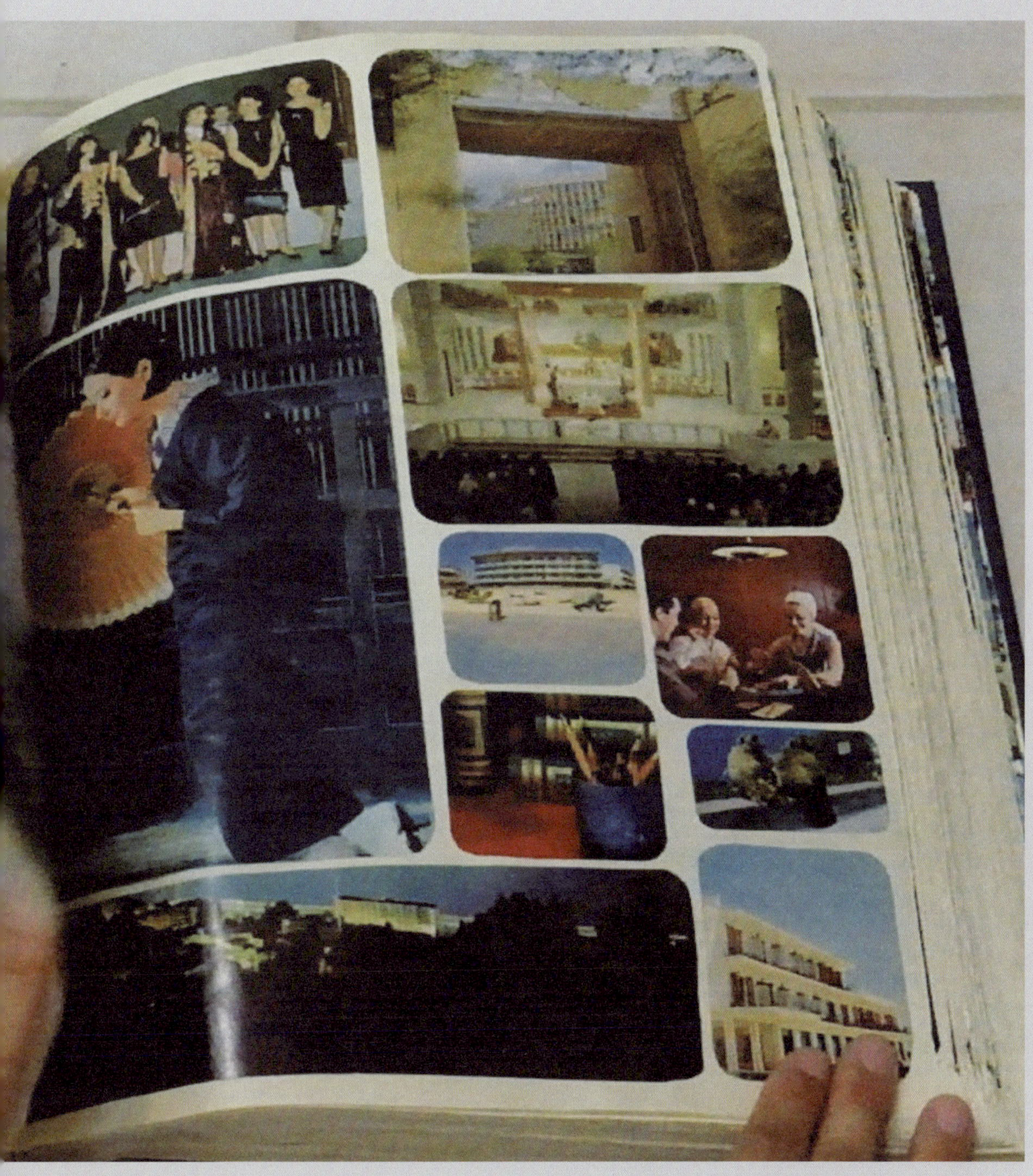

The memorial statue was meant to commemorate five women martyrs whose names and dates of birth and death were to feature on the monument: Asrar Mohammed (1959-14/1/1991); Suad Ali Hussein (1981-6/2/1991); Sana Abdulrahman (1969-8/8/1990); Ghalia Abdulrahman (1965-26/2/1991); and Wafa Ahmad Ali (1967-6/2/1991).

The monument was titled *Kuwaiti Women, Giving and Sacrifice.*

The artist had experienced the invasion first-hand.

Qattan drew sketches for a monument, with various motifs and figurative elements: a flower emblematic of both women and Kuwait; a soldier's helmet evoking the women and men who sacrificed their lives for the liberation of Kuwait; and a map of the country emerging from a helmet as a five-petalled Nuwaira flower.

On the back of the monument, a mark symbolised Iraq's betrayal or "stab in the back."

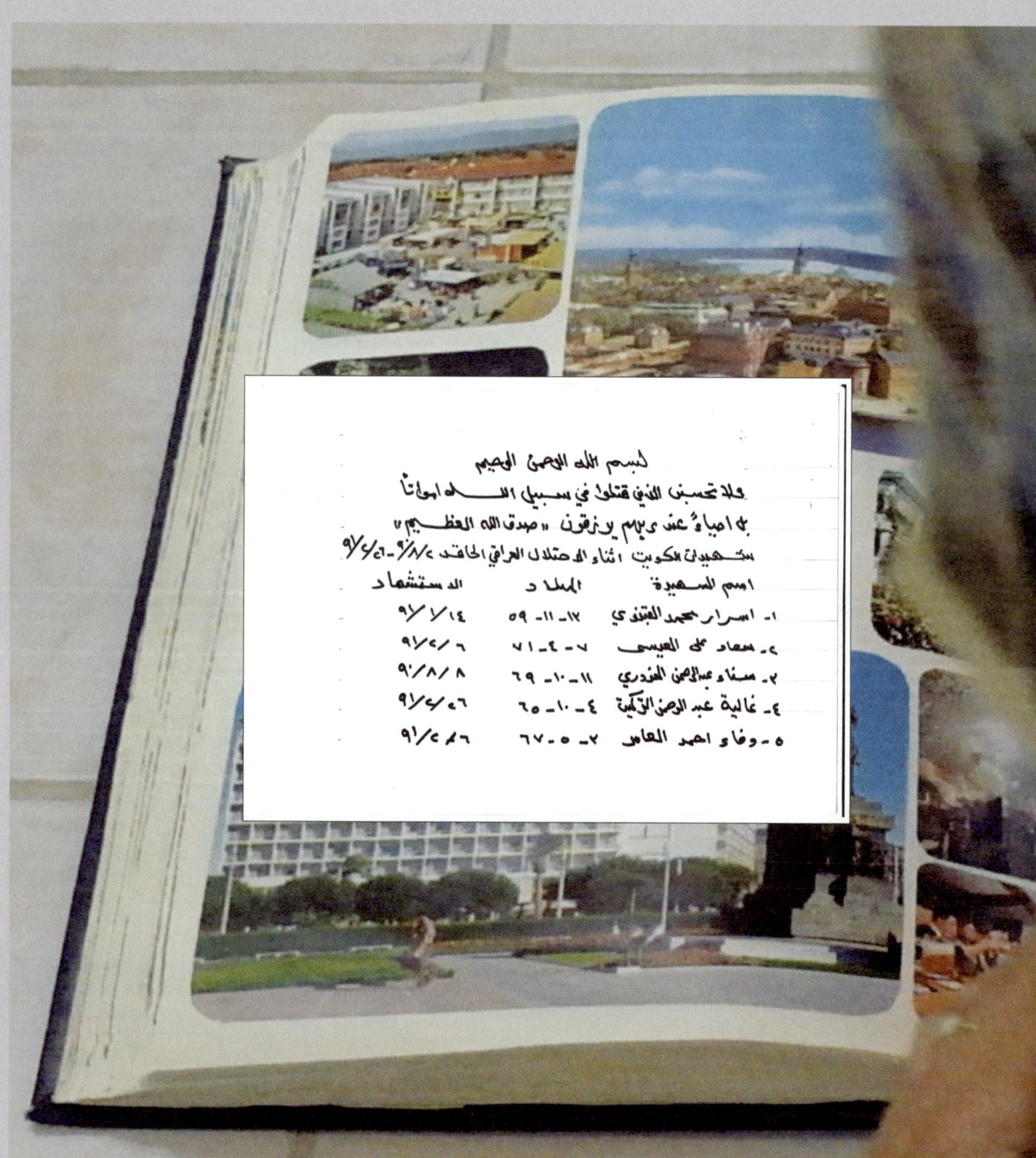

بسم الله الرحمن الرحيم

ولا تحسبن الذين قتلوا في سبيل الله امواتاً بل احياء عند ربهم يرزقون «صدق الله العظيم»

شهيدات الكويت اثناء الاحتلال العراقي الحاقد ٢/٨/٩ - ٢٦/٤/٩١

اسم الشهيدة	الميلاد	الاستشهاد
١- اسرار محمد العتيبي	١٧-١١-٥٩	٩١/١/١٤
٢- سعاد علي العيسى	٧-٢-٧١	٩١/٤/٦
٣- سناء عبدالرحمن الغندري	١١-١٠-٦٩	٩٠/٨/٨
٤- غالية عبد الرحمن الزكية	٤-١٠-٢٥	٩١/٤/٢٦
٥- وفاء احمد العامر	٢-٥-٧٦	٩١/٤/٢٦

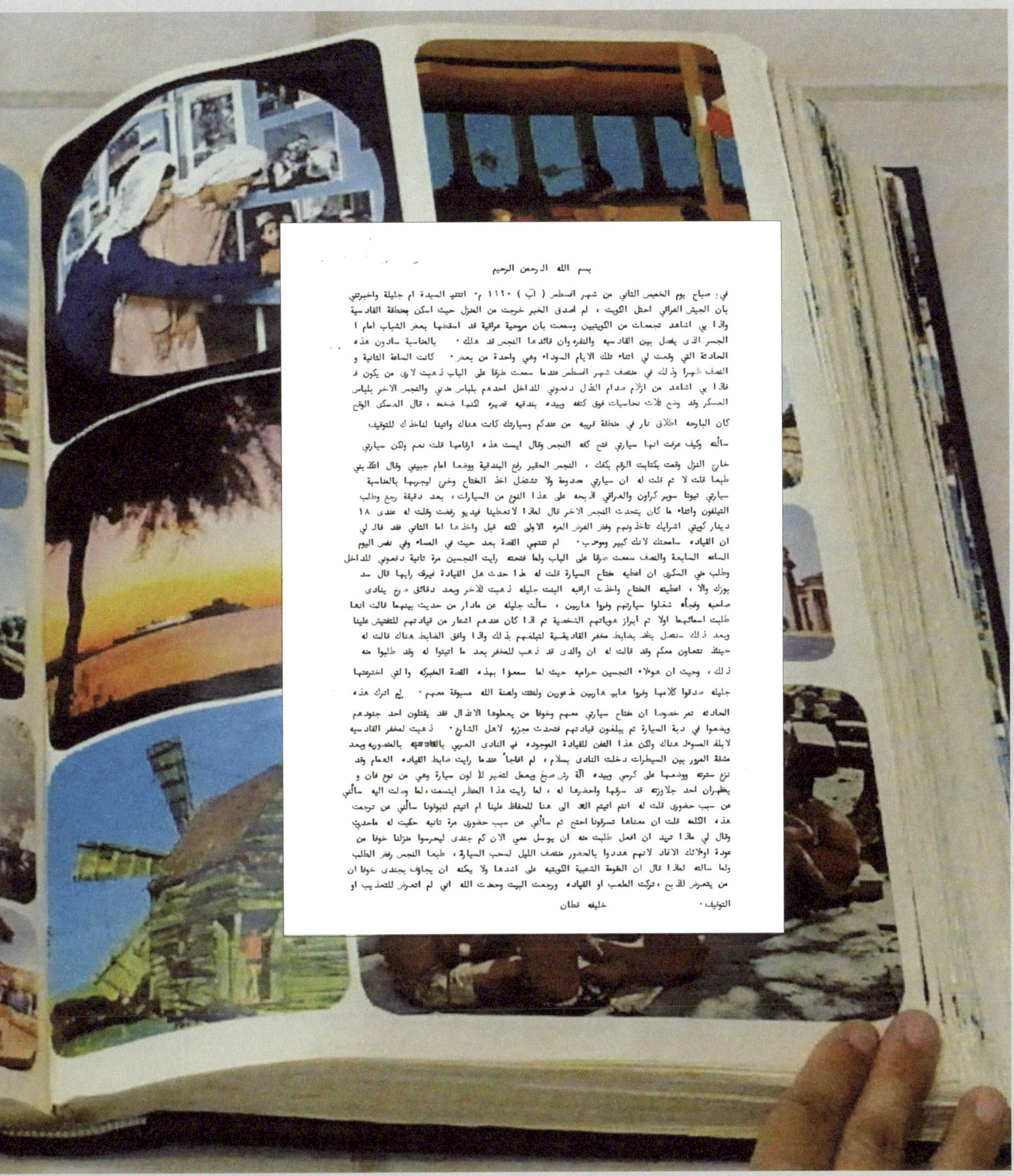

بسم الله الرحمن الرحيم

في صباح يوم الخميس الثاني من شهر اغسطس (آب) ١١٩٠ م٠ اتتني السيدة ام جليلة واخبرتني
بان الجيش العراقي احتل الكويت ، لم اصدق الخبر خرجت من المنزل حيث اسكن بمنطقة القادسية
واذا بي اشاهد تجمعات من الكويتيين وسمعت بان مروحية عراقية قد اسقطها بعض الشباب امام
الجسر الذي يفصل بين القادسيه والنقره وان قائدها النجم قد هلك ٠ بالمناسبة سادون هذه
الحادثة التي وقعت لي اثناء تلك الايام السوداء وهي واحدة من بحر ٠ كانت الساعة الثانية و
النصف ظهرا وذلك في منتصف شهر اغسطس عندما سمعت طرقا على الباب ذهبت لارى من يكون ف
فاذا بي اشاهد من ازلام صدام الذل دعوني للداخل احدهم بلباس مدني والنجم الاخر بلباس
العسكر وقد وضع ثلاث نحاسيات فوق كتفه وبيده بندقيه قصيره لكنها ضخمه ، قال العسكري الوقح
كان البارحه اطلاق نار في منطقة قريبه من عندكم وسيارتك كانت هناك واتينا لناخذك للتوقيف
سألته وكيف عرفت انها سيارتي فتح كفه النجم وقال ايست هذه ارقامها قلت نعم ولكن سيارتي
خارج المنزل وقمت بكتابت الرقم بكفك ، النجم الحقير رفع البندقية ووضعها امام جبيني وقال اتكذب بني
طبعا قلت لا ثم قلت له ان سيارتي مصدومة ولا تشتغل اخذ المفتاح وخرج ليجربها بالمناسبة
سيارتي تيوتا سوبر كراون والعراقي اذبحه على هذا النوع من السيارات ، بعد دقيقة رجع وطلب
التيلفون واثناء ما كان يتحدث النجم الاخر قال لماذا لاتعطينا فيديو رفضت وقلت له عندى ١٨
دينار كويتي اشرايك تاخذ ونهم وفر الغرض المره الاولى لكنه قبل واخذها اما الثاني فقد قال لي
ان القياده سامحتك لانك كبير وموهب ٠ لم تنتهي القصة بعد حيث في المساء وفي نفس اليوم
الساعه السابعة والنصف سمعت طرقا على الباب ولما فتحته رايت النجمين مرة ثانية دعوني للداخل
وطلب مني السكري ان اعطيه مفتاح السيارة قلت له هذا حدث هل القيادة نيرك رايها قال سد
بوزك والا ، اعطيه المفتاح واخذت اراقبه البت جليله ذهبت للاخر وبعد دقائق رح ينادى
صاحبه وفجاه شغلوا سيارتهم وفروا هاربين ، سألت جليله عن مادار من حديث بينهما قالت انها
طلبت اسمائهما اولا ثم ابراز هوياتهم الشخصية ثم اذا كان عندهم اشعار من قيادتهم للتفتيش علينا
وبعد ذلك نتصل يظن بضابط مخفر القادسية لتبلغهم بذلك والا وافق الضابط هناك قالت ه
حيكم نتعاون معكم وقد قالت له ان والدى قد ذهب للمخفر بعد ما اتيتوا له وقد طلبوا منه
ذلك ، وحيث ان هولاء النجمين حرامي حيث لما سمعوا بهذه القصة الكبيره والتي اخترعتها
جليله عدلوا كلامها وقبوا عابي هاربين ذعورين ولعنت ولعنة الله مسبوة معهم ٠ لم اترك هذه
الحادثه تمر خصوصا ان خدموا سيارتي معهم وخوفا من يعطلوها الاطفال فقد يظنون احد جنودهم
وضعوا في دبة السيارة ثم يلغمون قيادتهم تحدث مجزره لاهل الشارع ٠ ذهبت لمخفر القادسيه
لابلغ المسوول هناك ولكن هذا الضن للقيادة الموجوده في النادى العربي بالقادسيه بالصحوديه وبعد
مشقة المرور بين السيطرات دخلت النادى بسلام ، لم افاجئا عندما رايت ضابط القياده العام وقد
نزع سترته ووضعها على كرسي وبيده آلة رش صغ يعمل لتغير لا لون سيارة وهي من نوع فان و
يظهران احد جلاوزته قد سرقها واحضرها له ، لما رايت هذا المنظر ابتسمت، لما وصلت اليه سألني
عن سبب حضوري قلت له انتم احتم العا الى عنا للحفاظ علينا ام احتم لتبولونا سألني عن ترجمت
الكلمه قلت له مناها تصرلونا احتي ثم سألني عن سبب حضوري مرة ثانية حكيت له ماحدث
وقال لي ماذا تريد ان افعل طلبت منه ان يوصل معي الان ثم جندى ليحرسوا منزلنا خوفا من
عودة اولائك الافاد لانهم عددوا بالحضور منتصف الليل لسحب السيارة ، طبعا النجم رفض الطلب
ولما سألته لماذا قال ان القوة الشعبية الكويتية على اندها ولا يمكنه ان يجاوب جندى خوفا ان
من يحضر للآبي ، تركت الملعب او القياده ورجعت البيت وحمدت الله اني لم اتعرض للتعذيب او
التوقيف ٠

خليفه قطان

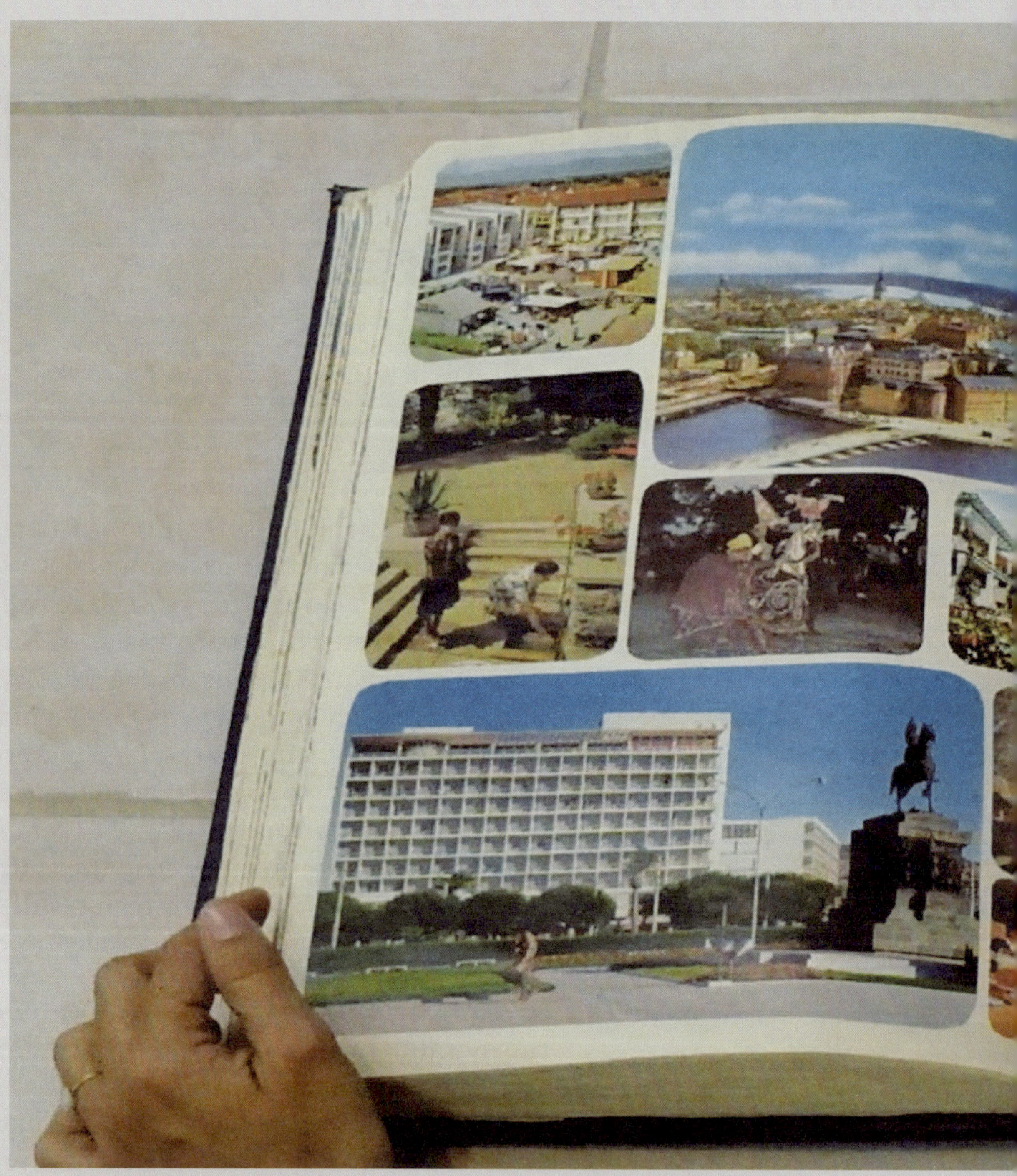

A few months after the end of Iraq's invasion of Kuwait (1990-1991), Narjes al-Shatti and Layla al-Ghanim, two members of the Women's Cultural and Social Society, asked artist Khalifa Qattan (1934-2003) to design a monument commemorating Kuwaiti women's resistance during the invasion.

Anahi Alviso-Marino

A Monument Once Called 'Kuwaiti Women, Giving and Sacrifice'

Researcher Anahi Alviso-Marino's visual essay draws on the personal archive of renowned Kuwaiti artist Khalifa Qattan (1934 – 2003). At the close of the 1990 Gulf War triggered by Iraq's invasion of Kuwait, Qattan conceived of a monument for the country's liberation, that was also a memorial to its female martyrs. His monument experienced a troubled history: over the years, references to women were removed, and the work was renamed and displaced several times across Kuwait City. These changes echo the shifting political contexts in Kuwait and the broader Gulf, drawing attention to contested public spaces and sites of memory.

Alviso-Marino uses Qattan's archive to retrace the monument's many lives. As a backdrop to her contribution, she used notebooks chock-full of collaged photographs and postcards meticulously collected by Qattan, including the many monuments and cityscapes worldwide that shaped his imagination and visual landscape.

باسل عباس وروان أبو رحمة

ولكن قناعي منيع

يقدم الفنانان باسل عباس وروان أبو رحمة اقتباساً من عملهما المستمر بعنوان "ولكن قناعي منيع" (2016 – متواصل)، ويتضمن مجموعةً من الأقنعة النيوليثية التي وُجدت في فلسطين والتي جرى استخراجها في ظروف مشبوهة، ومن ثم حفظها في متاحف إسرائيلية وغربية بعيدًا عن أعين الفلسطينيين. يرتدي هذه الأقنعة التي أعاد الفنانان إنتاجها بواسطة برمجيات النمذجة ثلاثية الأبعاد، أشخاصٌ يتجولون في قرى هجّرت ودُمّرت إبان نكبة 1948.

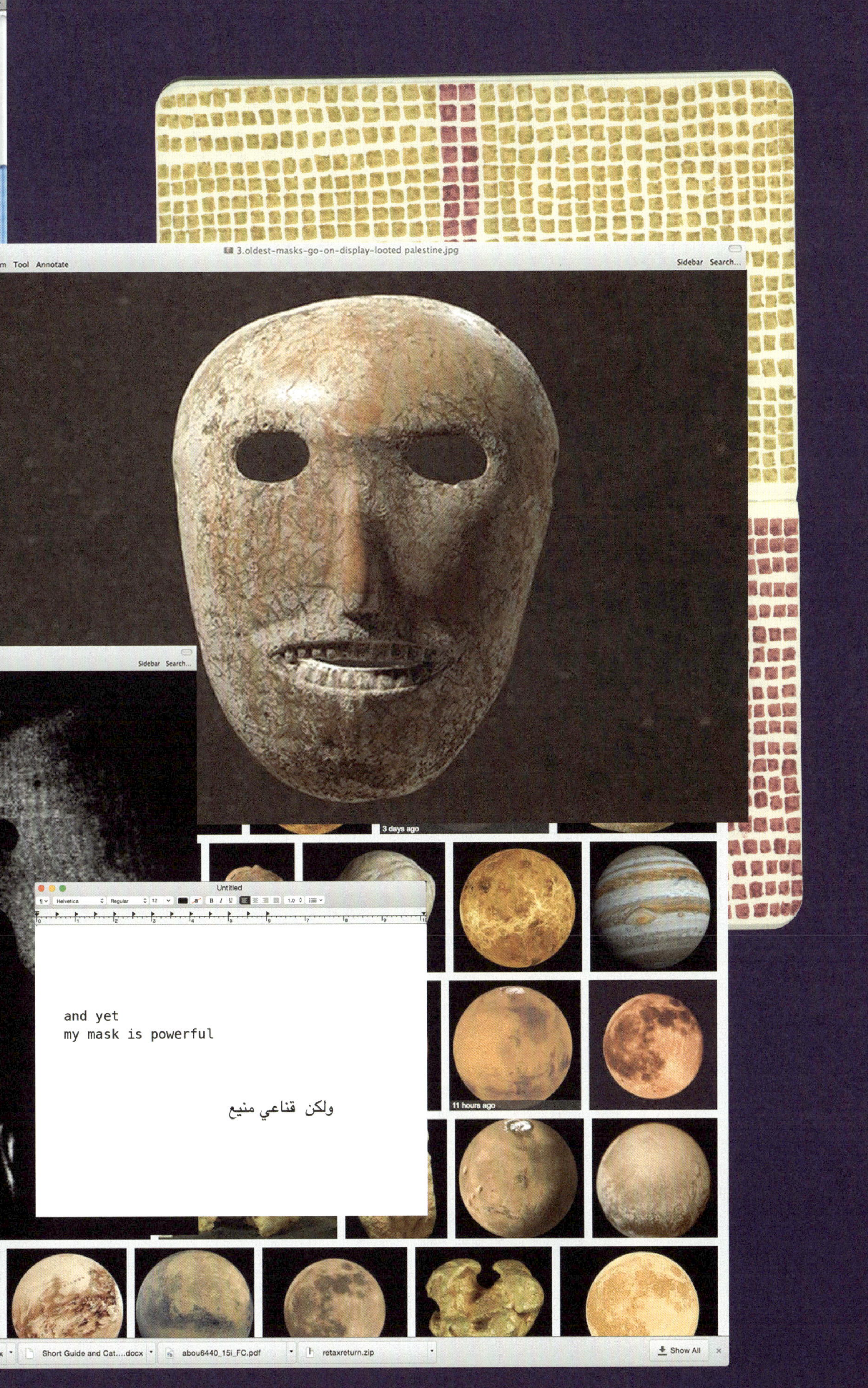
3.oldest-masks-go-on-display-looted palestine.jpg
and yet
my mask is powerful
ولكن قناعي منيع

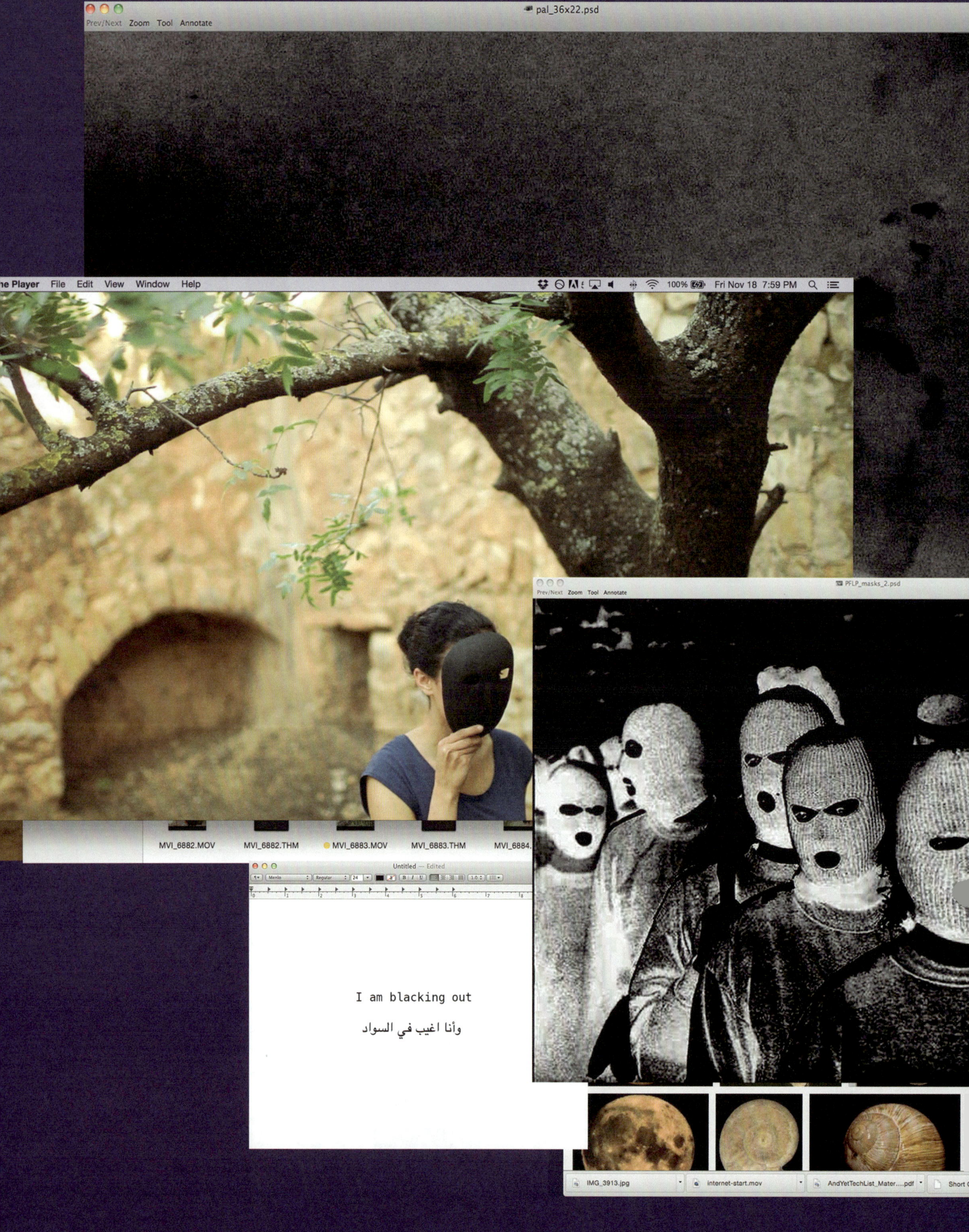

pal_36x22.psd
Prev/Next Zoom Tool Annotate
e Player   File   Edit   View   Window   Help   100% Fri Nov 18 7:59 PM
PFLP_masks_2.psd
Prev/Next Zoom Tool Annotate
MVI_6882.MOV   MVI_6882.THM   MVI_6883.MOV   MVI_6883.THM   MVI_6884.
Untitled — Edited
Menlo   Regular   24
I am blacking out
وأنا اغيب في السواد
IMG_3913.jpg   internet-start.mov   AndYetTechList_Mater....pdf   Short C

Symbolic Code – The Iconography of the Masks

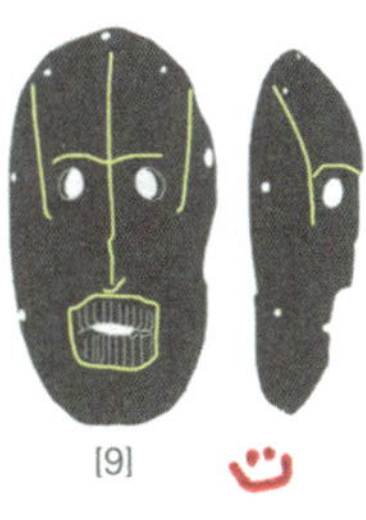
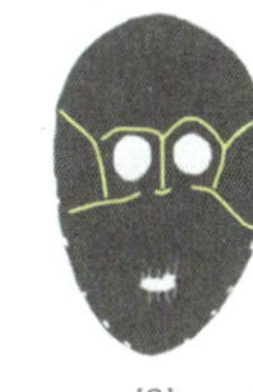
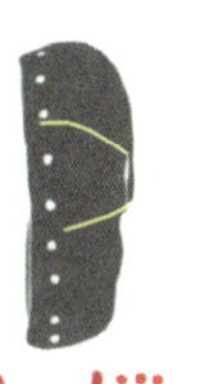
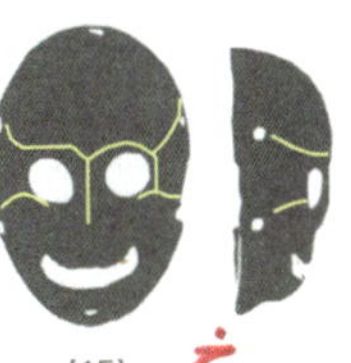
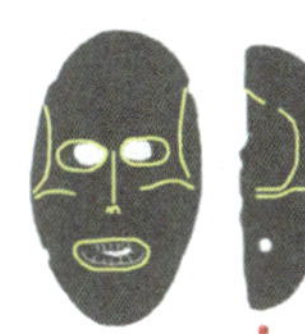
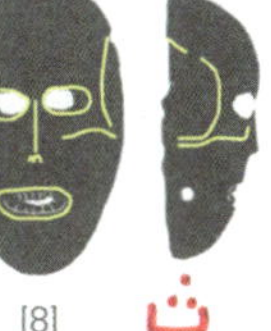

[9] ت   قناع وادي حيمر [2]   [15] خ   [8] ت

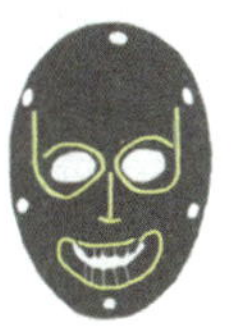
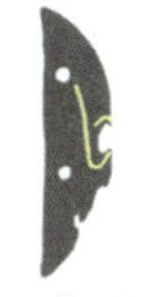
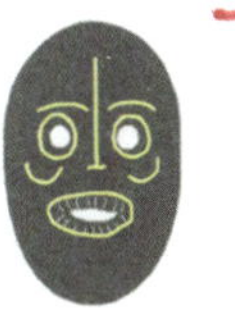
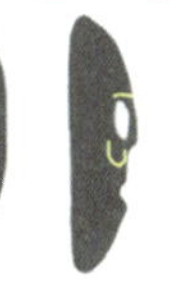
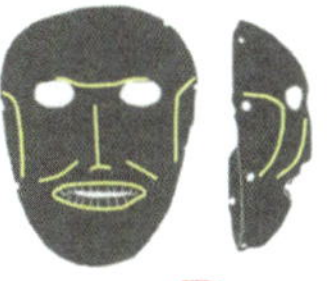

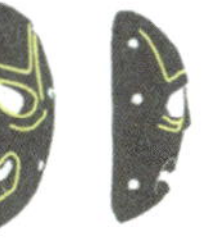
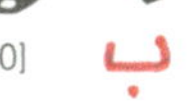

قناع الصلب [1]   [14] د   [13] ج   [10] ب

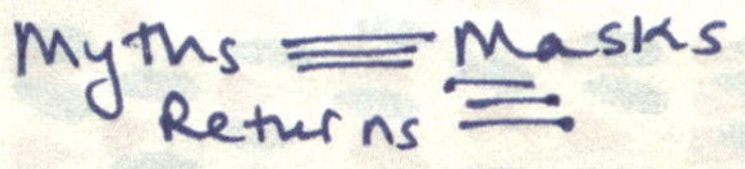

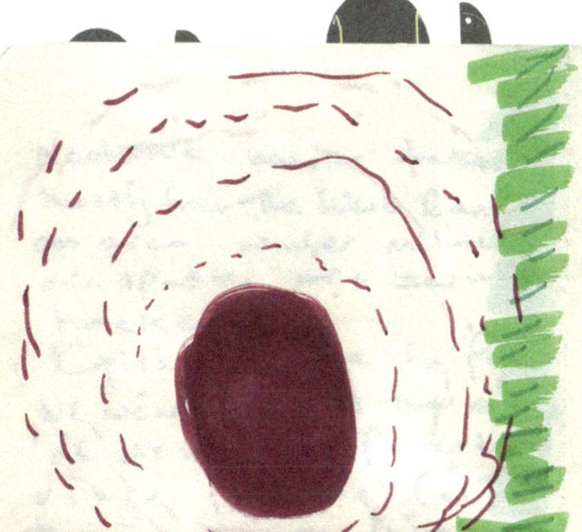

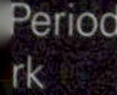

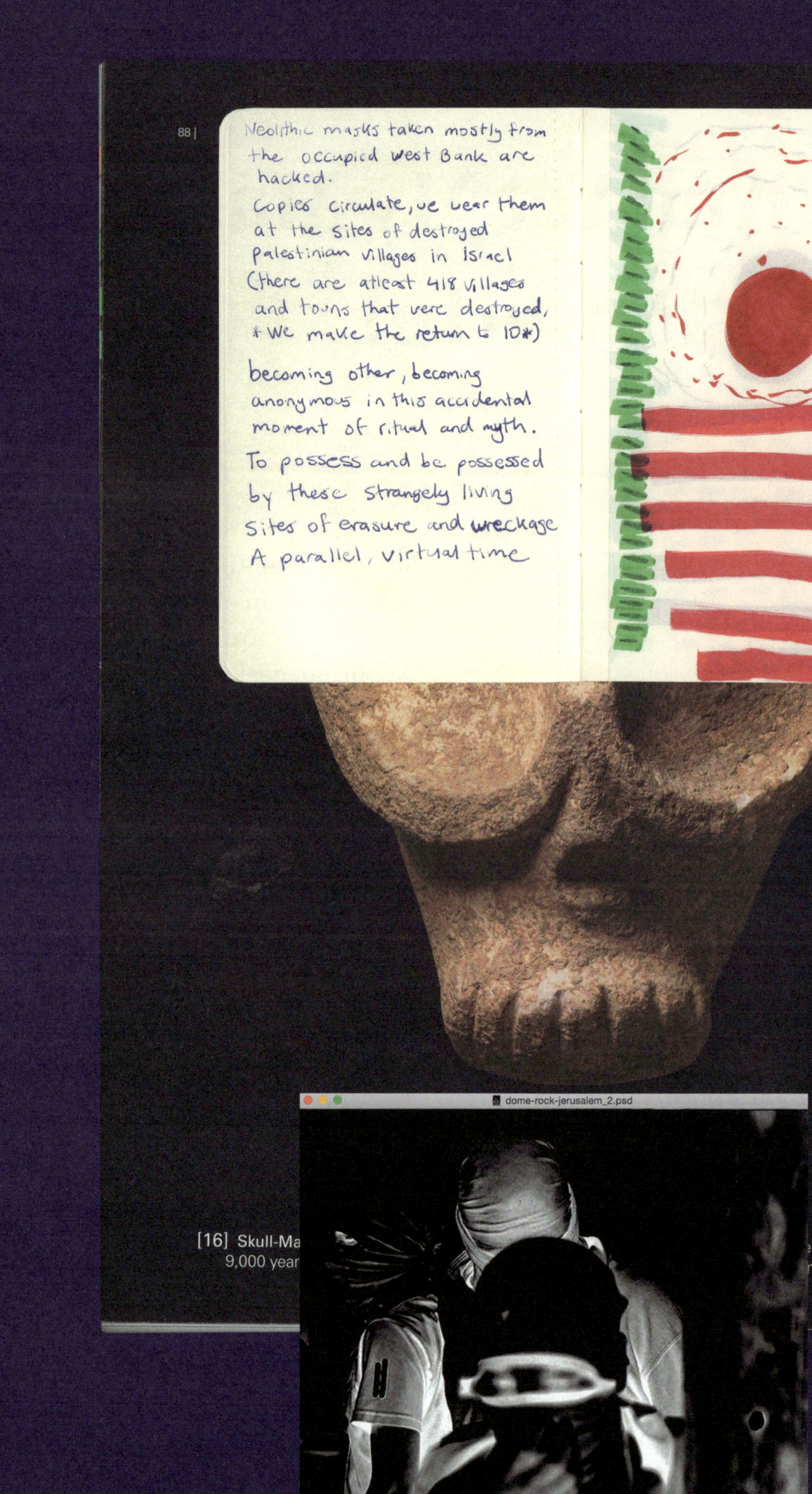
Neolithic masks taken mostly from the occupied West Bank are hacked.
Copies circulate, we wear them at the sites of destroyed Palestinian villages in Israel (there are atleast 418 villages and towns that were destroyed, * We make the return to ID*)
becoming other, becoming anonymous in this accidental moment of ritual and myth.
To possess and be possessed by these strangely living sites of erasure and wreckage
A parallel, virtual time
dome-rock-jerusalem_2.psd
[16] Skull-Ma
9,000 year

Basel Abbas and Ruanne Abou-Rahme

And Yet My Mask
Is Powerful

Artists Basel Abbas and Ruanne Abou-Rahme present
an adaptation of their body of work *And Yet My Mask
Is Powerful* (2016 – ongoing), which features several
Neolithic masks unearthed in Palestine. Often excavated
in dubious circumstances and subsequently stored in
Israeli and Western museums, the masks are all but inac-
cessible to Palestinians. Reproduced using 3D modelling
software, the masks adorn the faces of those wandering
in villages that were emptied and destroyed in the
1948 Nakba.

نورا البدري
الرؤية البابلية:
سلسلة تماثيل عصبونية قديمة

تندرج صور نورا البدري ضمن مشروع أكبر بعنوان "الرؤية البابلية" كانت قد بدأته عام 2019 بالتعاون مع طلاب التعلم الآلي في معهد البوليتيكنيك الفدرالي بلوزان (EPEFL). استخدمت الفنانة والطلاب المشاركون قاعدة بياناتٍ من 10 آلاف صورة لآثارٍ من بلاد ما بين النهرين وآثار نيو سومرية وأشورية، موجودةٍ في متحف المتروبوليتان للفن بنيويورك ومتحف كليفلند للفن، بهدف تدريب الذكاء الاصطناعي. وقد خرجوا بخوارزمية قادرة على تخليق صورٍ جديدةٍ لقطع أثرية مع إمكانيات لامتناهية من الاحتمالات لنمذجة قطع أثرية أصلية، وذلك ردًّا على رغبة البعض في خلق نسخٍ أو بدائل عن قطعٍ فُقدت أو سُرقت، وفي إطار يسعى إلى زعزعة المفاهيم السائدة عن التاريخانية والأصالة.

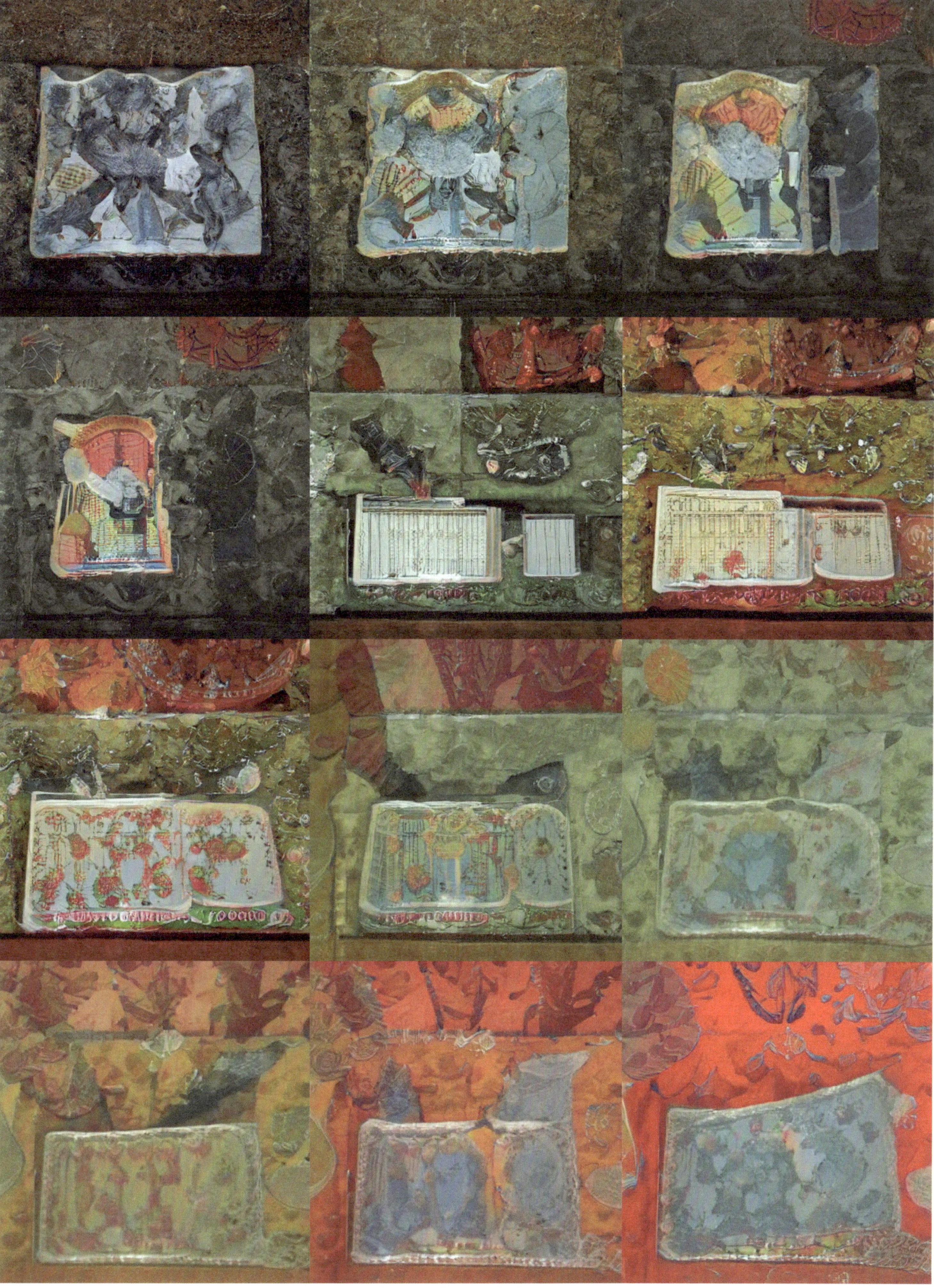

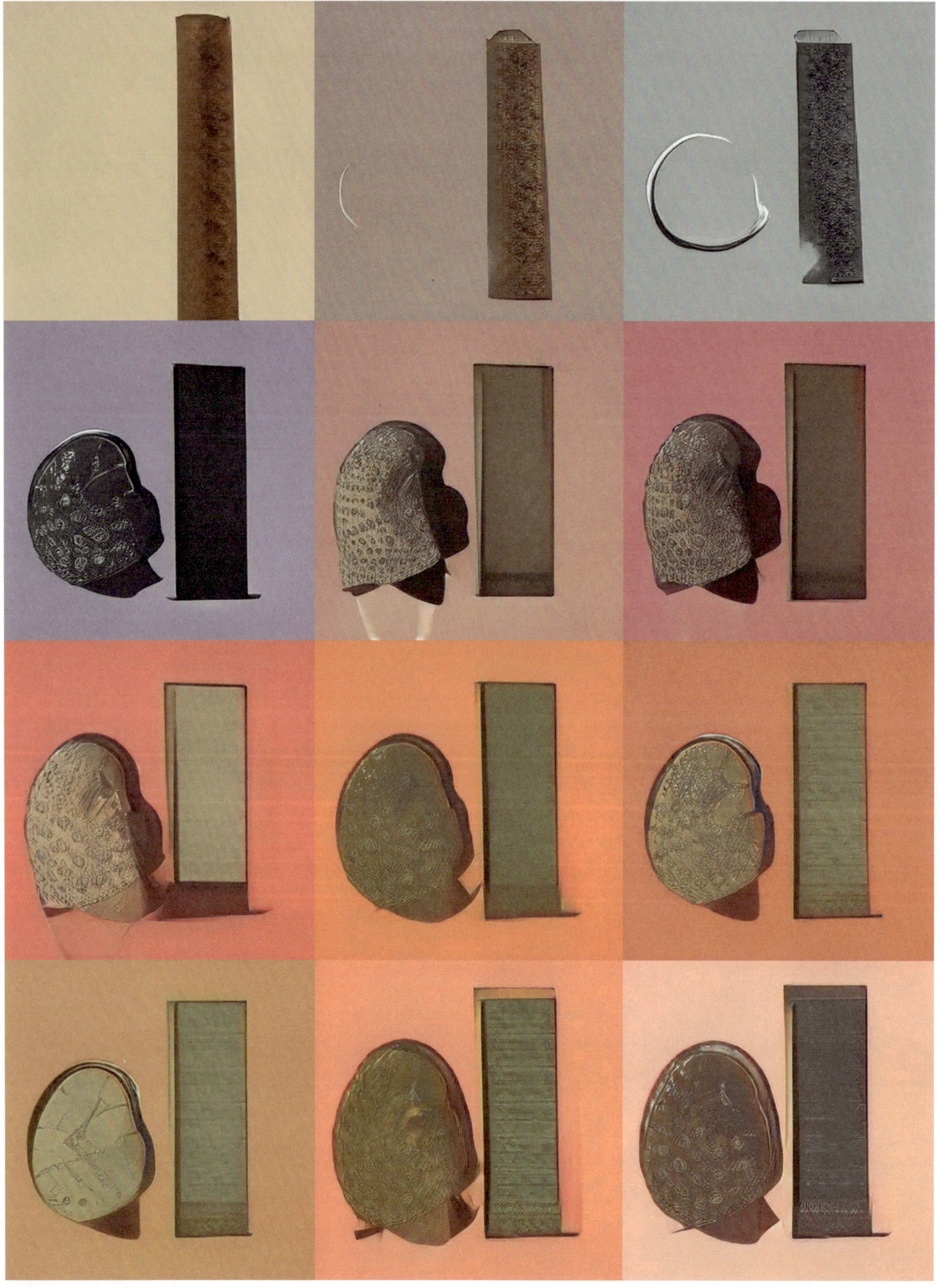

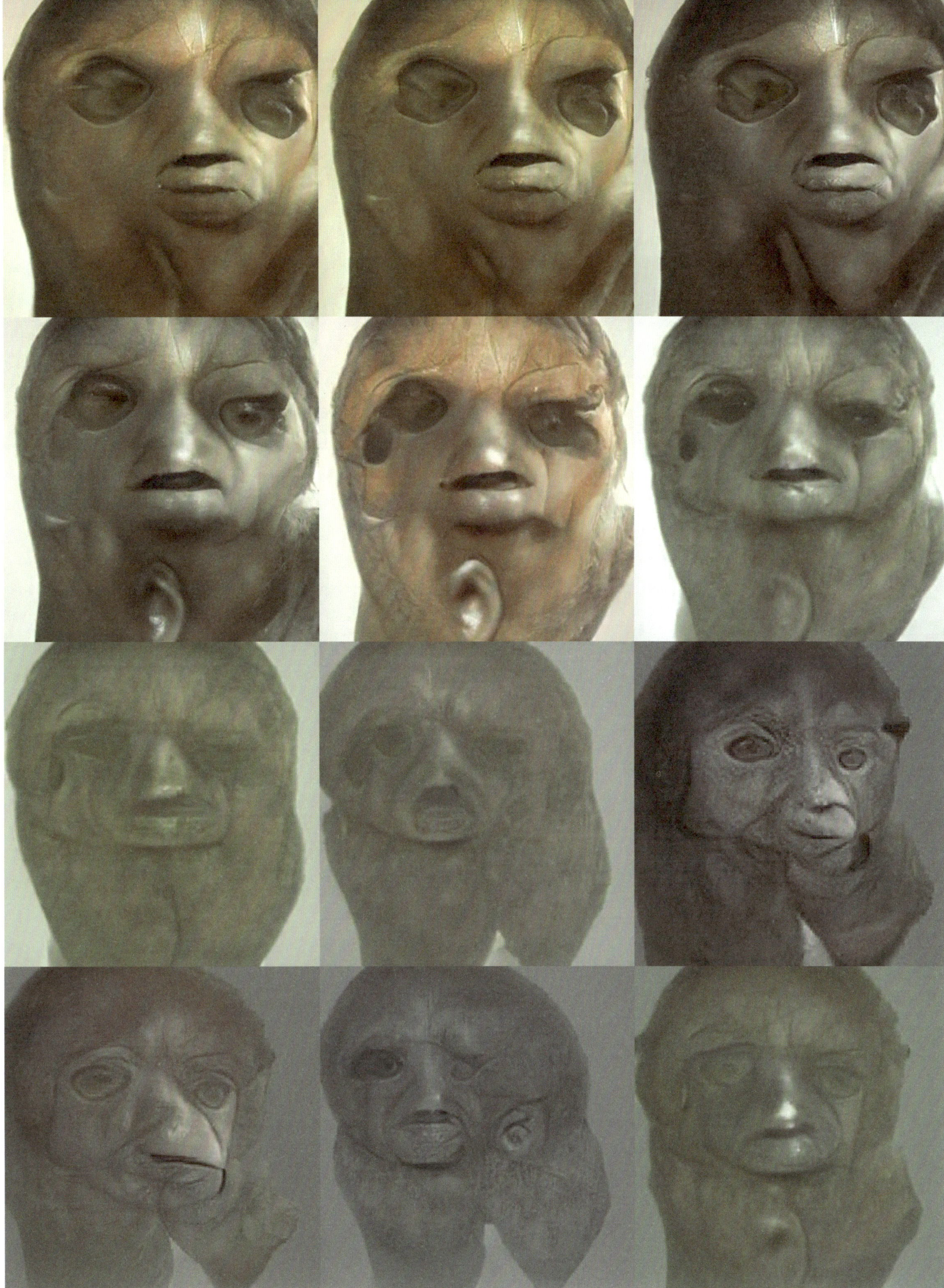

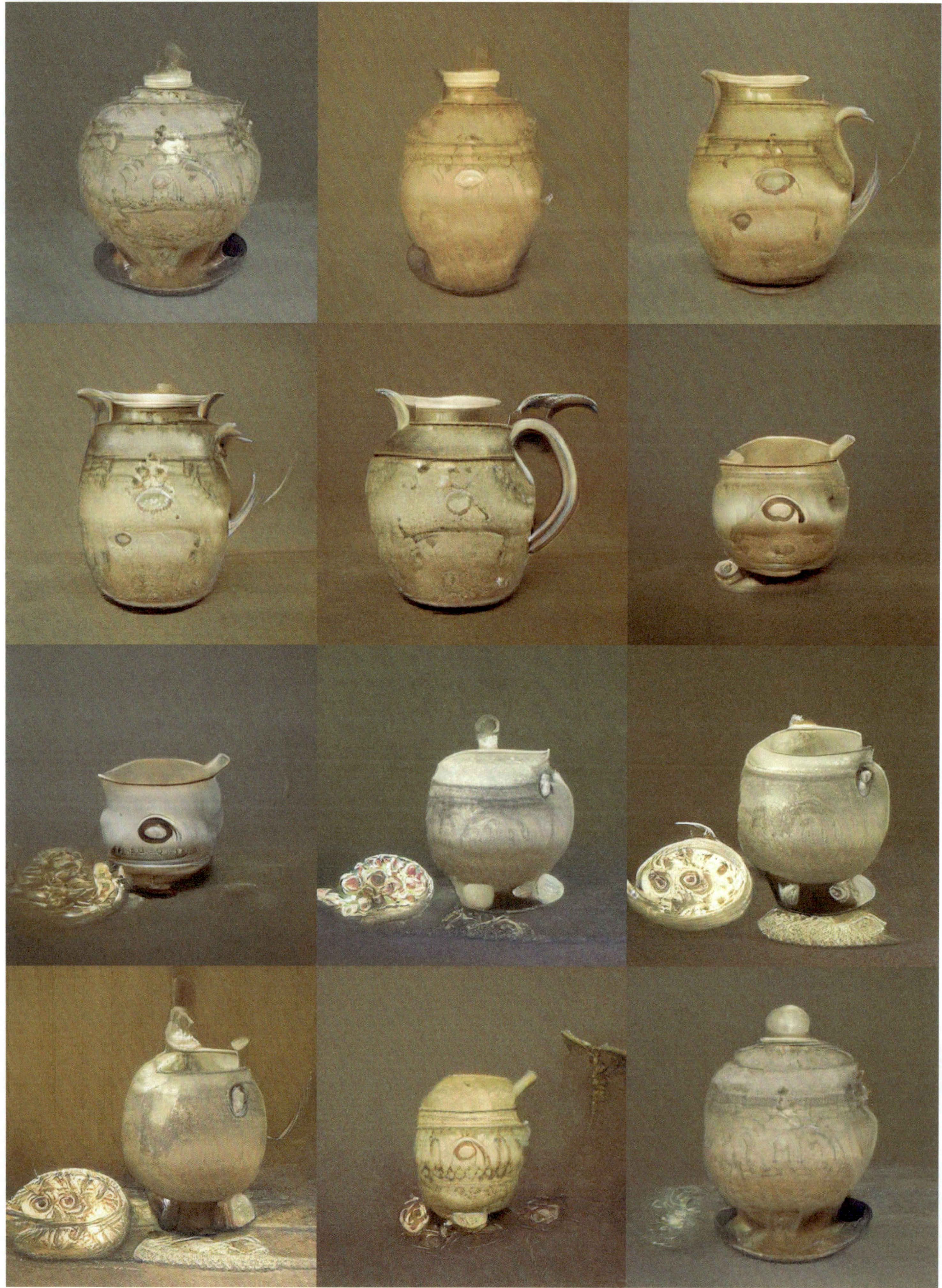

Nora Al-Badri

Babylonian Visions: Neuronal Ancestral Sculptures Series

Nora Al-Badri's images are part of a larger project titled *Babylonian Visions*, initiated in 2019 in collaboration with machine-learning students at the École polytechnique fédérale de Lausanne (EPFL). The artist and her collaborators used a database of 10,000 images of Mesopotamian, Neo-Sumerian and Assyrian artefacts – accessible through museums such as the Metropolitan Museum of Art in New York and the Cleveland Museum of Art – to train an artificial intelligence. It created an algorithm that produced new synthetic images of archaeological objects, with the potential to generate an infinite number of conceivably authentic artefacts, answering the desire of some to create surrogates for lost and stolen objects while troubling notions of historicity and authenticity.

ديمة سروجي

سبسطية: لمحة عن كثب حول الفصل العنصري

تتتبّع الفنانة والمعمارية ديمة سروجي في مقالتها البصرية التاريخ الطويل لتحويل علم الآثار إلى سلاحٍ وأداةٍ للاستغلال والنهب، بدءًا من الحفريات التوراتية في أوائل القرن العشرين تحت إشراف جامعة هارفرد، وصولًا إلى المساعي المستمرة من سلطات الآثار الإسرائيلية للاستيلاء على الآثار والأرض الفلسطينية بصورةٍ غير شرعية. تستند المقالة إلى مجموعة من الحوارات مع زيد أزهري، أحد سكان سبسطية في الضفة الغربية، لتسلط الضوء على تفاصيل النضال اليومي الذي تخوضه البلدة للتمسك بتراثها وأرضها.

"This is the same land that was affected by sewage water. So on top
of the sewage limitations, you also have these policies around timing and
access to harvest your own trees."

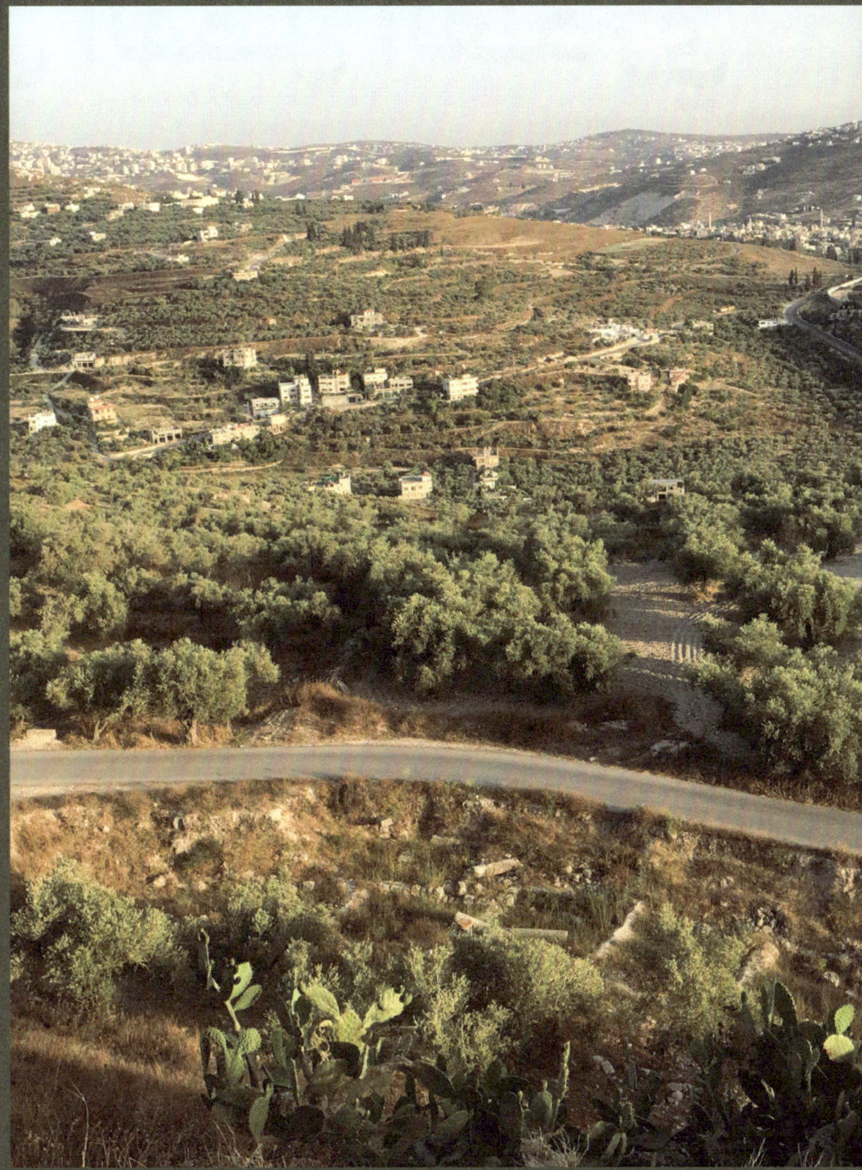

"The Israelis take issue with any intervention on the site undertaken
by Palestinian authorities. The residents started a watch group for the site to
make sure that, every night, no intruders enter the site."

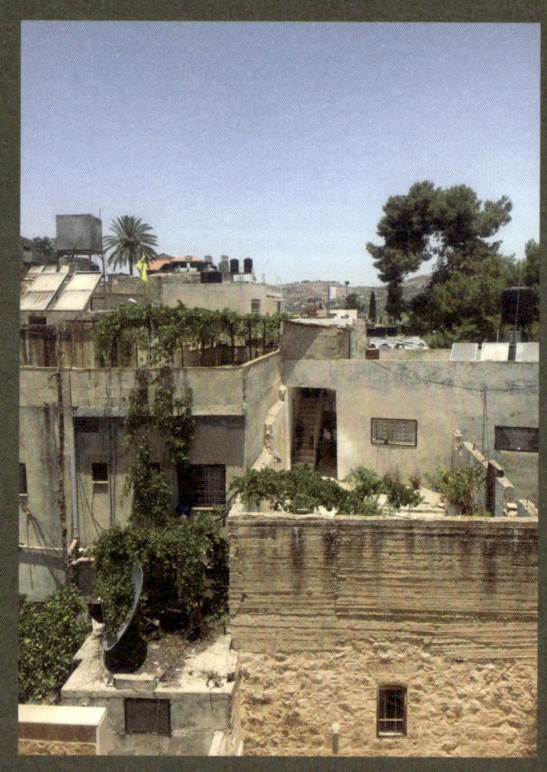

"IN THE   OLIVE SEASON,
IT WOULD TAKE
AT LEAST   15 DAYS
TO   HARVEST
THE   OLIVES"

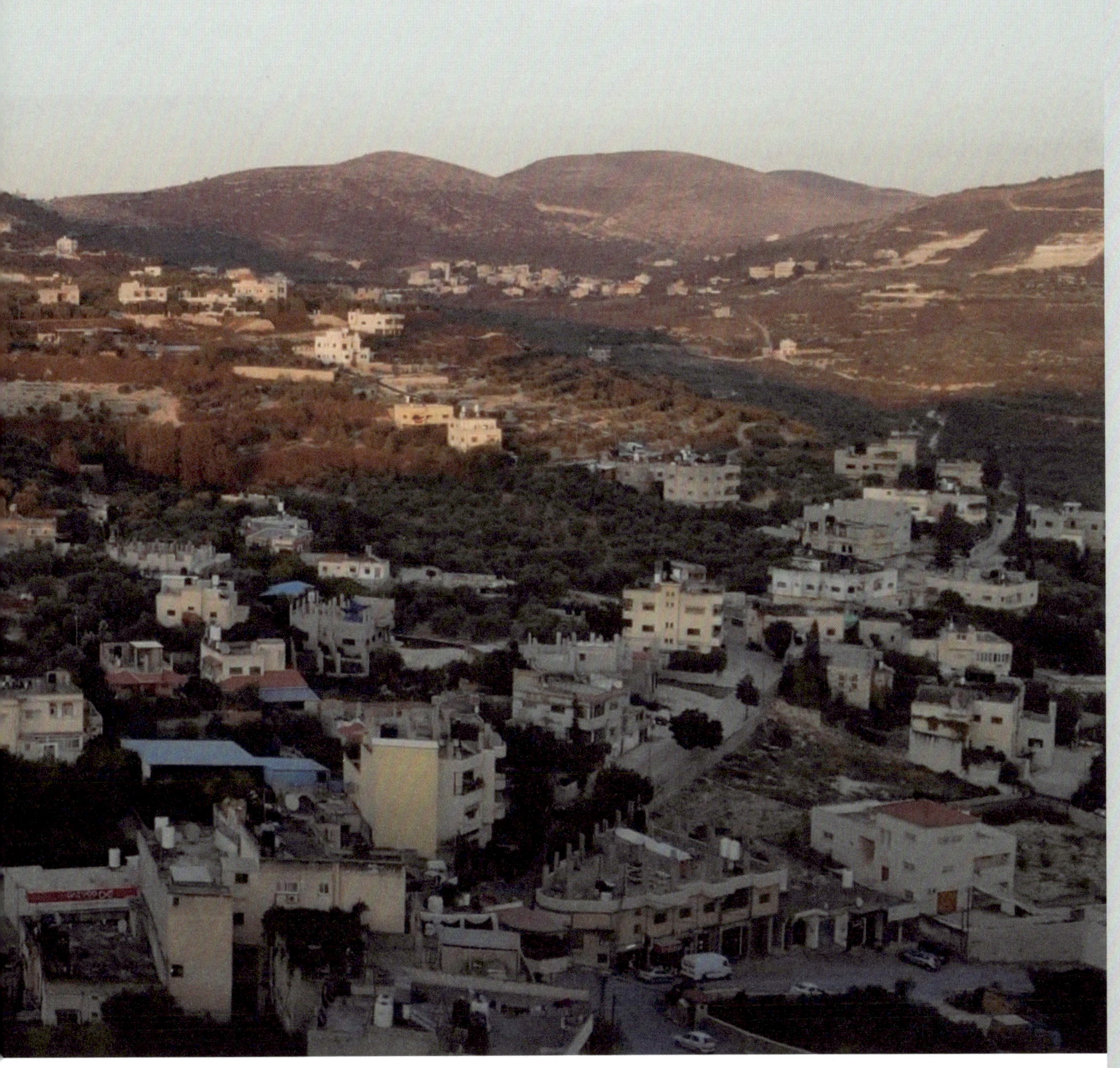

"It's not easy to sleep at night if you live in a house on the main street. You're constantly looking out your window. Someone has to stay awake to make sure settlers do not attack the house."

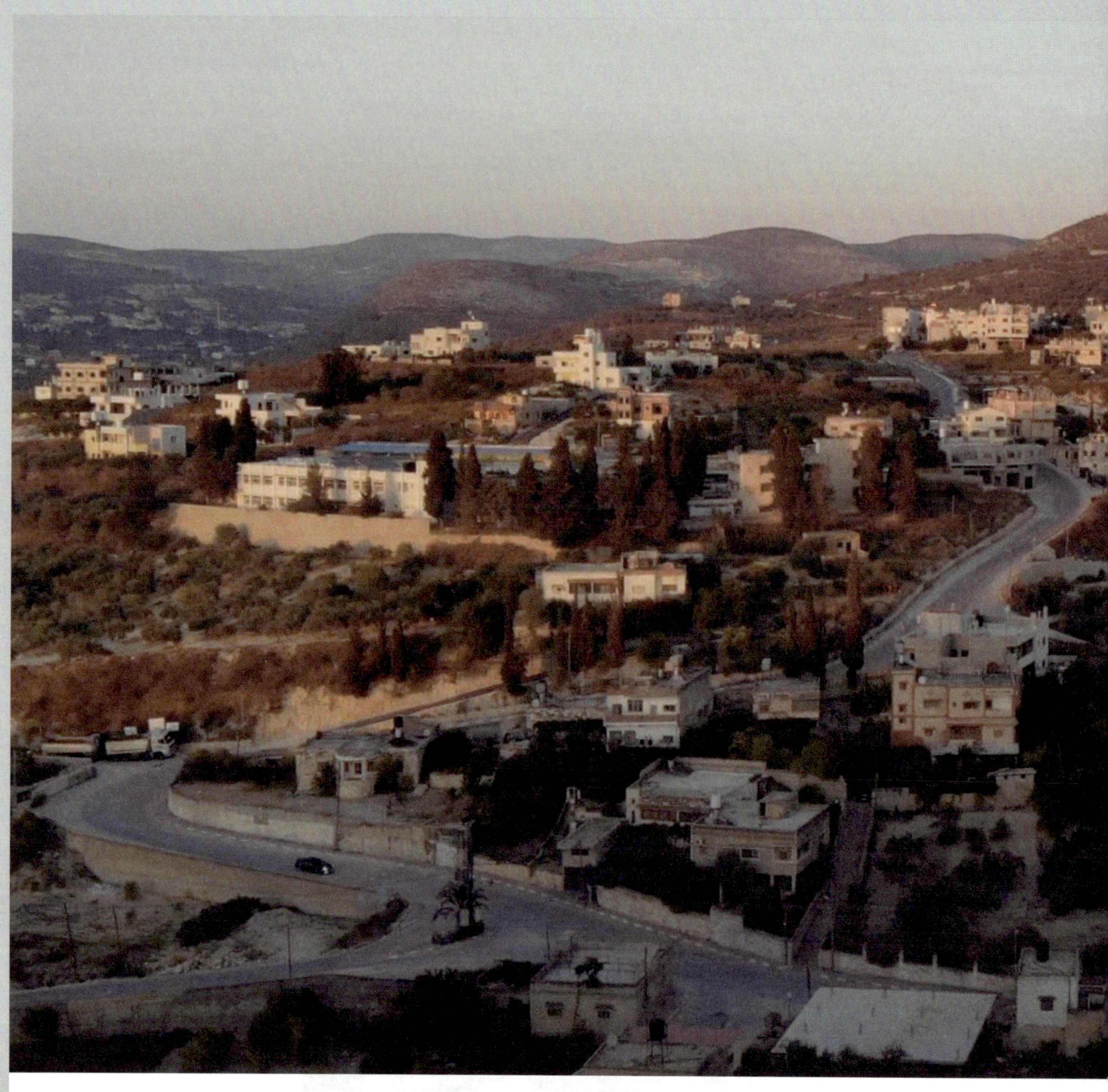

"The landscape itself is diminishing with further expansion of the Shavei Shomron settlement after then-US president Donald Trump gave settlers the permission to expand their operations, and with settler forms of terrorism and claiming ownership like burning trees and cutting them down prevailing."

In 1908, Harvard University excavated the archaeological site in Sebastia, exploiting
Palestinian women and child labour. The heaviness carried on this child's head is still
carried by her great-grandchildren. Using Palestinian labour to excavate the ground
they own is a common occurrence when it comes to Israeli excavations. This is a
less conspicuous form of forced labour.

"They asked the Palestinian residents of Sebastia to be part of the excavations. It is not
easy to protest work that your neighbours are doing themselves. [They were] convincing
Palestinian labourers that they were doing good by preserving or conserving the area for
their own community."

"After a few years of investing in making the public space more accessible to the
Palestinian residents, we are now on full-defence mode. This is because of the urgency
caused by settler violence and the recent, deliberate sabotage."

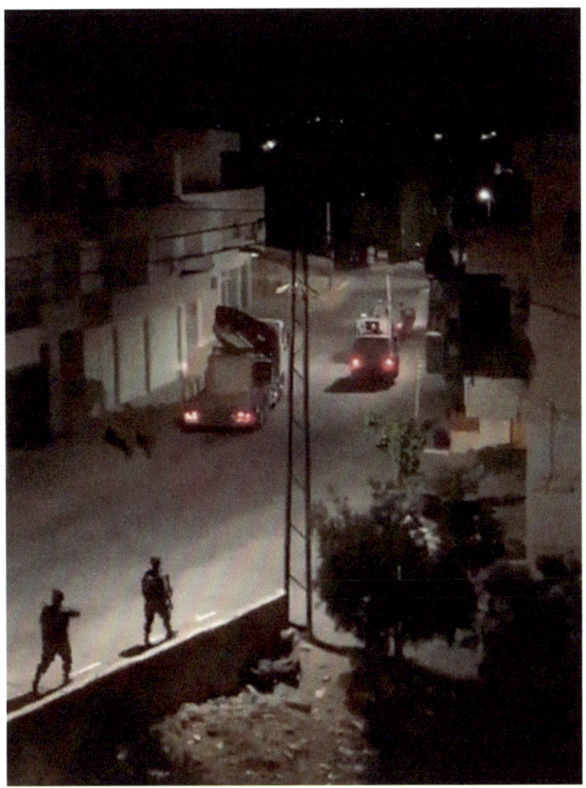

The Israeli military has an archaeology department supported by the Ministry
of Defense called the Archaeology Department of the Civil Administration. They
frequently loot artefacts from the West Bank and store them in military ware-
houses, occasionally displaying those objects in Israeli museums. This image
is of the looting of a baptismal font from Taqu, which took place in July 2020.
Israeli soldiers carrying machine guns snuck into a Palestinian site and carried
the artefact away on a truck.

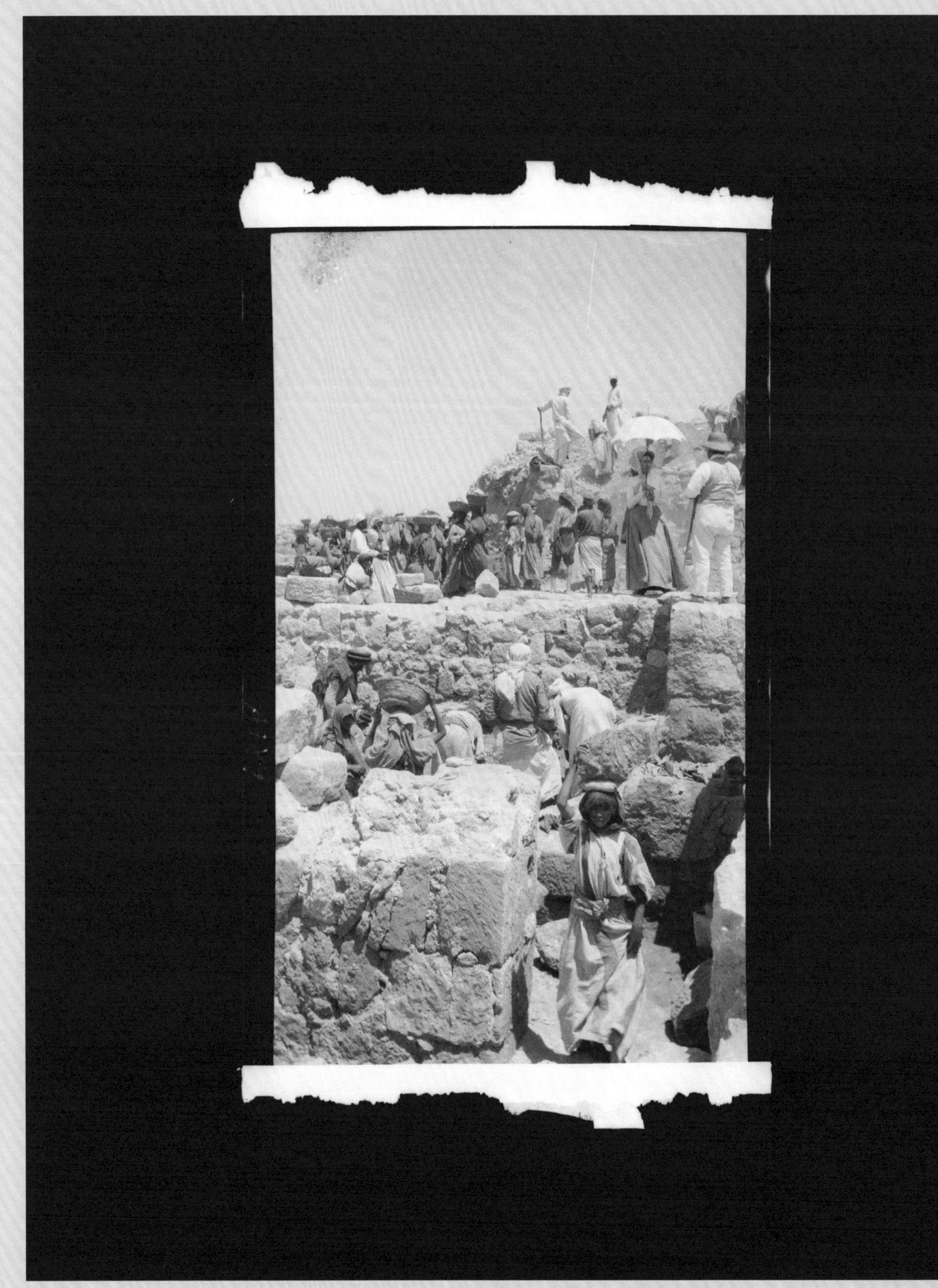

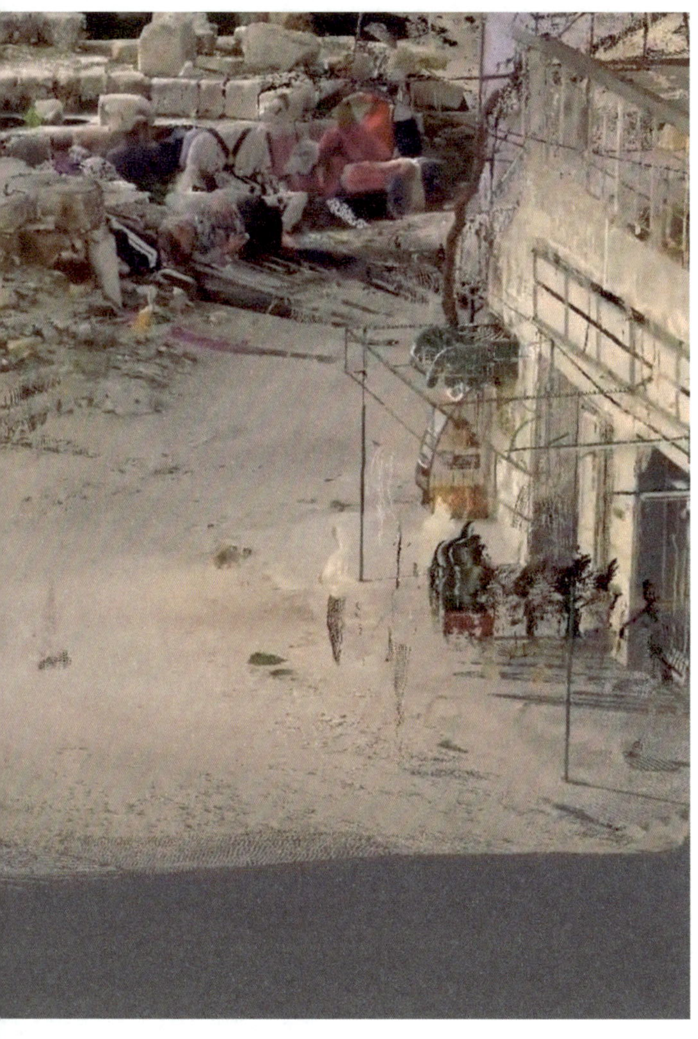

"This archaeological site has always been a big part of my life, especially during the Second Intifada, which began in the year 2000. This was an important period for us in Sebastia, and the after-effects of the Intifada were deeply felt for all of us for a full decade, from 2001 until 2011. Following the revolution in 2011, which in some ways is still ongoing, the Israeli settlers defended by the Israeli army began to take control of the archaeological site in Sebastia in a much more aggressive and targeted manner."

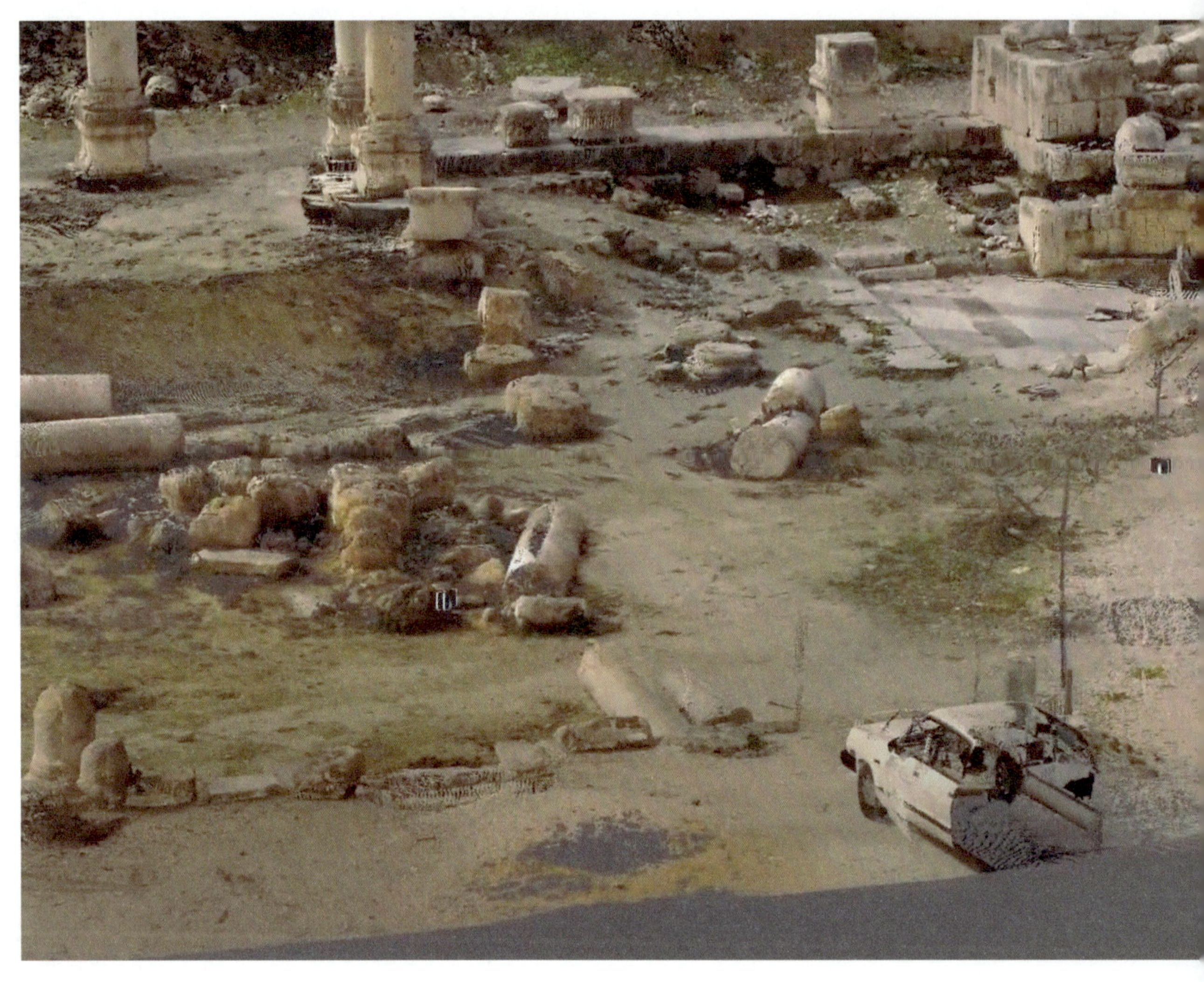

“I GREW UP
BETWEEN

THE RUINS”

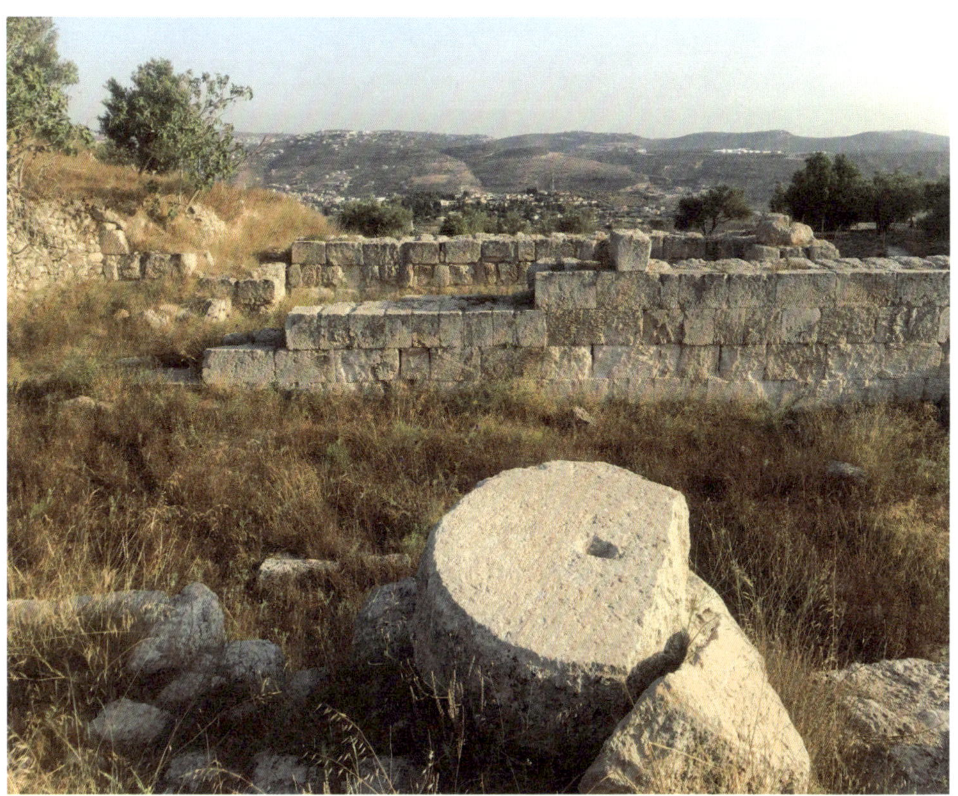

Surrounded by Israeli settlements, the city is struggling with intentional dumping of factory sewage in the agricultural valleys, and frequent attacks by settlers guarded by the Israel Defense Forces.

But the efforts to control the narrative by settler-colonial powers didn't begin with the occupation of the land by Israeli settlers. It began with colonial archaeology in 1908.

Sebastia is an archaeological site in the West Bank,
Palestine, northwest of the city of Nablus.

The site is a living and breathing city, not a mound of frozen
monuments. The city is alive and the monuments are used as public
spaces for weddings, performances, festivals, walks, and even as a
soccer field.

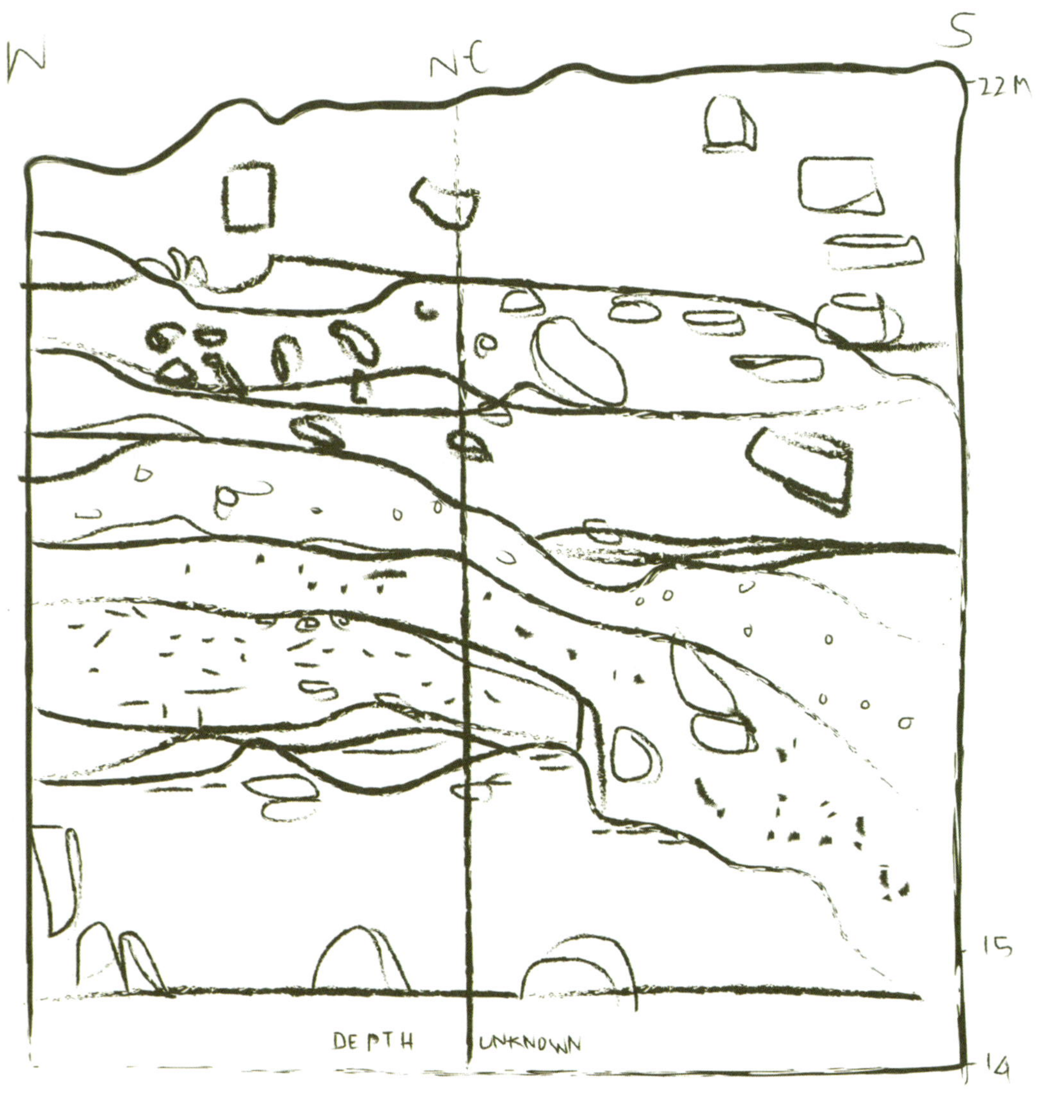

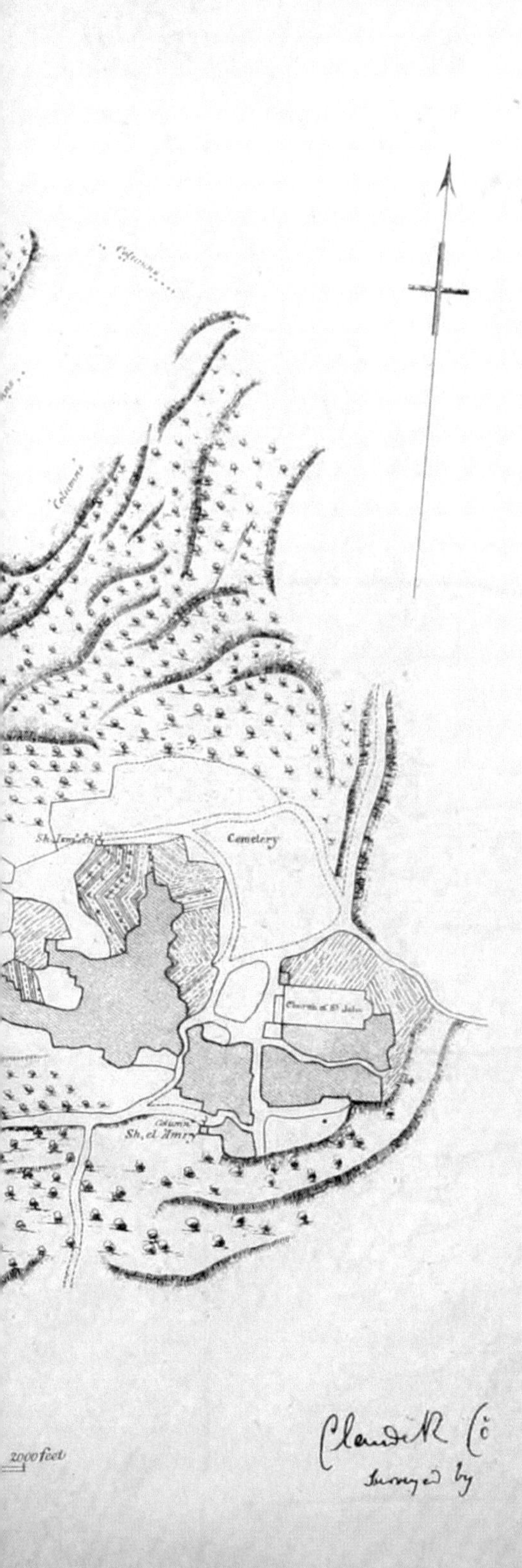

93% of all land in occupied Palestine is owned and managed by the Israeli state, with the exception of Gaza and the West Bank.

In the West Bank, the Israeli government controls 60% of the land. 23% of the territory has also been illegally declared to be state-owned.

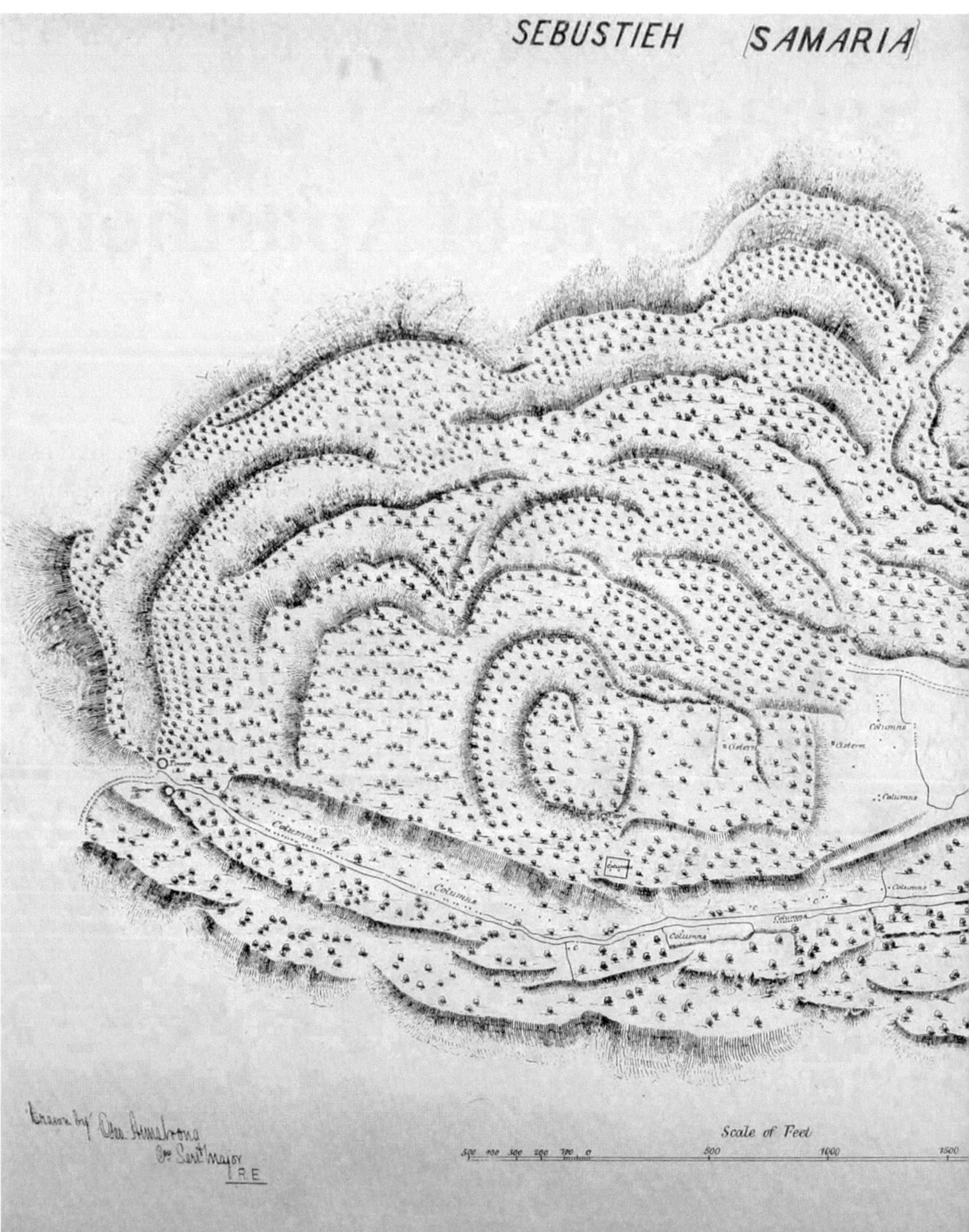

SEBUSTIEH [SAMARIA]
Columns
Cistern
Cistern
Columns
Columns
Columns
Columns
Columns
Columns
Columns
Cistern
Drawn by Chas. Armstrong
Cor. Sert. Major
R.E.
Scale of Feet
500 400 300 200 100 0
500
1000
1500

Dima Srouji

Sebastia: A Vignette of Apartheid from Below

Artist and architect Dima Srouji's visual essay traces the long lineage of archaeology's weaponisation as a tool of exploitation and dispossession, from early 20th-century Biblical excavations supervised by Harvard University to the ongoing illegal dispossession of Palestinian artefacts and land by Israeli archaeological authorities. Drawing on conversations with Zaid Azhari, a resident of the city of Sebastia in the West Bank, Palestine, the essay is a window into the town's daily struggle to hold on to its heritage and land.

رند عبد الجبار

اقتفاء الجذور

تَنظُم الفنانة والمصممة رند عبد الجبار مقالتها البصرية في مديح الأشياء التي تسكن في يوميات بيوت المهجر. تحمل هذه المجموعات البيتية من أقمشة وآنية فضية ولوحات وخزفيات قصصًا عن الهجرة والشتات، فتتحول إلى خزانات للذاكرة ووصلات مع أماكن وأناس غائبين. تقول رند إن بقايا الماضي لا تنتمي إلى المتحف بالضرورة، بينما يمكن للتاريخ أن يُستخلص على نطاق أصغر عابر للأجيال بواسطة اللغة والمقتنيات اليومية.

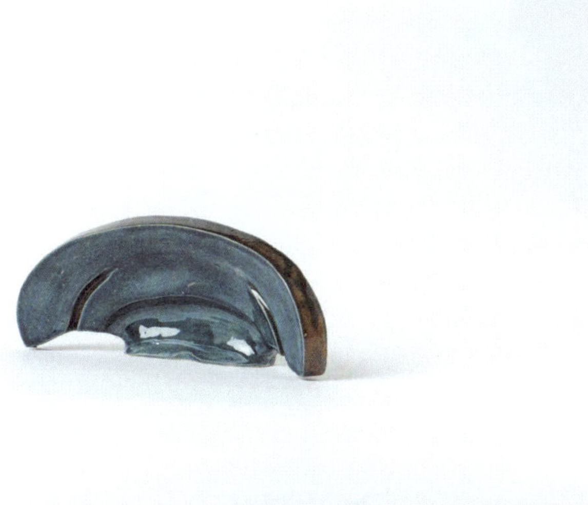

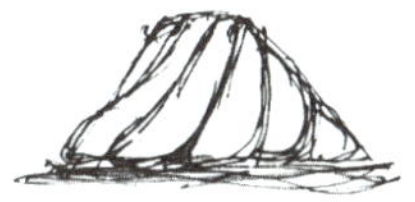

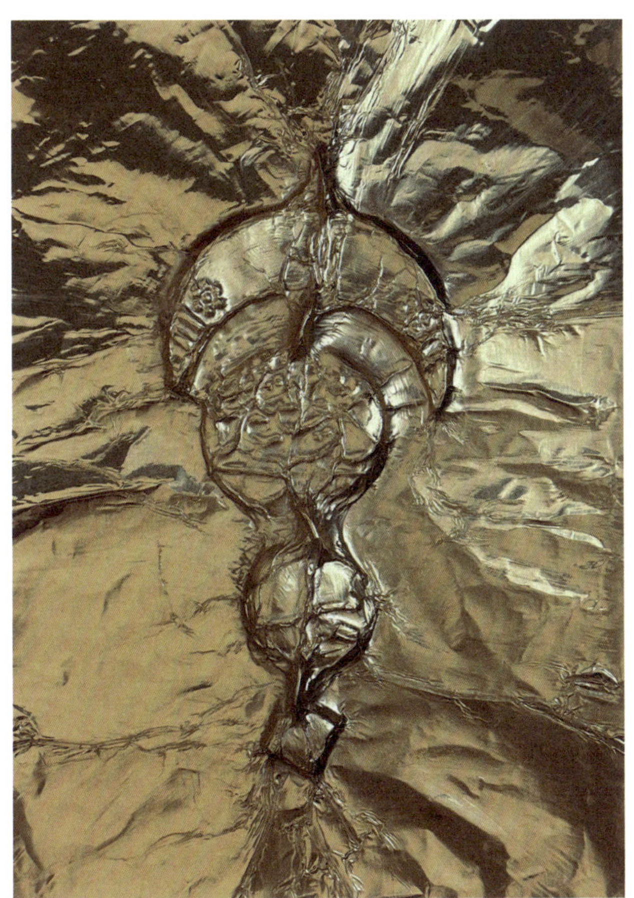

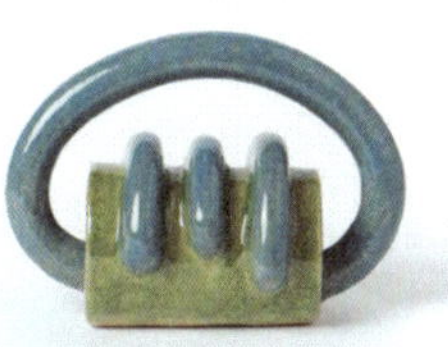

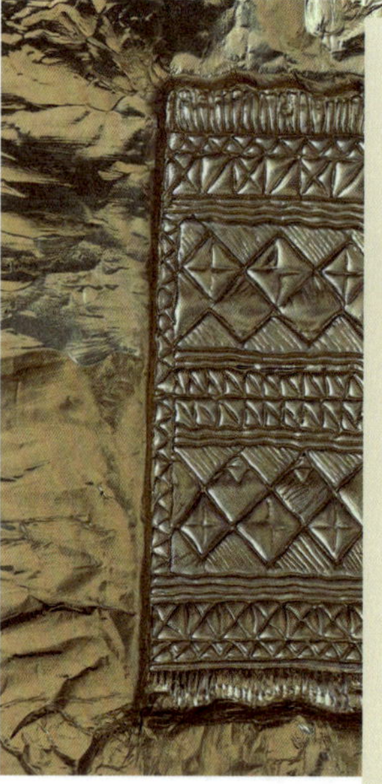

My mother maintains a collection of ceramic objects which dominate wall space within our home. As a child, I'd study their engraved depictions of reed houses and spiralling minarets, run my fingers over their smooth, glazed surfaces to trace the outlines of archways and overhanging balconies, and feel the textured grooves of palm fronds. These artefacts accompanied us on multiple journeys across continents, surviving cracks and breakages, after careful restoration by my father. I used to consider their value as stemming purely from their visual artistry and intricate colour compositions; however, over time, I have come to recognise their embodiment of our material culture, of our land itself.

From household vessels to temple offerings, mud-brick houses to the grand processional walls of the Ishtar Gate, clay has been our primary medium of expression for millennia. Shaping clay connects me to my ancestry and the embodied knowledge held within my hands. Every repetitive action recalls a gesture transmitted across generations, a legacy sustained through objects and heirlooms preserved as an act of resistance against the looming threat of forgetting – or being forgotten. In my research, in encounters with these ancient vestiges, sitting out of reach and encased in glass, I contemplate their makers. How far back does this cycle of intergenerational dialogue extend? I search for the knowledge imbued within their boundaries.

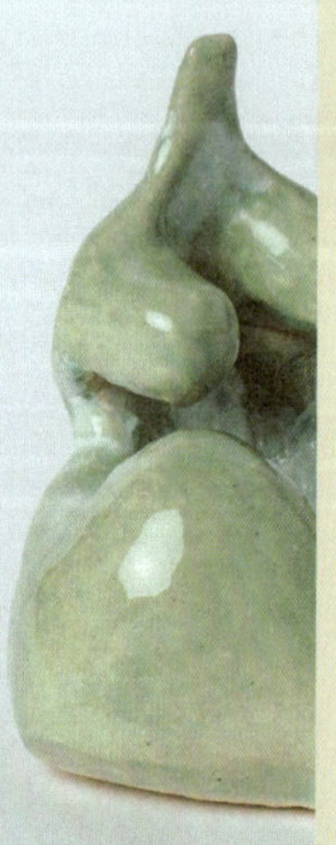

I was brought up in a diaspora household with
a pronounced presence and acute awareness
of my Iraqi heritage. For my parents, our displacement
was temporary – a present unsettled by a resistance
to laying roots. In an effort to instil within us a deep
sense of connection to our homeland, they filled our
house with a wide range of objects, pictorial and
abstract representations of 'home' that took the form
of paintings, ceramics, silverware, and tapestries; some
smaller items they carried with them when we left,
others they collected over the years. To them, these
were relics of a lived experience. To me, they marked
an absence, a liminal space that straddled a past beyond
reach and a longing for the future, an uncertain return.

'One day...'

I pieced together these visual fragments to construct
a spatial and temporal imaginary as the setting for
all the stories shared and the memories recounted.
As time erodes memory and the rift of displacement
expands, the urgency to preserve intensifies. These
objects, remnants and memorabilia of the past, served as
mnemonic anchors and acted as portals that transported
me across spatial and temporal boundaries. Without its
vestiges, how can the remembered past maintain
its credibility?

This childhood experience was formative in my
understanding of the potential for relics to traverse
the past and present, creating a space of overlap
between their historical and contemporary positions.
I witnessed the power of these tangible remains to serve
as vessels through which the more ephemeral aspects of
history, namely memory, are enriched and affirmed. While
historic accounts and inherited narratives require filtering,
processing, or re-imagination, the physical remnants of
the past can be directly accessed and assessed by our
senses. Embedded within them are clues that help shape
our identity and sense of personal continuity.

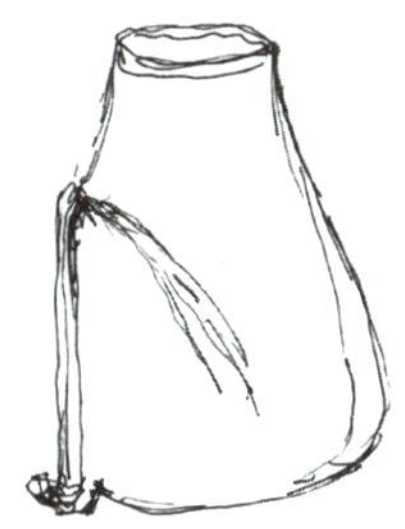

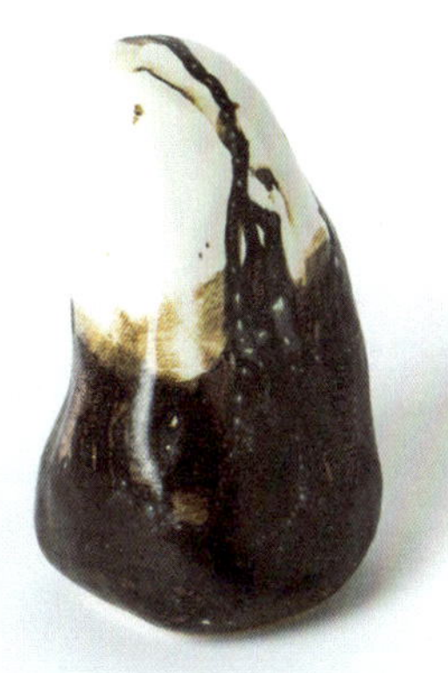

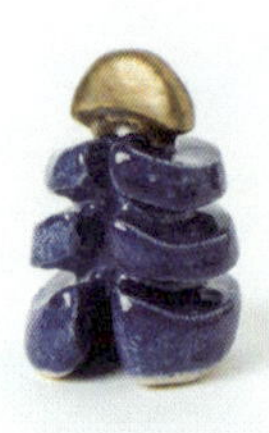

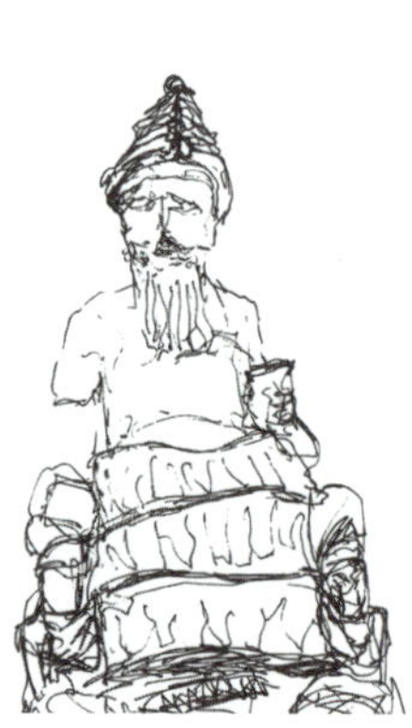

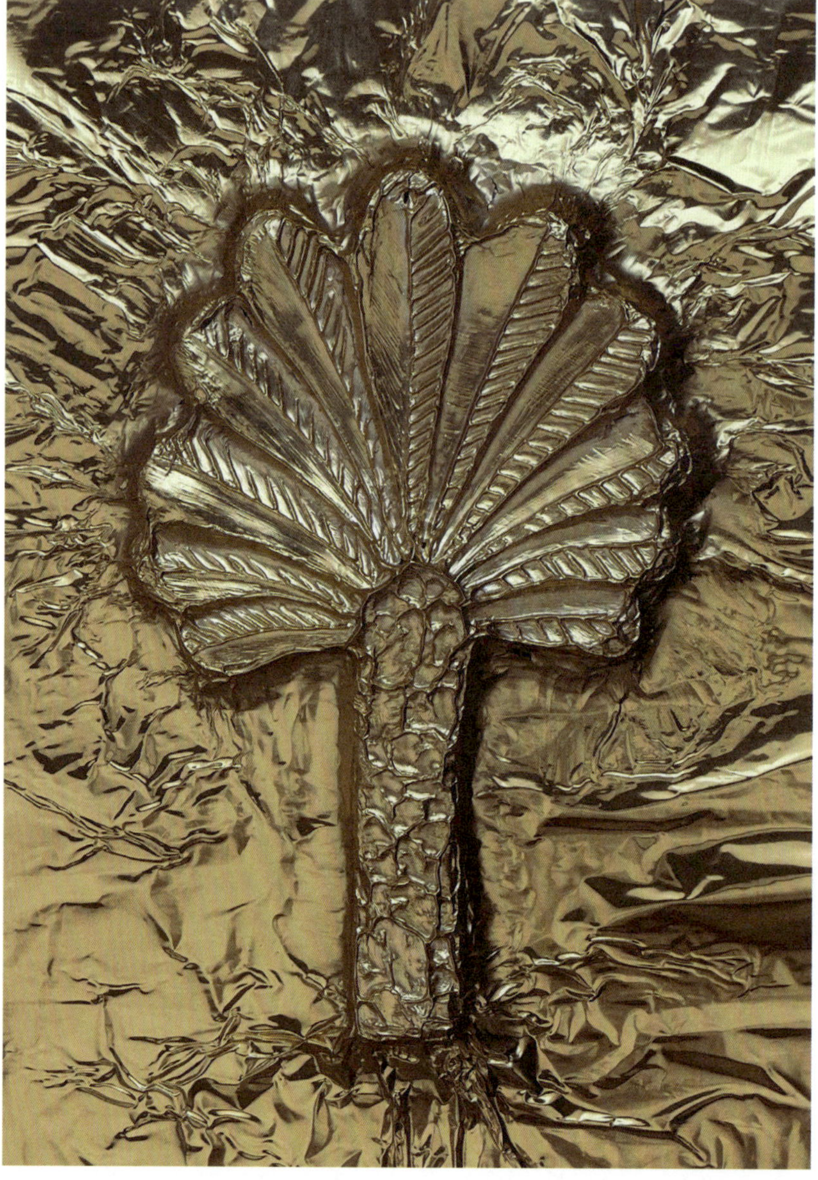